Andrew Radford's new textbook is written for students with little or no background in syntax, and introduces them to key concepts of Chomsky's minimalist program (e.g. merger and movement, checking, economy and greed, split VPs, agreement projections), as well as providing detailed analysis of the syntax of a range of different construction types (e.g. interrogatives, negatives, passives, unaccusatives, complement clauses). Illustrative material is mainly drawn from varieties of English (Standard English, Belfast English, Shakespearean English, Jamaican Creole and Child English). There is a substantial glossary at the end of the overall book, and an extensive integral *workbook section* at the end of each chapter with helpful hints and model answers, which aim to enable students to analyse phrases and sentences for themselves within a minimalist framework.

CAMBRIDGE TEXTBOOKS IN LINGUISTICS

General Editors: S. R. ANDERSON, J. BRESNAN, B. COMRIE, W. DRESSLER,
C. EWEN, R. HUDDLESTON, R. LASS, D. LIGHTFOOT, J. LYONS,
P. H. MATTHEWS, R. POSNER, S. ROMAINE, N. V. SMITH, N. VINCENT

SYNTACTIC THEORY AND THE STRUCTURE OF ENGLISH

In this series

SYNTACTIC THEORY AND THE STRUCTURE OF ENGLISH

A MINIMALIST APPROACH

ANDREW RADFORD

DEPARTMENT OF LANGUAGE AND LINGUISTICS, UNIVERSITY OF ESSEX

CAMBRIDGE
UNIVERSITY PRESS

PUBLISHED BY THE PRESS SYNDICATE OF THE UNIVERSITY OF CAMBRIDGE
The Pitt Building, Trumpington Street, Cambridge CB2 1RP, United Kingdom

CAMBRIDGE UNIVERSITY PRESS
The Edinburgh Building, Cambridge CB2 2RU, United Kingdom
40 West 20th Street, New York, NY 10011–4211, USA
10 Stamford Road, Oakleigh, Melbourne 3166, Australia

First published 1997

Printed in the United Kingdom at the University Press, Cambridge

Typeset in Times 8/10 pt

A catalogue record for this book is available from the British Library

Library of Congress Cataloguing in Publication data applied for

ISBN 0 521 47125 7 hardback
ISBN 0 521 47707 7 paperback

TAG

CONTENTS

Contents

PREFACE

The aim of this book is to provide an intensive introduction to recent work in syntactic theory (more particularly, to key concepts which are presupposed in works written within the broad framework of the minimalist program in the version outlined in Chomsky 1995b). There are six main features which mark this book out as different from other introductions to syntax currently available.

The first is that it does not presuppose any background knowledge of syntactic theory: it is suitable for use with true beginners, and does not presuppose that students have already done a course on generative syntax (though it is also suitable for false beginners who have already taken a course on an earlier model of syntax, and want to learn about more recent work).

The second is that it does not adopt a historical approach, or presuppose any historical knowledge (for example, there is no discussion of earlier work in the 1980s *government and binding* paradigm). Rather (for the most part), it deals directly with 1990s work within the *minimalist program*.

The third is that cross-linguistic variation is illustrated in terms of different varieties of English (e.g. Belfast English, Jamaican Creole, Child English, Shakespearean English, etc.), rather than in terms of different languages. Hence it does not make the unrealistic assumption that the reader knows (for example) Spanish, German, Arabic, Chinese and Chuckchee.

The fourth is that the book contains a substantial *workbook section* at the end of each chapter, containing exercise material designed to be used for class discussion, self-study or coursework assignments, with fully worked out *model answers* provided for key examples, and *helpful hints* for potentially problematic points. Where a particular exercise presupposes understanding of key concepts introduced in particular sections of the text, the relevant text sections are indicated in parentheses, after the exercise number.

The fifth is that there is an extensive *glossary* at the end of the overall book, intended to alleviate the terminological trauma of doing syntax.

The sixth is that the book is published alongside an abridged version called *Syntax: a Minimalist Introduction*. The two books cover roughly the same range of topics: the abridged version is intended for use as a nonintensive introduction on short syntax courses, and includes less theoretical and descriptive detail and less exercise material; the full-length version is intended for use as an intensive introduction on longer syntax courses, and contains twice as much text material and three times as much exercise material (as well as a slightly extended glossary and bibliography). The full-length version can be used as a follow-up to the abridged version (e.g. students who read the abridged version and get interested in the syntax of agreement projections can then turn to read the more detailed account given in chapter 10 of this book).

This book is divided into ten chapters, with each chapter (on average) comprising 25–35 pages of text (divided up into ten numbered sections) and 10–20 pages of exercise material. In general, chapters are written in such a way as to become progressively more difficult: the first half of the text of each chapter introduces key ideas in a relatively accessible way; the second half typically discusses rather more complex descriptive details or theoretical issues, and is often considerably more challenging. In addition, the chapters become cumulatively more complex as the book progresses; the last two chapters are particularly challenging and involve a far higher level of abstraction than the others.

Because each new chapter serves to introduce a new set of ideas, you will find that earlier anaylses are often revised in later chapters. Thus, the book introduces students to a range of different analyses of particular constructions (e.g. the analysis of double-object constructions presented in chapter 9 is substantially revised in chapter 10).

The extensive *workbook section* at the end of each chapter is designed as an integral part of the text: the *model answers* provided in some cases extend the analysis presented in the text, and are thus an essential part of the 'learning experience' provided by the book. As Sam Featherston remarked to me after teaching an earlier version of the book to a group of students: 'I wish I'd told the students to read all the *model answers* even if they don't tackle the relevant exercises – they contain a lot of important additional information.'

The *glossary* at the end of the book provides simple illustrations of how key terms (and abbreviations) are used – not just theory-specific technical terms like *enlightened self-interest*, but also more basic general terms such as *subject*.

I am grateful to Laura Rupp, Sam Featherston and Martin Atkinson (Essex), and Jon Erickson (Cologne) for helpful comments on an earlier draft of this manuscript; and above all to the series editor Neil Smith (University College London) for his patient and good-humoured comments on numerous ((re-)re-)revised drafts of the manuscript.

This book is dedicated to my father and my sister (who both died before I had time to thank them for all they did for me) and to my mother for battling so bravely against bereavement and blindness over the past couple of years, before finally passing away on 16 February 1997.

1
Principles and parameters

1.1 Overview

The aim of this chapter is to outline contemporary ideas on *the nature of grammar* and *the acquisition of grammar*. The approach adopted here is that associated with the **principles-and-parameters** model developed by Noam Chomsky during the 1980s and 1990s, in works ranging from his 1981 book *Lectures on Government and Binding* to his 1995c book *The Minimalist Program*.

1.2 Grammar

Grammar is traditionally subdivided into two different but inter-related areas of study – **morphology** and **syntax**. Morphology is the study of how words are formed out of smaller units (traditionally called *morphemes*), and so addresses questions such as 'What are the various component parts (= morphemes) of a word like *antidisestablishmentarianism*, and what kinds of principles determine the ways in which the parts are combined together to form the whole?' Syntax is concerned with the ways in which words can be combined together to form phrases and sentences, and so addresses questions like 'Why is it OK in English to say *Who did you see Mary with?*, but not OK to say **Who did you see Mary and?*' (A star in front of an expression means that it's ungrammatical.) 'What kinds of principles determine the ways in which we can and cannot combine words together to form phrases and sentences?'

However, grammar is traditionally concerned not just with the principles which determine the *formation* of words, phrases and sentences, but also with the principles which govern their *interpretation* – i.e. with the principles which tell us how to *interpret* (= assign meaning to) words, phrases and sentences. For example, any comprehensive grammar of English will specify that compound words like *man-eater* and *man-made* have very different interpretations: in compounds like *man-eater*, the word *man* is traditionally said to have a *patient* interpretation, in the sense that man is the patient/hapless victim on whom the act of eating is going to be performed; by contrast, in compounds like *man-made*, the word *man* is said to have an *agent* interpretation, in the sense that *man* is the agent responsible for the act of making. Thus, structural aspects of meaning are traditionally said to be part of the domain of grammar. We

1

might therefore characterize grammar as the study of *the principles which govern the formation and interpretation of words, phrases and sentences*. In terms of the traditional division of grammar into morphology and syntax, we can say that morphology studies the formation and interpretation of words, whereas syntax is concerned with the formation and interpretation of phrases and sentences.

In a fairly obvious sense, any native speaker of a language can be said to know the grammar of his or her native language. After all, native speakers clearly know how to form and interpret words, phrases and sentences in their native language. For example, any native speaker of English can tell you that the negative counterpart of *I like syntax* is *I don't like syntax*, and not e.g. **I no like syntax*: thus, we might say that native speakers know how to negate sentences in their language. However, it is important to emphasize that this grammatical knowledge is *tacit* (i.e. subconscious) rather than *explicit* (i.e. conscious): so, it's no good asking a native speaker of English a question such as 'How do you form negative sentences in English?', since human beings have no conscious awareness of the psychological processes involved in speaking and understanding a language. To introduce a technical term, we might say that native speakers have grammatical **competence** in their native language: by this, we mean that they have tacit knowledge of the grammar of their language – i.e. of how to form and interpret words, phrases and sentences in the language.

In work dating back to the 1960s, Chomsky has drawn a distinction between *competence* (the fluent native speaker's tacit knowledge of his language) and **performance** (what people actually say or understand by what someone else says on a given occasion). Competence is 'the speaker–hearer's knowledge of his language', while performance is 'the actual use of language in concrete situations' (Chomsky 1965, p. 4). Very often, performance is an imperfect reflection of competence: we all make occasional slips of the tongue, or occasionally misinterpret what someone else says to us. However, this doesn't mean that we don't know our native language, or don't have competence (i.e. fluency) in it. Misproductions and misinterpretations are *performance errors*, attributable to a variety of performance factors like tiredness, boredom, drunkenness, drugs, external distractions, and so forth. Grammars traditionally set out to tell you what you need to know about a language in order to have native speaker competence in the language (i.e. to be able to speak the language like a native speaker): hence, it is clear that grammar is concerned with *competence* rather than *performance*. This is not to deny the interest of *performance* as a field of study, but merely to assert that performance is more properly studied within the different – though related – discipline of psycholinguistics, which studies the psychological processes underlying speech production and comprehension. It seems reasonable to suppose that competence will play an important part in the study of performance, since you have to understand what native speakers tacitly know about their language before you can study the effects of tiredness, drunkenness, etc. on this knowledge.

If we say that grammar is the study of grammatical competence, then we are implicitly taking a *cognitive* view of the nature of grammar. After all, if the term *grammatical competence* is used to denote what native speakers tacitly know about the grammar of their language, then grammar is part of the more general study of cognition (i.e. human knowledge). In the terminology adopted by Chomsky (1986a, pp. 19–56), we're studying language as a cognitive system *internalized* within the human brain/mind; our ultimate goal is to characterize the nature of the internalized linguistic system (or *I-language*, as Chomsky terms it) which enables humans to speak and understand their native language. Such a cognitive approach has obvious implications for the descriptive linguist who is interested in trying to describe the grammar of a particular language like English. What it means is that in devising a grammar of English, we are attempting to describe the grammatical knowledge possessed by the fluent native speaker of English. However, clearly this competence is not directly accessible to us: as noted above, you can't ask native speakers to introspect about the nature of the processes by which they produce and understand sentences in their native language, since they have no conscious awareness of such processes. Hence, we have to seek to study competence *indirectly*. But how?

Perhaps the richest vein of readily available evidence which we have about the nature of grammatical competence lies in native speakers' intuitions about the *grammaticality* and *interpretation* of words, phrases and sentences in their native language. For example, preschool children often produce past tense forms like *goed*, *comed*, *seed*, *buyed*, etc. and any adult native speaker of (Modern Standard) English will intuitively know that such forms are ungrammatical in English, and will know that their grammatical counterparts are *went*, *came*, *saw* and *bought*. Similarly, any native speaker of English would intuitively recognize that sentences like (1a) below are grammatical in English, but that sentences like (1b) are ungrammatical:

(1) (a)   If you don't know the meaning of a word, look it up in a dictionary

     (b)   *If you don't know the meaning of a word, look up it in a dictionary

(Recall that a star in front of an expression means that it is ungrammatical; by convention, any expression which does not have a star in front of it is grammatical; note that stars go *before* – not *after* – ungrammatical words, phrases or sentences.) Thus, we might say that *intuitions about grammaticality* form part of the native speaker's grammatical competence. Equivalently, we can say that native speakers have the ability to make *grammaticality judgments* about words, phrases and sentences in their native language – i.e. the ability to judge whether particular expressions are grammatical or ungrammatical within their native language. An interesting implication of this fact is that if grammars model competence, a grammar of a language must tell you not only what you *can* say in the language, but also what you *can't* say, since native speaker competence includes not only the ability to make the judgment that certain types of

3

sentence (e.g. (1a) above) are grammatical, but also the ability to judge that others (e.g. (1b) above) are ungrammatical. Indeed, much of contemporary work in syntax is concerned with trying to explain why certain types of structure are ungrammatical: it would perhaps not be too much of an exaggeration to say that whereas traditional grammars concentrate on *grammaticality* (i.e. on telling you how to form grammatical phrases and sentences), work on grammar within the Chomskyan paradigm tends to focus much more on explaining *ungrammaticality* (i.e. on explaining why certain types of structures are ungrammatical).

A second source of introspective evidence about the nature of grammatical competence relates to native speaker intuitions about the *interpretation* of words, phrases and sentences in their native language. For example, any native speaker of English can tell you that a sentence such as:

(2) Sam loves you more than Jim

is ambiguous, and has two different interpretations which can be paraphrased as in (3a–b) below:

(3) (a) Sam loves you more than Jim loves you
     (b) Sam loves you more than Sam loves Jim

So, it seems that the native speaker's grammatical competence is reflected not only in intuitions about *grammaticality*, but also in intuitions about *interpretation*.

1.3 Criteria of adequacy

Given that a grammar of a language is a model of the competence of a fluent speaker of the language, and given that competence is reflected in intuitions about grammaticality and interpretation, an important criterion of adequacy for a grammar of any natural language is that of *descriptive adequacy*. We can say that a grammar of a given language is *descriptively adequate* if it correctly describes whether any given string (i.e. sequence) of words in a language is or isn't grammatical, and also correctly describes what interpretation(s) the relevant string has. So, for example, a grammar of English would be descriptively adequate in the relevant respects if it told us that sentences like (1a) above are grammatical in English but those like (1b) are ungrammatical, and if it told us that sentences like (2) are ambiguous as between the two interpretations paraphrased in (3a) and (3b): conversely, our grammar would be descriptively inadequate if it wrongly told us that both the sentences in (1a–b) are grammatical in English, or that (2) can be paraphrased as in (3a), but not as in (3b).

While the concern of the descriptive linguist is to devise grammars of particular languages, the concern of the theoretical linguist is to devise a *theory of grammar*. A theory of grammar is a set of hypotheses about the nature of possible and impossible grammars of *natural* (i.e. human) languages: hence, a theory of grammar answers questions like: 'What are the inherent properties which natural language grammars do and don't possess?' Just as there are *criteria of adequacy* for grammars, so too there are a number of criteria which any adequate theory of grammar must satisfy. One obvious criterion is *universality*, in the sense that a theory of grammar should provide us with the tools needed to describe the grammar of *any* natural language adequately; after all, a theory of grammar would be of little interest if it enabled us to describe the grammar of English and French, but not that of Swahili or Chinese. So, what we mean by saying that *universality* is a criterion of adequacy for a theory of grammar is that a theory of grammar must enable us to devise a descriptively adequate grammar for every natural language: in other words, our ultimate goal is to develop a *theory of Universal Grammar*. In the linguistic literature, it is a standard convention to abbreviate the term *Universal Grammar* to *UG*, and hence to talk of devising a *theory of UG*.

However, since the ultimate goal of any theory is *explanation*, it is not enough for a theory of Universal Grammar simply to list sets of universal properties of natural language grammars; on the contrary, a theory of UG must seek to *explain* the relevant properties. So, a key question for any adequate theory of UG to answer is: '*Why* do natural language grammars have the properties they do?' The requirement that a theory should *explain* why grammars have the properties they do is conventionally referred to as the criterion of *explanatory adequacy*.

Since the theory of Universal Grammar is concerned with characterizing the properties of *natural* (i.e. human) language grammars, an important question which we want our theory of UG to answer is: 'What are the essential defining characteristics of natural languages which differentiate them from, for example, artificial languages like those used in mathematics and computing (e.g. Basic, Prolog, etc.), or from animal communication systems (e.g. the tail-wagging dance performed by bees to communicate the location of a food source to other bees)?' It therefore follows that the descriptive apparatus which our theory of Universal Grammar allows us to make use of in devising natural language grammars must not be so powerful that it can be used to describe not only natural languages, but also computer languages or animal communication systems (since any such excessively powerful theory wouldn't be able to pinpoint the criterial properties of natural languages which differentiate them from other types of communication system). In other words, a third condition which we have to impose on our theory of language is that it be maximally *restrictive*: that is, we want our theory to provide us with technical devices which are so *constrained* in their expressive power that they can only be used to describe natural languages, and are not appropriate for the description of other communication systems. Any such restrictive theory would then enable us to characterize the very essence of natural language.

The neurophysiological mechanisms which underlie linguistic competence make it possible for young children to *acquire* language in a remarkably short period of time: children generally start to form elementary two-word structures at around 18 months of age, and by the age of 30 months have acquired a wide range of different grammatical constructions and are able to produce sentences of considerable grammatical complexity. Accordingly, a fourth condition which any adequate linguistic theory must meet is that of *learnability*: it must provide grammars which are learnable by young children in a relatively short period of time.

A related requirement is that linguistic theory should provide grammars which make use of the *minimal* theoretical apparatus required to provide a descriptively adequate characterization of linguistic phenomena: in other words, grammars should be as simple as possible. Much of the work in syntax in the 1980s involved the postulation of ever more complex structures and principles: as a reaction to the excessive complexity of this kind of work, Chomsky in the 1990s has made **minimalism** (i.e. the requirement to minimize the theoretical and descriptive apparatus used to describe language) the cornerstone of linguistic theory. The *minimalist program for linguistic theory* which he has been developing (cf. Chomsky 1995c) is motivated to a large extent by the desire to minimize the acquisition burden placed on the child, and thereby maximize the learnability of natural language grammars.

1.4 Language faculty

Our brief discussion of learnability leads us naturally to consider the goal of developing a *theory of the acquisition of grammar*. An acquisition theory is concerned with the question of how children acquire grammars of their native languages. One of the most fundamental questions which an acquisition theory seeks to answer is: 'How and when do children develop an initial grammar of the language they are acquiring, and what are the subsequent stages they go through in their grammatical development?'

Children generally produce their first recognizable word (e.g. *Mama* or *Dada*) by the age of 12 months. For the next 6 months or so, there is little apparent evidence of grammatical development, although the child's productive vocabulary typically increases by about three words a month until it reaches around a couple of dozen words at age 18 months. Throughout this *single-word stage*, children's utterances comprise single words spoken in isolation: e.g. a child may say *Apple* when reaching for an apple, or *Up* when wanting to get on her mother's knee. During the single-word stage, there is no evidence of the acquisition of grammar, in that children do not make productive use of *inflections* (e.g. they don't add the plural +*s* ending to nouns, or the past tense +*d* ending to verbs), and don't productively combine words together to form two- and three-word utterances. At around the age of 18 months, we find the first signs of the acquisition of grammar: children start to make productive use of inflections (e.g. using plural nouns like *doggies* alongside the singular form *doggy*, and participles like *going* alongside the uninflected verb form *go*), and similarly start to produce elementary two- and three-word utterances such as *Want Teddy*, *Eating cookie*, *Dolly go bed*, etc. From this point on, there is a rapid expansion in their grammatical development, so that by the age of around 30 months, children have typically acquired most of the inflections and core grammatical constructions used in English, and are able to produce adultlike sentences such as *Where's Mummy gone? What's Daddy doing? Can we go to the zoo, Daddy?* etc. (though of course occasional morphological or syntactic errors occur – cf. e.g. *We goed there with Daddy, What we can do?* etc.).

Thus, the central phenomenon which any theory of language acquisition must seek to explain is this: how is it that after a long drawn-out period of many months in which there is no obvious sign of grammatical development, at around the age of 18 months there is a sudden *spurt* as multiword speech starts to emerge, and a phenomenal growth in grammatical development then takes place over the next twelve months? This *uniformity* and (once the spurt has started) *rapidity* in the pattern of children's linguistic development are the central facts which a theory of language acquisition must seek to explain. But how?

Chomsky maintains that the most plausible explanation for the uniformity and rapidity of first language acquisition is to posit that the course of acquisition is determined by a biologically endowed innate *language faculty* (or *language acquisition program*, to borrow a computer software metaphor) within the brain, which provides children with a (genetically transmitted) algorithm (i.e. set of procedures) for developing a grammar, on the basis of their linguistic *experience* (i.e. on the basis of the speech input they receive). The way in which Chomsky visualizes the acquisition process can be represented schematically as in (4) below (where *L* is the language being acquired):

(4)

Children acquiring a language will observe people around them using the language, and the set of expressions in the language which the child hears – and the contexts in which they are used – in the course of acquiring the language constitute the child's linguistic *experience* of the language. This experience serves as input to the child's *language faculty*, which provides the child with a procedure for (subconsciously) analysing the experience in such a way as to devise a *grammar* of the language being acquired. Thus, the input to the language faculty is the child's experience, and the output of the language faculty is a grammar of the language being acquired.

The hypothesis that the course of language acquisition is determined by an innate language faculty is known popularly as the *innateness hypothesis*. Chomsky maintains that language acquisition is an activity unique to human beings, and different in kind from any other type of learning which human beings experience, so that learning a language involves mental processes entirely distinct from those involved in e.g. learning to play chess, or learning to ride a bicycle.

One piece of evidence which Chomsky adduces in support of positing an innate language faculty unique to humans is that language acquisition is a *species-specific* ability, possessed only by human beings: cf.

> Whatever evidence we do have seems to me to support the view that the ability to acquire and use language is a species-specific human capacity, that there are very deep and restrictive principles that determine the nature of human language and are rooted in the specific character of the human mind. (Chomsky 1972a, p. 102)

Moreover, he notes, language acquisition is an ability which all humans possess, entirely independently of their general intelligence: cf.

> Even at low levels of intelligence, at pathological levels, we find a command of language that is totally unattainable by an ape that may, in other respects, surpass a human imbecile in problem-solving activity and other adaptive behavior. (Chomsky 1972a, p. 10)

In addition, the apparent *uniformity* in the pattern of acquisition suggests that children have genetic guidance in the task of constructing a grammar of their native language: cf.

> We know that the grammars that are in fact constructed vary only slightly among speakers of the same language, despite wide variations not only in intelligence but also in the conditions under which language is acquired. (Chomsky 1972a, p. 79)

Moreover, there is similar *uniformity* in the types of grammars developed by different speakers of a given language: cf.

> Different speakers of the same language, with somewhat different experience and training, nonetheless acquire grammars that are remarkably similar. (Chomsky 1972a, p. 13)

Furthermore, the *rapidity* of acquisition (once the *grammar spurt* has started) also points to genetic guidance in grammar construction:

> Otherwise it is impossible to explain how children come to construct grammars . . . under the given conditions of time and access to data. (Chomsky 1972a, p. 113)

(The sequence 'under . . . data' means simply 'in so short a time, and on the basis of such limited linguistic experience'.) What makes the *uniformity* and *rapidity* of acquisition even more remarkable is the fact that the child's linguistic experience is often *degenerate* (i.e. imperfect), since it is based on the linguistic performance of adult speakers, and this may be a poor reflection of their competence: cf.

> A good deal of normal speech consists of false starts, disconnected phrases, and other deviations from idealized competence. (Chomsky 1972a, p. 158)

If much of the speech input which children receive is ungrammatical (because of performance errors), how is it that they can use this degenerate experience to develop a (competence) grammar which specifies how to form grammatical sentences? Chomsky's answer is to draw the following analogy:

> Descartes asks: how is it when we see a sort of irregular figure drawn in front of us we see it as a triangle? He observes, quite correctly, that there's a disparity between the data presented to us and the percept that we construct. And he argues, I think quite plausibly, that we see the figure as a triangle because there's something about the nature of our minds which makes the image of a triangle easily constructible by the mind. (Chomsky 1968, p. 687)

The obvious implication is that in much the same way as we are genetically predisposed to analyse shapes (however irregular) as having specific geometrical properties, so too we are genetically predisposed to analyse sentences (however ungrammatical) as having specific grammatical properties. A further argument Chomsky uses in support of the innateness hypothesis relates to the fact that language acquisition is an entirely subconscious and involuntary activity (in the sense that you can't consciously *choose* whether or not to acquire your native language – though you can choose whether or not you wish to learn chess); it is also an activity which is largely unguided (in the sense that parents don't *teach* children to talk): cf.

> Children acquire . . . languages quite successfully even though no special care is taken to teach them and no special attention is given to their progress. (Chomsky 1965, pp. 200–1)

The implication is that we don't *learn* to have a native language, any more than we learn to have arms or legs; the ability to acquire a native language is part of our genetic endowment – just like the ability to learn to walk.

1.5 Creativity

An essential tenet of Chomsky's theory is that the nature of the language acquisition process in humans is profoundly different in character from animal learning processes with which we are familiar – for instance, the process by which animals learn to respond to specific stimuli (e.g. learn to press buttons in specific combinations in order to get food), and so develop a *habit structure* (i.e. a conditioned response to a specific type of stimulus). If language acquisition involved this kind of conditioned response, we should expect it to be a purely *imitative* process – i.e. a process in which children simply memorize lists of sentences which they have heard people around them produce. However (Chomsky argues), language acquisition is not a purely imitative process, but rather an inherently *creative* process. Evidence which supports this conclusion is that when we acquire a language, we are capable of producing and understanding not only sentences we have previously heard, but also *novel sentences* which we have never encountered before: cf.

> The most striking aspect of linguistic competence is what we may call the *creativity* of language, that is, the speaker's ability to produce new sentences, sentences that are immediately understood by other speakers although they bear no physical resemblance to sentences which are familiar. (Chomsky 1966, p. 11)

(By *resemblance* here, Chomsky means *identity*: i.e. he is saying that we can produce and understand sentences which are not exact word-for-word repetitions of any sentences we have ever heard before.) To cite one of Chomsky's own examples (from p. 132 of the published version of *The Logical Structure of Linguistic Theory* – written in 1955 but published in 1975), you have probably never encountered any of the following sentences before:

(5) (a)   Look at the cross-eyed elephant
    (b)   Look at the cross-eyed kindness
    (c)   Look at the cross-eyed from

And yet – if you are a native speaker of English – you intuitively know that (5a) is perfectly OK in English (though of course, the zoo-keepers among you might object that elephants can't be cross-eyed). By contrast, (5b) is decidedly odd, and (5c) seems nonsensical. Any native speaker is capable of producing and understanding such *novel utterances*, or making judgments about their acceptability. What is the significance of the fact that all native speakers have the ability to produce, understand and make judgments about sentences that they have not come across before? Chomsky argues that this essential creativity of language shows that language can't simply be learned by imitation: i.e. learning a language doesn't simply involve rote-learning a list of sentences produced by others, and repeating them parrot-fashion. On the contrary, as Chomsky notes:

> The normal use of language is innovative in the sense that much of what we say in the course of normal language use is entirely new, not a repetition of anything that we have heard before, and not even similar in pattern – in any useful sense of the terms 'similar' and 'pattern' – to sentences or discourse that we have heard in the past. (Chomsky 1972a, p. 12)

The novelty of most sentences that we produce or hear provides a strong argument against the claim made by behavioural psychologists that language-learning is a purely imitative process which involves the acquisition of a set of *linguistic habits*.

Empirical studies of children acquiring their native languages would seem to bear out Chomsky's claim that language acquisition is not an imitative but a creative process. Consider, for example, the process by which children acquire grammatical inflections. On the *imitative* view, acquisition would involve memorization of a set of inflected forms which children have previously encountered (so that e.g. children would only be able to form the plural of a noun which they have previously heard used in the plural). By contrast, on the *creative* view, acquisition would be a very different kind of process: on the basis of hearing a set of singular/plural contrasts such as *dog/dogs, car/cars, bed/beds, ball/balls, pin/pins*, etc. the child would formulate (i.e. create) a generalization to the effect that 'You form the plural by adding an *+s* ending.' These two different views of acquisition would lead to entirely different predictions about whether or not children would be able to form *novel plurals* (i.e. plurals of words which they have not previously heard used in the plural). The most obvious way of testing whether or not children can form novel plurals is by seeing whether or not they can pluralize *nonsense words* (i.e. invented words which are not in general use). This is precisely what Jean Berko did in an experiment described in her classic 1958 paper 'The child's learning of English morphology'. She showed a group of young children a picture of an imaginary animal, and told them that it was called a *wug*; she then showed them a picture of two of the same animals, and asked the children what the animals were. The children replied 'Wugs'. The significance of this experiment is that it shows that children do not learn plurals by simple imitation, but rather have the ability to *create* novel plural forms. This suggests that the acquisition of grammatical inflections involves the creation of a set of hypotheses about how such inflections are used, and thus supports the *creative* rather than the *imitative* view of language acquisition.

Another source of evidence supporting the conclusion that children learn language by creating generalizations comes from *errors* that they produce. A case in point are overgeneralized past-tense forms like *comed, goed, seed, buyed, bringed*, etc. frequently used by young children. Such forms cannot have been learned by imitation of adult speech, since they do not occur in adult speech (instead, we find *came, went, saw, bought, brought*). So how is it that children produce such forms? The obvious answer is that, on the basis of pairs such as *love/loved, close/closed, use/used*, etc., children create for themselves a generalization to the effect that 'You form the past tense by adding *+d* to the stem of the verb'; the generalization is then applied to irregular verbs like *come, go, see, buy, bring*, etc.

The observations above suggest that children acquire grammatical inflections (e.g. past-tense endings, plural endings, etc.) by creating for themselves (albeit subconsciously) a set of generalizations about how such inflections are used. There is parallel evidence that the acquisition of syntax is similarly a creative rather than an imitative process. Part of the evidence for this comes from the fact that young children frequently produce *novel structures* (i.e. structures which cannot be word-for-word imitations of adult sentences, for the simple reason that the relevant structures are not found in adult speech). For example, Akmajian and Heny (1975, p. 17) report one group of three-year-old children producing questions like:

(6) (a)   Is I can do that?
     (b)   Is you should eat the apple?
     (c)   Is Ben did go?
     (d)   Is the apple juice won't spill?

Clearly, no adult English speaker would produce sentences like (6), so that they cannot be the product of simple imitation. How do the children come to produce them? The obvious answer is that on the basis of hearing adult sentences such as:

(7) (a)   Is Daddy going to the pub?

    (b)   Is he spending the night here?

    (c)   Is Mummy going shopping?

    (d)   Is Teddy in bed?

the children create for themselves the generalization that 'You form a question by putting *is* as the first word in the sentence.' Of course, the generalization is wrong (in the sense that this isn't how adults form questions) and will be corrected at a later stage of acquisition by the children. But these novel structures produced by young children provide evidence that acquiring a grammar involves formulating a set of generalizations about how inflections are used, and how words are combined together to form phrases and sentences. Thus, its inherently *creative* nature makes language acquisition a qualitatively different process from animal learning behaviour, so reinforcing Chomsky's view that language acquisition is the product of a species-specific language faculty.

1.6 Principles

If human beings do indeed have a genetically endowed *language faculty*, an obvious question to ask is what are the defining characteristics of the language faculty. An important point to note in this regard is that children can in principle acquire *any* natural language as their native language (e.g. Bosnian orphans brought up by English-speaking foster parents in an English-speaking community acquire English as their first language). It therefore follows that the language faculty must incorporate a set of **principles of Universal Grammar/UG** – in the sense that the language faculty must be such as to allow the child to develop a grammar of *any* natural language on the basis of suitable linguistic experience of the language (i.e. sufficient speech input). Experience of a particular language *L* (examples of words, phrases and sentences in L which the child hears produced by native speakers of L) serves as input to principles of UG which are an inherent part of the child's language faculty, and UG then provides the child with an algorithm for developing a grammar of L.

If the acquisition of grammatical competence is indeed controlled by a genetically endowed language faculty incorporating principles of Universal Grammar, then it follows that certain aspects of child (or adult) competence are known without experience, and hence must be part of the genetic blueprint for language with which we are biologically endowed at birth. Such aspects of language would not have to be learned, precisely because they form part of the child's genetic inheritance. If we make the (not unnatural) assumption that the language faculty does not vary significantly from one (normal) human being to another, then it follows that those aspects of language which are innately determined will also be *universal*. Thus, in seeking to determine the nature of the language faculty, we are in effect looking for universal principles which determine the very structure of language – principles which govern the kinds of grammatical operations which are (and are not) permitted in natural languages, principles of such an abstract nature that they could not plausibly have been learned on the basis of experience.

But how can we discover what these abstract universal principles are which constrain the range of grammatical operations permitted in natural language grammars? The answer is that since the relevant principles are posited to be universal, it follows that they will constrain the application of *every* grammatical operation in *every* language. Thus, detailed observation of even *one* grammatical operation in *one* language should reveal evidence of the operation of principles of UG (Universal Grammar). By way of illustration, let's consider how *yes–no questions* are formed in English (i.e. questions to which 'Yes' and 'No' are appropriate as one-word answers). If we compare a simple declarative sentence (= statement) like (8a) below with its interrogative (= question) counterpart (8b):

(8) (a)   *Memories* **will** fade away
    (b)   **Will** *memories* fade away?

we see that the yes–no question in (8b) appears to be formed by preposing the word *will* in front of the word *memories* (this particular grammatical operation is often referred to as *interrogative inversion*, the word *inversion* here serving to indicate a change of word order). We might therefore imagine that inversion involves some operation such as the following:

(9)   Move the second word in a sentence in front of the first word

However, it's easy enough to show that (9) is *descriptively inadequate*. For example, it would wrongly predict that the interrogative counterpart of (10a) below would be (10b):

(10) (a)   *Memories* **of** happiness will fade away
     (b)   ***Of** *memories* happiness will fade away?

Why is (9) wrong? The most principled answer which we can hope to give is that grammars of natural languages simply don't work like that. More specifically, we might suppose that what's wrong with an operation like (9) is that it is *structure-independent*, in the sense that it operates independently of (i.e. makes no reference to) the grammatical structure of the sentence, so that you don't need to know what the grammatical structure of the sentence is (i.e. which words belong to which grammatical categories, or which words modify which other words, etc.) in order to know how inversion works.

13

In fact, no linguist has ever claimed to have found any grammatical operation like (9) which operates in a completely structure-independent fashion in any natural language. It therefore seems reasonable to suppose that we would want to exclude structure-independent operations like (9) from our theory of grammar. One way of doing this would be to incorporate into our theory of Universal Grammar a principle such as (11) below:

(11)   STRUCTURE DEPENDENCE PRINCIPLE
         All grammatical operations are structure-dependent.

What this means is that grammatical operations only apply to certain types of grammatical structure, not others. Let's look briefly at what is meant by **grammatical structure** in this context.

It is traditionally said that sentences are structured out of words, and phrases, each of which belongs to a specific **grammatical category** and serves a specific **grammatical function** within the sentence containing it. (We shall turn to consider categories in detail in the next two chapters, so for the time being don't worry if you're not familiar with the terminology used here.) To see what we mean by this, consider the grammatical structure of our (pessimistic) sentence (10a) *Memories of happiness will fade away*. In traditional grammatical analysis, each of the words in the sentence would be assigned to a specific *grammatical category*: e.g. *memories* and *happiness* belong to the category of **noun**, *fade* is a **verb**, *will* is an **auxiliary** (so called because it provides additional – hence *auxiliary* – information about the action or process described by the verb, in this case indicating that the process of fading away will take place in the future), *of* is a **preposition**, and *away* is traditionally classed as an **adverb** (though might be analysed as a prepositional particle). Certain of the words in the sentence combine together to form phrases, and each of these phrases in turn belongs to a specific category: for example, the string *memories of happiness* is a **noun phrase**, and the string *fade away* is a **verb phrase**. These two phrases are joined together by the auxiliary *will*, thereby forming the overall **sentence** *Memories of happiness will fade away*. Each of the various constituents (i.e. component parts) of the sentence also serves a specific *grammatical function*. For example, the noun phrase *memories of happiness* serves the grammatical function of being the **subject** of the auxiliary *will*, whereas the verb phrase *fade away* serves the function of being the **complement** of *will*. (See the *glossary* if you are unfamiliar with these terms.)

Having looked briefly at some traditional assumptions about grammatical structure, let's now return to our earlier discussion and see how we might develop a *structure-dependent* approach to the phenomenon of interrogative inversion. In keeping with suggestions made in traditional grammars, we might suppose that inversion involves an operation such as the following:

(12)   Move an *auxiliary* in front of a preceding *noun expression* which
            functions as its subject.

(where *noun expression* can be glossed as 'expression comprising a noun together
with any expressions modifying the noun'). Such a characterization is overtly
structure-dependent in the sense that it presupposes knowledge of the grammatical
structure of a given sentence – i.e. knowledge of what grammatical categories the various
expressions in the sentence belong to (e.g. *noun expression* and *auxiliary*), and what
grammatical function they serve (e.g. *subject*). Consequently, in order to know whether
inversion can apply in a given sentence, we need to know whether the sentence
contains a subject noun expression followed by an auxiliary verb. In (8a), *memories* is
a noun expression (comprising the single noun *memories*), and serves the grammatical
function of being the subject of the auxiliary *will*. Thus, our structure-dependent characterization of inversion in (12) correctly predicts that (8b) *Will memories fade away?*
is the question counterpart of (8a) *Memories will fade away*. Likewise, it correctly
predicts that the question counterpart of (10a) *Memories of happiness will fade away* is
Will memories of happiness fade away?, in which we have an auxiliary (= *will*)
inverted with a noun expression (the noun phrase *memories of happiness*) which functions as its subject. Hence, the structure-dependent account makes correct predictions
about both sets of sentences.

But no less importantly, our structure-dependent description of inversion also
correctly predicts that inversion is not possible in cases such as:

(13) (a)   *Down* **will** come taxes
     (b)   ***Will** down* come taxes?

(14 (a)   *John* **received** a prize
     (b)   ***Received** John* a prize?

In (13b) we have the prepositional particle *down* inverted with the auxiliary *will*; and in
(14b) we have the noun expression *John* inverted with the verb *received*. Since in
neither case do we have inversion of a subject noun expression with an auxiliary, our
structure-dependent characterization of inversion correctly predicts that inversion
cannot take place here. By contrast, our structure-independent characterization of
inversion in (9) wrongly predicts that inversion should be possible in both cases.

So, the phenomenon of inversion in questions provides us with clear evidence in
support of incorporating into our theory of grammar the **structure dependence principle** (11), which specifies that all grammatical operations are sensitive to the grammatical structure of the sentences they apply to. It seems reasonable to suppose that (11) is
a fundamental principle of Universal Grammar, so that (11) holds for all grammars of
all natural languages. If (11) is universal, and if we assume that abstract grammatical
principles which are universal are part of our biological endowment, then the natural

15

conclusion to reach is that (11) is a principle which is incorporated into the language faculty, and which thus forms part of the child's genetic blueprint for a grammar. If so, the innate language faculty incorporates a set of universal grammatical principles (such as the structure dependence principle): these are conventionally referred to as **UG principles** or **principles of UG**. If the language faculty incorporates a theory of Universal Grammar which provides the child with an algorithm (i.e. set of procedures) for developing a grammar of any language, we can revise our earlier model of acquisition given in (4) above as (15) below:

(15)

In this (revised) model, the child's experience is processed by the UG module which is an integral part of the language faculty.

A theory of grammar which posits that the internal grammatical structure of words, phrases and sentences in natural language is determined by innate principles of UG offers the important advantage that it minimizes the burden of *grammatical learning* imposed on the child. This is a vital consideration, since we saw earlier that *learnability* is a criterion of adequacy for any theory of grammar – i.e. any adequate theory of grammar must be able to explain how children come to learn the grammar of their native language(s) in such a rapid and uniform fashion. The **UG theory** developed by Chomsky accounts for the rapidity of the child's grammatical development by positing that there is a universal set of innately endowed grammatical principles which determine the nature of grammatical structure and the range of grammatical operations found in natural language grammars. Since UG principles which are innately endowed do not have to be learned by the child, the theory of UG minimizes the learning load placed on the child, and thereby maximizes the learnability of natural language grammars.

1.7 Parameters

Thus far, we have argued that the language faculty incorporates a set of universal grammatical principles (= *UG principles*) which are invariant across languages, and which determine the nature and acquisition of grammatical structure. However, it clearly cannot be that *all* aspects of the grammatical structure of languages are determined by innate grammatical principles; if this were so, all languages would have precisely the same grammatical structure, and there would then be no *structural* learning involved in language acquisition (i.e. no need for children to learn anything about the grammatical structure of sentences in the language they are acquiring), only *lexical* learning (viz. learning about the *lexis* (= vocabulary) of the language – i.e. learning the words in the language and their idiosyncratic linguistic properties, e.g. whether a given item has an irregular plural form, etc.). However, it is quite clear that although there are universal principles which determine the broad outlines of the grammatical structure of words, phrases and sentences in every natural language, there are also language-particular aspects of grammatical structure which children have to *learn* as part of the task of acquiring their native language. Thus, language acquisition involves not only *lexical* learning, but also some *structural* learning. Our main concern here is to examine structural learning, and what it tells us about the language acquisition process.

Clearly, structural learning is not going to involve learning those aspects of structure which are determined by *universal* (hence innate) grammatical principles. Rather, structural learning will be limited to those **parameters** (i.e. 'dimensions' or 'aspects') of grammatical structure which are subject to language-particular variation (i.e. which vary from one language to another). In other words, structural learning will be limited to *parametrized* aspects of structure (i.e. those aspects of structure which are subject to parametric variation from one language to another). Thus, the obvious way to determine just what aspects of the grammatical structure of their native language children have to *learn* is to examine the range of parametric variation in grammatical structure between different (adult) natural languages.

We can illustrate one type of parametric variation across languages in terms of the following contrast between the Italian examples in (16 a–b) below, and their English counterparts in (16 c–d):

(16) (a) Maria parla francese
(b) Parla francese
(c) Maria speaks French
(d) *Speaks French

As we see from (16a/c), in both Italian and English, finite verbs (i.e. verbs which carry present/past etc. tense) like *parla/speaks* license (i.e. 'can have') an overt subject like *Maria*; the two languages differ, however, in that finite verbs also license a null (i.e. 'missing but understood') subject in Italian (as we see from the fact that (16b) is grammatical in Italian, and is understood as meaning '*He/she* speaks French'), but not in English (so that (16d) is ungrammatical in English). Thus, finite verbs in a language like Italian license either overt or covert (= null) subjects, but in a different kind of language like English, finite verbs license only overt subjects, not null subjects. We might describe the differences between the two languages by saying that Italian is a **null subject language**, whereas English is a **non-null subject language**. More generally, there appears to be parametric variation between languages as to whether or not they allow finite verbs to have null subjects. The relevant parameter (termed the **null subject parameter**) would appear to be a binary one, with only two possible settings, viz. 'does/doesn't allow finite verbs to have null subjects'. There appears to be no language which allows the subjects of some finite verbs to be null, but not others – e.g. no language in which it is OK to say *Drinks wine* (meaning 'He/she drinks wine') but not

OK to say *Eats pasta* (meaning 'He/she eats pasta'). The range of grammatical variation found across languages appears to be strictly limited: there seem to be just two possibilities – languages either do or don't systematically allow finite verbs to have null subjects.

A more familiar aspect of grammatical structure which is obviously parametrized relates to *word order*, in that different types of language have different word orders in specific types of construction. One type of word order variation can be illustrated in relation to the following contrast between English and Chinese:

(17) (a)   *What* do you think he will say?

    (b)   Ni   xiangxin ta hui shuo *shenme*

             you think   he will say *what*?

In English wh-questions (questions which contain a wh-word, i.e. a word like *what/where/when/why* beginning with *wh-*), the wh-expression is moved to the beginning of the sentence. By contrast, in Chinese, the wh-word does not move to the front of the sentence, but rather remains *in situ* (i.e. in the same place as would be occupied by a corresponding noninterrogative expression), so that *shenme* 'what' is positioned after the verb *shuo* 'say' because it is the complement of the verb, and complements are normally positioned after their verbs in Chinese. Thus, another parameter of variation between languages is the **wh-parameter** – i.e. the parameter which determines whether wh-expressions can be fronted (i.e. moved to the front of the overall interrogative structure containing them) or not. Interestingly, this parameter again appears to be one which is *binary* in nature, in that it allows for only two possibilities – viz. a language either does or doesn't allow **wh-movement** (i.e. movement of wh-expressions to the front of the sentence). Many other possibilities for wh-movement just don't seem to occur in natural language: for example, there is no language in which the counterpart of *who?* undergoes wh-fronting but not the counterpart of *what?* (i.e. no language in which it is OK to ask '*Who* did you see?' but not '*What* did you see?'). Likewise, there is no language in which wh-complements of some verbs can undergo fronting, but not wh-complements of other verbs (e.g. no language in which it is OK to ask 'What did he *see*?', but not 'What did he *hear*?'). It would seem that the range of parametric variation found with respect to wh-fronting is strictly limited to just two possibilities: viz. a language either does or doesn't allow wh-expressions to be systematically fronted.

A second type of word-order variation which we find concerns the relative position of **heads** and **complements** within phrases. It is a general (indeed, universal) property of phrases that every phrase has a head word which determines the nature of the overall phrase. For example, an expression such as *students of linguistics* is a plural noun phrase, because its **head** word (i.e. the key word in the phrase whose nature determines the properties of the overall phrase) is the plural noun *students*. The following expression *of linguistics* which combines with the head noun *students* to expand it into the noun phrase *students of linguistics* is said to be the **complement** of the noun *students*. In much the same way, an expression such as *in the kitchen* is a prepositional phrase which comprises the head preposition *in* and its complement *the kitchen*. Likewise, an expression such as *stay with me* is a verb phrase which comprises the head verb *stay* and its complement *with me*. And similarly, an expression such as *fond of fast food* is an adjectival phrase formed by combining the head adjective *fond* with the complement *of fast food*.

In English (and many other languages) head nouns, verbs, prepositions, adjectives, etc. precede their complements; however, there are also languages like Korean in which heads follow their complements. Thus, in informal terms, we might say that English is a **head-first** language, whereas Korean is a **head-last** language. The differences between the two languages can be illustrated by comparing the English examples in (18) below with their Korean counterparts in (19):

(18) (a)   Close the door

     (b)   desire for change

(19) (a)   Moonul dadala

             door   close

     (b)   byunhwa-edaehan kalmang

             change-for   desire

In the English verb phrase *close the door* in (18a), the head verb *close* precedes its complement *the door*; if we suppose that *the door* is a determiner phrase, then the head of the phrase (= the determiner *the*) precedes its complement (= the noun *door*). Likewise, in the English noun phrase *desire for change* in (18b), the head noun *desire* precedes its complement *for change*; the complement *for change* is in turn a prepositional phrase in which the head preposition *for* likewise precedes its complement *change*. Since English consistently positions heads before complements, it is a *head-first* language.

By contrast, we find precisely the opposite ordering in Korean. In the verb phrase *moonul dadala* (literally 'door close') in (19a), the head verb *dadala* 'close' follows its complement *moonul* 'door'; likewise, in the noun phrase *byunhwa-edaehan kalmang* (literally 'change-for desire') in (19b) the head noun *kalmang* 'desire' follows its complement *byunhwa-edaehan* 'change-for'; the complement *byunhwa-edaehan* 'change-for' is in turn a prepositional phrase whose head preposition *edaehan* 'for' follows its complement *byunhwa* 'change' (so that *edaehan* 'for' might more appropriately be called a *postposition*). Since Korean consistently positions heads *after* their complements, it is a *head-last* language. Given that English is *head-first* and Korean *head-last*, it is clear that the relative positioning of heads with respect to their complements is one word-order parameter along which languages will differ; the relevant parameter might be referred to as the **head (position) parameter**.

It should be noted, however, that word-order variation in respect of the relative positioning of heads and complements falls within narrowly circumscribed limits. There are many different logically possible types of word-order variation which just don't seem to occur in natural languages. For example, we might imagine that in a given language some verbs would precede and others follow their complements, so that (for example) if two new hypothetical verbs like *scrunge* and *plurg* were coined in English, then *scrunge* might take a following complement, and *plurg* a preceding complement. And yet, this doesn't ever seem to happen (rather, *all* verbs typically occupy the same position in a given language with respect to a given type of complement).

What all of this suggests is that there are universal constraints on the range of parametric variation found across languages in respect of the relative ordering of heads and complements. It would seem as if there are only two different possibilities which the theory of grammar allows for, so that a given language must be either *head-first* (and so consistently position all heads before all their complements) or *head-last* (and so consistently position all heads after all their complements). Many other logically possible orderings of heads with respect to complements simply appear not to be found in natural language grammars. The obvious question to ask is why this should be.

The answer given by Chomsky is that the theory of Universal Grammar which is wired into the language faculty imposes genetic constraints on the range of parametric variation permitted in natural language grammars. In the case of the **head parameter** (i.e. the parameter which determines the relative positioning of heads with respect to their complements), UG allows only a binary set of possibilities – namely that a language may either be consistently *head-first* or consistently *head-last*. If this is so, then the only structural learning which children have to undertake when learning the word-order properties of the relevant class of constructions is to choose (on the basis of their linguistic experience) which of the two alternative settings of the parameter allowed by UG (viz. *head-first* or *head-last*) is the appropriate one for the language being acquired.

1.8   Parameter-setting

We might generalize our discussion at this point in the following terms. If the **head parameter** reduces to a simple binary choice, and if the **wh-parameter** and the **null subject parameter** also involve binary choices, it seems implausible that binarity could be an accidental property of these particular parameters. Rather, it seems much more likely that it is an inherent property of parameters that they constrain the range of structural variation between languages, and limit it to a simple binary choice. Generalizing still further, let us suppose that *all* grammatical variation between languages can be characterized in terms of a set of parameters, and that for each parameter, UG (= Universal Grammar) specifies a binary choice of possible values for the parameter. If so, then the only *structural learning* which children face in acquiring their native language is the task of determining the appropriate value for each of the relevant structural parameters along which languages vary. (Of course, children also face the formidable task of *lexical learning* – i.e. building up their vocabulary in the relevant language.)

If our reasoning here is along the right lines, then it leads us to the following view of the language acquisition process. The central task which the child faces in acquiring a language is to construct a grammar of the language. The child's language faculty incorporates a theory of Universal Grammar which includes (i) a set of universal **principles** of grammatical structure, and (ii) a set of structural **parameters** which impose severe constraints on the range of structural variation permitted in natural languages (perhaps limiting the range of variation to a series of binary choices). Since universal principles of grammatical structure don't have to be learned, the child's structural learning task is limited to that of **parameter-setting** (i.e. determining an appropriate *setting* for each of the relevant structural parameters). For obvious reasons, the model outlined here has become known as the **principles-and-parameters theory** (= **PPT**) of language.

The PPT model clearly has important implications for the nature of the language acquisition process: more precisely, such a model would vastly reduce the complexity of the acquisition task which children face. It would lead us to expect that those structural principles of language which are invariant across languages will not have to be learned by the child, since they will be part of the child's genetic endowment: on the contrary, all that the child has to learn are those grammatical properties which are subject to parametric variation across languages. Moreover, the child's learning task will be further simplified if it turns out (as we have suggested here) that the values which a parameter can have fall within a narrowly specified range, perhaps characterizable in terms of a series of binary choices. This simplified parameter-setting conception of the child's acquisition task has given rise to a metaphorical acquisition model in which the child is visualized as having to *set* a series of switches in one of two positions (*up/down*) – each such switch representing a different structural parameter. In the case of the **head parameter** which we discussed above, we might hypothesize that if the switch is set in the *up* position, the language will be head-first, whereas if it is set in the *down* position, the language will be head-last. Of course, an obvious implication of the *switch* metaphor is that the switch must be set in *either* one position *or* the other, and so cannot be set in both positions. (This would preclude the possibility of a language having both head-first and head-last structures.)

The assumption that acquiring the syntax of a language involves the relatively simple task of setting a number of structural parameters provides a natural way of accounting for the fact that the acquisition of specific parameters appears to be a remarkably *rapid* and *error-free* process in young children. For example, young children acquiring English as their native language seem to set the **head parameter** at its appropriate *head-first* setting from the very earliest multiword utterances they produce (at around age 18 months), and seem to know (tacitly, not explicitly, of course) that English is a *head-first* language. For example, the earliest verb phrases and prepositional phrases produced by young children consistently show verbs and prepositions positioned before their complements, as structures such as the following indicate (produced by a young boy called Jem at age 20 months; head verbs or prepositions are italicized, and their complements are in non-italic print):

(20) (a) *Touch* heads. *Cuddle* book. *Want* crayons. *Want* malteser. *Open* door.
       Want biscuit. *Bang* bottom. *See* cats. *Sit* down

   (b) *On* mummy. *To* lady. *Without* shoe. *With* potty. *In* keyhole. *In* school. *On*
       carpet. *On* box. *With* crayons. *To* mummy

The obvious conclusion to be drawn is that children consistently position heads before their complements from the very earliest multiword utterances which they produce. They do not use different orders for different words of the same type (e.g. they don't position the verb *see* after its complement but the verb *want* before its complement), or for different types of words (e.g. they don't position verbs before and prepositions after their complements).

A natural question to ask at this point is how we can provide a principled explanation for the fact that from the very onset of multiword speech we find heads correctly positioned before their complements. The **principles-and-parameters** model of acquisition enables us to provide a principled explanation for why children manage to learn the relative ordering of heads and complements in such a rapid and error-free fashion. The answer provided by the model is that learning this aspect of word order involves the comparatively simple task of setting a binary parameter at its appropriate value. This task will be a relatively straightforward one if UG tells the child that the only possible choices are for a language to be uniformly *head-first* or uniformly *head-last*. Given such an assumption, the child could set the parameter correctly on the basis of minimal linguistic experience. For example, once the child is able to parse (i.e. grammatically analyse) an adult sentence such as *Help Daddy* and knows that it contains a verb phrase comprising the head verb *help* and its complement *Daddy*, then (on the assumption that UG specifies that *all* heads behave uniformly with regard to whether they are positioned before or after their complements), the child will automatically know that *all* heads in English are normally positioned before their complements.

1.9 Evidence

One of the questions posed by the parameter-setting model of acquisition outlined in the previous section is just how children come to arrive at the appropriate setting for a given parameter, and what kind(s) of evidence they make use of in setting parameters. As Chomsky notes (1981, pp. 8–9), there are two types of evidence which we might expect to be available to the language learner in principle – viz. *positive* and *negative* evidence. *Positive evidence* would comprise a set of observed sentences illustrating a particular phenomenon: for example, if children's experience (i.e. the speech input they receive) is made up of structures in which heads precede their complements, this provides them with positive evidence which enables them to set the **head parameter** appropriately. *Negative evidence* may be of two kinds – *direct* and *indirect*. Direct negative evidence comes from the correction of the child's errors by other speakers of the language. However, correction (contrary to what is often imagined) plays a fairly insignificant role in language acquisition, for two reasons. Firstly, correction is relatively infrequent: adults simply don't correct all the errors children make (if they did, children would soon become inhibited and discouraged from speaking); and secondly, children are notoriously unresponsive to correction, as the following dialogue (from McNeill 1966, p. 69) illustrates:

(21)   CHILD: Nobody don't like me
         ADULT: No, say: 'Nobody likes me'
         CHILD: Nobody don't like me
         (eight repetitions of this dialogue)
         ADULT: No, now listen carefully. Say 'Nobody likes me'
         CHILD: Oh, nobody don't likes me

Equally informative in this respect is the following conversation between me and my daughter Suzy when she was 49 months of age (as I was teasing her by drowning the toy duck she was playing with in the bath):

(22)   SUZY: Don't make me lost it!
         DADDY: No, don't make me *lose* it!
         SUZY: No, not *lose* . . . *losed*!

As you can see, when I attempted to correct Suzy, she responded by attempting to correct me.

Direct negative evidence might also take the form of *self-correction* by other speakers. Such *self-corrections* tend to have a characteristic intonation and rhythm of their own, and may be signalled by a variety of fillers (such as those italicized in (23) below):

(23) (a)   The picture was hanged . . . *or rather* **hung** . . . in the Tate Gallery
     (b)   The picture was hanged . . . *sorry* **hung** . . . in the Tate Gallery
     (c)   The picture was hanged . . . *I mean* **hung** . . . in the Tate Gallery

However, self-correction is arguably too infrequent a phenomenon to play a major role in the acquisition process.

Rather than say that children rely on direct negative evidence, we might instead suggest that they learn from *indirect negative evidence* (i.e. evidence relating to the *non-*

occurrence of certain types of structure). Suppose that a child's experience includes no examples of structures in which heads follow their complements (e.g. no prepositional phrases like **dinner after* in which the head preposition *after* follows its complement *dinner*, and no verb phrases such as **cake eat* in which the head verb *eat* follows its complement *cake*). On the basis of such *indirect negative evidence* (i.e. evidence based on the nonoccurrence of head-last structures), the child can infer that English is not a *head-last* language.

Although it might seem natural to suppose that indirect negative evidence plays some role in the acquisition process, there are potential *learnability* problems posed by any such claim. After all, the fact that a given construction does not occur in a given chunk of the child's experience does not provide conclusive evidence that the structure is ungrammatical, since it may well be that the nonoccurrence of the relevant structure in the relevant chunk of experience is an accidental (rather than a systematic) gap. Thus, the child would need to process a very large (in principle, *infinite*) chunk of experience in order to be sure that nonoccurrence reflects ungrammaticality. It seems implausible to suppose that children store massive chunks of experience in this way and search through it for negative evidence about the *nonoccurrence* of certain types of structure. In any case, given the assumption that parameters are binary, negative evidence becomes entirely unnecessary: after all, once the child hears structures like *with Daddy* in which the head preposition *with* precedes its complement *Daddy*, the child will have positive evidence that English licenses (i.e. allows) *head-first* structures; and given the assumption that the head parameter is a binary one, and that structures in a given language can be *either* uniformly head-first *or* uniformly head-last (but not both), then it follows (as a matter of logical necessity) that if English allows head-first structures, it will not allow head-last structures. Thus, in order for the child to know that English doesn't allow head-last structures, the child does not need negative evidence from the nonoccurrence of such structures, but rather can rely on positive evidence from the occurrence of the converse order in head-first structures (on the assumption that if a language is head-first, UG specifies that it cannot be head-last). And, as we have already noted, a minimal amount of positive evidence is required in order to identify English as a head-first language. Learnability considerations such as these have led Chomsky (1986a, p. 55) to conclude that 'There is good reason to believe that children learn language from positive evidence only.' The claim that children do not make use of negative evidence in setting parameters is known as the **no-negative-evidence** hypothesis; it is a hypothesis which is widely assumed in current acquisition research.

1.10 Summary

In this chapter, we have been concerned with the nature and acquisition of *grammar*. We began in §1.2 by arguing that a grammar of a language is a model of the grammatical competence of the fluent native speaker of the language, and that grammatical competence is reflected in native speakers' intuitions about grammaticality and interpretation. We suggested in §1.3 that, correspondingly, the main criterion of adequacy for grammars is that of *descriptive adequacy* (i.e. correctly accounting for grammaticality and interpretation). We noted that a theory of grammar is concerned with characterizing the general properties and organization of grammars of natural languages; we suggested that any adequate theory of language should be *universal, explanatory, restrictive, minimally complex* and should provide grammars which are *learnable* (in order to explain how children acquire grammars in such a rapid and error-free fashion). In §1.4 we outlined Chomsky's *innateness hypothesis*, under which the course of language acquisition is genetically predetermined by an innate *language faculty*. In §1.5 we argued that language acquisition is a *creative* process (which involves the child in formulating generalizations about how words, phrases and sentences are formed), not an imitative one. In §1.6 we argued that the language faculty must be assumed to incorporate a set of *principles of Universal Grammar/UG* (i.e. universal grammatical principles) if we are to account for children's ability to acquire the grammar of *any* language (on the basis of suitable exposure to the language). We argued that if principles of UG determine the nature of every grammatical process and structure in every natural language, close examination of any one type of grammatical structure or operation in any one language will reveal evidence for the operation of UG principles – and we saw that the operation of *inversion* in English provides evidence for postulating the **structure dependence principle**. In §1.7 we went on to suggest that languages differ in their structure along a range of different *grammatical parameters*. We looked at three such parameters – the **wh-parameter**, the **null subject parameter** and the **head parameter**. In §1.8 we argued that each of these parameters is inherently binary in nature, and that consequently the structural learning which the child faces involves *parameter-setting* – i.e. determining which of the two alternative settings provided by UG is the appropriate one for each parameter in the language being acquired. We further argued that if the only structural learning involved in language acquisition is parameter-setting, we should expect to find evidence that children correctly set parameters from the very onset of multiword speech: and we presented evidence to suggest that from their very earliest multiword utterances, children correctly set the **head parameter** at the *head-first* value appropriate for English. In §1.9 we asked what kind(s) of evidence children use in setting parameters, and concluded that they use *positive* evidence from their experience of the occurrence of some particular type of structure (e.g. head-first structures, or null-subject structures, or wh-fronted structures).

Workbook section
Exercise I

Say how many *morphemes* (i.e. grammatical units) each of the following words is composed of; identify the constituent morphemes, and say how you arrived at your answer:

Principles and parameters

1
    a unhappiness   b pleasurable   c redefinition
    d disturbances   e realistically   f impassivity
    g dematerialization   h hopelessness   i misery
    j antidisestablishmentarianism

[handwritten margin notes: Can't always answer many! how many depends on whether have a historical or modern view of it. We are interested in morphemes that + change part of speech]

For the purposes of this exercise, assume that a word is a compound of two or more morphemes if each of the potential constituent morphemes can occur with the same form, function and meaning when used as (part of) a different word.

Model answer for 1

The word *unhappiness* seems to be composed of three separate morphemes: a prefix *un+*, a stem *happy* and a suffix *+ness*. Each of these morphemes can occur elsewhere with essentially the same form, function and meaning. For example, the negative prefix *un+* can be attached to many other adjectives, giving compound forms such as *un+stable, un+popular, un+lucky, un+fair*, etc. The adjective stem *happy* can occur on its own as an independent word (cf. e.g. *She was very happy*). The suffix *+ness* can be added to many other adjectives to form nouns – cf. e.g. *sad+ness, clever+ness, devious+ness, thoughtless+ness*; it can also be attached to some adjectives carrying the negative prefix *un+*, as here: cf. *un+happi+ness, un+fair+ness, un+seemli+ness*, etc.

Exercise (II)

Discuss the interpretation(s) which the italicized expressions can have in the following sentences, giving an appropriate paraphrase for each interpretation:

1   He loves me more than *you*
2   *Who* do you want to/wanna help?
3   *John* is easy to recognize
4   Visiting *relatives* can be a nuisance *[handwritten: is/are]*
5   *Which DA* did the judge ask to investigate?
6   Italians like pasta, but not *fish*
7   *Your hair* needs cutting
8   *What* do you intend to do?
9   *The president* is eager to please *[handwritten: not "easy" like #3]*
10 *John* is certain to win the race

In particular, consider which word(s) the italicized expression is the subject or complement of, and whether it occupies the canonical (i.e. normal) position associated with a subject/complement. (See the entries for **subject** and **complement** in the glossary if these terms are unfamiliar.)

Model answer for 1

Sentence 1 is ambiguous as between two different interpretations which can be paraphrased as in (i) and (ii) below:

(i)   He loves me more than he loves you

(ii)   He loves me more than you love me

The ambiguity here seems to arise through *ellipsis* (i.e. the omission of one or more words which can be understood from the context): on interpretation (i), *he* and *loves* undergo ellipsis (i.e. are omitted); on interpretation (ii), *love* and *me* undergo ellipsis. On interpretation (i), *you* is interpreted as the complement of the ellipsed sequence *he loves*. On interpretation (ii), *you* is understood as the subject of the ellipsed expression *love me*.

Exercise III

Say whether you think each of the following sentences is (or is not) grammatical in (Modern Standard) English:

1a   I gave the book back to him
 b   I gave back the book to him
 c   I gave the book to him back
 d   I gave him the book back—
 e   I gave him back the book— we feel better about this one
 f   I gave back him the book

2a   He's someone whom I can't put up with
 b   He's someone with whom I can't put up
 c   He's someone up with whom I can't put
 d   He's someone who I can't put up with
 e   He's someone with who I can't put up
 f   He's someone up with who I can't put

3a   He's looking for a place where to stay
 b   He's looking for a place in which to stay
 c   He's looking for a place which to stay in
 d   He's looking for a place to stay in
 e   He's looking for a place to stay

4a   Why don't you ring Mary up? — different meanings (phone/cashier)
 b   Why don't you ring up Mary?
 c   Why don't you ring her up?
 d   Why don't you ring up her?

5a   Who didn't you know that they'd fired?
 b   Who didn't you know they'd fired?
 c   Who didn't you know that had been fired?
 d   Who didn't you know had been fired?
 e   Who didn't you know if they'd fired?
 f   Who didn't you know if had been fired?

6a   I very much want for you to be there

27

    b   I very much want you to be there

    c   I want very much for you to be there

    d   I want very much you to be there

Helpful hints

Don't assume that only one of the sentences in each set is grammatical, and that all the others are ungrammatical: bear in mind the possibility that all the sentences in each set may be grammatical (or indeed none); or, different sentences may be grammatical in different styles of English. In some cases, you may find it helpful to distinguish different degrees of grammaticality, e.g. using a prefixed *?* to indicate a sentence which is a bit forced, *??* to indicate a sentence which is unnatural, *?** to indicate a sentence which is pretty awful (while not being entirely ungrammatical), * to indicate a sentence which is completely ungrammatical, and ** to indicate a sentence which is doubly ungrammatical (etc.).

Exercise IV

Pedagogical grammarians (i.e. grammarians writing grammar books designed for teaching in schools) often take a *prescriptive* approach to grammar, in that they prescribe (i.e. lay down) grammatical norms for Standard English and brand all non-standard structures as deviations from supposedly *correct* usage. By contrast, contemporary linguists adopt a *descriptive* approach to language, and are concerned to describe what people actually say (rather than prescribe what they ought to say). Compare and contrast the *prescriptive* and *descriptive* approaches to the following set of sentences.

  1   The mission of the *USS Enterprise* is to boldly go where no man has gone before

  2   The weather will hopefully clear up by tomorrow

  3   It's me that gets the blame for everything

  4   John and Mary love one another

  5   What are you up to?

  6   You are taller than me

  7   Everyone loses their cool now and then

  8   Those kind of people get on my nerves

  9   If I was you, I'd complain

10   You and me were made for each other

Model answer for 1

Although splitting the atom has been one of our greatest achievements in the twentieth century, splitting the infinitive is regarded by prescriptive pedants as a sign of the linguistic decadence of twentieth-century society. The word *to* in a sentence like 1 is traditionally referred to as an *infinitive particle*, in that it takes after it a verb like *go* in the so-called *infinitive* form (which is the *base* or *uninflected* form of the verb – the form cited in dictionary entries). Prescriptive grammarians insist that it is 'bad grammar' to separate the infinitive particle *to* from the infinitive verb with which it is associated (in this case *go*): one of the golden rules of traditional prescriptive grammar is 'Never split an infinitive' (i.e. never separate infinitival *to* from its associated verb). In the case of 1, this prescriptive rule has been violated by virtue of the fact that *boldly* has been positioned between *to* and *go*. However, the *split infinitive* rule is purely prescriptive and in no sense reflects contemporary usage, given that in colloquial English infinitival *to* is frequently separated from its dependent verb (cf. e.g. *I want you to fully appreciate the gravity of the situation*): indeed, the very fact that the phrase *to boldly go where no man has gone before* is taken from the title sequence of the cult sci-fi television series *Star Trek* underlines the fact that split infinitives are characteristic of colloquial English (even Spock splits his infinitives when talking to humans).

Exercise V

Nonstandard varieties of English often differ from Standard English (SE) in respect of certain aspects of their grammar. Each of the sentences below is taken from a different (nonstandard) variety of English; identify how the sentences differ from SE in respect of their grammar. (The SE counterparts of the relevant constructions are given in parentheses where they are not immediately obvious.)

1   You a real cool dude, man
2   Your car wants mending (= 'Your car needs to be repaired')
3   Them's me mates (= 'Those are my friends')
4   I give it her (= 'I gave it to her')
5   Can the both of us come?
6   I ought to go there, didn't I?
7   Mine's bigger than what yours is
8   There's a man sells vegetables in the village
9   It were me what told her
10   Y'all got a drink, don't y'all?
11   Slow you up! (*Sign in Norfolk car park asking people to reduce speed*)
12   Ain't nobody gonna take me for a ride

Model answer

Sentence 1 is characteristic of a variety of English widely referred to as *African American English* (= AAE). One nonstandard grammatical feature here is the omission of *are*. A well-known characteristic of AAE is the omission of *are* and *is* (but not other forms of *be*) in contexts where speakers of Standard English (= SE) would use the contracted forms *'re* and *'s*: hence in place of SE *He's working* we find AAE *He workin'*. But where SE requires the full forms *are* and *is*, they cannot be omitted in AAE (e.g. in structures like *You sure are!*). A second grammatical characteristic of 1 is the use of the form *real* where SE would require the form *really* (cf. *real pretty* in place of the standard form *really pretty*): in SE, regular adverbs differ from the corresponding adjectives in that the adverbs end in +*ly* (hence we have the adjective *real* as in *They are **real** (people)*, and the adverb *really* as in *It was **really** great*); however, in AAE, regular adverbs do not end in +*ly*, and have the same form as the corresponding adjectives. Sentence 1 also shows interesting *lexical* (i.e. vocabulary) characteristics, in the nonstandard ways in which the words *cool*, *dude* and *man* are used.

Exercise (VI)

Sentences such as those given below are grammatical in one variety of Northern Irish English spoken in Belfast (as described in two interesting studies by Alison Henry, 1992, 1995), but are ungrammatical in standard varieties of English.

1 The eggs/*They is cracked
2 Us students/*We is very hardworking
3 Them oranges/*They doesn't look too fresh
4 How's her and them getting on together?
5 Tell you me the truth!
6 Be going you out of the door when they arrive!
7 I want <u>for</u> to meet them
8 I don't like the children for to be out late
9 I don't know where for to go
10 I wonder what street that he lives in
11 Nobody could tell me was there going to be a strike

Give their Standard English counterparts, and discuss the differences between Standard English and (the relevant variety of) Belfast English.

Model answer for 1

In Standard English, the +*s* ending on verbs is used only when the verb has a third person singular subject like *he/she/it/the egg*. However, in Belfast English, *s*-inflected verb forms can be used with plural subjects as well, except where the subject is a (nominative) plural personal pronoun like *we/they*. Hence, we find the following pattern of (un)grammaticality:

(i)   The eggs is cracked
(ii)   Them eggs is cracked
(iii)   These is cracked

30

(iv)   Themuns is cracked (= 'them ones' = 'those ones')

(v)   *They is cracked

For fuller discussion, see Henry 1995; for unfamiliar grammatical terminology, see the glossary.

Exercise Ⓥ︎Ⅱ (§1.2)

Chomsky argued in a number of works in the 1960s that native speakers can judge the *acceptability* (or otherwise) of sentences, but that it can often be difficult for native speakers to tell whether an unacceptable sentence is *ungrammatical* (i.e. *syntactically* ill formed), or ill formed in some other way (e.g. stylistically incongruous, semantically incoherent, pragmatically inappropriate, etc.). Discuss the (un)acceptability of the following examples, and attempt to determine in what way(s) – if any – they are 'odd':

1   I knew [*thought*] that she was ill, but I was wrong *contradictory to say you know & were wrong*

2   My goldfish thinks that I'm a lousy cook *goldfish don't think*

3   Whom was he trying to get off with? *Styles formal, informal*

4   I eat much chocolate

5   My wife is not my wife

6   You're a living dead man, marshal

7   It's I that's to blame for everything

8   You'll never come across a five-sided hexagon

9   This oats is of rather poor quality

10 He loves you more than me

11 You can see the taste in a Fox's glacier mint

12 The christian which we threw to the lions was as tough as old boots

13 Whom were you talking to?

14 I order you to know the answer

15 Machines Who Think (title of a book by Pamela McCorduck on computers)

16 My toothbrush is pregnant again

17 Colourless green ideas sleep furiously —— *Chomsky 1958, grammatical but anomalous.*

18 I was literally over the moon about it
    ↳ used for exaggeration

(Those from a culturally impoverished background might like to know in relation to 11 that Fox's glacier mints are colourless and transparent, rather like glass in their appearance.)

Model answer for 1–3

Sentence 1 appears to be *semantically incoherent*, in that it expresses a contradiction. It is part of the meaning of the verb *know* that if we say *I know that...*,

31

we presuppose that the proposition introduced by the word *that* is true; hence if we then go on to deny the truth of the proposition, we are implying that the proposition is both true and false, and thereby expressing a contradiction.

The oddity of sentence 2 seems to be largely *pragmatic*: *pragmatics* is the study of the relation between language and the world (and is concerned e.g. with the kinds of situations which a given sentence could be used to describe, and with the role played by nonlinguistic knowledge in our use of sentences). Thus, whether or not you find expressions like *My goldfish thinks that . . .* well formed depends on whether or not you believe that goldfish do (or might) possess powers of thought; a sentence like 2 implies that goldfish are capable of thought, and a person who rejects sentences like 2 is in effect rejecting the implied proposition that goldfish can think (because it conflicts with their *personal beliefs about the world*).

The oddity of 3 seems to be stylistic. The form *whom* is used only in very formal styles of English, whereas the colloquial expression *get off with* is used only in very informal styles. Hence, there is a clash of styles here, leading to stylistic incongruity.

Exercise VIII

The following sentences are all taken from various plays written by Shakespeare (around the year 1600):

1 Speak not you for him! (Prospero, *Tempest*, I.ii)
2 How came you hither? (Alonso, *Tempest*, V.i)
3 Hast any more of this? (Trinculo, *Tempest*, II.ii)
4 You are come to see my daughter Anne? (Mrs Page, *Merry Wives of Windsor*, II.i)
5 Whether had you rather lead mine eyes or eye your master's heels? (Mrs Page, *Merry Wives of Windsor*, III.ii)
6 Hath he not a son? (Duke, *Two Gentlemen of Verona*, II.iv)
7 What an ass art thou! I understand thee not (Speed, *Two Gentlemen of Verona*, II.v)
8 Yourself shall go first (Slender, *Merry Wives of Windsor*, I.ii)
9 I do repent me (Juliet, *Measure for Measure*, II.iii)
10 Friend hast thou none (Duke, *Measure for Measure*, III.i)
11 Our corn's to reap (Duke, *Measure for Measure*, IV.i)
12 A heavier task could not have been impos'd
   Than I to speak my griefs unspeakable (Aegeon, *Comedy of Errors*, I.i)
13 In our sight they three were taken up (Aegeon, *Comedy of Errors*, I.i)
14 Is there any ship puts forth tonight? (Antipholus of Syracuse, *Comedy of Errors*, IV.iii)
15 Who heard me to deny it? (Antipholus of Syracuse, *Comedy of Errors*, V.i)

Give the counterparts of these sentences in Modern Standard English, and describe the differences between the sentences above and their contemporary counterparts.

Model answer for 1

Example 1 is a type of sentence used to issue an order, traditionally known as an **imperative**. In present-day English, negative imperatives are formed by using *don't* followed by the subject (if overtly expressed), followed by the verb and any complements which the verb has – as illustrated by the following examples (where the subject, if overt, is italicized):

(i)   Don't *you* dare answer back!

(ii)   Don't *anybody* move!

(iii)   Don't give me any bullshit!

In Shakespearean English, however, negative imperatives could be of the form verb + *not* + subject + complement, as in 1 above and in the examples below:

(iv)   Fear not you that! (Mrs Page, *Merry Wives of Windsor*, IV.iv)

(v)   Clamber not you up to the casements! (Shylock, *Merchant of Venice*, II.v)

(vi)   Come not thou near me! (Phebe, *As You Like It*, III.v)

Exercise IX (§1.7)

In the text, we claimed that the **head parameter** always has a uniform setting in a given language: either it is *head-initial* (so that all heads precede their complements), or it is *head-final* (so that all heads follow their complements). However, although this would seem to be true of many languages (English included), there are other languages which don't show the same uniform setting for the **head parameter**. In this respect, consider the German phrases and sentences given below.

1   Hans muss stolz auf seine Mutter sein
       Hans must proud of his   mother be
       'Hans must be proud of his mother'

2   Hans muss auf seine Mutter stolz sein
       Hans must of his   mother proud be
       'Hans must be proud of his mother'

3   Hans geht den Fluss entlang
       Hans goes the river along
       'Hans goes along the river'

4   Hans muss die Aufgaben lösen
       Hans must the exercises do
       'Hans must do the exercises'

5   Ich glaube dass Hans die Aufgaben lösen muss
    I think that Hans the exercises do must
    'I think that Hans must do the exercises'

In relation to these sentences, make the following assumptions about their structure. In 1 and 2 *muss* is a verb, *Hans* is its subject and *stolz auf seine Mutter sein* is its complement; *sein* is a verb and *stolz auf seine Mutter* is its complement; *stolz* is an adjective, and *auf seine Mutter* is its complement; *auf* is a preposition and *seine Mutter* is its complement; *seine* is a determiner, and *Mutter* is its complement. In 3 *geht* is a verb, *Hans* is its subject and *den Fluss entlang* is its complement; *entlang* is a preposition (or, more precisely, a *postposition*) and *den Fluss* is its complement; *den* is a determiner and *Fluss* is its complement. In 4 *muss* is a verb, *Hans* is its subject and *die Aufgaben lösen* is its complement; *lösen* is a verb and *die Aufgaben* is its complement; *die* is a determiner and *Aufgaben* is its complement. In 5 *glaube* is a verb, *ich* is its subject and *dass Hans die Aufgaben lösen muss* is its complement; *dass* is a complementizer (i.e. a complement-clause-introducing particle) and *Hans die Aufgaben lösen muss* is its complement; *muss* is a verb, *Hans* is its subject, and *die Aufgaben lösen* is its complement; *lösen* is a verb and *die Aufgaben* is its complement; *die* is a determiner and *Aufgaben* is its complement.

Helpful hints

Look at which categories are positioned before their complements and which after. Which words always seem to occupy a fixed position in relation to their complements, and which occupy a variable position? In the case of categories which sometimes go before (and sometimes after) their complements, try and establish whether the position of the head word is determined by *structural factors* (i.e. the type of structure involved) or *lexical factors* (i.e. the choice of head word).

Exercise X (§§1.7–1.8)

Below are examples of utterances produced by a girl called Lucy at age 24 months. Comment on whether Lucy has correctly set the three parameters discussed in the text (the **head parameter**, the **wh-parameter** and the **null subject parameter**). Discuss the significance of the relevant examples for the parameter-setting model of acquisition.

	CHILD SENTENCE	ADULT COUNTERPART
1	What Daddy making?	'What's Daddy making?'
2	Want bye-byes	'I want to go to sleep'
3	Mummy go shops	'Mummy went to the shops'; this was in reply to 'Where did mummy go?'
4	Me have yoghurt?	'Can I have a yoghurt?'
5	Daddy doing?	'What's Daddy doing?'

6	Think Teddy sleeping	'I think Teddy's sleeping'; this was in reply to 'What d'you think Teddy's doing?'
7	What me having?	'What am I having?'; this followed her mother saying 'Mummy's having fish for dinner'
8	No me have fish	'I'm not going to have fish'
9	Where Daddy gone?	'Where's Daddy gone?'
10	Gone office	'He's gone to his office'
11	Want bickies	'She wants some biscuits'; this was her reply to 'What does Dolly want?'
12	What Teddy have?	'What can Teddy have?'
13	Where Mummy going?	'Where's Mummy going?'
14	Me go shops	'I want to go to the shops'
15	Daddy drinking coffee	'Daddy's drinking coffee'
16	What Nana eating?	'What's Grandma eating?'
17	Want choc'ate	'He wants some chocolate'; this was her reply to 'Teddy wants some more meat, does he?'
18	Dolly gone? +truncation	'Where's Dolly gone?'
19	Watch te'vision	'I'm going to watch television'
20	Me have more	'I want to have some more'
21	In kitchen	'In the kitchen' (reply to 'Where's Mummy?')
22	Me play with Daddy	'I want to play with Daddy'

Helpful hints

If Lucy has correctly set the **wh-parameter**, we should expect to find that she systematically preposes wh-expressions and positions them sentence-initially. If she has correctly set the **head parameter**, we should expect to find (for example) that she correctly positions the complement of a verb after the verb, and the complement of a preposition after the preposition; however, where the complement is a wh-expression, we expect to find that the complement is moved into sentence-initial position in order to satisfy the requirements of the **wh-parameter** (so that in effect the **wh-parameter** over-rides the **head parameter**). If Lucy has correctly set the **null subject parameter**, we should expect to find that she does not use null subjects. However, the picture here is complicated by the fact that young children often produce truncated sentence structures in which the first word of the sentence is omitted (just as in diary styles, adults truncate sentences by omitting the subject when it is the first word in a sentence: cf. *Went to a party. Had a great time. Got totally sozzled*). Hence, when a child sentence has a missing subject, it is important to determine whether we are dealing with a *null subject* (i.e. whether the child has

35

mis-set the null subject parameter), or a *truncated subject*. Since truncation occurs only sentence-initially (as the first word in a sentence), but null subjects can occur in any subject position in a sentence, one way of telling the difference between the two is to see whether children omit subjects only when they are the first word in the sentence (which would be the result of truncation), or whether they also omit subjects in non-initial positions in the sentence (as is the case in a genuine null-subject language like Italian). Another way of differentiating the two is that in null subject languages we find that overt pronoun subjects are only used for emphasis, so that in an Italian sentence like *L'ho fatto io* (literally 'It have done **I**') the subject pronoun *io* 'I' has a contrastive interpretation, and the relevant sentence is paraphraseable in English as 'It was *I* who did it': by contrast, in a non-null-subject language like English, subject pronouns are not intrinsically emphatic – e.g. *he* doesn't have a contrastive interpretation in an English diary-style sentence such as *Went to see Jim. Thought he might help*). A third way of differentiating between sentences with null and truncated subjects is that in truncation structures we sometimes find that expressions other than subjects can be truncated (e.g. preposed complements).

In relation to the sentences in 1–22, make the following assumptions (where I use the informal term *covert subject* to mean 'understood null or truncated subject'). In 1 *making* is a verb which has the subject *Daddy* and the complement *what*; in 2 *want* is a verb which has a covert subject and the complement *bye-byes*; in 3 *go* is a verb which has the subject *Mummy* and the complement *shops*; in 4 *have* is a verb which has the subject *me* and the complement *yoghurt*; in 5 *doing* is a verb which has the subject *Daddy*, and its complement is a covert counterpart of *what*; in 6 *think* is a verb with a covert subject and its complement is *Teddy sleeping* (with *Teddy* serving as the subject of the verb *sleeping*); in 7, *having* is a verb which has the subject *me* and the complement *what*; in 8 *no* is a negative particle which has the complement *me have fish* (assume that *no* is the kind of word which doesn't have a subject), and *have* is a verb which has the subject *me* and the complement *fish*; in 9 *gone* is a verb which has the subject *Daddy* and the complement *where*; in 10 *gone* is a verb which has a covert subject and the complement *office*; in 11 *want* is a verb which has a covert subject and the complement *bickies*; in 12 *have* is a verb which has the subject *Teddy* and the complement *what*; in 13 *going* is a verb which has the subject *Mummy* and the complement *where*; in 14 *go* is a verb which has the subject *me* and the complement *shops*; in 15 *drinking* is a verb which has the subject *Daddy* and the complement *coffee*; in 16 *eating* is a verb which has the subject *Nana* and the complement *what*; in 17 *want* is a verb which has a covert subject and the complement *choc'ate*; in 18 *gone* is a verb which has the subject *Dolly* and its complement is a covert counterpart of *where*; in 19 *watch* is a verb which has a covert subject and the complement *te'vision*; in 20 *have* is a verb which has the subject *me* and the complement *more*; 21 is a phrase in which the preposition *in* has the complement *kitchen* (assume that phrases don't have subjects); and in 22 *play* is a verb which has the subject *me* and the complement *with Daddy* (and in turn *Daddy* is the complement of the preposition *with*).

2
Categories and features

2.1 Overview

In the previous chapter, we saw that the **structure dependence principle** determines that all grammatical operations in natural language are category-based (so that any word-based operation will apply to whole categories of words rather than to specific individual words). In this chapter, we provide further evidence in support of this conclusion, and argue that a principled description of the grammar of any language (the language chosen for illustrative purposes being Modern Standard English) requires us to recognize that all words in the language belong to a restricted set of **grammatical categories**. We look at the main categories found in English and explore their nature, arguing that categories are composite elements, built up of sets of grammatical **features**.

2.2 Morphological evidence

A natural question to ask at this point is: 'What does it mean to say that words belong to grammatical *categories*?' We can define a grammatical *category* in the following way:

(1)   A *grammatical category* is a class of expressions which share a common set of grammatical properties.

For example, by saying that words like *boy, cow, hand, idea, place, team*, etc. belong to the grammatical category **noun**, what we are saying is that they all share certain grammatical properties in common: e.g. they have a plural form (ending in the suffix +*s*), they can all be premodified by *the*, and so forth. Likewise, by saying that words such as *see, know, like, understand, write, appear*, etc. belong to the grammatical category **verb**, what we imply is that they too have certain grammatical properties in common (e.g. they can take the progressive +*ing* suffix, they can occur after infinitival *to*, etc.). Similarly, by saying that *tall, hot, narrow, old, wise, sad*, etc. belong to the grammatical category **adjective**, we capture the fact that they share a number of grammatical properties in common (e.g. they can take the comparative +*er* suffix). In much the same way, by saying that words like *quickly, cleverly, urgently, truly, greatly, completely*, etc.

belong to the grammatical category of **adverb**, we aim to capture the grammatical properties which they share (not least the fact that they all end in the suffix +*ly*). And in addition, by saying that *up*, *down*, *over*, *under*, *across*, *between*, etc. belong to the grammatical category *preposition*, we are saying that they have certain grammatical properties in common (e.g. they can be intensified by a word like *right* or *straight*). As is implicit here, the bulk of the evidence in support of postulating that words belong to categories is *morphosyntactic* (i.e. morphological and/or syntactic) in nature.

The relevant morphological evidence relates to the **inflectional** and **derivational** properties of words: inflectional properties relate to different forms of the same word (e.g. the plural form of a noun like *cat* is formed by adding the plural inflection +*s* to give the form *cats*), while derivational properties relate to the processes by which a word can be used to form a different kind of word by the addition of another morpheme (e.g. by adding the suffix +*ness* to the adjective *sad* we can form the noun *sadness*). Although English has a highly impoverished system of inflectional morphology, there are none the less two major categories of word which have distinctive inflectional properties – namely *nouns* and *verbs*. We can identify the class of nouns in terms of the fact that they typically inflect for **number**, and thus have (potentially) distinct **singular** and **plural** forms – cf. pairs such as *dog/dogs*, *man/men*, *ox/oxen*, etc. Accordingly, we can differentiate a noun like *fool* from an adjective like *foolish* by virtue of the fact that only (regular) nouns like *fool* – not adjectives like *foolish* – can carry the noun plural inflection +*s*: cf. e.g.

(2)   They are *fools* [noun]/**foolishes* [adjective]

There are three complications which should be pointed out, however. One is the existence of irregular nouns like *sheep* which are invariable and hence have a common singular/plural form (cf. *one **sheep***, *two **sheep***). A second is that some nouns have no plural by virtue of their meaning: only those nouns (generally called **count nouns**) which denote entities which can be counted have a plural form (e.g. the noun *chair*: cf. *one chair*, *two chairs*, etc.); some nouns (like *furniture*) denote an uncountable mass (and for this reason are called **mass nouns** or **noncount nouns**) and so cannot be pluralized – hence the ungrammaticality of **one furniture*, **two furnitures*. A third complication is posed by noun expressions which contain more than one noun; only the head noun in such expressions can be pluralized, not any preceding noun used as a dependent or modifier of the head noun: thus, in expressions such as *car doors*, *wheel trims*, *policy decisions*, *skate boards*, *horse boxes*, *trouser presses*, *coat hangers*, etc. the second noun is the head noun and can be pluralized, whereas the first noun is a nonhead (i.e. is a modifier/dependent of some kind) and cannot be pluralized.

In much the same way, we can identify verbs by their inflectional morphology in English. In addition to their uninflected *base* form (= the form under which they are listed in dictionaries) verbs typically have up to four different inflected forms, formed by adding one of four inflections to the appropriate stem form: the relevant inflections are the past/perfective participle suffix +*n*, the past tense suffix +*d*, the third person singular present tense suffix +*s*, and the present/imperfective/progressive participle suffix +*ing* (see the *glossary* if these terms are unfamiliar), giving the range of forms illustrated in the table in (3) below:

(3)   TABLE OF VERB FORMS

BASE	+N	+D	+S	+ING
hew	hewn	hewed	hews	hewing
mow	mown	mowed	mows	mowing
sew	sewn	sewed	sews	sewing
show	shown	showed	shows	showing
strew	strewn	strewed	strews	strewing

Like most morphological criteria, however, this one is complicated by the irregularity of English inflectional morphology; for example, many verbs have irregular *past* or *perfective* forms, and in some cases either or both of these forms may not in fact be distinct from the (uninflected) base form, so that a single form may serve two or three functions (thereby *neutralizing* the relevant distinctions), as the table in (4) below illustrates:

(4)   TABLE OF TYPICAL IRREGULAR VERBS

BASE	PERFECTIVE	PAST	PRESENT	IMPERFECTIVE
go	gone	went	goes	going
speak	spoken	spoke	speaks	speaking
see	seen	saw	sees	seeing
———come———		came	comes	coming
wait	———waited———		waits	waiting
meet	———met———		meets	meeting
————————cut————————			cuts	cutting

(In fact, the largest class of verbs in English are those which have the morphological characteristics of *wait*, and thus form both their past and perfective forms by suffixing +(*e*)*d*.) The picture becomes even more complicated if we take into account the verb *be*, which has eight distinct forms (viz. the base form *be*, the perfective form *been*, the imperfective form *being*, the past forms *was/were*, and the present forms *am/are/is*). The most regular verb suffix in English is +*ing*, which can be attached to the base form of almost any verb (though a handful of defective verbs like *beware* are exceptions).

    The obvious implication of our discussion of nouns and verbs here is that it would not be possible to provide a systematic account of English inflectional morphology unless we were to posit that words belong to grammatical categories, and that a specific type of inflection attaches only to a specific category of word. The same is also true if we wish to provide an adequate account of *derivational morphology* in English (i.e. the processes by which words are derived from other words). For it turns out that particular derivational affixes can only be attached to words belonging to a particular category. For example, the negative prefixes *un+* and *in+* can be attached to adjectives to form a corresponding negative adjective (cf. pairs such as *happy/unhappy* and *flexible/inflexible*) but not to nouns (so that a noun like *fear* has no negative counterpart **unfear*), nor to prepositions (so that a preposition like *inside* has no negative antonym **uninside*). Similarly, the adverbializing (i.e. adverb-forming) suffix *+ly* in English can be attached only to adjectives (giving rise to adjective/adverb pairs such as *sad/sadly*) and cannot be attached to a noun like *computer*, or to a verb like *accept*, or to a preposition like *off*. Likewise, the nominalizing (i.e. noun-forming) suffix *+ness* can be attached only to adjective stems (so giving rise to adjective/noun pairs such as *coarse/coarseness*), not to nouns, verbs or prepositions (hence we don't find *+ness* derivatives for a noun like *boy*, or a verb like *resemble*, or a preposition like *down*). There is little point in multiplying examples here: it is clear that derivational affixes have categorial properties, and any principled account of derivational morphology will have to recognize this fact (see Aronoff 1976 and Fabb 1988).

Although the inflectional and derivational properties of items provide potential clues as to their categorial identity, in some cases they may not be conclusive. For example, in a language like English with a relatively impoverished system of inflections, inflectional morphology is of limited usefulness because many words are invariable in form, and so uninflected; moreover, derivational evidence poses the problem that derivational processes are often only of limited productivity (for example, there is no *+ly* adverb derivative of adjectives like *little*, *old*, *fat*, *unable*, etc.). For this reason, morphological criteria have to be used in conjunction with *syntactic* criteria.

2.3 Syntactic evidence

The *syntactic* evidence for assigning words to categories essentially relates to the fact that different categories of words have different *distributions* (i.e. occupy a different range of positions within phrases or sentences). For example, if we want to complete the four-word sentence in (5) below by inserting a single word at the end of the sentence in the position marked __:

(5)   They have no __

we can use an (appropriate kind of) noun, but not a verb, preposition, adjective or adverb, as we see from (6) below:

(6) (a)   They have no *car/conscience/friends/ideas* (nouns)
    (b)   **They have no *went* (verb)/*for* (preposition)/*older* (adjective)/
            conscientiously (adverb)

Thus, using the relevant syntactic criterion, we might define the class of nouns as the set of words which can terminate a sentence in the position marked __ in (5).

Using the same type of syntactic evidence, we could argue that only a verb (in its uninflected *infinitive/base* form) can occur in the position marked __ in (7) below to form a complete (non-elliptical) sentence:

(7)   They/it can __

And support for this claim comes from the contrasts in (8) below:

(8) (a)   They can *stay/leave/hide/die/starve/cry* (verb)
     (b)   *They can *gorgeous* (adjective)/*happily* (adverb)/*down* (preposition)/
             door (noun)

And the only category of word which can occur after *very* (in the sense of *extremely*) is an adjective or adverb, as we see from (9) below:

(9) (a)   He is *very* **slow**   (*very* + **adjective**)
     (b)   He walks *very* **slowly**   (*very* + **adverb**)
     (c)   **Very* **fools** waste time   (*very* + **noun**)
     (d)   **He *very* **adores** her   (*very* + **verb**)
     (e)   **It happened *very* **after** the party   (*very* + **preposition**)

(But note that *very* can only be used to modify adjectives/adverbs which by virtue of their meaning are *gradable* and so can be qualified by words like *very/rather/some-what* etc; adjectives/adverbs which denote an absolute state are *ungradable* by virtue of their meaning, and so cannot be qualified in the same way – hence the oddity of !*Fifteen students were very* **present**, *and five were very* **absent**, where ! marks semantic anomaly.) Moreover, we can differentiate adjectives from adverbs in syntactic terms. For example, only adverbs can be used to end sentences such as *He treats her* __, *She behaved* __, *He worded the statement* __: cf.

(10) (a)   He treats her *badly* (adverb)/**kind* (adjective)/**shame* (noun)
     (b)   She behaved *abominably* (adverb)/**appalling* (adjective)/**disgrace*
             (noun)/**down* (preposition)
     (c)   He worded the statement *carefully* (adverb)/**good* (adjective)/**tact* (noun)

And since adjectives (but not adverbs) can serve as the complement of the verb *be* (i.e. can be used after *be*), we can delimit the class of (*gradable*) adjectives uniquely by saying that only adjectives can be used to complete a four-word sentence of the form *They are very* __: cf.

(11) (a)   They are very *tall/pretty/kind/nice* (adjective)
     (b)   *They are very *slowly* (adverb)/*gentlemen* (noun)/*working* (verb)/
             outside (preposition)

Another way of differentiating between an adjective like *real* and an adverb like *really* in syntactic terms is that adjectives are used to modify nouns, whereas adverbs arc used to modify other types of expression: cf.

(12) (a) There is a *real* **crisis** (*real* + **noun**)

(b) He is *really* **nice** (*really* + **adjective**)

(c) He walks *really* **slowly** (*really* + **adverb**)

(d) He is *really* **down** (*really* + **preposition**)

(e) He must *really* **squirm** (*really* + **verb**)

Adjectives used to modify a following noun (like *real* in *There is a real crisis*) are traditionally said to be *attributive* in function, whereas those which do not modify an immediately following noun (like *real* in *The crisis is real*) are said to be *predicative* in function.

As for the syntactic properties of prepositions, they alone can be intensified by *right* in the sense of 'completely', or by *straight* in the sense of 'directly':

(13) (a) Go *right* **up** the ladder

(b) He went *right* **inside**

(c) He walked *straight* **into** a wall

(d) He fell *straight* **down**

By contrast, other categories cannot be intensified by *right/straight* (in Standard English): cf.

(14) (a) *He *right/straight* **despaired** (*right/straight* + **verb**)

(b) *She is *right/straight* **pretty** (*right/straight* + **adjective**)

(c) *She looked at him *right/straight* **strangely** (*right/straight* + **adverb**)

(d) *They are *right/straight* **fools** (*right/straight* + **noun**)

However, there are two minor *caveats* which should be noted here. Firstly, since *right/straight* serve to intensify the meaning of a preposition, they can only be combined with those (uses of) prepositions which express the kind of meaning which can be intensified in the appropriate way (hence they cannot be used to intensify ungradable prepositions like *of/with/for* as they are used in phrases such as **a man* *right/straight of great courage*, **a house right/straight with shattered windows*, **a present right/straight for Mary* – though in other uses *for* can be intensified, cf. *He made right/straight for the exit*). A second caveat to note is that in some varieties of English (e.g. Northern British English) *right* can be used to intensify adjectives, adverbs and nouns, so that (14b–d) are grammatical with *right* in these varieties, though not with *straight*.

A further syntactic property of some prepositions (namely those which take a following (pro)nominal complement (traditionally called *transitive prepositions*)) which they share in common with (transitive) verbs is the fact that they permit an immediately following *objective pronoun* as their complement (i.e. a pronoun in its object form, like *me/us/him/them*): cf.

(15) (a)   She was *against* **him**   (*transitive preposition* + **pronoun**)

    (b)   She was *watching* **him**   (*transitive verb* + **pronoun**)

    (c)   *She is *fond* **him**   (*adjective* + **pronoun**)

    (d)   *She works *independently* **him**   (*adverb* + **pronoun**)

    (e)   *She showed me a *photo* **him**   (*noun* + **pronoun**)

Even though a preposition like *with* does not express the kind of meaning which allows it to be intensified by *right* or *straight*, we know it is a (transitive) preposition by virtue of the fact that it is invariable (so not a *verb*) and permits an objective pronoun as its complement, e.g. in sentences such as *He argued with **me/us/him/them***.

Given that different categories have different *morphological* and *syntactic* properties, it follows that we can use the morphological and syntactic properties of a word to determine its categorization (i.e. what category it belongs to). The morphological properties of a given word may provide an initial rough guide to its categorial status: in order to determine the categorial status of an individual word, we can ask whether it has the inflectional and derivational properties of a particular category of word. For example, we can tell that *happy* is an adjective by virtue of the fact that it has the derivational properties of typical adjectives: it can take the negative prefix *un*+ (giving rise to the negative adjective *unhappy*), the adverbializing suffix +*ly* (giving rise to the adverb *happily*), the comparative/superlative suffixes +*er*/+*est* (giving rise to the forms *happier/happiest*), and the nominalizing suffix +*ness* (giving rise to the noun *happiness*).

However, we cannot always rely entirely on morphological clues, owing to the fact that inflectional morphology is sometimes irregular, and derivational morphology often has limited productivity: this means that a word belonging to a given class may have only *some* of the relevant morphological properties, or even (in the case of a completely irregular item) *none* of them. For example, although the adjective *fat* has comparative/superlative forms in +*er*/+*est* (cf. *fat/fatter/fattest*), it has no negative *un*+ counterpart (cf. **unfat*), no adverb counterpart in +*ly* (cf. **fatly*), and (for many speakers) no noun counterpart in +*ness* (cf. **fatness*): even more exceptional is the adjective *little*, which has no negative *un*+ derivative (cf. **unlittle*), no adverb +*ly* derivative (cf. **littlely/*littly*), no productive noun derivative in +*ness* (cf. the awkwardness of ?*littleness*), and no productive +*er*/+*est* derivatives (the forms *littler/ littlest* are not usual – at least, for me).

What makes morphological evidence even more problematic is the fact that many morphemes may have more than one use. For example, we noted earlier that +*n* and +*ing* are inflections which attach to verbs to give perfective or imperfective verb forms (traditionally referred to as *participles*). However, certain +*n*/+*ing* forms seem to function as *adjectives*, suggesting that +*ing* and +*n* can also serve as adjectivalizing morphemes. Thus, although a word like *interesting* can function as a verb (in sentences like *Her charismatic teacher was gradually interesting her in syntax*), it can also function as an adjective (used attributively in structures like *This is an interesting book*, and predicatively in structures like *This book is very interesting*). In its use as an adjective, the word *interesting* has the negative derivative *uninteresting* (cf. *It was a rather uninteresting play*), and the +*ly* adverb derivative *interestingly* (though, like many other adjectives, it has no noun derivative in +*ness*, and no comparative/superlative derivatives in +*er*/+*est*). Similarly, although we earlier identified +*n* as a verbal inflection (in forms like *grown/shown/blown/thrown* etc.), it should be noted that many words ending in +*n* can also function as adjectives. For example, the word *known* in an expression such as *a known criminal* seems to function as an (attributive) adjective, and in this adjectival use it has a negative *un*+ counterpart (cf. expressions like *the tomb of the unknown warrior*). Similarly, the form *expected* can function as a perfective verb form in structures like *We hadn't expected him to complain*, but seems to function as an (attributive) adjective in structures such as *He gave the expected reply*; in its adjectival (though not in its verbal) use, it has a negative *un*+ derivative, and the resultant negative adjective *unexpected* in turn has the noun derivative *unexpectedness*.

So, given the potential problems which arise with morphological criteria, it is unwise to rely solely on morphological evidence in determining categorial status: rather, we should use morphological criteria in conjunction with *syntactic* criteria (i.e. criteria relating to the range of positions that words can occupy within phrases and sentences). One syntactic test which can be used to determine the category that a particular word belongs to is that of **substitution** – i.e. seeing whether (in a given sentence) the word in question can be substituted by a regular noun, verb, preposition, adjective or adverb. We can use the *substitution* technique to differentiate between comparative adjectives and adverbs ending in +*er*, since they have identical forms. For example, in the case of sentences like:

(16) (a)   He is *better* at French than you
     (b)   He speaks French *better* than you

we find that *better* can be replaced by a *more* + *adjective* sequence like *more fluent* in (16a) but not (16b), and conversely that *better* can be replaced by a *more* + *adverb* sequence like *more fluently* in (16b) but not in (16a): cf.

(17) (a)   He is *more fluent/*more fluently* at French than you
     (b)   He speaks French *more fluently/*more fluent* than you

Thus, our *substitution* test provides us with syntactic evidence that *better* is an adjective in (16a), but an adverb in (16b).

2.4 Functional categories: determiners and pronouns

For reasons set out below, the five categories which we have looked at so far (viz. noun, verb, preposition, adjective and adverb) are known as **lexical categories**; we now go on to look at a rather different set of categories found in English termed **functional categories**. The lexical/functional dichotomy is rooted in the distinction drawn by descriptive grammarians (cf. e.g. Bolinger and Sears 1981, pp. 59–70) between two different types of words – namely (i) **contentives** or **content words** (which have idiosyncratic *descriptive content* or *sense* properties), and (ii) **function words** (or **functors**), i.e. words which serve primarily to carry information about the grammatical properties of expressions within the sentence, for instance information about number, gender, person, case, etc.

One test of whether words have descriptive content is to see whether they have *antonyms* (i.e. opposites): if a word has an antonym, it is a contentive (though if it has no antonym, you can't be sure whether it is a functor or a contentive). For example, a noun/N such as *loss* has the antonym *gain*; a verb/V such as *rise* has the antonym *fall*; an adjective/A such as *tall* has the antonym *short*; an adverb/ADV such as *early* (as in *He arrived early*) has the antonym *late*; and a preposition/P such as *inside* has the antonym *outside*. This reflects the fact that nouns, verbs, adjectives, adverbs and prepositions typically have descriptive content, and so are contentives. By contrast, a particle like infinitival *to*, or an auxiliary like *do* (cf. *Do you want to smoke?*), or a determiner like *the*, or a pronoun like *they*, or a complementizer (i.e. complement-clause-introducing particle) like *that* (cf. *I said that I was tired*) have no obvious antonyms, and thus can be said to lack *descriptive content*, and so to be *functors*. Using rather different (but equivalent) terminology, we might say that contentives have *lexical content* (i.e. idiosyncratic descriptive content which varies from one lexical item/word to another), whereas functors have *functional content*. We might then say that nouns, verbs, adjectives, adverbs and prepositions are **lexical categories** (because the words belonging to these categories have lexical/descriptive content) whereas particles, auxiliaries, determiners, pronouns and complementizers are **functional categories** (because words belonging to these categories have an essentially grammatical function). Having briefly outlined the characteristics of functional categories, let's take a closer look at the main functional categories found in English.

The first type of functional category which we shall deal with is the category of **determiner** (abbreviated to **D**, or sometimes **DET**). Items such as those bold-printed in (18) below (as used here) are traditionally said to be determiners (because they determine the referential or quantificational properties of the italicized noun expression which follows them):

(18) (a) I bought **a** *new battery* from **the** *local garage*

    (b) I prefer **this** *painting* to **that** *photo*

(c)　　**My** *studio apartment* is no bigger than **your** *garage*

(d)　　**All** *good comedians* tell **some** *bad jokes*

(Quantifying determiners are determiners like *all/some* which denote quantity, and are sometimes said to belong to the subcategory *quantifier*; referential determiners are determiners like *the/this/that/my* which are used to introduce referring expressions – e.g. an expression like *the car* in a sentence like *Shall we take the car?* is a referring expression in the sense that it refers to a specific car whose identity is assumed to be known to the hearer.) Since determiners are positioned in front of nouns (cf. *the* boys), and adjectives can similarly be positioned prenominally (cf. *tall* boys), an obvious question to ask at this point is why we couldn't just say that the determiners in (18) have the categorial status of adjectives. The answer we shall give is that any attempt to analyse determiners as adjectives in English runs up against a number of serious descriptive problems. Let's see why.

One reason for not subsuming determiners within the category of adjectives is that adjectives and determiners are syntactically distinct in a variety of ways, in respect of their *distribution*. For example, adjectives can be recursively (i.e. repeatedly) stacked in front of the noun they modify (in that you can go on putting more and more adjectives in front of a given noun), whereas determiners cannot be stacked in this way, in that you can generally only have one determiner (of a given type – e.g. one referential determiner and one quantificational determiner) premodifying a noun:

(19) (a)　ADJECTIVES:　men; *handsome* men; *dark handsome* men; *tall dark handsome* men; *sensitive tall dark handsome* men; *intelligent sensitive tall dark handsome* men, etc.

(b)　DETERMINERS:　*the* car; **a my* car; **that the* car; **that his the* car; **a that* car, etc.

Moreover, both determiners and adjectives can be used together to modify a noun, but when they do so, any determiner modifying the noun has to precede any adjective(s) modifying the noun: cf. e.g.

(20) (a)　　**my** *nice new* clothes　　(**determiner** + *adjective* + *adjective* + noun)

(b)　　**nice* **my** *new* clothes　　(*adjective* + **determiner** + *adjective* + noun)

(c)　　**nice new* **my** clothes　　(*adjective* + *adjective* + **determiner** + noun)

Thus, determiners seem to form a distinct distributional class (hence belong to a different category) from adjectives.

A further difference between determiners and adjectives can be illustrated by what speaker B can – and cannot – reply in the following dialogue:

(21)　　SPEAKER A: What are you looking for?

SPEAKER B: **Chair/*Comfortable* chair/**A** chair/**The** chair/**Another** chair **This** chair/**My** chair

As already noted, nouns like *chair* have the property that they are *countable* (in the sense that we can say *one chair, two chairs*, etc.), and in this respect differ from nouns like *furniture* which are *uncountable* (hence we cannot say **one furniture, *two furnitures*, etc.). As we see from (21), a singular count noun like *chair* cannot stand on its own as a complete noun expression, nor indeed can it function as such even if premodified by an adjective like *comfortable*; rather, a singular count noun requires a premodifying determiner like *a/the/another/this/my* etc. This provides us with clear evidence that determiners in English belong to a different category from adjectives.

Indeed, a more general property which differentiates determiners from adjectives is that determiners tend to be restricted to modifying nouns which have specific *number/countability* properties. For example, the determiner *a* modifies a singular count noun, *much* modifies a (singular) mass noun, *several* modifies a plural count noun, *more* modifies either a plural count noun or a (singular) mass noun: cf.

(22) (a)   Can you pass me **a** *chair/*chairs/*furniture*?

(b)   He doesn't have **much** *furniture/*chair/*chairs* of his own

(c)   He bought **several** *chairs/*chair/*furniture* in the sale

(d)   Do we need **more** *furniture/chairs/*chair*?

By contrast, typical adjectives like *nice, simple, comfortable, modern*, etc. can generally be used to modify all three types of nominal: cf.

(23) (a)   We need a **nice, simple, comfortable, modern** *chair*

(b)   We need some **nice, simple, comfortable, modern** *chairs*

(c)   We need some **nice, simple, comfortable, modern** *furniture*

(It should be noted, however, that a handful of determiners like *the* can also be used to modify singular/plural count and noncount nouns alike.)

It seems reasonable to suppose that determiners constitute a *functional* category (whereas adjectives are a *lexical* category). After all, there is an obvious sense in which adjectives (e.g. *thoughtful*) have descriptive content but determiners do not – as we can illustrate in terms of the following contrast (**?** and **!** are used to denote increasing degrees of semantic/pragmatic anomaly)

(24) (a)   a *thoughtful* friend/?cat/??fish/?!pan/!problem

(b)   **a/the/another/this/my** friend/cat/fish/pan/problem

As (24a) illustrates, an adjective like *thoughtful* can only be used to modify certain types of noun; this is because its descriptive content is such that it is only compatible with (for example) an expression denoting a rational entity. By contrast, determiners like those bold-printed in (24b) lack specific descriptive content, and hence can be used to premodify any kind of noun (the only restrictions being *grammatical* in nature – cf. e.g. the fact that *a(n)/another* can only be used to premodify a singular count noun).

Thus, it seems appropriate to conclude that determiners constitute a functional category and adjectives a lexical category.

Let's turn now to look at a second type of functional category, namely the category of **pronoun**. The most familiar kind of pronoun are **personal pronouns** like *I/me/we/us/you/he/him/she/her/it/they/them*. These are called personal pronouns not because they denote people (the pronoun *it* is not normally used to denote a person), but rather because they encode the grammatical property of **person**. In the relevant technical sense, *I/me/we/us* are said to be *first person* pronouns, in that they are expressions whose reference includes the person/s speaking; *you* is a second person pronoun, in that its reference includes the addressee/s (viz. the person/s being spoken to), but excludes the speaker/s; *he/him/she/her/it/they/them* are third person pronouns in the sense that they refer to entities other than the speaker/s or addressee/s. Personal pronouns differ morphologically from nouns in that they inflect for **case**, as we can see from contrasts such as:

(25) (a) *John* admires *Mary*, and *Mary* admires *John*

(b) **He/*Him** admires **her/*she**, and **she/*her** admires **him/*he**

Pronouns like *he/him* and *she/her* change their morphological form according to the position which they occupy within the sentence, so that the *nominative* forms *he/she* are required as the subject of a present-tense verb like *admires* (or a past-tense verb), whereas the *objective/accusative* forms *him/her* are required e.g. when used after (more precisely, as the **complement** of) a transitive verb or preposition: these variations are said to reflect different *case forms* of the pronoun. By contrast, nouns such as *John* and *Mary* don't overtly inflect for nominative/objective case in Modern English, and hence don't change their form according to whether they are used as subjects or complements.

Personal pronouns might be argued to be functors by virtue of the fact that they lack descriptive content: thus, whereas a noun like *dogs* denotes a specific type of animal, a personal pronoun like *they* denotes no specific type of entity, but has to have its reference determined from the linguistic or nonlinguistic context. Personal pronouns simply encode sets of **person**, **number**, **gender** and **case** properties – as represented in the table in (26) below:

(26)

PERSON	NUMBER	GENDER	CASE NOMINATIVE	OBJECTIVE
1	SG	–	I	me
1	PL	–	we	us
2	–	–	you	you
3	SG	M	he	him
3	SG	F	she	her
3	SG	N	it	it
3	PL	–	they	them

(Note: SG = singular; PL = plural; M = masculine; F = feminine; N = neuter; – indicates that the item in question carries no specific gender/number restriction on its use.) Since personal pronouns encode purely grammatical properties, it is reasonable to suppose that they too are *functors*.

Given that many items can belong to more than one category (and so are *polycategorial*), it is not surprising that some words can be used both as determiners and as pronouns. For example, the bold-printed items in (27) below serve as determiners (premodifying an italicized noun expression) in the first example in each pair, but as pronouns (standing on their own) in the second:

(27) (a)   **Both** *children* were ill/**Both** were ill

(b)   **Some** *people* say that he is dying/**Some** say that he is dying

(c)   I don't have **any** *cigarettes*/I don't have **any**

(d)   I prefer **this** *book*/**this**

Although most such items have the same form when used as determiners or pronouns, there are a few which have slightly different forms according to whether they are used as (italicized) determiners or as (bold-printed) pronouns: cf.

(28) (a)   *No* student has failed the test/**None** has failed the test

(b)   *My* house is bigger than *your* house/**Mine** is bigger than **yours**

Thus, *no* is a determiner whose pronoun counterpart is *none*, and similarly *my/your* are determiners whose pronoun counterparts are *mine/yours*. Consequently, one way of trying to decide whether a word which has dual determiner/pronoun status is being used as a determiner or as a pronoun in a given sentence is to use the familiar **substitution** test and see whether the word in question can be replaced by items like *no* and/or *my* (which can be used as determiners but not as pronouns), or by items like *none* and/or *mine* (which can be used as pronouns but not as determiners). If we apply this simple substitution test to sentences such as:

(29) (a)   *Neither* of the candidates was suitable for the post

(b)   *Neither* candidate was suitable for the post

we find that *neither* in (29a) can be replaced by *none* and hence is a pronoun, whereas in (29b) *neither* can be replaced by *no* and so is a determiner.

2.5   Auxiliaries and infinitival *to*

Thus far, we have looked at two types of functional category (**determiner** and **pronoun**) which are associated with noun expressions (in the sense that determiners typically modify nouns, and pronouns typically replace or refer back to noun expressions). We now turn to look at functional categories which are associated with verb expressions – beginning with the category **auxiliary**.

Categories and features

Traditional grammarians posit that there is a special class of items which once functioned simply as verbs, but in the course of the evolution of the English language have become sufficiently distinct from other verbs that they are now regarded as belonging to a different category of **auxiliary** (conventionally abbreviated to **AUX**). Auxiliaries differ from other verbs in a number of ways. Whereas a typical verb like *want* may take a range of different types of complement (e.g. a subjectless infinitival *to*-complement as in *I want [to go home]*, an infinitive with a (bold-printed) subject as in *I want [you to keep quiet]*, or a noun expression as in *I want [lots of money]*), by contrast auxiliaries typically take a verb expression as their complement, and have the semantic function of marking grammatical properties associated with the relevant verb, such as *tense*, *aspect*, *voice*, *mood* or *modality*. (See the *glossary* if you are not familiar with these terms.) The items italicized in (30) below (in the use illustrated there) are traditionally categorized as auxiliaries taking a [bracketed] verbal complement:

(30) (a) He *has/had* [gone]
    (b) She *is/was* [staying at home]
    (c) He *is/was* [seen regularly by the doctor]
    (d) He really *does/did* [say a lot]
    (e) You *can/could* [help]
    (f) They *may/might* [come back]
    (g) He *will/would* [get upset]
    (h) I *shall/should* [return]
    (i) You *must* [finish your assignment]

In the relevant uses, *have* is traditionally said to be a perfective auxiliary, *be* an imperfective/progressive auxiliary, *do* a dummy (i.e. meaningless) auxiliary, and *can/could/may/might/will/would/shall/should/must* are said to be modal auxiliaries. (See the *glossary* for glosses of these terms.) A minor complication is posed by the fact that the items *have* and *do* have other uses in which they function as *verbs* rather than auxiliaries.

There are clear syntactic differences between auxiliaries and verbs. For example (as we saw in §1.6), auxiliaries can undergo *inversion* (i.e. can be moved into presubject position) in questions – as illustrated by the following examples, where the auxiliary is italicized and the subject is bold-printed:

(31) (a) *Can* **you** speak Japanese?
    (b) *Do* **you** smoke?
    (c) *Is* **it** raining?

By contrast, typical verbs do not themselves permit inversion, but rather require what is traditionally called *do*-support (i.e. have inverted forms which require the use of the dummy auxiliary *do*): cf.

(32) (a)   **Intends* **he** to come?

    (b)   *Does* **he** intend to come?

    (c)   **Saw* **you** the mayor?

    (d)   *Did* **you** see the mayor?

    (e)   **Plays* **he** the piano?

    (f)   *Does* **he** play the piano?

A second difference between auxiliaries and verbs is that auxiliaries can generally be directly negated by a following *not* (which can usually contract down onto the auxiliary in the form of *n't*): cf.

(33) (a)   John *could not/couldn't* come to the party

    (b)   I *do not/don't* like her much

    (c)   He *is not/isn't* working very hard

    (d)   They *have not/haven't* finished

By contrast, verbs cannot themselves be directly negated by *not/n't*, but require indirect negation through the use of *do*-support: cf.

(34) (a)   **They *like not/liken't* me

    (b)   They *do not/don't* like me

    (c)   **I *see not/seen't* the point

    (d)   I *do not/don't* see the point

    (e)   **You *came not/camen't*

    (f)   You *did not/didn't* come

(Note that in structures such as *John decided not to stay* the negative particle *not* negates the infinitive complement *to stay* rather than the verb *decided*.) And thirdly, auxiliaries can appear in sentence-final tags, as illustrated by the examples below (where the part of the sentence following the comma is traditionally referred to as a *tag*): cf.

(35) (a)   You don't like her, *do* you?

    (b)   He won't win, *will* he?

    (c)   She isn't working, *is* she?

    (d)   He can't spell, *can* he?

In contrast, verbs can't themselves be used in tags, but rather require the use of *do*-tags: cf.

(36) (a)   You like her, *do/*like* you?

    (b)   They want one, *do/*want* they?

So, on the basis of these (and other) syntactic properties, it seems that we are justified in positing that auxiliaries constitute a different category from verbs.

A second type of functor which is associated with verbs is the **infinitive particle** *to* – so called because the only kind of complement it will allow is one containing a verb in the *infinitive* form. (The infinitive form of the verb in English is its uninflected base form – the form found in dictionary entries.) Typical uses of infinitival *to* are illustrated in (37) below:

(37) (a)   I wonder whether *to* [go home]
 (b)   Many people want the government *to* [change course]
 (c)   We don't intend *to* [surrender]

In each example in (37), the [bracketed] complement of *to* is an expression containing a verb in the infinitive form (viz. the infinitives *go*, *change*, and *surrender*). But what is the categorial status of infinitival *to*?

We are already familiar with an alternative use of *to* as a preposition, e.g. in sentences such as the following:

(38) (a)   He stayed *to* [the end of the film]
 (b)   Why don't you come *to* [the point]?
 (c)   He went *to* [the police]

In (38), *to* behaves like a typical (transitive) preposition in taking a [bracketed] determiner phrase (i.e. *the*-phrase) as its complement (viz. *the end of the film*, *the point* and *the police*). A natural suggestion to make, therefore, would be that *to* is a preposition in both uses – one which takes a following determiner phrase complement (i.e. has a determiner expression as its complement) in (38) and a following verbal complement in (37).

However, infinitival *to* is very different in its behaviour from prepositional *to* in English: whereas prepositional *to* is a contentive with intrinsic semantic content (e.g. it means something like 'as far as') infinitival *to* seems to be a dummy (i.e. meaningless) functor with no intrinsic semantic content. Because of its intrinsic semantic content, the preposition *to* can often be modified by intensifiers like *right/straight* (a characteristic property of prepositions) – cf.

(39) (a)   He stayed *right* **to** the end of the film
 (b)   Why don't you come *straight* **to** the point?
 (c)   He went *straight* **to** the police

By contrast, the dummy functor infinitival *to* (because of its lack of descriptive content) cannot be intensified by *right/straight*: cf.

(40) (a)   *I wonder whether *right/straight* **to** go home
 (b)   *Many people want the government *right/straight* **to** change course
 (c)   *We don't intend *right/straight* **to** surrender

Moreover, what makes the prepositional analysis of infinitival *to* even more problematic is that infinitival *to* takes an entirely different range of complements from prepositional *to* (and indeed different from the range of complements found with other prepositions in general). For example, prepositional *to* (like many other prepositions) takes a noun expression as its complement, whereas infinitival *to* requires a verbal complement – as we see from examples such as those below:

(41) (a) I intend to *resign* (= verb)/to **resignation* (= noun)

(b) She waited for John to *arrive* (= verb)/**to *arrival* (= noun)

(c) Try to *decide* (= verb)/**to *decision* (= noun)

Significantly, genuine prepositions in English (such as those bold-printed in the examples below) only permit following verbal complements when the verb is in the *+ing* form (known as the *gerund* form in this particular use), not where the verb is in the uninflected base/infinitive form: cf.

(42) (a) I am **against** *capitulating/*capitulate*

(b) Try and do it **without** *complaining/*complain*

(c) Think carefully **before** *deciding/*decide*

By contrast, infinitival *to* can only take a verbal complement when the verb is in the uninflected base (= infinitive) form, never when it is in the gerund form: cf.

(43) (a) I want to *go/*going* there

(b) You must try to *work/*working* harder

(c) You managed to *upset/*upsetting* them

A further difference between infinitival and prepositional *to* (illustrated in (44) below) is that infinitival *to* permits *ellipsis* (i.e. omission) of its complement, whereas prepositional *to* does not: cf.

(44) SPEAKER A: Do you want *to* go **to** the cinema?

SPEAKER B: No, I don't really want *to*   (infinitival)

No, I don't really want *to* go **to   (prepositional)

Thus, there are compelling reasons for assuming that infinitival *to* belongs to a different category from prepositional *to*. But what category does infinitival *to* belong to?

In the late 1970s, Chomsky suggested that there are significant similarities between infinitival *to* and a modal auxiliary like *should*. For example, they occupy the same position within the clause: cf.

(45) (a) It's vital [that John *should* show an interest]

(b) It's vital [for John *to*   show an interest]

We see from (45) that *to* and *should* are both positioned between the subject *John* and the verb *show*. Moreover, just as *should* requires after it a verb in the infinitive form (cf. *You should show/*should showing/*should shown more interest in syntax*), so too does infinitival *to* (cf. *Try to show/*to showing/*to shown more interest in syntax*). Furthermore, if *to* is analysed as an infinitival auxiliary, we can account for the fact that infinitival *to*, like auxiliaries (e.g. *should*) but unlike typical nonauxiliary verbs (e.g. *want*), allows ellipsis of its complement: cf.

(46) (a)   I don't really want to go to the dentist's, but I know I *should*

    (b)   I know I should go to the dentist's, but I just don't want *to*

    (c)   *I know I should go to the dentist's, but I just don't *want*

The fact that *to* patterns like the auxiliary *should* in several respects strengthens the case for regarding them as belonging to the same category. But what category?

Chomsky (1981, p. 18) suggested that the resulting category (comprising finite auxiliaries and infinitival *to*) be labelled **INFL** or **inflection**, though (in accordance with the standard practice of using single-letter symbols to designate categories) in later work (1986b, p. 3) he replaced **INFL** by the single-letter symbol **I**. The general idea behind this label is that finite auxiliaries inflect for tense/agreement, and infinitival *to* serves much the same function in English as infinitive inflections in languages like Italian which have overtly inflected infinitives (so that Italian *canta+re* = English *to sing*). We can then say (for example) that an auxiliary like *should* is a finite I/INFL, whereas the particle *to* is an infinitival I/INFL.

2.6 Complementizers

The last type of functional category which we shall look at is that of **complementizer** (abbreviated to **COMP** in earlier work and to **C** in more recent work): this is a term used to describe a special kind of (*italicized*) word which is used to introduce complement clauses such as those bracketed below:

(47) (a)   I think [*that* you may be right]

    (b)   I doubt [*if* you can help me]

    (c)   I'm anxious [*for* you to receive the best treatment possible]

Each of the bracketed clauses in (47) is a *complement clause*, in that it functions as the complement of the word immediately preceding it (*think/doubt/anxious*); the italicized word which introduces each clause is known in recent work (since 1970) as a *complementizer* (but would be known in more traditional work as a particular type of subordinating *conjunction*). Complementizers are *functors* in the sense that they encode particular sets of grammatical properties. For example, complementizers encode (non)finiteness by virtue of the fact that they are intrinsically *finite* or *nonfinite* (see the *glossary* if these terms are unfamiliar). Thus, the complementizers *that* and *if* are inherently finite in the sense that they can only be used to introduce a finite clause (i.e. a clause containing a present- or past-tense auxiliary or verb), and not e.g. an infinitival *to*-clause; by contrast, *for* is an inherently infinitival complementizer, and so can be used to introduce a clause containing infinitival *to*, but not a finite clause containing a tensed (i.e. present/past-tense) auxiliary like *should*; compare the examples in (47) above with those in (48) below:

(48) (a)   *I think [*that* you **to** be right]

    (b)   *I doubt [*if* you **to** help me]

    (c)   *I'm anxious [*for* you **should** receive the best treatment possible]

Complementizers in structures like (47) serve three grammatical functions: firstly, they mark the fact that the clause they introduce is the complement of some other word (*think/doubt/anxious*); secondly, they serve to indicate whether the clause they introduce is finite (i.e. contains a present/past-tense verb/auxiliary) or infinitival (i.e. contains infinitival *to*); and thirdly, they mark the *illocutionary force* (i.e. semantic/pragmatic function) of the clause they introduce (thus, *if* introduces an interrogative clause, whereas *that/for* introduce other types of clause: e.g. *that* typically introduces a declarative/statement-making clause).

However, an important question to ask is whether we really need to assign words such as *for/that/if* (in the relevant function) to a new category of complementizer, or whether we couldn't simply treat (for example) *for* as a preposition, *that* as a determiner and *if* as an adverb. The answer is 'No', because there are significant differences between complementizers and other apparently similar words. For example, one difference between the complementizer *for* and the preposition *for* is that the preposition *for* has intrinsic semantic content and so (in some but not all of its uses) can be intensified by *straight/right*, whereas the complementizer *for* is a dummy functor and can never be so intensified: cf.

(49) (a)   He headed *straight/right* **for** the pub   (= preposition)

    (b)   The dog went *straight/right* **for** her throat   (= preposition)

    (c)   *He was anxious *straight/right* **for** nobody to leave   (= complementizer)

    (d)   *It is vital *straight/right* **for** there to be peace   (= complementizer)

Moreover, the preposition *for* and the complementizer *for* also differ in their syntactic behaviour. For example, a clause introduced by the complementizer *for* can be the subject of an expression like *would be unthinkable*, whereas a phrase introduced by the preposition *for* cannot: cf.

(50) (a)   *For you to go there on your own* would be unthinkable   (= *for*-clause)

    (b)   **For you* would be unthinkable   (= *for*-phrase)

What makes it even more implausible to analyse infinitival *for* as a preposition is the fact that prepositions in English aren't generally followed by a [bracketed] infinitive complement, as we see from the ungrammaticality of:

55

(51) (a)　　*She was surprised *at* [there to be nobody to meet her]

　(b)　　*I'm not sure *about* [you to be there]

　(c)　　*I have decided *against* [us to go there]

On the contrary, as examples such as (42) above illustrate, the only verbal complements which can be used after prepositions are gerund structures containing a verb in
the +*ing* form.

　A further difference between the two types of *for* is that if we replace a noun expression
following the preposition *for* by an appropriate interrogative expression like *who?/what?/
which one?*, the interrogative expression can be preposed to the front of the sentence (with
or without *for*) if *for* is a preposition, but not if *for* is a complementizer. For example, in
(52) below, *for* functions as a preposition and the (distinguished) nominal *Senator
Megabucks* functions as its complement, so that if we replace *Senator Megabucks* by *which
senator?*, the wh-expression can be preposed with or without *for*: cf.

(52) (a)　　I will vote *for* **Senator Megabucks** in the primaries

　(b)　　**Which senator** will you vote *for* in the primaries?

　(c)　　*For* **which senator** will you vote in the primaries?

However, in (53a) below, the bold-printed expression is not the complement of the
complementizer *for* (the complement of *for* here is the infinitival clause *Senator
Megabucks to keep his cool*), but rather is the subject of the expression *to keep his
cool*: hence, even if we replace *Senator Megabucks* by the interrogative wh-phrase
which senator?, the wh-phrase can't be preposed:

(53) (a)　　They were anxious *for* **Senator Megabucks** to keep his cool

　(b)　　***Which senator** were they anxious *for* to keep his cool?

　(c)　　**For* **which senator** were they anxious to keep his cool?

Furthermore, when *for* functions as a complementizer, the whole *for*-clause which it
introduces can often be substituted by a clause introduced by another complementizer:
for example, the italicized *for*-clause in (54a) below can be replaced by the bold-
printed *that*-clause in (54b):

(54) (a)　　Is it really necessary *for there to be a showdown*?

　(b)　　Is it really necessary **that there should be a showdown**?

By contrast, the italicized *for*-phrase in (55a) below cannot be replaced by a *that*-
clause, as we see from the ungrammaticality of (55b):

(55) (a)　　We are heading *for a general strike*

　(b)　　*We are heading **that there (will/should) be a general strike**

Thus, there seems to be considerable evidence in favour of drawing a categorial distinction between the preposition *for*, and the complementizer *for*.

Consider now the question of whether the complementizer *that* can be analysed as a determiner. At first sight, it might seem as if such an analysis would provide a natural way of capturing the apparent parallelism between the two uses of *that* in sentences such as the following:

(56) (a)   I refuse to believe **that** [*rumour*]

(b)   I refuse to believe **that** [*Randy Rabbit runs Benny's Bunny Bar*]

Given that the word *that* has the status of a prenominal determiner in sentences such as (56a), we might suppose that it has the function of a preclausal determiner (i.e. a determiner introducing the italicized clause *Randy Rabbit runs Benny's Bunny Bar*) in sentences such as (56b).

However, there is strong empirical evidence against a determiner analysis of the complementizer *that*. Part of the evidence is phonological in nature. In its use as a complementizer (in sentences such as (56b) above), *that* typically has the vowel-reduced form /ðət/, whereas in its use as a determiner (e.g. in sentences such as (56a) above), *that* invariably has the unreduced form /ðæt/: the phonological differences between the two suggest that we are dealing with two different items here, one of which functions as a complementizer and typically has a reduced vowel, and the other of which functions as a determiner and always has an unreduced vowel.

Moreover, *that* in its use as a determiner (though not in its use as a complementizer) can be substituted by another determiner (such as *this/the*):

(57) (a)   Nobody else knows about **that/this/the** *accident*   (= determiner)

(b)   I'm sure **that/*this/*the** *you are right*   (= complementizer)

Similarly, the determiner *that* can be used pronominally (without any complement), whereas the complementizer *that* cannot: cf.

(58) (a)   Nobody can blame you for **that** *mistake*   (prenominal determiner)

(b)   Nobody can blame you for **that**   (pronominal determiner)

(59) (a)   I'm sure **that** *you are right*   (preclausal complementizer)

(b)   *I'm sure **that**   (pronominal complementizer)

The clear phonological and syntactic differences between the two uses of *that* argue strongly that the particle *that* which serves to introduce complement clauses should not be analysed as a determiner, but rather as a complementizer (hence assigned to the category **C** of complementizer).

The third item which we earlier suggested might function as a complementizer in English is interrogative *if*. However, at first sight, it might seem that there is a potential parallelism between the use of *if* and interrogative wh-adverbs like *when/where/whether*: cf.

(60)   I don't know [*where/when/whether*/**if** he will go]

Thus, we might be tempted to analyse *if* as a wh-adverb of some kind.

However, there are a number of reasons for rejecting this possibility. For one thing, *if* differs from interrogative adverbs like *where/when/whether* not only in its form (it isn't a *wh*-word, i.e. it doesn't begin with *wh*), but also in its distribution: for example, whereas typical wh-adverbs can occur in finite and infinitive clauses alike, the complementizer *if* is restricted to introducing finite clauses – cf.

(61)   (a)   I wonder [*when/where/whether*/**if** I should go]   (finite clause)

     (b)   I wonder [*when/where/whether*/***if** to go]   (infinitive clause)

Moreover, *if* is different from interrogative wh-adverbs (but similar to other complementizers) in respect of the fact that it cannot be used to introduce a clause which serves as the complement of a (bold-printed) preposition: cf.

(62)   (a)   I'm not certain **about** [*whether/when/where* he'll go]

     (b)   *I'm concerned **over** [*if* taxes are going to be increased]

     (c)   *I'm puzzled **at** [*that* he should have resigned]

     (d)   *I'm not very keen **on** [*for* you to go there]

Finally, whereas a wh-adverb can typically be coordinated with (e.g. joined by *or* to) another similar adverb, this is not true of *if*: cf.

(63)   (a)   I don't know [*where* or **when** to meet him]

     (b)   I don't know [*whether* or **not** he'll turn up]

     (c)   *I don't know [*if* or **not** he'll turn up]

For reasons such as these, then, it seems more appropriate to categorize *if* as an interrogative complementizer and *whether/where/when* as interrogative adverbs. More generally, our discussion highlights the need to posit an additional category C of complementizer, to designate clause-introducing items such as *if/that/for* which serve the function of introducing specific types of finite or infinitival clause.

2.7   Parsing

Having given an outline of the major lexical and functional categories found in English, we are now in a position where we can start to **parse** (i.e. analyse the grammatical structure of) phrases and sentences. The first step in parsing any expression is to **categorize** each of the words in the expression. A conventional way of doing this is to use the traditional system of **labelled bracketing**: each word is enclosed in a pair of square brackets, and the lefthand member of each pair of brackets is given an appropriate subscript category label to indicate what category the word belongs to. To save space, it is conventional to use the following (bold-printed) capital-letter abbreviations to represent categories:

(64) **N** = noun   **V** = verb

     A = adjective   **ADV** = adverb

     P = preposition **D/DET** = determiner

     PRN = pronoun **C/COMP** = complementizer

     I/INFL = finite inflected auxiliary or infinitival *to*

Adopting this notation, we can represent the categorial status of each of the words in a sentence such as *Any experienced journalist knows that he can sometimes manage to lure the unsuspecting politician into a cunning trap* as in (65) below:

(65) [$_D$ Any] [$_A$ experienced] [$_N$ journalist] [$_V$ knows] [$_C$ that] [$_{PRN}$ he]

    [$_I$ can] [$_{ADV}$ sometimes] [$_V$ manage] [$_I$ to] [$_V$ lure] [$_D$ the]

    [$_A$ unsuspecting] [$_N$ politician] [$_P$ into] [$_D$ a] [$_A$ cunning] [$_N$ trap]

What (65) tells us is that the words *journalist/politician/trap* belong to the category N (= noun), *he* to the category PRN (= pronoun), *any/the/a* to the category D (= determiner), *experienced/unsuspecting/cunning* to the category A (= adjective), *sometimes* to the category ADV (= adverb), *into* to the category P (= preposition), *knows/manage/lure* to the category V (= verb), *can/to* to the category I/INFL (since *can* is a finite present-tense auxiliary and *to* an infinitive particle) and *that* to the category C (= complementizer). It is important to note, however, that the category labels used in (65) tell us only how the relevant words are being used in this particular sentence. For example, the N label on *trap* in (65) tells us that the item in question functions as a noun in this particular position in this particular sentence, but tells us nothing about the function it may have in other sentences. So, for example, in a sentence such as *Greed can **trap** careless politicians*, the word *trap* functions as a verb – as represented in (66) below:

(66) [$_N$ Greed] [$_I$ can] [$_V$ trap] [$_A$ careless] [$_N$ politicians]

Thus, a labelled bracket round a particular word is used to indicate the grammatical category which the word belongs to in the particular position which it occupies in the phrase or sentence in question, so allowing for the possibility that the same word may have a different categorial status in other positions in other structures.

2.8 Subcategorial features

  So far, we have assumed that the grammatical properties of words can be described in terms of a system of grammatical categories, so that (for example) the fact that the word *fool* (but not the word *foolish*) has a plural form in +*s* (cf. They are *fools/*foolishes*) and can be used after *a* in a sentence such as *He is a fool/*a foolish* is attributable to the fact that *fool* belongs to the category N/noun, whereas *foolish* belongs to the category A/adjective. However, while a category-based model of syntax enables us to provide a description of those properties which different words belonging to the same category share in common, it provides us with no way of describing important grammatical *differences* between words belonging to the same category. For example, traditional grammars draw a distinction between two different subclasses of noun, traditionally called **common nouns** and **proper nouns**. The essential difference between the two is that proper nouns typically denote names of people (e.g. *Chomsky*), places (e.g. *Cambridge*), dates (e.g. *Tuesday*) or magazines (e.g. *Cosmopolitan*), and the first letter of a proper noun is generally capitalized; from a semantic viewpoint, proper nouns have the property of having *unique reference*. In terms of their syntactic properties, what differentiates proper nouns from common nouns is that common nouns can freely be modified by determiners like *the*, whereas proper nouns (perhaps because of their unique reference) generally cannot – cf. contrasts such as:

(67) (a)   I have never visited the *capital*   (= common noun)

   (b)   *I have never visited the *London*   (= proper noun)

An important theoretical question to ask is how we handle the distinction between proper nouns and common nouns. Within a purely categorial theory of grammar (i.e. a framework in which the only mechanism for describing the grammatical differences between words is to assign them to different grammatical categories), the only solution is to assign proper nouns and common nouns to two entirely different categories, say *PROPER* and *COMMON*. However, although such a solution would provide an obvious way of accounting for the *differences* between common and proper nouns, it would fail to provide any account of the *similarities* between the two – viz. the fact that both are species of *noun*. What we need is some technical device which will allow us to continue to maintain that both proper and common nouns have the categorial status of *nouns*, while recognizing the fact that they belong to different subclasses of noun. But how can we do this? Chomsky (1965, pp. 79–86) suggests that just as specific phonological properties are analysed in terms of *phonological features* (so that the distinction between *nasal* and *oral* sounds is described in terms of a feature such as [±NASAL]), so too specific grammatical properties can be described in terms of *grammatical features*. He suggests, for example, that the distinction between common nouns and proper nouns can be described in terms of a binary **grammatical feature** such as [±COMMON], so that a common noun like *capital* would carry the grammatical feature [+COMMON], whereas a proper noun like *London* would carry the feature [–COMMON].

A further traditional distinction (mentioned earlier) between two different subclasses of noun is that between **count nouns** and **mass/noncount nouns**. How can we handle this distinction? Within a purely category-based model of grammar, the only way of doing so is to assign count nouns and mass nouns to two entirely distinct categories (e.g. *COUNT* and *MASS*): however, although the *two-categories* approach would capture the differences between the two, it would fail to capture the essential similarity between them – namely that they are both types of *noun*. For this reason, Chomsky

(1965, p. 82) suggests that the distinction should be handled in terms of a grammatical feature such as [±COUNT] – i.e. countable/uncountable. We could then say that a count noun like *chair* and a mass noun like *furniture* have in common their categorial status as N words, but differ in respect of the grammatical feature [±COUNT] in that countable nouns like *chair* are [+COUNT], whereas mass nouns like *furniture* are [–COUNT].

We have noted that one of the characteristic properties of regular count nouns is that they have both *singular* and *plural* forms (cf. *chair/chairs*). However, our existing model of grammar provides no way of representing the difference between singular and plural nouns. Clearly, any proposal to handle the distinction in categorial terms (e.g. by assigning singular nouns to the category *SG*, and plural nouns to the entirely distinct category *PL*) would fail to capture the essential nominal properties which the two types of noun share. Hence, it would seem preferable to handle number in terms of a grammatical feature such as [±PLURAL] (i.e. plural/nonplural), so that a plural noun like *scissors* would carry the feature [+PLURAL], whereas an inherently singular noun like *news* would be specified as [–PLURAL]; by contrast, the lexical entry for a noun like *book* (which has both the singular form *book* and the plural form *books*) would assign it the number feature [±PLURAL].

Generalizing our discussion at this point, we might suppose that the *categorial* properties of words are specified by assigning each word to an appropriate category, and that their *subcategorial* properties are specified in terms of a set of grammatical features. So, for example, the (relevant parts of) the lexical entries for *news* and *scissors* might be as in (68) below:

(68)   *news*:   N, [+COMMON, –COUNT, –PLURAL]
            scissors: N, [+COMMON, –COUNT, +PLURAL]

The lexical entries in (68) say that *news* is a noncount common noun which is inherently singular (so has no plural form: cf. *The news is/*are bad*), and that *scissors* is a noncount common noun which is inherently plural (so has no singular form: cf. *These scissors are blunt/*This scissor(s) is blunt*). But note that two different technical devices are used to describe the relevant properties: thus, the nounhood properties of the two items are described in terms of the category label N, whereas their commonness, countability and number properties are described in terms of sets of grammatical features.

We might extend the use of features to handle the relation between quantifiers and determiners. In our discussion of the examples in (18) above, we suggested that quantifiers are a subclass of determiner. One way of handling the relation between the two would be in terms of a feature such as [±Q] (i.e. quantifying/nonquantifying), so that a determiner such as *many* would carry the feature [+Q], whereas a referential determiner such as *this* would carry the feature [–Q]. Similarly, we could use features as a way of capturing the traditional insight that adverbs are a subclass of adjectives, typically derived from adjectives by the addition of +*ly*, so that from the adjective *quiet* we form the adverb *quietly* by the addition of the suffix +*ly*. Some evidence that adverbs are a subclass of adjectives comes from the fact that the comparative form of an adverb like *quickly* is derived by adding the comparative suffix +*er* to the corresponding adjective stem *quick* (cf. *He runs quicker than me*, where *quicker* is an adverb paraphraseable as 'more quickly'). Moreover, in some nonstandard varieties of English, we find adjective forms used where Standard English requires an adverb form carrying the suffix +*ly* (e.g. in nonstandard sentences such as *Tex talks real slow*, corresponding to Standard English *Tex talks really slowly*). One way of capturing the inter-relation between adjectives and adverbs would be to say that they share the categorial properties of adjectives, but differ in respect of a subcategorial feature such as [±ADV], with adverbs like *quickly* being [+ADV] and hence adverbial, and adjectives like *quick* being [–ADV] and hence nonadverbial.

Chomsky (1965) argues that we can achieve a more unitary theory of syntax if we suppose that *all* grammatical properties of words are encoded as grammatical features. If so, then category labels such as N will be replaced by categorial features such as [+N], and the (relevant parts of the) lexical entries in (68) will be replaced by the sets of grammatical features in (69) below:

(69)   *news*:   [+N, +COMMON, –COUNT, –PLURAL]
         scissors: [+N, +COMMON, –COUNT, +PLURAL]

Of course, the wider implication of our discussion here is that the categorial and subcategorial properties of other categories of word can similarly be described in terms of a **feature matrix** (i.e. a set of features). We can illustrate this by a brief discussion of how we might differentiate the (various different uses) of verb forms such as *show/showing/shown/showed/shows*. (The set of features used here is based loosely on that proposed in Halle and Marantz 1993.)

Consider first of all how we might differentiate those (participle) verb forms which are overtly inflected for aspect (*shown/showing*) from those which are not. An obvious suggestion would be to handle this difference in terms of a feature such as [±ASPECT] or alternatively [±PARTICIPLE], with participles like *shown/showing* being positively specified for the relevant feature, and nonparticipial forms like *show/shows/showed* being negatively specified. In order to differentiate past-tense finite verbs from the corresponding present-tense forms, and to differentiate past (perfective) participles from present (imperfective) participles, we might make use of a feature such as [±PAST]. And in order to differentiate between those third person singular present-tense forms like *shows* which are overtly inflected for agreement from those like *show* which are not, we might posit a feature such as [±AGR] – or perhaps [±3SG]. The various uses of the italicized verb forms in the examples below will then have the tense/aspect/agreement feature specifications indicated:

(70) (a)　　He has *shown* improvement　　[+V, +PARTICIPLE, +PAST]

　　(b)　　He is *showing* improvement　　[+V, +PARTICIPLE, –PAST]

　　(c)　　He *showed* improvement　　[+V, –PARTICIPLE, +PAST]

　　(d)　　He *shows* improvement　　[+V, –PARTICIPLE, –PAST, +3SG]

　　(e)　　You *show* improvement　　[+V, –PARTICIPLE, –PAST, –3SG]

Correspondingly, we can say that different inflectional affixes encode different sets of tense/aspect/agreement features. For example, the *+s* affix encodes the properties *third person singular present tense*, and the affix *+n* encodes the properties *past participle*.

2.9　Cross-categorial features

　　Thus far, we have argued that we need to break down categories into sets of features in order to provide an adequate account of **subcategorial properties** (i.e. those grammatical properties which are associated with a subset of the members of a given category). However, a second advantage of a feature-based analysis is that it enables us to capture the fact that many grammatical properties are **cross-categorial**, in the sense that they extend across more than one category. For example, Stowell (1981, p. 57, fn. 17) notes that verbs and adjectives in English share the morphological property that they alone permit direct *un+* prefixation, as examples such as the following illustrate:

(71) (a)　　*un*do, *un*tie, *un*fold, *un*pack　　　　(*verbs*)

　　(b)　　*un*afraid, *un*friendly, *un*manly, *un*kind　　(*adjectives*)

　　(c)　　**un*fear, **un*friend, **un*woman, **un*convention　(*nouns*)

　　(d)　　**un*inside, **un*by, **un*on, **un*from　　(*prepositions*)

More extensive similarities between the two are found in Jamaican Creole, as we see from the examples below (from Bailey 1966):

(72) (a)　　Daag bait

　　　　　dog　bite

　　　　　'Dogs bite'

　　(b)　　Manggo swiit

　　　　　mango　sweet

　　　　　'Mangoes are sweet'

(73) (a)　　Tiicha　no kom　yet

　　　　　teacher no come yet

　　　　　'The teacher hasn't come yet'

　　(b)　　Dat-de　　kuoknut no gud

　　　　　that-there coconut no good

　　　　　'That coconut is no good'

(74) (a)   Mi kyaan dringk mi kaafi
             me can't drink me coffee
             'I can't drink my coffee'

     (b)   Di milk kyaan sowa
             the milk can't sour
             'The milk can't be sour'

The examples in (72) show that both a verb like *bait* 'bite' and an adjective like *swiit* 'sweet' (but not a preposition or noun) can function as a predicate in an independent sentence; those in (73) that both a verb like *kom* 'come' and an adjective like *gud* 'good' can be negated by *no*; and those in (74) that both a verb like *dringk* 'drink' and an adjective like *sowa* 'sour' can be the complement of a modal like *kyaan* 'can't'.

Similarly, <u>nouns and adjectives</u> share certain grammatical properties in common: e.g. in Russian, nouns and adjectives inflect for grammatical ***case***, but not verbs or prepositions: cf.

(75)   Krasiva*ya* dyevushk*a* vsunula chornuy*u* koshk*u* v pustuy*u* korobk*u*
          beautiful girl   put   black   cat   in empty box
          'The beautiful girl put the black cat in the empty box'

Thus, the nouns and adjectives in (75) carry (italicized) case endings (+*a* is a nominative case suffix, +*u* is an accusative/objective case suffix), but not the verb or preposition. How can we account for the fact that adjectives seem to share properties in common with verbs on the one hand, and with nouns on the other?

In work dating back to Chomsky 1970, Chomsky suggested that we can account for cross-categorial properties such as these by analysing categories as composites of binary grammatical features (with each feature value representing a set of shared grammatical properties). More specifically, he suggested that the four primary lexical categories noun, adjective, verb and preposition can be analysed as complexes of just two binary grammatical features, namely [±N] (nominal/non-nominal) and [±V] (verbal/non-verbal), and decomposed into feature matrices (= sets of features) in the manner indicated in (76) below:

(76)   verb = [+V, –N]   adjective = [+V, +N]
          noun = [–V, +N]   preposition = [–V, –N]

Within the feature-based analysis of categories outlined in (76) above, the fact that verbs and adjectives form a natural class (as we see from the fact that both allow *un*-prefixation) is not an accidental property, but rather follows from the assumption that they form a ***supercategory***, by virtue of sharing the feature [+V] (though of course they differ in respect of the feature [±N]). We could then specify in relation to the paradigm in (71) above that only [+V] words allow *un*-prefixation, so that words belonging to the

[+V] categories *verb/adjective* allow an *un+* prefix, but those belonging to the [–V] categories *noun/preposition* do not; likewise, in relation to the examples in (72–4), we could say that only [+V] categories in Jamaican Creole can function as predicates, can be negated by *no* and can occur as the complement of a modal. This would mean that the feature [±V] serves to *cross-classify* categories (in that it is a feature which cuts across traditional category boundaries). Likewise, the feature [±N] serves to cross-classify categories in a similar way, since it implies that the [+N] categories noun and adjective share certain properties in common (and hence in effect form a *supercategory*) which differentiate them from the [–N] categories verb and preposition. Given the feature analysis in (76) we could account for the data in (75) by positing that the property of inflecting for case in Russian is associated with the supercategory of [+N] constituents (viz. adjectives and nouns).

We can exploit the use of grammatical features to provide an interesting account of the inter-relations between lexical and functional categories. Each functional category seems to be closely related to a corresponding lexical category: auxiliaries appear to be related to verbs, pronouns to nouns, determiners to adjectives, and the complementizer *for* and the infinitive particle *to* to the corresponding prepositions.

To make our discussion more concrete, let's explore the relation between *auxiliaries* and *verbs*. In §2.5, we argued that auxiliaries and verbs should be assigned to the two separate categories *auxiliary* (= AUX) and *verb* (= V), on the grounds that the two show systematic syntactic differences (e.g. with respect to their behaviour in negatives, interrogatives and tags). However, any proposal that AUX and V should be analysed as two different categories predicts that auxiliaries should be utterly distinct from verbs in their morphosyntactic characteristics. And yet, this is not the case at all: on the contrary, auxiliaries behave just like verbs in some respects – and this fact is implicitly recognized in their classification as *auxiliary verbs* in traditional grammar. One such common property which is shared by verbs and auxiliaries (illustrated in the table in (77) below) is that both have potentially distinct past/present-tense forms:

(77)	VERB		AUXILIARY	
	PAST	PRESENT	PAST	PRESENT
	heard	hear(s)	had	have/has
	hid	hide(s)	did	do(es)
	saw	see(s)	was/were	am/is/are
	fled	flee(s)	would	will
	bought	buy(s)	might	may

Within a *feature-based* theory of syntax, a natural way of capturing the fact that auxiliaries are similar to verbs in some respects (e.g. in inflecting for tense) but different in others (e.g. in undergoing inversion) is to suppose that auxiliaries and verbs share the core features [+V, –N], but differ in respect of some other feature. Bearing in mind that auxiliaries are *functors* and verbs are not (verbs are *contentives*), one way of capturing the differences between them would be in terms of a *functionality* feature [±F]: auxiliaries would be [+F] and hence functors, and verbs would be [−F] and hence contentives. Given these twin assumptions, the respective feature specifications of verbs and auxiliaries would be as in (78) below:

(78)   auxiliary verb   = AUX = [+V, −N, +F]
          nonauxiliary verb = V   = [+V, −N, −F]

We could then identify the *supercategory* of verb/auxiliary constituents which inflect for tense as words carrying the features [+V, −N] (so that both auxiliaries and verbs would inflect for tense), and the class of words which undergo interrogative inversion (i.e. auxiliaries) as those carrying the features [+V, −N, +F].

If auxiliaries and verbs together form a supercategory of elements which share certain properties in common but differ in respect of a single functionality feature, we might handle the relation between other contentive/functor pairs in terms of the same feature [±F]. Clearly, the most general feature theory we could develop would be one in which each contentive category has a functional counterpart: as suggested earlier, we might suppose that pronouns (like *he*) are the functional counterparts of nouns, that determiners (like *the*) are the functional counterparts of adjectives and that particles like infinitival *to* and the complementizer *for* are the functional counterparts of prepositions. If this is so, lexical categories and their functional counterparts would have the respective feature composition in (79) below:

(79)   LEXICAL CATEGORIES   FUNCTIONAL CATEGORIES
          noun/N   = [+N, −V, −F]   pronoun/PRN   = [+N, −V, +F]
          adjective/A = [+N, +V, −F]   determiner/D = [+N, +V, +F]
          verb/V   = [−N, +V, −F]   auxiliary/AUX = [−N, +V, +F]
          preposition/P = [−N, −V, −F]   particle/C/I = [−N, −V, +F]

It would then follow that pronouns are *functional nominals* whereas nouns are *lexical nominals*, determiners are *functional adjectives* whereas descriptive adjectives are *lexical adjectives*, auxiliaries are *functional verbs* whereas nonauxiliary verbs are *lexical verbs*, and that particles (e.g. the infinitive particle *to* and the prepositional complementizer *for*) are *functional prepositions* whereas contentive prepositions are *lexical prepositions*.

A further relationship which is captured within the analysis in (79) is that between infinitival *to* and auxiliaries. (Recall from §2.5 that these are different exponents of the category INFL.) Under the analysis in (79), infinitival *to* has the feature specification [−V, −N, +F], whereas auxiliaries carry the feature specification [+V, −N, +F]: this means that the two share in common the features [−N, +F] (hence belong to the same category INFL), but differ in respect of the feature [±V], in that auxiliaries are [+V] (and hence carry verbal tense/agreement inflections), whereas infinitival *to* is [–V] (and so is an uninflected tenseless and agreementless particle).

Our discussion here provides a clear illustration of how a feature-based theory achieves a higher level of *descriptive adequacy*, in terms of capturing important descriptive generalizations about relations between categories (e.g. between auxiliaries and verbs). We have argued that the categorial and subcategorial properties of any given word can be described in terms of a matrix of categorial features [$\pm F_1$, $\pm F_2$, $\pm F_3$, $\pm F_4$ ... $\pm F_n$] which defines its feature specification (and hence its categorial properties). This being so, we can redefine the notion of *grammatical category* as follows:

(80)   A *grammatical category* is a set of elements which have the same
         value(s) for a given set of grammatical features

It then follows that traditional capital-letter category labels are nothing more than abbreviations for sets of features (in much the same way as a chemical symbol like *H* is simply a convenient abbreviation for the atomic properties of hydrogen).

An interesting (though not immediately obvious) corollary of the feature-based definition of categories given in (80) is that there is a variety of different category labels which we might attach to a given item on the basis of its feature specification, depending on how fine- or coarse-grained a system of category labels we choose: an analysis based on a small number of shared feature values will give us a relatively *coarse* categorization, whereas an analysis based on a much larger number of shared feature values will give us a much *finer* categorization. We can illustrate this point by considering what kind of category label we might give to *have* in its use as a perfective auxiliary (e.g. in sentences like *They have gone home*, where *have* marks the perfection – in the sense of 'completion' – of the activity of going home). Let's assume that perfective *have* is specified as [+V, –N, +F, +PERF], where the feature [+PERF] marks perfectivity. If we adopt a relatively coarse system of category labels based on the two features [$\pm V$] and [$\pm N$], then perfective *have* is labelled as a verb (= V) by virtue of being [+V, –N]. If we adopt a rather less coarse system of category labels based on the three features [$\pm V$], [$\pm N$] and [$\pm F$], then perfective *have* is categorized as an *auxiliary verb* (= AUX) by virtue of being [+V, –N, +F]. But if we adopt a much more finely differentiated set of category labels based on the four features [$\pm V$, $\pm N$, $\pm F$, $\pm PERF$], perfective *have* will be assigned the category label PERF, by virtue of being [+V, –N, +F, +PERF]. Thus, depending how coarse- or fine-grained a system of category labelling we use, perfective *have* can variously be labelled as V, AUX or PERF. Of course, within a category-based theory which regards categories as primitive (irreducible) elements, this would lead to an obvious contradiction: however, there is no contradiction within a feature-based theory if we adopt the definition of *category* given in (80) above, since each different category symbol (viz. V, AUX, PERF) simply picks out a different subset of the grammatical features associated with perfective *have*. For analogous reasons, the so-called progressive auxiliary *be* (as in *He may be working*) could variously be labelled as V, AUX or PROG; and the passive auxiliary *be* (as in *He may be arrested*) could variously be labelled as V, AUX or PASS. And, in the same way, a quantifier such as *many* could be labelled either as D (by virtue of being a determiner) or as Q (by virtue of being a quantifying determiner).

Since the feature-based analyses outlined in the last two sections are rather more abstract than the purely categorial analyses in earlier sections, you may feel (if you are a beginner) that you don't have a good grasp of feature-based analyses at this stage. Since the discussion in the next two chapters will be category-based, this doesn't matter for the time being. We return to consider grammatical features in chapter 5, and it may be a good idea for you to reread sections §2.8 and §2.9 in conjunction with chapter 5.

2.10 Summary

In this chapter, we have looked at the nature of grammatical categories. In §2.2 we defined a *category* as a class of expressions which share a common set of grammatical properties; we argued that inflectional and derivational morphology provide us with strong empirical evidence for categorizing words, in that certain types of inflectional or derivational affix attach only to certain categories of word. In §2.3 we argued that there is also syntactic evidence for categorization, in that different categories of word occur in a different range of positions within the phrase or sentence. We suggested that we can determine the categorial status of a word from its morphological and syntactic properties, with *substitution* being used as a test in problematic cases. For example, verbs (= V) have the morphological property that they can take a range of inflectional suffixes (+*s*/+*d*/+*n*/+*ing*), and have the syntactic property that they can be used as the complement of a word like *can*; nouns (= N) have the morphological property that they typically inflect for number (cf. *cat*/*cats*), and the syntactic property that they can be preceded by *a*/*the*; adjectives (= A) have the morphological property that they have +*ly* or +*ness* derivatives, and the distributional property that they can be modified by words like *very* and occur after the verb *be*; adverbs have the morphological property that they end in +*ly*, and the distributional property that they can follow a verb like *behave*; and prepositions have the morphological property that they are invariable, and the distributional property that they can be modified by *right*/*straight*. In §2.4 we suggested that verbs, nouns, adjectives, adverbs and prepositions are *lexical categories*, in that words belonging to these categories typically have descriptive content. We noted that English also has a number of *functional categories*, whose members lack descriptive content and serve to mark grammatical properties (e.g. number, person, tense, etc.). We argued that determiners (= D) constitute a functional category, and that they differ from their lexical (adjective) counterparts in that they precede (but don't follow) adjectives, they can't be stacked and they impose grammatical restrictions on the types of expression they can modify (e.g. *a* can only modify a singular count noun expression). We went on to look at the functional counterparts of nouns, namely pronouns (= PRN); we argued that these differ from nouns in that they have no descriptive content and simply serve to encode functional properties like person, number, gender and case. In §2.5 we looked at the functional counterparts of verbs, namely *auxiliaries*; we argued that these are functors in that (unlike verbs) they describe no specific action or event, but rather encode verb-related grammatical properties such as tense, mood and aspect; we noted that *auxiliaries* are syntactically distinct from verbs in that (for example) they undergo inversion. We showed that infinitival *to* is distinct from the preposition *to*, and shares a number of properties in common with finite auxiliaries (e.g. auxiliaries and infinitival *to* allow ellipsis of their complements, but prepositional *to* does not): we noted Chomsky's suggestion that finite auxiliaries and infinitival *to* are different exponents of the same category I (or INFL). In §2.6 we argued that complementizers (= C or COMP) like *that/if/for* form a further category of functors which mark the illocutionary force of a complement clause (e.g. indicate whether it is a statement or question), and that (for example) *if* is distinct from interrogative adverbs like *how/when/whether* in that it can only introduce a finite clause, and cannot introduce a clause which is used as the complement of a preposition. In §2.7 we showed how the labelled bracketing technique can be used to parse the words in a sentence. In §2.8 we argued that categories are not primitive elements, but rather are composites of grammatical features. We noted that in a category-based theory of grammar, we have no straightforward way of accounting for subcategorial properties (e.g. the fact that count nouns and mass nouns differ in certain respects), but that in a feature-based grammar we can handle these differences in terms of a feature such as [±COUNT]. In §2.9 we suggested that cross-categorial properties (i.e. properties which are shared by members of two or more different categories) can similarly be handled in a feature-based grammar: for instance, if we suppose that the four primary categories (noun, verb, adjective and preposition) are composites of two primitive features [±V] and [±N], so that nouns are [+N, –V], adjectives are [+N, +V], verbs are [–N, +V] and prepositions are [–N, –V], we can then say that only items which are specified as [+V] allow *un*-prefixation. We further suggested that each major class of contentive category has a functional counterpart, so that auxiliaries are the functional counterparts of verbs, determiners of adjectives, pronouns of nouns, and particles (e.g. complementizer *for* and infinitival *to*) of prepositions; and we suggested that the similarities between functors and their contentive counterparts are a consequence of their having shared values for certain features, and that the differences between them could be handled in terms of a functionality feature such as [±F], with functors being [+F] and contentives [–F]. We noted that within a feature-based theory, a *grammatical category* is no longer a primitive construct, but rather is defined as a set of elements which have the same value(s) for a given set of grammatical features. We pointed out that one consequence of this is that there can be a variety of ways of categorizing a given item on the basis of its feature specification, depending on how fine- or coarse-grained a categorization we choose: thus, perfective *have* can be variously labelled as a verb (= V) by virtue of being [+V, –N], or an auxiliary verb (= AUX) by virtue of being [+V, –N, +F], or a perfective auxiliary verb (= PERF) by virtue of being [+V, –N, +F, +PERF].

Workbook section
Exercise I (§§2.2–2.3)

Each of the words below is *polycategorial*, in that it is a member of more than one different grammatical category. What are the different categories that each word can belong to? Provide a different example sentence to illustrate each different use of each word, and give reasons in support of your proposed categorization.

1 people	2 desire	3 down	4 clean	5 well	6 outside
7 long	8 gross	9 late	10 back	11 like	12 sound

Model answer for 1

The word *people* can be used in three different ways. One use is as a verb meaning 'populate' (cf. *to people a continent*): in this use, it has three other inflected forms, viz. the imperfective/progressive form *peopling*, the third person singular present-tense form *peoples* and the past/perfective form *peopled*. A second use is as a singular count noun meaning 'tribe' or 'nation' (in which case it has the regular plural form *peoples* – cf. e.g. *Algerians are the descendants of several different peoples*). A third use is as a plural count noun meaning 'human beings': in this third function, it is morphologically irregular, in that it does not take the noun plural +*s* suffix, and has no singular form (e.g. we cannot use *a people* to mean 'a person', only to mean 'a tribe/nation').

Exercise II (§§2.2–2.3)

Below are some examples of Shakespearean English (dating back to around the year 1600) containing words which are no longer used (or which have a different use) in contemporary English:

1　I will *example* it (Armado, *Love's Labour's Lost*, III.i)
2　I can *gleek* upon occasion (Bottom, *Midsummer Night's Dream*, II.i)
3　I had rather he should *shrive* me than *wive* me (Portia, *Merchant of Venice*, I.ii)
4　We are now to *examination* these men (Dogberry, *Much Ado About Nothing*, III.i)
5　Then you'd *wanton* with us (Second Lady, *Winter's Tale*, II.i)
6　. . . a soldier . . . bearded like the *pard* (Jaques, *As You Like It*, II.vii)

7   What will you *adventure* to save this brat's life? (Leontes, *Winter's Tale*, II.iii)

8   He is not *like* to marry me well (Touchstone, *As You Like It*, III.iv)

9   I would *fain* prove so (Polonius, *Hamlet*, II.i)

10 An old black ram is *tupping* your white ewe (Iago, *Othello*, I.i)

11 I had as *lief* be wooed of a snail (Rosalind, *As You Like It*, IV.i)

12 I'll *pheeze* you (Sly, *Taming of the Shrew*, Induction)

13 I am no *breeching* scholar in the schools (Bianca, *Taming of the Shrew*, III.i)

14 He that *ears* my land spares my team (Clown, *All's Well That Ends Well*, I.iii)

15 Let thy tongue *tang* arguments of state (Malvolio, *Twelfth Night*, II.v)

Attempt to categorize each of the italicized words (saying how you arrived at your analysis), and (if they are still in use in contemporary English), compare and contrast their use in Shapespearean English with their use in contemporary English.

Model answer for 1

Syntactic evidence suggests that the word *example* in 1 is used as a transitive verb. The word *will* has to be followed by a verb in the infinitive form (cf. *I will **be** there*); hence *example* in 1 is an infinitival verb form. Since it is a property of *transitive* verbs that they take a pronoun or noun expression after them as their complement, and since *example* is followed by the pronoun *it* in 1, *example* must be a transitive verb. In present-day English, *example* can no longer be used as a verb, and instead is used only as a noun; in its noun use, it has a plural form in +*s* (cf. *I can think of several **examples***), though remains in the singular when used to modify another noun (cf. *I can think of several **example** sentences*).

Exercise III (§§2.2–2.3)

There seem to be three main classes of adverb in English. The largest class are those formed from adjectives by adding the suffix +*ly* (e.g. if we add the suffix +*ly* to the adjective *quick*, we form the corresponding adverb *quickly*). The +*ly* formation rule seems to be productive, in the sense that if we create a new adjective (e.g. *spondulous*), we expect to find a corresponding +*ly* adverb (cf. *spondulously*). If this is so, we can minimize redundancy in lexical entries by listing only the adjective form of such adjective–adverb pairs in the lexicon, and positing a *lexical redundancy rule* which will generate a corresponding +*ly* adverb for every adjective listed in the lexicon. A second class of adverbs are those (like *far*) which have the same form when used as adjectives (cf. *at the far end of the street*) and as adverbs (cf. *a far better idea*). We might suppose that such words are listed in the lexicon as having dual adjective/adverb status, and that a *blocking mechanism* (in the sense of Aronoff 1976)

71

prevents the generation of a +*ly* adverb for adjectives which already have an adverb counterpart listed in the lexicon (so that the existence of *far* as an adverb prevents the generation of **farly*). A third class of adverbs are those like *soon* (cf. *He'll arrive soon*) which have no adjective counterpart (cf. **his soon arrival*): we might suppose that these are listed in the lexicon as intrinsically adverbial.

For each of the words below (and any others which you care to consider), devise examples of your own to illustrate whether or not the word in question can function as an adjective (and if so whether it has an immediate adverb counterpart) or an adverb (and if so whether it has an immediate adjective counterpart). Say whether any of the relevant words pose problems for the tripartite classification of adverbs suggested here – and if so, which and why.

1 almost	2 lively	3 partly	4 prior	5 very
6 already	7 fat	8 hardly	9 ineligible	10 averagely
11 unlikely	12 old	13 yet	14 shortly	15 straight
16 often	17 only	18 purposely	19 humanitarian	20 last
21 weekly	22 present	23 well	24 poorly	25 afraid
26 always	27 sheer	28 quite	29 still	30 routinely

Helpful hints

One problem which arises is how to deal with adjectives which have no +*ly* counterpart. An *ad hoc* (lexical) solution to this problem would be simply to indicate in the lexical entry of the relevant words that they are exceptions to the +*ly* formation rule. However, given that linguistics is concerned with *explanation*, a more principled approach would be to see whether we can explain exceptions in phonological terms (e.g. in terms of avoiding certain sound sequences), or in morphological terms (e.g. avoiding certain sequences of suffixes), or semantic terms (only words with a certain meaning allow +*ly* suffixation), or in etymological terms (e.g. only words of Anglo-Saxon or Latinate origin permit +*ly* suffixation), or in terms of *blocking* (e.g. +*ly* adverb formation is blocked when the language already contains a related lexical item with the same adverbial function and meaning). A second problem which arises is how to deal with +*ly* adverbs which appear to be derived from a word other than an adjective. A third problem relates to the fact that some words have more than one meaning/use, and may behave differently in different uses: you may wonder whether to deal with each different use separately (i.e. by having a separate lexical entry for each use).

Exercise IV (§2.5)

On the basis of their behaviour in negatives, interrogatives and tags, determine whether each of the italicized items below (in each of its uses) can have the categorial status of an auxiliary and/or a verb (bearing in mind the possibility that some items in some uses may be polycategorial, and so may have dual auxiliary/verb status).

Give examples to illustrate the ways in which each item can *and cannot* be used, and discuss any problematic cases. The italicized labels in parentheses are provided purely as a way of helping you differentiate between different uses of a given item.

1a	John *got* a new car	(*transitive*)
b	John *got* arrested **Verb**	(*passive*)
c	John *got* to be famous	(*infinitival*)
2a	John *did* his duty	(*transitive*)
b	John *did* not understand	(*dummy*)
3a	John *needs* a haircut	(*transitive*)
b	John *needs* to think about it	(*to-infinitival*)
c	Nobody *need* say anything	(*bare infinitival*)
4a	Nobody *dares* to challenge him	(*to-infinitival*)
b	Nobody *dare* challenge him	(*bare infinitival*)
5a	John *is* to leave for Paris tomorrow	(*infinitival*)
b	John *is* a nice guy/very tall/in Paris	(*copula/predicative*)
c	John *is* working hard	(*progressive*)
d	John *is* sometimes seen in the bar	(*passive*)
6a	John *has* his car repaired locally	(*causative*)
b	John *has* no money	(*transitive*)
c	John *has* done it	(*perfective*)
d	John *has* to go there	(*infinitival*)
e̶ 7	John *used* to go there quite often	
f̶ 8	John *ought* to be more careful	

Helpful hint

When followed by a bare (*to*-less) infinitival complement, *need* and *dare* are restricted to occurring in a negative or interrogative structure – hence e.g. we don't say **He dare/need do it*, though we do have *I don't think he dare/need do anything* and *I wonder whether he dare/need do anything*.

Model answer for 1a

In its transitive use, *get* requires *do*-support in interrogatives, negatives and tags, as illustrated by the examples below:

TESTS

(i)	(a)	**Got John a new car?* interrog.
	(b)	*Did John get a new car?*
(ii)	(a)	**John gotn't a new car* neg.
	(b)	John *didn't* get a new car
(iii)	(a)	**John got a new car, got he?* tag.
	(b)	John got a new car, *did* he?

aux — verb
inversion — do support
neg. by not → No, do "
can app. in tags — do tags

73

Categories and features

Thus, transitive *get* patterns in all the relevant respects like a typical nonauxiliary verb, and thus belongs to the category V/verb.

Exercise V (§§2.5–2.6)

Discuss the categorization of the italicized words in each of the following examples, giving empirical arguments in support of your analysis.

1a It is important *for* parents to spend time with their children
  b He was arrested *for* being drunk
  c We are hoping *for* a peace agreement to be signed
  d Ships make *for* the nearest port in a storm
  e Congress voted *for* the treaty to be ratified
  f I would prefer *for* the lock to be changed
  g It would be unfortunate *for* the students to fail their exams
2a Executives like *to* drive *to* work
  b I look forward *to* learning *to* drive
  c It's difficult *to* get him *to* work
  d I've never felt tempted *to* turn *to* taking drugs
  e Better *to* yield *to* temptation than *to* submit *to* deprivation!
  f Failure *to* achieve sometimes drives people *to* drink
  g Try *to* go *to* sleep

Model answer for 1a and 2a

In 1a, *for* could be either a complementizer (introducing the infinitival clause *parents to spend time with their children*), or a preposition (whose complement is the noun *parents*). The possibility that *for* might be used here as a preposition is suggested by the fact that the string *for parents* (or an interrogative counterpart like *for how many parents?*) could be preposed to the front of its containing sentence, as in (i) below:

(i) (a)   *For parents*, it is important to spend time with their children
     (b)   *For how many parents* is it important to spend time with their children?

The alternative possibility that *for* might be used as a complementizer (with the infinitival clause *parents to spend time with their children* serving as its complement) is suggested by the fact that the *for*-clause here could be substituted by a *that*-clause, as in:

(ii)   It is important *that parents should spend time with their children*

Thus, 1a is structurally ambiguous as between one analysis on which *for* functions as a preposition and a second on which it functions as a complementizer.

In 2a, the first *to* is an infinitive particle, and the second *to* is a preposition. Thus, the second *to* (but not the first) can be modified by the prepositional intensifier *straight* (cf.

74

Executives like to drive straight to work, but not **Executives like straight to drive to work*). Moreover, the second *to* is a contentive preposition which has the antonym *from* (cf. *Executives like to drive from work*), whereas the first has no obvious antonym since it is a dummy infinitive particle (cf. **Executives like from drive/driving to work*). In addition, like a typical transitive preposition, the second *to* (but not the first) can be followed by an objective pronoun like *them* – cf. *Executives think the only way of getting to their offices is to drive to them*. Conversely, the first (infinitival) *to* allows ellipsis of its complement (cf. *Executives like to*), whereas the second (prepositional) *to* does not (cf. **Executives like to drive to*). Thus, in all relevant respects the first *to* behaves like a dummy infinitive particle, whereas the second *to* behaves like a contentive preposition.

Exercise VI (§§2.2–2.6)

Some linguists have argued that the word *of* has two different uses, illustrated in 1 and 2 below:

1   items of sentimental value
2   his criticism of the press

It has been suggested that *of* in expressions such as 1 belongs to the category **P** of prepositions, and is a contentive which is often paraphraseable by *with* (and hence which has the antonym *without*: cf. *items with/without sentimental value*). In this (contentive) use, an *of*-phrase can be modified by an appropriate adverb (cf. *items **purely** of sentimental value*), and can be (noncontrastively) negated by *not* – cf. *items **not** of much sentimental value*. By contrast, it is suggested that *of* in structures like 2 is a dummy functor belonging to the category **K** of **case particle**, and that its function is to link a noun (e.g. *criticism*) which cannot directly take a nominal or pronominal complement (cf *criticism [*the press/me*]) to a following nominal or pronominal complement (cf. *criticism of* [*the press/me*]). *Of* is required in structures like 2 because nominal/pronominal expressions like *the press/me* can only serve as the complement of a transitive item, and *of* is transitive whereas nouns are intransitive. One reason for supposing that *of* in structures like 2 is a meaningless functor is that *of* is not used in corresponding verbal constructions like *He criticizes the press*, suggesting that it has no intrinsic meaning. Moreover, *of*-phrases like those in 2 are not paraphraseable by *with*-phrases, cannot be modified by adverbs (cf. **his criticism **truly** of the press*), have no antonyms (e.g. whatever *his criticism without the press* may mean, it is not the opposite of *his criticism of the press*) and cannot be noncontrastively negated by *not* (cf. **his criticism **not** of the press*: this is only grammatical if we use contrastive negation, and continue with e.g. *but of the cinema*). On the basis of considerations such as these, determine how *of* should be categorized in each of the following:

1   The Queen is the head *of* state
2   It is a building *of* substantial architectural merit

   3   He was a composer *of* classical music
   4   He is a man *of* unlimited means
   5   This is a portrait *of* the president
   6   I am very appreciative *of* your assistance
   7   He is someone *of* a violent disposition
   8   He fell out *of* the window

Model answer for 1

In 1, *of* seems to function like a dummy case particle (= K) rather than like a contentive preposition (= P). One argument in support of this is that *of* is omitted in the corresponding verbal construction (*The queen **heads** the state*), and thus presumably has no intrinsic semantic content of its own. Moreover, the *of*-phrase has no obvious antonym here: an expression like *the head without a state* is not the antonym of *the head of state*. Moreover, the *of* phrase cannot be modified by an adverb (cf. **the head **truly/immensely/entirely/largely/purely** of state*) and cannot be (noncontrastively) negated (cf. **She is the head **not** of state*). All of these properties are consistent with the view that *of* here is a contentless dummy case particle, whose essential function is to allow the intransitive noun *head* to have a noun complement (*state*) which it could not otherwise have.

Exercise VII (§§2.2–2.7)

Parse the words in the sentences below, using the labelled bracketing technique to assign each word to a grammatical category which represents how it is being used in the position in which it occurs in the sentence concerned. Give reasons in support of your proposed categorization, highlight any analytic problems which arise, and comment on any interesting properties of the relevant words.

   1   He had obtained an average grade in the morphology exercise
   2   Student counsellors know that money troubles can cause considerable stress
   3   Opposition politicians are pressing for election debates to receive better television coverage
   4   One instinctively knows that good taste comes from a proper upbringing
   5   I think I would rather have the red dress than the green one
   6   Seasoned press commentators doubt if the workers will ever fully accept that substantial pay rises lead to runaway inflation
   7   Students often complain to their high school teachers that the state education system promotes universal mediocrity
   8   Some scientists believe that climatic changes result from ozone depletion due to excessive carbon dioxide emission

9   Linguists don't really know the extent to which peer group pressure shapes linguistic behaviour patterns in very young children

10   You don't seem to be too worried about the possibility that many of the shareholders may now vote against your revised takeover bid

Model answer for 1

[$_{PRN}$ He] [$_I$ had] [$_V$ obtained] [$_D$ an] [$_A$ average] [$_N$ grade] [$_P$ in] [$_D$ the] [$_N$ morphology] [$_N$ exercise]

An issue of particular interest which arises here relates to the status of the words *average* and *morphology*. Are these nouns or adjectives – and how can we tell? Since nouns used to modify other nouns are invariable in English (e.g. we say *skate boards*, not **skates boards*), we can't rely on morphological clues here. However, we can use syntactic evidence. If (as we claim), the word *average* functions as an adjective in 1, we should expect to find that it can be modified by an adverb like *relatively* which can be used to modify adjectives (cf. *relatively good*); by contrast, if *morphology* serves as a noun in 1, we should expect to find that it can be modified by the kind of adjective (e.g. *inflectional*) which can be used to modify such a noun. In the event, both predictions are correct, as we see from (i) below:

(i)   She had obtained a *relatively average* grade in the *inflectional morphology* exercise

Some additional evidence that *average* can function as an adjective comes from the fact that it has the +*ly* adverb derivative *averagely*, and (for some speakers at least) the noun derivative *averageness* (cf. *The very averageness of his intellect made him a natural choice for prime minister*).

Helpful hint

In structures such as *morphology exercises*, you will not always find it easy to determine whether the first word (in this case, *morphology*) is a noun or an adjective. As a rule of thumb, where the item concerned is clearly a noun in other uses, assume that it has the categorial status of a noun in this type of structure as well, unless (as in the case of *average* in the expression *average grade*) you have clear evidence that it is an adjective.

Exercise VIII (§2.8)

In the text, we suggested that the grammatical properties of different subclasses of noun could be described in terms of features such as [±COMMON], [±COUNT] and [±PLURAL]. In the light of this, specify which subclass(es) of noun the following words belong to, and what their feature composition would be in their various uses:

describe the grammatical properties of each word as a whole, rather than the properties of the particular form of the word cited below.

1 data	2 criteria	3 oats	4 syntax	5 sadness
6 poem	7 poetry	8 goods	9 coffee	10 advice
11 biceps	12 finance	13 dice	14 granny	15 christmas
16 phenomena	17 schema			

In addition, say what subclasses of noun the following determiners can (and can't) be used to modify

18 little	19 what?	20 no	21 many	22 another
23 the	24 both	25 less	26 each	27 few
28 some	29 that	30 which?	31 neither	32 most
33 all	34 any	35 every	36 this	37 much

Model answers for 1 and 18

Prescriptive grammars of English tell us that *data* is a plural count noun, and that the corresponding singular form is *datum* (a word borrowed from Latin): accordingly, to prescriptivists, the words should be used as in (i) below:

(i)   (a)   This is an interesting *datum*
      (b)   My experiments have yielded several interesting *data*

However, this does not correspond to the kind of usage we find in linguistics textbooks. The word *datum* is generally not used at all, and the word *data* is used primarily as a singular mass noun, though can also be used as a plural count noun (but not as a singular count noun): cf.

(ii) (a)   We don't have *much data* to go on   (singular mass noun)
     (b)   We don't have *many data* to go on   (plural count noun)
     (c)   *I don't have *a single data* to go on   (singular count noun)

(Note also that (ii)(a) is more natural than (ii)(b) for many people.) When a singular count expression is required, a phrase such as *an interesting piece of data* is used (rather than the pedantic form *a datum*). Thus, in this variety of English, *data* carries the two alternative feature specifications [+COUNT, +PLURAL], and [−COUNT, −PLURAL]. The esoteric form *datum* would be [+COUNT, −PLURAL].

The word *little* has two different uses in English: it can function either as an adjective meaning 'small in size', or as a quantifier meaning 'a small quantity of'. In its quantifier use, it can generally modify only a singular mass noun: cf.

(iii)   We had *little food* left   (*little* + mass noun)
(iv)   *He had *little car*   (*little* + singular count noun)
(v)   *We had *little supplies* of water left   (*little* + plural count noun)

Apparent counterexamples such as:

(vi) *Little people* are called leprechauns *plur count noun*

(where *little* might seem to be quantifying the plural count noun *people*) involve *little* used as an adjective meaning 'small in size', and so are not genuine counterexamples to the claim that when used as a quantifier, *little* can only modify a singular mass noun.

Exercise (IX) *(§2.8)*

In the text, we suggested that different inflectional affixes carried by verb forms encode different sets of tense/aspect/agreement features. Identify the affixes in the italicized verb forms in the examples below, and discuss the grammatical features which they encode.

1a He has *deceived* her
 b He *deceived* her
2a They *beat* him every time he misbehaves
 b They once *beat* him because he came home late
3a I *come* here twice a week
 b I have never *come* here before
4a They *strewed* flowers everywhere
 b They have *strewed/strewn* flowers everywhere
5a You sometimes *hurt* the one you love
 b He once *hurt* someone he loved
 c He has never *hurt* anyone he loves

In addition, consider how in a feature-based analysis we might account for the following dialect variation in the paradigms for the present tense of regular verbs like *love* in three varieties of British English (table adapted from Cheshire 1989):

6

STANDARD ENGLISH	EAST ANGLIAN ENGLISH	SOUTH-WESTERN ENGLISH
I love	I love	I love*s*
we love	we love	we love*s*
you love	you love	you love*s*
he/she love*s*	he/she love	he/she love*s*
they love	they love	they love*s*

What features are encoded by the present-tense forms *love/loves* in each of these varieties? Finally, provide a feature-based account of the difference between the standard and nonstandard past-tense forms illustrated below (where % marks a nonstandard form):

7a We *saw*/%*seen* him yesterday
 b I *did*/%*done* it for you

Helpful hints

Assume that apparently uninflected verb forms carry a null (i.e. inaudible) inflection ∅. Also, examine the possibility that where a single affix marks more than one property, it may encode some single feature shared between the various forms. (To take a nonoccurring example, suppose that the past- and present-participle forms of some verb carried the same affix; we could then say that the relevant affix simply encodes the feature [+PARTICIPLE].)

Exercise X (§2.8)

Young children might be said to acquire the grammar of words 'one feature at a time'. Two-year-olds have generally acquired some (but not all) of the grammatical properties of words, so that (from an adult perspective) particular child words might be said to be *underspecified* in respect of particular sets of grammatical features. On the basis of what you are told below, try to develop a feature-based account of the child's acquisition of English verb forms, using the system of features introduced in the text.

At the very earliest stage of development (stage I), children typically use only uninflected verb forms like *go*: these are used with any choice of subject (e.g. *Me/Daddy go home*). At stage II, we see the emergence of +*ing* forms of verbs, so that at this point we have a two-way contrast (cf. e.g. *Daddy go/going home*). At stage III, we find past-participle forms ending in +*n* (e.g. *gone*) being acquired alongside past-tense forms (e.g. *went*), so that we now have a four-way contrast (cf. *Daddy go/going/gone/went home*). At stage IV, we see the emergence of agreement in present-tense forms, so that there is a distinction between *He/she* **goes** *there* and *I/we/you/they* **go** *there*: at this point, we have a five-way contrast between *go/going/gone/went/goes*.

Model answer for stage I

In the text we argued that adult verb forms are differentiated in terms of subcategorial features such as [±PARTICIPLE], [±PAST] and [±AGREEMENT]. We might suppose that at stage I, none of these features has yet been acquired, so that verb forms like *go* simply carry the categorial features [+V, –N]. Each of the subsequent stages in the child's development is marked by the acquisition of a new feature. (*You* take over at this point, and say which features are acquired in which order. Also, show how the specification of each verb form gradually becomes more complex at each successive stage of development.)

TURN IN ### Exercise XI (§2.8)

English might be said to have the following system of *personal pronouns* (note that although we analysed forms like *my/our/your* etc. in the text as determiners, here we are following an alternative traditional analysis of them as genitive case forms of pronouns):

	1SG	1PL	2	3MSG	3FSG	3NSG	3PL
nominative	I	we	you	he	she	it	they
objective	me	us	you	him	her	it	them
genitive	my	our	your	his	her	its	their

These pronouns inflect for **case** (nominative, objective or genitive), **number** (SG = singular, PL = plural), **gender** (M = masculine, F = feminine, N = neuter) and person (1 = first person, 2 = second person, 3 = third person). It might be argued that the grammatical differences between these various pronoun forms could be described in terms of a system of binary person/number/animacy/gender/case features such as the following:

[±1 PERSON] = including/excluding the speaker/s in its reference

[±2 PERSON] = including/excluding the addressee/s in its reference

[±PLURAL] = denoting more than one entity (or not)

[±ANIMATE] = denoting animates or inanimates

[±FEMININE] = denoting females or others

[±NOMINATIVE] = carrying nominative case (or not)

[±GENITIVE] = carrying genitive case (or not)

Using this feature system, discuss the feature composition of each of the eighteen different pronoun forms in the table above.

Helpful hints

Make the following set of assumptions. The feature [±1 PERSON] differentiates first person pronouns like *I/we* from others, and pronouns which are [−1 PERSON] would be further differentiated in terms of the feature [±2 PERSON], so *he* would be [−1 PERSON, −2 PERSON] because it excludes both speaker and addressee, whereas *you* would be [−1 PERSON, +2 PERSON] because it excludes the speaker but includes the addressee. The feature [±PLURAL] would be used to differentiate e.g. a [+PLURAL] pronoun like *we* (which includes the speaker and someone else) from its [−PLURAL] counterpart *I* (which includes only the speaker). The feature [±ANIMATE] would differentiate between pronouns like *he/she* which can be used to denote animate beings, and pronouns like *it* which are used to denote inanimates; pronouns which carry the feature [+ANIMATE] would be further differentiated into [±FEMININE] forms. Thus, *she* would be [+ANIMATE, +FEMININE], *he* would be [+ANIMATE, −FEMININE] and *it* would be simply [−ANIMATE]. The case feature [±NOMINATIVE] would be used to differentiate nominative pronouns from others, and the feature [±GENITIVE] would be used to differentiate genitive pronouns from others: since no pronoun can carry two positive case features, pronouns cannot be both [+GENITIVE] and [+NOMINATIVE]: hence, it follows that any pronoun which is [+NOMINATIVE] will automatically be [−GENITIVE] (so need not be specified as nongenitive), and conversely that any pronoun which is [+GENITIVE] will automatically be [−NOMINATIVE] (so again need not be specified as non-nominative).

Categories and features

Objective pronouns (by virtue of being neither nominative nor genitive) carry the features [–NOMINATIVE, –GENITIVE]. Thus, *they* would be [+NOMINATIVE], *their* would be [+GENITIVE] and *them* would be [–NOMINATIVE, –GENITIVE]. Analyse pronoun forms like *you* which serve two different nominative/objective functions as a single item (not as two different items, one nominative and the other objective). Assume that some pronouns are *unspecified* with respect to certain features. For example, the pronoun *you* might be argued to be unspecified (i.e. not morphologically marked) for number, gender or the nominative/non-nominative case distinction, so that – in terms of its case properties – *you* is a nongenitive form.

Model answer for *we*

The pronoun *we* includes the speaker in its reference and so carries the person feature [+1 PERSON]; it denotes more than one single individual, so is [+PLURAL]. It carries nominative case, and so is [+NOMINATIVE]. It is unspecified with respect to the feature [±2 PERSON], since English draws no morphological distinction between inclusive and exclusive first person plural pronouns (i.e. pronouns which include the speaker and addressee and so mean 'you and I' and pronouns which include the speaker and some third person/s and so mean 'I and he/she/they'). The pronoun *we* is not morphologically marked for either animacy or gender, and so can be presumed to be unspecified for the features [±ANIMATE] and [±FEMININE]. Thus, its overall feature specification is [+1 PERSON, +PLURAL, +NOMINATIVE].

Exercise XII (§2.9)

Say which of the following generalizations can (or cannot) be captured straightforwardly in terms of the feature-based analysis of lexical categories outlined in (76) in the main text – and why.

In Dutch (according to Hoekstra 1984, p. 31), prepositions and nouns take following complements, whereas adjectives and verbs take preceding complements; cf. his examples:

1a voor [de maaltijd]
    before the meal

 b een verhaal [over vogels]
    a story about birds

 c ... dat hij [dat gezeur] moe is
    ... that he that drivel weary is
    'that he is weary of that drivel'

 d ... dat hij [een fout] maakte
    ... that he a mistake made
    'that he made a mistake'

82

In English, (transitive) verbs and prepositions can have a noun expression as their complement (immediately following them), but not nouns or adjectives:

    2a   He enjoys [syntax] (verb+noun)
     b   He is against [vivisection] (preposition+noun)
     c   *He is a supporter [monetarism] (noun+noun)
     d   *He is fond [chocolate] (adjective+noun)

In Italian, nouns and adjectives are inflected for (masculine or feminine) gender, but not verbs or prepositions: cf.

3   Giorgio parlava di cose   stupide
               Giorgio spoke   of things stupid
               'Giorgio talked about silly things'

where *e* is a *feminine* plural affix.

In German (according to Stowell 1981, p. 24), adjectival or verbal expressions can be positioned in front of a noun and used to premodify the noun, but not nominal or prepositional expressions: cf.

4a   der [*seiner Freundin überdrüssige*] Student   (adjectival modifier)
               the of-his girlfriend weary   student
               'the student weary of his girlfriend'
 b   ein [*sein Studium seit   langem hassender*] Student   (verbal modifier)
               a   his   studies since long   hating   student
               'a student hating his studies for a long time'

In English, adverbs like *really* can be used to modify adjectives, prepositions and verbs, but not nouns (instead, the corresponding adjective *real* must be used to modify a noun): cf.

    5a   He is really nice   (really + adjective)
     b   He is feeling really down   (really + preposition)
     c   He will really squirm   (really + verb)
     d   *There is a really crisis   (really + noun)

In questions in English, a nominal (= noun-containing), prepositional or adjectival expression containing a question-word like *who?*, *what?*, *which?*, *how?*, etc. can be positioned at the front of a sentence, but not a verbal expression:

    6a   Which girl does he seem most keen on?   (nominal expression)
     b   In which town does he live?   (prepositional expression)
     c   How fond of you is she?   (adjectival expression)
     d   *Live in which town does he?   (verbal expression)

83

Helpful hints

You should look at the question of whether a given set of expressions which behave similarly share a given (positive or negative) feature specification: e.g. whether all the words which behave in a certain way have the feature value [+F] (or alternatively have the value [–F]) for some feature *F*. So, in 1, you look to see whether (in terms of the feature analysis in (76) in the main text), prepositions and nouns form a natural supercategory in that they share some feature specification in common, in 2 whether verbs and prepositions share a common feature specification, in 3 whether nouns and adjectives constitute a supercategory, in 4 whether adjectives and verbs have a common feature specification, in 5 whether adjectives, prepositions and verbs have some common set of featural properties and in 6 whether nouns, prepositions and adjectives form a natural supercategory.

Exercise XIII (§2.9)

In the text, we argued that the major lexical and functional categories found in English can be analysed as composites of the three binary features [±V], [±N] and [±F]. Jane Grimshaw (1991) proposes a rather different componential theory of categories based on the two binary features [±V] and [±N], and a third functionality feature [F] which has three values [0, 1, 2] and so is *ternary*. Grimshaw suggests that nouns and verbs (not being functors) have the value [F0]; determiners and auxiliaries (which precede nouns and verbs) have the value [F1], and prepositions/complementizers (which precede determiners and auxiliaries) have the value [F2]. Under Grimshaw's analysis, these six categories have the following feature specifications:

V = verb = [+V, –N, F0]	N = noun = [–V, +N, F0]
I = inflected auxiliary = [+V, –N, F1]	D = determiner = [–V, +N, F1]
C = complementizer = [+V, –N, F2]	P = preposition = [–V, +N, F2]

Consider whether Grimshaw's analysis (or that proposed in the text) could better account for the following facts:

1 Items such as *for, to, have, this* and *that* have more than one use. (Are these different uses of the same item related or unrelated in the two analyses?)
2 Verbs and auxiliaries inflect for tense/agreement in English, nouns and (some) determiners inflect for (singular/plural) number (cf. *this book*/*these books*), but prepositions and complementizers are invariable.
3 Prepositions in Irish inflect for person, number and gender (e.g. *leis* = 'with him', *léithi* = 'with her'); finite complementizers in West Flemish inflect for agreement with the subject of the auxiliary/verb following them (e.g. *Kpeinzen **dan** Valère en Pol morgen goan* = 'I think *that+3PL* Valère and Pol will go tomorrow', from Haegeman 1992).

4   Adjectives in English take a preposition to link them to a nominal complement and a complementizer to link them to a verbal complement (cf. *anxious **about** the race, anxious **that** he should win,* **anxious **about** that he should win*).

Model answer for this

The word *this* can function both as a determiner (cf. *I like **this** book*) and as a pronoun (cf. *I like **this***). If we suppose that Grimshaw would treat pronouns as a subclass of nouns (e.g. as nouns which lack descriptive content), then *this* will carry the features [–V, +N, F0] in its pronoun use, but will carry the features [–V, +N, F1] in its determiner use. Thus, the two uses of *this* will share the lexical features [–V, +N], and will differ only in their value for the functionality feature, the pronoun *this* having the value [F0], and the determiner *this* having the value [F1]. The fact that the two share the specification [–V, +N] may account for the fact that in both uses, *this* inflects for singular/plural number (the corresponding plural form being *these*). In terms of the analysis presented in (79) in the text, pronouns and determiners would share the specification [+N, +F] but would differ in that pronouns are [–V] and determiners (counterintuitively) [+V].

3
Syntactic structure

3.1 Overview

In the previous chapter, we looked at the way in which the grammatical properties of words can be described in terms of grammatical categories or grammatical features. In this chapter, we turn to address the rather different question of the ways in which words can be combined together to form phrases and sentences, and we look at how we can represent the structure of the phrases and sentences thereby formed.

3.2 Forming phrases

To put our discussion on a concrete footing, let's consider how an elementary two-word phrase such as that produced by speaker B in the following mini-dialogue is formed:

(1)   SPEAKER A: What's the government planning to do?
        SPEAKER B: *Privatize hospitals*

As speaker B's utterance illustrates, the simplest way of forming a phrase is by combining two words together: for example, by combining the word *privatize* with the word *hospitals* in (1), we form the phrase *privatize hospitals*.

An important question to ask, however, is the following: 'When two words combine together to form a phrase, what grammatical properties does the resulting phrase have, and how are they determined?' There is clear evidence that the grammatical properties of phrases are determined by one of the two words in the phrase. For example, when we combine a verb like *privatize* with a noun like *hospitals*, the resulting phrase *privatize hospitals* seems to have verbal (= verblike) rather than nominal (= nounlike) properties. This we can see from the fact that the phrase *privatize hospitals* can occupy the same range of sentence positions as a verb like *reconsider*, and hence e.g. occur after the infinitive particle *to*: cf.

(2) (a)   The government is intending to *reconsider*
    (b)   The government is intending to *privatize hospitals*

By contrast, *privatize hospitals* cannot occupy the kind of position occupied by a plural noun such as *hospitals*, as we see from (3) below:

(3) (a)   *Hospitals* are at the heart of the debate about policy

(b)   **Privatize hospitals* are at the heart of the debate about policy

So, it seems clear that the grammatical properties of a phrase like *privatize hospitals* are determined by the verb *privatize*, and not by the noun *hospitals*. We might say that the verb *privatize* is the *head* of the phrase *privatize hospitals*, and conversely that the phrase *privatize hospitals* is a <u>*projection*</u> (i.e. 'phrasal expansion') of the verb *privatize*. More specifically, we can say that a phrase like *privatize hospitals* is a *verb phrase*: and in the same way that we abbreviate category labels like *verb* to *V*, we can abbreviate the category label *verb phrase* to *VP*. If we use the traditional labelled bracketing technique to represent the category of the overall phrase *privatize hospitals* and of its component words *privatize* and *hospitals*, we can represent the structure of the resulting phrase as in (4) below:

(4) $[_{VP} [_V$ privatize] $[_N$ hospitals]]

What (4) tells us is that the overall phrase *privatize hospitals* is a verb phrase/VP, and that it comprises the verb/V *privatize* and the noun/N *hospitals*. The verb *privatize* is the **head** of the overall phrase, and the noun *hospitals* is traditionally said to fulfil the grammatical role of being the **complement** of the verb *privatize*.

Although we have used our familiar technique of labelled bracketing to represent the structure of the verb phrase *privatize hospitals* in (4), an alternative way of representing the structure of phrases is in terms of a **labelled tree diagram** such as (5) below (you have to imagine that the tree has been uprooted in a storm, hence it is upside down):

(5)

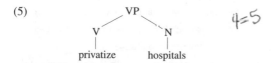

We might say that each of the category labels in a tree diagram is a different **node** in the tree, and that the words are the **leaves** on the tree. The tree diagram in (5) is entirely equivalent to the labelled bracketing in (4), in the sense that the two provide us with precisely the same information about the structure of the phrase *privatize hospitals*: the differences between the two are purely notational (e.g. each category is represented by a single *node* in a tree diagram, but by a *pair of brackets* in a labelled bracketing), and not of any theoretical significance. In general, we shall use tree diagrams to represent phrase structure in our discussions below (though where we only want to indicate part of the structure of a given phrase or sentence, we shall sometimes use labelled bracketings).

Given that our ultimate goal is to determine the principles of phrase formation, an important question for us to ask at this juncture is whether our analysis of the verb phrase *privatize hospitals* leads to any wider conclusions about the way in which phrases are formed. We might generalize our discussion of (5) and hypothesize that all phrases are formed by a process of **merger** whereby two categories are merged together to form a new (phrasal) category. The phrase which is thereby formed is (to use a traditional technical term) **endocentric** (i.e. headed), in that it is a **projection** of a **head** word. In the case of (5), the resulting phrase is formed by combining two words together. However, not all phrases are formed by combining two words – as we see if we look at the structure of B's utterance in (6) below:

(6)   SPEAKER A: What's the health minister's principal objective?

           SPEAKER B: *To privatize hospitals*

The phrase in (6) would seem to be formed by combining the infinitive particle *to* with the verb phrase *privatize hospitals*. What's the head of the resulting phrase *to privatize hospitals*? A reasonable guess would be that the head is the infinitive particle *to*, so that the resulting string (i.e. sequence of words) *to privatize hospitals* is an infinitive phrase. If this is so, we'd expect to find that infinitive phrases have a different distribution from verb phrases; and indeed this does seem to be the case, as sentences such as (7) and (8) below illustrate:

(7) (a)   They ought [*to privatize hospitals*]
      (b)   *They ought [*privatize hospitals*]

(8) (a)   They should [*privatize hospitals*]
      (b)   *They should [*to privatize hospitals*]

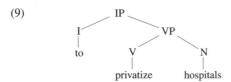

diff. distrubion from verb phrases.

If we assume that *privatize hospitals* is a verb phrase whereas *to privatize hospitals* is an infinitive phrase, we can then account for the contrasts in (7) and (8) by saying that *ought* is the kind of auxiliary which requires an infinitive phrase after it as its complement, whereas *should* is the kind of auxiliary which requires a following verb phrase complement.

Ought → inf.P
Should → VP

The infinitive phrase *to privatize hospitals* is formed by merging (i.e. combining) the infinitive particle *to* (which in §2.5 we argued to belong to the category I or INFL) with the verb phrase *privatize hospitals*. Assuming that the verb phrase *privatize hospitals* has the structure (5) above, the structure formed by merging infinitival *to* with the VP in (5) will be (9) below:

(9)

```
                    IP
            ┌────────┴────────┐
            I                 VP
            │           ┌──────┴──────┐
            to          V             N
                        │             │
                    privatize     hospitals
```

The structure (9) is formed by two different merger operations; one merging the verb *privatize* with the noun *hospitals* to form the verb phrase/VP *privatize hospitals*, and

88

the other merging the infinitive particle *to* with the verb phrase *privatize hospitals* to form the infinitive phrase/IP *to privatize hospitals*.

What is implicit in our discussion here is that we can build up complex structures in a stepwise fashion by merging successive pairs of constituents together to form even larger phrases. For example, by merging the infinitive phrase *to privatize hospitals* with the noun *plans*, we can form the phrase *plans to privatize hospitals*, as in speaker B's reply in (10) below:

(10)   SPEAKER A: What are the rebel ministers unhappy about?

         SPEAKER B: *Plans to privatize hospitals*

The resulting phrase would seem to be headed by the plural noun *plans*, and so requires plural agreement if used as the subject of an auxiliary like *be*: cf.

(11)   [Plans to privatize hospitals] *are/*is* being drawn up

So, it seems clear that *plans* is the head of the bracketed phrase in (10), and the infinitive phrase *to privatize hospitals* is the complement of the noun *plans*. This being so, the bracketed phrase in (11) has the structure (12) below:

(12)

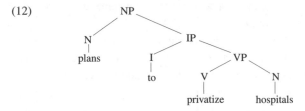

The structure (12) is the product of three different merger operations – one merging the verb *privatize* with the noun *hospitals* to form the verb phrase *privatize hospitals*: another merging the infinitive particle *to* with the verb phrase *privatize hospitals* to form the infinitive phrase *to privatize hospitals*; and a third merging the noun *plans* with the infinitive phrase *to privatize hospitals* to form the noun phrase *plans to privatize hospitals*.

3.3 Specifiers

So far, all examples of the **merger** operation which we have looked at have involved merging a head word with a complement (the complement being either a word, or a phrase which is itself formed by one or more merger operations). This might lead us to wonder whether phrases are always of the form *head + complement*, with the complement being positioned after the head (because English has a head-first setting for the **head parameter**, as noted in §1.7). However, this seems unlikely, as we can show in relation to phrases such as that produced by speaker B in (13) below:

(13)   SPEAKER A: What is making the health minister so unpopular?

         SPEAKER B: *Government plans to privatize hospitals*

89

If (contrary to what we are suggesting here) all phrases were formed by combining a head with a following complement, then we would have to posit that the italicized phrase in (13) was a noun phrase formed by merging the head noun *government* with the noun phrase complement *plans to privatize hospitals*. But this can't be right because the overall phrase is clearly plural in number, as we see from the pattern of agreement in (14) below:

(14)   [Government plans to privatize hospitals] *are/*is* making the health minister very unpopular

If the singular noun *government* were the head of the bracketed phrase in (14), we'd wrongly predict that the singular auxiliary *is* would be required. The fact that the plural form *are* is required makes it clear that the head of the overall phrase is the noun *plans*. Since this noun has a complement of its own (namely the infinitive phrase *to privatize hospitals*) and since in any case complements *follow* their heads in English, the noun *government* which precedes the head *plans* cannot be the complement of *plans*. So what grammatical function does it serve? Introducing a new term at this point, let's say that the noun *government* functions as the **specifier** of the noun *plans* (since it specifies who has devised the plans in question).

The obvious question to ask at this point is 'What is a specifier, and how can we tell whether a given expression functions as a specifier or not?' This is not a straightforward question to answer, since although the notion **specifier** is central to much contemporary work in syntax, it is hard to identify any common set of properties which all specifiers share (and indeed there is sometimes disagreement between linguists about whether one expression does or doesn't function as the specifier of another). For the time being, rather than attempt to give a unitary definition of *specifier*, we shall simply illustrate some of the ways in which the term is used in the contemporary linguistic literature. In this connection, consider the syntax of the following phrases and sentences:

(15) (a)   *straight* **to** bed
     (b)   *such* **a** pity
     (c)   *Each* **teasing** the other (in reply to 'What were they doing?')
     (d)   *They* **have** finished
     (e)   *Why* **are** we waiting?

One way of analysing the relevant expressions is as follows. In (15a) the preposition *to* is the head of the relevant structure, the noun *bed* is the complement of *to* and the adverb *straight* is the specifier of *to*. In (15b), the determiner *a* is the head of the structure, the noun *pity* is its complement and the degree adjective *such* is its specifier.

90

In (15c), the verb *teasing* is the head of the structure, the expression *the other* is its complement and the quantifier *each* is its specifier. In (15d), the auxiliary *have* is the head of the structure, the verb *finished* is the complement of *have* and the pronoun *they* is the specifier of *have*. And in (15e), the inverted auxiliary *are* is the head of the structure, the expression *we waiting* is the complement of *are* and the adverb *why* is the specifier of *are*. If these assumptions are correct, each of the structures in (15) is of the form *specifier + head + complement*, suggesting that heads are generally positioned before complements in English, and specifiers positioned before heads (so that English might be said to be not only a **head-first** language because it positions heads before complements, but also a **specifier-first** language because it positions specifiers before heads). We should underline once again, however, that there is by no means universal agreement among linguists as to the nature and function of specifiers (e.g. the analysis of (15d–e) presented here is generally accepted, but the analysis of (15a–c) is more controversial). Since there is no universally agreed definition of what a specifier is, it is only to be expected that you yourself won't at first be very clear about whether this or that expression should be analysed as a specifier or not. Hopefully, it will become clearer as our exposition unfolds just how the term is used in this book; and the justification for analysing particular expressions as specifiers is ultimately *empirical* – i.e. it resides in the fact that if we posit that a particular expression serves as a specifier in a given construction, we can begin to make sense of various aspects of the syntax of the construction (in ways which will gradually become clearer in subsequent chapters).

Returning now to our discussion of the bracketed expression *government plans to privatize hospitals* in (14), let's assume that the noun *government* here serves as the specifier of the noun *plans* (setting aside any unclarity about what the term *specifier* means). If this is so, the relevant expression will be a noun phrase/NP built up out of three different constituents – namely the head noun *plans*, its complement *to privatize hospitals* and its specifier *government*. Now, if we assume that the **merger** operation which forms phrases combines *pairs* of constituents into successively larger phrases, then it follows that the overall noun phrase *government plans to privatize hospitals* must be formed by two different merger operations. Reasoning along these lines, we might suppose that the head noun *plans* combines with its infinitive phrase complement *to privatize hospitals* to form an intermediate nominal expression which (following the terminology introduced in Chomsky's *Remarks on Nominalization* paper in 1970) we might call an $\bar{N}$ (also written as **N'** or as **N-bar**, but in all three cases pronounced *en-bar*); let's also suppose that the resulting N-bar is then merged with the noun *government* which serves as its specifier, so forming the full noun phrase/NP constituent *government plans to privatize hospitals*. Given these assumptions, the resulting NP will have the structure (16) below:

(16)

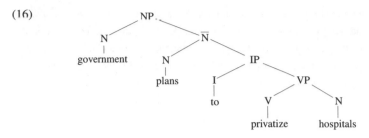

What (16) tells us is that the head noun *plans* merges with its IP complement *to privatize hospitals* to form the N-bar *plans to privatize hospitals*, and the resulting N-bar then merges with its N/noun specifier *government* to form the overall NP/noun phrase *government plans to privatize hospitals*.

It's important to be clear about the system of category labels which we are employing at this point. We are using the category label **N-bar** to designate an **intermediate** nominal projection – i.e. to designate a nominal expression which is larger than a noun, but which itself projects into an even larger nominal structure (this larger nominal structure being designated as **NP**). By contrast, the category label NP denotes a nominal expression which is larger than a noun, but which doesn't project into an even larger type of nominal expression. Thus, the expression *plans to privatize hospitals* is an NP constituent in (10) (since it doesn't project into a larger nominal structure), but is an N-bar in (13) (since it projects into the larger nominal expression *government plans to privatize hospitals*).

Given the assumptions we have made so far, there are two different types of phrase: on the one hand, there are phrases of the schematic form (17a) below which comprise just a head **X** (where X represents a word category of some kind – e.g. a noun, or verb, or preposition, etc.) and its complement; while on the other hand, there are more complex phrases of the schematic form (17b) below which comprise a specifier, a head (= X) and a complement:

(17) (a)   (b)

On this view, specifiers differ from complements not only in respect of the fact that they are positioned to the left (rather than the right) of the head, but also in respect of the structural position they occupy (specifiers are sisters to an intermediate (X-bar) projection, whereas complements are sisters to a head (as we shall see shortly)).

Having looked at the internal structure of the noun phrase *government plans to privatize hospitals*, let's now consider the structure of the more complex phrase produced by speaker B in the dialogue below:

(18) SPEAKER A: Which way is Lord Lacklustre going to vote?

SPEAKER B: *Against government plans to privatize hospitals*

The italicized structure in (18) would seem to be formed by merging the preposition *against* with the noun phrase (16), so forming the **prepositional phrase (= PP)** constituent (19) below:

(19)

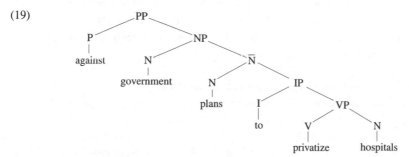

The resulting structure (19) is formed by five separate merger operations, viz. one merging the V *privatize* with the N *hospitals* to form the VP *privatize hospitals*; a second merging the I *to* with the VP *privatize hospitals* to form the IP *to privatize hospitals*; a third merging the N *plans* with the IP *to privatize hospitals* to form the N-bar *plans to privatize hospitals*; a fourth merging the N *government* with the N-bar *plans to privatize hospitals* to form the NP *government plans to privatize hospitals*; and a fifth merging the preposition *against* with the NP *government plans to privatize hospitals* to form the PP *against government plans to privatize hospitals*.

Now consider speaker B's response in (20) below:

(20) SPEAKER A: What will the rebel ministers do?

SPEAKER B: *Vote against government plans to privatize hospitals*

The italicized structure in (20) is arguably a verb phrase/VP, formed by merging the verb *vote* with the prepositional phrase *against government plans to privatize hospitals* in (19), and so has the structure (21) below:

(21)

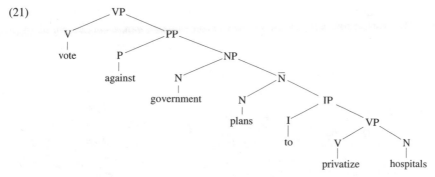

As should be obvious, (21) is the result of six separate merger operations.

93

3.4 Forming sentences

Thus far, we have restricted our discussion to the question of how **phrases** are formed. However, an obvious question to ask is how **sentences** (or **clauses**) are formed. We might argue on theoretical grounds (in terms of our desire to develop a unified and internally consistent theory) that the optimum answer is to posit that sentences are formed by exactly the same **merger** operation which leads to the formation of phrases. To make our discussion more concrete, let's suppose that speaker B had chosen to use the sentence italicized in (22) below to reply to speaker A, rather than the phrase (21):

(22)   SPEAKER A: What will the rebel ministers do?
          SPEAKER B: *They will vote against government plans to privatize*
                          hospitals

What's the structure of the sentence produced by speaker B in (22)? Let's make the (unifying) assumption that sentences are formed by the same merger operation as phrases (merging categories together in a pairwise fashion to form larger categories). This being so, we might suppose that speaker B's reply in (22) is formed by merging the auxiliary *will* with the verb phrase *vote against government plans to privatize hospitals*, and then subsequently merging the pronoun *they* with the resulting structure. Since the sentence thereby formed is finite, it seems reasonable to take the finite auxiliary *will* to be the head of the clause. Moreover, given that complements follow heads and specifiers precede them, we might suggest that the VP *vote against government plans to privatize hospitals* is the complement of *will*, and that the pronoun *they* is its specifier. If we adopt the suggestion made in §2.5 that finite auxiliaries are I/INFL constituents (by virtue of being inflected for finiteness), we can offer the following account of how the italicized sentence in (22) is formed. The I constituent *will* is merged with its VP complement *vote against government plans to privatize hospitals* to form the intermediate projection $\bar{I}$ (= I' = **I-bar**, pronounced *eye-bar*) *will vote against government plans to privatize hospitals*. The resulting I-bar is then merged with the pronoun *they* which serves as its specifier (and subject) to form the full IP (= inflected auxiliary phrase) *They will vote against government plans to privatize hospitals*. Given these assumptions, the italicized sentence in (22) will have the structure (23) below:

94

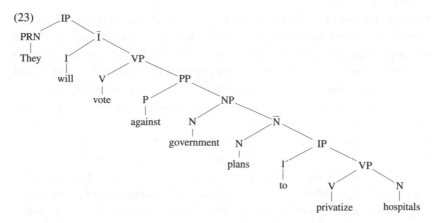

(23)

The overall sentence is headed by the auxiliary (= I constituent) *will*, and thus has the status of an **auxiliary phrase** (= IP).

But now consider the reply given by speaker B in the following dialogue:

(24)   SPEAKER A: What is the prime minister expecting of the rebels?
          SPEAKER B: *That they will vote against government plans to privatize hospitals*

In speaker B's reply in (24), it would seem that the auxiliary phrase (IP) *they will vote against government plans to privatize hospitals* has been merged with the complementizer *that* to form an even larger type of structure, which (in work since 1970) has been termed a **complementizer phrase** (= **CP**). Given this assumption, speaker B's reply in (24) will have the structure (25) below:

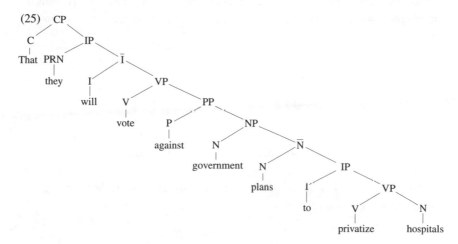

(25)

Following this line of reasoning, we might suggest that clauses introduced by complementizers like *that/if/for* are CP constituents (i.e. complementizer phrases). This analysis (which takes the complementizer to be the head of the structure containing it) implies that complementizers determine the nature of the clause they introduce; and this is in keeping with the observation we made in §2.6 that a complementizer like *that* indicates that the clause it introduces is a finite declarative (i.e. statement-making) clause.

So far, all the examples of merger operations which we have discussed have involved merging a word with another word, or merging a word with a phrase. However, if we take the simplest characterization of merger as an operation which forms phrases by combining pairs of categories, we should expect to find that merger can also involve combining *two projections* (i.e. two expressions larger than a word). In this connection, compare (26a) and (26b) below:

specifer

(26). (a)   They will vote against privatization

(b)   The opposition will vote against privatization

Det. phrase

Given the assumptions we have been making, (26a) is formed by merging the preposition *against* with the noun *privatization* to form the prepositional phrase *against privatization*; the resulting PP is then merged with the verb *vote* to form the verb phrase *vote against privatization*; this VP is then merged with the I constituent *will* to form the I-bar *will vote against privatization*; and the I-bar is then merged with its specifier/subject (the pronoun *they*) to form the IP *They will vote against privatization*.

However, in the case of (26b), the subject which merges with I-bar is not the pronoun *they*, but rather the phrase *the opposition*. This is formed by merging the determiner *the* with the noun *opposition* to form a type of constituent which is termed a **determiner phrase (= DP)** in recent work; the resulting DP has the structure (27) below:

(27)

This being so, the overall clause (26b) is formed by merging the I-bar *will vote against privatization* with a phrase which has itself been formed by another merger operation – namely the determiner phrase *the opposition*. Thus, the resulting IP is formed by merging the DP subject *the opposition* with the I-bar *will vote against privatization*, and so has the structure (28) below:

(28)

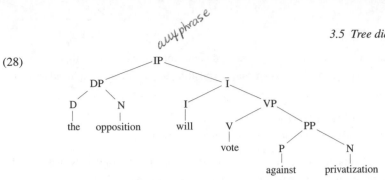

So, (28) illustrates the possibility of forming a phrase by merging one *projection* (i.e. expression larger than a word) with another (in this case, merging DP with I-bar).

3.5   Tree diagrams

Our discussion has led us to the conclusion that phrases and sentences are formed by successive merger operations, and that the resulting structures can be represented in the form of tree diagrams. Because they mark the way that words are combined together to form phrases of various types, tree diagrams are referred to in the relevant technical jargon as **phrase-markers** (conventionally abbreviated to **P-markers**). It is instructive to ask just what is represented in phrase-markers such as (28). The answer is that such diagrams show us how the overall sentence is built up out of **constituents** (i.e. syntactic units, or structural building blocks) of various types: hence, we might say that a tree diagram provides a visual representation of the **constituent structure** of the corresponding sentence. Each **node** in the tree (i.e. each point in the tree which carries a category label like N, V, N̄, Ī, PP, etc.) represents a different constituent of the sentence; thus, there are as many different constituents in any given phrase or sentence structure as there are nodes carrying category labels. Nodes at the bottom of the tree are called **terminal nodes**, and other nodes are **nonterminal nodes**: thus, the two N nodes and the D, I, V and P nodes in (28) are terminal nodes, and the IP, I-bar, DP, VP and PP nodes are nonterminal. The topmost node in any given tree structure (i.e. IP in the case of (28) above) is said to be its **root**. (Remember that the tree has been uprooted in a storm, so is upside-down.) As we noted earlier, the words on the tree are its **leaves**; it should be obvious from (28) that only terminal nodes carry leaves (i.e. words). So, for example, the word *against* in (28) is not itself a node, but rather is the leaf carried by the P node.

A tacit assumption made in our discussion of the **merger** operation which leads to the formation of syntactic structures is that categories are combined in a *pairwise* fashion to form larger categories. One consequence of this is that phrases and sentences have an intrinsically **binary** structure, since the merger operation which forms projections combines *two* categories together, and never combines e.g. three, four or five categories together at one go. This amounts to positing the following constituent structure principle:

(29)   BINARITY PRINCIPLE
         All nonterminal nodes are binary-branching.

Principle (29) claims that all nonterminal nodes branch into two and only two immediate constituents, never more than two, and never fewer than two. This is a controversial assumption (in that not all syntacticians accept it), though it is widely adopted in much recent work (and will be assumed throughout the rest of this book).

Given a tree diagram such as (28), there is a relatively informal procedure which we can use in order to determine whether a given string (i.e. sequence of words) does or doesn't form a constituent of the relevant structure. Imagine that you're the kind of anti-social and environmentally unfriendly individual who gets their kicks out of breaking branches off trees. Let's also suppose that *nodes* are the weak points of trees, and that you can only break branches off at nodes. (Recall that a node is a point of a tree which carries a category label.) We might then say that any part of a tree (any substructure) which comes away when you break the tree off at a particular node is a constituent (of the structure containing it), and that the category of the relevant substructure is represented by the category label carried by the root (= topmost) node in the structure. For example, if we break the tree off at the I-bar node in (28), the part of the tree that will come away is:

(30)
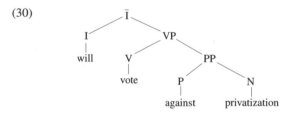

What this act of environmental vandalism tells us is that the string *will vote against privatization* is a constituent of the structure (28), and that it belongs to the category I-bar (and so is an intermediate auxiliary projection), since the topmost node in the substructure (30) carries the category label I-bar. Of course, if we had been in a rather less destructive mood, we could have chosen simply to break off a branch at the V node in (28); all we would have pulled away would have been the poor twig in (31) below:

(31)   V
              |
            vote

What we learn from this vandal-like *break-off-a-branch* game is that every part of a tree structure which you can break off at a node is a *constituent* of the overall structure.

The obvious conclusion is thus that there are as many constituents in a tree structure as there are nodes carrying category labels. Hence, there are eleven different constituents in (28) – namely [$_N$ *privatization*], [$_P$ *against*], [$_{PP}$ *against privatization*], [$_V$ *vote*], [$_{VP}$ *vote against privatization*], [$_I$ *will*], [$_{\bar{I}}$ *will vote against privatization*], [$_N$ *opposition*], [$_D$ *the*], [$_{DP}$ *the opposition*] and [$_{IP}$ *the opposition will vote against privatization*].

3.6 Configurational relations

We can also determine whether or not a given string of words forms a constituent in a rather more formal way, by using a simple **algorithm** (i.e. mechanical procedure) which exploits the geometrical properties of trees. Why do we need to invoke the formal properties of tree structures? Well, any adequate description of any phenomenon in any field of enquiry (in our present case, syntax) must be fully *explicit*, and to be explicit, it must be *formal* – i.e. make use only of theoretical constructs which have definable formal properties. The use of formal apparatus (involving a certain amount of technical terminology) may seem confusing at first to the beginner, but as in any other serious field of enquiry (e.g. molecular biology) no real progress can be made unless we try to construct formal models of the phenomena we are studying. It would clearly be irrational to accept the use of formalism in one field of enquiry (e.g. molecular biology) while rejecting it in another (e.g. linguistics): hence our excursus on the formal properties of phrase-markers.

Essentially, a P-marker is a graph comprising a set of points (represented by the **labelled nodes** in the tree), connected by **branches** (represented by solid lines). Any given pair of nodes contained in the same P-marker will be related by one of two different types of relation, namely either (i) by **dominance** (i.e. hierarchical/top-to-bottom ordering), or (ii) by **precedence** (i.e. linear/left-to-right ordering). We can illustrate what these terms mean in terms of the following abstract tree structure (where A, B, C, D, E, F, G H and J are labelled nodes):

(32)

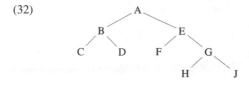

The *dominance* relations between nodes (relating to whether one node occurs higher up in the structure than another) are indicated by the branches (i.e. solid lines) in the tree; the *precedence* relations between nodes (i.e. whether one node occurs to the left of another or not) are indicated by the relative left-to-right ordering of nodes on the printed page. (We can say that one node X *precedes* another node Y if X occurs to the left of Y, and if neither node dominates the other.) A simple way of understanding the relation *dominates* is to think of tree diagrams like (32) as train networks, with each of the labelled nodes being different stations in the network, and with the solid lines representing the tracks linking the various stations in the network. We can then say that X dominates Y if it is possible to get from X to Y on a *southbound* train. So, for example, A dominates H in (32) because it is possible to get from A to H on a southbound train (via E and G). By contrast, B does not dominate H because it is not possible to get from B to H on a southbound train: on the contrary, to get from B to H, you first have to catch a *northbound* train to A, and then from A catch a southbound train to H (via E and G). As you should be able to work out for yourself, node A in (32) dominates nodes B, C, D, E, F, G, H and J; node B dominates only nodes C and D; node E dominates nodes F, G, H and J; node G dominates nodes H and J; and nodes C, D, F, H and J are terminal nodes and so dominate no other nodes (i.e. in train terms, they represent the terminus at the end of each line).

We can make use of *dominance* relations to provide a configurational definition of the term *constituent* as in (33) below (i.e. a definition couched in terms of tree configurations, viz. the relative positions occupied by different nodes in a tree):

(33)   A set of words forms a *constituent* of category Z if the terminal nodes carrying them are all dominated by the same Z node, and if there are no other terminal nodes dominated by the relevant Z node.

Let's see how this definition can be applied in relation to a structure such as (34) below:

(34)

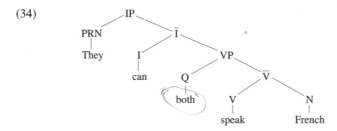

The quantifier *both* (in this kind of use) is referred to as a **floating quantifier** because although it quantifies *they*, it is *floating* in a position where it is separate from *they*. We have assumed in (34) that the verb *speak* combines with its noun complement *French* to form a $\bar{\mathbf{V}}$ (= **V'** = **V-bar**, in each case pronounced *vee-bar*) constituent *speak French*, and that (as suggested in recent work – e.g. Sportiche 1988) the floating quantifier *both* is the specifier of this V-bar, and combines with it to form the **VP** *both speak French*. Given these assumptions, it follows from the definition in (33) that the string (of words) *speak French* is a V-bar constituent, since [$_V$ speak] and [$_N$ French] are both dominated by V-bar, and are the only terminal nodes dominated by V-bar. For analogous reasons, *both speak French* is a VP constituent, *can both speak French* is an I-bar constituent, and *They can both speak French* is an IP constituent. By contrast, the string *They speak French* is not a constituent of the structure (34), since although [PRN *they*], [V *speak*] and [N *French*] are all dominated by the IP node, they are not the only terminal nodes dominated by IP: after all, [I *can*] and [Q *both*] are also terminal nodes dominated by IP. Similarly, the string *They both speak French* is not a constituent of the structure (34), nor are strings such as *can speak French, They both speak, both French*, etc.

Given the obvious resemblance between the tree diagrams like (34) above used to represent the syntactic structure of sentences, and *family tree* diagrams (representing who is related to whom in a given family), it has become a standard convention in the linguistic literature to use kinship terminology to denote relationships between constituents within a given tree structure. We can illustrate how this terminology is used in terms of an abstract tree diagram of the following form (where A, B, C, D and E are labelled nodes):

(35)

A here is said to be the **mother** of B and C (by virtue of being the next node up in the tree from B and C); conversely, B and C are the two **daughters** of A; and B and C are **sisters**. Likewise, C is the **mother** of D and E; in addition, D and E are the **daughters** of C; and similarly D and E are **sisters**. (Interestingly, the corresponding tree relations in Italian are *father, son* and *brother*: I leave the sociologists among you to ponder on the hidden significance of this transcultural terminological transvestism.)

We can use these family relations to define the property of **complementhood** as follows:

(36)   A constituent X is the complement of a head H (and, by extension, of any H-bar or HP constituent which is a projection of H) if X and H are sisters, and the mother of X is a projection of H.

Returning now to our tree diagram (34), it follows from (36) that [N *French*] is the complement of [V *speak*], since the relevant V and N nodes are sisters, and the mother of N is a V-bar constituent *speak French* which is a projection of the verb *speak*; and, by extension, we might say that *French* is also the complement of the V-bar *speak French*, and of the VP *both speak French*. Similarly, [VP *both speak French*] is the complement of [I *can*] in (34), since the two are sisters, and the mother of VP is an I-bar *can both speak French* which is a projection of the I constituent *can*; by extension, we might say that the relevant VP is also the complement of the I-bar *can both speak French*, and of the IP *They can both speak French*. By contrast, [V̄ *speak French*] is not the complement of [Q *both*] in (34) because although the two are sisters, the mother

This is a little confusing even though it seems to make sense!

of [$_\bar{V}$ *speak French*] is a VP constituent *both speak French* which is not a projection of the floating quantifier *both* (but rather of the verb *speak*). For analogous reasons [$_T$ *can both speak French*] in (34) is not the complement of [$_{PRN}$ *they*], because the mother of the relevant I-bar is an IP *They can both speak French* which is not a projection of the pronoun *they* (but rather of the auxiliary *can*).

In much the same way, we can define the property of **specifierhood** in kinship terms, along the following lines:

(37)   A constituent Y is the *specifier* of a head H (and, by extension, of the H-bar and HP constituents into which H projects) if Y is the sister of H-bar and the daughter of HP.

In terms of the definition in (37), we can say that [$_Q$ *both*] is the specifier of [$_V$ *speak*] in (34), since [$_Q$ *both*] is the sister of [$_\bar{V}$ *speak French*] and the daughter of [$_{VP}$ *both speak French*]; and by extension, we can say that [$_Q$ *both*] is also the specifier of [$_\bar{V}$ *speak French*] and of [$_{VP}$ *both speak French*]. In much the same way, [$_{PRN}$ *they*] is the specifier of [$_I$ *can*], since [$_{PRN}$ *they*] is the sister of [$_\bar{I}$ *can both speak French*] and the daughter of [$_{IP}$ *they can both speak French*]; and by extension, [$_{PRN}$ *they*] is also the specifier of [$_\bar{I}$ *can both speak French*] and of [$_{IP}$ *They can both speak French*]. By contrast, [$_I$ *can*] is not the specifier of [$_Q$ *both*] since *can* is not the sister or daughter of a projection of *both*; and similarly, [$_V$ *speak*] is not the specifier of [$_N$ *French*], since *speak* is not the sister or daughter of a projection of *French*.

3.7   Testing structure

Thus far, we have argued that sentences are built up by merging successive pairs of constituents into larger and larger structures, and that the resulting structure can be represented in terms of a labelled tree diagram, with notions such as *constituent*, *complement* and *specifier* being defined in configurational terms. The tree diagrams which we use to represent syntactic structure make specific claims about how sentences are structured out of successive layers of constituents. But this hypothesis raises the question of how we know (and how we can test) whether the claims made about structure in tree diagrams are true. So far, we have relied entirely on intuition in arriving at structural representations – we have in effect guessed at the structure. However, it is unwise to rely solely on our intuitions in attempting to determine the structure of a given string in a given language. For while experienced linguists over a period of years tend to acquire fairly strong intuitions about structure, novices by contrast tend to have relatively weak, uncertain and unreliable intuitions; moreover, even the intuitions of supposed experts may sometimes turn out to be based on little more than personal prejudice.

For this reason, it is more satisfactory (and more accurate) to regard *constituent structure* as having the status of a *theoretical construct*. That is to say, it is part of the theoretical apparatus which linguists find they need to make use of in order to explain certain facts about language (just as *molecules*, *atoms* and *subatomic particles* are constructs which physicists find they need to make use of in order to explain the nature of matter in the universe). It is no more reasonable to rely wholly on intuition to determine syntactic structure than it would be to rely on intuition to determine molecular structure. Inevitably, then, much of the evidence for syntactic structure is of an essentially **empirical** character (i.e. evidence based on the observed grammatical properties of words, phrases and sentences). The evidence typically takes the form 'Unless we posit that such-and-such a sentence has such-and-such a constituent structure, we shall be unable to provide a principled account of the observed grammatical properties of the sentence.' Thus, structural representations ultimately have to be justified in *empirical* terms, i.e. in terms of whether or not they provide a principled account of the grammatical properties of words, phrases and sentences.

To put our discussion on a more concrete footing, let's consider the structure of a sentence such as:

(38)   He might have been watching television

Example (38) contains the lexical verb *watching* and three auxiliary verbs, viz. the modal auxiliary *might*, the perfective auxiliary *have* and the progressive auxiliary *been*. What we shall claim here is that each of these four (auxiliary or nonauxiliary) verbs heads a separate phrasal projection, with *watching* projecting into the phrase *watching television*, *been* projecting into the phrase *been watching television*, *have* projecting into the phrase *have been watching television*, and *might* projecting into the overall phrase/sentence *He might have been watching television*. More specifically, we shall claim that (38) has a structure along the lines of (39) below:

(39)

The label **PERF** here is used to denote a perfective auxiliary, and **PERFP** to denote a perfective phrase – i.e. a phrase headed by a perfective auxiliary. Similarly, **PROG** denotes a progressive auxiliary, and **PROGP** denotes a progressive phrase. Of course, given our observation in §2.9 that (at a relatively coarse level of categorization) auxiliaries like *have/be* can be classified as *verbs*, an alternative labelling for the relevant constituents in (39) would be to suppose that *been* and *have* belong to the category V (verb), and that correspondingly their phrasal projections *been watching television* and *have been watching television* belong to the category VP (verb phrase). We assume that the modal auxiliary *might* occupies the head INFL position of IP because it is finite (hence inflected for tense, as we can see from the fact that it carries the past-tense suffix +*t*); the auxiliaries *have* and *been* do not occupy an INFL position here because they are not finite (*have* is an infinitive form and *been* a perfective participle form).

Our structural representation (39) has the status of a *hypothesis* (i.e. untested and unproven assumption) about the structure of the corresponding sentence (38). So how can we test our hypothesis and determine whether (39) is or isn't an appropriate representation of the structure of (38)? The answer is that there are a number of standard heuristics (i.e. 'tests') which we can use to determine structure. One such test relates to the phenomenon of **coordination**. English and other languages have a variety of *coordinating conjunctions* (which we might designate by the category label **CONJ** or **J**) like *and/but/or* which can be used to coordinate (= conjoin = join together) expressions such as those bracketed below:

(40) (a)   [*fond of cats*] and [**afraid of dogs**]
      (b)   [*slowly*] but [**surely**]
      (c)   [*to go*] or [**to stay**]

In each of the phrases in (40), a coordinating conjunction has been used to conjoin the bracketed pair of expressions. Clearly, any adequate grammar of English will have to provide a principled answer to the question: 'What kinds of strings (i.e. sequences of words) can and cannot be coordinated?'

Now, it turns out that we can't just coordinate any random set of strings, as we see by comparing the grammatical reply produced by speaker B in (41) below:

(41)   SPEAKER A: What did he do?
         SPEAKER B: Run *up the hill* and *up the mountain*

with the ungrammatical reply produced by speaker B in (42) below:

(42)   SPEAKER A: What did he do?
         SPEAKER B: *Ring *up his mother* and *up his sister*

Why should it be possible to coordinate the string *up the hill* with the string *up the mountain* in (41), but not possible to coordinate the string *up his mother* with the string *up his sister* in (42)? We might seek to provide a principled answer to this question in terms of *constituent structure*. More specifically, we might argue that the italicized string *up the hill* in (41) is a constituent of the phrase *run up the hill* (*up the hill* is a prepositional phrase, in fact), and so can be coordinated with another similar type of prepositional phrase (e.g. a PP such as *up the mountain*, or *down the hill*, or *along the path*, etc.). Conversely, however, we might claim that the string *up his mother* in (42) is not a constituent of the phrase *ring up his mother*, and so cannot be coordinated with another similar string. (Traditional grammarians say that *up* is associated with *ring*, and that the expression *ring up* forms a complex verb which carries the sense of 'telephone'.) On the basis of contrasts such as these, we might suggest that:

(43)   Only *like constituents* can be conjoined; nonconstituent strings cannot be   *Constraint*
            conjoined.

A constraint (i.e. structural restriction) along the lines of (43) is assumed in most work in traditional grammar.

Having established the constraint (43), we can now make use of this constraint as a *heuristic* (i.e. diagnostic test) for evaluating the structural representation (i.e. testing the tree diagram) in (39) above. A crucial claim made in (39) is that the strings *watching television, been watching television, have been watching television* and *might have been watching television* are all constituents (of various different types). Some empirical evidence for this assumption comes from coordination facts in relation to paradigms (i.e. sets of examples) such as:

(44) (a)   He might have been [*watching television*] or [**playing pool**]

     (b)   He might have [*been watching television*] or [**been playing pool**]

     (c)   He might [*have been watching television*] or [**have been playing pool**]

     (d)   He [*might have been watching television*] or [**might have been playing pool**]

Given the crucial premise (43) that only strings of like constituents can be conjoined, example (44a) provides empirical support for analysing *watching television* as a VP, since it can be conjoined with another verb phrase like *playing pool*; likewise, (44b) provides empirical evidence for analysing *been watching television* as a PROGP, (44c) for analysing *have been watching television* as a PERFP, and (44d) for analysing *might have been watching television* as an I-bar. In other words, the analysis in (39) correctly predicts that all of the sentences in (44) are grammatical (though for pragmatic reasons they become increasingly more unwieldy as more and more information is repeated, since the longer sentences like (44d) violate Grice's (1975) conversational maxim 'Be concise!' by virtue of repeating redundant words which could have been omitted).

The type of coordination discussed above might be called *simple coordination*. However, there is a second type of coordination test which we can use, and this relates to coordination structures such as that produced by speaker B in the following dialogue:

(45)   SPEAKER A: What did your lawyer advise you to do?

          SPEAKER B: Try to appeal (but try not to beg) *for clemency*

In an intuitively obvious sense, what speaker B says seems to be an abbreviated form of *Try to appeal **for clemency** but try not to beg **for clemency***: in this fuller form of the sentence, we see that the bold-printed string is shared (so to speak) between the two conjuncts (i.e. between the two expressions conjoined by *but*). We can represent what this means in diagrammatic form in (46) below:

(46) *try to appeal*
but } **for clemency**
try not to beg

Schema (46) is intended to show that we have coordinated two *try*-phrases, and that the bold-printed string ***for clemency*** is the shared complement both of the verb *appeal* and of the verb *beg*. We might suppose that when a string is shared between two or more conjuncts in this way, it need be mentioned only once – hence the fact that it occurs only once in speaker B's utterance in (45). For obvious reasons, we might refer to this type of coordination as *shared string coordination*, and to the bold-printed sequence in (46) as the *shared string*.

However, there are interesting restrictions on the kinds of sequences which can function as the *shared string* in such cases: although the reply given by speaker B in (45) above is grammatical, the reply in (47) below is not: cf.

(47) SPEAKER A: What was he so undecided about?
This sounds ok → SPEAKER B: *Whether to ring (or not to ring) *up his mother*

So I'm having trouble following

Why should the sequence *for clemency* be able to function as the shared string in (45), but not the sequence *up his mother* in (47)? A natural answer would be to suppose that this is because the string *for clemency* is a constituent of the verb phrases *appeal for clemency/beg for clemency* (it is a prepositional phrase, in fact), whereas the sequence *up his mother* is not a constituent of the verb phrase *ring up his mother*; and we might further suppose that:

(48) Only a *constituent* can function as the shared string in the relevant type of coordinate structure.

Given (48), it follows that speaker B's reply in (45) is grammatical because the italicized shared string is a constituent, whereas speaker B's reply in (47) is ungrammatical because the shared string is a nonconstituent sequence.

In the light of (48), we might suggest that one way of testing whether a given expression is or is not a constituent of a given structure is by seeing whether or not the relevant expression can function as the *shared string* in elliptical coordinate structures. In this connection, consider the following:

(49) (a) He might have been (or might not have been) *watching television*
(b) He might have (or might not have) *been watching television*

(c)   He might (or might not) *have been watching television*

(d)   Some say that **she** (and others claim that **he**) *might have been watching television*

Given the premise (48) that the shared string in this type of coordinate structure must be a constituent, the fact that *watching television* in (49a) can function as a shared string is consistent with the analysis of it as a verb phrase in (39); similarly, the fact that *been watching television* is the shared string in (49b) is consistent with the claim in (39) that it is a progressive phrase constituent; likewise, the fact that *have been watching television* is the shared string in (49c) lends some empirical support to the claim in (39) that it is a perfective phrase constituent; and finally, the fact that *might have been watching television* is the shared string in (49d) is consistent with the assumption in (39) that it is an I-bar constituent.

3.8   Additional tests

A further type of test which we can use to try and establish whether a given string of words is a constituent or not is the **sentence fragment test**. The underlying premise of the test is that there are restrictions on the types of expression which can (or can't) be used as sentence fragments (i.e. which can be used as free-standing phrases, e.g. in answer to a question). This premise seems to be justified by contrasts such as the following:

(50)   SPEAKER A: Who were you talking to?
         SPEAKER B: *To my girlfriend* — *Constituent of VP "talking to my girlfriend"*

(51)   SPEAKER A: Who were you ringing up?
         SPEAKER B: **Up my girlfriend*

Why should it be that *to my girlfriend* can serve as a sentence fragment in (50), but not *up my girlfriend* in (51)? The traditional answer is (52) below:

(52)   Only *constituents* can serve as sentence fragments.

Given the postulate in (52), we can account for the contrast between (50) and (51) in a straightforward fashion if we maintain that *to my girlfriend* is a constituent of the verb phrase *talking to my girlfriend*, whereas *up my girlfriend* isn't a constituent of the verb phrase *ringing up my girlfriend*.

In the light of our premise (52), consider the following mini-dialogue (paying particular attention to the various replies which SPEAKER B can give):

(53)   SPEAKER A: What d'you think she might have been doing?
         SPEAKER B: *Watching television/Been watching television/Have been watching television*

(Or course, given Grice's *conciseness* maxim, the longer the replies in (53), the more cumbersome they are, since they repeat redundant information: but all of the replies in (53) are grammatical.) In the light of our premise in (52) that only constituents can be used as sentence fragments, speaker B's replies in (53) are consistent with the analysis in (39), in that when B replies *watching television* he is using a VP, when he replies *been watching television* he is using a PROGP, and when he replies *have been watching television*, he is using a PERFP. Thus, the analysis in (39) correctly predicts that all three replies produced by speaker B in (53) are grammatical.

But wait! Doesn't the analysis in (39) also predict that we should be able to use the I-bar (= auxiliary expression) *might have been watching television* as a sentence fragment? However, this is not the case, as we see from the ungrammaticality of (54) below:

(54)   SPEAKER A: What d'you think she might have been doing?
         SPEAKER B: *Might have been watching television*

Surely (54) is a counterexample to the analysis in (39), since (39) specifies that *might have been watching television* is an I-bar constituent, and a core assumption of the sentence fragment test is that constituents can serve as sentence fragments? The answer is 'No', since the claim in (52) that *only* constituents can serve as fragments does not entail that *all* constituents can serve as fragments. More specifically, we might hypothesize that:

(55)   Only *maximal projections* can serve as sentence fragments.

Following Chomsky (1995a, p. 396) we might define the term **maximal projection** informally as follows:

(56)   A category that does not project any further is a maximal projection.

(Note that *further* here means 'into a larger structure with the same head'.) We could then say that *might have been watching television* can't be used as a sentence fragment in (54) because it is an intermediate projection: by this we mean that although it is a projection of the I constituent *might*, it isn't the *maximal* (i.e. largest) projection of I, since I projects further into the IP *He might have been watching television*. Hence, if speaker B in (54) wants to reply with a structure headed by *might*, he has to use the full IP *He might have been watching television*.

Our revised premise (56) has interesting implications for how we analyse speaker B's reply in (57) below:

(57)   SPEAKER A: What do you think she might have been watching?
         SPEAKER B: *Television*

Given the definition of *maximal projection* in (56), the noun *television* is a maximal projection in the structure (39) above, precisely because it does not project into a larger

NP constituent. Thus a word which has no complement or specifier of its own functions as a *maximal projection* – and hence can serve as a sentence fragment.

A fourth structural diagnostic which we can use to test structures like (39) relates to the syntax of a class of items which are sometimes referred to collectively as **proforms**. These are items which can be used to replace (or refer back to) a constituent of an appropriate kind, as in (58) below:

(58) (a)   *The Vice-President* is giving away freebies to anyone promising to vote for **him**

(b)   They say *that he is guilty*, though I personally don't think **so**

(c)   If John does *quit his job* (**which** he might), who will replace him?

In (58a), the proform *him* is used to replace the determiner phrase *the vice-president*, in order to avoid repetition (equivalently, we might say that *the vice-president* is the **antecedent** of *him*, i.e. the expression that *him* refers back to); in (58b) the proform *so* replaces/refers back to the complementizer phrase *that he is guilty*; and in (58c) the proform *which* replaces/refers back to *quit his job*.

Of course, if different kinds of proform can be used to replace (or serve as the antecedent of) different kinds of constituent, another way in which we can test the structure in (39) is to see whether the various constituents in (39) can be replaced by (or serve as the antecedent of) an appropriate type of proform. In this connection, consider the use of *so* in (59) below:

(59)   He suggested that she might have been watching television, and . . .

(a) *so* she might have been

(b) *so* she might have

(c) *so* she might

(d) **so* she

The proform *so* replaces (or has as its antecedent) the verb phrase *watching television* in (59a), the progressive phrase *been watching television* in (59b) and the perfective phrase *have been watching television* in (59c). Given that (as noted in §2.9) lexical verbs like *watch* and auxiliary verbs like *have/be* share in common the features [+V –N], we could say that *so* can replace a projection of a [+V, –N] head (i.e. a projection of an auxiliary or nonauxiliary verb). However, what remains to be accounted for is why (59d) should be ungrammatical – i.e. why *so* can't replace the I-bar *might have been watching television*. One reason might be that proforms can only be used to replace *maximal projections*, and I-bar is an intermediate projection. An alternative possibility might be to suppose that *so* has to be used as the complement of an appropriate auxiliary or nonauxiliary verb and there is no such verb here. Thus, *proform* facts work out much as we expect, and lend further empirical support to our postulated structure (39).

The fifth and final constituent structure test which we'll make use of here relates to a phenomenon traditionally referred to as **ellipsis** – a term used to designate the process by which redundant information in a sentence is *ellipsed* (i.e. omitted) if it can be inferred from the context (e.g. if it has been previously mentioned in the preceding discourse). There are two rather different kinds of ellipsis – one involving the ellipsis of *head words*, and the other of *projections* (i.e. of expressions comprising more than just a head word). We can see the difference by comparing the two sentences in (60a–b) below:

(60) (a)   He can speak French better than she can German

    (b)   He can speak French better than she can

Example (60a) is understood as an elliptical (i.e. abbreviated) form of *He can speak French better than she can **speak** German*, and so is a structure in which the head verb *speak* of the verb phrase *speak German* has undergone ellipsis (it has been ellipsed/omitted because it was already mentioned earlier in the sentence): this type of ellipsis is often referred to as **gapping** because it has the effect of leaving a gap in the middle of a sentence. However, (60b) involves a different kind of ellipsis: it is understood as an elliptical form of *He can speak French better than she can **speak French***, and in this type of structure, a whole projection has undergone ellipsis (viz. the verb phrase *speak French* which serves as the complement of *can*).

If (certain types of) projections can undergo ellipsis, an obvious way of testing the constituent structure of (39) is to see whether or not the various projections it contains can undergo ellipsis. In this connection, consider the examples in (61) below (where bold-printing on (**s**)**he** marks contrastive stress):

(61) (a)   **She** might have been watching television more often than **he** might have been

    (b)   **She** might have been watching television more often than **he** might have

    (c)   **She** might have been watching television more often than **he** might

    (d)   **She** might have been watching television more often than **he**

(Of course, given Grice's *conciseness* maxim, the longer sentences like (61a) which repeat redundant words are more cumbersome than the corresponding shorter sentences – but they are none the less grammatical.) An analysis such as (39) above can provide a straightforward account of the ellipsis facts in (61), since what has been ellipsed is the VP *watching television* in (61a), the PROGP *been watching television* in (61b), the PERFP *have been watching television* in (61c) and the I-bar *might have been watching television* in (61d). Thus, ellipsis facts provide further empirical support for the analysis in (39).

3.9   C-command

We have argued at some length here that heuristics such as our two *coordination tests*, the *sentence fragment test*, the *proform test* and the *ellipsis test* provide empirical evidence in support of our claim that any phrase or sentence in a language has a complex *hierarchical categorial constituent structure* which can be represented in terms of a labelled tree diagram such as (39). In this section, we look at a further type of evidence, based on the assumption that certain **syntactic constraints** (i.e. restrictions on the use of particular kinds of constituents) can be given a straightforward characterization in structural terms. As a case in point, consider the syntax of the quantifier *any* (and its compounds like *anyone, anything, anywhere*, etc.). This has two uses. One is as a *universal quantifier* with a meaning similar to that of *every/all*, as in *Any policeman can tell you the time*. The second use (and the one which concerns us here) is as an *existential* (or *partitive*) *quantifier* with a meaning similar to that of *some*, e.g. in sentences such as *Is there any coffee left?* (where the speaker is asking a question about the existence of coffee). In its existential use, *any* (and its compounds) can occur in negatives like (62a) below, interrogatives like (62b), conditionals like (62c) and degree structures like (62d) – but not (for example) in ordinary declaratives like (62e):

(62) (a)   Nobody will say anything
   (b)   I doubt whether anyone will say anything
   (c)   If anyone should ask for me, say I've gone to lunch
   (d)   He was too lazy to do anything
   (e)   *He has found anything interesting

Edward Klima (1964, p. 313) conjectured that negative words like *nobody*, interrogatives like *whether*, conditionals like *if* and degree expressions like *too* share 'a common grammatico-semantic feature to be referred to as *affective*': in his terms, *nobody/whether/if/too* are affective constituents. (By this, he seems to mean that they are all non-assertive.) Given this terminology, we can say that existential *any* is restricted to occurring in a structure containing an *affective* constituent. It turns out that numerous other expressions (e.g. *ever, care a damn, lift a finger,* etc.) are similarly restricted to occurring in affective contexts: cf.

(63) (a)   I didn't think I would *ever* pass syntax
   (b)   *I thought I would *ever* pass syntax

(64) (a)   He's too selfish to *care a damn* about what happens to you
   (b)   *I know that he *cares a damn* about what happens to you

(65) (a)   I doubt whether he would *lift a finger* to help you
   (b)   *He would *lift a finger* to help you

(Note that the asterisk on (65b) indicates that it is not grammatical on the intended idiomatic interpretation of 'He would do something to help you.') Expressions which are restricted in this way are referred to as *polarity expressions*, because they seem to have an inherent affective polarity (in the sense that they are restricted to occurring in affective contexts).

However, it's not enough simply to say that a polarity expression must occur in a phrase or sentence containing an affective constituent, as contrasts such as the following illustrate:

(66) (a)   The fact that he has resigned won't change anything
     (b)   *The fact that he hasn't resigned will change anything

In both cases, the polarity item *anything* occurs after a negative auxiliary (after *won't* in (66a), and after *hasn't* in (66b)), and yet only the first of these two examples is grammatical. Why? The traditional answer is that *anything* falls within the **scope** (i.e. 'sphere of influence') of the negative auxiliary *won't* in (66a), but does not fall within the scope of the negative auxiliary *hasn't* in (66b). Implicit in this account is the assumption that a polarity item must fall within the scope of an affective constituent; and it has been suggested that the relative *scope* of constituents can be defined in terms of the structural relation **c-command** (a conventional abbreviation of 'constituent-command'). Given these assumptions, the restriction on the distribution of polarity items can be given the following structural characterization:

(67)   C-COMMAND CONDITION ON POLARITY EXPRESSIONS
         A polarity expression must be c-commanded by an affective constituent.

The relation **c-command** can be defined *configurationally* (i.e. in terms of the relative positions occupied by the constituents concerned within a given tree) in the following manner:

(68)   A node X c-commands another node Y if the mother of X dominates Y, and X and Y are disconnected (X and Y are disconnected if X ≠ Y and neither dominates the other).

(If you prefer to think of structural relations in terms of networks of train stations, (68) amounts to claiming that X c-commands Y if you can get from X to Y by catching a northbound train, getting off at the first station and catching a southbound train on a different line – i.e. you can't travel south on the line you travelled north on.)

To see how the **c-command condition** in (67) works, consider the structure of (66a) above given in (69) below:

(69)

```
                              IP
              DP                          I
        D          NP               I          VP
       The      N        CP        won't    V       PRN
              fact    C        IP         change  anything
                    that   PRN      I
                            he    I      V
                                 has  resigned
```

The crucial question here is whether the pronoun *anything* is c-commanded by the negative auxiliary *won't*. Since the mother of the I node containing *won't* is the encircled I-bar node containing *won't change anything*, and since the relevant I-bar node dominates the PRN node containing *anything* (and the relevant I and PRN nodes are disconnected), it follows that *won't* does indeed c-command *anything* in (69). (You can reach the same conclusion if you think of (69) as a network of train stations: you can get from the I-node containing *won't* to the PRN node containing *anything* by travelling north, getting off at the station represented by the I-bar node containing *won't change anything*, then catching a southbound train to the station represented by the PRN node containing *anything*.) Since *anything* is c-commanded by *won't* in (69), the c-command condition (67) is satisfied, and sentence (66a) is correctly predicted to be grammatical.

Now consider why, by contrast, (66b) is ungrammatical. Example (66b) has the structure (70) below:

(70)

```
                              IP
              DP                          I
        D          NP               I          VP
       The      N        CP        will     V       PRN
              fact    C        IP         change  anything
                    that   PRN      I
                            he    I      V
                                hasn't  resigned
```

Since the only affective constituent in (70) is the negative auxiliary *hasn't*, the question which we need to ask here is whether the polarity expression *anything* is c-commanded by *hasn't*. The mother of the I-node containing *hasn't* is the encircled I-bar node containing *hasn't resigned*: since the relevant I-bar node does not dominate the PRN node containing *anything*, *hasn't* doesn't c-command *anything*. But since there is no other affective constituent in the sentence, this in turn means that *anything* does not fall within the scope of an affective constituent, thereby violating the c-command condition in (67); hence, we correctly predict that (66b) is ungrammatical.

The overall conclusion which we reach is that the restricted distribution of polarity expressions can be given a *configurational* characterization in terms of the relation **c-command**. Of course, it goes without saying that such an account is only tenable if we suppose that sentences have a hierarchical categorial constituent structure: in other words, the fact that the restriction on polarity items can be given a straightforward characterization in structural terms lends empirical support to the more general claim that sentences have an abstract syntactic structure which can be represented in the form of tree diagrams like (69) and (70).

A second class of expressions whose distribution can be accounted for in structural terms are so-called **anaphors**. These include reflexives (i.e. *+self* forms) like *myself/yourself/themselves* etc., and reciprocals like *each other* and *one another*. Such anaphors have the property that they cannot be used to refer directly to an entity in the outside world, but rather must be **bound** by (i.e. take their reference from) an **antecedent** elsewhere in the same phrase or sentence. Where an anaphor has no (suitable) antecedent to bind it, the resulting structure is ungrammatical – as we see from contrasts such as that in (71) below:

(71) (a)   He can feel proud of *himself*

 (b)   *She can feel proud of *himself*

 (c)   **Himself* help me?! You've got to be kidding

In (71a), the third person masculine singular anaphor *himself* is bound by a suitable third person masculine singular antecedent (*he*), with the result that (71a) is grammatical. But in (71b), *himself* has no suitable antecedent (the feminine pronoun *she* is obviously not a suitable antecedent for the masculine anaphor *himself*), and so is **unbound** (with the result that (71b) is ungrammatical). In (71c), there is no potential antecedent of any kind for the anaphor *himself*, with the result that the anaphor is again unbound.

There seem to be structural restrictions on the binding of anaphors by their antecedents, as we can illustrate in terms of the following contrasts:

(72) (a)   **The president** can congratulate *himself*

 (b)   *Supporters of **the president** can congratulate *himself*

(73) (a)   **They** may finger *each other*

(b)   *The evidence against **them** may finger *each other*

As a third person masculine singular anaphor, *himself* must be bound by a third person masculine singular antecedent like *the president*; similarly, as a plural anaphor, *each other* must be bound by a plural antecedent like *they/them*. However, it would seem from the contrasts above that the antecedent must occupy the right kind of position within the structure in order to **bind** the anaphor, or else the resulting sentence will be ungrammatical. The question of what is the *right position* for the antecedent can be defined in terms of the following structural condition:

(74)   C-COMMAND CONDITION ON BINDING

A bound constituent must be c-commanded by an appropriate antecedent.

The relevant bound constituent is the reflexive anaphor *himself* in (72), and its antecedent is *the president*; the bound constituent in (73) is the reciprocal anaphor *each other*, and its antecedent is *they/them*. Let's also suppose that (72a) has the structure (75) below, and that the DP *the president* is the antecedent of the anaphoric PRN *himself* (as is indicated below by the fact that the two carry the same subscript letter index *i*):

(75)

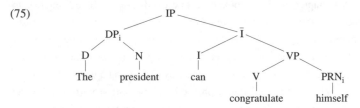

If the **c-command condition on binding** (74) is to be satisfied, it follows that the DP node containing *the president* must c-command the PRN node containing *himself*. Since the mother of DP is IP, and since IP dominates PRN, it should be clear that the c-command requirement is met, and hence that *himself* is bound by *the president*. We therefore correctly predict that (72a) is grammatical, with *the president* interpreted as the antecedent of *himself*.

But now consider why *the president* can't be the antecedent of *himself* in (76) below (cf. (72b) above):

(76)

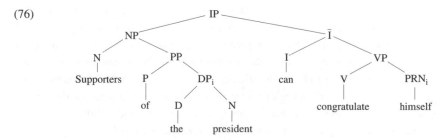

The answer is that the DP node containing *the president* doesn't c-command the PRN node containing *himself*, because the mother of DP is the PP node, and PP doesn't dominate PRN. Since there is no other potential antecedent for *himself* within the sentence (e.g. although the NP *supporters of the president* c-commands *himself*, it is not a suitable antecedent because it is a plural expression, and *himself* requires a singular antecedent), the anaphor *himself* remains *unbound* – in violation of the c-command requirement. Thus, (72b) is correctly predicted to be ungrammatical. However, the binding condition which the sentence violates is one which crucially involves the structural relation **c-command** – and this relation is defined in terms of the relative structural positions occupied by the anaphor and its antecedent. The fact that the relevant restriction on the binding of anaphors can be given a straightforward characterization in structural terms provides further (indirect) support for our claim that sentences have a hierarchical constituent structure. There's much more to be said about binding, though we shan't pursue the relevant issues here. (For a recent discussion, see Roberts 1996, chapter 3: don't attempt to read it until you have finished this book.)

3.10 Summary

In this chapter, we have looked at how words are combined together to form phrases and sentences, and at how we can represent the structure of the phrases and sentences thereby formed. In §3.2 we hypothesized that phrases and sentences are formed by a binary **merger** operation which combines pairs of constituents to form larger and larger structures. We suggested that one way of forming a larger structure is to project (i.e. expand) a head word into a phrase by combining it with a following complement, so that e.g. by combining the verb *privatize* with the complement noun *hospitals*, we form the verb phrase *privatize hospitals*, and by combining this verb phrase with the infinitive particle *to* we in turn form the infinitive phrase *to privatize hospitals*. In §3.3 we argued that some phrases have a more complex structure and contain a *specifier* as well as a head and a complement: we suggested that in a noun phrase such as *government plans to privatize hospitals*, the head noun *plans* merges with the infinitive phrase *to privatize hospitals* to form the intermediate nominal constituent (N-bar) *plans to privatize hospitals*, and that the resulting N-bar then merges with its specifier (the noun *government*) to form the full noun phrase *government plans to privatize hospitals*. In §3.4 we suggested that sentences are formed by the same binary merger operation as phrases: for example, a sentence such as *The government might privatize hospitals* is formed by merging the past-tense-inflected auxiliary (= I) *might* with the verb phrase complement *privatize hospitals* to form the intermediate auxiliary projection (= I-bar) *might privatize hospitals*; the resulting I-bar is then projected into an IP (i.e. complete auxiliary phrase) by merging it with the determiner phrase *the government* which serves as its specifier (or, more traditionally, its subject), thereby forming the clause or sentence *The government might privatize hospitals*. We noted that the resulting IP can in turn be merged with a complementizer like *that* to form the complementizer phrase (CP) *That the government might privatize hospitals* (which could be used e.g. as a reply to a sentence such as *What's the latest rumour?*). In §3.5 we looked at the structure of tree diagrams, and presented a simple (break-off-a-branch) procedure for determining which strings of words in a tree do and don't form constituents. In §3.6 we looked rather more closely at the formal properties of syntactic trees, suggesting that they are sets of nodes interconnected by *precedence* and *dominance* relations. We showed how terms such as *complement* and *specifier* can be defined configurationally (i.e. in relation to the position occupied by a given expression in a given structure). In §3.7 we noted that tree diagrams embody specific claims about syntactic structure which must be tested empirically; and we argued that *simple coordination* and *shared string coordination* could be used as ways of testing structure. In §3.8, we presented further constituent structure tests relating to *sentence fragments*, *proforms* and *ellipsis*. In §3.9 we saw that the distribution of *affective polarity items* and *anaphors* could be characterized in structural terms (via the relation *c-command*), so providing further evidence for positing that sentences have a hierarchical categorial constituent structure.

Workbook section

Exercise I (§§3.2–3.8)

In the text, we argued that the terms *constituent, specifier* and *complement* can be defined configurationally. In the light of the text definitions, look at the structure immediately below:

and answer the following questions about this structure (giving reasons for your answer):

1 Is *a meeting* a constituent, and if so of what kind? yes DP
2 Is *hold a meeting* a constituent, and if so of what kind? yes VP

3   Is *The Dean may expect to hold a meeting* a constituent, and if so of what kind? *No*

4   Is *to hold* a constituent, and if so of what kind? *No*

5   Is *may expect you to hold a meeting* a constituent, and if so of what kind? *Yes, I*

6   Is *expect a meeting* a constituent, and if so of what kind? *No*

7   Is *expect you* a constituent, and if so of what kind? *No*

8   Is *you to hold a meeting* a constituent, and if so of what kind? *Y, IP*

9   Is *may expect you* a constituent, and if so of what kind? *No*

10 Is *you* a constituent, and if so of what kind? *Yes, NRN*

11 Is *the* the specifier of *Dean*? *No*

12 Is *the Dean* the specifier of *may*? *Yes*

13 Is *may* the specifier of *expect*? *No*

14 Is *expect* the specifier of *you*? *No*

15 Is *you* the specifier of *to*? *yes*

16 Is *you* the specifier of *hold*?

17 Is *to* the specifier of *hold*?

18 Is *hold* the specifier of *a meeting*?

19 Is *Dean* the complement of *the*?

20 Is *may* the complement of *Dean*?

21 Is *may expect you to hold a meeting* the complement of *the Dean*?

22 Is *expect* the complement of *may*?

23 Is *you* the complement of *expect*?

24 Is *to hold a meeting* the complement of *you*?

25 Is *hold* the complement of *to*?

26 Is *a meeting* the complement of *to hold*?

27 Is *a* the complement of *meeting*?

In addition, in the light of the text definition, say:

28 Which of the nodes are (or are not) *maximal projections*?

Model answers for 1, 11 and 28

In terms of the definition of constituency given in (33) in the text, the string *a meeting* forms a DP constituent by virtue of the fact that *a* and *meeting* are both dominated by the DP node, and they are the only words dominated by the DP node. In terms of the definition of specifierhood given in (37) in the text, *the* cannot be the specifier of *Dean* because *the* is neither a sister nor a daughter of a projection of the noun *Dean*: on the contrary, the expression *the Dean* is a projection of the determiner *the*, and so is a determiner phrase, with *the* serving as its head determiner. The noun *Dean* here is the complement of *the* in terms of definition (36) in the text, since the N node containing *Dean* and the D node containing *the* are sisters, and since their mother is a

[handwritten margin note: if have V', I then you expect to be a specifier.]

DP node which is a projection of the determiner *the*. In terms of the definition of *maximal projection* given in (56) in the text, the N-node containing *meeting* is a maximal projection, since it is the largest constituent headed by the noun *meeting*; however, the D-node containing *a* is not a maximal projection, since it projects into a larger structure (= the DP *a meeting*) which is headed by the same determiner *a*; the DP *a meeting*, by contrast, is a maximal projection (viz. the maximal projection of the determiner *a*).

Exercise II (§§3.2–3.8)

Discuss the derivation of the following sentences, showing how their structure is built up in a pairwise fashion by successive merger operations, and showing how constituent structure tests can be used to support your analysis.

1 He has been writing to her
2 John may need to ask for help
3 Inflation is threatening to undermine government plans to reflate the economy
4 They will expect you to stay in Rome
5 I would imagine that they must have arrested him
6 I should like to know if you would feel able to support me
7 They may all suspect that Sam was cheating at syntax
8 They do both seem anxious for you to see a doctor

Helpful hint

Assume that the sentences are derived by first merging the last two words in the sentence to form a constituent, then merging the constituent thereby formed with the third-from-last word to form an even larger constituent, then merging this even larger constituent with the fourth-from-last word . . . and so on. (It should be noted, however, that while this simple parsing procedure will work with the sentences in this exercise, it requires modification to handle more complex sentences.)

Model answer for 1

Merging the preposition *to* with the pronoun *her* derives the prepositional phrase in (i) below:

(i)
```
        PP
       /  \
      P    PRN
      |     |
      to   her
```

Merging the PP in (i) with the verb *writing* immediately to its left in turn forms the verb phrase (ii) below:

(ii)

```
              VP
           /     \
         V         PP
         |        /   \
      writing    P     PRN
                 |      |
                 to    her
```

Merging the VP in (ii) with the progressive auxiliary *been* derives the progressive auxiliary phrase (iii) below:

(iii)

```
                   PROGP
                 /        \
            PROG            VP
             |           /      \
           been        V          PP
                       |         /   \
                    writing     P     PRN
                                |      |
                                to    her
```

Merging the PROGP in (iii) with the finite (third person singular present tense) auxiliary *has* forms the incomplete intermediate projection *has been writing to her* (which is incomplete in the sense that it cannot stand on its own as a sentence fragment, but rather requires a subject like *he*). If finite auxiliaries are I/INFL constituents, and intermediate auxiliary projections have the status of I-bar constituents, merging *has* with the VP in (iii) will derive the I-bar (iv) below:

(iv)

```
               Ī
            /      \
          I          PROGP
          |        /        \
         has    PROG          VP
                 |          /     \
               been        V        PP
                           |       /   \
                        writing   P     PRN
                                  |      |
                                  to    her
```

Merging the I-bar in (iv) with the subject pronoun *he* will in turn derive the IP (i.e. inflected auxiliary phrase) (v) below:

(v)

```
                   IP
                /      \
            PRN          Ī
             |         /    \
            He       I        PROGP
                     |       /      \
                    has   PROG        VP
                           |        /    \
                         been      V       PP
                                   |      /   \
                                writing  P     PRN
                                         |      |
                                         to    her
```

On this view, syntactic structures are derived in a *bottom–up* fashion, i.e. by building up trees in successive layers from bottom to top.

Evidence in support of positing that the PP, VP, PROGP and I-bar in (v) are constituents comes from simple coordination facts in relation to sentences such as (vi) below:

(vi) (a)   He has been writing *to her* and **to her sister**

    (b)   He has been *writing to her* and **phoning her**

    (c)   He has *been writing to her* and **been phoning her**

    (d)   He *has been writing to her* and **has been phoning her**

Moreover (for reasons which should be evident to you), the fact that the italicized sequences in (vii) below can serve as the shared string in the appropriate kind of coordinate structure provides further empirical evidence in support of the same conclusion (bold print marks contrastive stress):

(vii) (a)   Has he been writing or talking *to her*?

    (b)   Has he been – or hasn't he been – *writing to her*?

    (c)   Has he – or hasn't he – *been writing to her*?

    (d)   Could it be that **she** – or perhaps that **he** – *has been writing to her*?

Furthermore, as we can see from (viii) below, the PP, VP and PROGP constituents (by virtue of being maximal projections) can serve as sentence fragments:

(viii) (a)   Who has he been writing to? *To her?*

    (b)   What has he been doing to stay in touch? *Writing to her?*

    (c)   What has he been doing to stay in touch? *Been writing to her?*

(though (viii)(b) is more concise than (viii)(c), and so preferred). In addition, VP and PROGP can serve as the antecedent of a pronoun like *which*: cf.

(ix) (a)   If he has *been writing to her* (**which** he has), why doesn't she write back?

    (b)   If he has been *writing to her* (**which** he has been), why doesn't she write back?

and VP and PROGP (by virtue of being the complements of auxiliaries) can undergo ellipsis, as we see from (x) below:

(x) (a)   I wonder why he has been *writing to her* as often as he has been

    (b)   I wonder why he has *been writing to her* as often as he has

Thus, there is considerable empirical evidence in support of analysis (v).

Exercise III (§§3.2–3.8)

Consider the following set of sentences:

1 John has been taking drugs
2 They are both feeling tired
3 Congress is expecting the president to back down
4 She must be keen for him to win
5 The bullet has gone right through his skull
6 You might fall out of the window
7 The government has rejected opposition demands for legislation
8 The answers to this exercise may baffle you

Below are incorrect analyses of these sentences suggested by some of my students (their names have been withheld to protect the innocent and incompetent). Say what's wrong with each of the diseased trees below, and draw an alternative tree diagram representing the right structure (giving reasons for preferring your analysis):

9

```
        NP
       /  \
      N    IP
      |   /  \
   John  I    VP
         |   /  \
       has  PROG  V̄
            |    / \
          been  V   N
                |   |
             taking drugs
```

10

```
         PRNP
        /    \
      PRN    IP
      |     /  \
    They   I    QP
           |   /  \
          are  Q   VP
               |   / \
             both  V   A
                   |   |
               feeling tired
```

11

```
          NP
         /  \
        N    IP
        |   /  \
   Congress I   VP
            |  /  \
           is V    DP
              |   /  \
          expecting D   NP
                    |  /  \
                  the N    IP
                      |   /  \
                 president I   VP
                          |   / \
                         to  V   P
                             |   |
                           back down
```

12

```
          PRNP
         /    \
       PRN    IP
       |     /  \
     She    I    V̄
            |   /  \
          must V    AP
               |   /  \
              be  A    PP
                  |   /  \
               keen P    PRNP
                    |   /   \
                   for PRN   IP
                       |    / \
                      him  I   V
                           |   |
                          to  win
```

13
```
        DP
       /  \
      D    NP
    The    / \
          N   IP
       bullet / \
             I   VP
            has  / \
               V    ADVP
             gone   /  \
                  ADV   PP
                right  /  \
                      P    DP
                 through  /  \
                         D    N
                        his  skull
```

14
```
          IP
         /  \
       PRN   Ī
      You   / \
           I   VP
         might / \
              V   PP
            fall / \
                P   P̄
               out / \
                  P   DP
                 of  /  \
                    D    N
                  the  window
```

Model answer for 9

There are three respects in which the analysis in 9 proves problematic. Firstly, it claims that the whole structure is a noun phrase; and yet it doesn't have the distribution of an NP, as we see from the fact that (unlike a typical noun expression such as *John*) it can't occur as the complement of a preposition like *about*: cf.

(i)   She complained about *John*

(ii)   *She complained about *John has been taking drugs*

Secondly, 9 provides no principled account of the fact that *has* agrees with *John*, since the two are contained within different projections (*John* within NP and *has* within IP), and agreement typically involves a *local* relation between the head and specifier of the same projection (typically, IP). Thirdly, 9 wrongly predicts that the string *taking drugs* should not be able to serve as a sentence fragment, since it is not a maximal projection (it is a V-bar, not a VP); but this prediction is wrong, as we see from the grammaticality of speaker B's reply in (iii) below:

(iii)   SPEAKER A: What has John been doing?
        SPEAKER B: *Taking drugs*

In place of 9, we might posit the structure (iv) below:

(iv)
```
          IP
         /  \
       N     Ī
     John   / \
           I   PROGP
          has  /  \
            PROG   VP
            been   / \
                  V   N
               taking drugs
```

The analysis in (iv) correctly predicts that (as a finite IP), the relevant structure can be used as the complement of a finite complementizer like *if* or *that*: cf.

(v)   He might ask if *John has been taking drugs*
(vi)   She may suspect that *John has been taking drugs*

Moreover, since *has* is the head and *John* the specifier of IP in (iv), we correctly predict that the two enter into a local specifier–head agreement relation. And since *taking drugs* is a maximal projection (more specifically, a VP) in (iv), we correctly predict that it can serve as a sentence fragment, as in (iii).

Only
look
at!

Exercise IV (§§3.2–3.8)

Below are a number of alternative analyses of the structure of the sentence *He might have been watching television* which have been proposed in the linguistic literature over the past four decades. (Some of the category labels have been adapted to make them compatible with those used here.)

1   Chomsky, *Syntactic Structures* (1957)

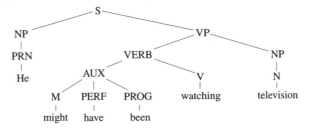

2   Chomsky, *The Logical Structure of Linguistic Theory* (1955/1975)

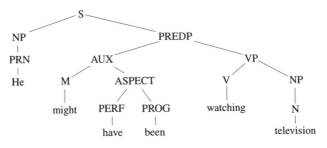

3   Chomsky, *Studies on Semantics in Generative Grammar* (1972b)

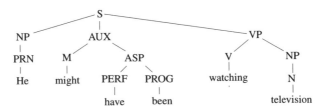

4   Jackendoff, *Semantic Interpretation in Generative Grammar* (1972)

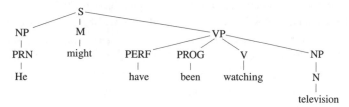

5   Emonds, *A Transformational Approach to English Syntax* (1976)

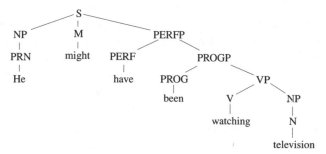

(Some of the less familiar abbreviations used above are as follows: S = sentence/clause; M = modal auxiliary; ASP = aspectual auxiliary; PREDP = predicate phrase.) Comment on significant structural differences between the analysis for the relevant sentence proposed in (39) in the text, and those in 1–5 above. In addition, for each of the five analyses outlined above, say whether it would account for the (un)grammaticality of the sentences in (44), (49), (53), (54), (59) and (61) in the text.

Model answer for 1

One obvious difference between the analysis in the text and the exercise analysis 1 above is that the text analysis posits that the relevant clause is a projection of the finite modal auxiliary *might*, whereas the exercise analysis 1 assumes that clauses are formed by a different process of *predication* under which a VP is predicated of a subject NP, and the two combine together to form a (headless) S constituent. The S analysis leads to an asymmetrical theory in which phrases and clauses are formed by different processes – phrases being the result of the *projection* of a head, and clauses being the result of a *predication* relation between two phrases. A second difference is that the text analysis posits a binary-branching structure (i.e. a structure in which all nonterminal nodes are binary-branching), whereas the exercise analysis 1 implicitly rejects the binarity principle, since the AUX node is ternary-branching (i.e. it branches down into M, PERF and PROG), and the two NP nodes are unary-branching (in that both branch down into a single PRN node: note that it was assumed in earlier work that

125

all maximal projections were phrases, and hence that (for example) a noun or pronoun could not serve as a maximal projection unless it projected into NP).

The exercise analysis in 1 above correctly predicts that sentences like (44d) in the text are grammatical (since the string *might have been watching television* is analysed as a VP which can therefore be coordinated with another similar VP), but wrongly predicts that (44a–c) are ungrammatical by virtue of the fact that the strings *watching television*, *been watching television* and *have been watching television* are not constituents according to the exercise analysis 1. In much the same way, the exercise analysis in 1 correctly predicts that (49d) in the text is grammatical (since the shared string *might have been watching television* is analysed as a VP constituent), but wrongly predicts that (49a–c) are all ungrammatical (because the shared string in each case is a nonconstituent sequence). Moreover, the exercise analysis 1 wrongly predicts that *watching television*, *been watching television* and *have been watching television* cannot be used as sentence fragments in (53) in the text (since they are not constituents), and conversely wrongly predicts that the string *might have been watching television* should be able to function as a sentence fragment in (54) in the text, since it is a VP constituent and hence a maximal projection. In much the same way, the exercise analysis 1 wrongly predicts that *might have been watching television* should be able to function as the antecedent of *so* in (59) in the text (since it is a VP), and also wrongly predicts that the strings *watching television*, *been watching television* and *have been watching television* should not (since they are nonconstituents). Finally, the exercise analysis 1 correctly predicts that *might have been watching television* can undergo ellipsis in (61) in the text, but wrongly predicts that *watching television*, *been watching television* and *have been watching television* cannot. Overall, then, the exercise analysis 1 is *descriptively inadequate*, since it makes grossly inaccurate predictions about the (un)grammaticality of the relevant sentences.

Exercise V (§§3.2–3.9)

As noted in the text, a number of words in English are said to be *polarity items*, in the sense that they seem to have an inherently *affective* polarity, and so are restricted to occurring in a position where they are c-commanded by an affective (e.g. negative or interrogative) constituent. One such polarity item (as we saw in the text) is existential *any* (and its compounds like *anyone/anything/anywhere*). Two other polarity items are *need* and *dare*, when used with a bare (*to*-less) infinitive complement, as in *I don't think he dare/need say anything*. (Note that when *need/dare* are used with a *to* complement as in *He needs to see a specialist*, they are not polarity items.) Show how the c-command condition would account for the (un)grammaticality of the following:

1   You mustn't talk to anyone
2   Nobody need do anything

3 She has refused to go anywhere

4 Who dare say anything?

5 They might ask if anyone has seen anything

6 We wouldn't want anything to happen to anyone

7 I don't think that anyone need feel guilty about anything

8 He may have no desire to change anything

9 *Anyone couldn't find anything

10 *Anyone dare do nothing

Helpful hints

Assume that *need/dare* (when they take a bare infinitive complement) are modal auxiliaries which occupy the head I position of IP, and that they take a VP complement. Assume that pronominal quantifiers like *anyone/anything/anywhere/nobody* belong to the category PRN. Likewise, assume that *no* in 8 is a quantifier (= Q) which heads a quantifier phrase (= QP) constituent which has a noun phrase (= NP) comple ment. Finally, assume that *mustn't/wouldn't/don't/couldn't* are negative auxiliaries occupying the head I position of IP.

Model answer for 1

Given the arguments in the text, 1 will have the structure (i) below:

(i)

The I node containing the negative auxiliary *mustn't* here c-commands the PRN node containing the polarity item *anyone*, because the two are disconnected, and the mother of the I node is I-bar, and I-bar dominates [$_{PRN}$ *anyone*]. Thus, since the polarity item *anyone* is c-commanded by the negative auxiliary *mustn't*, the *c-command condition* on the use of polarity items is satisfied, so sentence 1 is grammatical.

Exercise VI

A distinction which we overlooked in the text is that between phrases and compound words. It is traditionally claimed that an expression such as *prone to accidents* is an adjectival phrase with the structure 1a below, whereas an expression such as *accident prone* is a compound adjective with the structure 1b:

127

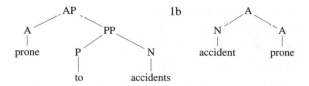

1a   AP: A (prone) — PP: P (to) — N (accidents)

1b   A: N (accident) — A (prone)

Let's say that in both cases, *prone* is the *head* of the phrase or (compound) word containing it (which is why both expressions are adjectival in nature), and that *accident(s)* is its complement noun. (Strictly speaking, we should say that the complement of *prone* in 1b is the prepositional phrase *to accidents*.) Try and identify the phonological, morphological and syntactic differences between compounds and phrases illustrated in the examples below (note that the capital letters in 2 mark syllables which carry primary stress):

2a   They are PRONE to ACcidents
 b   They are ACcident prone
3a   They are prone to accidents/*They are prone to accident
 b   They are accident prone/*They are accidents prone
4a   They are prone to accidents/*They are to accidents prone
 b   They are accident prone/*They are prone accident
5a   People who have lots of accidents must be prone to them
 b   *People who have lots of accidents must be them prone
6a   Accidents, I've always been prone to
 b   *Accident, I've always been prone

In addition, draw tree diagrams representing the structure of the two expressions in (7a–b) below:

7a   manufacturers of pianos
 b   piano manufacturers

and highlight phonological, morphological and syntactic differences between the two.

Helpful hints

Look at the stress properties of the head and its complement; at the number (singular/plural) properties of the complement noun; at whether the relevant structures are right- or left-headed (i.e. whether the head word is positioned on the left or right of the structure); at whether the complement can be a pronoun rather than a noun; and at whether the complement noun can be extracted (i.e. moved) out of its containing expression. Don't attempt to draw tree diagrams representing the structure of sentences (2–6), since some parts of these sentences involve constructions we haven't yet looked at: focus on the adjectival structures we are concerned with.

Exercise VII (§§3.2–3.5)

In the text, we noted that the syntactic structure of any phrase or sentence can be represented either by a labelled tree diagram or by a labelled bracketing; each constituent is represented by a single node in a tree diagram, but by a pair of brackets (the lefthand one of which carries the relevant category label) in a labelled bracketing. The labelled bracketings given below represent the structure of a number of different sentences. Label each of the righthand brackets in the structure, and then convert each of the labelled bracketings into an equivalent tree diagram.

1   [$_{IP}$ [$_{PRN}$ We] [$_{\bar{I}}$ [$_I$ have] [$_{VP}$ [$_V$ made] [$_N$ progress]]]]]

2   [$_{IP}$ [$_{PRN}$ She] [$_{\bar{I}}$ [$_I$ won't] [$_{VP}$ [$_V$ succumb] [$_{PP}$ [$_P$ to] . . .

        . . . [$_{NP}$ [$_N$ threats] [$_{PP}$ [$_P$ of] [$_N$ violence]]]]]]]]

3   [$_{IP}$ [$_{DP}$ [$_D$ The] [$_N$ opposition]] [$_{\bar{I}}$ [$_I$ are] [$_{VP}$ [$_V$ pointing] . . .

        . . . [$_{PP}$ [$_P$ to] [$_{NP}$ [$_N$ press] [$_{\bar{N}}$ [$_N$ allegations] . . .

        . . . [$_{PP}$ [$_P$ of] [$_N$ corruption]]]]]]]]]

4   [$_{IP}$ [$_{PRN}$ They] [$_I$ [$_I$ arc] [$_{VP}$ [$_V$ anticipating] [$_{CP}$ [$_C$ that] . . .

        . . . [$_{IP}$ [$_{PRN}$ he] [$_{\bar{I}}$ [$_I$ will] [$_{VP}$ [$_V$ resign] [$_{PP}$ [$_P$ from] . . .

        . . . [$_{DP}$ [$_D$ his] [$_N$ post]]]]]]]]]]]]

(Note that the dots (. . .) in 2–4 are simply a graphic device to indicate that the structure continues on (or from) the following line: thus, each structure in 2–4 should be treated as if it were on one continuous line.)

Model answer for 1

In order to label the righthand brackets, we work as follows. Proceeding from left to right, we pick out the first unlabelled righthand bracket in the structure, and we pair it with (i.e. assign it the same category label as) the nearest unpaired labelled bracket to its left. Since we haven't labelled any of the righthand brackets in 1, the first unlabelled bracket we come to (if we proceed from left to right) is the bracket immediately following the word *we*. We then pair this with the nearest unpaired labelled bracket to its left (i.e. with the PRN bracket which immediately precedes the word *we*) – as in:

(i)   [$_{IP}$ [$_{PRN}$ We $_{PRN}$] [$_{\bar{I}}$ [$_I$ have] [$_{VP}$ [$_V$ made] [$_N$ progress]]]]]

The lefthand bracket round *we* marks the beginning of the pronoun constituent *we*, and the righthand bracket marks the end of the same PRN constituent. Proceeding from left to right, we now look for the next unlabelled righthand bracket (= the bracket immediately following *have*) and we pair it with the nearest unpaired lefthand bracket to its left (= the I bracket immediately preceding *have*) – as in (ii) below:

(ii)   [$_{IP}$ [$_{PRN}$ We $_{PRN}$] [$_{\bar{I}}$ [$_I$ have $_I$] [$_{VP}$ [$_V$ made] [$_N$ progress]]]]]

We then find the next unlabelled righthand bracket (= that immediately following *made*), and we pair it with the nearest unpaired lefthand bracket to its left (= the V bracket to the immediate left of *made*), giving:

(iii) $[_{IP} [_{PRN}$ We $_{PRN}] [_{\bar{I}} [_{I}$ have $_{I}] [_{VP} [_{V}$ made $_{V}] [_{N}$ progress]]]]

The next unlabelled righthand bracket in the structure (iii) is that immediately following the word *progress*, which we pair with the nearest unpaired lefthand bracket to its left (= the N bracket to the immediate left of *progress*), so resulting in:

(iv) $[_{IP} [_{PRN}$ We $_{PRN}] [_{\bar{I}} [_{I}$ have $_{I}] [_{VP} [_{V}$ made $_{V}] [_{N}$ progress $_{N}]]]]$

We now find the next unlabelled righthand bracket, which is the third bracket from the end of the overall structure. We then pair it with the nearest *unpaired* lefthand bracket to its left (i.e. that labelled VP), as in (v):

(v) $[_{IP} [_{PRN}$ We $_{PRN}] [_{\bar{I}} [_{I}$ have $_{I}] [_{VP} [_{V}$ made $_{V}] [_{N}$ progress $_{N}]$ $_{VP}]]]$

The next unlabelled righthand bracket in (v) is the last-but-one bracket: the nearest *unpaired* bracket to its left is the I-bar bracket preceding *have*, so the two are paired as in (vi) below:

(vi) $[_{IP} [_{PRN}$ We $_{PRN}] [_{\bar{I}} [_{I}$ have $_{I}] [_{VP} [_{V}$ made $_{V}] [_{N}$ progress $_{N}]$ $_{VP}]$ $_{\bar{I}}]]$

The one remaining unlabelled righthand bracket (= the rightmost bracket) is then paired with the one remaining unpaired lefthand bracket (= the leftmost IP bracket), as in (vii) below:

(vii) $[_{IP} [_{PRN}$ We $_{PRN}] [_{\bar{I}} [_{I}$ have $_{I}] [_{VP} [_{V}$ made $_{V}] [_{N}$ progress $_{N}]$ $_{VP}]$ $_{\bar{I}}]$ $_{IP}]$

What (vii) tells us is (for example) that the VP comprises all the constituents which are contained within the lefthand and righthand VP brackets – i.e. the verb *made* and the noun *progress*. The resulting structure (vii) can equivalently be represented in terms of the tree diagram in (viii) below:

(viii)

I leave it to you to devise an algorithm (i.e. set of procedures) of your own for converting a labelled bracketing into a labelled tree diagram, and conversely for converting a labelled tree diagram into a corresponding labelled bracketing: this is an interesting exercise in itself.

4

Empty categories

4.1 Overview

So far, our discussion of syntactic structure has tacitly assumed that all constituents in a given structure are *overt*. However, we now turn to argue that syntactic structures may also contain *empty* (= *covert* = *null*) categories – i.e. categories which have no overt phonetic form, and hence which are inaudible or silent. As we shall see, empty categories play a central role in the theory of grammar which we are outlining here.

4.2 PRO subjects

We begin by looking at the structure of clauses which might be argued to contain an empty subject. In this connection, compare the structure of the bracketed infinitive clauses in the (a) and (b) examples below:

(1) (a)   We would like [*you* to stay]
    (b)   We would like [to stay]
(2) (a)   We don't want [*anyone* to upset them]
    (b)   We don't want [to upset them]
(3) (a)   They will expect [*students* to pass the exam]
    (b)   They will expect [to pass the exam]

Each of the bracketed infinitive complement clauses in the (a) examples in (1–3) contains an overt (italicized) subject. By contrast, the bracketed complement clauses in the (b) examples appear to be subjectless. However, we shall argue that apparently subjectless infinitive clauses contain an understood **null subject**. (By saying that a constituent is *null* or *empty* or *covert*, we mean that it has no overt phonetic form and so is silent.) The kind of null subject found in the bracketed clauses in the (b) examples has much the same grammatical and referential properties as pronouns, and hence is conventionally designated as **PRO**. (The fact that English allows infinitives to have null subjects does not mean that English is a null subject language, since null subject languages are languages which allow *finite* verbs to have a null subject.)

Given this assumption, sentences such as (1a–b) have essentially the same structure, except that the bracketed IP has an overt pronoun *you* as its subject in (1a), but a covert pronoun subject *PRO* in (1b) – as represented in (4a–b) below:

(4)

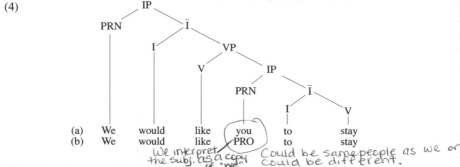

Using the relevant technical terminology, we can say that the null subject PRO in (4b) is **controlled** by (i.e. refers back to) the subject *we* of the matrix (= containing = next highest) clause – or, equivalently, that *we* is the **controller** or **antecedent** of PRO. Verbs (such as *like*) which allow an infinitive complement with a PRO subject are said to function (in the relevant use) as **control predicates**. An important corollary of the analysis in (4b) is that apparently subjectless infinitive clauses have essentially the same structure as infinitive clauses with overt subjects, in that both are IPs: the two types of infinitive clause differ only in respect of whether the infinitive subject is an overt or covert pronoun.

An obvious question to ask at this juncture is why we should posit that apparently subjectless infinitive complements like those bracketed in (1–3b) above have a null PRO subject. Part of the motivation for positing PRO is semantic in nature. In traditional grammar it is claimed that subjectless infinitive clauses have an *understood* or *implicit* subject – and positing a **PRO** subject in such clauses is one way of capturing the relevant intuition. The implicit subject becomes explicit if the relevant clauses are paraphrased by a finite clause, as we see from the paraphrases for the (a) examples given in the (b) examples below:

(5) (a) I am sorry [to have kept you waiting]
    (b) I am sorry [*I* have kept you waiting]
(6) (a) It is important [to carry your passport with you]
    (b) It is important [*you* should carry your passport with you]
(7) (a) Dumbo has promised [to come to my party]
    (b) Dumbo has promised [*he* will come to my party]

The fact that the bracketed clauses in the (b) examples contain an overt (italicized) subject makes it plausible to suppose that the bracketed clauses in the synonymous (a) examples have a covert PRO subject.

There is also a considerable body of syntactic evidence in support of claiming that subjectless infinitive clauses have a covert PRO subject. Part of the relevant evidence comes from the syntax of reflexive anaphors (i.e. *+self/+selves* forms such as *myself/yourself/himself/themselves* etc.). As examples such as the following indicate, reflexives generally require a **local** antecedent:

(8) (a)   They want [John to help *himself*]

(b)   *They want [John to help *themselves*]

In the case of structures like (8), a *local* antecedent means 'an antecedent contained within the same [bracketed] clause as the reflexive'. Example (8a) is grammatical because it satisfies this *locality* requirement: the antecedent of the reflexive *himself* is the noun *John*, and *John* is contained within the same [bracketed] *help*-clause as *himself*. By contrast, (8b) is ungrammatical because the reflexive *themselves* does not have a local antecedent (i.e. it does not have an antecedent within the bracketed clause containing it); its antecedent is the pronoun *they*, and *they* is an immediate constituent of the *want* clause, not of the [bracketed] *help*-clause. In the light of the requirement for reflexives to have a local antecedent, consider now how we account for the grammaticality of the following:

(9)   John wants [**PRO** to prove *himself*]

Given the requirement for reflexives to have a local antecedent, it follows that the reflexive *himself* must have an antecedent within its own [bracketed] clause. This requirement is satisfied in (9) if we assume that the bracketed complement clause has a PRO subject, and that PRO is the antecedent of *himself*. Since PRO in turn is controlled by *John* (i.e. *John* is the antecedent of PRO), this means that *himself* is coreferential to (i.e. refers to the same person as) *John*.

We can formulate a further argument in support of positing a PRO subject in apparently subjectless infinitive clauses in relation to the syntax of **predicate nominals**: these are nominal (i.e. noun-containing) expressions used as the complement of a copular (i.e. linking) verb such as *be*, *become*, *remain* (etc.) in expressions such as *John was/became/remained my best friend*, where the property of 'being my best friend' is predicated of *John*. Predicate nominals in copular constructions have to agree with the subject of their own clause, as we see from examples such as the following:

(10) (a)   They want [**their son** to become *a millionaire/*millionaires*]

(b)   He wants [**his sons** to become *millionaires/*a millionaire*]

As examples like (10) illustrate, the italicized predicate nominal has to agree with the (bold-printed) subject of its own [bracketed] *become*-clause, and cannot agree with the subject of the *want*-clause. In the light of this clause-internal agreement requirement, consider now how we account for the agreement pattern in (11) below:

(11) (a) They want [**PRO** to become *millionaires/*a millionaire*]

  (b) He wants [**PRO** to become *a millionaire/*millionaires*]

If we posit that the *become* clause has a PRO subject which is controlled by the subject of the *want* clause, the relevant agreement facts can be accounted for straightforwardly: we simply posit that the predicate nominal (*a*) *millionaire(s)* agrees with PRO (since PRO is the subject of the *become* clause), and that PRO in (11a) is plural because its controller/antecedent is the plural pronoun *they*, and conversely that PRO in (11b) is singular because its antecedent/controller is the singular pronoun *he*. It goes without saying that it is far from obvious how we would handle the relevant agreement facts if we didn't posit a PRO subject for the bracketed infinitive complements in sentences such as (11).

There is a range of additional empirical evidence which supports the claim that apparently subjectless infinitive clauses have an understood PRO subject. Some of this evidence is given in the paradigms (12–15) below:

(12) (a) Do you want [**John** to use *his own* car]?

  (b) *Does John want [**you** to use *his own* car]?

  (c) John wants [**PRO** to use *his own* car]

(13) (a) I don't want [**you** to lose *your* cool]

  (b) *I don't want [**you** to lose *my* cool]

  (c) I don't want [**PRO** to lose *my* cool]

(14) (a) The president doesn't want [**the congressmen** to fight *each other*]

  (b) *The congressmen don't want [**the president** to fight *each other*]

  (c) The congressmen don't want [**PRO** to fight *each other*]

(15) (a) John wants [**his parents** to live *together*]

  (b) *They want [**John** to live *together*]

  (c) They want [**PRO** to live *together*]

The examples in (12a–b) suggest that in expressions like *one's own*, the possessive *one's* requires a local antecedent: this requirement will only be met in (12c) if the bracketed infinitive complement has a PRO subject which is controlled by *John*. The examples in (13a–b) show that in expressions such as *lose one's cool*, the possessor *one's* must agree with the subject of *lose*; this requirement will only be met in (13c) if we assume that the bracketed *lose* clause contains a PRO subject controlled by *I*. The examples in (14a–b) and (15a–b) show that expressions like *each other* and *together* require a local plural antecedent; this requirement will only be met in (14c) and (15c) if we posit that the bracketed complement clause has a PRO subject which is plural by virtue of the fact that it is controlled by the plural expressions *the congressmen/they*.

Examples such as (5–15) above provide empirical evidence in support of positing that apparently subjectless infinitive clauses have a PRO subject. In examples such as those discussed above, PRO has a controller in a higher clause (generally the subject of the higher clause). However, in examples such as (16) below, PRO has no obvious controller within the sentence containing it:

(16) (a)   [Why **PRO** kid *myself*]? I know she doesn't love me any more

    (b)   [**PRO** kill *himself*]?! He hasn't got the guts!

    (c)   It's important [**PRO** to rid *ourselves* of private prejudices]

    (d)   SPEAKER A: What is their greatest ambition?

             SPEAKER B: [**PRO** to see *themselves* on television]

Clearly we need to posit a PRO subject for the bracketed clauses in (16) in order to satisfy the requirement that each of the italicized reflexives have a local antecedent. In examples like (16), PRO has no antecedent within the sentence containing it; instead, the reference of PRO seems to be discourse-determined (i.e. PRO seems to denote some specific individual or set of individuals who is talking, being talked to or being talked about in the relevant discourse). By contrast, in sentences such as (17) below:

(17)   It's wrong [**PRO** to blame *oneself* for other people's misfortune]

PRO seems to denote an arbitrary individual (i.e. it means 'any arbitrary person you care to choose'), and thus might be said to have *arbitrary reference*. There is a great deal more that could be said about the referential properties of PRO, but we won't pursue the matter further here.

4.3   Null auxiliaries

So far, all the clauses we have looked at in this chapter and the last have contained an IP projection headed by a finite auxiliary or infinitival *to*. The obvious generalization suggested by this is that all clauses are IPs. An important question begged by this assumption, however, is how we are to analyse finite clauses which contain no finite auxiliary. In this connection, consider the construction illustrated in (18) below:

(18)   *He* could have left, and [*she* have stayed]

Both clauses here (viz. the *left*-clause and the *stayed*-clause) appear to be finite, since both have nominative subjects (*he/she*). If all finite clauses contain an IP projection headed by a finite INFL, it follows that both clauses in (18) must be IPs containing a finite I/INFL constituent. This is clearly true of the *left*-clause, which contains the finite modal auxiliary *could*; however, the *stayed*-clause doesn't seem to contain any finite auxiliary constituent, since *have* is an infinitive form (the corresponding finite form being *has*). How can we analyse finite clauses as projections of an INFL constituent when clauses like that bracketed in (18) contain no finite auxiliary?

An intuitively plausible answer is to suppose that the string *she have stayed* in (18) is an elliptical variant of *she could have stayed*, and that the I constituent *could* undergoes head-ellipsis (alias **gapping**) in the second clause. If this is so, then the second clause will have the structure (19) below (where *e* marks the ellipsed auxiliary):

(19)

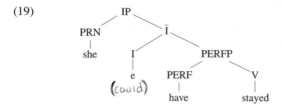

The head I position of IP would then be filled by an ellipsed auxiliary. We can think of ellipsis as a process by which a constituent (in this case, *could*) is given a null phonetic form, but retains its grammatical and semantic properties (so that *e* in (19) is a silent counterpart of *could*). The *null auxiliary* analysis in (19) provides a principled account of three sets of facts. Firstly, the bracketed clause in (18) is interpreted as an elliptical form of *she could have stayed*: this can be straightforwardly accounted for under the analysis in (19), given that *e* is an elliptical form of *could*. Secondly, the subject is in the nominative case form *she*: this can be attributed to the fact that the I position in (19) is filled by a null counterpart of *could* and so is finite (and thereby requires a nominative specifier). Thirdly, the perfective auxiliary *have* is in the uninflected infinitive form: this is because *e* (being an elliptical form of *could*) has the same grammatical properties (hence the same complement-selection properties) as *could*, so that *e* (like *could*) requires a complement headed by a word (like *have*) in the infinitive form.

A further argument in support of the analysis in (19) comes from facts relating to **cliticization** (a process by which one word attaches itself in a leechlike fashion to another). The perfective auxiliary form *have* has a range of different allomorphs (i.e. variant forms) in the spoken language. When unstressed, it loses its initial /h/ segment and has its vowel reduced to schwa /ə/, and so is pronounced as /əv/ e.g. in sentences such as *You should have been there*. (Because *of* is also pronounced /əv/ when unstressed, some people write this as *You should **of** been there* – not *you*, of course!) However, when *have* is used with a subject ending in a vowel or diphthong (e.g. a subject pronoun like *I/we/you/they*), it can lose its vowel entirely and be contracted down to /v/; in this form, it is phonetically too insubstantial to survive as an independent word, and **cliticizes** (i.e. attaches itself) to its subject, e.g. in structures such as:

(20) (a)   *You've* done your duty

  (b)   *We've* seen the Mona Lisa

  (c)   *I've* forgotten to lock the door

  (d)   *They've* shown no interest in my idea

However, note that *have* cannot cliticize onto *she* in (21):

(21)   *He could have left and *she've* stayed

Why should cliticization of *have* onto *she* be blocked here? The *null auxiliary* analysis in (19) provides us with an obvious answer, if we make the reasonable assumption that *have* can only cliticize onto an *immediately preceding* word ending in a vowel or diphthong. We can then say that *have* is blocked from cliticizing onto *she* in (19) by the presence of the null auxiliary which intervenes between *have* and *she*. Thus, the *null auxiliary* analysis seems entirely appropriate for elliptical finite clauses like the *stayed-*clause in (18) – i.e. clauses which contain an ellipsed auxiliary.

A rather different kind of *null auxiliary* constituent is found in *African American English* (AAE), in sentences such as the following (from Labov 1969, p. 717):

(22)   He just feel like he gettin' cripple up from arthritis

In AAE, specific forms of *be* have null variants (so that we find null allomorphs of *are* and *is* in contexts where Standard English (SE) would require the contracted forms *'s* and *'re*). Hence, in place of SE *He's getting crippled* we find AAE *He gettin cripple* (with a null counterpart of *'s*). Evidence in support of the assumption that AAE sentences like (22) incorporate a null variant of *is* comes from the fact that the missing auxiliary *is* may surface in a *tag*, as in sentences such as the following (where the sequence following the comma is the *tag*):

(23)   He gonna be there, I know he *is* (Fasold 1980, p. 29)

Given the general assumption that the auxiliary found in the tag is a copy of the auxiliary used in the main clause, it follows that the main *gonna*-clause in (23) must contain a null variant of *is*. Interestingly, the form *am* (contracted to *'m*) has no null counterpart in AAE, nor do the past-tense forms *was/were*. It would seem, therefore, that the only finite forms of *be* which have a null counterpart in AAE are the specific auxiliary forms *are* and *is*. No less interestingly, Wolfram (1971, p. 149) reports that in nonstandard southern white English the use of null auxiliaries is even more restricted, and that the only form of *be* with a null counterpart is *are*, not *is*; cf. the parallel observation by Fasold (1980, p. 30) that 'There are many southern whites who delete only *are*.'

4.4   Unfilled INFL

Our analysis of apparently auxiliariless clauses like those in (18) and (22) above suggests an interesting analysis of finite clauses such as the following, which contain a finite verb, but no auxiliary:

(24) (a)   He hates syntax
     (b)   He failed syntax

Why not treat auxiliariless finite clauses in much the same way as we analysed structures like (19) which contain an ellipsed auxiliary – namely as IP structures headed by a null I constituent? More specifically, let's suppose that auxiliariless finite clauses like those in (24) above are IP constituents which have the structure (25) below:

(25)

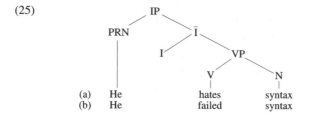

(a)	He	hates	syntax
(b)	He	failed	syntax

The fact that the INFL node in (25) contains no *leaf* (not even an invisible *empty* one) is meant to represent the assumption that the head I position of IP is simply *unfilled*; that it is to say, the INFL position in (25) is neither occupied by an overt item, nor occupied by a covert item – it is simply *unoccupied*.

However, one apparent problem posed by the analysis in (25) is that of how we account for the fact that *he* agrees with *hates*. After all, agreement (e.g. between *he* and *has* in *He has gone*) typically involves a local (phrase-internal) spec(ifier)–head relation between INFL and its specifier: since the verb *hates* is an immediate constituent of VP and *he* is an immediate constituent of IP, the two are clearly not in a local specifier–head relation, so would not be expected to agree. How can we deal with this problem? One possible solution would be to suppose that when INFL is unfilled, the tense and agreement properties of the head V of VP **percolate** up to INFL. Since *hates* is a third person singular present-tense verb form, the features of INFL (inherited from *hates*) will indicate that it is a third person singular present-tense form, and so will require it to have a third person singular nominative subject. Thus, the fact that the subject in (25) surfaces in the nominative form *he* and agrees with the verb *hates* is unproblematic.

'But why on earth would we want to pretend that clauses which obviously don't contain an auxiliary actually contain an unfilled auxiliary position?' you might wonder. Well, from a theoretical point of view, an obvious advantage of the *unfilled INFL* analysis is that it provides a unitary characterization of the syntax of clauses, since it allows us to say that all clauses contain an IP projection, and that the subject of a clause is always in **spec-IP** (i.e. always occupies the specifier position within IP), that INFL in a finite clause always has a nominative subject, and always agrees with its subject. Lending further weight to theory-internal considerations such as these is a substantial body of empirical evidence. A direct consequence of the *unfilled INFL* analysis (25) of auxiliariless finite clauses is that finite auxiliaries and finite verbs occupy different positions within the clause: finite auxiliaries (being functors) occupy the head I position of IP, whereas finite nonauxiliary verbs (being contentives) occupy the head V position of VP. An interesting way of testing this hypothesis is in relation to the behaviour of polycategorial items which have the status of auxiliary verbs in some uses, but of nonauxiliary verbs in others. One such word is *have*. In the kind of use illustrated in (26) below, it functions as a perfective auxiliary:

(26) (a)   She *has* gone to Paris

    (b)   I *have* been working on my assignment

    (c)   They *had* been warned about syntax

However, in the uses illustrated in (27) below, *have* functions as a causative or experiential verb (i.e. a verb carrying much the same meaning as 'cause' or 'experience'):

(27) (a)   The doctor *had* an eye-specialist examine the patient

    (b)   The doctor *had* the patient examined by an eye-specialist

    (c)   The teacher *had* three students walk out on her

    (d)   I've never *had* anyone send me flowers

By traditional tests of auxiliarihood, perfective *have* is an auxiliary, and causative/experiential *have* is a lexical (i.e. nonauxiliary) verb: e.g. perfective *have* can undergo inversion (***Has** she gone to Paris?*) whereas causative/experiential *have* cannot (***Had** the doctor an eye-specialist examine the patient?*). In terms of the assumptions we are making here, this means that finite forms of *have* are positioned in the head I position of IP in their perfective use, but in the head V position of VP in their causative or experiential use.

Evidence in support of this claim comes from facts about *cliticization*. We noted earlier in relation to our discussion of (20) and (21) above that *have* can cliticize onto an immediately preceding word ending in a stressed vowel or diphthong, provided that no (overt or covert) constituent intervenes between the two. In the light of this, consider contrasts such as the following:

(28) (a)   *They've* seen a ghost   (= perfective *have*)

    (b)   **They've* their car serviced regularly   (= causative *have*)

    (c)   **She'd* three students walk out on her (= experiential *have*)

How can we account for this contrast? If we assume that perfective *have* in (28a) is a finite auxiliary which occupies the head I position of IP, but that causative *have* in (28b) and experiential *had* in (28c) are nonauxiliary verbs occupying the head V position of a VP complement of an unfilled INFL, then prior to cliticization the three clauses will have the respective (simplified) structures indicated by the labelled bracketings in (29) below (where $[_I$ ___ $]$ denotes an INFL position which is unfilled):

(29) (a) $[_{IP}$ They $[_I$ have] $[_{VP}$ $[_V$ seen] a ghost]]

    (b) $[_{IP}$ They $[_I$ ___ $]$ $[_{VP}$ $[_V$ have] their car serviced regularly]]

    (c) $[_{IP}$ She $[_I$ ___ $]$ $[_{VP}$ $[_V$ had] three students walk out on her]]

(In labelled bracketings like (29) which give a partial representation of structure, we omit intermediate projections like I-bar and V-bar in order to simplify exposition: of course, if we wanted to be more precise, we should indicate that e.g. *seen a ghost* is a V-bar in (29a), and *have seen a ghost* is an I-bar.) If *have*-cliticization is subject to an *adjacency* condition (to the effect that cliticization is only possible when *have* immediately follows the expression to which it cliticizes and is blocked by the presence of an intervening constituent), it should be obvious why *have* can cliticize onto *they* in (29a) but not *have/had* onto *they/she* in (29b–c): after all, *have* is immediately adjacent to *they* in (29a), but *have/had* is separated from *they/she* by a null INFL constituent in (29b–c). A crucial premise of this account is the assumption that (in its finite forms) *have* is positioned in the head I of IP in its perfective use, but in the head V of a VP complement of an IP headed by an unfilled I in its causative and experiential uses. Thus, *have* cliticization facts suggest that finite clauses which lack a finite auxiliary are IPs headed by an unfilled I constituent.

A further piece of empirical evidence in support of the IP analysis comes from *tag questions*. As we see from the examples below, sentences containing (a finite form of) perfective *have* are tagged by *have*, whereas sentences containing (a finite form of) causative *have* are tagged by *do*:

(30) (a)   She has gone to Paris, *has/*does* she?

(b)   She has her hair styled by Vidal Sassoon, *does/*has* she?

Given the I-analysis of perfective *have* and the V-analysis of causative *have* and the assumption that all clauses are IP constituents, the main clauses in (30a–b) will have the respective (simplified) structures indicated in (31a–b) below (where __ denotes an unfilled position):

(31) (a) $[_{IP}$ She $[_I$ has] $[_{VP}$ $[_V$ gone] to Paris]]

(b) $[_{IP}$ She $[_I$ __] $[_{VP}$ $[_V$ has] her hair styled by Vidal Sassoon]]

If we assume that the I constituent which appears in the tag must carry the same semantic and grammatical properties as the I constituent in the main clause, the contrast in (30) can be accounted for in a principled fashion. In (31a), the head I position of IP is filled by the perfective auxiliary *has*, and so the tag contains a copy of this auxiliary. In (31b), however, the head I position of IP is unfilled (and hence contains no meaning-bearing constituent), and so can only be tagged by the *dummy* auxiliary *does* (which carries the same present-tense feature as the unfilled I constituent in the main clause). Note, incidentally, that the assumption that auxiliaries in tags carry the same grammatical properties as the I constituent in the main clause provides us with evidence for positing that the unfilled I constituent in a structure such as (31b) carries tense-features (since these are copied in the auxiliary in the tag); the relevant tense-features percolate up from V to I when I is unfilled, so that I in (31b) inherits the present-tense feature carried by *has*.

Thus, the different behaviour of perfective and causative *have* provides us with strong empirical evidence in support of the IP analysis of auxiliariless finite clauses. We can adduce a further piece of evidence in support of the IP analysis from facts relating to the syntax of *floating quantifiers* in sentences such as:

(32)   The students *all* hate syntax

Although the quantifier *all* here is interpreted as quantifying *the students*, it seems clear that it is a separate constituent from *the students*. One reason for thinking this is the fact that a string such as *the students all* cannot serve as a sentence fragment – as we see from the ungrammaticality of speaker B's reply in (33) below:

(33)   SPEAKER A: How many of them hate syntax?
            SPEAKER B: **The students all*

Moreover, *all* can be separated from *the students* by (for example) an intervening adverb such as *definitely*; cf.

(34)   *The students* definitely *all* hate syntax

But if *all* is separate from *the students* (and is floating somewhere internally within the structure of the sentence – hence its designation as a *floating quantifier*), where is *all* positioned? At this point, it is timely to recall our suggestion in §3.6 that floating quantifiers occupy the specifier position within VP in sentences such as *They can **both** speak French*. It would seem natural to extend that suggestion to sentences such as:

(35)   They don't all hate syntax

and maintain that the floating quantifier *all* occupies spec VP (i.e. the specifier position within VP). If we extend the spec-VP analysis of floating quantifiers to sentences such as (32), we might suggest that (32) has a structure along the lines of (36) below:

(36)

The IP analysis in (36) enables us to say that *the students* occupies spec-IP, whereas the floating quantifier *all* occupies spec-VP. We can then say that floating quantifiers and the expressions they quantify have in common the fact that they both occupy *specifier* positions within the clause. (We shall return to consider the syntax of floating quanti-

fiers in more detail in chapter 8.) However, a crucial premise of the analysis in (36) is
that auxiliariless finite clauses are headed by an unfilled INFL constituent.

We can adduce a further piece of evidence in support of the IP analysis from facts
relating to the syntax of **adjuncts**. A traditional distinction is drawn between **arguments** (which are expressions which typically denote the participants in the activity or
event described by a verb) and **adjuncts** (which are expressions providing additional
information about the relevant activity/event, e.g. its location, the time at which it took
place, the manner in which it took place, etc.). Thus, in sentences such as:

(37) (a)   [They] ignored [her] *completely*

    (b)   [They] ignored [her] *on the boat*

    (c)   [They] ignored [her] *during the visit*

the bracketed subject *they* and the bracketed complement *her* are arguments of the verb
ignored, while the italicized expressions are *adjuncts*. (The term *adjunct* describes the
function of the italicized expressions, not their categorial status, since *completely* is an
adverb, and *on the boat* and *during the visit* are prepositional phrases.)

On distributional grounds, we might suggest that there are (at least) two different
kinds of adverbial adjunct; the difference between the two can be illustrated by examples such as the following:

(38) (a)   They **certainly** have [ignored her *completely*]

    (b)   They **certainly** have [*completely* ignored her]

    (c)   *They *completely* have [**certainly** ignored her]

    (d)   *They *completely* have [ignored her **certainly**]

In (38), the adverb *certainly* seems to be associated with the IP headed by *have*, since it
can be positioned between the specifier (= *they*) and head (= *have*) of the relevant IP;
hence, we might say that *certainly* is an **IP-adverb** (i.e. an adverb which is positioned
internally within IP). Conversely, the adverb *completely* seems to be associated with
the bracketed VP headed by *ignored*, and can be positioned at the beginning or end of
the bracketed VP; thus, *completely* seems to function as a **VP-adverb** (i.e. as an adverb
positioned internally within VP). Evidence that *completely* is a constituent of the
bracketed VP in (38) comes from sentences such as the following:

(39)   It seems incredible that they should have ignored her completely, but . . .

    (a)   [*ignored her completely*], they certainly have

    (b)   they certainly have

The fact that the adverb *completely* is fronted when the bracketed VP is fronted in
(39a) and is ellipsed (i.e. omitted) when the VP is ellipsed in (39b) suggests that *completely* is a constituent of the bracketed VP. The assumption that *certainly* is an IP

adverb which must be positioned internally within IP and that *completely* is a VP adverb which must be positioned internally within VP accounts for the ungrammaticality of sentences such as (38c–d).

An obvious question to ask at this point is what position adverbial adjuncts occupy within the expressions containing them. In this connection, consider the following:

(40)   They **certainly** have both *completely* ignored her

The IP-adverb *certainly* in (40) is positioned between the head I constituent *have* of IP and its specifier *they*; likewise, the VP-adverb *completely* is positioned between the head V *ignored* of VP and its specifier *both*. If we assume that all projections are binary-branching and that all intermediate projections are single-bar constituents, (40) will have the structure (41) below:

(41)

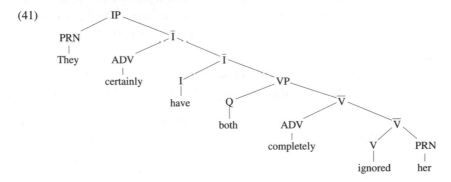

The VP-adverb *completely* in (41) attaches to the V-bar *ignored her* and expands it into the extended V-bar *completely ignored her*; we might therefore say that *completely* is a **V-bar adjunct**. Similarly, the IP-adverb *certainly* in (41) expands the I-bar *have both completely ignored her* into the extended I-bar *certainly have both completely ignored her*, and hence is an **I-bar adjunct**. Example (41) illustrates two properties of the relevant kind of adverbial adjuncts: firstly, they merge with intermediate projections (like V-bar and I-bar); and secondly, they serve to expand a category of a given type into an extended category of the same type (e.g. *completely* expands V-bar into an extended V-bar, and *certainly* expands I-bar into an extended I-bar).

In the light of our discussion of adverbial adjuncts, consider now how we account for examples such as the following:

(42)   They certainly ignored her

Given that *certainly* is an I-bar adjunct, it follows that (42) must be an IP; and since the relevant IP contains no overt I constituent, it must contain a covert I. In other words, (42) must have the structure (43) below:

(43)

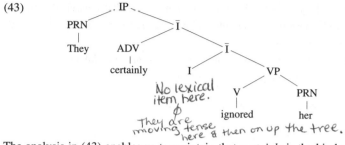

The analysis in (43) enables us to maintain that *certainly* is the kind of adverb which merges with an I-bar to form an extended I-bar. But a crucial premise of the analysis in (43) is the assumption that auxiliariless finite clauses are IPs headed by an unfilled I constituent.

We can formulate a further empirical argument in support of the IP analysis in relation to facts about sentence fragments. In this connection, consider the two alternative replies which might be given by speaker B in the dialogue in (44) below:

(44)   SPEAKER A: What does Egbert Ego do to attract attention?
         SPEAKER B: (a) *He blows his nose*
                     (b) *Blows his nose*

Under the IP analysis which we are arguing for here, speaker B's reply in (44a) will have the structure (45) below:

(45)

Recall that in §3.8, we noted that maximal projections can serve as sentence fragments: since the VP *blows his nose* is the maximal projection of the V *blows* in (45), and the IP *He blows his nose* is the maximal projection of the empty INFL constituent, the IP analysis in (45) correctly predicts that both can be used as sentence fragments – precisely as we find in (44).

4.5   Bare infinitives

The more general conclusion to be drawn from our discussion in the previous section is that there is empirical evidence that auxiliariless finite clauses are IP constituents headed by an unfilled INFL. Given that clauses containing a finite auxiliary are also IPs, the natural conclusion to draw is that all finite clauses are IPs. Since *to* infinitive clauses are also IPs, can we generalize still further and say that all finite and infinitival clauses are IPs? Well, this depends on how we analyse a class of *bare* (i.e. *to*-less) infinitive complement clauses such as those bracketed below:

(46) (a) I have never known [*Tom criticize him*]

(b) They heard [*the prime minister berate his wet colleagues*]

(c) You mustn't let [*the pressure get to you*]

(d) The students watched [*the acid turn the litmus paper red*]

(e) A reporter saw [*Senator Sleaze leave Benny's Bunny Bar*]

If (as we are suggesting) all finite and infinitival clauses are indeed IPs, bare infinitive clauses like those in (46) will be IPs headed by an abstract INFL constituent. More specifically, we might suppose that the relevant clauses are IPs headed by a null counterpart of infinitival *to* (below denoted as **ø**), so that (e.g.) the bracketed infinitive in (46a) would have the structure (47) below:

(47)

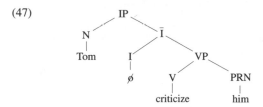

We have assumed in (47) that rather than being unfilled, INFL is filled by a null variant of infinitival *to*. One reason for thinking this is that the head V in a bare infinitive complement is always in the *infinitive* form – i.e. the same form as is required after infinitival *to*: we can account for this if we assume that the null infinitive particle ø has the same complement-selection properties as infinitival *to*, and thus selects a complement headed by a verb like *criticize* in the infinitive form. We could then say that verbs like *know/hear/let/watch/see* as used in (46) above select an IP complement headed by the null infinitive particle ø, whereas verbs like *expect, judge, report, consider, want*, etc. select an IP complement headed by *to*, as in (48) below:

(48) (a) I expect [him *to* win]

(b) I judged [him *to* be lying]

(c) They reported [him *to* be missing]

(d) I consider [her *to* have behaved badly]

(e) I want [you *to* help me]

It would then follow that all infinitive clauses contain an IP headed by *to* or by its covert counterpart ø.

145

What lends plausibility to the suggestion that bare infinitive complements are headed by a null counterpart of *to* is the fact that many bare infinitive complements have *to* infinitive counterparts – cf.

(49) (a)   I've never known [Tom criticize him]

(b)   I've never known [Tom *to* criticize him]

(50) (a)   They heard [the prime minister berate his wet colleagues]

(b)   The prime minister was heard [*to* berate his wet colleagues]

(51) (a)   A reporter saw [Senator Sleaze leave Benny's Bunny Bar]

(b)   Senator Sleaze was seen [*to* leave Benny's Bunny Bar]

Moreover, many bare infinitive complements in present-day English have *to* infinitive counterparts in Early Modern English – as illustrated by the following Shakespearean examples:

(52) (a)   I saw [her coral lips *to* move] (Lucentio, *Taming of the Shrew*, I.i)

(b)   My lord your son made [me *to* think of this] (Helena, *All's Well That Ends Well*, I.iii)

(c)   What would you have [me *to* do]? (Lafeu, *All's Well That Ends Well*, V.ii)

(d)   I had rather hear [you *to* solicit that] (Olivia, *All's Well That Ends Well*, III.i)

The fact that bare infinitives sometimes have *to* infinitive counterparts (in particular types of construction) makes it all the more plausible to suppose that they are headed by a covert counterpart of *to*, and hence are IPs.

Further evidence in support of the IP analysis comes from cliticization facts in relation to sentences such as the following (% = acceptable in some varieties, e.g. mine):

(53) (a)   %I wouldn't let [*you have* done it]

(b)   *I wouldn't let [*you've* done it]

If we suppose that the bracketed infinitive complement in (53b) is an IP headed by the null infinitive particle ø, as in (54) below:

(54)   I wouldn't let [$_{IP}$ you [$_I$ ø] [$_{VP}$ [$_V$ have] done it]]

we can account for the fact that *have* cannot cliticize onto *you* by positing that the presence of the null infinitive particle ø between *you* and *have* blocks cliticization.

Another argument leading to the same conclusion comes from structures like:

(55) (a)   Let [there be light]

(b)   I've never known [there be so many complaints about syntax]

It has been argued by Safir (1993) that the pronoun *there* (in this use as a contentless *dummy* pronoun) is restricted to occurring in the specifier position within IP. Such a restriction would account for contrasts such as:

(56) (a)   I don't consider [there to be any good reason why I should do it]

  (b)   *I don't consider [there any good reason why I should do it]

since the first bracketed complement is an IP headed by infinitival *to*, and the second is a type of verbless clause sometimes referred to as a **small clause** which appears not to be headed by INFL (since it contains no auxiliary or infinitival *to*, and no VP). If dummy *there* can only occur as the specifier of an IP, it follows that the bracketed complements in (55) must be IPs (headed by the null infinitive particle ø).

Our discussion here leads us to the wider conclusion that both *to* infinitive clauses and bare infinitive clauses are IP (infinitive phrase) constituents headed by an infinitival INFL; INFL is filled by *to* in structures like (48), but is filled by the null infinitive particle ø in bare infinitive complements like those bracketed in (46). Given that we have also argued that all finite clauses contain an IP projection (headed by an INFL which is either filled or unfilled), the overall conclusion which we reach is that all finite and infinitival clauses contain an IP, and that INFL is filled in clauses containing a finite auxiliary or infinitival *to*/ø, but unfilled elsewhere. One obvious advantage of this analysis is that it enables us to attain a uniform characterization of the syntax of (finite and infinitival) clauses as structures which contain an IP with a VP complement.

4.6 Null complementizers

Thus far, we have argued that all clauses contain an overt or covert INFL constituent which projects into IP (with the subject of the clause positioned in spec-IP). However, given that clauses can be introduced by complementizers such as *if*, *that* or *for*, a natural question to ask is whether all apparently complementizerless clauses are CPs headed by a null complementizer. In this connection, consider the following:

(57) (a)   Phyllis Stein thinks [*that* money can buy happiness]

  (b)   Phyllis Stein thinks [money can buy happiness]

(58) (a)   We didn't intend [*for* that to happen]

  (b)   We didn't intend [that to happen]

The question we are asking is whether all four bracketed complement clauses in (57–8) are CPs, or whether the (a) sentences containing an overt complementizer are CPs, and the complementizerless (b) sentences are IPs. In more concrete terms, this amounts to asking (for example) whether the complement clause in (57b) is a CP with the structure (59a) below headed by a null declarative complementizer ∅, or simply an IP with the structure (59b) below:

147

(59)(a)

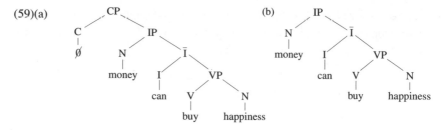

What kind of theoretical or empirical considerations might lead us to favour one analysis over the other?

At first sight, it might seem as if semantic considerations favour the *null complementizer* analysis (59a). After all, the bracketed *that*-clause in (57a) is *declarative* in illocutionary force (i.e. is used to make a statement), and we might argue that its declarative force is attributable to the presence of the declarative complementizer *that*. More generally, we might suppose that complementizers serve the function of marking the illocutionary force of clauses. We could go on from there to argue that because the bracketed complement clause in (57b) is also interpreted as declarative in force, the relevant clause must be a CP headed by a null (declarative) complementizer ∅. This would then enable us to arrive at a structurally uniform characterization of all clauses as CPs in which the illocutionary force of the clause is indicated by the choice of (overt or covert) complementizer heading CP: for obvious reasons, we might refer to the claim that all clauses are CPs as the **structural uniformity hypothesis**.

Unfortunately, however, this type of illocutionary force argument carries little conviction. After all, we might equally account for the declarative force of the bracketed complement clause in (57b) by supposing that clauses which do not contain an interrogative head or specifier are interpreted as declarative *by default*: there would then be no reason not to analyse the bracketed complement clause in (57b) as a simple IP with the structure (59b), interpreted as declarative by default (e.g. by virtue of not containing an interrogative constituent). Some evidence in favour of the *default* analysis comes from nonstandard structures such as:

(60)   I don't know [which street that he lives in]

found in many varieties of English (e.g. Belfast English). Since the bracketed CP in (60) is interrogative in force, the complementizer *that* clearly cannot be declarative in force and cannot determine the illocutionary force of the bracketed CP (which is in fact determined by the interrogative expression *which street?*), but rather must simply serve to mark the CP containing it as finite. So, the fact that the bracketed CP in (57a) is declarative in force might not be attributable to the presence of *that* but rather to the absence of an interrogative constituent preceding *that*.

Consequently, the *illocutionary force* argument in favour of the CP analysis in (59a) is unpersuasive. By contrast, there are a number of alternative arguments which seem to favour the IP analysis (57b). One such can be formulated in relation to **economy** considerations. Recall from our discussion in §1.3 that one criterion of adequacy for linguistic theory is that we *minimize* the theoretical and descriptive apparatus we use to describe the syntax of phrases and sentences. In this connection, it is interesting to note the suggestion made by Chomsky that UG incorporates what he calls *a least effort condition* to the following effect:

(61)   ECONOMY PRINCIPLE

Derivations and representations . . . are required to be minimal . . . with no superfluous steps in derivations and no superfluous symbols in representations. (Chomsky 1989, p. 69)

(where *minimal* means 'as economical/short as possible'). Peggy Speas (1995) has proposed a related principle to the effect that UG does not license *contentless projections* (i.e. projections whose head and specifier have no independent content of their own). Since CP in structures such as (59a) has no specifier and contains a head with no phonetic, semantic or grammatical properties, it follows that CP is a *contentless projection*, and so violates the **no-contentless-projections constraint**. So, *economy* considerations favour analysing the (a) sentences in (57–8) as CPs, and the (b) sentences as IPs.

There seems to be some supporting empirical evidence in favour of the *economy* (IP) analysis of clauses such as those in (57–8b). One such piece of evidence comes from coordination facts. Bošković (1994) argues that complementizerless clauses such as those italicized in (62) below cannot (idiomatically) be coordinated with clauses containing an overt complementizer such as *that*, cf.

(62) (a)   *John said [*Peter left*] and [**that Bill kissed Mary**]
     (b)   *John reckoned [*Peter left*] and [**that Bill kissed Mary**]

If this is so (and the grammaticality judgments are very subtle), why should it be? If we suppose that the italicized *that*-less complement clauses are IPs but that the bold-printed *that*-clauses are CPs, we can attribute the ungrammaticality of sentences like (62) to the fact that we have coordinated an IP with a CP, thereby violating the condition that we can only (idiomatically) conjoin constituents belonging to the same category. By contrast, if we claim that italicized complementizerless clauses in (62) are CPs, we would have no obvious account of why they can't be coordinated with the bold-printed CPs.

A further piece of evidence leading to the same conclusion comes from facts relating to *preposing*. As we see from the examples below, we can prepose the subject of a complementizerless clause (to emphasize it in some way by moving it into a more prominent position at the front of the sentence), but not the subject of a clause introduced by a complementizer like *that*:

149

(63) (a)   She thinks [*money* can buy happiness]

    (b)   *Money* she thinks [can buy happiness]

(64) (a)   She thinks [that *money* can buy happiness]

    (b)   **Money* she thinks [that can buy happiness]

If we adopt the *economy* analysis and assume that the bracketed clauses in (63) are IPs but those in (64) are CPs, we can provide a (somewhat simplified: cf. Culicover 1992) account of the facts if we posit a *constraint* (i.e. structural restriction) to the effect that the subject cannot be extracted out of a CP. Example (64b) will then be ungrammatical because the subject *money* has been extracted out of the CP *that money can buy happiness*; but (63b) will correctly be predicted to be grammatical because the subject *money* has been extracted out of the IP *money can buy happiness*, not out of a CP. However, if we (wrongly) suppose that the bracketed clause in (63b) is a CP, we wrongly predict that (63b) is ungrammatical (because under the CP analysis, (63b) would involve extracting a subject out of a CP). The provisional conclusion which our discussion leads us to is that complementizerless clauses are IPs – not CPs headed by a covert complementizer. Thus, all clauses are IPs, but only some clauses (viz. those containing a complementizer like *that/if/for*) project further into CP.

A further argument leading us to the same conclusion comes from facts relating to the *cliticization* of *is* (in the guise of its variant *'s*) onto the preceding verb (*think*) in structures such as:

(65) (a)   Who do you think is helping him?

    (b)   Who do you *think's* helping him?

Under the IP analysis of complementizerless clauses, (65a) would have the structure (66a) below, whereas under the CP analysis it would have the structure (66b):

(66) (a)   Who do you think [$_{IP}$ [$_I$ is] helping him]?

    (b)   Who do you think [$_{CP}$ [$_C$ $\emptyset$] [$_{IP}$ [$_I$ is] helping him]]?

However, given that we earlier saw in relation to sentences such as (21), (28b–c) and (53b) above that an intervening null head blocks cliticization, we should expect the intervening null complementizer $\emptyset$ in (66b) to block cliticization of *is* onto *think*. The fact that cliticization is indeed possible in (65b) suggests that the CP analysis in (66b) can't be right, and that the more economical IP analysis in (66a) is more plausible.

We can provide a parallel cliticization argument against the claim made in earlier work (e.g. Radford 1988) that infinitive complements with null PRO subjects are CPs headed by a null complementizer. If this were so, it would be difficult to account for the fact that *to* can cliticize onto *want* (forming *wanta/wanna*) in structures such as:

(67) (a)   I want to go home

    (b)   I wanna go home

since we would expect that the presence of a complementizer between *want* and *to* would prevent *to* from cliticizing onto *want*. After all, cliticization of *to* onto *want* is not possible in varieties of English (like Belfast or Ozark English) which allow *for to* infinitives: cf.

(68)   (a)   %I *want* for *to* go home (% = OK in the relevant varieties)

     (b)   *I *wanna* for go home

and it seems reasonable to suppose that this is because *to*-cliticization is blocked by the presence of an intervening complementizer (in this case, *for*). But if this is so, the fact that cliticization is possible in sentences like (67b) *I wanna go home* would argue that there cannot be a complementizer intervening between *want* and *to* in sentences like (67) – hence that the infinitive complement *to go home* has the status of an IP rather than a CP.

So, the overall conclusion which our discussion of examples such as (57–68) leads us to is that all clauses are IPs, but that only clauses which contain an overt complementizer (like *that/if/for*) project further into CP. For additional evidence pointing to this conclusion, see Bošković 1995, chapter 2.

4.7   Null determiners

Having arrived at a unitary characterization of clauses as IPs, we now turn our attention to the syntax of *nominal* structures. (We shall use the term *nominal* here to describe any structure containing a noun or pronoun.) Let's begin by considering the structure of the italicized nominal arguments below:

(69)   *We* don't expect *students* to enjoy *the course*

Given the assumptions we have made so far, (69) will have the structure (70) below:

(70)

However, (70) presupposes a curiously asymmetric analysis of the status of nominals (i.e. of expressions containing nouns or pronouns). Some (like *we*) have the status of PRN;

others (like *students*) have the status of N; and others (like *the course*) are DPs. Given our earlier arguments that clauses have a uniform status as IP constituents, it would seem natural to ask whether we can attain a uniform characterization of the syntax of nominals. But how? What we shall suggest here (following ideas developed by Abney 1987 and Longobardi 1994) is that all nominals are projections of a head determiner constituent.

What this implies in the case of *bare* nominals (i.e. noun expressions used without any modifying determiner) is that such nominals are DPs headed by a null determiner (below symbolized as ∅). This means (for example) that the bare noun *students* in (69) is not simply an N, but rather a DP like (71) below:

(71)

The assumption that bare nominals contain a null determiner is a traditional one – for example, Chomsky (1965, p. 108) suggests that the noun *sincerity* in a sentence such as *Sincerity may frighten the boy* is premodified by a null determiner. If this is so, then empty categories play just as central a role in the syntax of nominals as they do in the syntax of clauses: in the same way as auxiliariless finite clauses are IPs headed by an empty INFL, so too bare nominals are DPs headed by an empty determiner.

However, an important question to ask about the *empty determiner* analysis of bare nominals is whether it is consistent with a *minimalist* approach to syntax which posits an **economy principle** like (61) which prohibits superfluous projections. More specifically, we might ask whether a DP analysis of bare nominals is consistent with the **no-contentless-projections constraint** proposed by Peggy Speas (1995). The answer is that it is, by virtue of the fact that the null determiner ∅ in structures like (70) – although lacking phonetic content – has clear semantic and grammatical properties of its own, and thus has intrinsic content.

Let's look first at the semantic properties of the null determiner ∅. In this connection, consider the interpretation of the italicized bare nominals in sentences such as:

(72) (a)   *Eggs* are fattening
     (b)   *Bacon* is fattening
(73) (a)   I had *eggs* for breakfast
     (b)   I had *bacon* for breakfast

The nouns *eggs/bacon* in (72) have a *generic* interpretation, and hence are interpreted as meaning 'eggs/bacon in general'. In (73) they have an *existential* (= *partitive*) interpretation, roughly paraphraseable as '*some* eggs/bacon'. If we say that bare nominals are DPs headed by a null generic/existential determiner ∅, we can say that the semantic properties of ∅ determine that bare nominals will be interpreted as generically or existentially quantified.

152

Moreover, there is evidence to suggest that the null determiner ∅ carries *person* properties – and in particular, is a third person determiner. In this respect, consider sentences such as:

(74) (a) We syntacticians take **ourselves/*yourselves/*themselves** too seriously, don't *we/*you/*they*?

　　 (b) You syntacticians take **yourselves/*ourselves/*themselves** too seriously, don't *you/*we/*they*?

　　 (c) Syntacticians take **themselves/*ourselves/*yourselves** too seriously, don't *they/*we/*you*?

The examples in (74a) show that a first person expression such as *we syntacticians* can only bind a first person reflexive like *ourselves*, and can only be tagged by a first person pronoun like *we*. The examples in (74b) show that a second person expression like *you syntacticians* can only bind a second person reflexive like *yourselves*, and can only be tagged by a second person pronoun like *you*. The examples in (74c) show that a bare nominal like *syntacticians* can only bind a third person reflexive like *themselves* and can only be tagged by a third person pronoun like *they*. One way of accounting for the relevant facts is to suppose that the nominals *we syntacticians/you syntacticians/ syntacticians* in (74) are DPs with the structure (75) below:

(75)

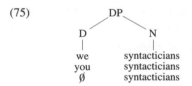

and that the person properties of the DP are determined by those of its head determiner. If we suppose that *we* is a first person determiner, *you* is a second person determiner and ∅ is a third person determiner, the facts in (74) above are precisely as the analysis in (75) would lead us to expect.

In addition to having quantificational properties and person properties, the null determiner ∅ also has specific *complement-selection* properties – as can be illustrated by the following set of examples:

(76) (a) I write *poems*

　　 (b) I write *poetry*

　　 (c) *I write *poem*

If we suppose that each of the italicized bare nouns in (76) is the complement of the null determiner ∅, the restrictions in (76) would seem to suggest that ∅ can select as its complement an expression headed by a plural count noun like *poems*, or a singular mass noun like *poetry* – but not by a singular count noun like *poem*. The complement-selection properties of the null determiner ∅ would seem to be parallel to those of the overt determiner *enough*: cf.

(77) (a)   I've read *enough poetry*

(b)   I've read *enough poems*

(c)   *I've read *enough poem*

The fact that the null generic/existential determiner ∅ has much the same quantificational, person and complement-selection properties as a typical overt determiner such as *enough* strengthens the case for positing the existence of a null determiner ∅, and for analysing bare nominals as DPs headed by a null determiner.

4.8   Pronouns

The conclusion we have arrived at so far is that both nominals containing an overt determiner and bare nominals are DPs headed by a determiner which is overt in the former case and covert in the latter. This leads us towards the conclusion that all nominal arguments are projections of a head D constituent (a conclusion argued for at length by Longobardi 1994). But can we extend this analysis to pronouns – and if so, how?

The answer is that there is some evidence (from studies by Postal 1966, Abney 1987, Longobardi 1994 and Uriagereka 1995) to suggest that pronouns have the categorial status of determiners. We have already implicitly suggested in (75) that in structures such as *we/you syntacticians*, the so-called pronouns *we* and *you* function as determiners which take the noun *syntacticians* as their complement. It therefore seems natural to suppose that simple pronouns like *we* and *you* could be analysed as determiners used without any noun complement. If this is so, sentences such as:

(78) (a)   We psychologists don't trust you linguists

(b)   We don't trust you

would have the respective structures (79a–b) below:

(79) (a)

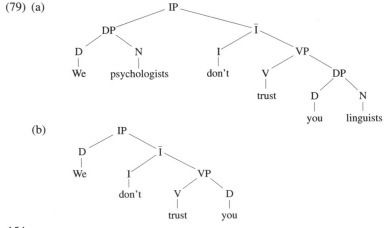

(b)

The analysis in (79) would enable us to provide a unitary account of the syntax of nominals, and to suppose that they are all projections of a head determiner constituent. In structures such as (79a), the determiner *we* is used *prenominally* (with a following noun as its complement), whereas in structures such as (79b) it is used *pronominally* (i.e. on its own, without any following noun complement). The determiner analysis of pronouns would also provide us with a straightforward answer to the question of why (as noted in §2.4) most determiners have pronoun counterparts.

The determiner analysis of pronouns might also help us understand why two-year-old children sometimes produce structures such as the following (reported by McNeill 1970, p. 28):

(80)   Get it ladder!

One answer might be that children analyse *it* as a determiner, and wrongly assume that (like most determiners) it can be used not only pronominally, but also prenominally; this would mean that *it ladder* in (80) is a DP with the structure (81) below:

(81)   DP
              ╱   ╲
          D   N
          | |
          it   ladder

The analysis in (81) assumes that the child uses the definite pronoun *it* in (80) in much the same way as an adult would use the definite prenominal determiner *the*.

However, the analysis in (81) raises the interesting question of why *it* can be used pronominally but not prenominally in adult English, and conversely why *the* can be used prenominally but not pronominally – in other words, how we account for contrasts such as (82) below:

(82) (a)   I walked under *the ladder*
     (b)   *I walked under *it ladder*
     (c)   I walked under *it*
     (d)   *I walked under *the*

The answer lies in the specific *complement-selection* properties of individual words. More specifically, let us say that it is a selectional property of most determiners that they can be used with or without a following noun complement: however, a determiner like *the* has the selectional property that it requires a complement headed by a noun; and conversely, a determiner like *it* has the selectional property that it doesn't allow a complement of any kind.

The assumption that pronouns are determiners (as noted above) leads us towards our goal of attaining a unitary characterization of the syntax of nominal arguments as projections of a head determiner constituent: nominals modified by an overt determiner are DPs, bare nominals are DPs headed by a null determiner, and pronouns are determiners used without a complement. We can then conclude that all nominal and pronominal arguments are projections of an (overt or covert) D constituent, and so arrive at a uniform characterization of nominals as **D-projections**. Given this assumption, our earlier sentence (69) above will no longer have the asymmetric structure (70) above, but rather the more uniform structure (83) below:

(83)

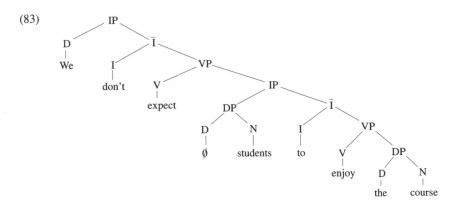

in which the three nominal arguments *we*, *students* and *the course* are all analysed as D-projections.

The conclusion to be drawn from our discussion here is that all nominal and pronominal expressions are D-projections. However, there are reasons for thinking that this is only true of nominal expressions used as **arguments** (i.e. as subjects or complements), not of **nonargument nominals** (e.g. nominals which have a vocative, predicative or exclamative use). Examples such as those in (84) below would suggest that nonargument nominals can be N-projections lacking a determiner:

(84) (a)   Do all syntacticians suffer from asteriskitis, *doctor*?

    (b)   Dick Head is *head of department*

    (c)   *Poor fool!* He thought he'd passed the syntax exam

The italicized nominal expression serves a *vocative* function (i.e. is used to address someone) in (84a), a *predicative* function in (84b) (in that the property of being head of department is predicated of the unfortunate Dick Head) and an *exclamative* function in (84c). Each of the italicized nominals in (84) is headed by a singular count noun (*doctor/head/fool*): in spite of the fact that such nouns require an overt determiner when used as arguments, here they function as nonarguments and are used without any determiner. This suggests (as noted by Longobardi 1994) that nonargument nominals can be N-projections, whereas argument nominals are always D-projections.

The analysis we have presented here points to significant potential parallels between the internal structure of clauses and that of nominal arguments. Just as clauses are projections of an overt or covert I constituent, so too nominal arguments are projections of an overt or covert D constituent. Using the terminology suggested by Jane Grimshaw (1991), we can say that V has an **extended projection** into IP in the same way as N has an extended projection into DP (so that IP is an extended projection of V, and DP is an extended projection of N). The parallels between IP and DP may go even further – as we can illustrate in terms of the following examples:

(85) (a)   We can arrange [for the accountants to audit the books]

    (b)   We can arrange [for an audit of the books]

In (85a), the verb *audit* has a direct projection into the VP *audit the books*, an extended projection into the IP *the accountants to audit the books*, and might be argued to have a further extended projection into the CP (complementizer phrase) *for the accountants to audit the books*. In (85b) the noun *audit* has a direct projection into the NP *audit of the books*, an extended projection into the DP *an audit of the books*, and a further extended projection into the PP (prepositional phrase) *for an audit of the books*. Thus, CP and PP might be analysed as (secondary) extended projections of V and N respectively.

4.9   Attributive adjectives

One topic which we have not touched on so far is the syntax of prenominal attributive adjectives (i.e. adjectives which attribute some property to the noun expression which follows them). Although adjectives do not overtly inflect for (singular/plural) number in English, some adjectives (like *numerous* and *various*) carry an intrinsic plural number feature by virtue of their meaning – as we see from the fact that *various* can only modify the plural noun *attempts* in (86) below, not the singular noun *attempt*:

(86)   [The *various* government **attempts/*attempt** to gag the press] have/*has been unsuccessful

If we suppose that agreement canonically involves a relation between a functional head and its specifier (e.g. subject–verb agreement in a sentence like *He has gone* involves a relation between the INFL constituent *has* and its specifier *he*), one way in which we might handle adjective–noun agreement in structures such as (86) is to suppose (following Cinque 1994) that the adjective *various* serves as the specifier of a higher functional head (let's call it **F**) which occupies a position between D and N. Given this assumption, the bracketed DP in (86) would have a structure along the lines of (87) below (where the noun *government* is the controller of PRO):

Ronnie does not like PP use it. doesn't use it. She hasn't read or heard of it before.

(87)

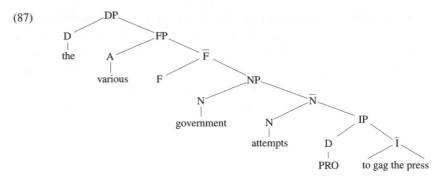

We could then suppose (cf. our earlier discussion of (25) above) that the plural number feature of the noun *attempts* percolates up from N to F, and there is checked against the number feature of the inherently plural adjective *various*.

Further evidence that the grammatical properties of nouns percolate from N to F comes from phrases such as that bracketed in (88) below:

(88)   She bought [a new *chair/*chairs/*furniture*]

As this example illustrates, the determiner *a* requires a complement headed by a singular count noun. Given Cinque's analysis of attributive adjectives as specifiers of a functional head *F*, the bracketed nominal expression in (88) will be a determiner phrase with the structure (89) below:

(89)

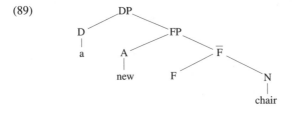

However, the requirement for the determiner *a* to have a complement headed by a singular count noun would appear not to be met in (89), because the complement of *a* is headed by F (FP is the complement of D, and FP is headed by F), not by N. However, we can overcome this problem if we suppose that the grammatical properties of the N *chair* (more specifically, its properties as a singular count noun) percolate up from N to F: the requirement for *a* to have a complement headed by a singular count noun would then be met (by virtue of the fact that FP is the complement of *a*, FP is headed by F, and F inherits the grammatical properties of the singular count noun *chair*).

If Cinque's analysis is along the right lines, it follows that attributive adjectives are contained within a functional projection (here symbolized as **FP**) which has an empty functional head, so providing us with evidence of the existence of a further type of empty category. In Grimshaw's terminology, FP is a further *extended projection* of N. We shall have little more to say about the syntax of attributive adjectives here, however.

4.10   Summary

In this chapter, we have seen that empty categories (i.e. categories which have no overt phonetic form) play a central role in syntactic theory. In §4.2 we argued that apparently subjectless *to*-infinitive clauses have an empty **PRO** subject which is typically controlled by an antecedent in a higher clause. In §4.3 we argued that elliptical clauses like that bracketed in *He could have left and* [*she have stayed*] are IPs headed by a null (ellipsed) finite auxiliary. In §4.4 we argued that clauses like *He hates syntax* containing a finite nonauxiliary verb are IPs headed by a null INFL constituent, and that the tense/agreement properties of the verb *hates* percolate from V to INFL. In §4.5 we claimed that bare infinitive clauses are also IPs, headed by a null counterpart of infinitival *to*. In §4.6 we considered the possibility of adopting a symmetrical analysis of clause structure under which all clauses would be analysed as CPs, with complementizerless clauses (i.e. clauses which do not contain an overt complementizer) being analysed as CPs headed by a null complementizer whose properties determine the illocutionary force of the clause. However, we rejected the CP analysis of complementizerless clauses in favour of a simpler IP analysis, supporting the IP analysis on the basis of considerations relating to economy, coordination, subject extraction and cliticization. In §4.7 we turned to look at the syntax of nominal arguments, suggesting that bare nominals should be analysed as DPs headed by a null determiner $\emptyset$ which has a generic or existential interpretation, and which has the complement-selection property that it can only be used to quantify a singular mass noun or plural count noun. In §4.8 we went on to argue that pronouns (e.g. personal pronouns like *we/you/they* etc.) are simply determiners used without a complement. We concluded from this that all nominal arguments are D-projections: e.g. in a sentence such as *We don't expect students to enjoy the course, we* is a pronominal (i.e. complementless) determiner, *students* is a projection of the null determiner $\emptyset$, and *the course* is a projection of the overt determiner *the*. We suggested that there are significant parallels between the syntax of clauses and that of nominal arguments, in that just as verbs have an extended projection into IP (and in some structures may have a further extended projection into CP) so too nouns have an extended projection into DP (and in some structures may have a further extended projection into PP). In §4.9 we briefly discussed the syntax of attributive adjectives, suggesting that these serve as the specifiers of an empty functional category **F** which is positioned between D and N.

Workbook section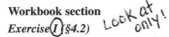
Exercise(I)(§4.2)

In the text, we made no mention of **imperative clauses** (i.e. clauses used to issue a command). In English, imperatives can have overt (usually second person) subjects such as those italicized in (1) below:

    1a   *You* be quict, John!

    b   Don't *you* dare answer me back!

But more often, they are apparently subjectless, as in 2 below:

    2a   Do be careful!

    b   Mind the step!

Subjectless imperative clauses have traditionally been assumed to have an understood second person subject which might be regarded as a null counterpart of the overt *you* subject that appears in imperatives such as 1. What reasons are there for supposing that seemingly subjectless imperatives have an understood second person null subject, and what differences can you see between null imperative subjects and PRO?

> *Model answer*
>
> Empirical evidence in support of positing a null second person subject in imperatives comes from tag sentences such as the following:

(i) (a)   Shut the window, could *you*!

     (b)   Don't say anything, will *you*!

Tags typically contain a pronominal copy of the subject of the tagged clause (cf. ***Harry likes pasta, doesn't he***?). The fact that imperative sentences always carry a *you* tag suggests that imperatives have an understood null second person (singular or plural) subject. Further support for positing a null second person subject in imperatives comes from evidence of essentially the same type as that which we adduced in support of positing a PRO subject in apparently subjectless infinitives in §4.2. (*You* take over at this point, and devise relevant examples and supporting arguments.)

Exercise II (§§4.3–4.4)

In the stylized construction illustrated by the examples in (1) below:

    1a   The prosecutor demanded [that he *be* banned from driving]

    b   The major ordered [that he *have* completed the operation by midnight]

    c   The Dean insisted [that he *tell* the truth]

the italicized items are traditionally said to be finite verbs in their **subjunctive** form. If we assume that finite auxiliaries occupy the head I position of IP, then this might suggest that the bracketed complement clause in 1a has the structure 2 below:

2

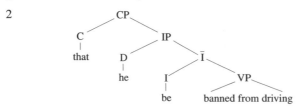

However, an alternative possibility which has been suggested in the relevant literature is that the IP constituent in subjunctive clauses is headed by a null modal (e.g. a null counterpart of *should*). If this were so, the bracketed complement clause in 1a would have the alternative structure 3 below:

3

```
                    CP
              C         IP
              |
            that    D        Ī
                    |
                    he   I        PASSP
                         |
                         ∅   PASS       VP
                              |
                              be    banned from driving
```

(where ∅ denotes a null modal, PASS denotes a passive auxiliary and PASSP denotes a passive phrase – i.e. a phrase headed by a passive auxiliary). Discuss whether either or both of the analyses could provide a principled account of relevant aspects of the morphosyntax of subjunctive clauses.

Helpful hints

Some points which you might like to look at include how to account for the fact that subjunctive clauses require *nominative* subjects like *he*, and for the fact that so-called subjunctive verb forms are homophonous with the corresponding infinitive forms. You might also try and account for why *have* cannot cliticize onto *he* in 1b – as we see from the ungrammaticality of **The major ordered that he've completed the operation by midnight*. Also look at how subjunctive clauses are negated: ordinary finite clauses are negated by positioning *not* after the finite auxiliary (cf. *He was not arrested*), whereas subjunctive clauses seem to require preauxiliary negation (cf. *The defence counsel asked that he not be banned from driving*).

Exercise III (§4.4)

Discuss the syntax of the adverbs in the following sentences:

1a They will all severely censure him
  b *They will severely all censure him
  c *They severely will all censure him
2a The students all fully appreciate the situation
  b *The students fully all appreciate the situation
3a The students all really enjoyed the course
  b The students really all enjoyed the course
4a They probably all desperately need help
  b *They desperately all probably need help

161

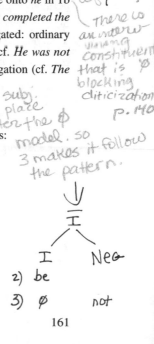

  5a You mustn't let them ever both publicly humiliatc you
  b   *You mustn't let them publicly both ever humiliate you

Which adverbs are VP-adverbs, which are IP-adverbs – and which can serve both functions? Draw tree diagrams for each of the sentences in 1–5 to illustrate your answer, and give arguments in support of your analysis.

Model answer for 1a

  The data in 1 suggest that *severely* is a VP-adverb which merges with a V-bar constituent to form an extended V-bar, as in (i) below:

(i)

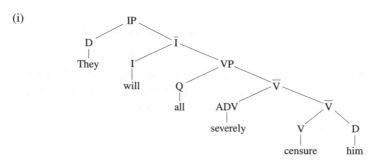

The analysis in (i) assumes that *severely* is a V-bar adjunct, and hence merges with the V-bar *censure him* to form the extended V-bar *severely censure him*, which then merges with the floating quantifier *all* (which we assume to occupy spec-VP, i.e. the specifier position within VP) to form the maximal projection (VP) *all severely censure him*. Some evidence that this string is indeed a maximal projection comes from the fact that it can serve as a sentence fragment, e.g. in a discourse such as:

(ii)   SPEAKER A: What will they do?
         SPEAKER B: All severely censure him

Exercise IV (§4.7)

  Discuss the syntax of the italicized nominal expressions in the following Jamaican Creole sentences (from Bailey 1966), commenting on differences with Modern Standard English.

1   *Manggo* swiit
         mango   sweet
         'Mangoes are sweet'
2   *Di manggo* swiit
         the mango   sweet
         'The mango is sweet'

3   *Di manggo-dem* swiit
the mango-them sweet
'The mangoes are sweet'

4   Jan   mash *di eg-dem*
John smash the egg+them
'John broke the eggs'

5   *Jien-dem* naa   kom
Jane+them no+are come
'Jane and her friends aren't coming'

6   *Wan daag* bait mi
one dog bite me
'A dog bit me'

7   Dat a   *plom*
that are plum
'That is a plum'

8   Mi a   *tiicha*
me are teacher
'I am a teacher'

9   *Tiicha* no kom yet
teacher no come yet
'The teacher hasn't come yet'

10   *Fait* brok out
fight broke out
'A fight broke out'

11   *Disya*   *bwai* niem Piita
this+here boy   name Peter
'This boy is called Peter'

12   *Dis bwai-ya* niem Piita
this boy+here name Peter
'This boy is called Peter'

13   *Dem-de*   *manggo* swiit
them+there mango   sweet
'Those mangoes are sweet'

14   *Dem manggo-de*   swiit
them mango+there sweet
'Those mangoes are sweet'

15   Im waip *im mout*
him wipe him mouth
'He wiped his mouth'

16   Dat a   *Rabat hous*
          that are Robert house
          'That is Robert's house'
17   *Di uman   biebi* sik
          the woman baby sick
          'The woman's baby is sick'
18   *Dat-de   wan* a   *fi-mi*
          that-there one are for-me
          'That one is mine'
19   *Fi-tiicha   hous* big
          for teacher house big
          'The teacher's house is big'
20   *Fi-yu   gyal-de* a   debl
          for-you girl-there are devil
          'That girl of yours is a devil'

Model answer for 3

The suffix +*dem* is traditionally classified as a noun suffix which marks plural number and definiteness. If we assume that the definite determiner *di* 'the' occupies the head D position of DP, the italicized nominal in 3 will have a structure along the lines of (i) below:

(i)
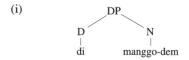

In order to account for the fact that a plural definite noun like *manggo-dem* can only be modified by a definite determiner like *di* (which can be used in a plural function – as well as having a singular use), not (for example) by an indefinite singular determiner like *wan* 'one' (as we see from the ungrammaticality of *wan manggo-dem 'one mangoes'), we clearly have to suppose that the determiner must agree with its noun complement in number and definiteness. One way of handling agreement between the noun and its determiner (which we shall discuss in more detail in the next chapter) is to assume that the number/definiteness features of the noun *percolate* from N to D, and are thereby checked against the features of the determiner.

Helpful hints

The nominals in sentences 15–20 all involve prenominal possessive structures not discussed so far in the text. There are a number of alternative analyses of prenominal possessives in English. However, for the purposes of this exercise, assume the following analysis. Prenominal possessives (like *the president's* or *my*) are DP/D constituents which function as specifiers of a null determiner Ø (cf. Abney 1987), and carry genitive case (marked by the suffix *'s* on nominal expressions like *the president*, and by using the genitive form in pronouns like *I/me/my* which inflect for case). Thus, expressions like *the president's car* and *my car* have the respective structures indicated below:

(ii) (a)   (b)

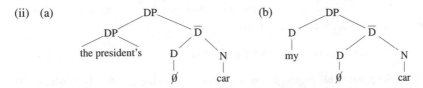

where the null determiner Ø has a genitive specifier (in much the same way as a finite auxiliary has a nominative specifier). Assume that prenominal possessives in Jamaican Creole occupy the same spec-DP position as their English counterparts – though don't assume that they necessarily have the same case properties.

Exercise V *(§4.8)* Turn in sent. 1-4 ONLY!

Discuss the syntax of the italicized items as they are used in the bracketed nominal expressions below:

1a [*No* student/**None* student] ever fails syntax

b [*None/*No*] ever will fail syntax

2a I like [*your* car/**yours* car]

b I like [*yours/*your*]

3a The Dean spoke to [*each* student/*every* student]

b The Dean spoke to [*each/*every*]

4a I can't do [*this* exercise/*the* exercise/**it* exercise]

b I can't do [*this/it/*the*]

In addition, say what problems (if any) are posed for the analysis in the text by the italicized items in the bracketed expressions in the examples below (some of which are taken from nonstandard varieties of English):

5 [The new *one*] outperforms [the old *ones*]

6 You wouldn't shoot [little old *me*], would you?

7 [*Us* students] should stick together

8 [*Usuns*] hates syntax (Belfast English: *usuns* = 'us ones' = 'we')

9 Tell Cooper to shift [*they* stones there] (Devonshire, from Harris 1991, p. 23)

10 It was like this in [*them* days], years ago, you see (Somerset, from Ihalainen 1991, p. 156)

165

11   [Poor *me* one]! (Jamaican Creole)

Where variety-specific pronouns are being used in a way which is different from their use in Standard English, specify the nature of the differences.

> *Model answer for 1 and 5*
> The quantifier *no* functions as a prenominal determiner used to quantify singular or plural count nouns and mass nouns: cf.

(i)   I have [*no chair/no chairs/no furniture*] to sit on

None is the pronominal counterpart of *no*, and correspondingly can only be used on its own, without a following nominal complement. Thus, both *no* and *none* are determiners, but they differ in their complement-selection properties: *no* has the property that it requires a nominal complement, while *none* has the property that it cannot have a nominal complement (though it can have a complement headed by *of* – cf. *none of us*). Given these assumptions, *no student* and *none* will have the respective structures indicated in (ii) below:

(ii)   (a)   (b)

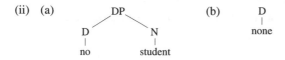

However, an alternative possibility (not discussed in the text) would be to assume that *none* is a determiner which takes an empty N or empty NP as its complement, so that *none* has the structure (iii) below (where N^{max} denotes a maximal projection of N – i.e. an N on its own, or an NP – and $\emptyset$ is an empty category):

(iii)

The problem of interpreting *none* would then amount to that of determining what *none* quantifies – i.e. determining the antecedent of $\emptyset$. In sentences such as (iv) below:

(iv)   I was looking for [a *chair*/some *chairs*/some *furniture*], but found *none*

we could say that the antecedent of $\emptyset$ is *chair/chairs/furniture*.

In sentences like 5, the pronoun *one(s)* seems to have the morphosyntactic properties of a typical noun. For one thing, like most nouns (and unlike pronouns such as *he*) it has a regular noun plural form in +*s* (cf. *one/ones*). Secondly, it has the *countability* property of many nouns, and so cannot have a mass noun as its antecedent: cf.

(v)   *I was looking for *furniture* but couldn't find *one*

and cannot be used without a premodifying determiner: cf.

(vi) (a)   She bought [a/the red *one*]
      (b)   *I bought [blue *one*]

Moreover, like a typical noun such as *fish* (but unlike a typical pronoun such as *him*), *one* can be modified by a preceding adjective: cf.

(vii) (a)   They caught [a *big* fish]
      (b)   They caught [a big *one*]
      (c)   *They caught [(a) big *him*]

If *one* is indeed a pronominal noun, it follows that it cannot be the case that all pronouns are pronominal determiners (though a determiner analysis might be argued to be appropriate for most pronouns).

Exercise VI (§§4.2–4.8)

Draw tree diagrams representing the structure of the following sentences, giving arguments in support of your analysis, and commenting on points of interest.

    1   I want to become chairman of the board
    2   People say he had a breakdown
    3   She seems keen for him to become president
    4   We expected him to back her
    5   I would prefer you to stay at home
    6   They decided to try to contact her
    7   %He wouldn't let me have done it
    8   I have never known him be rude to anyone

Helpful hints

Assume that *wouldn't* is a single word, with much the same syntax as *would*. Try and account for why *he had* can't become *he'd* in 2, and why *me have* can't become *me've* in 7.

Model answer for 1

Given the assumptions made in the text, 1 will have the structure (i) below:

(i)

A key assumption made in 1 is that the *become* clause has a null PRO subject. This can be justified in terms of agreement facts. As we see from examples like (10) in the text, predicate nominals have to agree with the subject of their own clause (i.e. with the subject of their own IP). Only if we assume that the *become* clause has a null PRO subject which is controlled by *I* and so first person singular can we account for why the predicate nominal *chairman of the board* has to be singular in 1 – cf. the ungrammaticality of:

(ii)   *I want to become *chairmen of the board*

Given the PRO analysis in (i), we can say that *chairman of the board* agrees with the PRO subject of the IP containing it, and so has to be singular because PRO is singular (since PRO is controlled by *I*).

In the text, it was claimed that argument nominals are D-projections (i.e. expressions headed by a determiner), and that pronouns are determiners. If this is so, then both the overt pronoun *I* and the covert pronoun PRO will be determiners. We can account for the fact that neither can have a noun complement after it (cf. **I* deputy*) by positing that it is a complement-selection property of inherently pronominal determiners that they can't have a noun complement.

Although argument nominals are D-projections, nonargument nominals (used in a vocative, predicative or exclamative function) can simply be N-projections. In this respect, it is interesting to note that the nominal *chairman of the board* is headed by the singular count noun *chairman*: when used as arguments, singular count noun expressions must contain an overt determiner in English. The fact that there is no determiner preceding *chairman of the board* in 1 suggests that it is here being used in a nonargument function: in traditional terms, *chairman of the board* is a *predicate nominal* (by virtue of being used as the complement of a predicative verb such as *be*, *become*, *stay*, *remain* etc.). Since predicative nominals are not arguments, and non-arguments are not required to contain a D-projection, *chairman of the board* can be analysed as a bare NP.

In the text, it is claimed that all clauses contain an I-projection. The complement clause *PRO to become chairman of the board* is clearly an IP headed by infinitival *to*. Some evidence that it isn't a CP headed by a null complementizer comes from *wanna*-contraction facts in relation to sentences such as (iii) below, where *to* cliticizes onto *want*:

(iii)   I *wanna* become chairman of the board

If (contrary to what we are suggesting here) the *to*-clause were a CP, (iii) would have the structure (iv) below prior to cliticization of *to* onto *want*:

(iv)   I want [$_{CP}$ COMP [$_{IP}$ PRO to become chairman of the board]]

Such an analysis would wrongly predict that *to* cannot cliticize onto *want*, because the intervening null COMP would block cliticization (in the same way as the intervening null INFL blocks cliticization in sentences such as (21), (28b-c) and (53b) in the main text).

The analysis in (i) also assumes that the *want*-clause is an IP, but one headed by an unfilled I constituent (with the *first person singular present-tense* features carried by *want* percolating up to I). Some empirical support for the claim that there is a null present-tense I constituent in (i) comes from the fact that the sentence is tagged by a present-tense form of the dummy auxiliary *do* in sentences such as:

(v)   I want to become chairman of the board, *don't/*didn't* I?

5

Checking

5.1 Overview

In chapters 3 and 4, we discussed the ways in which words are projected into syntactic structures. In this chapter, we shall be concerned with the principles which determine the morphological form of words. The kinds of question we shall ask here include (for example) why we say *We are winning* not **Us are winning*, or **We is winning*, or **We are win*. Why is it that we require *we* rather than *us* here, *are* rather than *is*, and *winning* rather than *win*? We shall suggest that the morphological properties of words can be characterized in terms of sets of **grammatical features**, and features must be **checked** in an appropriate manner: this chapter thus provides an introduction to the concept of **checking**. It should be noted that work on checking theory is as yet in its infancy, so that many of the ideas and descriptive details in this chapter are inevitably somewhat sketchy and speculative.

5.2 Interpretable and uninterpretable features

Before we explore *feature-checking*, however, let's first consider the overall organization of a grammar, and the role which features play in it. We assume that the sentence structures formed by successive merger operations must ultimately be **mapped** (i.e. converted) into two different kinds of structural representation for the sentence: (i) a representation of those aspects of the structure of the sentence which determine its **phonetic form** (= **PF**); and (ii) a representation of those aspects of the structure of the sentence which determine its **logical form** (= **LF**, i.e. linguistic aspects of the meaning of the sentence). Accordingly, for any given sentence, a descriptively adequate grammar should provide us with a **PF representation** on the one hand (specifying how it is pronounced), and an **LF representation** on the other (specifying what it means). There are thus two different output levels in a grammar: **PF** (= phonetic form) and **LF** (= logical form). The **derivation** of a sentence (i.e. the series of operations by which it is formed) involves a set of linguistic operations (or *computations*) which **generate** (i.e. produce) syntactic structures, together with a set of **PF operations** which convert syntactic structures into PF representations, and a set of

LF operations which convert syntactic structures into LF representations. LF and PF are said to be the two **interface levels** in the grammar, since they are the levels at which the grammar interfaces (i.e. connects) with other systems which lie outside the domain of the theory of grammar: i.e. PF representations serve as input to articulatory–perceptual systems, and LF representations serve as input to conceptual–intentional systems.

Let us assume that the phonetic, grammatical and semantic properties of words are described in terms of sets of features. Let us also suppose that it is in the nature of PF representations that they contain only phonetically interpretable features, and in the nature of LF representations that they contain only semantically interpretable features. This requirement is imposed by a UG constraint known as the **principle of full interpretation** (= PFI). This specifies that a representation for a given expression must contain all and only those elements which contribute directly to its interpretation at the relevant level: thus, the only features which the PF representation of an expression can contain are those relevant to determining its phonetic form, and likewise the only features which the LF representation of an expression can contain are those relevant to determining its logical form. If a derivation results in a PF representation which satisfies PFI (and hence contains only phonetically interpretable features), it is said to **converge at PF**; if the derivation results in an LF representation which satisfies PFI (and hence contains only semantically interpretable features), it is said to **converge at LF**. If both the PF and LF representations for some expression satisfy PFI, the associated derivation is said to **converge** (and the relevant expression is grammatical). If the PF and/or LF representations of an expression violate PFI, the resulting derivation is said to **crash** (and the relevant expression is ungrammatical).

One obvious implication of the **principle of full interpretation** is that PF representations must contain phonetically but not semantically interpretable features, and conversely that LF representations must contain semantically but not phonetically interpretable features. This suggests that at some stage derivations split into two paths, one computing PF representations which *spell out* the phonetic form of phrases and sentences, and the other computing their LF representation. Accordingly, we might envisage the derivation of a sentence as involving the following steps. By an operation of **selection**, lexical items are taken from the lexicon (each item comprising sets of phonetic, semantic and grammatical features). By the process of **merger**, constituents are combined together in a pairwise fashion to form a phrase structure tree (with each word in the tree comprising a set of phonetic, semantic and grammatical features). After **spellout**, the phonetic and semantic features of items are processed separately, the former being processed by PF operations which compute PF representations, and the latter being processed by LF operations which compute LF representations. We can represent this model in diagrammatic terms as in (1) below:

[Handwritten annotations:]

ERASED FEATURES
Case : Nom, Accus, GEN, DATIVE

Not erased — interpretable things
grammatical: person, gender, number

171

(1)

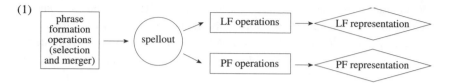

Spellout is the point at which the phrase structures generated by the processes of selection and merger feed into two different components – a PF component which processes their phonetic features, and an LF component which processes their grammatical and semantic features. We shall have little to say about PF representations here, and will focus mainly on how LF representations are computed.

The assumption that PF representations contain only phonetically interpretable features and LF representations only semantically interpretable features raises interesting questions about the status of *grammatical features* (which Chomsky 1995b terms *formal features*, since they determine the morphological form of items). The first question to ask is: 'What are *grammatical features*?' Informally, we can define them as features which play a role in grammatical (i.e. morphological or syntactic) processes. So, grammatical features include number (singular/plural) features, since these play an obvious role in the syntax of agreement (cf. *these/*this books*). They also include gender (masculine/feminine/inanimate) features, since these play a role in the syntax of reflexive anaphors (cf. *He/*She/*It turned himself into a giant*). Likewise, they include person features, which play a role in the syntax of subject–verb agreement (cf. *He/*I/*You likes syntax*). They also include features which determine the morphological form of items – for example, the case features of pronouns (cf. *He/*Him likes me/*I*), or the inflectional features of verbs (cf. *He has gone/*go/*going*). But they do not include features which have no morphological or syntactic correlate: for example, although words such as *calf, foal, kitten, puppy*, etc. share the feature [YOUNG], this is a purely semantic feature which plays no role in any grammatical process, and so is not a grammatical/formal feature. (By convention, features are enclosed in square brackets, and are often written in capital letters.)

However, the distinction between *grammatical* and *semantic* features is not always clearcut, since many grammatical features have clear semantic content, as we can illustrate in terms of the following sentence:

(2)   She has gone

The grammatical features of *she* indicate that it is third person feminine singular nominative determiner, those of *has* indicate that it is third person singular present-tense auxiliary, and those of *gone* indicate that it is an *n*-participle. Some of these grammatical features are *interpretable* at LF (in the sense that they have semantic content and so contribute to determining meaning), whereas others are *uninterpretable* at LF (in that they have no semantic content and so make no contribution to meaning). For example, the fact that *she* is a third person singular expression plays a role at LF (since it tells us e.g. that *she* can refer to *the girl next door* but not to *the curtains next door*). By contrast, the fact that *she* is *nominative* does not – as we can see from sentences such as the following:

(3) (a)   They expect [*she* will win]
     (b)   They expect [*her* to win]

The fact that the italicized subject of the bracketed complement clause plays the same semantic role in both sentences (as the subject of the *win*-clause), even though it has the nominative form *she* in (3a) and the objective form *her* in (3b), suggests that case is an uninterpretable feature. In much the same way, the fact that *has* is a present-tense auxiliary has a role to play at LF (since a sentence like *She had gone* containing the past-tense auxiliary *had* has a different interpretation), but the fact that *has* is third person singular seems to play no role at LF (it is simply a consequence of the grammatical requirement for *has* to agree with its subject *he*). Likewise, the fact that *gone* is a participle seems to have no role to play at LF (but rather is simply a consequence of the fact that *have* requires a complement headed by a verb in the +*n* participle form). It would seem that the case-features of pronouns and the agreement/participial inflections of verbs have no role to play in semantic interpretation, and thus are purely *formal* features.

So, the problem we face is that *some* of the grammatical features of words are interpretable at LF (i.e. contribute to meaning), but *others* are uninterpretable at LF (i.e. do not contribute to meaning). If we assume that (in consequence of the **principle of full interpretation**) LF representations contain only semantically interpretable features, it follows that uninterpretable features must somehow be eliminated in the course of deriving an LF representation, in order to ensure that the derivation converges at LF. Since phonetic features are processed by the PF component (and hence do not input into the LF component), the problem we face is how to eliminate uninterpretable grammatical features from LF representations.

Before we try and answer this question, let's consider a second problem posed by grammatical features – namely that of how to deal with grammatical restrictions which heads impose on their choice of specifier and complement. In this connection, consider the restrictions on the choice of specifier (i.e. subject) and complement for *has* illustrated in the following sentences:

(4) (a)   *He/*Him/*They* has gone
     (b)   He has *gone/*going/*go*

The examples in (4a) show that *has* can have a third person singular nominative pronoun like *he* as its specifier, but not a third person singular objective pronoun like *him*, or a third person plural nominative pronoun like *they*: in other words, a finite auxiliary like *has* imposes person/number/case restrictions on its specifier/subject. The examples in (4b) show that *has* allows as its complement a verb in the *n*-participle form, but not a verb in the *ing*-participle form, or a verb in its infinitive form: in other words, *has* imposes morphological restrictions on its complement.

5.3 Checking

Thus, grammatical features pose two sets of problems: one is how to eliminate uninterpretable features; the other is how to ensure that specifiers and complements carry the appropriate features for a given type of head. We can deal with both types of problem in a unified way within the framework of (feature-) **checking theory**. Let us suppose that items carry three different sets of grammatical features: **head-features** (which determine their intrinsic grammatical properties), **specifier-features** (which determine the kinds of specifier which they allow), and **complement-features** (which determine the kinds of complement which they can take). Let us further assume (following Chomsky 1995b) that all uninterpretable features must be checked in an appropriate checking configuration within an appropriate checking domain, and that checked uninterpretable features are erased (in much the same way as when checking a shopping list, you cross off the items which you have bought). I shall assume (following Bobaljik 1995) that a head checks features of its specifier and its complement. I shall further assume that all specifier- and complement-features are uninterpretable, as are purely formal head-features (i.e. head-features with no intrinsic semantic content). We can assume that UG specifies which head-features are interpretable and which are not – e.g. that number-features are interpretable, but case-features are not.

To put our discussion on a concrete footing, let's look at how checking works in the case of our earlier sentence (2) *She has gone*. Consider first the grammatical features carried by each of the three words in the sentence. (Throughout our discussion in this chapter, we shall only be concerned with *grammatical features*: hence, phrase structure trees are simplified by ignoring phonetic and semantic features, and LF representations are simplified by ignoring semantic features.) The head-features of *has* indicate its categorial properties (i.e. that it is an auxiliary verb) and its tense properties (i.e. that it is present tense): its specifier-features tell us that it requires a third person singular nominative subject; and its complement-features indicate that it requires a complement headed by a verb in the *n*-participle form. The head-features of *she* tell us that it is third person feminine singular determiner: and the head-features of *gone* indicate that it is an *n*-participle form. Since neither *she* nor *gone* has a specifier or complement here, we can assume that in the relevant uses their head- and complement-features specify that they can be used without any specifier or complement. Given these assumptions, (2) *She has gone* will have the grammatical structure (5) below (as noted above, we only show grammatical/formal features):

(5)

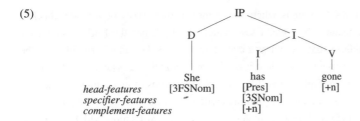

	She	has	gone
head-features	[3FSNom]	[Pres]	[+n]
specifier-features	—	[3SNom]	
complement-features		[+n]	

(3 = third person, F = feminine, S = singular, Nom = nominative case, Pres = present tense, +n = *n*-participle; the blank entries for the specifier- and complement-features of *she* and *gone* mean that (in this use) they don't have a specifier or complement.) The information within the square brackets in (5) provides an informal indication of the fact that *she* carries the head-feature 'third person feminine singular nominative'; *has* carries the head-feature 'present tense', the specifier-feature 'requires third person singular nominative subject' and the complement-features 'takes an *n*-participle complement'; and *gone* carries the head-feature '*n*-participle'. The head-features of each item also include its categorial features (which tell us that *she* is a determiner, *has* is an auxiliary verb, and *gone* is a nonauxiliary verb), but these are represented by the category-labels (D, I and V) carried by the relevant nodes in the tree.

Now consider how the process of (feature-) checking works in (5). For concreteness, let's make the following assumptions about checking:

(6)   The specifier-features of a head are checked against the head-features of its specifier; likewise, the complement-features of a head are checked against the head-features of its complement.

If there is compatibility between **checker** and **checked** in respect of a given feature, the relevant specifier- or complement-feature is erased (because specifier- and complement-features are uninterpretable), and the corresponding head-feature is erased if purely formal and so uninterpretable (but is not erased if interpretable). If there is incompatibility between checker and checked in respect of some feature, the relevant feature cannot be erased from either.

Consider first what happens when the specifier-features of *has* are checked against the head-features of *she* in (5). The [3] (third person) and [S] (singular) specifier-features of *has* exactly match the [3S] head-features of *she*: since the relevant features play a role in the interpretation of *she* but not in that of *has*, the [3S] specifier-features of *has* are erased, but the [3S] head-features of *she* are not. The [Nom] (nominative case) specifier-feature of *has* exactly matches the [Nom] head-feature of *she*, and since case-features play no role in semantic interpretation, both [Nom] features are erased. Thus, checking the specifier-features of *has* against the head-features of *she* in (5) erases all the specifier-features of *has*, together with the nominative case-feature of *she*, but leaves the interpretable [3FS] features on *she*.

Now consider what happens when the complement-features of *has* are checked against the head-features of *gone*. These match exactly, since the [+n] complement-feature of *have* tells us that it requires a complement headed by an *n*-participle, and the [+n] head-feature of *gone* tells us that it is an *n*-participle. If we assume that the inflectional properties of nonfinite verbs (like the case properties of pronouns) play no role in semantic interpretation, both [+n] features will be erased.

So, checking in (5) will mean that the only grammatical features which survive in the LF representation are those in (7) below:

(7)

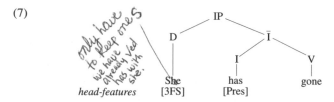

All specifier- and complement-features have been erased (because they play no role in semantic interpretation). Likewise, purely formal head-features (e.g. the nominative case-feature of *she* and the [+n] inflectional feature of *gone*) have also been erased, because they too are uninterpretable. The only grammatical features which survive at LF are *interpretable head-features*. Since all the features in (7) are interpretable, (7) satisfies the **principle of full interpretation**, and so the derivation converges at LF.

Of course, (7) is only a *partial* LF-representation: because we are concerned here with how grammatical features are checked, we have not included purely semantic features in (7); a full LF representation for *She has gone* would clearly have to include the semantic features of *has* (e.g. the fact that it is a perfective auxiliary) and *gone* (e.g. the fact that it is a verb of motion). Hence, the orthographic representations of the words *she*, *has* and *gone* in (7) should be understood as a shorthand abbreviation for the *semantic features* of the relevant items: we could make this explicit e.g. by using capital letters for the words which appear in LF representations (so that e.g. GONE denotes the semantic features carried by the word *gone*) – but rather than do this, we shall simply take it as implicit in what follows (so that e.g. *gone* in (7) should be understood as representing the set of semantic features which characterize its meaning).

Now let's turn to consider how checking breaks down in an ungrammatical structure such as:

(8)

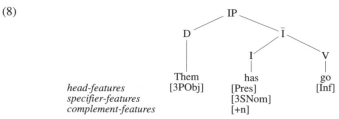

176

(3 = third person, P = plural, S = singular, Obj = objective case, Nom = nominative case, Pres = present tense, Inf = infinitival, +n = *n*-participle.) Here, the [3] specifier-feature of *has* (requiring it to have a third person subject) can be erased because its specifier *them* is a third person pronoun. But the [S] specifier feature of *has* (requiring it to have a singular subject) cannot be erased because the subject of *has* is the plural pronoun *them*, and so remains unchecked. Similarly, the [Nom] specifier-feature of *has* (requiring it to have a nominative subject) remains unchecked because it is incompatible with the objective case-feature [Obj] carried by *them*. In addition, the [+n] complement-feature of *has* (requiring it to have a participial complement) cannot be checked because of a mismatch with the [Inf] head-feature carried by the infinitive verb form *go*. Checking therefore results in the (partial) LF representation (9) below (*partial* because – as noted earlier – we are concerned here only with grammatical features, and so do not represent purely semantic features):

(9)

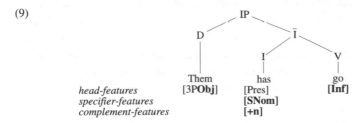

	Them	has	go
head-features	**[3PObj]**	[Pres]	**[Inf]**
specifier-features		**[SNom]**	
complement-features		**[+n]**	

But since numerous (**bold-printed**) uninterpretable features remain in (9) (viz. the **[Obj]** case-feature of *them*, the **[Inf]** inflectional feature of *go*, the **[SNom]** specifier-features of *has*, and the **[+n]** complement-feature of *has*), the resulting LF representation violates PFI by virtue of containing uninterpretable features and so crashes at LF.

As we see in relation to structures such as (5) and (7–9), one set of features carried by a finite auxiliary like *has* which have to be checked are its (third person singular) agreement-features. However, since modal auxiliaries (such as *can/could*, *may/might*, *will/would*, *shall/should* and *must*) never take the third person singular +*s* inflection in their present-tense forms, an interesting question which arises is what kind of specifier-features modals carry. To make our discussion more concrete, consider the specifier-features of the present-tense modal *can* in a sentence such as:

(10)   They *can* swim

It is clear that *can* imposes case restrictions on its choice of subject, since it requires a nominative subject like *they*, not an objective subject like *them* or a genitive subject like *their*. However, *can* doesn't seem to impose any person/number restrictions on its choice of subject, since it allows (for example) a first person singular/plural subject like *I/we*, a second person subject like *you* or a third person singular/plural subject like *he/they*. We shall therefore make the simplifying assumption that the only specifier-

177

feature carried by a modal like *can* is the case-feature [Nom], indicating that it requires a nominative subject. This being so, a sentence like (10) will have the grammatical structure (11) below:

(11)

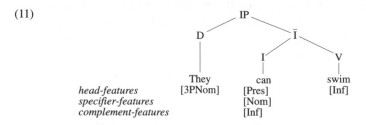

(3 = third person; P = plural; Nom = nominative case; Pres = present tense; Inf = infinitive.) The [Nom] specifier-feature of *can* will be checked against the [Nom] head-feature of *they*, and both [Nom] case-features erased thereby (since case-features are uninterpretable). The [Inf] complement-feature of *can* will be checked against the [Inf] head-feature of *swim*, and both [Inf] features thereby erased (on the assumption that inflectional features of nonfinite verbs are uninterpretable). Thus, the only features which survive at LF are the interpretable [3P] *third person plural* head-features carried by *they*, and the [Pres] *present-tense* head-feature carried by *can*.

5.4 Phrases

So far, we have only looked at elementary structures in which complements and specifiers consist of single words rather than phrases. But consider how checking works in more complex sentences such as (12) below, where the complement of *are* is a [bracketed] phrase:

(12)   They are [getting old]

Let's assume that (12) has the grammatical structure (13) below:

(13)

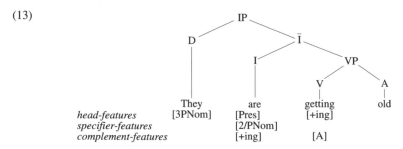

The head-features of the relevant items here indicate that *they* is a third person plural nominative determiner (recall that the head-features of items include their categorial features, indicated by the category-label they carry), *are* is a present-tense auxiliary, *getting* is a verb in its *+ing* form, and *old* is an adjective. The [2/PNom] specifier-features of *are* tell us that it requires a second person or plural nominative specifier; the [+ing] complement-feature of *are* specifies that it requires an *+ing* complement; and the [A] complement-feature of *get* specifies that it requires an adjectival complement. Consider now how the relevant complement-features are checked.

The [A] complement-feature of *getting* (requiring it to have an adjectival complement) can be checked (and erased) straightforwardly, since the complement of *getting* is *old*, and its head-features (which include its categorial features, represented by the category label A in the tree) indicate that it is an adjective. But now consider how the [+ing] complement-feature of the auxiliary *are* is checked. We earlier noted in (6) above that the complement-features of a head are checked against the head-features of its complement. The complement of *are* in (12) is the verb phrase *getting old*, which is a projection of the head *getting*. Since getting is an *ing*-head, we might suppose that its projection *getting old* is correspondingly an *ing*-projection, and hence can check the [+ing] complement-feature of *are* (requiring *are* to have an *ing*-complement), so that both [+ing] features can be erased. What we are tacitly assuming here is that it is in the very nature of the **merger** operation by which phrases are formed that the head-features of a head are shared by all projections of the head (e.g. a phrase headed by an infinitive verb form is an infinitival verb phrase). If so, what a complement-feature such as [+ing] effectively means is 'requires a complement headed by an *+ing*-participle form'.

We can treat phrasal specifiers in a similar fashion. In this connection, consider the structure in (14) below:

(14)

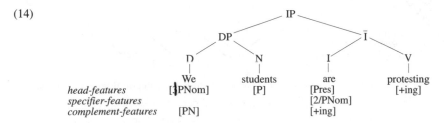

The [1PNom] head-features of *we* indicate that it is a first person plural nominative determiner; its [PN] complement-feature indicates that it requires a plural noun as its complement in this type of use, not a singular noun (cf. *we student). The head-features of *students* indicate that it is a plural noun. The head-features of *are* tell us that it is a present-tense auxiliary; its specifier-features indicate that it requires a second person or plural nominative expression as its specifier; and its complement-features indicate that it requires an *ing*-complement. Finally, the head-features of *protesting* indicate that it is an *ing*-participle.

Now consider the specific problem of checking the [2/PNom] specifier-features of the auxiliary *are* (requiring it to have a second person or plural nominative specifier).

Checking

We suggested in (6) above that the specifier-features of a head are checked against the head-features of its specifier. Since the specifier of *are* is the DP *we students*, and this is a projection of the first person plural nominative determiner *we*, it follows (from our assumption that phrases share the same head-features as their heads) that the DP *we students* will also be a first person plural nominative expression; as such, it can check (and erase) the [2/PNom] specifier-features of *are* (with the uninterpretable nominative case-feature carried by *we (students)* being erased at the same time). Thus, what a specifier-feature like [2/PNom] in effect means is 'requires a specifier with a second person or plural nominative head'.

Having looked at how specifier- and complement-features are checked in simple phrases, let's consider how checking works in more complex structures such as:

(15)(a)   He might have been helping them

    (b)   *Him might having be helped they

We can assume that (15a) has the following grammatical structure:

(16)

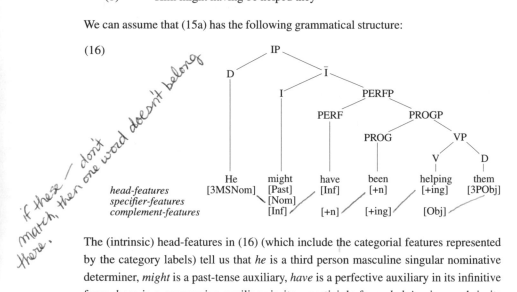

The (intrinsic) head-features in (16) (which include the categorial features represented by the category labels) tell us that *he* is a third person masculine singular nominative determiner, *might* is a past-tense auxiliary, *have* is a perfective auxiliary in its infinitive form, *been* is a progressive auxiliary in its *n*-participle form, *helping* is a verb in its *ing*-participle form and *them* is a third person plural objective determiner. But let's concentrate on the specifier- and complement-features of the relevant items, and how they are checked.

The [Nom] specifier-feature of *might* (telling us that it requires a nominative subject) is checked against the corresponding [Nom] head-feature of *he*, leading to erasure of both [Nom] case-features (since case-features are uninterpretable). The [Inf] complement-feature of *might* tells us that it requires an infinitival complement (i.e. a complement

180

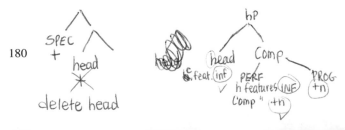

headed by an infinitival auxiliary or nonauxiliary verb): this requirement is satisfied by virtue of the fact that the head word *have* of its complement *have been helping them* carries the head-feature [Inf], and phrases carry the same head-features as their heads (hence *have been helping them* is an infinitival expression). The [+n] complement-feature of *have* indicates that it requires an *n*-participle complement (i.e. a complement headed by an *n*-participle): this requirement is satisfied because its complement *been helping them* is headed by *been*, and hence carries the same intrinsic [+n] feature as *been*. The [+ing] complement-feature of *been* tells us that it requires an *ing*-complement (i.e. a complement headed by an *ing*-participle form): this requirement is met, since the complement of *been* is *helping them*, which is headed by the *ing*-participle *helping* and hence is an *ing*-participle expression. If we assume that the only inflectional head-features of verbs which play a role in semantic interpretation are the tense-features of finite verbs (and that nonfinite inflections are purely formal), then all the [Inf], [+n] and [+ing] inflectional features will be erased. Finally, the [Obj] complement-feature of *helping* is checked against the corresponding [Obj] objective-case head-feature of *them*, and both features thereby erased.

So, checking derives the (partial) LF representation (17) below:

(17)

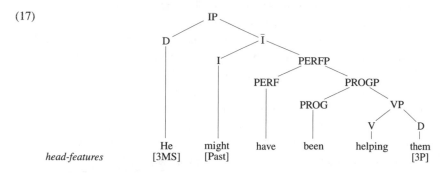

All purely formal features (e.g. case-features on pronouns and inflectional features on nonfinite verbs) have been erased, so that the only grammatical features which remain are interpretable person/number/gender/tense-features and interpretable categorial features such as PERF (indicating perfective aspect) and PROG (indicating progressive aspect). (As already noted, we are concerned here only with *grammatical/formal* features and so omit purely semantic features from partial LF representations like (17) above.)

Now let's consider the corresponding ungrammatical example (15b) **Him might having be helped they*, and see what goes wrong there. We can assume that (15b) has the (partial) grammatical structure (18) below (simplified by ignoring phonetic and semantic features):

(18)

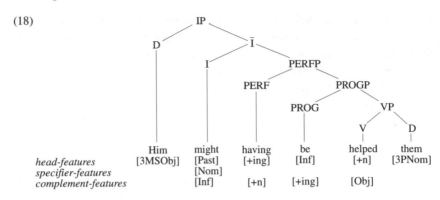

head-features	Him [3MSObj]	might [Past] [Nom] [Inf]	having [+ing] [+n]	be [Inf] [+ing]	helped [+n] [Obj]	them [3PNom]
specifier-features						
complement-features						

The head-features in (18) tell us that *him* is a third person masculine singular objective determiner, *might* is a past-tense auxiliary, *having* is an *ing*-participle, *be* is an (irregular) infinitive form, *helped* is an *n*-participle (it could of course also be a past-tense form) and *they* is a third person plural nominative determiner. The specifier- and complement-features of the relevant items are as in our earlier discussion of (16) above.

Now consider how the various specifier- and complement-features in (18) are checked. In fact, none of the specifier- and complement-features can be erased. Thus, the [Nom] specifier-feature of *might* (requiring it to have a nominative subject) is incompatible with the [Obj] head-feature carried by the objective pronoun *him*, so neither case-feature can be erased. Likewise, the [Inf] complement-feature of *might* (requiring an infinitive complement) is incompatible with the [+ing] head-feature of the phrase headed by *having*; the [+n] complement-feature of *having* is incompatible with the [Inf] head-feature of the phrase headed by *be*; the [+ing] complement-feature of *be* is incompatible with the [+n] head-feature of the phrase headed by *helped*; and the [Obj] objective-case complement-feature of *helped* is incompatible with the [Nom] head-feature of the nominative pronoun *they*. Since all of these unerased features are uninterpretable case or inflectional features, the resulting LF representation violates the **principle of full interpretation**, so causing the derivation to crash at LF.

The distinction between interpretable and uninterpretable features has an interesting correlate in the case of *creole* (i.e. hybrid) languages. It is often said that English-based creoles have a simplified morphology compared to that of English. But simplified in what ways? One way is by eliminating uninterpretable head-features, thereby simplifying the process of checking. For example, in Jamaican Creole (as described in Bailey 1966) personal pronouns inflect for person, number and (in the third person singular only) gender, but not for case, so that pronouns have the following head-features (*1/2/3* denote person, *S/P* denote singular/plural number, and *In* denotes inanimate gender; English counterparts are given in inverted commas):

(19)   *mi* [1S] = 'I/me/my'

          we [1P] = 'we/us/our'

          yu [2S] = 'you/your' (singular)

          unu [2P] = 'you/your' (plural = you-and-you)

          im [3S] = 'he/him/his; she/her; it/its'

          i [3SIn] = 'it/its'

          dem [3P] = 'they/them/their'

The features which have been lost (compared to English) are uninterpretable case-features; those which have been retained are interpretable person-, number- and gender-features. We find much the same picture in relation to verb morphology, with the loss of uninterpretable agreement inflections. For example, in a sentence such as:

(20)   Mi/Im/Dem a rait

          me/him/them are write

          'I am/(S)he is/They are writing'

the auxiliary *a* is invariable, and so doesn't inflect for agreement at all. (I have glossed *a* here by English *are*: it should be noted, however, that Rickford 1986 and Harris 1986 posit that *a* is a reduced form of *does* – though this seems implausible for sentences like *Mi a tiicha*, 'I am (a) teacher'.) It would seem that in Jamaican Creole, only inter-pretable head-features survive.

The distinction between interpretable and uninterpretable features also has an inter-esting developmental correlate. We should expect that interpretable features (which have semantic content) would be acquired more easily than uninterpretable features (which are purely formal and have no intrinsic semantic content). In this connection, it is interesting to note that young children acquiring English have problems in mastering the case properties of pronouns and the agreement properties of finite verbs – as the following child utterances illustrate:

(21) (a)   *Me* can fly

     (b)   Teddy *want* ice-cream

In (21a) we find the objective pronoun *me* used where an adult requires the nominative pronoun *I*; and in (21b) we find the uninflected verb form *want* where an adult requires the agreement-inflected form *wants*. It seems to be uninterpretable features which pose particular acquisition problems, in that (for example) the interpretable singular/plural number features in nouns like *dog/dogs* are typically acquired before the uninter-pretable case-features of pronouns like *I/me*, and the interpretable past-tense feature in verbs like *went* is typically acquired before the uninterpretable third person singular agreement-features in forms like *goes*. There are interesting potential parallels between *agh!!* Child English and Creole English, in that in both cases uninterpretable features are 'lost'.

5.5 Percolation

After a brief look at Jamaican Creole and Child English, let's now return to Standard English. Thus far, we have considered how checking works in clauses headed by a finite auxiliary. But what about auxiliariless finite clauses such as the following?

(22)   She hates him

In the previous chapter, we argued that sentences like (22) are IPs headed by an unfilled INFL constituent. If we further assume that the head-features of *hates* tell us that it is a present-tense form, its complement-features tell us that (in this transitive use) it requires an objective complement like *him* (cf. *She hates he*), and its specifier-features tell us that it requires a third person singular nominative subject (cf. *Her/*They hates him*), (22) will have the grammatical structure (23) below:

(23)

head-features	She	hates	him
specifier-features	[3FSNom]	[Pres]	[3MSObj]
complement-features		[3SNom]	
		[Obj]	

It is clear that the objective complement-feature of *hates* can be checked against the objective head-feature of *him* here (with both objective features thereby being erased, because case-features are uninterpretable at LF), since *him* is the complement of *hates*. But if we assume (as in (6) above) that the specifier-features of a head are checked against the head-features of its specifier, we cannot check the specifier-features of *hates* against the head-features of *she* here – for the obvious reason that the two are contained within different phrases, *she* being the specifier of IP, and *hates* being the head of VP (so that *she* is not the specifier of *hates*). However, if the relevant features remain unchecked, the derivation will crash at LF, so wrongly predicting that sentences like (22) *She hates him* are ungrammatical. How are we to overcome this problem?

In §4.4, we outlined a possible solution. We suggested that in auxiliariless finite clauses, the grammatical features carried by the verb *percolate* from V to I. However, clearly we don't want to assume that the *complement-features* of the verb *hates* (which tell us that it requires an objective complement) percolate to I, since these are checked internally within VP. So, let's assume that the complement-features of *hates* are first checked internally within VP and erased, and then the remaining unchecked features of *hates* (i.e. its head- and specifier-features) percolate from V to INFL, as shown by the arrows in (24) below (where we assume that the objective complement-feature of *hates* and the objective head-feature of *him* have already been checked and erased internally within VP):

(24)

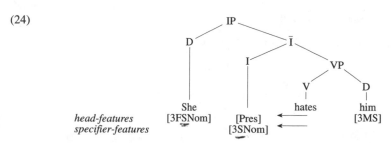

	She	hates	him
head-features	[3FSNom]	[Pres]	[3MS]
specifier-features		[3SNom]	

We can suppose that the [Pres] present-tense head-feature of *hates* percolates from V to INFL in order to ensure LF convergence: if we make the reasonable assumption that INFL is only interpretable at LF if it carries a tense-feature, percolation of the [Pres] feature from V to I provides a way of ensuring that INFL acquires a tense-feature and can therefore be interpreted at LF. The assumption that the present-tense head-feature of *hates* percolates up to INFL accounts for the fact that the corresponding tag-sentence *She hates him, **doesn't** she?* contains a present-tense auxiliary (*doesn't*), since the auxiliary in a tag generally carries the same tense-features as the head INFL constituent of the clause to which the tag is attached (cf. e.g. *She **has** finished, **hasn't** she?*).

In much the same way, we might suppose that the [3SNom] specifier-features of *hates* also percolate to INFL in order to ensure LF convergence: since specifier-features are uninterpretable, they must be checked and erased in the course of deriving the relevant LF representation. But since *hates* and *she* are contained within different phrases (*hates* is the head V of VP, and *she* is the specifier of IP), the only way for the specifier-features of *hates* to be checked is for them to percolate up to INFL, where they can then be checked against the corresponding [3SNom] head-features of *she* (by virtue of being in the same IP-projection as *she*): checking will result in erasure of the uninterpretable [3SNom] specifier-features of *hates*, and of the uninterpretable [Nom] head-feature of *she*.

Erasing the relevant uninterpretable checked features in (24) yields the (partial) LF representation (25) below (all surviving features are head-features):

(25)

IP
D — Ī
I — VP
V — D
She hates him
[3FS] [Pres] [3MS]

185

And (25) is essentially the same LF representation (in relevant respects) as is required for a sentence such as:

(26)   She does hate him

which has the grammatical structure (27) below:

(27)

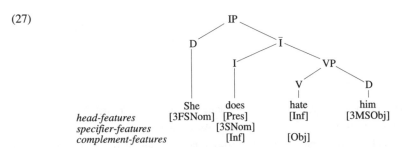

	She	does	hate	him
head-features	[3FSNom]	[Pres]	[Inf]	[3MSObj]
specifier-features		[3SNom]		
complement-features		[Inf]	[Obj]	

Erasure (via checking) of the specifier- and complement-features in (27) along with nominative/objective-case head-features of *she/him* and the infinitival head-feature of the verb *hate* derives the LF representation (28) below:

(28)

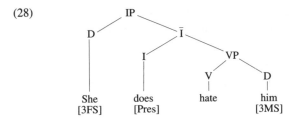

And (28) is the same in the relevant respects as (26) – the difference in semantic interpretation between the two lying in whatever (contrastive or emphatic) content *does* has.

An interesting question which arises from our discussion here is why sentences such as (29) below should be ungrammatical:

(29)   *She does hates him

Let's assume that (29) has the morphosyntactic structure (30) below:

(30)

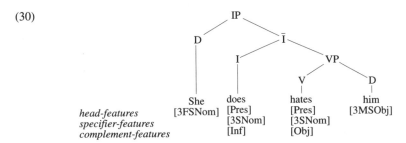

	She	does	hates	him
head-features	[3FSNom]	[Pres]	[Pres]	[3MSObj]
specifier-features		[3SNom]	[3SNom]	
complement-features		[Inf]	[Obj]	

186

One factor which causes the derivation to crash at LF is the fact that the [Inf] complement-feature of *does* (requiring a complement headed by a verb in the infinitive form) cannot be checked, since the [Pres] head-feature of *hates* indicates that it is a present-tense form, hence not an infinitive. Another is that the specifier-features of *does* and *hates* require them each to have a (third person singular) nominative subject, and the single subject pronoun *she* can't serve as the subject of both verbs. Why not? Because if the nominative-case specifier-feature of *does* is checked against the nominative-case head-feature of *she*, the nominative case-feature of *she* will thereby be erased (because it is uninterpretable); and this will mean that the nominative specifier-feature of *hates* cannot be erased (even if it percolates from V to INFL), because the nominative head-feature of *she* has already been erased.

We can summarize our discussion so far in the following terms. The morphological properties of lexical items can be described in terms of sets of head-, complement- and specifier-features: uninterpretable features need to be checked in an appropriate domain. Checking involves either a local specifier–head relation whereby the specifier-features of a head are checked against the head-features of its specifier, or a local head–complement relation whereby the complement-features of a head are checked against the head-features of its complement. Where a feature carried by the head word of a phrase cannot be checked within its containing phrase it may *percolate* up to the next highest head position in the structure for checking purposes. Checking erases features which are uninterpretable – hence, it erases all specifier- and complement-features, along with those head-features (e.g. case-features of pronouns and inflectional features of nonfinite verbs) which play no role in semantic interpretation. Any uninterpretable features which are not erased by checking cause a derivation to crash.

5.6 Determiner phrases

The structures which we have looked at so far have mainly involved arguments which are personal pronouns. But how are we to deal with nominal arguments such as that italicized in (31) below?

(31)   *The students* are complaining

Since the specifier-features of *are* (like those of all finite auxiliary and nonauxiliary verbs) include the fact that *are* requires a nominative specifier, it is clear that the DP *the students* must be nominative. Moreover, since it contains the plural noun *students*, it is clearly plural (as we also see from the fact that it is used as the subject of *are*, and *are* requires a plural or second person subject like *we/you/they* etc.). The DP *the students* must also be a third person expression, since a DP headed by the determiner *the* can only bind a third person reflexive anaphor like *themselves*, not a first or second person reflexive: cf.

(32)   *The students* take **themselves/*ourselves/*yourselves** too seriously

187

So, the DP *the students* in (31) must carry the features [3PNom], indicating that it is a third person plural nominative expression. Since phrasal categories are projections of the head-features of their heads, and since the DP *the students* is a projection of the determiner *the*, it follows that *the* must carry the head-features [3PNom], and so be third person plural nominative.

While it is plausible to suppose (on the basis of sentences like (32) above) that *the* is intrinsically third person, we clearly can't claim that it is intrinsically plural (since it is singular in sentences such as *The coursebook is boring*), or that it is intrinsically nominative (since it is objective in sentences like *I hate the coursebook*). One solution would be to suppose that *the* has variable number and case properties, and hence can be either singular or plural in number, and either nominative or objective in case. This seems a reasonable assumption: after all, determiners like *this/these* carry overt number properties (*this* being singular and *these* plural), and pronominal determiners like *I/me, he/him*, etc. carry overt case properties (*I* being nominative and *me* objective): hence, it is by no means implausible to suppose that determiners like *the* carry covert (variable) number and case properties, since this enables us to arrive at a unitary characterization of the feature specification of determiners as constituents which carry overt or covert person/number/case properties.

One way in which we might think of variable feature-values is in the following terms. Let's suppose that when an item which has variable values for one or more features is selected, it is pulled out of the lexicon with *one* fixed value for each such variable feature. So, for example, if we use *the* as a nominative plural determiner in a sentence like (31) above and *are* as a plural (rather than second person) auxiliary, (31) will have the grammatical structure (33) below:

(33)

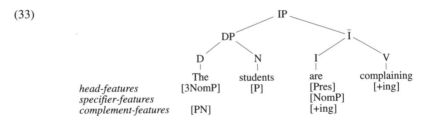

The [NomP] specifier-features of *are* indicate that (in this particular use), it requires a nominative plural subject. The subject/specifier of *are* is the DP *the students*: since this is a projection of the determiner *the*, and since the [3NomP] head-features of *the* indicate that (in this particular use) it is a third person nominative plural determiner, it follows that the specifier-features of *are* can be checked and erased, along with the uninterpretable nominative case-feature carried by *the* (*students*). It goes without saying that if (for example) we used *the* as an objective singular determiner in (33), the relevant case- and agreement-features carried by *the students* and *are* would be incompatible, so could not be checked. (An interesting question of detail arising from the analysis in (33) is whether we need to assume that the plural head-feature carried by *students* is erased prior to LF, since it is redundant if *the* carries a plural head-feature: an alternative way of dealing with this problem would be to suppose that *the* carries no intrinsic number feature at all, and that the plural number-feature of *students* percolates from N to D.)

this is what people go by today.

It should be evident that our discussion here can be generalized from overt determiners like *the* to covert determiners like the null determiner quantifying *students* in sentences such as:

(34)   Students are complaining

Given our arguments in §4.7 that bare nominal arguments like *students* are DPs headed by a null determiner ∅ with a generic or partitive interpretation, it follows from our assumption that all determiners in English have person/number/case properties that the null determiner ∅ must have person/number/case properties of its own. It seems clear that the relevant null determiner must be intrinsically third person, since a bare nominal like *students* can only bind a third person reflexive like *themselves* – as we see from sentences like:

(35)   *Students* are preparing **themselves/*ourselves/*yourselves** for exams

It is also clear that the null determiner must be nominative plural in (34), since otherwise the DP ∅ *students* would not be able to satisfy the requirements for *are* to have a nominative plural subject. Thus, (34) has essentially the same structure as (33) above, save for the fact that the head D position of DP is occupied by the null determiner ∅ rather than by the overt determiner *the*.

One matter which we haven't yet discussed concerns the checking of features internally within determiner phrases. In this connection, consider the syntax of the bracketed subject DP in:

(36)   [*The numerous opposition allegations of incompetence*] are unsettling the prime minister

If we assume Cinque's (1994) analysis of the syntax of attributive adjectives (briefly outlined in §4.9) under which they serve as specifiers of an abstract functional head F, the bracketed DP in (36) will have the structure (37) below:

(37)

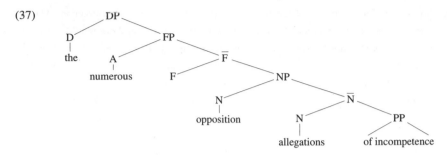

Let's consider first the *number* features of relevant constituents of the DP in (37). It is clear that the noun *allegations* is plural in number, since it carries the plural suffix +*s*. Moreover, the adjective *numerous* is intrinsically plural (by virtue of its meaning). In addition, the determiner *the* (as used here) must be plural, in order that the overall phrase which it heads (*the numerous opposition allegations of incompetence*) should be plural and so agree with the (third person plural) auxiliary *are* (cf. our earlier discussion of (31) above). The fact that *the*, *numerous* and *allegations* are all plural would suggest that there is an agreement relation between them (hence the resulting sentence becomes ungrammatical if the plural noun form *allegations* is replaced by its singular counterpart *allegation*).

Consider first how we can account for the fact that the adjective *numerous* agrees in number with the plural noun *allegations*. One answer (suggested in §4.9) is to suppose that the plural number-feature carried by *allegations* percolates up the tree to the head F position of FP, as indicated informally in (38) below (where the arrow indicates feature percolation):

(38)

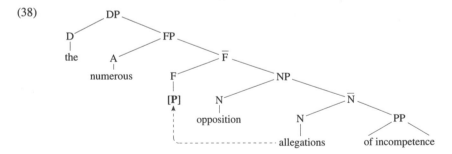

The **[P]** plural number-feature which the functional head F acquires via percolation can then be checked against the plural number-feature carried by *numerous* (checking here involving a spec–head relation between F and its specifier). Thus, percolation ensures that *allegations* agrees with *numerous*.

But of course we also need to ensure that *allegations* agrees with *the* (and, more generally, that determiners agree with the nouns they modify – cf. *this/*these ridiculous* *allegation*, where the determiner *this/these* has to agree with *allegation*). One way of doing this would be to extend the percolation analysis and to suppose that the plural number-feature of the noun *allegations* percolates first from N to F (as in (38) above), and then from F to D – as in (39) below:

(39)

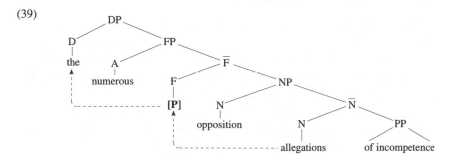

Once the plural number-feature of the noun *allegations* has percolated from N (through F) to D, it can be checked against the plural number-feature carried by the determiner *the* (as used here), and thereby erased. (An alternative to the analysis sketched here would be to suppose that *the* has no number-feature of its own, and acquires its plural number-feature by percolation from the noun *allegations*.) It will be apparent from (39) that *percolation* (like *movement*) always proceeds in an *upwards* direction, never *downwards*.

It goes without saying that many details of this account of the internal syntax of DPs remain to be filled in. For example, while it is clear that the determiner *the* carries (covert) nominative case in sentences such as (36), it is less clear whether the noun *allegations* and the adjective *numerous* also carry nominative case. In languages (like Latin or Russian) with a much richer case morphology than English, nouns, attributive adjectives and determiners all inflect overtly for case: hence, we might conclude (on universalist grounds) that the determiner *the*, the adjective *numerous* and the noun *allegations* all carry covert nominative case in (36), and that they agree with each other in case as well as number (with case agreement being treated via percolation, as in (39) above). On the other hand, since no nouns or adjectives overtly inflect for case in English, it might be argued to be against the spirit of *minimalism* to posit that nouns and adjectives carry case properties which are never overtly marked: on this alternative view, we might say that the noun *allegations* and the adjective *numerous* carry (plural) number-features, but no case-features (case being a property carried only by determiners in English). For obvious reasons, it is hard to find compelling empirical evidence that nouns and adjectives do (or don't) have covert case properties in English: hence, we shall leave the issue open here.

5.7 PRO subjects

In the previous section, we briefly discussed how the features carried by the null prenominal determiner ∅ are checked in sentences such as (34). This raises the interesting question of what features are carried by the null PRO subject in control structures such as (40) below (where PRO is controlled by *they*), and how they are checked:

(40)   They were trying [**PRO** to escape]

If PRO is a null pronoun, and if pronouns carry **case** properties, an obvious conclusion to draw is that PRO must carry case. Chomsky and Lasnik (1995, pp. 119–20) suggest that just as PRO has a null phonological form, so too it carries **null case**. If so, how is the null case carried by PRO checked? Chomsky and Lasnik suggest that it is checked by infinitival *to*. What this implies is that infinitival *to* carries a null-case specifier-feature which is checked against the null-case head-feature of PRO. So, for example, we might suppose that the bracketed infinitive complement in (40) has the (simplified) morphosyntactic structure (41) below:

(41)

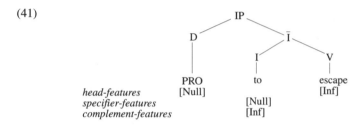

The [Null] specifier-feature of *to* indicates that it requires a specifier with null case; and the corresponding [Null] head-feature of PRO indicates that it carries null case. The two [Null] case-features are checked against each other and thereby erased, since case-features are uninterpretable.

There are potential parallels here with how nominative case is checked in finite-clause structures such as (5) above, repeated as (42) below:

(42)

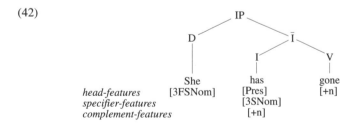

In (42), the [Nom] nominative-case specifier-feature carried by the finite INFL constituent *has* is checked against the corresponding [Nom] head-feature carried by its subject *she*. Likewise, in (41) the [Null] null-case specifier-feature carried by the nonfinite INFL constituent *to* is checked against the corresponding [Null] head-feature carried by its PRO subject. In both types of structure, checking involves a spec–head relation (more specifically, a relation between INFL and its specifier), in that the case of the subject is checked by the INFL constituent heading the IP containing the subject. We might suppose that a finite INFL constituent checks nominative case (and so requires a nominative subject), whereas an infinitival INFL checks null case (and so requires a PRO subject).

However, the overall picture is more complicated than this, since some verbs (like those bold-printed in (43–4) below) which take a *to* infinitive complement don't allow their complement to have a PRO subject, and instead require it to have an objective subject like *him*: cf.

(43) (a)   They **believe** [*him* to be wrong]

   (b)   *They **believe** [*PRO* to be wrong]

(44) (a)   They **consider** [*him* to have cheated]

   (b)   *They **consider** [*PRO* to have cheated]

One way of handling the relevant facts is to suppose that the infinitive particle *to* has two different uses. In its use in control structures like (40) above, infinitival *to* checks null case, and so requires a PRO subject with null case. But in its very different use in structures like (43–4), *to* does not check null case and so does not allow a PRO subject. We might further suppose that it is a lexical (i.e. word-specific) property of verbs like *try* that they select (i.e. 'take') an IP complement headed by null-case *to* (i.e. the kind of *to* which can check null case), and conversely a lexical property of verbs like *believe* that they do not. Thus, (40) is grammatical because *try* is a control verb (i.e. the kind of verb which selects an IP complement headed by null-case *to*), and (43b) is ungrammatical because *believe* is not a control verb (and so does not select an IP complement headed by null-case *to*). On this account, verbs like *try* and *believe* differ in their complement-features (more specifically, in respect of whether they do or don't select an infinitive complement headed by null-case *to*). Of course, a second premise of the analysis is that there are two different uses of infinitival *to* – one on which it checks null case, and one on which it does not.

5.8 Objective subjects

As noted in relation to examples like (43–4) above, alongside infinitival IPs with null PRO subjects we also find infinitival IPs with objective subjects like those bracketed in (45) below (where the italicized pronoun is the subject of the bracketed clause):

(45) (a)   They had **expected** [*us* to counterattack]

   (b)   We don't **consider** [*him* to be suitable]

   (c)   He would have **liked** [*me* to reconsider]

   (d)   We are keen **for** [*them* to take part]

An interesting property of IPs with objective subjects is that they occur only as the complement of a transitive verb (like *expect/consider/like*), or of the transitive complementizer *for*. Since transitive verbs and complementizers have the property that they check objective case, it seems reasonable to suppose (for example) that the objective case of *us* is checked by the transitive verb *expected* in (45a), and likewise that the objective case of *them* in (45d) is checked by the transitive complementizer *for*. Such an analysis would correctly predict that sentences such as (46) below are ungrammatical:

(46) (a) *[*Them* to abandon syntax] would be a mistake

(b) *He may be anxious [*them* to make amends]

(c) *Brigadier Blunderbuss gave the order [*them* to cease fire]

This is because in none of the relevant examples is the bracketed infinitive clause the complement of a transitive verb or complementizer: in (46a), the bracketed IP is the subject of *would*; in (46b) it is the complement of the adjective *anxious* (adjectives are intransitive); and in (46c) it is the complement of the noun *order* (nouns too are intransitive).

If what we are suggesting here is along the right lines, it follows that the case of a null PRO subject is checked in a different way from the case of an objective subject. More specifically, the null case of a PRO subject is *internally* checked (from within IP) by the null-case infinitive particle *to*; but the case of an objective subject is *externally* checked (from outside IP) by a transitive matrix verb or complementizer (i.e. by a transitive verb or complementizer which takes the relevant IP as its complement). Since it is exceptional for a subject to have its case externally checked from outside its containing IP, the relevant phenomenon is widely referred to as **exceptional case-marking** (conventionally abbreviated to **ECM**): similarly, an infinitive complement with an objective subject is referred to as an **ECM complement**; and a verb which selects an infinitive complement with an objective subject is referred to as an **ECM verb**. As we shall see, the different ways in which the case properties of null and objective subjects are checked are reflected in systematic asymmetries between control infinitives with PRO subjects and ECM infinitives with objective subjects.

One such asymmetry relates to the behaviour of the relevant complements in active and passive structures. A verb like *decide* (when used as a control verb taking an IP complement headed by null-case *to*) allows a PRO subject irrespective of whether (as in (47a) below) it is used as an active verb or (as in (47b) below) as a passive participle:

(47) (a) They had **decided** [*PRO* to postpone the meeting]

(b) It had been **decided** [*PRO* to postpone the meeting]

By contrast, a verb like *believe* can function as an ECM verb taking an infinitive complement with an objective subject only when used actively (as in (48a) below), not when used passively (as in (48b) below):

(48) (a)   People genuinely **believed** [*him* to be innocent] transitive

      (b)   *It was genuinely **believed** [*him* to be innocent] nontransitive

Why should this be? If (as we suggest) the null case of PRO in control structures like (47) is checked by infinitival *to*, it makes no difference whether the matrix verb *decide* is used in an active or passive form. By contrast, if (as we also suggest) the objective case carried by the subject of an ECM infinitive clause is externally checked by a transitive matrix verb (or complementizer), we correctly predict that only when the matrix verb is used in an active form (and hence is transitive) will it allow an ECM complement with an objective subject – not when used in a passive form (given the traditional assumption that passive participles are intransitive).

A second asymmetry between control infinitives and ECM infinitives relates to adverb position. An adverb modifying a control verb can be positioned between the control verb and its IP complement, as we see from (49) below (where the adverb *hard* modifies the verb *tried*):

(49)   He tried *hard* [PRO to convince her]

By contrast, an adverb modifying an ECM verb cannot be positioned between the ECM verb and its IP complement, as we see from (50) below (where the adverb *sincerely* modifies the verb *believes*):

(50)   *She believes *sincerely* [him to be innocent]

How come? If we suppose that the case of PRO in control structures like (49) is checked by infinitival *to*, we correctly predict that an adverb positioned between the matrix verb and its IP complement will not prevent the case of PRO from being checked. By contrast, if we posit that the case of *him* in (50) is checked by the transitive verb *believes*, we could conjecture that the presence of an intervening adverb between the matrix verb and the objective subject will prevent the objective case of *him* from being checked by the transitive verb *believes*. Since the transitive verb *believes* in (50) does not immediately precede the pronoun *him*, *believes* cannot check the objective case of *him* (with the consequence that the resulting sentence is ungrammatical by virtue of containing an unchecked case-feature).

Independent evidence that intervening adverbs block a verb from checking the objective case of its complement (so that objective case can only be checked by *an immediately preceding transitive head*) comes from contrasts such as the following:

(51) (a)   He plays chess *well*

      (b)   *He plays *well* chess

In (51a), the transitive verb *plays* immediately precedes (and hence can check the objective case carried by) its complement *chess* (which is a DP headed by the null determiner $\emptyset$); however, in (51b), the adverb *well* intervenes between the transitive

195

verb *plays* and its complement *chess*, so that the *strict adjacency* requirement for checking objective case is not met, and case-checking cannot take place (so causing the derivation to crash, since case-features are uninterpretable at LF).

We thus have a substantial body of empirical evidence that the objective case carried by the subject of an ECM infinitive is externally checked from outside the infinitive complement by an immediately preceding transitive matrix verb or complementizer. One consequence of this is that infinitival *to* in ECM structures does not check the objective case carried by the infinitive subject, but rather is a *caseless* particle. If *to* in ECM structures is indeed caseless (and cannot check the case of its subject), it follows that the objective case of an ECM infinitive subject cannot be checked from inside IP by infinitival *to*, and hence (exceptionally) has to be checked from outside IP by an immediately preceding transitive matrix verb or complementizer. By contrast, in *control* structures (as we saw in the previous section) *to* carries a null-case specifier-feature (and hence requires a PRO subject); but in all other uses (e.g. in ECM structures) infinitival *to* functions as a caseless particle which cannot check the case of its subject.

In the light of these observations, let's now consider how we handle the syntax of three different types of verb which take infinitival IP complements. Consider first verbs like *hope* which allow a *to* complement with a PRO subject, but not one with an objective subject like *him*: cf.

(52) (a)   She was hoping [*PRO* to win]
     (b)   *She was hoping [*him* to win]

One way of describing the data in (52) is to specify in the *lexical entry* (i.e. dictionary entry) for *hope* that it is an intransitive verb which selects an infinitival IP headed by null-case *to*; since null-case *to* requires a PRO subject, this accounts for the pattern in (52). An alternative possibility would be to suppose that *hope* selects an IP headed by either type of *to*, but that (by virtue of being intransitive) *hope* can't check the case of an objective subject like *him* in sentences like (52b).

Now consider what we say about verbs like *believe*, which allow an IP complement with an objective subject like *him*, but not one with a PRO subject: cf.

(53) (a)   She believes [*him* to be innocent]
     (b)   *She believes [*PRO* to be innocent]

One way of handling the relevant data is to suppose that *believe* (in this use) is a transitive verb which selects an IP complement headed by caseless *to*: hence, since it doesn't allow an infinitive complement headed by null-case *to*, it doesn't allow a complement with a null-case PRO subject. An alternative possibility would be to posit that *believe* can select an IP complement headed by either kind of *to*, but that it is always transitive when it takes an infinitival IP complement: this will mean that *believe* has to check objective case, and this it clearly cannot do in a structure such as (53b) – at any rate, if we make the plausible assumption that neither infinitival *to* nor *PRO* can carry objective case. (Of course, if the objective case-checking feature carried by *believe* is not checked and erased, it will cause the derivation to crash at LF, since all case-features are uninterpretable.)

Now consider a third class of verbs like *expect* which allow an infinitival IP complement with either a PRO subject or an objective subject: cf.

(54) (a)   She expects [*PRO* to win]
     (b)   She expects [*him* to win]

One way of handling the data would be to suppose that *expect* has a dual use: in sentences like (54a) it is an intransitive verb selecting an IP complement headed by null-case *to*, whereas in sentences such as (54b) it is a transitive verb selecting an IP complement headed by caseless *to*. Another possibility would be simply to say that *expect* can select a complement headed by either kind of *to*, and can be either transitive (and hence carry an objective case-checking feature) or intransitive.

Thus, the analysis of infinitival IPs presented here makes four crucial assumptions: firstly, that there are two different kinds of infinitival *to* (one which checks null case, and another which has no case-checking properties); secondly, that different items select different kinds of infinitive complement (some select an IP headed by null-case *to*, others an IP headed by caseless *to*); thirdly, that some items are transitive (and in the relevant use have to check objective case), others are intransitive, and yet others can be either transitive or intransitive; and fourthly, that the case of an infinitive subject is checked externally (by an immediately preceding transitive matrix verb or complementizer) in structures where it cannot be checked internally.

Summary of this section

If there are indeed two different uses of infinitival *to* (one which checks null case, and another which is caseless), we should expect to find that they differ not only in their case-checking properties, but also in other respects. A number of linguists have suggested that the two different uses of infinitival *to* differ in their *tense* properties (cf. Stowell 1982, Martin 1992, Watanabe 1993, Bošković 1995 and Felser 1995). In this connection, compare the bracketed control infinitive in (55a) below with the bracketed ECM infinitive in (55b):

(55) (a)   Mary hopes [*PRO* to be an actress]
     (b)   He believes [*her* to be an actress]

In (55a), the *to*-clause seems to carry different temporal properties from the *hopes*-clause. (The *hopes*-clause refers to the present whereas the *to*-clause refers to the future – hence (55a) is paraphraseable as 'Mary hopes she will be an actress'.) By contrast, the *to*-clause in (55b) seems to have the same temporal properties as the *believes*-clause (both have present time-reference, as we see from the fact that (55b) can be paraphrased as 'He believes that she is an actress'). More generally, we might suggest that *to* in control infinitives has tense properties independent of those in the matrix clause (Stowell 1982 notes that *to* in control infinitives often has future time-reference), whereas *to* in ECM infinitives has tense properties determined by (and typically simultaneous with) those of the matrix clause. If this is so, there is a correlation between the tense properties of infinitival *to* and its case-checking properties, in that *to* only checks null case in (control) structures where it has independent tense properties. However, the proposed correlation between the tense and case properties of *to* is far from unproblematic (e.g. it is not clear that *to* has different tense properties in (54a) from those which it has in (54b)), so we shall not pursue this matter any further here.

To summarize: we have suggested in this section that infinitive complements with objective subjects are IPs headed by caseless *to*, and that consequently the objective case of the subject can only be checked from outside IP by an immediately preceding transitive matrix verb or complementizer. We shall return in chapter 10 to consider the precise way in which the exceptional objective case carried by the subject of an ECM infinitive is checked, so for the time being we shall have no more to say about it here.

5.9   Bare phrase structure

We end this chapter with some speculative remarks about phrase structure. Within the framework used so far, a sentence such as *She has gone* will have the grammatical structure (5) above, repeated as (56) below:

(56)

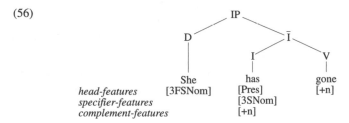

However, there is a potential notational inconsistency here, in that the categorial properties of words are represented by category labels attached to terminal nodes, whereas other grammatical properties of words are represented by sets of features attached to the words themselves. For example, the fact that *she* has the categorial status of a determiner is indicated by the label D attached to the terminal node carrying the word *she*, whereas the fact that *she* is third person feminine singular nominative is indicated by the bracketed [3FSNom] head-features carried by *she*.

One way of eliminating this notational inconsistency would be to incorporate the categorial properties of words into the head-features of the relevant items. This would mean that terminal nodes would no longer carry category labels. In the true minimalist spirit (seeking to get rid of all redundant apparatus), we might then go further and ask whether the category labels carried by nonterminal nodes should also be eliminated.

Perhaps (as suggested by Chomsky 1995a, 1995b) the only information which we need about the constituents represented by nonterminal nodes is what is the head of each such constituent. One way of providing this information would be for nonterminal nodes to carry an indication of which item is the head of the relevant constituent – as in (57) below (where the [D] head-feature of *she* indicates its categorial status as a determiner, the [I] head-feature of *has* indicates its categorial status as an auxiliary and the [V] head-feature of *gone* indicates its categorial status as a verb):

(57)

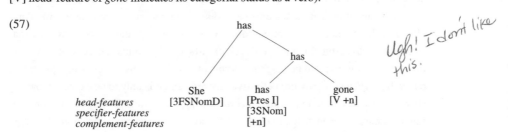

Ugh! I don't like this.

head-features	She [3FSNomD]	has [Pres I] [3SNom] [+n]	gone [V +n]
specifier-features			
complement-features			

A structure like (57) tells us that *has gone* and *she has gone* are both projections of *has*.

What our discussion here illustrates is that the **economy principle** (which proscribes the use of superfluous symbols in structural representations) leads us to question whether category labels play an essential role in syntactic representations, or whether they are superfluous because the information which they encode is redundant. Of course, we might go even further than in (57) and question whether nonterminal nodes need to carry any labels at all, or whether structure can't simply be represented in terms of unlabelled tree diagrams such as (58) below:

(58)

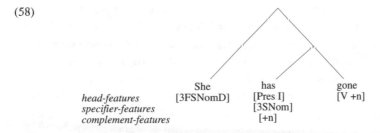

head-features	She [3FSNomD]	has [Pres I] [3SNom] [+n]	gone [V +n]
specifier-features			
complement-features			

We might argue that the fact that *has gone* is a projection of *has* (not of *gone*) is predictable from the lexical entries for the relevant items: that for *has* tells us that it takes an *n*-participle complement, and that for *gone* does not allow for it to take an auxiliary as its specifier. Similarly, we might argue that the fact that *she has gone* is not a projection of *she* follows from the fact that *she* does not allow a complement of any kind.

An interesting question which arises in the wake of the *bare phrase structure* model proposed by Chomsky relates to the question of whether (if nodes no longer carry labels such as X/X̄/XP) the distinction between an XP (i.e. a phrase) and an X (i.e. a head/word) can be defined in purely structural terms or not: in this connection, it is interesting to note that Carnie (1995, chapter 6) argues that indefinite complex nominal predicates in Irish (e.g. the Irish counterpart of the bold-printed string in *John is a big man*) behave like heads rather than phrases in respect of their syntax (though their English counterparts behave like phrases rather than heads).

As is all too apparent from our discussion here, many key theoretical questions remain unresolved for the moment; and indeed it must be apparent that many of the descriptive assumptions we have made in our exposition here are also questionable (e.g. the assumption that the features carried by *n/ing*-participles are purely formal and play no role in semantic interpretation). To a large extent, this reflects the fact that research in **checking theory** is only in its infancy. The initial success of any new research paradigm should be judged in terms of whether it raises interesting questions, rather than whether it provides definitive answers; and it is only to be expected that the answers to many descriptive and theoretical questions must await the outcome of future research. Given that the eventual outcome of questions about node labels is uncertain, we shall continue to use traditional trees (in which each node carries an appropriate category label) throughout the rest of the book – but the potential redundancy embodied in such conventional tree diagrams should be apparent.

5.10 Summary

In this chapter, we have discussed how the grammatical features carried by words are checked. In §5.2 we suggested that the phonetic, grammatical and semantic properties of words can be described in terms of sets of features. We argued that grammars generate two types of structural representation for sentences – a PF representation (a representation of their phonetic form) and an LF representation (a representation of their logical form). We noted that the **principle of full interpretation** requires that PF representations should contain only phonetic features, and that LF representations should contain only semantic features; a derivation which satisfies this requirement *converges*, whereas one which does not *crashes*. We noted that some grammatical features (e.g. the person/number/gender-features of pronouns like *she*) have semantic content and so are interpretable (at LF), whereas others (e.g. the case-features of pronouns and the inflectional features of nonfinite verbs) are uninterpretable and so must be erased in the course of the derivation (in order to ensure that they do not appear in LF representations). In §5.3 we argued that words carry three sets of grammatical features: *head-features* (which determine their intrinsic grammatical properties), *specifier-features* (which determine the kinds of specifier which they allow) and *complement-features* (which determine the kinds of complement they can take): so, for example, the head-features of perfective *has* indicate that it is a present-tense form, its specifier-features indicate that it requires a third person singular nominative subject and its complement-features indicate that it requires an *n*-participle complement. We suggested that specifier- and complement-features (as well as those head-features which are purely formal and hence have no semantic content) are uninterpretable, and so must be erased by a process of *checking*. For example, in a sentence such as *She has gone* the [3SNom] specifier-features of *has* (requiring it to have a third person singular nominative subject) are checked against the corresponding head-features of *she*, and thereby erased; similarly, the [+n] complement-feature of *has* (requiring it to have an *n*-participle complement) is checked against the corresponding head-feature of *gone*, and both [+n] features thereby erased. The grammatical features which survive at LF (after checking) are thus the interpretable [3FS] 'third person feminine singular' head-features of *she* and the [Pres] 'present-tense' head-feature of *has*. In §5.4 we looked at how checking works in structures containing a phrasal specifier or complement, and argued that it is in the nature of the *merger* process by which phrases are formed that projections carry the same head-features as their heads: hence in a sentence such as *They are getting old*, the requirement for *are* to have an *ing*-complement is satisfied by virtue of the fact that its VP complement *getting old* is a projection of the *ing*-verb *getting*, and hence is an *ing*-projection. In §5.5 we discussed the problems posed by finite nonauxiliary verbs like *hates* in *She hates syntax*, noting that the [3SNom] specifier-features of *hates* cannot be checked directly against the head-features of *she* because the two are contained in different phrases (*hates* being the head V of VP, and *she* being the specifier of IP). We suggested that one way of resolving the problem would be to suppose that the specifier-features of a finite nonauxiliary verb *percolate* from V to INFL, so that the head-features of the subject *she* can then be checked against the specifier-features of INFL (inherited from the verb *hates*). We also argued that the head-features (i.e. tense specification) of finite nonauxiliary verbs also percolate up to INFL, in order to ensure that INFL has tense properties and so is interpretable at LF. This means that INFL will acquire the present-tense head-feature of *hates* in *She hates syntax*, thereby accounting for the fact that the sentence is tagged by a present-tense auxiliary (cf. *She hates him, **doesn't** she?*). In §5.6 we discussed how the features carried by determiners, attributive adjectives and nouns are checked. We suggested that determiners like *the* (and the null quantifier ∅) carry fixed person properties (in that they are third person determiners), but variable number and case properties, so that (for example) *the* is third person nominative plural in a sentence like *The students are revolting*, but third person objective singular in a sentence like *Sack the Dean!* We suggested that one way of ensuring that determiners and attributive adjectives agree in number with the nouns they modify (e.g. in structures like *these numerous allegations*) would be to suppose that the number-feature carried by the noun percolates up to the head F constituent of the FP containing the adjective, and from there to the head D constituent of DP. We noted that while determiners carry case in English (overtly in the case of pronominal determiners like *I/me*, covertly in the case of prenominal determiners like *the*), it is unclear whether attributive adjectives and nouns carry covert case properties in English. In §5.7 we noted Chomsky and Lasnik's suggestion that PRO carries null case, and that its case is checked by infinitival *to* (so that PRO carries a null-case head-feature, and infinitival *to* carries a null-case specifier-feature in the relevant type of infinitive structure). In §5.8 we looked at the syntax of *exceptional case-marking* (= ECM) structures containing an infinitival IP with an objective subject. We argued that the infinitival IP in such structures is headed by a caseless infinitive particle, and that the objective case carried by the infinitive subject is checked by an immediately preceding transitive matrix verb or complementizer. In §5.9, we noted that the category labels carried by terminal nodes (i.e. heads) in tree diagrams can be eliminated if the relevant categorial properties are instead described in terms of head-features. We went on to speculate that the category labels carried by nonterminal nodes (i.e. intermediate and phrasal projections) might also be eliminated (by virtue of being redundant), so enabling us to develop a system of *bare phrase structure* in which syntactic structure is represented by *unlabelled* tree diagrams (i.e. tree diagrams in which nodes carry no category labels).

Workbook section

Exercise I (§§5.2–5.4)

Draw tree diagrams representing the grammatical structure of the following sentences, and say how the features carried by each of the words in each sentence are checked.

1   I helped him
2   She helps them
3   It may help him
4   They had helped us
5   You were helping me
6   We have been helping her
7   This could have helped you
8   He might be helping them
9   Someone must have been helping her
10   She might have been being blackmailed

Model answer for 1

Given the assumptions made in the text, 1 will have the grammatical structure (i) below:

(i)

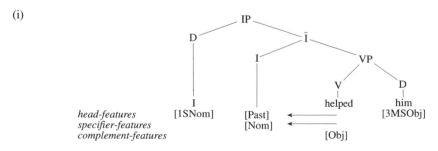

The verb *helped* (being transitive) carries an [Obj] objective-case complement-feature: this is checked against the matching objective-case head-feature carried by *him*, and both objective features are thereby erased. The [Past] head-feature of *helped* (indicating that it is a past-tense form) percolates up to INFL, in order to ensure LF convergence (i.e. in order to ensure that INFL has tense properties and so is interpretable at LF). The [Nom] specifier-feature of *helped* (indicating that it requires a nominative subject) also percolates up to INFL, and there checks the [Nom] head-feature carried by *I*, resulting in the erasure of both [Nom] case-features, since case-features are uninterpretable at LF. The grammatical features which survive into LF are those in (ii) below (all of which are interpretable head-features):

(ii)

```
            IP
        /        \
       D          Ī
       |        /    \
       |       I      VP
       |       |     /   \
       I       |    V     D
      [1S]  [Past] helped him
                          [3MS]
```

Since all features in (ii) are interpretable, the derivation satisfies the **principle of full interpretation** and converges at LF.

Exercise II (§§5.2–5.4) ~~looked at~~ in class

The sentences below (based on examples given in Miller 1989 and Brown 1991) illustrate some of the ways in which modals can be used in Scottish English:

have double modals

1 They might can come
2 He should can do it
3 He'll can help us
4 You'll have to can drive a car
5 They might could be working
6 I would like to could swim
7 I would have could have done it
8 He would could do it
9 He'll might can go to the disco
10 He'll should can find her
11 He'll might could do it
12 You might would like to come with us
13 You might should claim your expenses

(handwritten annotations)
He should do it.

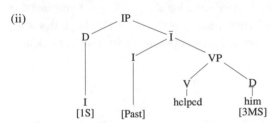

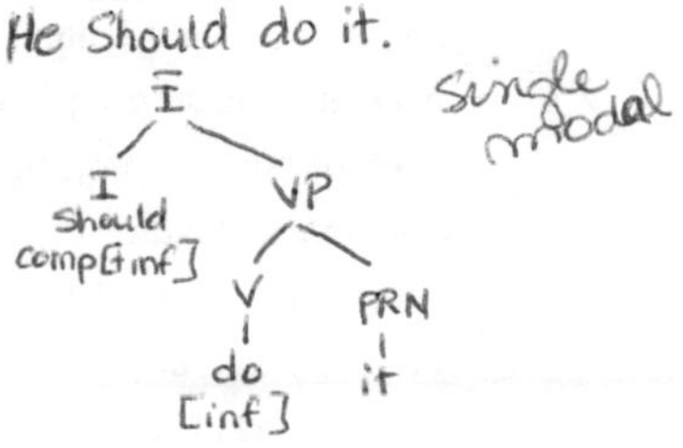

#2 Should & can could both be I's but will have other features left over.

or can make should can be 1 modal.

Comment on the ways in which the morphosyntax of Scottish modals differs from that of their Standard English counterparts.

Model answer for 1

The complement-features of the modal *might* in Standard English require it to have an infinitival complement (i.e. a complement headed by an auxiliary or nonauxiliary verb in the infinitive form). It is a morphological property of modals in Standard English that they have no infinitive form (cf. **I would like to can speak French*). It follows, therefore, that Standard English does not allow double-modal strings (i.e. strings in which one modal auxiliary is used as the complement of another). The fact that double-modal strings such as *might can* occur in Scots suggests either that modals have different complement-selection properties in Scots, or that they have different morphological properties. Pursuing the second possibility, we could suggest that modals in Scots serve not only as finite forms but also as infinitive forms, and that the form *can* in 1 is used as an infinitive, paraphraseable as 'be able to'. If this is so, 1 will have the morphosyntactic structure (i) below (where Mod = modal, and ModP = modal phrase):

(i)

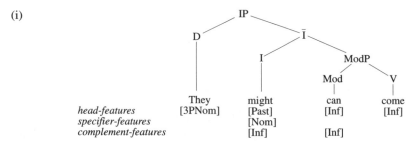

	They	might	can	come
head-features	[3PNom]	[Past]	[Inf]	[Inf]
specifier-features		[Nom]		
complement-features		[Inf]	[Inf]	

The [Nom] specifier-feature of *might* (requiring it to have a nominative specifier) and the corresponding [Nom] head-feature of *they* are erased under checking: similarly, the [Inf] complement-feature of *might* (requiring it to have an infinitive complement) is checked against the [Inf] head-feature which its complement *can come* carries by virtue of being a projection of *can*, and both [Inf] features erased; likewise, the [Inf] complement-feature of *can* (requiring it too to have an infinitive complement) is checked against the [Inf] head-feature of *come*, and both [Inf] features erased. So, after checking, the only features which survive at LF are the [3P] head-features of *they* and the [Past] head-feature of *might*. Since these are interpretable features, the derivation converges at LF.

Exercise III (§§5.2–5.5)

Discuss how the features of each of the words in the following Jamaican Creole sentences (adapted from Bailey 1966) are checked:

1   Dem en si we
        them been see we
        'They saw us'

2   Im a kom
    him are come
    'He/she/it is coming'

3   Dem ena kos mi (*ena = en+a* = 'been + are')
    them been+are curse me
    'They were cursing me'

4   Yu shudn en tel dem
    you shouldn't been tell them
    'You shouldn't have told them'

5   Im shuda en a ron
    him should been are run
    'He should have been running'

6   Im wuda mos hafi priti (*hafi = ha+fi* = 'have + for')
    him would must have+for pretty
    'She would have to (be) pretty'

7   Mi en nuo se im wudn kom
    me been know say him wouldn't come
    'I knew that he wouldn't come'

8   Mi miin se yu fi go
    me mean say you for go
    'I mean that you should go'

9   Mi waan yu fi sel i
    me want you for sell it
    'I want you to sell it'

10   Im waan fi haid dem
    him want for hide them
    'He wants to hide them'

11   Yu fi tikya dem
    you for take-care them
    'You should be wary of them'

Model answer for 1

  As noted in the text, both pronouns and verbs in Jamaican Creole (= JC) are invariable (uninflected) forms: there is thus no overt morphological marking of the distinction between (for example) nominative and objective pronouns, or finite and non-finite verb forms. Since verbs don't inflect for tense, past tense is indicated by the use of the past-tense auxiliary *en* (cognate with English *been*, but used with roughly the same sense as English *did*). If we adopt a radically minimalist view of JC, we can suggest that the specifier- and complement-features of verbs and auxiliaries pick out *categorial* rather than *morphological* properties: e.g. finite verbs simply require a D-projection as their subject (i.e. a D or DP) rather than a nominative subject, and transitive verbs require a D-projection as their complement rather than an objective complement. On this (minimalist) view, 1 would have the morphosyntactic structure (i) below:

(i)

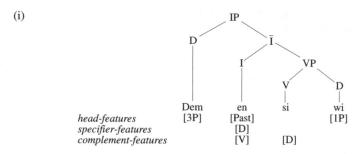

	head-features	Dem [3P]	en [Past]	si	wi [1P]
	specifier-features		[D]		
	complement-features		[V]	[D]	

The bracketed head-features indicate that *dem* is third person plural, *en* is past tense and *wi* is first person plural. (The categorial head-features of the words are indicated by their category labels.) The [D] specifier-feature of *en* (indicating that it requires a subject which is a projection of the category D) can be checked and erased, because its subject *dem* belongs to the category D. The [V] complement-feature of *en* (requiring it to have a complement which is a projection of the category V) can be checked and erased because its complement is the VP [*si wi*], and this is headed by the V *si*. The [D] complement-feature of *see* (requiring it to have a complement which is headed by the category D) can be checked and erased because its complement is the D *wi*. So, checking yields the LF representation (ii) below:

(ii)

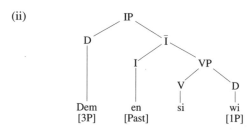

Since the only surviving grammatical features are interpretable head-features, (ii) satisfies the **principle of full interpretation**, so the derivation converges at LF.

If the analysis in (i–ii) above is along the right lines, it suggests that all head-features in JC are interpretable (e.g. there are no uninterpretable case-features or agreement-features), and that all specifier- and complement-features are purely categorial in nature. However, this analysis may be oversimplistic in that it ignores the distinction between overt pronouns like *mi* 'me' and the covert pronoun PRO. It may be that rather than say that JC has *no* case-system, we should instead say that it has a two-way distinction between *overt* case and *covert/null* case, so (for example) *mi* 'me' carries overt case, and PRO carries null case. Since the distinction between overt and covert forms is one which is visible in the PF component (because overt items have phonetic features, but covert items do not), we might argue that the *overt/covert* distinction is the minimal case distinction we should expect to find in any language.

Helpful hints

The form *ena* glossed as 'were' is composed of the past-tense auxiliary *en* 'been' and the progressive auxiliary *a* 'are'; treat them as separate words heading separate projections in the syntax. (They subsequently fuse together to become a single word in the PF component, we might suppose.) Although *fi* is cognate with English *for*, assume that in JC its function is more akin to that of the English infinitive particle *to*: likewise, assume that the form *hafi* is composed of the verb *ha* 'have' and the infinitive particle *fi* 'for', and that they are separate words heading separate projections in the syntax (subsequently fusing together to form a single word in the PF component). Recall from §2.9 that adjectives have verblike properties in JC (e.g. they can serve as predicates, occur as the complement of a modal, etc.). The word *se* (cognate with English *say*) is generally assumed to serve as a complementizer (corresponding roughly to English *that*) in JC.

Exercise IV (§§5.2–5.5)

The utterances below (edited in minor ways) were produced by children acquiring English as their native language (the names of the children producing the examples are given in parentheses, together with their age in *years;months* at the point when the examples were produced). Comment on the nature of errors made by the children in the way they use auxiliaries.

1   Don't fighting me! (Adam 2;7)
2   I can building a tower with you (Peter 3;0)
3   He doesn't likes to be unhappy (Ross 3;0)
4   She won't makes me (Adam 4;7)
5   That didn't went down (Peter 2;10)
6   We didn't saw cartoons (Sarah 4;2)
7   Marky could have went to school (Ross 4;8)
8   You should saw it! (Sarah 4;8)
9   He was cried (Nina 2;6 = 'He was crying')
10   He will wound it up (Sarah 4;11)
11   My tummy will fell off (Mark 3;1)
12   This one doesn't fell down either (Peter 2;10)

Model answer for 1

Auxiliaries in adult English have complement-features which determine the range of complements which they allow. For example, the dummy auxiliary *do* (here used in its negative imperative form *don't!*) has the complement-feature [Inf], and so requires an infinitive complement (i.e. a complement headed by a verb which carries the head-feature [Inf]). However, the complement of *don't* in 1 is a verb (*fighting*) in the *ing*-participle form, suggesting that Adam has not mastered the complement-features of auxiliaries as yet. This is consistent with the suggestion made in the text that children have problems in acquiring uninterpretable features, and that the inflectional features of nonfinite verbs are purely formal (hence uninterpretable, and therefore difficult to acquire). In this particular case, it may be that Adam has confused the negative imperative *don't!* with its positive imperative synonym *stop!* (cf. *Stop fighting me!*).

Exercise V (§5.7)

Discuss the derivation of the following sentences, drawing tree diagrams to illustrate your answers.

1a They had planned to escape
 b *They had planned him to escape (intended as synonymous with 'They had planned that he should escape')
2a They want to leave
 b They want him to leave
3a She seems keen for them to participate
 b *She seems keen for to participate
4a He received a request to help the refugees
 b *He received a request they to help the refugees
5a It was agreed to review the policy
 b *It was agreed them to review the policy
6a Congress decided to ratify the treaty
 b *Congress decided for the president to ratify the treaty
7a We consider him to be right
 b *We consider to be right (intended as synonymous with 'We consider ourselves to be right')
8a He felt himself to be ageing
 b *He felt himself was ageing
9a You must let yourself have a break
 b *You must let have a break (intended as synonymous with 9a)
10a For him to resign would be disastrous
 b *He/*Him to resign would be disastrous

Pay particular attention to how grammatical properties of subjects are checked.

Model answer for 1

Given the IP analysis of subjectless infinitive complements presented in the text of this chapter and the last, (1a–b) will have the respective syntactic structures (ia–b) below:

(i)

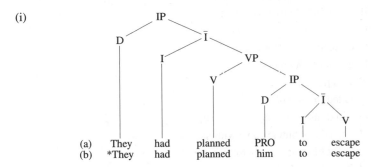

(a)	They	had	planned	PRO	to	escape
(b)	*They	had	planned	him	to	escape

In the text, we suggested that infinitival *to* can function either as a null-case particle or as a caseless particle, and that some verbs select an IP complement headed by null-case *to*, and others select a complement headed by caseless *to*. On the basis of data like 1, we might suppose that it is a lexical (= word-specific) property of the verb *plan* (when used with an infinitive complement) that it is an intransitive verb which selects an IP headed by null-case *to*, but not an IP headed by caseless *to*. If so, the null-case head-feature carried by PRO will be checked against the null-case specifier-feature of *to* in (i)(a), with both case-features thereby being erased. Example (i)(b) will be ungrammatical because the null-case specifier-feature of *to* is incompatible with the objective-case head-feature of *him*, with the result that both case-features remain unchecked and cause the derivation to crash at LF (since case-features are uninterpretable).

Evidence that the null case carried by PRO is checked by the infinitive particle *to* (rather than by the verb *planned*) comes from the fact that even when used as a passive participle, the verb *planned* still allows an IP complement with a PRO subject: cf.

(ii)   It had been planned [PRO to escape]

Moreover, an adverb modifying *plan* can freely be positioned between *plan* and its complement: cf.

(iii)   They had planned meticulously [PRO to escape]

In these respects, *plan* behaves like a typical control verb, and unlike an ECM verb.

Exercise VI (§5.7)

The following examples (cf. Henry 1995) illustrate infinitive constructions with *for* found in (one variety of) Belfast English:

1 [For him to win] would be amazing
2 [For to win] would be amazing
3 Mary seems keen [for them to come]
4 Mary seems keen [for to come]
5 I tried [for to get them]
6 *I tried [for him to get them]
7 I wanted [for to go]
8 I wanted [him for to come with me]
9 *I wanted [for him to come with me]
10 I wanted [them definitely for to be there]
11 I believe [them for to have done it]
12 *I believe [for them to have done it]
13 *I believe [for to have done it]
14 *I don't know [whether for to go]

Discuss the syntax of the bracketed infinitive complement in each of these examples, paying particular attention to the morphosyntax of its subject.

Model answer for 1 and 2

Sentence 1 would seem to have essentially the same structure (i) below as its Standard English counterpart:

(i)

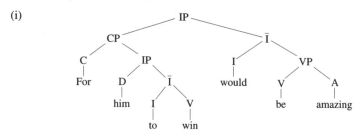

We might suppose that (as in Standard English) *for* takes an IP complement headed by caseless *to*, and that the objective-case head-feature of *him* is checked by the immediately preceding transitive complementizer *for*.

At first sight, it would seem as if 2 has much the same structure as (i), save that the infinitive subject is PRO rather than *him*. If this were so, 2 would have the structure (ii) below:

(ii)

```
                        ___IP___
                   ____/        \____
                  CP                  Ī
              ___/  \___          ___/ \___
             C        IP         I'        VP
             |      __/\__       |       __/ \__
            For    D      Ī    would    V       A
                   |     / \            |       |
                  PRO   I   V           be   amazing
                        |   |
                        to  win
```

We could then say that *for* in Belfast English (unlike Standard English) can serve as an intransitive head taking an IP complement headed by null-case *to*, and that the null case of PRO is checked by infinitival *to*.

However, an alternative possibility is to suppose that (via a process of cliticization similar to that by which *want to* becomes *wanna*) *forto* has become a compound infinitive particle in Belfast English, with a syntax similar to that of Standard English *to*. On this alternative analysis, 2 would have the very different structure (iii) below:

(iii)

```
                      ___IP___
                 ____/        \____
                IP                  Ī
            ___/  \___          ___/ \___
           D         Ī         I'        VP
           |       __/\__      |       __/ \__
          PRO     I      V   would    V       A
                  |      |            |       |
                forto   win           be   amazing
```

If we assume that *forto* in (iii) has essentially the same case properties as Standard English null-case *to*, it can check the case of a null PRO subject. One potential complication with this analysis is that we need to account for the fact that *forto* isn't used in infinitive structures like 1 which are introduced by the infinitival complementizer *for*, as we see from the ungrammaticality of:

(iv)   *[For him forto win] would be amazing

However, this can be accounted for if we suppose that overt complementizers in Belfast English require an IP complement headed by *to*, not by *forto* (so that *forto* only occurs in IP infinitives, not in CP infinitives).

> *Helpful hint*
>
> Consider the possibility that *whether* functions as an interrogative complementizer in Belfast English (even though it isn't a complementizer in Standard English).

TURN IN

Exercise VII (§§5.2–5.8)

Discuss the morphosyntax of the following utterances produced by a boy called Knox at age 3;6 (= 3 years 6 months):

1   I be a lion
2   I got my coke
3   I got you coke (= 'I got your coke')
4   She drink she bottle
5   She don't pick she food (= 'She shouldn't pick at her food')
6   We got we drink
7   Him don't want it
8   Him need sit down (= 'He needs to sit down')
9   Him hasn't got him supper, he haven't
10   Me can mix it
11   She said she want the net
12   I don't want she help me

Helpful hints

In the text, we didn't discuss how genitive case is checked. For the purpose of this exercise, make the following assumptions. Just as nominative case is associated with the specifier of a functional head (INFL) which is often null, so too genitive case (in adult English) is associated with the specifier of a null determiner constituent. More concretely, assume that the bracketed DPs in sentences such as:

(i)   (a)   It may be faster than [*my* car], but [*mine*] has more class
      (b)   [*The queen's* car] is faster than [*the king's*]

have the respective structures indicated in (ii) below (where *e* is an empty category whose antecedent is the noun *car*):

(ii)

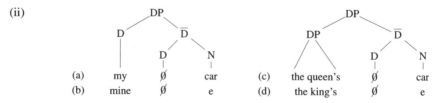

Assume that the null determiner Ø has the specifier-feature [Gen], and so requires a specifier with genitive case – i.e. a genitive determiner like *my/mine*, or a genitive DP like *the queen's/the king's* (carrying the genitive suffix *'s*).

Model answer for 9

In the text, we suggested that children have problems in acquiring the morphosyntax of uninterpretable features (e.g. the case-features of pronouns, and the agreement-features of finite verbs and auxiliaries). The fact that Knox uses *him* as the subject of *hasn't* in 9 suggests that he hasn't yet fully acquired the specifier-features of finite verbs: he seems to think that finite verbs allow either a nominative or an objective subject (and some children also use genitive subjects: cf. *My did get my leg dry*, produced by a girl called Betty at age 2;6). The fact that Knox uses *he* as the subject of *haven't* may suggest that he analyses forms like *haven't* as imposing no person/number restrictions on their choice of specifier (like adult modals); by contrast, in adult English, *have(n't)* allows only a first person, second person or plural subject). It may well be that *s*-inflected forms are correctly specified for agreement (e.g. forms like *has*, *wants*, etc. are only used with third person singular subjects), but that uninflected forms like *have*, *want*, etc. are unspecified for agreement (i.e. they carry no agreement features, and so impose no person/number restrictions on their choice of subject).

The use of the objective pronoun *him* in *him supper* (where adult English would require the genitive form *his*) might be accounted for along similar lines. Assuming the analysis in the *helpful hints*, *him supper* will have the structure (i) below·

(i)

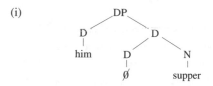

We could then say that Knox hasn't yet mastered the specifier-features of the null possessive determiner ∅, since he allows it to have an objective specifier like *him* (whereas adults require a genitive specifier like *his*). It may be that Knox assumes that ∅ has the categorial specifier-feature [D], and so allows a specifier which is a D-projection, irrespective of whether it has nominative, objective, genitive or even null case: this would lead us to expect that Knox alternates between e.g. *Teddy eat he dinner*, *Teddy eat him dinner*, *Teddy eat his dinner* and perhaps even *Teddy eat PRO dinner*.

At any rate, what our analysis here suggests is that children like Knox have problems in acquiring the specifier-features of items (viz. the case and agreement restrictions which finite verbs and auxiliaries impose on their choice of specifier, and the case restrictions which the possessive determiner ∅ imposes on its choice of specifier). More generally, it would seem that such items are *underspecified* with respect to their specifier-features at the relevant stage of development.

Exercise VIII (§§5.2–5.8)

The following sentences produced by SLI children (i.e. children suffering from *specific language impairment*) show a number of grammatical errors (the data are adapted from Gopnik and Crago 1991, Bishop 1994 and Schaeffer 1994):

1 Him want some
2 Me want a cookie
3 I eats an apple
4 I am go
5 Carol is cry in the church
6 He didn't took his ladder
7 A Patrick is naughty
8 He sawed mine brother
9 He take Bernard teddy
10 My sister use my dad car

Discuss the nature of the errors made by SLI children.

Helpful hints
See those for the previous exercise.

Model answer for 1
 The verb *want* might be argued to be a present-tense form here (since it lacks the past-tense suffix +*d*); however, it lacks the third person singular agreement suffix +*s* required in Standard English. The pronoun *him* in 1 carries objective case, though the corresponding Standard English sentence *He wants some* would require a nominative subject. This might suggest that SLI children simply confuse nominative and objective pronouns: however, this is not entirely true, since Bishop notes that only objective pronouns are used as complements of transitive verbs, never nominative pronouns. Thus, SLI children make errors with the case of subjects, but not with the case of complements. One way of accounting for both the agreement error and the case error in 1 is to suppose that the child concerned has not yet mastered the specifier-features of finite verb forms like *want*, and assumes that they impose no person/number restrictions on their choice of subject, and allow a subject with variable (nominative or objective) case properties. This would mean that 1 would have the grammatical structure (i) below:

(i)

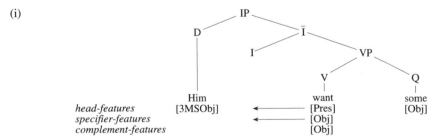

The head-features in (i) indicate that *him* is a third person masculine singular objective pronoun, *want* is a present-tense verb and *some* is an objective pronominal quantifier (as used here). The [Obj] specifier-feature of *want* indicates that it allows an objective subject; its [Obj] complement-feature indicates that it takes an objective complement. The [Obj] complement-feature of *want* can be checked against the [Obj] head-feature of *some*, with both case-features being erased in consequence. The head- and specifier-features of *want* percolate up from V to I, as indicated by the arrows in (i). Percolation of the [Pres] head-feature of *want* from V to INFL ensures that INFL carries a tense-feature, and so is interpretable at LF. Once the [Obj] specifier-feature of *want* percolates to INFL, it can be checked against the [Obj] objective-case head-feature of *him*, resulting in the erasure of both case-features. Thus, the only grammatical features which survive at LF are those indicated below:

(ii)

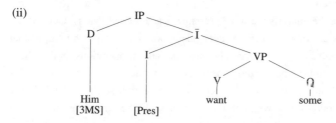

Since the surviving grammatical features are all interpretable, (ii) converges at LF.

On this view, the major deficit in the SLI child's grammar in respect of sentences like 1 relates to the specifier-features of finite verbs like *want*. In English, a present-tense form like *want* requires a nominative subject which is first person, second person, or plural (i.e. which is not third person singular). The child has thus not yet mastered the case/person/number specifier-features of uninflected finite verb forms. It may be that the child's initial hypothesis is that only verbs which carry overt agreement inflections impose person/number restrictions on their choice of subject: by contrast, in Standard English, the present-tense form *want* contains a null agreement inflection which requires a first or second person or plural nominative subject. Since specifier-features are uninterpretable, the more general conclusion we reach is that SLI children have problems in acquiring uninterpretable features.

6

Head movement

6.1 Overview

So far, the analysis we have presented has assumed that syntactic structures are derived by a series of binary **merger** operations. We now go on to argue that
derivations may involve not only merger, but also **movement** operations. In this chapter, we look at two similar types of movement operation, one which affects auxiliaries
in Modern English, and another which affected verbs in earlier stages of English. We
shall argue that both types of movement involve essentially the same **head movement**
operation, involving movement from one head position to another. We begin by looking at the syntax of so-called *auxiliary inversion* in English.

6.2 Auxiliary inversion

In chapters 3–5, we saw that complementizers are positioned in front of
subjects in the clauses they introduce. More specifically, we suggested that complementizers head a separate layer of functional superstructure in clauses, which we
termed a *complementizer phrase* (= CP), with the head C (= COMP) position of CP
being filled by complementizers like *that/for/if*. However, complementizers are not the
only kinds of constituent which can precede subjects in clauses. After all, in our brief
discussion of *auxiliary inversion* in §1.6, we saw that auxiliaries can also precede subjects in inversion structures (e.g. in yes–no questions such as *Can you help me?*). In
this respect, inverted auxiliaries seem to resemble complementizers – as the following
(love-struck, soap-operesque) dialogue illustrates:

(1)   SPEAKER A: Honey-buns, there's something I wanted to ask you

                SPEAKER B: What, sweetie-pie?

                SPEAKER A: **If you will marry me**

                SPEAKER B: (*pretending not to hear*): What d'you say, darlin'?

                SPEAKER A: **Will you marry me?**

What's the structure of the two bold(-printed) proposals which speaker A makes in (1)? The answer is straightforward enough in the case of *If you will marry me*: it's a clause introduced by the complementizer *if*, and so is a CP (complementizer phrase) constituent, with the structure (2) below:

(2)

```
              CP
          /        \
       C            IP
       |         /      \
       if      D          Ī
               |       /      \
              you     I        VP
                      |       /    \
                     will   V       D
                            |       |
                          marry    me
```

But now consider the more problematic question of the structure of the second proposal, *Will you marry me?* Here we have an auxiliary inversion structure, in which the auxiliary *will* appears in front of the subject *you*. What position is being occupied by the inverted auxiliary *will*? Since *will* appears to occupy the same presubject position that the complementizer *if* occupies in (2), a natural suggestion to make is that the inverted auxiliary actually occupies the head C position of CP. If this is so, then we'd expect to find that *will* and *if* are mutually exclusive (on the assumption that we can only insert *one* word in a given head position like C, not *two* words): in other words, if both complementizers and inverted auxiliaries occupy the head C position of CP, we'd expect to find that a clause can be introduced *either* by a complementizer *or* by a preposed auxiliary – but not by the two together. This is indeed the case, as we see from the ungrammaticality of speaker B's reply in (3) below:

(3)   SPEAKER A: What d'you want to ask me?
        SPEAKER B: ***If** *will* you marry me

The fact that no clause can contain both a complementizer and an inverted auxiliary provides us with strong empirical evidence that inverted auxiliaries occupy the same structural position as complementizers – i.e. that both occupy the head COMP position in CP.

But how can it be that a finite auxiliary (which normally occupies the head INFL position within IP) comes to be positioned in the head COMP position of CP? The answer provided by descriptive grammarians is that auxiliaries move out of their normal postsubject position into presubject position, by an operation traditionally referred to as *inversion*. In terms of the framework being used here, this would mean that an inverted auxiliary moves from the head I position in IP into the head C position in CP, as in (4) below:

(4)

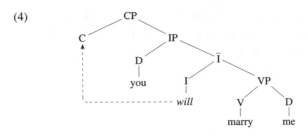

This type of *inversion* operation involves movement of a word from the head position in one phrase into the head position in another phrase (in this case, from the head I position of IP into the head C position of CP), and so is known more generally as **head-to-head movement** (or **head movement**).

An obvious question which is begged by the head movement analysis is *why* auxiliaries should undergo inversion in questions. Using a metaphor developed by Chomsky (1995c), let's say that COMP in an interrogative clause is a **strong** head, and that a strong head has to be filled. In a complement-clause yes–no question like that bracketed below, COMP can be filled by the complementizer *if*:

(5)   He asked [*if* I would marry him]

(Speaker A's first proposal in (1) can be regarded as an elliptical form of *I wanted to ask you **if you will marry me***, with *if* introducing the bold-printed complement clause.) However, complementizers can't be used to introduce main clauses in English, so some other way has to be found of filling the strong COMP node in main-clause questions. A strong COMP node has the power to lure an auxiliary from INFL to COMP (as in (4) above), thereby satisfying the requirement for a strong COMP to be filled.

The assumption that some categories are **strong** (and conversely others are **weak**) provides us with an interesting account of an otherwise puzzling property of questions in English – namely the fact that the question counterpart of a statement which contains no auxiliary requires the use of the (dummy or expletive) auxiliary *do*, as we can see from sentences such as the following:

(6) (a)   They know him
     (b)   *Do* they know him?

Why should this be? One answer would be to suppose that an interrogative COMP is strong in present-day English (and so has to be filled) whereas INFL is weak (and so doesn't have to be filled). Since INFL is weak, it can be left empty in sentences such as (6a), which has the structure (7) below:

(7)

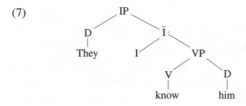

However, if we assume that interrogative clauses are CPs headed by a strong C, and that complementizers can't be used to fill COMP in main clauses, the only way of filling COMP is to resort to generating the auxiliary *do* in INFL and then raising it from INFL to COMP (to satisfy the requirement for a strong COMP to be filled) as in (8) below:

(8)

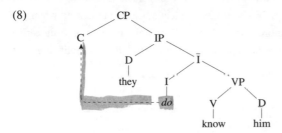

The auxiliary *do* can't be directly generated in COMP here because *do* requires a VP complement, and will only have a VP complement if it originates in INFL. Chomsky (1995c) suggests that dummy *do* is only used as a **last resort** – i.e. only where needed in order to satisfy some grammatical requirement which would not otherwise be satisfied (the relevant requirement in (8) being the need to fill a strong COMP). The *last resort* condition follows from the more general **economy principle** banning the use of super-fluous constituents and operations: from this principle it follows that a dummy item like *do* or an operation like *inversion* is used only when there is no other way of satisfying some grammatical requirement (e.g. the need to fill a strong interrogative COMP).

6.3 Traces

An interesting question which arises from the assumption that auxiliaries in questions move from I to C is what happens to the head I position in IP once it is vacated by movement of the inverted auxiliary into C. What we shall argue here is that the head I position of IP remains in place, but in the form of an **empty category**. What properties does this empty category have? It seems clear that the empty category left behind in the head I position of IP in a structure such as (4) must have the same head-features as *will*, since (like *will* in (2) above) it occupies the head I position of IP. Likewise, the empty I in (4) must have the same specifier-features as *will*, since (like *will*) it requires a nominative

219

spccificr (cf. *Will **she/*her** marry me?*). Moreover, the empty I must have the same complement-features as *will,* since the head V constituent of the VP has to be in the infinitive form *marry* (and cannot e.g. be in the *+ing* form, cf. **Will you **marrying** me?*).

So, it would seem that the empty category left behind in I by movement of *will* from I to C in (4) has the same head-features, specifier-features and complement-features as *will.* The empty category would therefore seem to be a silent copy of *will* – i.e. a constituent which has the same grammatical properties as *will*, and which differs from *will* only in that it has no phonetic content. To use the relevant terminology, we can say that when the auxiliary *will* moves, it leaves behind (in the position out of which it moves) an empty **trace** of itself, and that this trace (by virtue of being a silent copy of *will*) has precisely the same grammatical features as *will.* (The romantics among you can think of *traces* as being like the footprints you leave behind in the sand when you walk along the beach in Mallorca or Malibu.) Given this assumption, our earlier question *Will you marry me?* has the superficial structure (9) below (simplified e.g. by not representing features):

(9)

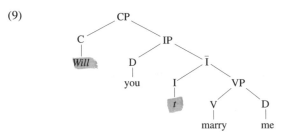

in which the head I position of IP is filled by an abstract trace *t* of the moved auxiliary *will*. The assumption that moved constituents leave behind a (silent) trace of themselves is the cornerstone of what became known in the 1970s as **trace theory**. Using the relevant terminology, we might say that a moved constituent is the **antecedent** of its trace, and that the antecedent of an empty trace serves to **bind** the trace – i.e. to determine its properties. (This involves a slightly extended use of the terms *antecedent/bind* compared with our earlier use of them in §3.9.) We might further posit that a moved constituent and its trace together form a (movement) **chain**, so that C and I form a chain in (9). Extending the chain analogy still further (to gratify the bikers among you), let's say that the moved auxiliary *will* in C and its empty trace *t* in I are the two different **links** of the relevant movement chain. Let's also say that the moved constituent is the **head** of the associated movement chain, and the trace is the **foot** of the chain. In our ensuing discussion, we shall adopt the convention of using the same type-face to denote a trace and its antecedent (hence both the trace *t* and its antecedent *will* are printed in italics in (9) above): the general convention used in the literature is to mark the binding relation between a trace and its antecedent by attaching identical subscript letters – called **indices** – to them (e.g. $will_i$ and t_i).

'Why on earth should we want to assume that moved constituents leave behind an invisible empty category *trace*?' you might wonder at this point. There is both theoretical and empirical evidence in support of this assumption. The relevant theoretical evidence comes from the fact that trace theory enables us to explain an otherwise puzzling property of movement operations. It will become more evident as our exposition unfolds that moved constituents always move from a lower to a higher position in any given structure, never from a higher to a lower position: for example, the moved auxiliary *will* in (9) moves from the head I position in IP into the head C position in CP, and thereby moves from a lower to a higher position in the structure. Why should movement always be from a lower to a higher position? Trace theory provides us with a natural explanation for the fact that movement is always *upwards*, never *downwards*. If we assume that a moved constituent leaves behind a trace which it binds, then the *upward* nature of movement is a direct consequence of the **c-command condition on binding** which we posited in our brief discussion of anaphors in §3.9 (where we saw that a reflexive anaphor like *himself* must be c-commanded by its antecedent) If a moved constituent has to bind its trace, and if a bound constituent has to be c-commanded by its antecedent, it follows that a moved constituent must always move into a position where it c-commands (and hence occurs higher up in the structure than) its trace: hence, movement will always be in an *upwards* direction. For example, in (9) above the moved auxiliary *will* in C c-commands its trace in I by virtue of the fact that (using our train analogy) if you travel one stop on a northbound train from C you arrive at CP, and from there you can catch a southbound train to I (via IP and $\overline{\text{I}}$). So, one theoretical argument in support of trace theory is that it explains the *upward* nature of movement.

A second theoretical reason for positing that a moved constituent leaves behind an empty category trace (and hence e.g. that there is an empty I constituent in inversion structures such as (9) above) relates to the *headedness* property of projections. If all phrases and clauses are projections of a head word category (as we argued in chapters 3 and 4), then IP must be headed by an I constituent; and if there is no overt I constituent in (9), there must be a *covert* one.

In addition to theory-internal considerations such as these, there is also empirical evidence for claiming that a moved constituent (e.g. the moved auxiliary *will* in (9) above) leaves behind an empty category trace. Part of this evidence comes from familiar facts about *have*-cliticization. In this connection, note that *have* cannot cliticize onto the immediately preceding pronoun *we/I/you/they* in inversion structures such as the following:

(10) (a)   Will *we have/*we've* finished the rehearsal?

    (b)   Should *I have/*I've* called the police?

    (c)   Would *you have/*you've* wanted to come with me?

    (d)   Could *they have/*they've* done something to help?

(*'ve* represents the vowel-less clitic form /v/ here.) The sequence *we've* in (10a) doesn't rhyme with *weave* (in careful speech styles), since *we have* can be reduced to /wiəv/ but not /wiv/: similarly, *I've* doesn't rhyme with *hive* in (10b), nor *you've* with *groove* in (10c), nor *they've* with *grave* in (10d). Why should cliticization of *have* onto the pronoun be blocked here? We can give a straightforward answer to this question if we posit that inverted auxiliaries move from I to C, and leave behind an empty category trace *t* in the I position out of which they move. Given this assumption, a sentence such as (10a) will have the structure (11) below. (To simplify exposition, details not of direct relevance to the discussion at hand are omitted – e.g. all features have been omitted, and the internal structure of the VP *finished the rehearsal* is not shown.)

(11)

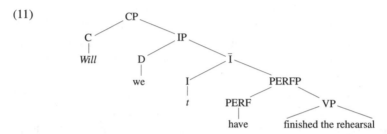

It would seem natural to suggest that the fact that there is an empty trace *t* intervening between *have* and *we* prevents *have* from cliticizing onto *we* in structures such as (11), since cliticization is subject to an **adjacency condition** (in that the clitic must be immediately adjacent to its host in order for cliticization to be possible). More generally, cliticization facts lend empirical support to the claim that auxiliary inversion results in an IP headed by an I constituent which is filled by a trace of the moved auxiliary.

Our discussion of auxiliary inversion here has interesting implications for the derivation of sentences (i.e. the way in which they are formed). More specifically, it implies that derivations may involve both **merger** and **movement** operations. For example, our earlier sentence *Will you marry me?* is formed by merging *marry* with *me* to form the VP *marry me*; merging this VP with the auxiliary *will* to form the I-bar *will marry me*; merging the resulting I-bar with *you* to form the IP *you will marry me*; and finally merging this IP with a C constituent into which the auxiliary *will* moves, forming the CP *Will you marry me?* (and leaving a trace behind in I, as in (9) above).

6.4 Verb movement

Having looked briefly at *auxiliary inversion* in English, we now turn to look at another type of **head movement** operation, which we shall refer to simply as **verb movement** or **V movement**, since it involves movement of a finite nonauxiliary verb from the head V position of VP into the head I position of IP. We shall see that this kind of V movement operation was productive in the Early Modern English (= EME) period when Shakespeare was writing (around the year 1600), but is no longer productive in Modern Standard English (= MSE). Since part of the evidence for V movement involves negative sentences, we begin with a brief look at the syntax of negation in EME.

In Shakespearean English, clauses containing a finite auxiliary are typically negated by positioning *not* between the auxiliary and the verb: cf.

(12) (a)   You may *not* deny it (Princess, *Love's Labour's Lost*, V.ii)

    (b)   I would *not* lose you (Portia, *Merchant of Venice*, III.ii)

    (c)   Thou shalt *not* die for lack of a dinner (Orlando, *As You Like It*, II.vi)

    (d)   I will *not* hear thy vain excuse (Duke, *Two Gentlemen of Verona*, III.i)

It would seem plausible to suppose that *not* in EME is an adverb which is positioned internally within VP, to the left of the verb. If so, (12a) will have a structure along the lines of (13) below:

(13)

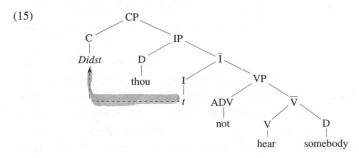

An analysis such as (13) accounts for the position which *not* occupies in front of the verb *deny*. It also enables us to provide a straightforward account of interrogatives such as:

(14) (a)   Didst thou not hear somebody? (Borachio, *Much Ado About Nothing*, III.iii)

    (b)   Will you not dance? (King, *Love's Labour's Lost*, V.ii)

    (c)   Have I not heard the sea rage like an angry boar? (Petruchio, *Taming of the Shrew*, I.ii)

If interrogatives involve movement from INFL to COMP, then a sentence such as (14a) will have the derivation (15) below:

(15)

Head movement

As (15) shows, the auxiliary *didst* originates in I and moves to C, leaving behind a trace *t* in the position out of which it moves. The assumption that *not* is contained within VP provides a straightforward account of the fact that *not* remains positioned in front of the verb *hear* when *didst* is preposed.

However, what is particularly interesting about negative sentences in Shakespearean English is that in auxiliariless finite clauses, the main verb is positioned in front of the negative *not*: cf.

(16) (a)   He heard *not* that (Julia, *Two Gentlemen of Verona*, IV.ii)

   (b)   I care *not* for her (Thurio, *Two Gentlemen of Verona*, V.iv)

   (c)   My master seeks *not* me (Speed, *Two Gentlemen of Verona*, I.i)

   (d)   I know *not* where to hide my head (Trinculo, *The Tempest*, II.ii)

   (e)   Thou thinkest *not* of this now (Launce, *Two Gentlemen of Verona*, IV.iv)

   (f)   She lov'd *not* the savour of tar (Stephano, *The Tempest*, II.ii)

   (g)   My charms crack *not* (Prospero, *The Tempest*, V.i)

   (h)   Demetrius loves her and he loves *not* you (Lysander, *Midsummer Night's Dream*, 3.ii)

If we assume that *not* in EME occupied a preverbal position internally within VP, how can we account for the fact that the verb (which would otherwise be expected to follow the negative *not*) ends up positioned in front of *not* in sentences like (16)? An obvious answer is to suggest that when INFL is not filled by an auxiliary, the verb moves out of the head V position in VP into the head I position in IP. If this is so, (16a) *He heard not that* will have the derivation (17) below:

(17)

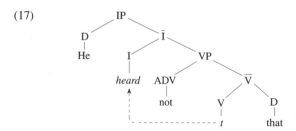

Thus, the verb *heard* originates in the head V position within VP, and then moves across *not* into the head I position in IP, so accounting for the fact that *heard* is positioned in front of *not*.

There would seem to be significant parallels between **V-to-I movement** in (17) and **I-to-C movement** in (15). For one thing, in both cases movement is from one head position to another, and so is an instance of the more general operation of **head movement**. Moreover, in both cases movement is from a *lower* to a *higher* position, and so results in a structure in which the moved head c-commands its trace (thereby satisfying the **c-command condition on binding**). Furthermore, in both cases move-

224

ment is **local**, with the moved head being moved into the head position in the next highest phrase within the structure; and in both cases, the moved head can move across an intervening nonhead constituent. Thus, *didst* in (15) moves from the head I position in IP into the head position within the next highest phrase in the structure (into the head C position in CP), and in doing so moves across its specifier *thou*; likewise, *heard* in (17) moves from the head V position in VP into the head position in the next highest phrase in the structure (= the head I position of IP), and in doing so moves across the adverb *not*. Since both **V-to-I movement** and **I-to-C movement** are local operations, it seems reasonable to suppose that their *locality* property is not accidental, but rather reflects the operation of some principle of Universal Grammar. Lisa Travis (1984) suggested that the relevant principle is a **head movement constraint** (= HMC) to the effect that a head can only move from the head position in one phrase to the head position in the immediately containing (i.e. next highest) phrase in the structure.

As we see from the examples in (14) above, questions in EME (= Early Modern English) involved the same *inversion* operation as in MSE (= Modern Standard English). Given our assumption that *inversion* involves movement from I to C, an obvious prediction made by the assumption that verbs move from V to I in EME is that they can subsequently move from I to C, so resulting in sentences such as:

(18) (a)   *Saw* you my master? (Speed, *Two Gentlemen of Verona*, I.i)

    (b)   *Heard* you this, Gonzalo? (Alonso, *The Tempest*, II.i)

    (c)   *Speakest* thou in sober meanings? (Orlando, *As You Like It*, V.ii)

    (d)   *Call* you this gamut? (Bianca, *Taming of the Shrew*, III.i)

    (e)   *Came* you from the church? (Tranio, *Taming of the Shrew*, III.ii)

    (f)   *Know* you not the cause? (Tranio, *Taming of the Shrew*, IV.ii)

    (g)   *Spake* you not these words plain? (Grumio, *Taming of the Shrew*, I.ii)

If so, a typical Early Modern English question such as (18f) *Know you not the cause?* would be derived in the manner represented in (19) below:

(19)

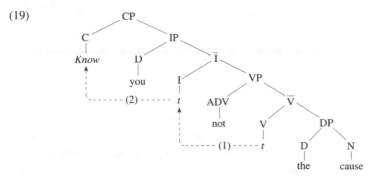

The fact that the verb *know* is positioned to the left of the subject *you* suggests that it is raised first from V to I and then from I to C by two successive applications of head movement (numbered (1) and (2) respectively). In structures like (19), head movement is said to apply in a **successive cyclic** fashion, moving the verb *know* (in successive steps) first into INFL, then into COMP. Each separate movement operation is local (in that it moves *know* only into the head position in the next highest phrase containing it in the tree).

6.5 Strong and weak features

It is interesting to reflect on the significance of the fact that negatives like (16) and interrogatives like (18) are no longer grammatical in MSE (Modern Standard English). What is the nature of the change that has taken place in the course of the evolution of the language? The answer seems to be that it was possible for finite (nonauxiliary) verbs to move to INFL in EME, but that this is no longer possible in MSE; hence (for example) nonauxiliary verbs could move to INFL in EME sentences such as (16), and from INFL subsequently move to COMP, so giving rise to interrogatives such as (18) – but no movement to INFL (and thence to COMP) is possible for nonauxiliary verbs in MSE.

Why should finite nonauxiliary verbs be able to move to INFL in Early Modern English, but not in present-day English? Using Chomsky's *strength* metaphor, we might suggest that finite verbs carried *strong* agreement-features (i.e. strong person/number specifier-features) in EME, whereas their counterparts in MSE carry *weak* agreement-features. And we might further suppose that only verbs which carry strong agreement features are strong enough to move into INFL – hence that verbs carrying weak agreement-features are too weak to move into INFL.

One question raised by this account is: 'What determines whether finite verbs carry strong or weak agreement features?' A plausible answer is that this is correlated with the relative *richness* of the agreement inflections carried by finite verbs, in that finite verbs have strong agreement-features in languages in which they carry rich agreement inflections, and weak agreement-features in languages in which they carry relatively impoverished agreement inflections. In this connection, it is interesting to note that whereas third person singular +*s* is the only regular agreement inflection found on (present-tense) verbs in Modern Standard English, in Shakespearean English we find three present-tense inflections, viz. second person singular +*st* and third person singular +*th* and +*s*: cf.

(20) (a)   Thou see*st* how diligent I am (Petruchio, *Taming of the Shrew*, IV.iii)

    (b)   Thou say*st* true (Petruchio, *Taming of the Shrew*, IV.iii)

    (c)   The sight of love feed*eth* those in love (Rosalind, *As You Like It*, III.v)

    (d)   She take*th* most delight in music, instruments and poetry (Baptista, *Taming of the Shrew*, I.i)

    (e)   Winter tame*s* man, woman and beast (Grumio, *Taming of the Shrew*, IV.i)

    (f)   It look*s* ill, it eat*s* drily (Parolles, *All's Well That Ends Well*, I.i)

Accordingly, we might argue that finite verbs have strong agreement features in EME by virtue of the relatively rich system of agreement inflections they carry; and conversely that finite verbs have weak agreement features in MSE by virtue of their relatively impoverished agreement morphology in present-day English. (See Rohrbacher 1994 and Vikner 1995 for interesting attempts to explore the correlation between the strength of agreement-features and the relative richness of agreement inflections in a range of different languages.)

The different strength of the agreement-features carried by finite verbs in EME on the one hand and MSE on the other is reflected in a further syntactic difference between them. Early Modern English was a **null subject language**, as we see from sentences such as the following:

(21) (a) Hast any more of this? (Trinculo, *The Tempest*, II.ii)

    (b) Sufficeth, I am come to keep my word (Petruchio, *Taming of the Shrew*, III.ii)

    (c) Would you would bear your fortunes like a man (Iago, *Othello*, IV.i)

    (d) Lives, sir (Iago, *Othello*, IV.i, in reply to 'How does Lieutenant Cassio?')

Since the null subject in sentences like (21) occurs in a nominative position (by virtue of being the subject of a finite clause), it has different case properties from the PRO subject of infinitives (which has null case), and hence is generally taken to be a different kind of null subject conventionally designated as **pro** (affectionately known as *little pro*, whereas its big brother is affectionately known as *big PRO*). By contrast, MSE is a **non-null subject language**, as we see from the fact that the present-day counterparts of (21) require (italicized) overt subjects: cf.

(22) (a) Have *you* any more of this?

    (b) *It* is enough that I have come to keep my word

    (c) *I* wish you would bear your fortunes like a man

    (d) *He* is alive, sir

It would seem, therefore, that finite verbs can have a null *pro* subject in a language like EME where they carry strong agreement features, but not in a language like MSE where they carry weak agreement-features. Why should this be? An obvious suggestion is that in a language with a rich system of agreement inflections, the agreement inflections on the verb serve to **identify** the null subject (e.g. the +*st* inflection on *hast* in (21a) is a second person singular inflection, and hence allows us to identify the null subject as a second person singular subject with the same properties as *thou*). But in a weak agreement language like MSE, agreement morphology is too impoverished to allow identification of a null *pro* subject (e.g. if we asked **Can help?*, we'd have no way of telling from the agreementless form *can* whether the missing subject is *I*, *you*, *he*, *they* or whatever).

What our discussion here suggests is that there is parametric variation across languages in respect of whether finite verbs carry strong or weak agreement features, and that the relative strength of these features determines whether nonauxiliary verbs can raise to INFL, and whether null subjects are permitted or not. However, this still poses the question of why finite verbs should raise out of V into I in languages like EME where they carry strong agreement-features. One answer to this question is provided by **checking theory:** let us suppose that *movement* is a *last resort* mechanism by which heads can check features which would otherwise remain unchecked. As we have seen, finite verbs in EME carry strong agreement-features; hence a finite verb raises to INFL in order to *check* its strong agreement-features (i.e. its person/number specifier-features) against those of the subject occupying the specifier position within IP. To see how this might work, consider the syntax of a sentence such as *Thou thinkest not of this* (cf. (16e) above). The verb *thinkest* originates in the head V position of VP, and (because it contains strong agreement-features) then raises to INFL as in (23) below (the [2SNom] features of *thou* mark the second person singular nominative head-features of *thou*, the [Pres] feature of *thinkest* marks its present-tense head-feature, and the [2SNom] features carried by *thinkest* are specifier-features which mark the fact that it requires a second person singular nominative subject as its specifier; all other features are omitted, to simplify exposition):

(23)

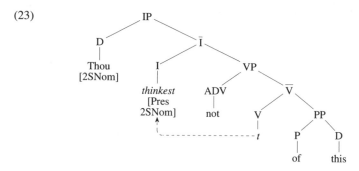

Since subject-verb agreement involves a local checking relation between INFL and its specifier, an obvious consequence of moving *thinkest* from V into I in (23) is that it enables the specifier-features of *thinkest* to be checked: this is because *thinkest* ends up in INFL, and from there can check its [2SNom] specifier-features against the corresponding [2SNom] head-features of *thou*. Since the two sets of features match, the specifier-features of *thinkest* are erased along with the nominative case-feature of *thou* (because the relevant features are uninterpretable), so ensuring that the derivation does not crash. Using a metaphor developed by Chomsky, we can say that movement from V to INFL is motivated by considerations of **greed** – i.e. by the selfish desire of the verb to check its own morphological features. Movement of *thinkest* to INFL also ensures that INFL carries a tense-feature (viz. the present-tense head-feature of *thinkest*), and so is interpretable at LF (i.e. at the level of logical form).

228

As we have seen, the agreement properties of finite nonauxiliary verbs in EME are checked by moving the verb into INFL, so that the verb is in a local spec–head relation with its subject, and its person/number/case specifier-features can be checked. But recall (from our discussion in the previous chapter) that the specifier-features of finite nonauxiliary verbs are checked in a rather different way in MSE – as we can illustrate in relation to a simple sentence such as:

(24)   She mistrusts him

Example (24) is an IP headed by an empty INFL constituent, with the verb *mistrusts* occupying the head V position of VP, and the subject *she* occupying the specifier position within IP. We suggested in the previous chapter that the head- and specifier-features of finite nonauxiliary verbs percolate from V to INFL in MSE, to satisfy the requirement that INFL carry a tense-feature (in order to be interpretable at LF), and to enable the specifier-features of the verb to be checked. In the case of (24), percolation will work in the manner indicated in (25) below (to simplify exposition, we show only the features directly relevant to our discussion here):

(25)

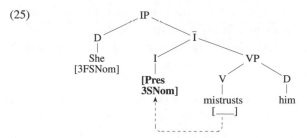

Once the bold-printed head- and specifier-features of *mistrusts* have percolated up to INFL, its [3SNom] specifier-features (requiring it to have a third person singular nominative subject) can then be checked for compatibility with the [3FSNom] head-features of *she*, and thereby erased (along with the uninterpretable nominative head-feature of *she*). Chomsky (1995c) refers to the relevant process of feature percolation as **attraction** (the idea being that INFL in structures like (25) *attracts* the relevant features carried by *mistrusts*).

So, it would appear that EME and MSE make use of two very different ways of checking the agreement properties of finite (nonauxiliary) verbs: EME makes use of **movement** of the verb from V to INFL; MSE makes use of **attraction** of the head- and specifier-features of the verb from V to INFL. These two different ways of checking the relevant features of finite verbs correlate directly with the relative **strength** of the agreement-features carried by the verbs. In a language like EME in which verbs carry strong agreement-features, agreement is checked by movement; in a language like MSE where verbs carry weak agreement-features, agreement is checked by attraction (= percolation). Since the ultimate goal of any theory is to *explain* why things are the way they are, an important question for us to ask is *why* strong features should be checked by movement, and weak features by attraction. The answer to this question may lie in the nature of the two different operations. **Attraction** involves movement of a set of *grammatical features* carried by a head on their own (without movement of the corresponding phonetic features) – more specifically, movement of those grammatical features which could not be checked otherwise. For example, in (25) above, the tense/agreement-features of *mistrusts* are attracted to INFL, but its phonetic features (represented by the spelling form *mistrusts*) remain attached to the V-node. By contrast, **head movement** involves movement of the *phonetic and grammatical* features of a head together (our discussion here is simplified by leaving *semantic features* to one side): thus, in (23) above not only do the tense/agreement-features of *thinkest* move to INFL, but so too do its phonetic features (represented by the spelling form *thinkest*). We might conjecture that what it means for a word like *thinkest* in (23) to carry strong agreement-features is that these strong agreement-features cannot be separated from the phonetic features carried by the relevant word: hence, the only way of checking the strong agreement-features of *thinkest* is to move the whole word (i.e. the whole set of phonetic and grammatical features carried by the word). Conversely, what it means to say that a verb like *mistrusts* in (25) has weak grammatical features is that the relevant grammatical features can move to INFL on their own, with the phonetic features carried by the word being stranded (i.e. left behind) in the head V position of VP.

We might further suppose that in consequence of the **economy principle**, only the minimal set of features needed to satisfy some grammatical requirement undergo movement in a given structure. Thus, because INFL requires a tense-feature and the [3SNom] specifier-features of *mistrusts* cannot be checked unless they move to INFL, the relevant tense/agreement-features percolate to INFL in (25); because these features are weak, they can be separated from the phonetic features carried by *mistrusts*, and hence the economy principle requires that only these tense/agreement-features should move. By contrast, the verb *thinkest* in (23) carries strong [2SNom] agreement features, with the result that not just these features but also the phonetic features carried by *thinkest* move to INFL (so that in effect the whole word *thinkest* moves to INFL). Attraction is more economical than movement, since movement affects both the phonetic and the grammatical features carried by a word, whereas attraction involves movement of grammatical features alone: hence, the economy principle will ensure that attraction will be preferred to movement wherever possible (e.g. in structures like (25)), with movement only being forced where the relevant features being checked are strong (e.g. in (23)).

6.6   Negation

An unexpected complication is raised by contrasts such as the following:

(26) (a)   She never trusts him

    (b)   *She not trusts him

It seems reasonable to suppose (on the basis of examples such as (27) below) that *never* can function as a VP adverb:

(27) (a)   He will [*never admit defeat*]

    (b)   SPEAKER A: What did he advise you to do?

              SPEAKER B: [*Never admit defeat*]

    (c)   One thing you must do is [*never admit defeat*]

This assumption provides a straightforward account of the fact that *never* is positioned in front of the verb *admit* in (27a), and of the fact that the bracketed string *never admit defeat* behaves like a typical VP in being able to occur as a sentence fragment in (27b), and as the complement of *be* in (27c).

If we assume that *never* is a VP-adverb, (26a) can be derived straightforwardly as in (28) below, with the tense- and agreement-features of *trusts* being attracted to INFL (to simplify exposition we show only features directly relevant to the discussion at hand):

(28)

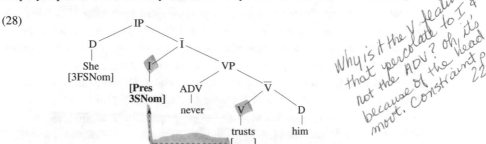

Why is it the V features that percolate to I & not the ADV? Oh, it's because of the Head movt. Constraint p. 225.

As a result, the [3SNom] specifier-features which are attracted to INFL (requiring INFL to have a third person singular nominative subject) can be checked for compatibility with the [3FSNom] head-features of *she* and thereby erased (along with the [Nom] nominative head-feature of *she*).

But if we assume that *not* is also a VP-adverb, we should expect to find that (26b) **She not trusts him* can be derived in exactly the same way, and so should be grammatical. The fact that (26b) is ungrammatical suggests that *not* must be different from *never* in some way. But how? A suggestion made in recent work is to assume that *not* (in present-day English) is not a VP-adverb at all, but rather belongs to the separate category **NEG**(ation), and functions as a syntactic head which projects into a **NEGP** (negation phrase). Given this assumption, (26b) will have the structure (29) below (as before, we show only the head-features of *she* and the head- and specifier-features of *trusts*):

(29)

```
                    IP
           D              Ī
           |          I       NEGP
          She            NEG        VP
        [3FSNom]          |      V      D
                         not     |      |
                               trusts  him
                               [Pres
                               3SNom]
```

If the uninterpretable [3SNom] specifier-features of *trusts* and the [Nom] head-feature of *she* are to be erased, it's clear that the tense- and agreement-features of *trusts* must be attracted to INFL. However, the fact that the corresponding sentence (26b) **She not trusts him* is ungrammatical suggests that *not* somehow prevents percolation of the relevant features up to INFL. Why should this be?

A reasonable suggestion to make would be that **attraction** (like **head movement**) is a purely *local* process whereby features can only percolate up from one head onto the head of the next highest phrase containing it in the tree. This seems plausible, given our earlier observation that both movement and attraction involve movement of sets of features (movement affecting both phonetic and grammatical features alike, and attraction affecting only grammatical features). If so, it would follow that the bold-printed tense- and agreement-features in (29) can't percolate directly from V to I: rather, the only way they can get from V to I is first to percolate from V to NEG, and then to percolate from NEG to I. But let's suppose that percolation of the [3SNom] specifier-features of *trusts* from V to NEG is blocked because NEG simply isn't the kind of head which can have a subject (and hence NEG can't carry subject-related specifier-features). In the terminology of Roberts 1993, we might say that while INFL is an **A-head** (i.e. an argumental head – the kind of head which can have an argument as its specifier), NEG is an **Ā-head** (an *A-bar head*, i.e. a non-argumental head which can't have an argument as its specifier: note that the *bar* symbol here is used in a way similar to the prefix *non-*, viz. as a negation operator). This would mean that the [3SNom] specifier-features of *trusts* cannot be checked because they cannot move directly to INFL (since percolation is a *local* operation), and cannot move to INFL via NEG (because NEG is an A-bar head, and hence can't carry subject-features). Consequently, the derivation crashes at LF, since the unchecked [3SNom] specifier-features of *trusts* and the [Nom] head-feature of *she* are uninterpretable at LF (so violating the **principle of full interpretation**).

But this isn't quite the end of the story, since the ungrammatical (26b) *She not trusts him* has the grammatical counterpart (30) below involving the use of *do*-support:

(30)   She does not trust him

Why should it be that use of *do*-support in (30) results in a grammatical sentence? Since *do* is an auxiliary which carries an [Inf] complement-feature (by virtue of requiring an infinitive complement), and since *trust* (as used in (30) above) carries an [Inf] head-feature (by virtue of being an infinitive form), let's suppose that the bold-printed **[Inf]** head-feature carried by *trust* can percolate up from V to NEG, as shown by the arrow in (31) below:

(31)

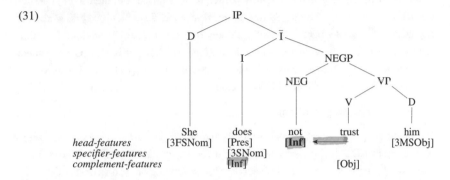

	She	does	not	trust	him
head-features	[3FSNom]	[Pres]	**[Inf]** ←		[3MSObj]
specifier-features		[3SNom]			
complement-features		[Inf]		[Obj]	

Since the NEGP *not trust him* is a projection of NEG, it follows that the NEGP string *not trust him* is a *negative infinitive phrase*, and hence can check the [Inf] complement-feature of *does* (which requires *does* to have an infinitival complement), leading to erasure of both [Inf] features. We might suppose that *not* (by virtue of its traditional status as a *preverbal particle*) can attract the *head-features* of the head verb of its complement, (though by virtue of being an A-bar head, it cannot attract the *specifier-features* of a finite verb). Since the verb *trust* here is nonfinite, it has no specifier-features to percolate up to NEG. Instead, the choice of subject is dictated by the finite auxiliary *does*: the [3SNom] specifier-features of *does* are checked for compatibility with the [3FSNom] head-features of *she* and thereby erased (along with the nominative case-feature of *she*). In addition, the objective complement-feature of *trust* is checked for compatibility with the objective head-feature of *him*, and both objective case-features erased. So, after checking, the only grammatical features which survive at LF are the [3FS] head-features of *she*, the [Pres] head-feature of *does* and the [3MS] head-features of *him*. (Of course, we are overlooking purely semantic features here – e.g. the negation feature carried by *not*.) Since no uninterpretable features remain after checking, the derivation satisfies the **principle of full interpretation** and converges at LF. Thus, the use of *do*-support provides a way of rescuing a derivation which would otherwise crash if *do* were not used. Our analysis thus provides a principled account of the observation made by

233

Williams (1994) that *not* can modify a nonfinite verb, but not a finite verb. What still remains to be accounted for, however, is why *do* can't be used in sentences such as:

(32)   *She does never trust him.*

The answer is that (as we saw in relation to our earlier discussion of the examples in (6) above) *do* is used only as a *last resort* – i.e. only in cases where some morphological feature would remain unchecked if *do* were not used. There is simply no need to use *do* with *never*, since sentences such as *She never trusts him* are grammatical, for reasons given in our earlier discussion of (28). So, *do* is only used where it has to be, and is avoided otherwise. The *last resort* condition on the use of *do* can be argued to be a consequence of the more general **economy principle**, which rules out the use of superfluous constituents: since dummy *do* has no intrinsic semantic content, it follows that its use must be avoided wherever possible. At any rate, the *last resort* condition (together with our earlier assumption that *never* is a VP-adverb but *not* is a NEG constituent which heads a NEGP) enables us to account for the data in (26), (30) and (32) above.

Consider now how we deal with contracted negative structures such as:

(33)   She *doesn't* trust him

We might suppose that (33) has essentially the same structure as (31) above, except that the head NEG position in NEGP is occupied by *n't* rather than *not*. Since *n't* is a suffix (and cannot be used as an independent word standing on its own), *n't* cliticizes to the preceding auxiliary *does*, adjoining to *does* in the manner represented in (34) below:

(34)

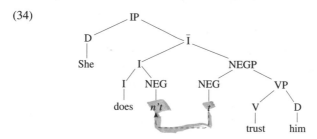

What (34) suggests is that when *n't* is attached to the auxiliary *does*, it forms a complex head comprising the auxiliary *does* and the negative suffix *n't* (thereby forming a negative auxiliary). The resulting negative auxiliary behaves like any other auxiliary in being able to undergo inversion, e.g. in questions such as:

(35)   *Doesn't* she trust him?

It would appear that attachment of *n't* to *does* is motivated by **greed**, since it is a morphological property of *n't* that it is a suffix, and hence must be suffixed to an appropriate host (the host in this case being *does*).

234

An interesting complication is posed by contrasts such as the following:

(36) (a)   She *mightn't* come

(b)   *She *mayn't* come

Such data suggest that *n't* can be suffixed to some items, but not others. How can we account for this? One way would be to invoke the traditional morphological distinction between *free* and *bound* forms – i.e. forms which can and can't stand on their own as independent words. (In these terms, *not* would be a free form, and *n't* a bound form.) We could then say that *may* can only serve as a free form, and so does not allow *n't* to be suffixed to it; by contrast, *might* can be used either as a free form (cf. *She might not come*), or as a bound form (cf. *She mightn't come*). In order to account for an item like *will* (which has the irregular contracted negative form *won't*), we might suppose that its lexical entry indicates that it has the free form *will* and the bound form *wo+* (the + symbol here indicating that a suffix like *+n't* needs to be added to it – and the + symbol on *+n't* indicating that it needs to be suffixed to a bound finite verb form).

To summarize: a sentence such as *She trusts him* cannot be negated by *not* alone (cf. *She not trusts him*), because the presence of *not* prevents the agreement features of *trusts* percolating from V to I, so leaving the agreement features of the verb and the nominative case-feature of its subject unchecked. Instead, such sentences have to be negated by the use of *do*-support (cf. *She does not trust him*), which provides a way of ensuring that the nominative case-feature carried by *she* can be checked. Thus, *do* is used because it is needed in order to check the case properties of the subject. Since *does* can function either as a free form or as a bound form to which *n't* can be suffixed, an alternative possibility is for *n't* to be used in place of *not* – in which case, *n't* is adjoined to *does* to form the negative auxiliary *doesn't* (which can undergo inversion like any other auxiliary).

6.7   The syntax of *have*

We have assumed in our discussion hitherto that although finite verbs moved from V to INFL in Early Modern English, this type of movement is no longer found in Modern English. However, this assumption is oversimplistic in one important respect. Consider, in this connection, the behaviour of the verb *have* (in its *possessive* use, i.e. where it has a meaning roughly paraphraseable as 'possess') in the following memorable line from the traditional nursery-rhyme *Baa Baa Black Sheep*:

(37)   Have you any wool?

– a type of structure which is still current in some (e.g. British) varieties of English, but which has fallen out of use in other (e.g. American) varieties. In (37), *have* behaves like an auxiliary in respect of undergoing inversion. And yet *have* in this use otherwise seems to have the properties of a typical transitive verb – e.g. it has much the same meaning as other transitive verbs like *own* or *possess*, and (like them) takes a DP complement (*any wool*). It seems plausible, then, to suppose that *have* (in this possessive use) is a transitive verb which originates in the head V position of VP, and which (being transitive) selects a DP complement. Such an assumption will, in any case, be required for structures such as:

(38)   Do you [have any wool]?

where it is clear that *have* occupies the head V position within the bracketed VP.

But if transitive *have* originates in the head V position of VP, how does it end up in the head C position of CP in sentences like (37) *Have you any wool?* Given that head movement is a strictly *local* operation, the answer must be that *have* in (37) moves first from V to I, then from I to C in a successive cyclic fashion, as represented by the arrows in (39) below:

(39)

Movement of the transitive verb *have* from V to INFL (and from there into COMP) in *Baa Baa Black Sheep* varieties of English would then be a last vestige of a once productive V-to-I movement process (whereby all finite verbs moved from V to INFL in EME). In many (e.g. American) varieties of English this type of movement of *have* from V to I is no longer possible, and (38) is grammatical in such varieties, but (37) is not (I leave the sociologists among you to ponder on whether this might be because politically correct parents no longer sing *Baa Baa Black Sheep* to their children in the relevant varieties, because of its racist and animalist overtones).

Independent evidence for claiming that possessive *have* can move out of V into I comes from the fact that *have* can cliticize onto its subject in structures such as:

(40)   *They've* no wool

If (as we claim) *have* moves from V to I in such structures, (40) will have the derivation (41) below:

236

(41)

```
              IP
          ___/  \___
         D          Ī
         |        __/ \__
        They    I'         VP
              __|__      _/  \_
            have   V        DP
               ↑   |       /  \
               └------ t  no wool
```

and we correctly predict that *have* (in the guise of its clitic variant *'ve*) can cliticize onto *they*, since the two are immediately adjacent. By contrast, if *have* always remains in the head V position of VP, we wrongly predict that cliticization of *have* onto *they* will be blocked by the intervening INFL constituent, since *have* and *they* will never be immediately adjacent. (Recall that in §4.4, we noted that cliticization requires adjacency, and is blocked by an intervening empty category.)

However, it should be noted that movement of possessive *have* from V to I is optional in *Baa Baa Black Sheep* varieties, as indicated by the syntax of the floating quantifier *both* in sentences such as the following:

(42) (a)   They (probably) *both* have very little wool
     (b)   They've *both* very little wool

If we assume (as in §3.6) that floating quantifiers are in spec-VP, we can account for the data in (42) by supposing that in (42a) the verb *have* remains in V (and so follows *both* which is in spec-VP), whereas in (42b) the verb *have* moves from V into I (thereby moving across *both*), and (once in I) can then cliticize onto the subject *they* in spec-IP. (For obvious reasons, sentences like (42b) are only grammatical in *Baa Baa Black Sheep* varieties of English – not in varieties in which transitive *have* always remains in V.)

Now consider a second (at first sight, rather puzzling) aspect of the syntax of possessive *have*. As the examples below illustrate, possessive *have* can be directly negated by the contracted negative *n't*, but not by the full negative *not*: cf.

(43) (a)   We have*n't* any wool
     (b)   *We have *not* any wool

How can we account for the puzzling contrast in (43)? The answer to this question turns out to provide us with a potential clue to the nature of **head movement**.

Consider first how we account for (43a) *We haven't any wool*. If we assume (as before) that *n't* originates as the head NEG of NEGP, (43a) will have the structure (44) below, if *have* remains *in situ* in the head V position in VP:

Head movement

[handwritten: not - attraction is enough n't - requires movement.]

(44)

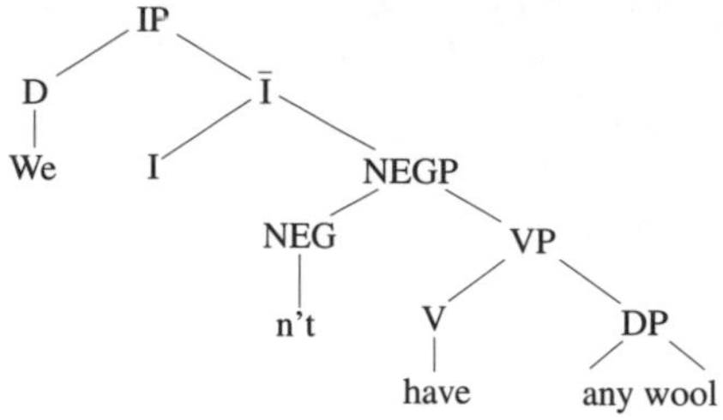

Let's assume that *have* adjoins to *n't*; since *n't* is a suffix, *have* will adjoin to the left of *n't*, as in (45) below:

(45)

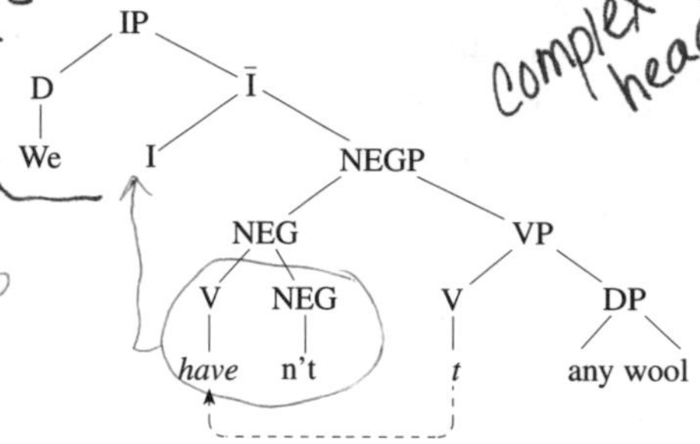

[handwritten: complex head of NEG]

[handwritten: after it moves to I it can invert & move into C.]

This process of adjoining one head to another leads to the formation of a complex head which comprises both *have* and *n't*, and which combines properties of both heads (e.g. *have* is a finite verb, *n't* is negative, so *haven't* is a negative finite verb). The next step in the derivation is for the resulting complex head *haven't* to move into INFL (so that the agreement features of *have* can be checked against those of *we*). Once *haven't* is in INFL, it can move from there to COMP, e.g. in questions such as:

(46)   Haven't we any wool?

Thus, the grammaticality of sentences like (43a) can be accounted for in a principled fashion.

But now consider how we account for the ungrammaticality of (43b), *We have not any wool* (with the independent negative *not* rather than the suffixal negative *n't*). We might expect this to be derived in the same way as (43a), with *have* first adjoining to *not* as in (45), and the resulting compound head *have* + *not* then moving to INFL. But since the resulting sentence (43b) is ungrammatical, something must prevent such a derivation. What could it be? The obvious answer is that the first step in the derivation (adjunction of *have* to *not*) is blocked because *not* is a free form (not a bound form), and so doesn't allow another word to adjoin to it. So, while adjoining *have* to NEG is possible where NEG contains the bound form *n't* (as in (45) above), it is not possible where NEG contains the free form *not*. For this reason, it is not possible to derive (43b)

238

We have not any wool by first adjoining *have* to *not*, and then adjoining *have + not* to INFL.

But isn't there a more direct way of generating (43b) – namely by moving *have* directly into INFL, as in (47) below?

(47)

If the derivation in (47) were possible, we would wrongly expect (43b) **We have not any wool* to be grammatical. The fact that (43b) is ungrammatical means that some principle of Universal Grammar must rule out the possibility of *have* skipping across NEG in (47). But what principle?

The answer is provided by the familiar **head movement constraint** (= HMC) proposed by Lisa Travis (1984) to the effect that a head can only move to the head position within the immediately containing (i.e. 'next highest') phrase in the tree: since the next highest phrase above the VP containing *have* in (47) is NEGP (not IP), this means that *have* can only adjoin to NEG, not to INFL. Such a constraint would ensure that head movement can only apply in a strictly *local* fashion – in precisely the same way as we earlier saw that **attraction** (i.e. movement of grammatical features) is local.

Given that HMC determines that head movement can only apply in a strictly *local* fashion, direct movement of *have* to INFL in (47) is ruled out. Since successive cyclic movement (adjoining *have* first to *not* then to INFL) is also ruled out (because *not* is a free form), both derivations crash. The only way of negating the sentence with *not* is to use *do*-support as a *last resort*, yielding the sentence:

(48)   We do not have any wool

And if the bound form *+n't* is used together with the bound form *do+* (which rhymes with *doe/dough*), *+n't* will adjoin to *do+*, giving:

(49)   We *don't* have any wool

Thus, we can provide a principled account of why in *Baa Baa Black Sheep* varieties of English, we find (48), (49) and (43a) – but not (43b).

Our discussion of negation here suggests that *not* and *n't* complement each other: *not* is a free form which can be used to negate a following nonfinite verb (in structures such as (31) above) but not a finite verb (as we see from the ungrammaticality of structures such as (29) above). By contrast, *n't* is a bound form which must be suffixed to a finite verb, and which cannot be suffixed to a nonfinite verb (perhaps because nonfinite verbs are free forms), as we see from the ungrammaticality of (50b) below (where *have* is an infinitive form):

(50) (a)   He may *not have* left

      (b)   *He may *haven't* left

Thus, we might characterize *not* informally as a free nonfinite form, and *n't* as a bound finite form.

6.8   Tense affix

A question which still remains to be answered is why it is possible for finite forms of transitive *have* to move from V to INFL in *Baa Baa Black Sheep* varieties – but not possible for other verbs. What is special about *have*: why does it move to INFL, when other nonauxiliary verbs don't? Given the assumption (embodied in Chomsky's **greed** principle) that head movement is triggered by the morphological properties of heads, one possibility is that *have* has some special morphological property which other verbs don't have. But what property?

A clue to this comes from the fact that *have* adjoins to *n't* in structures such as (45), yielding the form *haven't*. This suggests that finite forms of *have* can serve as *bound forms*. The fact that *have* can also cliticize onto its subject e.g. in structures such as (40) *They've no wool* provides additional evidence that *have* has the morphological property that it can be a bound form. Thus, we see that *have* has two distinctive properties: (i) the morphological property of being able to serve as a bound form (or a free form), and (ii) the syntactic property of being able to raise to INFL (or remain in V). Clearly, we should like to be able to relate these two properties somehow – but how?

One possibility would be to suppose (following Chomsky 1995c) that INFL contains an abstract (present or past) **tense affix**. If (as Fabb 1988 argues) affixes have specific categorial properties, we can assume that the relevant tense affix is a *finite verbal* affix, and hence must attach to a finite (auxiliary or nonauxiliary) verb. We might further suppose that (when used as a bound form) *have* raises to INFL to adjoin to this abstract tense-affix in the manner indicated below (where *T* denotes the category **tense**, and *Pres* denotes a null present-tense affix):

(51)

IP
├─ D
│ └─ They
└─ Ī
   ├─ I
   │ ├─ V
   │ │ └─ *have*
   │ └─ T
   │   └─ Pres
   └─ VP
      ├─ V
      │ └─ *t*
      └─ DP
         └─ no wool

240

Movement of *have* to I would then satisfy the requirement for the bound form *have* to be attached to an affix (though, of course, the present-tense affix it is attaching to here is null, and so has no overt phonetic form). One consequence of raising *have* from V to INFL is that the present-tense head-feature carried by *have* can thereby be checked against that of the present-tense affix T. (Let's assume that as a result of checking, the tense-feature of *have* is erased, but that of the T affix in INFL is not erased, since INFL must carry tense in order to be interpretable at LF.) Once *have* adjoins to INFL, it can then undergo further movement to COMP (e.g. in sentences like (37) *Have you any wool?*), or can cliticize onto *they* (as in (40) *They've no wool*).

However, there is an interesting hidden complication which arises out of the analysis in (51) above. It has standardly been assumed (in work over the past three decades) that adjoining one head X to another head Y produces a structure of the form (52) below:

(52)

```
      Y
     / \
    X   Y
```

In other words, adjunction of X to Y forms a *split-segment* category Y. (Hence there are two segments of the category Y in (52), the upper one and the lower one.) This assumption has obvious implications for the structure formed by adjoining *have* to the tense-affix T in (51). What it means is that adjoining *have* to T will result in the formation of a split-segment T category with the structure (53) below:

(53)

```
        T
       / \
      V   T
      |   |
    have Pres
```

The resulting string *have+Pres* thus has the status of a *T* constituent – not (as we had hitherto assumed) of an *INFL* constituent.

But this assumption in turn has even further ramifications. Since the head of the overall clause *They have no wool* is the T constituent *have+Pres* in (53), this means that the string *have no wool* must have the status of a T-bar constituent (not an I-bar), and likewise that the overall clause *They have no wool* must have the status of a TP constituent (not an IP). Thus, the overall sentence *They have no wool* will not be an IP with the structure (51) above, but rather a TP with the structure (54) below:

(54)

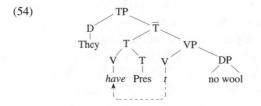

Ugh! So, what have we been doing up to this pt, saying every thing is an IP?

More generally, the assumption that finite clauses are headed by an abstract tense affix leads us to the conclusion that they have the status of TP (rather than IP) constituents.

So far, we have considered how to derive *Baa Baa Black Sheep* sentences in which possessive *have* moves out of the head V position in VP, and adjoins to an abstract tense affix (perhaps, as we suggested, because *have* is a bound form in this kind of use). But now consider how we account for the fact that all other lexical verbs in present-day English remain in the head V position of VP. If we suppose that clauses are headed by an abstract tense affix T, it follows that T must have some element affixed to it. Exploiting Chomsky's *strength* metaphor, let's suppose that the relevant tense affix is a *weak* affix in present-day English, and so is only strong enough to attract *grammatical features*, not phonetic features (i.e. not strong enough to trigger movement of the whole item). What this means (e.g. in the case of our earlier sentence (24) *She mistrusts him*) is that the head- and specifier-features of the verb (i.e. the tense/agreement-features of *mistrusts*) will adjoin to the tense affix T, as in (55) below, but its phonetic features (represented by the spelling form *mistrusts*) remain in V:

(55)

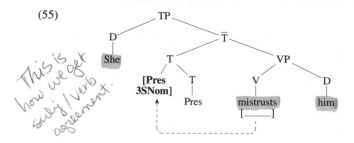

Attraction of the bold-printed head- and specifier-features (indicating that *mistrusts* is a present-tense verb which requires a third person singular nominative subject) to the tense affix T which heads the clause enables the tense and agreement properties of *mistrusts* to be checked.

An important question to ask about the derivation in (55) is why agreement can't be checked by movement of the whole word *mistrusts* (i.e. its phonetic and grammatical features together) from V to T. The answer lies in considerations of economy. As we noted in §6.5, attraction is more economical than movement since attraction affects grammatical features, whereas movement affects both grammatical and phonetic features. So, the **economy principle** determines that attraction will always be preferred to movement unless (strong) morphological properties force movement.

A second question which is posed by the assumption that finite clauses are headed by a weak T affix is how we account for the curious behaviour of possessive *have* in *Baa Baa Black Sheep* varieties. As we know, this can either behave like a typical lexical verb (remaining *in situ* in the head V position of VP and so requiring *do*-support in questions and negatives like (56a–b) below), or can raise from V to INFL (and from

242

there to COMP in questions), thereby forming questions and negatives without *do*-support (as in (57a–b) below): cf.

(56) (a)   *Do* you have any wool?

    (b)   We *don't* have any wool

(57) (a)   *Have* you any wool?

    (b)   We *haven't* any wool

In its use as a lexical verb requiring *do*-support, possessive *have* behaves like any other typical lexical verb (e.g. *mistrusts* in (55) above) in remaining *in situ* in the head V position of VP, and so is unproblematic. More puzzling is how we account for the fact that possessive *have* can adjoin to T as in (54) above. Why should this be? After all, we have said that T is *weak* in present-day English, and hence is only strong enough to trigger attraction of grammatical features, not strong enough to trigger movement of the whole set of phonetic and grammatical features carried by a head.

One answer which we could explore is along the following lines. Let's assume that possessive *have* in *Baa Baa Black Sheep* varieties has the idiosyncratic morphological property that when its tense/agreement-features adjoin to T, they can drag along with them all the other (e.g. phonetic and semantic) features carried by *have*. In terms of the metaphor used by Chomsky (1995c), we might say that the phonetic features of *have* are *pied-piped* along with its tense/agreement-features. (If you were brought up on a diet of nursery stories rather than virtual-reality videos, you may remember that the Pied Piper in the village of Hamelin induced the rats to follow him out of the village by playing his pipe.) We can then say that even though the weak tense affix T is only strong enough to attract the tense/agreement-features of verbs in present-day English, *have* has the peculiar property (in the relevant use) that its grammatical features are inseparable from the other features it carries, so if the tense/agreement-features of *have* are adjoined to T for checking purposes, its phonetic features are adjoined as well (hence, in effect, the whole word *have* adjoins to T). In terms of our discussion in §6.5, this amounts to claiming that *have* (in the relevant use) carries *strong* tense/agreement-features. (The relevant tense/agreement-features are *strong* in the sense that they are strongly bound to and hence inseparable from the phonetic features carried by *have*.) Of course, since *have* can also behave like a typical lexical verb (as in (56a–b) above), we have to suppose that the tense/agreement-features carried by *have* can either be *weak* (as for other lexical verbs in English), or (exceptionally) *strong*. Since *have* is the only verb which allows pied-piping in this way, it is clearly anomalous in the relevant respect: hence it comes as no surprise that this use of *have* is no longer found in most varieties of English, and is dying out even in those varieties of British English in which it survived longest. (In Radford 1992, I reported that preschool British children invariably use *do*-support with possessive *have*, hence treating it like a typical lexical verb which carries *weak* tense/agreement-features.)

An obvious question raised by our assumption that finite clauses in present-day English are headed by a weak tense affix (so that lexical verbs generally remain in the head V position of VP) is how we then account for the claim we made in §6.4 that finite verbs in Early Modern English (EME) raised from V to INFL (or, in terms of the rather different apparatus used in this section, adjoined to the head T constituent of TP). One answer (suggested in §6.5) would be to suppose that finite verbs carried *strong* tense/agreement features in EME, so that when the tense/agreement features of a verb adjoin to the tense affix T for checking purposes, the phonetic features carried by the verb are pied-piped along with its tense/agreement-features (thereby triggering adjunction of the whole verb to T). However, an alternative (rather different) analysis would be to suppose that finite clauses in EME were headed by a *strong* tense affix, and that a *strong* affix has the defining characteristic that it must have *phonetic* (as well as grammatical) features adjoined to it. It would then follow that a tense affix heading finite clauses in EME would always have to have an overt item adjoined to it: this could come about either by *merging* an auxiliary directly with the tense-affix T, or by *moving* a nonauxiliary verb from the head V position in VP to adjoin to the tense affix T heading TP.

This analysis leads us towards the following set of assumptions. Finite clauses are headed by an abstract (present or past) tense affix T. There is parametric variation across languages with respect to whether T is a *strong* or *weak* affix (T was strong in Early Modern English/EME, but is weak in Modern Standard English/MSE). A *weak* tense affix must have an appropriate set of tense/agreement-features attached to it; a *strong affix* must additionally have a set of phonetic features attached to it. Consider first how the requirements of the weak tense affix found in MSE can be satisfied. One possibility is by **attraction** – i.e. by adjoining the tense/agreement-features of a finite nonauxiliary verb to T, as in (55) above. A second (exceptional) possibility is by **movement**, as in (54) above, where possessive *has* has idiosyncratic pied-piping properties. However, a third possibility is by **merger** (more specifically, merging the tense affix with a finite auxiliary). We can illustrate this third possibility in terms of sentences containing finite auxiliaries such as the following:

(58) (a)   She has seen it
      (b)   She could see it

Let's suppose that (58a) is formed by merging the auxiliary *has* with a present-tense affix *Pres* to form a T constituent *has+Pres* which in turn merges with the VP *seen it* to form the T-bar *has+Pres seen it*, and that this T-bar in turn merges with *she* to form the TP in (59a) below. Similarly, let's suppose that (58b) is derived by merging the auxiliary *could* with a past-tense suffix *Past* to form the T constituent *could+Past* which in turn merges with the VP *see it* to form the T-bar *could+Past see it*, and that this T-bar then merges with *she* to form the TP (59b) below:

(59) (a)

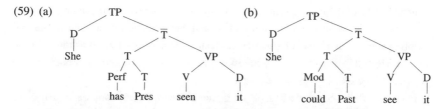

The requirement for the weak tense affixes *Pres/Past* to have a set of tense/agreement features adjoined to them is then met by virtue of the fact that *has* (which is a third person singular present-tense perfective auxiliary) merges with *Pres* in (59a), and *could* (which is a past-tense modal auxiliary) merges with *Past* in (59b).

Although we shall not enter into relevant details here, it may be that we can extend the analysis in (59) from finite clauses headed by auxiliaries to infinitival clauses headed by *to* (especially in view of Stowell's 1982 claim that *to* carries tense properties). If so, an infinitival *to*-clause would have essentially the same TP structure as (59b) above, save that in place of *could* we find *to*.

Now consider how the requirements of the strong tense affix heading finite clauses in Early Modern English can be satisfied (recall that we are assuming that a strong affix must have an overt item attached to it). One possibility is for an auxiliary to merge with the tense affix (much as in (59a–b) above). A second possibility is for a nonauxiliary verb to raise from V to adjoin to T, e.g. as in (60) below:

(60)

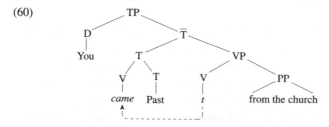

Once the verb *came* adjoins to T in (60), it can move from there to COMP, so deriving the structure associated with the question (61) below:

(61)   *Came* you from the church? (Tranio, *Taming of the Shrew*, III.ii)

However, adjunction of tense/agreement features of the verb to T alone (as in (55) above) would clearly not satisfy the requirement for a strong affix to have a set of phonetic features adjoined to it.

6.9   Question affix

As we noted earlier, our discussion here has important implications for the nature of **head movement**. We have suggested that suffixation in structures like (45) involves adjunction of a verb to a negative suffix; that overt head-movement in structures like (54) involves adjunction of (the set of phonetic and grammatical features carried by) a verb to a null tense affix; and that attraction in structures like (55) involves adjunction of a set of grammatical features to a tense affix. The wider generalization which this would seem to suggest is that movement and attraction both involve adjunction of a set of features to an affix.

However, if we conclude that all head movement is adjunction, we clearly have to revise our earlier analysis of *inversion* in questions. Rather than *moving into* COMP, it must be the case that an inverted auxiliary *adjoins to* an affix in COMP. If we assume (as earlier) that affixes have specific semantic and categorial properties (e.g. T has the semantic property that it denotes tense, and the categorial property that it is a verbal affix), we might suppose that the affix in COMP in questions has the semantic property that it marks the *illocutionary force* of the sentence (i.e. marks it as interrogative rather than declarative or imperative), and has the categorial property that it is a *verbal* affix. Given these assumptions, COMP will be filled by a question affix in interrogative sentences, and *inversion* will involve movement of a verb from T to adjoin to the question affix in COMP. The assumption that inversion in questions involves adjunction to a question affix gains cross-linguistic plausibility from Latin examples such as:

(62)   *Necavitne* Brutus Caesarem?
         killed+**Q**   Brutus Caesar (**Q** = 'question particle')
         'Did Brutus kill Caesar?'

where it would seem that the verb *necavit* 'killed' has been adjoined to the overt question suffix +*ne* in COMP. (Verbs are normally positioned at the end of clauses in Latin.) An obvious way of providing a unitary account of the two types of head-movement operation found in English and Latin questions is to assume that both types of structure involve adjunction of the preposed (auxiliary or nonauxiliary) verb to an (overt or covert) affixal question-particle in COMP. For concreteness, let's use the symbol **Q** to denote the null question affix found in English questions (following work in an earlier framework by Katz and Postal 1964 and Baker 1970). You can think of Q as the syntactic counterpart of the question-mark **?** used in the spelling system to indicate that a sentence is a question.

In the light of this assumption, consider now how we derive a question such as:

(63)   Can you help me?

The modal auxiliary *can* merges with a present-tense affix *Pres* to form the T constituent *can+Pres*; this in turn merges with the VP *help me* to form the T-bar *can+Pres help me*; the resulting T-bar merges with *you* to form the TP *You can+Pres help me*. This TP is then merged with a C constituent containing the strong question affix Q, so forming the CP (64) below:

(64)

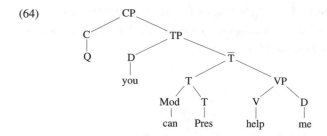

However, Q is a strong affix, and so needs an overt head (i.e. a non-null head with overt phonetic features) attached to it. The **economy principle** requires us to move the minimal constituent which will satisfy the requirement for Q to be attached to an overt head (and any other relevant grammatical requirements). The minimal overt head which we can adjoin to Q is the modal *can*; hence, we might suppose that the modal *can* adjoins to Q as in (65) below:

(65)

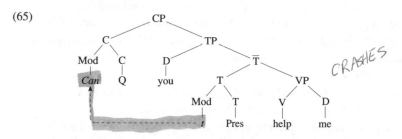

CRASHES

How does this happen? How does it skip over you??

In (65), the auxiliary *can* is said to **excorporate** out of the T constituent containing it, thereby detaching itself from the tense affix *Pres* (see Roberts 1991 for a technical discussion of excorporation).

However, an apparent problem posed by the excorporation analysis is that it presupposes that the tense affix *Pres* can be *stranded* by movement of the modal *can* on its own (without *Pres*). This might be argued to be potentially problematic because affixes can't generally be stranded (cf. Lasnik 1981), as we see from the fact that the negative affix *n't* attached to *couldn't* in (66a) below can't be stranded by inversion of *could*:

(66) (a)   He *couldn't* find it
     (b)   *Couldn't* he find it?
     (c)   **Could* he *n't* find it?

When *could* undergoes inversion, the negative affix *n't* must be inverted along with *could* (as in (66b)), and can't be left behind and thereby stranded – hence the ungrammaticality of (66c). So since *Pres* is a tense affix, and affixes can't be stranded, the derivation in (65) will crash.

How can we ensure that the tense affix *Pres* isn't stranded in (65)? One answer is to posit that it is *pied-piped* along with *can*, so that the whole T constituent *can+Pres* adjoins to the question affix Q, as in (67) below:

(67)

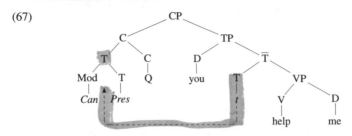

Since *Pres* remains adjoined to *can*, there is no violation of the constraint against *affix-stranding* in (67). Moreover, since (the T constituent containing) *can* is adjoined to (the C constituent containing) Q, the requirement for the strong affix Q to be attached to a set of phonetic features (i.e. to an overt item like *can*) is satisfied in (67).

So, the assumption that affixes can't be stranded would seem to favour the *pied-piping* analysis of inversion in (67) (whereby the tense affix *Pres* is pied-piped along with *can*, so that the whole T constituent *can+Pres* is moved) over the *excorporation* analysis in (65) (whereby only the modal auxiliary *can* is moved): accordingly, the T movement analysis in (67) has become the standard analysis of inversion (in one form or another) in the linguistic literature over the past two decades.

However, the conclusion that the *pied-piping* analysis is superior to the *excorporation* analysis is only as strong as the assumption on which it is based – namely that affixes can *never* be stranded. But is this necessarily so? After all, we earlier drew a distinction between *strong* and *weak* affixes, to the effect that a *strong* affix must be bound to a set of phonetic features (i.e. affixed to an overt item), whereas a weak affix need not be. (A weak affix serves simply to check an appropriate set of grammatical features.) In these terms, (66c) **Could he n't find it?* is ungrammatical because *n't* is a strong affix which needs to be attached to an overt finite form (like *could*). However, since we earlier argued that the T constituent heading finite clauses in Modern Standard English contains a *weak* tense affix, it follows that there is little reason to assume that the weak affix *Pres* cannot be separated from (phonetic features of) the modal *can* in (65). After all, if *can* raises to T in order to check its present-tense head-feature and its nominative specifier-feature, there would seem to be no obvious reason why *can* should not subsequently raise on its own to adjoin to Q once the relevant head- and specifier-features carried by *can* have been checked (and erased). Indeed, if we posit that the tense affix *Pres* remains in T (as in (65) above) after adjunction to Q takes place, this will facilitate LF convergence (if we assume that T is the locus of tense at LF). Thus, the choice between the *pied-piping* analysis in (67) and the *excorporation* analysis in (65) is far from straightforward (and depends heavily on theory-internal assumptions): as already noted, the *pied-piping* analysis is the one standardly adopted in the relevant literature (though it is usually *assumed* rather than *argued for*).

Our assumption that interrogative clauses contain a Q affix raises obvious questions about the syntax of the interrogative complementizer *if* in a complement clause such as that bracketed in (68) below:

(68)   I wonder [*if* you can help me]

If all interrogative clauses contain a Q affix, it seems plausible to suppose that the complementizer *if* is merged with the affix Q, so that the bracketed clause in (68) has the structure (69) below (where the symbol *Comp* is used to categorize the complementizer *if*):

(69)

This implies that the requirement for the strong interrogative affix Q to be attached to an overt item can be satisfied either by **merger** (i.e. by merging Q with a complementizer like *if* as in (69) above) or by **movement** (by adjoining an auxiliary/T-constituent to Q as in (65/67) above). One minor problem posed by the analysis in (69) is that it would seem to call in question our earlier claim that Q is a purely *verbal* affix, since the complementizer *if* doesn't seem to be a verbal head.

Since we have seen that there are **movement** operations in which the grammatical and phonetic features carried by a head are adjoined to another head, and also **attraction** operations which affect grammatical (but not phonetic) features, an obvious question to ask is whether there is a third type of movement operation by which phonetic features alone are adjoined to another head (leaving behind the corresponding grammatical features). This seems a plausible assumption in relation to the kind of *cliticization* phenomena illustrated below:

(70) (a)   *Who's* he dating?

(b)   *She's* losing weight

(c)   *They've* gone

(d)   They *wanna* leave

At first sight, it might seem plausible to suppose that cliticization here involves a movement operation adjoining (the grammatical and phonetic features of) one word to the other (as in the case of *n't*-suffixation). But such a *movement* analysis would wrongly predict that a compound head is thereby formed which can itself undergo movement as a single syntactic unit. However, this assumption is false – as we see from examples such as (71) below:

(71) (a)   You think *who's* winning?

  (b)   **Who's* do you think winning?

  (c)   *Who* do you think *'s* winning?

If cliticization of *'s* onto *who* in (71a) involved a movement operation by which *'s* adjoins to *who*, we'd expect the two to form a single constituent and hence to be able to move to the front of the sentence together in (71b): however, the fact that *who* can only be preposed to the front of the sentence on its own (as in (71c)) suggests that this type of cliticization is a purely phonological process, so that *who* and *is* remain separate words throughout the syntax, and only fuse together in the PF component, by a phonological process which adjoins the *phonetic features* of one item to those of the other. For the sake of concreteness, let's call this type of operation (whereby the phonetic features of one item are adjoined to those of another) **PF movement** (since it involves movement of phonetic features).

If our speculation here is along the right lines, it follows that we find three types of displacement operation: **attraction** (whereby grammatical features are moved without phonetic features); **PF movement** (whereby phonetic features are moved without grammatical features); and **movement** (whereby phonetic and grammatical features are moved together). It is clear that **movement** takes place in the syntactic component (prior to **spellout**), and that **PF movement** takes place in the PF component; and it may be that **attraction** is an operation which takes place in the LF component (and hence is an **LF movement** operation). If this is so, we find a remarkable symmetry in the types of operation found in all three components of the grammar, since all three may involve movement operations.

6.10   Summary

In this chapter, we have been concerned with the syntax of **head movement**. In §6.2 we looked at auxiliary inversion in questions in English, arguing that this involves an **I movement** operation whereby an auxiliary moves from INFL to COMP. We suggested that an interrogative COMP is *strong* (and so has to be filled), and that moving an auxiliary from INFL into COMP in questions serves to fill COMP. In §6.3, we argued that an inverted auxiliary leaves behind a trace (i.e. a silent copy of itself) in the INFL position out of which it moves when it moves to COMP. In §6.4 we saw that finite verbs in Early Modern English (EME) could move from V to INFL by an operation of **V movement** (as is shown by word-order facts in negative sentences like *I care not for her*), but that this kind of movement is generally no longer possible in Modern Standard English (MSE). We argued that **I movement** and **V movement** are two different reflexes of a more general **head movement** operation, and that **head movement** is subject to a strict locality constraint (the **head movement constraint**) which requires it to apply in a successive cyclic fashion. In §6.5 we suggested that verbs in EME had strong agreement-features (by virtue of the relatively rich agreement inflections they carried) and consequently allowed a null **pro** subject, whereas their counterparts in MSE have weak agreement-features (by virtue of their impoverished agreement morphology) and so do not license a **pro** subject. We noted that the strong agreement features of finite verbs in EME were checked by movement of the verb (along with its features) from V to INFL, whereas the weak agreement features of finite verbs in MSE are checked by **attraction** (i.e. percolation) of the relevant agreement features from V to INFL (with the verb itself remaining *in situ* in the head V position of VP). We went on to argue that movement and attraction are two different reflexes of a common *feature movement* operation which moves grammatical features from one constituent to another, and which in the case of **movement** also has the effect of *pied-piping* the phonetic features of the head along with its grammatical features. In §6.6 we looked at the syntax of negation in MSE, arguing that the negative particle *not* functions as a syntactic head NEG which projects into a NEGP constituent, and suggested that *not* can attract the head-features of (the head verb of) its complement, but not the specifier-features of a finite verb; we also suggested that *n't* differs from *not* in that *not* is a free form whereas *n't* is a bound form which can only attach to other bound forms. In §6.7 we looked at the syntax of possessive *have* in those (*Baa Baa Black Sheep*) varieties of English in which it can behave like an auxiliary. We argued that possessive *have* originates in the head V position of VP and from there can raise to INFL. We noted that possessive *have* can be directly negated by *n't*, but not by *not*. We suggested that this is because *have* can serve as a bound form, and hence can adjoin to the bound negative *n't* (but not to the free form *not*). More generally, we suggested that adjunction can only adjoin one bound form to another, and cannot target a free form like *not*. In §6.8 we went on to speculate that all head movement may involve adjunction to an affix, so that V-to-I movement involves adjunction of V to an abstract tense affix **T**: we noted that one consequence of this is that clauses are projections of a tense affix **T**, and hence have the status of **TP** (= tense phrase) constituents. We argued that T is a *weak* affix in MSE, but was a *strong* affix in EME; and we suggested that weak affixes have the property that they check grammatical features, whereas strong affixes must be attached to a set of phonetic features. We noted that the requirements of the weak T in MSE are generally satisfied either by *merging* an auxiliary with T, or by attraction of the tense/agreement-features of a nonauxiliary verb to T. By contrast, the requirements of the strong T in EME are satisfied either by *merger* with an auxiliary, or by *movement* of a nonauxiliary verb to adjoin to T. In §6.9 we suggested that questions are CP constituents headed by a C node containing a strong **Q** affix; we noted that the requirement for Q to be attached to a set of phonetic features is satisfied in main clauses by adjoining a preposed (auxiliary or nonauxiliary) verb to Q, and in complement clauses by merging the complementizer *if* with Q. We went on to speculate that grammars may contain three different types of movement operations: **PF movement** operations which affect phonetic features, **attraction** which affects grammatical features, and (syntactic) **movement** which affects phonetic and grammatical features. We speculated that each different type of movement operation might apply in a different component of the grammar – **movement** in the syntactic component (prior to spellout), **PF movement** in the PF component, and **attraction** in the LF component.

Workbook section
Exercise I (§§6.2–6.3)

Discuss the derivation of the following sentences, saying why each derivation crashes or converges.

1 Can he help us?
2 *If he can help us?
3 I wonder if he can help us
4 *I wonder if can he help us
5 *Could he've helped us?
6 Was he helping her? moves from I to C
7 Did he help her? did from I to C
8 *Did he be helping her?

Model answer for 1

Using the CP/IP analysis of clauses presupposed in §§6.2–6.3, we can derive 1 as follows. The verb *help* merges with the pronominal determiner *us* to form the VP (i) below:

(i)

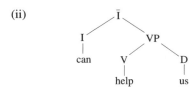

Since *us* is an objective pronoun, it satisfies the requirement for the verb *help* (when used transitively, as here) to have an objective complement.

The VP in (i) in turn merges with the auxiliary (I constituent) *can* to form the I-bar (ii) below:

(ii)

Since the VP *help us* is headed by the infinitive verb *help*, it satisfies the requirement for *can* to have an infinitive complement.

The pronoun *he* in turn merges with the I-bar in (ii), forming the IP in (iii) below:

(iii)

The nominative pronoun *he* satisfies the requirement for *can* to have a nominative subject.

The IP in (iii) is then merged with a C constituent into which the auxiliary *can* moves (leaving behind a trace in the position out of which it moves), so forming the CP (iv) below:

(iv)

(where *t* is a trace of the auxiliary *can* which moves from INFL to COMP).

Exercise II (§§6.4–6.5)

Discuss the syntax of the following Early Modern English (EME) sentences taken from various plays by Shakespeare:

1 Thou marvell'st at my words (Macbeth, *Macbeth*, III.ii)
2 Macbeth doth come (Third Witch, *Macbeth*, I.iii)
3 Wilt thou use thy wit? (Claudio, *Much Ado About Nothing*, V.i)
4 Wrong I mine enemies? (Brutus, *Julius Caesar*, IV.ii)
5 Do you fear it? (Cassius, *Julius Caesar*, I.ii)
6 I doubt not of your wisdom (Mark Antony, *Julius Caesar*, III.i)
7 I do not like thy look (Dogberry, *Much Ado About Nothing*, IV.ii)
8 Didst thou not say he comes? (Baptista, *Taming of the Shrew*, III.ii)
9 Knows he not thy voice? (First Lord, *All's Well that Ends Well*, IV.i)
10 Can'st not rule her? (Leontes, *Winter's Tale*, II.iii)

Model answer for 1 and 2

In terms of the framework outlined in §§6.4–6.5, sentence 1 will be derived as follows. The determiner *my* merges with the noun *words* to form the DP *my words*; this in turn merges with the preposition *at* to form the PP *at my words*. The verb *marvell'st* merges with this PP to form the VP (i) below:

(i)

```
              VP
         ____/  \____
        V           PP
        |       ___/  \___
    marvell'st  P         DP
                |      __/  \__
                at    D       N
                      |       |
                      my    words
```

The VP in (i) then merges with an abstract INFL constituent to form an I-bar constituent which in turn merges with the pronoun *thou* to form an IP. The verb *marvell'st* raises from V to INFL as in (ii) below:

(ii)

```
                    IP
            _____/  _____
           D                Ī
           |          _____/  \_____
         Thou        I             VP
                     |        ____/  \____
                 marvell'st   V          PP
                     ▲        |      ___/  \___
                     └--------t      P        DP
                                     |     __/  \__
                                     at   D       N
                                          |       |
                                          my    words
```

Why should finite verbs like *marvell'st* raise from V to INFL in EME? The answer suggested in §6.5 is that finite verbs in EME carry strong tense/agreement-features – i.e. features which are strongly bound to (and hence inseparable from) the corresponding phonetic features carried by the word. The [Pres] present-tense head-feature of *marvell'st* needs to raise to INFL in order to ensure that INFL is interpretable at LF (by virtue of carrying a tense-feature); the [2SNom] specifier-features of *marvell'st* need to raise to INFL in order to check whether the requirement for *marvell'st* to have a second person singular nominative specifier is satisfied by *thou*. (Checking erases the specifier-features of *marvell'st* and the nominative-case head-feature of *thou*.) Since the tense/agreement-features of *marvell'st* are strong, they cannot raise to INFL on their own by **attraction**; instead, they carry the phonetic features of *marvell'st* along with them, so that the whole word *marvell'st* undergoes **head-movement** and thereby moves into INFL – as in (ii) above.

Given the assumptions made in §§6.4–6.5, sentence 2 will be derived as follows. The verb *come* merges with the auxiliary/INFL constituent *doth* to form an I-bar which in turn merges with the subject *Macbeth* to form the structure (iii) below (*doth* is a regional variant of *does*):

(iii)

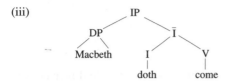

(We are assuming here, on the basis of the arguments presented in §4.7, that *Macbeth* is a DP headed by a null determiner; this is not implausible, given that we find overt determiners used with proper names in many languages – cf. Italian *la Callas*, literally 'the Callas'.)

A potential problem for the analysis in the text posed by sentences like 2 is that they might seem to call into question the assumption that dummy verbs like *do* are used purely as a last resort. We might suppose that if *do*-support were purely a last resort, sentences like 2 would be ungrammatical, since they have the *do*-less counterpart *Macbeth cometh* (which involves raising *cometh* from V to INFL). However, one way of maintaining the last resort account would be to suppose that *do* in EME was not a dummy auxiliary at all, but rather had independent semantic content of some kind. One possibility is that *do* in EME served the function of marking *aspect*. After all, there are varieties of present-day English in which *do* is an aspectual auxiliary: for example, in Caribbean creoles (according to Rickford 1986 and Harris 1986) we find the auxiliary *do* being used in sentences like:

(iv)   He does be sick

to mark habitual aspect (so that (iv) has much the same meaning as *He is usually sick*). Likewise, *do* functions as a habitual aspect marker in Irish English (cf. Guilfoyle 1983, Harris 1986) and in south-western varieties of British English (cf. Wakelin 1977, pp. 120–1). However, since sentence 2 *Macbeth doth come* doesn't have the habitual sense of *Macbeth usually comes*, it's implausible that *doth* functions as an aspectual auxiliary here. An alternative possibility is that *do* in EME had a *performative* sense, and thus meant something like *perform the action of*... This performative use of *do* in EME may be connected to its use in present-day British English in sentences such as:

(v)   He can read books quicker than I can *do*

where *do* might be glossed as *perform the relevant action* (i.e. of reading books). If *do* had independent semantic content in EME, it would clearly not be subject to the last resort condition (since the latter applies only to dummy or expletive items with no semantic content of any kind).

Head movement

An alternative possibility would be to suppose that the use of *do* here is determined by the need to satisfy *metrical* requirements. This becomes clearer if we look at the context in which 2 was uttered, viz.

(vi)   A drum! A drum!
              Macbeth doth come

Since the second line must contain four syllables and end in a word rhyming with *drum*, and since the three-syllable utterance *Macbeth cometh* satisfies neither requirement, the four-syllable utterance *Macbeth doth come* (which satisfies both) is used instead.

Overall, the precise function and content of *do* in EME is anything but clear. As noted by Tieken-Boon van Ostade (1988, p. 1) the origin of *do* 'may truly be called one of the great riddles of English linguistic history'.

Exercise III (§§6.6–6.9)

Discuss the derivation of the following sentences, saying why each derivation converges or crashes:

1   He smokes
2   *Smokes he?
3   Does he smoke?
4   *He not smokes
5   *He smokesn't
6   He does not smoke
7   Does he not smoke?
8   *Does not he smoke?
9   He doesn't smoke
10 Doesn't he smoke?

Model answer for 1

Given the assumptions made in the text, 1 will be derived as in (i) below (3 = third person; S = singular; M = masculine; Nom = nominative; Pres = present tense):

(i)

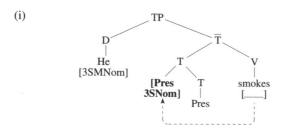

256

The head of the clause is a weak tense affix T. Since weak affixes trigger **attraction** but not **movement**, the (bold-printed) head- and specifier-features of *smokes* (its head-features indicating that it is present tense, its specifier-features that it requires a third person singular nominative specifier) are adjoined to present-tense affix T, as indicated by the arrow in (i) – though the verb *smokes* remains in V (more specifically, its phonetic features remain in V). The tense properties of *smokes* can then be checked against those of T, and its agreement properties (requiring it to have a third person singular nominative specifier) checked against those of *he*. Checking erases all grammatical features except the [3SM] head-features of *he* and the [Pres] present-tense head-feature of T.

One question which arises in relation to (i) is why it is not possible to check the agreement features of *smokes* by **movement** – i.e. by adjoining (the grammatical and phonetic features of) *smokes* to the tense affix T. The answer is provided by the **economy principle**: attraction is more economical than movement (since attraction involves movement of grammatical features alone, whereas movement involves pied-piping of phonetic features along with grammatical features), so attraction applies unless movement is forced by morphological considerations. Since T is a weak affix (which therefore only serves to check grammatical features), there is no morphological requirement for movement here, hence (by the **economy principle**) no possibility of movement.

A second question which arises in relation to (i) is why *do*-support is not required here. The answer is that the derivation in (i) converges without the use of *do*-support, so that the **economy principle** (in the guise of the **last resort** condition) determines that *do* cannot be used because it is not required. In this respect, it is interesting to note the following contrast (where DOES denotes a form carrying contrastive stress, and *d's* denotes the unstressed form /dəz/):

(ii) (a)   He DOES smoke
     (b)   *He *d's* smoke

The *last resort* account correctly predicts that the unstressed form *d's* cannot be used here. But how are we to account for the fact that the stressed form DOES can be used in (ii)(a)? One possible answer is to suppose that stressed forms of *do* have an emphatic or contrastive function, and so have intrinsic semantic content – and that (by virtue of their semantic content) they are not subject to the *last resort* condition on the use of contentless dummy items.

Helpful hints

Consider two alternative derivations for 2 – one in which *smokes* raises from V to T to C in successive cyclic fashion, and the other in which *smokes* raises directly from V to C: say why both derivations crash.

Exercise IV (§§6.6–6.9)

The following data (kindly provided by Larry Lamb) illustrate three different uses of *have* in a particular *Baa Baa Black Sheep* variety of English:

1   He has some sheep
2   Have you any sheep?
3   *They have not any sheep
4   They haven't any sheep
5   *Has he not any sheep?
6   *Has not he any sheep?
7   Hasn't he any sheep?
8   *Has hen't any sheep?
9   Do you have any sheep?
10   We do not have any sheep
11   We don't have any sheep
12   Do they not have any sheep?
13   *Do theyn't have any sheep?
14   *Do not they have any sheep?
15   He had a shower (= 'He took a shower')
16   *He'd a shower (= 'He took a shower')
17   *Had he a shower? (= 'Did he take a shower?')
18   Did he have a shower? (= 'Did he take a shower?')
19   *He hadn't a shower (= 'He didn't take a shower')
20   He did not have a shower (= 'He did not take a shower')
21   Did he not have a shower? (= 'Did he not take a shower?')
22   *Did not he have a shower? (= 'Did he not take a shower?')
23   He didn't have a shower (= 'He didn't take a shower')
24   Didn't he have a shower? (= 'Didn't he take a shower?')
25   He's lost the key
26   Has he lost the key?
27   *Does he have lost the key?
28   He's not lost the key
29   Has he not lost the key?
30   *Has not he lost the key?
31   He hasn't lost the key
32   Hasn't he lost the key?

The use of *have* illustrated in 1–14 might be called its *possessive* use (since *have* in this use can roughly be paraphrased by 'possess' or 'own'), that in 15–24 its *activity* use (since *have* in this use can be paraphrased by the activity verb 'take'), and that in 25–32 its *perfective* use. (Note that the grammaticality judgments in 15–24 are relative to the activity use of *have* where it is paraphraseable by 'take', not to the different possessive use of *have* where it is paraphraseable by 'own'.) Discuss the derivation of each of these sentences, and say why each derivation converges or crashes.

Model answer for 1

In its possessive use, *have* in most varieties of English behaves like a typical lexical verb, in that it occupies the head V position of VP. Its tense- and agreement-features are checked by **attraction** (i.e. by adjunction to the weak tense affix heading finite clauses), as indicated by the arrow in (i) below (where [Pres] denotes the present-tense head-feature carried by *has*, and [3SNom] are agreement-features indicating that *has* agrees with/requires a third person singular nominative specifier/subject):

(i)

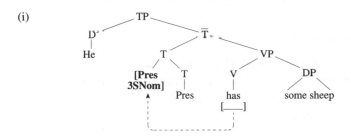

The phonetic features of *has* remain in the head V position of VP. There is no **movement** of *has* to T, since T is a weak affix (i.e. the kind of affix which requires grammatical rather than phonetic features to be attached to it), and hence the **economy principle** dictates that attraction is preferred to movement. Since T is empty here, we expect the relevant structure to be tagged by *do*, as in:

(ii)   He has some sheep, *doesn't* he?

However, it is a peculiarity of *Baa Baa Black Sheep* varieties that possessive *have* also has a second use, on which it appears to behave like an auxiliary (in not requiring *do*-support in questions and negatives). This cannot be because T can (e.g. optionally) be a strong affix in the relevant varieties, since otherwise all other lexical verbs would behave like *have*. Rather, it must be an idiosyncrasy of possessive *have*. The nature of this idiosyncrasy would appear to be that possessive *have* has the property that its phonetic features can optionally be pied-piped along with its tense/agreement-features. Movement of the tense/agreement-features of *has* alone will give rise to the derivation (i) above; pied-piping of other features along with the tense/agreement-features will cause the whole (set of features carried by the) item *has* to adjoin to T as in (iii) below:

259

(iii)

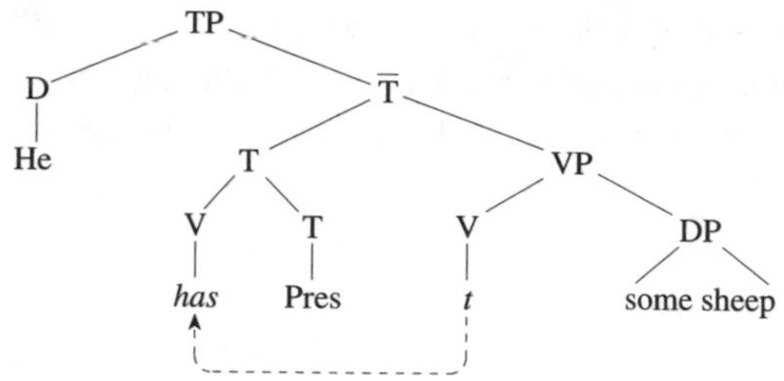

Since T is occupied by *has* in (iii), we correctly predict that the resulting structure will be tagged by *has* in sentences such as:

(iv)   He has some sheep, *hasn't* he?

We also correctly predict that (because the two are immediately adjacent) *has* can cliticize to *he* in (iii), giving:

(v)   *He's* some sheep

It may well be that *have*-cliticization involves **PF movement** (i.e. adjunction of the phonetic features of the clitic form *'s* to those of *he*), since there is no evidence that *he* and *'s* form a single constituent in the syntax (e.g. they can't undergo any kind of movement operation together).

Helpful hints

Consider the possibility that activity *have* is a transitive verb which is directly generated in V and cannot adjoin to T (why?), and that perfective *have* is merged with T.

Exercise V (§§6.6–6.9)

Discuss the derivation of the following sentences, saying what determines whether they are grammatical or not.

1   He cannot do anything
2   *Cannot he do anything?
3   Can he not do anything?
4   He has not returned
5   He's not returned
6   He hasn't returned
7   *He'sn't returned
8   He will not survive
9   *He willn't survive
10   He won't survive
11   Will he not survive?

12   *Will not he survive?

13   Won't he survive?

not–attraction
n't–movement

Model answer for 1–3

In the text, we suggested that *not* can't adjoin to an auxiliary, because *not* is a free form. However, one problem posed by this assumption is that *can* has the *not*-form *cannot*: the fact that this is written as a single word suggests that *not* adjoins to *can* at some stage of derivation. But where?

If *not* were to adjoin to *can* by a syntactic movement operation, 1 would be derived by adjunction of *not* to *can* in the syntactic component, as in (i) below (where we assume that *can* is a **Mod**(al auxiliary) which is merged with T):

(i)

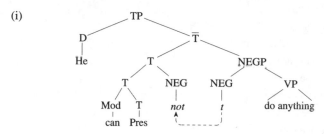

Such an analysis would result in the formation of a compound present-tense negative auxiliary *cannot*, which would then be expected to be able to undergo auxiliary inversion like other similar auxiliaries (e.g. *doesn't*). However, the fact that 2 **Cannot he do anything?* is ungrammatical suggests that this cannot be so – i.e. that *not* doesn't adjoin to *can* by a syntactic movement operation.

An alternative possibility is to assume that *not* (in this use) is a PF clitic which adjoins to *can* by a (postsyntactic) **PF movement** operation which adjoins the phonetic features of *not* to those of *can*, thereby forming *cannot* (whose PF status as a single word is recognized in the English spelling system). Under this alternative account, *can* and *not* would remain separate words in the syntax, and 1 would have the syntactic structure (ii):

(ii)

```
              TP
           ___/  \___
          D          T̄
          |       __/  \__
          He     T        NEGP
              __/ \__    __/  \__
            Mod   T    NEG      VP
             |    |     |     __/  \__
            can  Pres  not   do anything
```

Since *can* remains a separate word from *not* in the syntax, we correctly predict that, in questions, only *can* will be inverted (i.e. move from T to C), not *cannot* (since the latter remains two separate words in the syntax): this accounts for why the negative counterpart of 1 is 3, not 2. However, because *not* can serve as a PF clitic and *can* is able to serve as host for a PF clitic, *not* cliticizes to *can* in the PF component (with the phonetic features of *not* adjoining to those of *can*), so forming *cannot* (which therefore represents one word at PF, and two words in the syntax and at LF).

Exercise VI (§§6.6–6.9)

The sentences below illustrate the use of *be* as a copular verb linking a subject like *he* to a nonverbal (i.e. adjectival, nominal, or – as in this case – prepositional) predicate like *in the army*:

1   He has been in the army
2   He is in the army
3   Is he in the army?
4   He has not been in the army
5   He is not in the army
6   He isn't in the army
7   Is he not in the army?
8   Isn't he in the army?
9   *Is not he in the army?
10   . . . on condition that he not be in the army

Discuss the derivation of these sentences.

Helpful hints

A traditional analysis of copular *be* (dating back in spirit to Klima 1964) is that it originates in the head V of VP, and (in finite indicative forms) raises from V to T (but in nonfinite or subjunctive forms, remains in V). An alternative *minimalist* analysis would be to suppose that copular *be* is a dummy or expletive item with no semantic content, which serves purely to encode morphological features: for example, we might suppose that *been* is required in 1 because perfective *have* requires a complement headed by a perfective participle verb form. Say how the sentences above would be analysed on these two accounts, and whether either (or both) analyses run into problems in accounting for any of the examples. Note that *be* in 10 is a subjunctive form (cf. the discussion of such forms in exercise II of chapter 4).

Model answer for 2

Under the traditional *be*-raising account, *is* originates in the head V position of VP, and then raises up to adjoin to T as in (i) below:

(i)

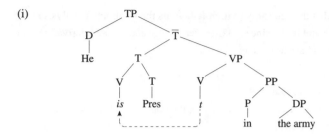

Once *be* is in T, it can then raise further to COMP, e.g. in questions such as 3 *Is he in the army?* However, what is puzzling is why *be* should raise to T (rather than remaining in the head V position within the VP), since the tense affix T in present-day English is *weak*: in order to account for why *be* raises to T we have to suppose that the tense/agreement-features of finite forms like *is* are strong (i.e. they are strongly bound to the phonetic features of *is*, so that movement of one triggers pied-piping of the other), so that the whole (set of features carried by the) item *is* has to adjoin to T.

Under the alternative minimalist analysis, the form *is* is directly *merged* with the tense affix T in INFL, as in (ii) below:

(ii)

```
              TP
          ___/  \___
         D          T̄
         |       __/  \__
        He      T        PP
              _/ \_     _/  \_
            Aux   T    P      DP
             |    |    |     /  \
            is   Pres  in   the army
```

Why should *is* be required here? One answer could be that T is a weak verbal affix, and so must either be merged with an auxiliary (like *is*), or associated with a set of verbal features which are attracted to T and thereby percolate up from the head V in VP: but since there is no VP (and hence no V) in (ii), the only possibility is to merge the affix with an auxiliary. On this account, *be* is a dummy auxiliary used only as a *last resort* (to satisfy the categorial requirements of the tense affix T – i.e. the requirement that it be attached to a verbal stem): it is used in structures with a nonverbal predicate (whereas dummy *do* is used as a last resort in structures with a verbal predicate). An alternative possibility would be to suppose that tense-features must be *visible* at PF – which amounts to claiming that every finite clause in English must contain an overt tensed auxiliary or nonauxiliary verb (though clearly this claim would have to be modified in relation to clauses where a finite verb undergoes ellipsis/gapping).

It might be argued that the **economy principle** favours the minimalist analysis in (ii) over the *be*-raising account in (i), since (ii) involves a more economical derivation (one with no VP projection and no movement).

Exercise VII (§§6.6–6.9)

In African American English (AAE), the copular verb *be* is used as illustrated in the following examples:

1 Rastus be happy
2 Rastus don't be happy
3 *Rastus ben't happy
4 Do Rastus be happy?
5 *Be Rastus happy?

Discuss the derivation of each of the sentences 1–5 in AAE.

Model answer for 1

Examples like 1–5 suggest that *be* in AAE behaves like a typical nonauxiliary verb in that it always occupies the head V position of VP. In terms of the analysis given in the text, this implies that the tense affix T is weak, and *attracts* the head- and specifier-features (i.e. tense/agreement-features) of *be* to adjoin to T, as represented by the dotted arrow in (i) below:

(i)

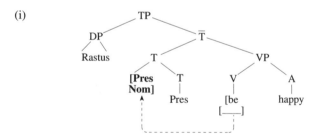

The head-feature [Pres] of *be* tells us that it is a present-tense form, and its [Nom] specifier-feature tells us that it requires a nominative subject: its tense-feature is checked against that of T, and its specifier-feature against those of the DP *Rastus*. (Given the claim in §4.7 that all argument nominals are DPs, *Rastus* will be a DP headed by a null nominative determiner.)

Exercise VIII (§§6.6–6.9)

Children acquiring English as a first language sometimes have problems with the syntax of auxiliaries in questions. Typical examples of sporadic errors made by children aged 2–4 years are given below (the name of the child producing each utterance is given in parentheses):

1 Did I be a good girl? (Sarah)
2 Does it doesn't move? (Nina)
3 Do she don't need that one? (Adam)
4 Did we went to somebody's house? (Adam)
5 Does his nose goes there? (Adam)
6 Does it opens? (Adam)
7 Is the clock is working? (Shem)
8 Is this is a dog? (Nina)

Akmajian and Heny (1975, p. 17) report a three-year-old girl producing interrogative structures such as:

9 Is I can do that?
10 Is you should eat the apple?
11 Is Ben did go?
12 Is the apple juice won't spill?

A similar pattern is noted by Davis (1987), who reports the following examples of child yes–no questions:

13 Are you want one?
14 Are you got some orange juice?
15 Are this is broke?
16 Are you don't know what Sharon's name is?
17 Are you sneezed?

Discuss how *do/be* appear to be used by the children concerned in each of the examples, highlighting differences with the corresponding adult utterances.

Helpful hints

You might find it useful to bear in mind the **helpful hints/model answers** given in relation to the two previous exercises.

Model answer for 1

In the text, we noted Chomsky's suggestion that dummy *do* is used only as a *last resort*, in structures which require an auxiliary but which would otherwise not have one: in other structures, it is superfluous (since it has no semantic content) and so the **economy principle** determines that it cannot be used. COMP in adult English questions contains a strong Q affix, and so must have an overt item attached to it. The adult counterpart of (1) in (standard varieties of) English is (i) below:

(i)   Was I a good girl?

Here, *was* is a copular (i.e. 'linking') verb which moves from T to adjoin to the strong question affix Q which occupies the head C position of CP. Since adult *be* can itself adjoin to Q in this way, *do* would be superfluous in *be* questions, and so cannot be used (since the **economy principle** bars the use of superfluous elements in syntactic representations).

The fact that Sarah uses *do* in (1) might suggest that she misanalyses *be* (in the relevant use) as a lexical verb with intrinsic semantic content (so that e.g. *be* in 1 is synonymous with 'behave like'); if so, it will originate (and remain) in the head V position of VP, and cannot adjoin to T (and thence to Q) because T is a weak affix in English. If *be* is prevented from moving out of the head V position of VP, it follows that (like typical nonauxiliary verbs) *be* (in the relevant use) will require *do*-support in interrogative sentences: thus, in 1, *do* will be merged with a past-tense affix T, and will then adjoin to Q (perhaps pied-piping the past-tense affix along with it, so that it is the whole T constituent rather than just *do* which adjoins to Q: see the discussion of *excorporation* in §6.9).

7
Operator movement

7.1 Overview

In the previous chapter, we looked at a particular kind of movement operation found in English, called **head movement**. In this chapter, we look at a very different kind of movement operation, known as **operator movement** because it applies to expressions which contain an (e.g. negative or interrogative) **operator** of some kind. Our discussion in the text will be concerned solely with interrogative operators (though we shall look at other types of operator construction in the exercises).

7.2 Wh-operators

To get our discussion underway, consider the syntax of the following wh-questions (i.e. questions containing an interrogative wh-word):

(1) (a)   **What languages** *can* you speak?
   (b)   **Which road** *should* we take?
   (c)   **Where** *were* you going?
   (d)   **Who** *have* they arrested?

Each of the sentences in (1) contains an (italicized) inverted auxiliary occupying the head C position of CP, preceded by a (bold-printed) interrogative expression. Each of the bold-printed pre-auxiliary phrases contains an **interrogative operator** (viz. *what?*, *which?*, *where?* or *who?*). Expressions containing an operator are – for obvious reasons – called *operator expressions*; hence *what languages?*, *which road?*, *where?* and *who?* are all (interrogative) operator expressions in (1a–d).

It seems clear that each of the operator expressions in (1) functions as the complement of the verb at the end of the sentence. One piece of evidence leading to this conclusion comes from the fact that each of the examples in (1) has a paraphrase in which the operator expression occupies the canonical (i.e. 'typical') complement position after the relevant verb: cf.

(2) (a)   You can speak *what languages?*
   (b)   We should take *which road?*

(c)   You were going *where*?

(d)   They have arrested *who*?

Structures like those in (2) are sometimes referred to as *wh-in-situ* questions, since the italicized wh-expression does not get preposed, but rather remains *in situ* (i.e. 'in place') in the canonical position associated with its grammatical function (e.g. *what languages* in (2a) is the complement of *speak*, and complements are canonically positioned after their verbs, so *what languages* is positioned after the verb *speak*). Structures like (2) are used primarily as *echo questions*, to echo and question something previously said by someone else (e.g. if a friend boasts 'I just met Nim Chimpsky', you could reply – with an air of incredulity – 'You just met *who*?'). Sentences such as (2) make it seem plausible to suppose that the italicized operator expressions in (1) originate as complements of the relevant verbs, and subsequently get moved to the front of the overall sentence. But what position do they get moved into?

The answer is obviously that they are moved into some position preceding the inverted auxiliary. Now, if inverted auxiliaries occupy the head C position of CP (adjoined to a question affix Q), we might suppose that preposed operator expressions are moved into some prehead position within CP. Given that *specifiers* are canonically positioned before heads, a natural suggestion to make is that preposed operator expressions occupy the *specifier position within CP* (= *spec-CP*). If this is so, a sentence such as (1a) will be derived as in (3) below (simplified by ignoring the possibility that *can* originates adjoined to a tense affix in T):

(3)

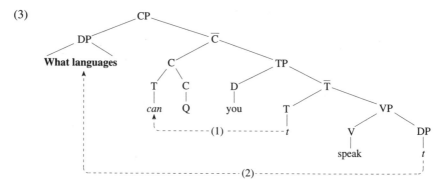

Two different kinds of movement operation (indicated by the arrows) are involved in (3): (1) involves movement of *can* from T to adjoin to the C position occupied by the question affix Q, and is an instance of **head movement.** By contrast, (2) involves movement of an operator expression (viz. the determiner phrase *what languages?* containing the interrogative operator *what?*) from complement position within VP into specifier position within CP: since this second type of operation involves movement of operator expressions, it is standardly referred to as **operator movement** (sometimes abbreviated to **O movement**).

A tacit assumption made in our analysis of operator movement in (3) is that just as a moved head (e.g. an inverted auxiliary) leaves behind a *trace* in the position out of which it moves, so too a moved operator expression leaves behind a trace at its *extraction site* (i.e. in the position out of which it is extracted/moved). The assumption that moved operator expressions leave a trace behind can be defended on empirical grounds. One piece of evidence comes from facts relating to a phenomenon generally known as *wanna contraction*. In colloquial English, the string *want to* can generally contract to *wanna* (through cliticization of *to* onto *want*, assimilation of /nt/ to /nn/, and degemination reducing /nn/ to /n/), so that alongside (4a) below we find (4b):

(4) (a)   I *want to* go home

    (b)   I *wanna* go home

In nonsloppy speech styles, however, the sequence *want to* cannot contract to *wanna* in a sentence such as (5a) below, as we see from the ungrammaticality of (5b):

(5) (a)   Who would you *want to* help you?

    (b)   *Who would you *wanna* help you?

Why should this be? Well, let's assume that *who* originates as the subject (and specifier) of the IP (infinitive phrase) *to help you* – as seems plausible in view of the fact that (5a) has the echo question counterpart:

(6)   You'd want *who* to help you?

Let's also assume that the wh-pronoun *who* (being an interrogative operator) undergoes movement from its underlying spec-IP position to the spec-CP position at the front of the clause, and that it leaves behind a trace in spec-IP. Assuming that auxiliary inversion also takes place, the resulting structure will then be along the lines of (7) below (where *t* is the trace of *who*; we omit the trace of *would* for simplicity):

(7)   *Who* would you want *t* to help you?

Why should *wanna* contraction then be blocked in a structure such as (7)? Since we have already seen in earlier chapters that cliticization is subject to an *adjacency* condition (and hence is only possible when the two words involved are immediately adjacent), the presence of the intervening trace *t* between *to* and *want* will prevent *to* from cliticizing onto *want*, and hence blocks *wanna-contraction*. (We might suppose that in sloppy speech styles, intervening traces are ignored, and so do not suffice to block contraction.)

A similar kind of argument in support of claiming that moved operator expressions leave behind a trace comes from facts about *have*-cliticization. The perfective auxiliary form *have* has the clitic variant /v/ and can cliticize to an immediately preceding word

269

which ends in a vowel or diphthong. Significantly, however, cliticization is not possible (in nonsloppy speech styles) in sentences such as (8a) below, as we see from the fact that the sequence *say have* in (8a) cannot contract to *say've* in (8b):

(8) (a)   Which students would you *say have* got most out of the course?
    (b)   *Which students would you *say've* got most out of the course?

(Hence the sequence *say've* is not homophonous with *save*.) Why should *have* be prevented from cliticizing onto *say* here? We might assume that prior to being moved to the front of the sentence by **operator movement**, the operator phrase *which students* was the subject of *have* – as in the echo question counterpart (9) below:

(9)   You would say *which students* have got most out of the course?

If we also assume that when the phrase *which students* is fronted, it leaves behind a trace (= *t*) in the position out of which it moves, then the superficial structure of (8b) will be (10) below (simplified by omitting the trace of *would*):

(10)   *Which students* would you say *t* have got most out of the course?

This being so, we can say that *have* cannot cliticize onto *say* in (10) because it is not immediately adjacent to *say*, the two words being separated by the intervening trace *t* in (10) – so accounting for the ungrammaticality of (8b).

The analysis presented here correctly predicts that while *have* cliticization is not possible in structures like (8b) above, it is indeed possible in structures like (11b) below:

(11) (a)   *Who have* they arrested?
    (b)   *Who've* they arrested?

Given our twin assumptions that preposed operators move into spec-CP and inverted auxiliaries adjoin to a question affix Q in COMP, (11b) will have the derivation (12) below (where movement (1) is **head movement**, and (2) is **operator movement**):

(12)

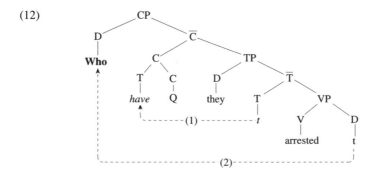

270

(Note that (12) is simplified by ignoring the possibility that *have* may be merged with a tense affix.) Since *who* is immediately adjacent to *have* here, our analysis correctly predicts that PF cliticization should be possible: the fact that the resulting sentence (11b) is grammatical makes it all the more plausible to posit that spec-CP is the *landing-site* for preposed operator expressions (i.e. spec-CP is the position into which they move).

Additional support for the claim that operator expressions move into spec-CP comes from the fact that in some varieties of English, preposed wh-expressions can precede a complementizer like *that*. This is true, for example, of Belfast English structures such as the following (from Henry 1995, p. 107):

(13) (a)   I wonder [**which dish** *that* they picked]

(b)   They didn't know [**which model** *that* we had discussed]

If we assume that the complementizer *that* occupies the head C position of CP, it seems reasonable to suppose that the wh-expressions *which dish/which model* that precede the complementizer *that* are in spec-CP (i.e. occupy the specifier position within CP) – and this is what Alison Henry argues.

7.3   Enlightened self-interest and shortest movement

Given that our ultimate goal is *explanation*, an important question to ask is *why* interrogative operator expressions should move to spec-CP. Howard Lasnik (1995) suggests that movement is driven by a principle which he terms **enlightened self-interest**: this specifies that constituents move in order to check features carried by other constituents, so that movement is motivated by a form of *altruism*. A natural implementation of the altruism analysis would be to suppose that the question affix Q which occupies the head C position of an interrogative CP carries an interrogative specifier-feature, and that (correspondingly) wh-operators like *who?* carry an interrogative head-feature. We could then say that wh-operators move to spec-CP in order to check the interrogative specifier-feature carried by Q: since interrogative operators in English generally begin with *wh* (cf. *who?, what?, which?, where?, when?, why?*, etc.), let's use **[wh]** to designate the relevant interrogative feature.

To see how this works, consider how we might derive a sentence such as:

(14)   What was he doing?

What originates as the complement of *doing*; merging *doing* with *what* forms the VP (15) below:

(15)

```
         VP
        /  \
       V    D
       |    |
     doing what
```

Operator movement

The progressive auxiliary *was* is merged with a past-tense affix T as in (16) below:

(16)

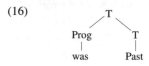

The resulting T constituent in (16) is then merged with the VP in (15) to form the T-bar (17) below:

(17)

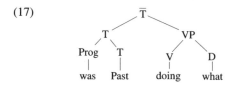

The subject *he* is then merged with the overall T-bar constituent in (17) to form the TP (18) below:

(18)

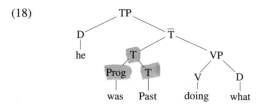

This in turn is merged with the interrogative complementizer Q, to form:

(19)

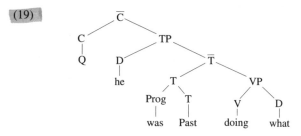

Since Q is a strong affix, the T constituent *was+Past* adjoins to the C-node containing Q, as in (20) below:

(20)

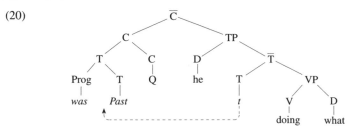

272

(In the context of our discussion in §6.9, note that we are assuming here that the whole T constituent adjoins to C, rather than just progressive *was* – though this is a question of detail of no direct relevance to our discussion of **operator movement** here.) Since Q also carries a [wh] specifier-feature, *what?* (which is an interrogative determiner containing the head-feature [wh]) raises to become the specifier of C-bar, as indicated by the arrow in (21) below:

(21)

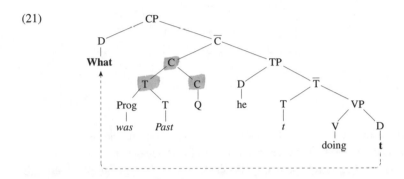

The [wh] specifier-feature of Q can then be checked by the [wh] head-feature carried by *what*, and is thereby erased, since specifier-features are uninterpretable at LF. (However, the [wh] head-feature carried by *what* is not erased, since it plays a role at LF in identifying *what* as an interrogative operator.) Checking here will involve a local spec–head relation (between the head and specifier of CP) if we assume that the [wh] feature of Q is carried by both C segments of the split-segment C constituent. On this account, movement of *what* to spec-CP is motivated by altruism (i.e. enlightened self-interest), in that this enables the specifier-feature of Q to be checked. (We shall consider why the relevant feature must be checked by movement rather than attraction in §7.7.)

The assumption that *what* moves to spec-CP for altruistic reasons (to check and erase the [wh] specifier-feature of Q) provides an interesting account of why in multiple wh-questions (i.e. questions containing more than one wh-operator) such as (22) below, only one wh-operator can be preposed, not both:

(22) (a)   **Who** do you think will say *what*?
     (b)   **What* **who** do you think will say?

Example (22a) has the derivation (23) below. (Here and throughout the rest of this chapter, we simplify the internal structure of T and C constituents for ease of exposition; fuller structures for T and C are given in (18) and (21) above.)

(23)

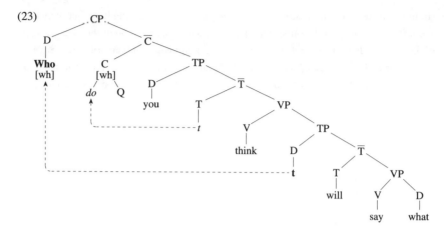

The [wh] specifier-feature of the C-node (which is associated with the question affix Q contained in C) is erased once it has been checked by movement of *who* into spec-CP. If we assume that **operator movement** is motivated purely by the altruistic desire to erase the [wh] specifier-feature of the C-node containing Q, it is clear that once this [wh] feature has been erased by movement of *who* to spec-CP, there is no motivation for the second wh-operator to be preposed, since the [wh] specifier-feature of Q has already been checked and erased. Thus, the principle of **enlightened self-interest** provides us with a neat account of the fact that only one wh-operator is preposed in multiple wh-questions in English.

However, a question not answered by our existing account is why it should be possible to prepose *who* on its own in a multiple wh-question like (22a), but not *what* – i.e. why we can't say:

(24)   *What* do you think who will say?

Example (24) would have the derivation (25) below (simplified in respect of the internal structure of T and C):

(25)

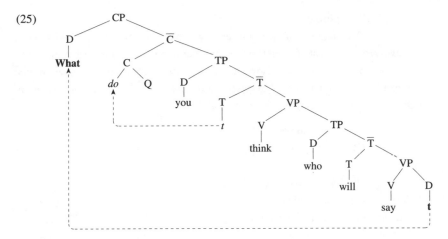

Since movement of *what* into spec-CP would enable the [wh] specifier-feature of Q to be checked, why does the derivation in (25) crash? Why should *who* be able to move to spec-CP in (23), but not *what* in (25)?

A natural suggestion to make is that this is because *who* is closer to Q than *what*, and the **economy principle** favours shorter movements over longer ones. So, Q lures the nearest wh-operator into spec-CP: since *who* is nearer to Q in (23/25) than *what*, it is *who* which must move to spec-CP, not *what*. The relevant condition (favouring shorter moves over longer ones) is known as the **shortest movement principle** (cf. Chomsky 1995b). Since the effect of the principle is to favour the formation of movement chains with minimal (i.e. the smallest/shortest possible) links, it is also referred to as the **minimal link condition** (or the **minimality condition**). It should be apparent that the **head movement constraint** discussed in the previous chapter (which holds that head movement is only possible from a complement head into a matrix head position) can be subsumed under the shortest movement principle (or the equivalent minimal link/minimality condition).

7.4 Pied-piping

Thus far, most of the instances of wh-movement which we have looked at have involved movement of a single wh-determiner (a pronominal wh-determiner such as *who?* or *what?*) into spec-DP. However, in sentences such as (26–8) below, we find movement of a whole DP headed by a wh-determiner into spec-CP, with movement of the determiner alone leading to ungrammaticality:

(26) (a) *Which film* did you see?
     (b) **Which* did you see *film*?
(27) (a) *Which of them* can you trust?
     (b) **Which* can you trust *of them*?
(28) (a) *What reason* did he give?
     (b) **What* did he give *reason*?

To use the familiar *pied-piping* metaphor, it would seem that when the wh-determiner *which?/what?* moves to spec-CP in (26–8), its complement (*film/of them/reason*) has to be pied-piped along with the moved wh-operator. Why should this be?

Consider first why moving the wh-determiner without its complement leads to ungrammaticality. Sentence (26b) will have the simplified derivation (29) below:

(29)

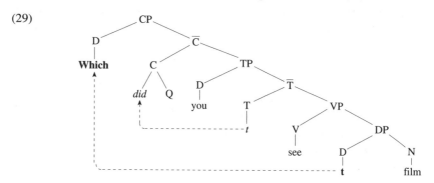

Why should the derivation in (29) crash? One possibility is that movement of *which* on its own into spec-CP results in the formation of a chain *which . . . t* which is *nonuniform* in that *which* and its trace differ in respect of their phrase structure status. To see why, consider the immediate structures containing *which* and its trace, given in (30a–b) below:

(30) (a)   (b)

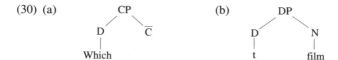

In (30a) the D-node containing *which* is a maximal projection (i.e. it is the largest category headed by *which*), whereas in (30b) the D-node containing its trace *t* is not a maximal projection (since the maximal projection of the D-node containing *t* is the DP *t film*). If (following Chomsky 1995a, p. 406) we assume the following principle governing the well-formedness of chains:

(31)   CHAIN UNIFORMITY PRINCIPLE
         A chain must be uniform with regard to phrase structure status.

the ungrammaticality of the (b) examples in (26–8) above can be accounted for in a principled fashion, since the (b) examples all result in a nonuniform chain whose head (= the preposed wh-word *which?/what?*) is a maximal projection, but whose foot (= the trace of the preposed wh-word) is not.

But now consider what happens if we prepose the whole DP *which film?* in (26a), in the manner indicated in (32) below:

(32)

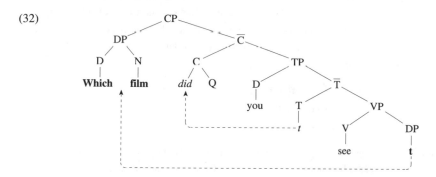

Here the resulting chain is uniform, since its head is the DP *which film* (which is a maximal projection) and its foot is a DP trace (hence also a maximal projection). Thus, it would seem that operator movement moves a D alone wherever possible (e.g. in structures like (25) above), but moves a DP when movement of D alone would violate the **chain uniformity principle** (e.g. in structures like (32) above). The more general principle which this suggests is that movement operations move only the *minimal* constituent required to satisfy UG principles: this can be argued to be a particular instance of the more general **economy principle**, which in effect tells us to move features rather than constituents whenever possible, and (when moving constituents) to move the smallest constituent possible the smallest distance possible.

We can extend the account given here from contrasts such as (26–8) above to those such as (33) below:

(33) (a)   *Whose car* did you borrow?
     (b)   **Whose* did you borrow car?
     (c)   **Who* did you borrow *'s car*?

Operator movement

Following a suggestion attributed to Richard Larson in Abney 1987, we might conjecture that genitive *'s* in English is a head determiner which takes a D projection as its specifier, so that *whose car* has the structure (34) below:

(34)

If we assume that *'s* is a PF clitic (and hence cliticizes to *who* in the PF component, forming *who's*, written as *whose*), we cannot prepose *who* on its own in (33c) since this will result in the suffix *'s* being stranded (*'s* is unable to attach to *who*, since *who* has been moved to the front of the sentence and is no longer adjacent to *'s*). Nor can we move the sequence *who's* (= *whose*) in (33b), since this is not a constituent. So, the minimal constituent which can be preposed is the whole DP *whose car* – as in (33a).

We can extend the *economy* account to handle contrasts such as the following in colloquial English:

(35) (a)   *Who* were you talking to?

    (b)   **To who were you talking?*

    (c)   **Talking to who were you?*

Each of the sentences in (35) is derived by preposing a wh-expression into the spec-CP position indicated by the question-mark in (36) below (and moving the auxiliary *were* from T to adjoin to Q):

(36)

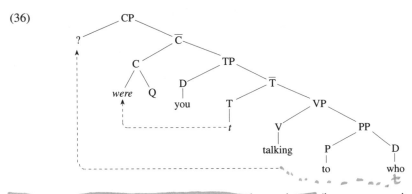

Since Q has a [wh] specifier-feature, some wh-constituent (i.e. some constituent containing a wh-operator) must move into the spec-CP position indicated by *?* in (36), in order to check this [wh] feature. If we move the determiner *who* on its own, the resulting chain *who . . . t* will be uniform, since both its head and foot will be D constituents which do not project into DP (and so are maximal projections). Of course, this

278

will also be true if the PP *to who* moves into spec-CP, since the result will be a uniform chain whose head and foot are both maximal (PP) projections; and the same is likewise true if the VP *talking to who* moves into spec-CP, since this will again result in a uniform chain whose head and foot are both maximal (VP) projections. So, since preposing the D *who*, the PP *to who* and the VP *talking to who* all result in the formation of a uniform chain, why should preposing D be preferred to preposing PP, or preposing VP? The obvious answer is that the D *who* is smaller than the PP *to who*, which in turn is smaller than the VP *talking to who*. And if we assume that (in consequence of the **economy principle**) operator movement moves only the minimal constituent needed to check the [wh] specifier-feature of Q, the relevant facts fall out much as we expect.

However, our discussion here overlooks an important *stylistic* variable. In formal styles of English (i.e. in styles where the objective form of the relevant pronoun is *whom* rather than *who*), things are rather different, as we see from the sentences below:

(37) (a)   **Whom* were you talking to?

  (b)   *To whom* were you talking?

  (c)   **Talking to whom* were you?

As these examples show, in formal English, the wh-pronoun *whom* cannot be preposed on its own; rather, the preposition *to* must be pied-piped along with *whom* (though the verb *talking* cannot be pied-piped in the same way). What is going on here?

Consider first why (37a) is ungrammatical. What's happened here is that the preposition *to* has been *stranded* or *orphaned* (i.e. separated from its complement *whom*); the fact that (37a) is ungrammatical suggests that there is a constraint against *preposition-stranding* in formal styles of English – a constraint rather inaccurately encapsulated in the traditional rule of prescriptive grammar: 'Never end a sentence with a preposition.' The fact that prepositions can be stranded in colloquial English but not in formal English would seem to correlate with the fact that we find the overtly case-inflected form *whom* in formal English (where +*m* marks objective case), but the uninflected form *who* in colloquial English. How might these two sets of facts be related?

Speculating at this point, let's conjecture that in formal styles of English, the overtly case marked form *whom* checks its case in sentences like (37) above by attraction to the transitive preposition *to*. If we suppose that attraction of overt case-features takes place in the overt syntax (prior to spellout), and triggers pied-piping of other unchecked grammatical features along with the attracted case-feature, it follows that not only will the objective case-feature of *whom* percolate to *to*, but so too will the wh-feature carried by *who* (with the result that the wh-feature is attached to *to*). The preposition *to* cannot be preposed on its own (since this would result in violation of the **chain uniformity principle**), so its complement *whom* is pied-piped along with it, and consequently the whole PP *to whom* moves to spec-CP in order to check the wh-feature of COMP, as in (37b) above.

But what of colloquial English? Here, we might suppose that (since it does not overtly inflect for objective case) *who* carries covert case, and that its case properties are checked after spellout in the covert syntax (i.e. in the LF component). Because there is no attraction of the case properties of *who* to *to* in the overt syntax, there is no pied-piping of the wh-feature carried by *who*, with the result that only *who* is moved to spec-CP to check the wh-feature carried by COMP. (A more radical and heretical variant of this analysis is to suppose that the colloquial form *who* has no case properties to be checked: for a different view of preposition pied-piping and stranding, see Salles 1995.)

Given the **preposition-stranding constraint**, we can begin to make sense of the data in (37). Movement of *whom* alone will violate the constraint, and so leads to ungrammaticality in (37a). The minimal constituent which can be preposed without violating the constraint is the PP *to whom*, in which *to* is pied-piped along with *whom*: hence, (37b) is grammatical. In (37c), the whole VP *talking to whom* has been preposed, with the verb *talking* being pied-piped as well; but this violates the **economy principle** (which requires that only the *minimal* constituent required to ensure convergence should be preposed). So, the contrasting patterns of grammaticality found in colloquial English sentences like (35) on the one hand and formal English sentences like (37) turn out to be reducible to the fact that the constraint against preposition-stranding holds in formal English (and many other languages – e.g. French, Italian, Spanish, etc.), but not in colloquial English. Everything else about the relevant data follows from UG principles.

Our discussion here suggests that pied-piping of additional material along with wh-operators occurs only when it is forced by the need to ensure convergence. This assumption offers us an interesting account of the otherwise puzzling set of data in (38) below (cf. Chomsky 1995b):

(38) (a)　　*Whose* did you think pictures of mother were on the mantelpiece?

　　　(b)　　*Whose mother* did you think pictures of were on the mantelpiece?

　　　(c)　　*Of whose mother* did you think pictures were on the mantelpiece?

　　　(d)　　*Pictures of whose mother* did you think were on the mantelpiece?

Here, the expression *pictures of whose mother* is a DP (headed by a null determiner) which originates as the subject of *were*; and the issue which concerns us here is which of the wh-constituents can be moved into the spec-CP position indicated by **?** in (39) below – and why:

(39)

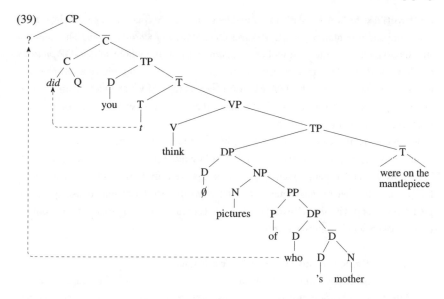

Whose cannot be preposed on its own, for reasons already familiar from our earlier discussion of (33) above – i.e. it is not a constituent, given the analysis in (39). More puzzling is why the whole DP *whose mother* can't be extracted in (38b). This is all the more puzzling in view of the fact that *whose mother* can indeed be extracted in sentences such as:

(40)   *Whose mother* was he taking/exhibiting/collecting pictures of?

How come *whose mother* can be extracted in (40), but not in (39)?

The answer would seem to lie in the different positions occupied by the DP *pictures of whose mother* prior to extraction. In (40), it is the complement of the verb *taking/exhibiting/collecting*; but in (39) it is the subject of *were*. It would seem that (to use a colourful metaphor suggested by Ross 1967) subjects are *islands* – i.e. they are constituents which nothing can be extracted out of. Or, to put matters the other way round, we might say – following the **condition on extraction domains** (= CED) suggested by Huang 1982 – that complements are the only types of constituent which allow extraction out of them. In the light of this constraint, we can begin to make sense of the data in (38). Moving the DP *whose mother* in (38b) or the PP *of whose mother* in

281

(38c) will lead to violation of the CED, since the DP/PP concerned are being moved out of the larger containing subject expression *pictures of whose mother*. The minimal structure which can be moved without violating CED is the whole subject DP *pictures of whose mother*. Thus, pied-piping of the rest of the DP along with the wh-pronoun *who* is a last resort, forced by the need to avoid violation of CED. Once again, we find that *pied-piping* is used only as a last resort, when needed to ensure convergence (i.e. to ensure a grammatical outcome).

We can summarize the assumptions we have made about **wh-movement** (i.e. movement of wh-operator expressions) in the following terms. Wh-questions are CPs headed by a C constituent containing an interrogative affix Q which has a [wh] specifier-feature checked by movement of a wh-word to spec-CP. Other constituents are pied-piped along with the wh-word only if this is required for convergence – i.e. only if the derivation would otherwise crash.

7.5 Embedded questions in Belfast English

So far, we have only dealt with *root wh-questions*. (Since the *root* of a tree is the topmost node in the tree, a root question is in effect an interrogative sentence – i.e. one in which the root/topmost node in the structure is interrogative.) An obvious question to ask is whether our analysis can be extended from root wh-questions to embedded wh-questions (i.e. question clauses which are embedded as the subject or complement of some other expression). In this connection, consider how we might deal with [bracketed] embedded wh-questions such as the following, found in (one variety of) Belfast English (cf. Henry 1995, p. 106):

(41) (a)   She asked [who had I seen]

 (b)   They wondered [what had John done]

 (c)   They couldn't understand [how had she had time to get her hair done]

 (d)   He didn't say [why had they come]

It seems natural to suppose that we should treat embedded wh-questions such as those bracketed in (41) in precisely the same way as we treated their root-clause counterparts. More concretely, we might suppose that the embedded clause *who had I seen* in (41a) is a CP whose head C position contains the question morpheme Q, and that Q is a strong (affixal) head with a [wh] specifier-feature, so that *had* adjoins to Q and *who* moves to spec-CP, as in (42) below. (Here and subsequently, we simplify the internal structure of C, and show only those aspects of the derivation which are of immediate concern, and not e.g. the fact that the head- and specifier-features of *asked* are attracted to T.)

(42)

Such an analysis would offer the obvious advantage that it requires us to posit no additional descriptive apparatus or theoretical assumptions over and above what we already need to handle root-clause wh-questions.

Moreover, the analysis can be extended in a fairly straightforward fashion to deal with *wh+that* questions in Belfast English such as those in (13) above, repeated in (43) below:

(43) (a)   I wonder [**which dish** *that* they picked]
     (b)   They didn't know [**which model** *that* we had discussed]

Given that the greed of a strong affix (i.e. its need to attach to an overt head) can be satisfied either by movement or by merger, an obvious suggestion to make about structures such as (43) is that they involve *merger* of the complementizer *that* with the interrogative affix Q, together with movement of the wh-DP *which dish* from VP-complement position to CP-specifier position, as in (44) below (simplified by showing only movement, not feature attraction):

Operator movement

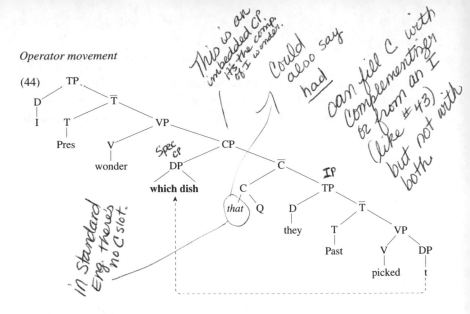

We could then say that the requirement for the strong affix Q to be bound to an overt head is satisfied in structures like (42) by *movement* (i.e. adjunction of *had* to Q), and in structures like (44) by *merger* (of *that* with Q); in both cases, the [wh] specifier-feature of Q is checked by movement of *who/which dish* to spec-CP. Since it is a lexical property of overt complementizers like *that/if/for* that they occur only in embedded clauses and not in root clauses, it follows that C in root-clause questions will always be filled by movement (i.e. adjunction of an auxiliary to Q), not by merger of Q with a complementizer like *that* (cf. the ungrammaticality of *Which dish that they picked?* as a root clause).

Interestingly, we find that inversion is also permitted (in the relevant variety of Belfast English) in noninterrogative clauses from which an italicized interrogative operator has been extracted, such as those bracketed in (45) below (cf. Henry 1995, p. 108):

(45) (a) **Who** did he hope [*would* he see]?

(b) **What** did Mary claim [*did* they steal]?

It is clear that the bracketed complement-clauses are declarative rather than interrogative, since *hope/claim* don't select interrogative complements (as we see from the ungrammaticality of sentences such as **I hoped/claimed whether he was coming*). Thus, the bracketed complement-clauses in (45) must be CPs headed by a null declarative COMP. Since declarative COMP constituents generally have *weak* head-features in all varieties of present-day English (and so don't trigger inversion), we would therefore not expect to find inversion in declarative complement clauses like those bracketed in (45). So what triggers inversion in such cases?

Since inversion in declarative clauses is only found in clauses out of which an interrogative operator has been extracted, an obvious suggestion to make is that the extrac-

284

tion of the operator somehow triggers inversion. But how? Well, since inversion is found in CPs with an interrogative specifier, let's suppose that when the interrogative operator is extracted out of the bracketed complement clauses in (45), it moves first to the front of the complement clause (thereby triggering inversion in the complement clause), and then to the front of the root clause (thereby triggering inversion in the root clause). This would mean that a sentence such as (45a) would have the (simplified) derivation (46) below:

(46)

He did hope he would see who

What is being claimed in (46) is that the wh-determiner *who* moves to the front of the overall sentence in two successive steps, numbered (1) and (2). On its first movement, *who* moves into the spec-CP position within the *would* clause; and on its second movement, *who* moves into spec-CP in the *did* clause. Thus, operator movement applies in a *successive cyclic* fashion, moving the operator to the front of the sentence one clause at a time. We might suppose that successive cyclicity is forced by the **shortest movement principle**, since this will require that a moved operator expression should move into the nearest spec-CP position above it (each time it moves).

However, this still leaves the question of why *did* and *would* undergo inversion in (46), and thereby move to COMP. In the case of *did*, the answer is straightforward, since the root (i.e. topmost) clause is interrogative, and so the head C position within CP contains the strong interrogative affix Q: thus, inversion of *did* is simply adjunction of *did* to Q. But inversion of *would* is more problematic, since the *would*-clause is declarative, and a declarative C is normally weak (and so cannot trigger movement of an auxiliary to COMP). What is going on here? One answer is to suggest that any C which has an interrogative specifier always has strong head-features (and so behaves like an affix, triggering movement of an auxiliary into C). This means that although the embedded COMP filled by *would* in (46) is noninterrogative, it is strong by virtue of the fact that it comes to have an interrogative specifier at the point in the derivation at which *who* moves into the specifier position in the embedded clause (i.e. immediately after movement (1) takes place). Thus, a declarative COMP is generally weak in Belfast English, but is strong where it has an interrogative specifier. It may be that the auxiliary *would* in (46) adjoins to an abstract declarative affix **Dec** (which would be the declarative counterpart of the question affix Q found in interrogatives).

7.6 Embedded questions in Standard English

So far, our discussion of embedded wh-questions has related entirely to one particular variety of Belfast English (BE). But since Standard English (SE) doesn't allow constructions such as (41), (43) and (45), an obvious question to ask is how – and why – complement-clause questions in SE differ from their BE counterparts. Consider first why SE doesn't allow *wh+that* questions such as (13/43) above, repeated as (47) below (the prefixed star indicates that they are ungrammatical in SE):

(47) (a)   *I wonder [**which dish** *that* they picked]
     (b)   *They didn't know [**which model** *that* we had discussed]

A simple answer is to suppose that the head-features of *that* indicate that it is an inherently *noninterrogative* finite-clause complementizer in SE. Because it is noninterrogative, SE *that* can't be merged with the question affix Q – hence the ungrammaticality of structures such as (44) in SE. By contrast, the head-features of its Belfast English counterpart indicate that it is simply *finite*, and so can be used in interrogative and noninterrogative clauses alike.

More problematic is how we account for the fact that Standard English doesn't allow auxiliary inversion in embedded wh-questions like those in (48) below (cf. (41) above):

(48) (a)   %She asked [who had I seen]
     (b)   %They wondered [what had John done]

(% = 'grammatical in the relevant variety of Belfast English, but ungrammatical in Standard English'). Given the assumption that movement is morphologically driven, the most principled answer we could give to this question is that the differences between SE and BE in respect of structures like (48) reduce to morphological properties of the head COMP node in the bracketed CP.

One possibility along these lines is to suggest that the COMP node in the bracketed CP has strong head-features in BE (so triggers auxiliary inversion), but has weak head-features in SE (so doesn't allow auxiliary inversion). However, this apparently simple solution is fraught with hidden complications. If embedded questions contain the same Q morpheme as root questions, how come Q isn't strong (since it is strong in root clauses, where it triggers inversion)? We could try saying that Q can be either strong or weak, and that verbs like *ask/wonder* which select an interrogative complement always select a complement headed by a weak Q. But this then poses the problem of how we account for why Q is always strong (and triggers inversion) in root clauses. Clearly, we can't say that principles of UG determine that Q universally has strong head-features in root clauses with an interrogative operator in spec-CP, since (for example) in Jamaican Creole we find root wh-questions with no inversion – as the following examples (from Bailey 1966) illustrate:

> *By this he rejects strong feature analysis. In main clause here, it's not a strong feature root clause (there's no inversion in the root clause).*
>
> *So, all root clauses aren't strong!*

(49) (a) Wa   Anti   sen fi me?
          What Auntie send for me?
          'What did Auntie send for me?'

   (b) Homoch   kuoknut im gat?
        How-much coconut him got?
        'How many coconuts has he got?'

   (c) We   da pikini-ya kom fram?
        Where that child-here come from?
        'Where has this child come from?'

So what are we to do?

One suggestion is to capitalize on the fact that inversion is not possible in *wh+that* questions in Belfast English – as we see from the ungrammaticality of sentences such as the following (from Henry 1995, p. 108):

(50) (a) *I wondered [which dish **that** *did* they pick]
   (b) *I wondered [which model **that** *had* they discussed]

Why is inversion not possible here? The answer is that the morphological requirements of the affix Q are satisfied by merger of *that* with Q, so that there is no necessity for (and hence no possibility of) adjoining the auxiliary to Q. Suppose we further posit that Standard English has a null complementizer ø which can adjoin to Q in complement-clause questions (in much the same way as *that* adjoins to Q in Belfast English) – though not in root questions (since it is a lexical property of complementizers like *that* and ø that they only occur in complement questions). It follows that a Standard English sentence such as:

(51)   I wondered [which dish they picked]

will have the (simplified) derivation (52) below:

287

(52)

The fact that the null complementizer ø merges with Q satisfies the requirement for Q to be affixed to an appropriate host, and thereby blocks any form of auxiliary inversion – hence, *do*-support is neither necessary nor possible in (52). A minor complication posed by the analysis is that we have to assume that a *null* constituent (in this case, the null complementizer ø) can satisfy the morphological requirements of a strong affix, whereas in the previous chapter we assumed that only an *overt* constituent could do so. This means we have to posit that the defining characteristic of strong affixes is that they require an (overt or covert) lexical item to be attached to them.

In order for the null complementizer account to work, however, we have to posit that all embedded CPs in Standard English must be headed by an (overt or covert) complementizer: in a finite declarative CP in SE, the complementizer will be the overt complementizer *that*; in a wh-question complement clause in SE, it will be the covert complementizer ø. It may be (as suggested by Kayne 1982) that the head C of an embedded CP is always nonverbal in Standard English (as is suggested by the fact that *for* is a prepositional complementizer), and hence does not allow a verb to be adjoined to it: by contrast, a root-clause C is not restricted in the same way, and hence allows an inverted auxiliary to be adjoined to it. The obvious drawback to this analysis is that it is *stipulative* rather than *explanatory* (i.e. it doesn't offer us any account of why C should be nonverbal in embedded clauses in Standard English, though not in Belfast English).

We can assume that the Q affix to which the null complementizer ø adjoins has the interrogative specifier-feature [wh]: in structures like (52), the [wh] specifier-feature of *Q* is checked by movement of *which dish* into spec-CP. However, in embedded *whether*-questions such as:

(53)   He asked [*whether* ø Q I was leaving]

there seems little reason to suppose that *whether* moves to spec-CP from somewhere lower down in the sentence. Rather, it seems more likely that *whether* is directly generated in spec-CP, and thus *merges* with C-bar, so that the bracketed complement clause in (53) has the structure (54) below:

(54)

Thus, spec-CP may be filled either by merger (as in (54)), or by movement (as in (52)).

We argued earlier in relation to the derivation outlined in (46) above that operator movement applies in a successive cyclic fashion in Belfast English. If we assume that this is in consequence of a principle of Universal Grammar (e.g. Chomsky's 1995b **shortest movement principle** or Rizzi's 1990 **relativized minimality principle**), it follows that the same must also be true in other varieties of English (and indeed in all natural languages). This in turn means that in a Standard English question such as:

(55)   How do you think that he is feeling?

operator movement applies in a successive cyclic fashion, moving *how* first into the spec-CP position in the *that*-clause, and then into spec-CP in the *do*-clause, as indicated by the (simplified) derivation in (56) below:

(56)

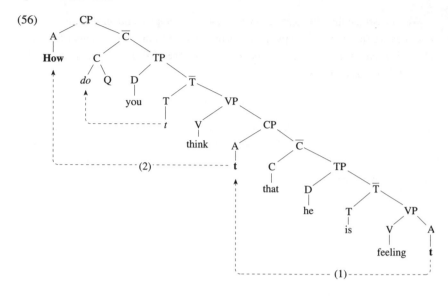

(We have assumed here that *how* is an adjectival wh-proform, since it is the complement of *feel*, and *feel* typically selects an adjectival complement, like *fine* in *I feel fine*: although *how* doesn't begin with *wh*, it is standardly classified as a wh-word because it exhibits the same syntactic behaviour as other wh-words.) Thus, *how* first becomes the specifier of the COMP containing *that*, and then moves on to become the specifier of the COMP node containing *do*.

At first sight, a successive cyclic derivation such as (56) might seem to be potentially problematic, in that it requires us to posit an intermediate stage of derivation (immediately after movement (1) has applied) in which the complementizer *that* has the wh-specifier *how*. What might seem to be problematic about this is that Standard English doesn't allow *wh+that* structures, as we see from the ungrammaticality of sentences such as:

(57)   *I don't know [**how** *that* he is feeling]

But this objection turns out to have little force. After all, one might counter that what the ungrammaticality of (57) actually illustrates is not that the complementizer *that* can never have an interrogative specifier at any stage of derivation in Standard English, but rather that it can't be the head of an interrogative clause (i.e. can't attach to Q) – as we noted earlier in relation to our discussion of (44/47) above. So, since *that* heads a declarative clause in (56), the relevant derivation converges.

The assumption that operator movement applies in a successive cyclic fashion provides us with a principled account of why a sentence such as (58a) below doesn't have a grammatical interrogative counterpart like (58b):

(58) (a)   I wonder [whether he is feeling *okay*]

    (b)   *How* do you wonder [whether he is feeling]?

If (as we claim) *whether* occupies the specifier position within the bracketed comple-ment clause, it is clear that we can't derive (58b) by moving *how* first into the specifier position within the bracketed CP, and then into the specifier position within the main clause (for the obvious reason that the specifier position within the bracketed CP is already occupied by *whether*). So, the only way of deriving (58b) is by *long movement* of *how* directly into the main clause spec-CP position, as in (59) below:

(59)

```
              CP
         /          \
        A            C̄
        |         /      \
      How       C          TP
             /    \      /    \
           do     Q    D'      T̄
                  ↑    |      /    \
                 you  ...    T      VP
                  └----t     |    /    \
                            ...  V       CP
                                |      /    \
                             wonder  ADV     C̄
                                     |     /    \
                                 whether  C      TP
                                        /   \   /   \
                                       ∅    Q  D     T̄
                                              |    /    \
                                             he   T      VP
                                                  |    /    \
                                                 is   V      A
                                                      |      |
                                                  feeling    t
```

Why should the resulting sentence (58b) be ungrammatical? The answer is that the **shortest movement principle** prohibits *long movement* of *how* directly into the main clause spec-CP position, since this isn't the nearest spec-CP position above the (VP-complement) position in which *how* originates (rather, the complement-clause spec-CP position occupied by *whether* is the nearest spec-CP position). So, since successive cyclic movement is blocked by the fact that the complement-clause spec-CP position is filled by *whether*, and the long movement in (59) is blocked because it violates the **shortest movement principle**, there is no way of deriving a sentence like (58b). More generally, the ungrammaticality of sentences like (58b) provides empirical support for the claim that operator movement applies in a successive cyclic fashion, moving a moved operator into the next highest spec-CP position within the structure containing it. (For an interesting minimalist account of locality constraints on operator movement, see Manzini 1994.)

7.7 Subject questions

Hitherto, we have assumed that all wh-questions (apart from *whether* questions) involve movement of a wh-operator expression into spec-CP. However, this assumption proves potentially problematic in relation to subject questions (i.e. interrogative clauses with an interrogative subject) such as:

(60)   Who helped you?

If we assume that all wh-questions (excluding *whether* questions) are CPs containing a wh-operator which moves into spec-CP, (60) will involve movement of *who* from its underlying position in spec-TP into its superficial position in spec-CP, and so will have the (simplified) derivation (61) below:

(61)

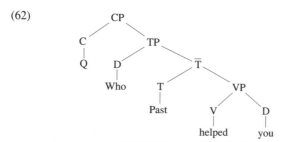

But what is problematic about the derivation in (61) is that Q is a strong affix in English, and so triggers auxiliary inversion in root clauses. If (61) were the right analysis for (60), we would therefore expect to find that *do*-support is required as a *last resort* here, to provide a verbal host for the strong Q affix to attach to. The absence of any inverted auxiliary in (60) calls into question the assumption that the subject *who* moves into spec-CP in (61).

If *who* doesn't move to spec-CP, it must remain *in situ* in spec-IP. If we continue to assume that all questions are CPs headed by a question affix Q, the structure of (60) must be along the lines of (62) below:

(62)

But an analysis like (62) poses two problems: (i) how is the wh-feature of Q checked; and (ii) why is there no *do*-support and no auxiliary inversion?

292

Since there are three different types of operation by which grammatical features can be checked (viz. merger, movement and attraction) and since *who* doesn't merge with Q in (43) and doesn't move to spec-CP, we might follow Chomsky (1995b, p. 293) in supposing that in this type of structure the [wh] feature of Q here is checked by attraction, with the [wh] head-feature of *who* adjoining to the C node containing Q, thereby enabling the [wh] feature of Q to be checked and erased. Thus, the [wh] feature of Q in an interrogative clause with an interrogative subject is checked by **wh-attraction**, not by **wh-movement**. Feature attraction is preferred to movement in such structures because (as noted in the previous chapter) attraction is more economical than movement. If we suppose that attraction is a strictly *local* operation whereby a head can only attract the features of the head or specifier of its complement, it follows that only the subject of an interrogative clause can check the strong [wh] feature of Q by attraction: other types of constituent can only check the strong [wh] feature of Q by moving to spec-CP.

So, our analysis provides a principled account of why we don't find wh-movement in interrogative clauses with interrogative subjects. But why don't we find auxiliary inversion in such sentences? One possible answer is to suppose that Q is only a strong affix when the CP headed by Q has an interrogative operator-specifier of its own. Since the CP headed by Q in (62) contains no specifier, it follows that Q in (62) is weak, and so does not trigger auxiliary inversion/*do*-support. An alternative possibility is to posit that T in interrogative clauses carries a [wh] specifier-feature; it follows that T would move to C (for example) in complement questions like (3) above (where *what languages* is in spec-CP); but in subject questions like (62), T could check its interrogative specifier-feature by remaining *in situ*, since TP has an interrogative specifier of its own (namely *who*).

Thus far, we have assumed (following Chomsky 1995b) that all interrogative clauses are CPs headed by an abstract question affix Q. But now let's consider an alternative possibility – namely that the defining characteristic of an interrogative clause is that it must contain an *interrogative specifier* in order to be interpretable as a question at LF. Let's also assume that COMP is strong in a CP with an interrogative specifier in Modern Standard English, but INFL is always weak. This alternative (*interrogative specifier*) analysis of questions offers a subtly different account of the syntax of wh-questions. In the case of sentences such as (1a) *What languages can you speak?*, we can say that the wh-DP *what languages?* raises to spec-CP in order to ensure LF convergence (i.e. to ensure that the sentence is interpretable as a question at LF by virtue of having an interrogative specifier). In multiple wh-questions like (22), only one of the wh-operator expressions will raise to spec-CP (as in (23) above), since the **economy principle** specifies that we move the minimal material required in order to ensure convergence. (The requirement for an interrogative clause to have an interrogative specifier can be met by moving only one of the wh-constituents to spec-CP.) But where

alternate

the *interrogative specifier* analysis differs most from Chomsky's *interrogative head* analysis is in the analysis of subject questions like (60) *Who helped you?* Under Chomsky's interrogative head analysis, this is a CP with the structure (62) above. But under the alternative *interrogative specifier* analysis, (60) is instead a simple TP, with the structure (63) below:

(63)

```
                TP
              /    \
           D          T̄
           |         /  \
          Who      T       VP
                   |      /   \
                  Past   V      D
                         |      |
                       helped  you
```

Since *who* occupies spec-TP, the resulting TP satisfies the requirement for a question to contain an interrogative specifier; hence there is no need to project the structure further into CP, and therefore (by the **economy principle**) no possibility of doing so. (For a TP analysis of subject questions, see Grimshaw 1993a, 1993b.)

7.8 Yes–no questions

The *interrogative specifier* analysis outlined in the previous section raises interesting questions about the syntax of root-clause yes–no questions such as:

(64)   Is it raining?

If questions are structures containing an interrogative operator, it follows (as argued in Grimshaw 1993a, 1993b and Roberts 1993) that these too contain an interrogative operator of some kind – perhaps a null counterpart of *whether*. (We might designate this null yes–no question operator as **Op**.) If so, a yes–no question such as (64) will have the (simplified) derivation (65) below. (I have not made any assumptions about what category **Op** belongs to here; perhaps it belongs to the same adverb category as its overt counterpart *whether*.)

(65)

```
              CP
            /    \
          Op       C̄
                 /    \
               C        TP
              /  \     /   \
            Is    Q   D      T̄
            ↑         |     /  \
            |        it    T    V
            |              |    |
            | - - - - - -  t   raining
```

From a historical perspective, the null-operator analysis is by no means implausible, since in Early Modern English we found root yes–no questions introduced by the overt

294

yes–no question operator *whether* – as illustrated by the following Shakespearean examples:

(66) (a)   *Whether* had you rather lead mine eyes or eye your master's heels? (Mrs Page, *Merry Wives of Windsor*, III.ii)

(b)   *Whether* dost thou profess thyself a knave or a fool? (Lafeu, *All's Well That Ends Well*, IV.v)

Given the null-operator analysis, we could posit that root yes–no questions have essentially the same syntax in present-day English as in Early Modern English, save that they could be introduced by the overt operator *whether* in Early Modern English, but are introduced by a covert operator *Op* in present-day English.

A further piece of evidence in support of assuming that inversion questions contain a null counterpart of *whether* comes from the fact that root yes–no questions can be introduced by *whether* when they are transposed into reported speech (and so occur in a complement clause): cf.

(67) (a)   'Are you feeling better?' he asked

(b)   He asked *whether* I was feeling better

A third piece of evidence is that root inversion questions resemble *whether*-questions in that in both cases *yes/no* are appropriate answers: cf.

(68) (a)   When he asked *whether* we voted for Larry Loudmouth, I said 'Yes' and you said 'No'

(b)   When he asked 'Did you vote for Larry Loudmouth?', I said 'Yes' and you said 'No'

A fourth argument is that main-clause yes–no questions can be tagged by *or not* in precisely the same way as complement-clause *whether* questions: cf.

(69) (a)   Has he finished *or not*?

(b)   I don't know *whether* he has finished *or not*

Moreover, from a theoretical point of view, the null-operator analysis offers the advantage that it allows us to arrive at a unitary analysis of the syntax of questions as clauses which contain an (overt or covert) interrogative operator as their specifier.

A natural question to ask at this juncture is how we deal with embedded *if* questions such as that bracketed in (70) below:

(70)   I wonder [*if* he is feeling better]

If (as we argued in §2.6) *if* is a complementizer (and so merges with Q), and if we further assume that all interrogative clauses contain an interrogative operator-specifier, it follows that *if*-questions (like root clause yes–no questions) must also contain a null operator, so that (70) will have the simplified structure (71) below:

(71)

```
              TP
         ／        ＼
        D           T̄
        |        ／    ＼
        I       T        VP
                |     ／    ＼
               Pres  V        CP
                     |     ／    ＼
                   wonder  Op      C̄
                                ／    ＼
                               C        TP
                               |     ／    ＼
                               if    D        T̄
                                     |     ／    ＼
                                     he   T        VP
                                          |     ／    ＼
                                          is   V        A
                                               |        |
                                            feeling   better
```

If we suppose that it is a lexical property of *if* that it only licenses the null yes–no question operator *Op* as its specifier, we can account for the fact that *if* is never used in wh-questions (as we see from the ungrammaticality of sentences like **I wonder how if he's feeling*).

Empirical evidence in support of claiming that *if*-questions contain a null interrogative operator comes from data relating to operator movement. If we replace the adjective *better* in (71) by the corresponding interrogative operator *how*, we find that *how* cannot be moved to the front of the overall sentence – as we see from the ungrammaticality of:

(72)   **How* do you wonder if he is feeling?

(though note that it's OK to ask *How do you think that he's feeling?*). Why should it be ungrammatical to extract a wh-operator out of an *if*-clause? If we suppose that *if*-questions have an abstract yes–no question operator (a null counterpart of *whether*) in spec-CP, we can give precisely the same answer as we earlier gave in relation to the impossibility of extracting a wh-operator out of a *whether*-clause in sentences like (58b) **How do you wonder whether he is feeling?* That is, a successive cyclic derivation like (73) below:

(73)   [CP*How* do you wonder [CP **Op** if he is feeling *t*]]

is ruled out by the fact that *how* can't move into the specifier position within the embedded (righthand) CP because this position is already occupied by the null operator **Op**. Moreover, (single-step) long movement of *how* directly into the main-clause (lefthand) CP as in (74) below:

(74)   [CP*How* do you wonder [CP **Op** if he is feeling *t*]]

is also ruled out, since it would lead to violation of the **shortest movement principle** (which requires *how* to move into the spec-CP position immediately above it). As should be apparent, a crucial assumption underpinning the argumentation here is that the *if*-clause contains a null operator-specifier which prevents successive cyclic movement.

On the analysis presented here, English has two interrogative complementizers (*if* and ∅). They differ in their specifier-features, in that the overt complementizer *if* requires a null yes–no question operator as its specifier, and the covert complementizer ∅ requires an overt interrogative specifier. They also differ in their selectional properties, as we see from contrasts such as the following:

(75) (a)   I didn't know [whether ∅ I should go]
     (b)   I didn't know [whether ∅ to go]
(76) (a)   I didn't know [Op if I should go]
     (b)   *I didn't know [Op if to go]

The null complementizer ∅ which heads wh-questions selects a TP complement headed by a finite T constituent like *should*, or by infinitival *to*; however, *if* can only select a finite TP complement, not an infinitival TP complement.

But there is a second, less immediately obvious, difference between the two interrogative complementizers: this relates to the *distribution* of clauses containing them, and can be illustrated by the following contrasts:

(77) (a)   She was curious about [whether ∅ I was wearing one]
     (b)   *She was curious about [Op if I was wearing one]
(78) (a)   [Whether ∅ 007 was a double-agent] will remain a secret
     (b)   *[Op if 007 was a double-agent] will remain a secret

The bracketed embedded clauses in (77) occur as the complement of the transitive preposition *about*; those in (78) occur as the subject of the finite auxiliary *will*. To put matters rather differently; the bracketed clauses occupy an *objective* case position in (77), and a *nominative* case position in (78). It would seem from the contrast between the (a) and (b) examples in (77–8) that a CP headed by the null complementizer ∅ can occur in a (nominative or objective) case position, whereas a CP headed by *if* cannot. To use the terminology of Stowell 1981, *if* is a *case-resistant* complementizer, whereas ∅ is not. Since it is typically a property of D-constituents (e.g. pronouns like *you*) that they carry case (and so occupy case positions), what this might suggest is that the null complementizer ∅ is actually a null determiner – and that the structure into which it projects is a DP rather than a CP. However, this can't be the whole story, since wh-question clauses (headed by ∅) can also occur (as can *if*-clauses) as the complement of an intransitive adjective like *sure*: cf.

(79) (a) I wasn't sure [whether ø she would agree]

(b) I wasn't sure [Op *if* she would agree]

There's clearly a lot more to be said about the different properties of the overt interrogative complementizer *if* and its covert counterpart ø, but we shan't attempt to probe the relevant issues any further here.

7.9 Nonoperator questions

Our analysis in the last two sections has suggested that questions are clauses which contain an interrogative operator-specifier. However, the *interrogative-specifier* analysis proves potentially problematic in relation to root noninversion (*in situ*) questions such as:

(80) (a) You're leaving?

(b) He said what?

Sentences such as (80) differ from typical operator questions in a number of ways – for example, they don't show auxiliary inversion or wh-movement. Moreover (unlike a typical auxiliary-inversion operator question such as (81a) below), they can't contain polarity items such as *any* – as we see from the ungrammaticality of *any* in (81b) below:

(81) (a) Have you ordered the/any drinks?

(b) You've ordered the/*any drinks?

If we assume that root yes–no questions with auxiliary inversion contain an abstract yes–no question operator *Op*, (81a) will have the (simplified) derivation (82) below:

(82)

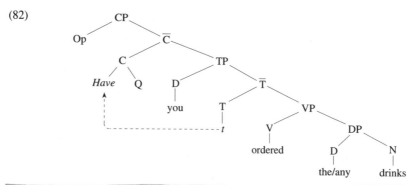

Since the quantifying determiner *any* is a polarity item, it must be c-commanded by a (negative, interrogative or conditional) operator. This condition is met in (82) in that the interrogative operator *Op* c-commands *any* (by virtue of the fact that the mother of *Op* is CP, and CP dominates *any*).

But why should *any* be ungrammatical in (81b)? Since they don't show auxiliary inversion and don't license polarity items, let's suppose that such questions don't contain the interrogative operator *Op* (and thus are **nonoperator questions**), so that (81b) is simply a TP with the (simplified) structure (83) below (cf. Grimshaw 1993a, 1993b):

(83)

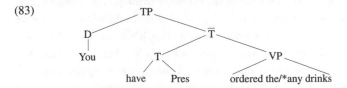

We could then say that *any* is ruled out by virtue of the fact that (83) is a *nonoperator question*, and thus does not contain an interrogative operator c-commanding *any*.

However, what a TP analysis such as (83) fails to account for is the fact that sentences like (80) are questions, as is shown orthographically by the question-mark at the end of the sentence, lexically by the use of the interrogative pronoun *what* in (80b) and phonetically by their intonation. One way of marking them as questions is to suppose that the head T constituent of TP carries an interrogative feature of some kind in the relevant structures. An alternative possibility (in keeping with Chomsky's assumption that all questions are CP constituents headed by a question affix Q) would be to suppose that they are CPs headed by Q, so that (81b) would have the structure (84) below:

(84)

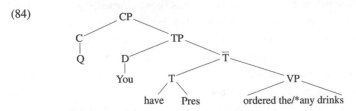

If we suppose that Q is only a strong affix when it has an (overt or covert) interrogative operator-specifier (as we earlier assumed in relation to subject-question structures like (62) above), it follows that Q in (84) will be weak (since (84) is a nonoperator question), and so will not trigger auxiliary inversion. Since (84) contains no interrogative operator, we correctly predict that the polarity item *any* is ungrammatical.

7.10 Summary

In this chapter, we have looked at the syntax of interrogative operators. In §7.2 we argued that wh-questions like *What did you say?* involve moving an interrogative wh-operator like *what?* into the specifier position within CP, and argued that the moved wh-operator leaves behind a trace in the position it moves out of. In §7.3 we suggested that movement of operators into spec-CP is motivated by Lasnik's principle of **enlightened self-interest**, and that operator movement serves to check the [wh] specifier-feature carried by the question affix Q which heads interrogative clauses. We noted that such an analysis predicts that in multiple wh-questions, only one of the wh-operator expressions will move to spec-CP, and that the **shortest movement principle** determines that it is the nearest wh-operator expression which moves. In §7.4 we argued that (in consequence of the **economy principle**) movement operations affect the *minimal* constituent which will suffice to check the features triggering their movement. We noted that in simple questions like *What did he say?* the wh-operator *what* is moved on its own, but that movement of *what* alone in sentences like **What did he give reason?* would violate Chomsky's **chain uniformity principle**, and that in consequence the complement of *what* (i.e. the noun *reason*) has to be pied-piped along with *what*, so deriving *What reason did he give?* We also noted that Huang's **condition on extraction domains** (which allows extraction only out of complements) prevents *what* from being extracted out of a subject expression in sentences like **Which country did you say the capital of was bombed during the war?*, and requires the whole subject constituent to be pied-piped along with *which*, so deriving *The capital of which country did you say was bombed during the war?* In §7.5 we looked at the syntax of embedded questions in Belfast English, noting that these allow the head C position of CP to be filled either by an inverted auxiliary or by the complementizer *that*, so deriving sentences like *I asked which street did he live in* and *I asked which street that he lived in*. We also noted that inversion takes place in noninterrogative clauses from which an interrogative operator has been extracted, e.g. in sentences like *Who did he hope would he see?* We suggested that this could be accounted for by positing that operator movement applies in a successive cyclic fashion (moving an operator expression into the nearest spec-CP position above it on each of its movements), and by positing that a C which has an interrogative specifier is a strong (affixal) head, and hence can trigger auxiliary inversion. In §7.6 we turned to look at Standard English, and argued that C is always filled by a null interrogative complementizer ø in Standard English complement-clause questions, with spec-CP being filled either by merging the adverb *whether* with C-bar, or by moving an operator expression from some position within TP into spec-CP. We argued that operator movement applies in a successive cyclic fashion, and that this accounts for why wh-operators can't be extracted out of wh-questions (i.e. why sentences like **How do you wonder whether he is feeling?* are ungrammatical), since successive cyclic movement is blocked by the fact that *whether* occupies spec-CP in the embedded clauses, and long (one-step) movement violates the **shortest movement principle**. In §7.7 we looked at subject questions like *Who helped him?* We noted Chomsky's claim that such sentences are CPs headed by the question-affix Q, and that the subject *who* is in spec-IP, with the wh-feature of *who* being attracted to Q. We saw that Chomsky's CP analysis would enable us to provide a unitary characterization of questions as CPs with an interrogative Q head. However, we suggested an alternative characterization of questions as clauses with an *interrogative specifier*, noting that this would allow us to posit that subject questions like *Who helped him?* are TPs which are questions by virtue of the fact that they have an interrogative specifier (= *who*); in questions such as *What did you say?*, movement of *what* into spec-CP would be motivated by the need to generate a structure with an interrogative specifier. In §7.8 we noted that the *interrogative specifier* analysis would entail positing that yes–no questions like *Is it raining?* contain an abstract yes–no question operator *Op* in spec-CP, and we saw that there were significant parallels between the syntax of such questions and *whether* questions which made it plausible to posit that they contain a null-operator counterpart of *whether*. We went on to suggest that embedded yes–no questions headed by the complementizer *if* also have a null yes–no question operator-specifier, and we argued that this assumption accounts for the fact that operators can't be extracted out of *if*-question clauses (cf. **How do you wonder if he is feeling?*), since successive cyclic movement is blocked by the null operator and long movement is blocked by the **shortest movement principle**. In §7.9 we argued that noninversion questions like *You're leaving?* and *He said what?* do not contain an interrogative operator, and hence are *nonoperator questions*. We suggested that they could be analysed as TPs headed by an interrogative T, or perhaps as CPs headed by a question particle Q which is weak by virtue of lacking an interrogative operator in spec-CP.

Workbook section
Exercise I (§§7.2–7.4)
Discuss the syntax of the following sentences in Standard English:

1a   What did he wanna do?
 b   *What did he wanna happen?
2a   What colour did you choose?
 b   *What did you choose colour?
3a   Whose jewels did they steal?
 b   *Whose did they steal jewels?
4a   Who've they been talking to?
 b   *To who've they been talking?
5a   The author of which book do you think will win the prize?
 b   *Which book do you think the author of will win the prize?
6a   What did he think would happen to who?
 b   *Who did he think what would happen to?

Model answer for 1a
   Given the assumptions made in the text, 1a will have the superficial syntactic structure (i) below (simplified in respect of the internal structure of T and C), where *arrows* indicate movement of *what* and *did*:

301

(i)

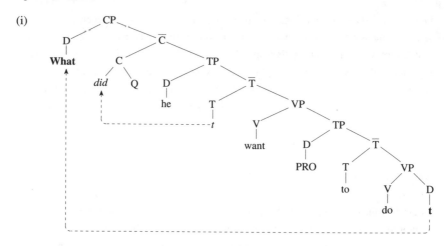

The wh-operator *what* moves to spec-CP to check the [wh] specifier-feature carried by Q (movement of *what* being motivated by **enlightened self-interest**); the auxiliary *did* adjoins to Q because Q is a strong affix.

What remains to be accounted for in (i) is how *to* can cliticize onto *want*, ultimately giving rise to *wanna*. This is not an entirely straightforward question to answer, since the two are separated by the intervening empty category *PRO*, and we have seen on numerous occasions that an intervening trace or empty INFL constituent blocks cliticization. For the time being, let's simply stipulate that an intervening *PRO* doesn't block cliticization but other empty categories do. (We shall provide a principled answer to the question of why *PRO* doesn't block cliticization in the next chapter.)

Exercise II (§7.5)

Discuss the syntax of the following sentences in (one variety of) Belfast English (cf. Henry 1995):

1a They wondered which one that he chose
 b They wondered which one did he choose
 c *They wondered which one that did he choose
2a They wondered if/whether (*that) we went
 b *They wondered if/whether did we go
 c They wondered did we go
3a Who did he say did she meet?
 b *Who did he say that did she meet?
 c I wonder who did he say did she meet

Why do you think Alison Henry (1995) argues that *whether* functions as a complementizer in Belfast English?

Model answer for 1a

Given the assumptions made in the text, 1a will have the (simplified) derivation (i) below:

(i)

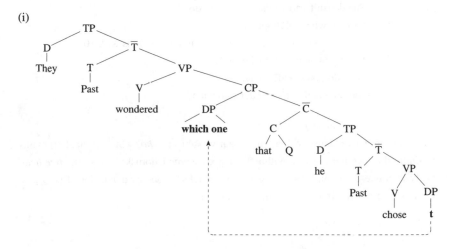

The [wh] specifier-feature of Q cannot be checked by wh-attraction here (since the DP *which one* does not originate as the specifier of the TP complement of Q), and so is checked by wh-movement. The wh-determiner *which* cannot move on its own (since this would violate the **chain uniformity principle**, resulting in a chain whose head is a maximal projection, but whose foot is not), so its N complement *one* is pied-piped along with it, to ensure convergence (i.e. satisfaction of the requirement for chains to be uniform: the resulting chain in (i) is uniform because it contains a maximal DP projection at its head and foot). If we suppose that (in Belfast English) Q is always strong (and indeed that any C which has an interrogative specifier is strong), the strong affixal head-features of Q will be satisfied by merger with the complementizer *that*. If we further suppose that the head-features of *that* in Belfast English simply indicate that it is finite, it follows that there is no reason why it cannot be adjoined to Q in interrogative clauses (unlike in Standard English, where *that* is inherently noninterrogative).

Exercise III (§§7.6–7.7)

Discuss the syntax of the following sentences in standard varieties of English:

1 Who upset you?
2 Who'd upset you? (*'d = had/would ≠ did*)
3 Who'd you upset? (*'d = had/would/did*)
4 Who said what?
5 *What did who say?

6　I wonder who said what
7　*I wonder what who said
8　She doesn't know what to do
9　*She doesn't know what (for) us to do
10　I wonder what will happen
11　*I wonder what to happen (intended as synonymous with 10)
12　*What do you wonder who said?
13　*Who do you wonder what said?
14　Who do you think/*wonder said what?

Model answer for 1

1 is an interrogative clause with an interrogative subject (*who*) which arguably remains *in situ* in the specifier position within TP. If we assume Chomsky's *interrogative head* analysis of questions (under which questions are CPs headed by a question affix Q), we might suppose that 1 is a CP with the structure (i) below:

(i)

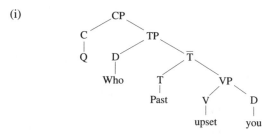

The [wh] feature of Q can be checked by *wh-attraction* (i.e. by percolation of the [wh] feature of *who* from D to C), since *who* is sufficiently close to Q to satisfy the locality restriction on attraction (to the effect that a head can only attract features of the head/specifier of its complement). Because it is more economical, wh-attraction is preferred to wh-movement – hence there is no movement of *who* into spec-CP. If we suppose that Q is only a strong affix when it has an operator-specifier in spec-CP, Q will be weak here (because there is no operator-specifier in spec-CP), and so not trigger *do*-support and auxiliary inversion.

On the other hand, if we adopt the alternative *interrogative specifier* analysis of questions outlined in §7.7, sentence 1 will simply be a TP of the form (ii) below:

(ii)

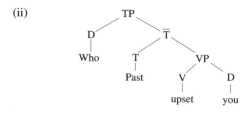

The resulting structure will be interpretable as a question at LF by virtue of the fact that it contains an interrogative operator-specifier (since *who* occupies the specifier position within TP). Since T is a weak affix in English, the past-tense head-features of *upset* are checked by attraction to T, not by movement.

Helpful hints

In 8, assume that the *to* clause has a *PRO* subject; in 9, ask yourself why *for* can't be used to head an interrogative CP (bearing in mind the text discussion of *wh+that* structures), and why the case of *us* can't be checked if *for* is not used. Similarly, in 11 say why the case of *what* can't be checked. Consider also whether any of these examples might lead you to modify some of the assumptions made in the text.

Exercise IV (§§7.6–7.7)

Clauses like those bracketed in the examples below are traditionally referred to as **relative clauses**, because they contain a (bold-printed) **relative pronoun** which relates to (i.e. has as its antecedent) an (italicized) expression outside the bracketed relative clause:

1a   He is *someone* [**who** we can identify with]
 b   He said *something* [**which** I didn't understand]
 c   There are *places* [**where** you can hide]
 d   There are *times* [**when** I feel like giving up syntax]

Relative pronouns (like their interrogative counterparts) usually begin with *wh* (cf. *who/which/where/when*). However, English also has two other types of relative clause. The first are structures like (2) below which contain no *wh* pronoun but contain *that*:

2a   He is *someone* [**that** we can identify with]
 b   He said *something* [**that** I didn't understand]

The second are relative clauses which contain neither a relative pronoun nor *that*: cf.

3a   He is *someone* [we can identify with]
 b   He said *something* [I didn't understand]

Relative *that* is generally taken to be a complementizer rather than a relative pronoun – for a number of reasons. Firstly, like the complementizer *that*, it has the vowel-reduced form /ðət/; secondly, like a typical complementizer but unlike a relative pronoun such as *who*, it has no possessive form (cf. *someone whose/*that's mother died*); and thirdly, like a typical complementizer but unlike a pronoun, it can't be used as the complement of a preposition (cf. *something about which/*about that he had complained*). It is generally suggested that *wh*-less relative clauses like those bracketed in 2–3 above contain a

305

null relative operator (a silent counterpart of *who/which* etc.) which originates internally within the sentence and is then moved to the spec-CP position at the front of the bracketed relative clause. Given these assumptions, discuss how the bracketed relative clauses in the examples below might be derived, saying why they are (un)grammatical:

4a She's the only person [that I wanna work with]

  b *She's the only person [that I wanna work with me]

  c Where are the prisoners [they've recaptured]?

  d *Where are the prisoners [they say've escaped]?

5a He is someone [who we can trust]

  b *He is someone [who that we can trust]

  c He is someone [that we can trust]

  d He is someone [we can trust]

6a Guy Sly is the candidate [for whom he voted]

  b *Guy Sly is the candidate [for whom that he voted]

  c *Guy Sly is the candidate [for that he voted]

  d *Guy Sly is the candidate [for he voted]

7a He is someone [who has impressed me]

  b *He is someone [who that has impressed me]

  c He is someone [that has impressed me]

  d *He is someone [has impressed me]

8a I'm looking for someone [for us to collaborate with]

  b *I'm looking for someone [who for us to collaborate with]

  c *I'm looking for someone [who to collaborate with]

  d I'm looking for someone [to collaborate with]

9a I'm looking for someone [with whom to collaborate]

  b *I'm looking for someone [with whom for us to collaborate]

  c *I'm looking for someone [with for us to collaborate]

  d *I'm looking for someone [with to collaborate]

10a I'm looking for someone [to collaborate with us]

  b *I'm looking for someone [who to collaborate with us]

Finally, say what's interesting about the bracketed Shakespearean relative clauses in 11 below, and how and why they differ from their contemporary counterparts:

11a I have an answer ^(that)[will serve all men] (Clown, *All's Well That Ends Well*, II.ii)

  b There's little ^(there)[can be said in't] (Parolles, *All's Well That Ends Well*, I.i)

  c You are the man ^(that)[must stead us all] (Tranio, *Taming of the Shrew*, I.ii)

  d I am he ^(that is)[am born to tame you] (Petruchio, *Taming of the Shrew*, II.i)

  e Youth's a stuff [will not endure] ^(that)(Clown, *Twelfth Night*, II.iii)

Model answer for 4a

One possible analysis of the bracketed relative clause in 4a would be to assume that it is a CP headed by a C containing a null relative clause affix **R** (with which the complementizer *that* merges), and that a null relative operator (below symbolized as *Op*) originates as the complement of *with*, and then moves into the spec-CP position within the relative clause, as in (i) below:

(i)

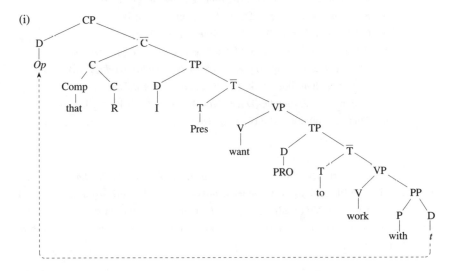

If we suppose that the null relative pronoun-operator *Op who* carries the head-feature [rel] (indicating its status as a relative operator) and that the null relative-clause head R carries the specifier-feature [rel] (indicating that it requires a relative pronoun as its specifier), we can say that movement of *who* into spec-CP is motivated by **enlightened self-interest** – i.e. by the requirement to check the [rel] specifier-feature of R (which cannot be checked by attraction, because *Op* is not the specifier of the TP complement of R). Thus, movement of the null relative operator *Op* to spec-CP is used as a last resort, as the only way of checking the [rel] specifier-feature of R. In relation to the cliticization of *to* onto *want* (ultimately forming *wanna*), see the model answer for exercise I.

Helpful hints

In 7a, consider whether the subject moves at all. In relation to the contrast between 7d and the sentences in 11, consider whether (and if so, how and why) this might be related to the fact that Early Modern English was a null subject language whereas present-day English is not. Are there puzzling differences between finite relative clauses like those in 4–7 and infinitival relative clauses like those in 8–10?

Exercise V (§§7.6–7.7)

Discuss the syntax of the following Early Modern English (EME) sentences taken from various plays by Shakespeare:

1 What sayst thou? (Olivia, *Twelfth Night*, III.iv)
2 What didst not like? (Othello, *Othello*, III.iii)
3 Who knows not that? (Curtis, *Taming of the Shrew*, IV.i)
4 Saw you my daughter? (Duke, *Two Gentlemen of Verona*, V.ii)
5 Can'st not rule her? (Leontes, *Winter's Tale*, II.iii)
6 What visions have I seen! (Titania, *Midsummer Night's Dream*, V.i)
7 What a caterwauling do you keep! (Maria, *Twelfth Night*, II.iii)
8 Seawater shalt thou drink (Prospero, *The Tempest*, I.ii)
9 Welcome shall they be (Duke, *All's Well That Ends Well*, III.i)
10 This fail you not to do! (Othello, *Othello*, IV.i)

Model answer for 1

The verb *sayst* in 1 originates as the head V of VP, with *what* as its complement. Since INFL contains a strong tense affix in EME, the verb *sayst* moves out of the head V position in VP to adjoin to T (and thereby check the tense and agreement properties of *sayst*), and the resulting T-bar then merges with the subject *thou* to form the TP (i) below:

(i)

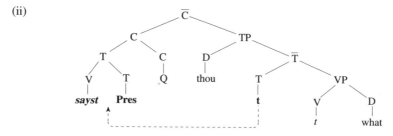

The TP in (i) then merges with the strong question affix Q, and the T constituent containing the verb *sayst* raises to adjoin to Q as in (ii) below:

(ii)

The wh-operator *what* then moves into spec-CP, as in (iii) below:

(iii)

If we assume that T and Q are strong affixes in EME, movement of *sayst* from V to T to C will be motivated by **enlightened self-interest**, driven by the desire to satisfy the requirement for the strong affixes T and Q to be attached to a lexical item. Since T is a strong affix, we might assume that it cannot be separated from *sayst*, so that when *sayst* moves from T to C as in (ii) above, the tense affix T is pied-piped along with it.

The movement of *what* into spec-CP might similarly be said to be motivated by **enlightened self-interest**, since it enables the [wh] specifier-feature carried by Q to be checked (and erased) by the [wh] head-feature carried by *what*. It is not possible for the relevant [wh] feature to be checked by attraction here, since *what* is too far away from Q to satisfy the locality restriction on attraction (which specifies that a head can only attract features from the head or specifier of its complement): hence, movement of *what* to spec-CP is a *last resort* strategy.

However, an alternative account of why *what* moves into spec-CP would be to suppose that this is in order to ensure LF convergence i.e. to ensure that the resulting structure contains an interrogative operator-specifier, and hence can be interpreted as an (operator) question at LF.

Helpful hints

Sentences like those in 6–7 are traditionally referred to as *exclamatives*: 8 might be called a *topic* sentence, in that the constituent *seawater* has been made into the topic of the sentence by being moved to the front of the sentence; sentence 10 is an *imperative*. Assume for the purposes of the exercise that all the sentences in 1–10 are CP structures in which the initial (auxiliary/nonauxiliary) verb in the sentence is adjoined to (an exclamative/topic/imperative affix in) C.

Exercise VI (§§.6–7.8)

Discuss the syntax of the following questions in Jamaican Creole (in sentences 1–3, the b sentence is intended to be synonymous with the corresponding a sentence):

1a   Yu gat eni fish?
    you got any fish
    'Have you got any fish?'

  b   *Gat yu eni fish?
    Got you any fish

2a   Homoch   kuoknat im en   sel?
    how-much coconut him been sell
    'How many coconuts did he sell?'

  b   *Homoch im en   sel kuoknat?
    how-much him been sell coconut?

3a   Huu yu a   taak bout?
    who you are talk about
    'Who are you talking about?'

  b   *Bout huu yu a   taak?
    about who you are talk

4a   Im aks ef mi en   si eniting
    him ask if me been see anything
    'He asked if I saw anything'

  b   Im aks wa mi en   si
    him ask what me been see
    'He asked what I saw'

Model answer for 1a

If we suppose (as suggested in §7.8) that root yes–no questions contain a null yes–no question operator, 1a will have the structure (i) below:

(i)

Since *eni* 'any' is a polarity item (and so must be c-commanded by an affective operator), we might argue that *eni* here is licensed by the null yes–no question operator *Op* (a null counterpart of English *whether*), since *Op* c-commands *eni* (by virtue of the fact that the mother of *Op* is CP, and CP dominates *eni*). The fact that there is no auxiliary inversion in 1a suggests that Q is weak in Jamaican Creole (though its counterpart in Standard English is strong).

Exercise VII (§§7.8–7.9)

Discuss the syntax of the following sentences:

1a   Has anyone seen anything?
  b   *Anyone has seen anything?
2a   I don't know whether/if anyone can do anything
  b   I don't know what anyone can do
3a   He can't decide whether to take the exam
  b   *He can't decide if to take the exam
4a   He seems unsure about what he should do
  b   He seems unsure about whether/*if he should do anything
5a   How do you think that he will behave?
  b   *How do you wonder whether/if he will behave?

In addition, comment on the nature of the ungrammaticality of the following sentence (from a letter written to me by a Spanish student):

6   I don't even know whether if they'll *give me some credits for the courses*

(but don't try and analyse the internal structure of the italicized VP headed by *give*, since this presupposes familiarity with assumptions about structure not introduced until chapter 9).

Model answer for 1

Given the suggestion made in §7.8 that root yes–no questions with auxiliary inversion contain an abstract yes–no question operator **Op**, 1a will have the (simplified) derivation (i) below:

(i)

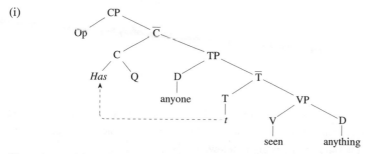

Since the partitive/existential quantifier *any* (and its compounds like *anyone/anything*) is a polarity item, it must be c-commanded by a (negative, interrogative or conditional) operator. This condition is met in (i) in that the yes–no question operator *Op* c-commands

311

anyone and *anything* by virtue of the fact that the mother of *Op* is CP, and CP dominates *anyone/anything*.

Exercise VIII

Discuss the syntax of the following **topic** structures in present-day Standard English:

1   This kind of behaviour we cannot tolerate
2   *This kind of behaviour cannot we tolerate
3   You know that this kind of behaviour we cannot tolerate
4   *You know this kind of behaviour that we cannot tolerate
5   This kind of behaviour you know that we cannot tolerate
6   *Can this kind of behaviour we tolerate?

Model answer for 1

In sentences such as 1, the DP *this kind of behaviour* serves as the complement of the verb *tolerate*, and is moved to the front of the sentence by an operation traditionally called **topicalization** (since it has the effect of moving the relevant constituent into a more prominent position at the front of the relevant clause, thereby marking it out as the *topic* of the sentence). However, the question raised by this assumption is what kind of movement operation is involved in topicalization.

One possibility is that the topicalized expression moves into the specifier position of a CP whose head C constituent contains a null **Top** (= topic) particle as represented in (i) below (simplified *inter alia* by treating *cannot* as a single head):

(i)

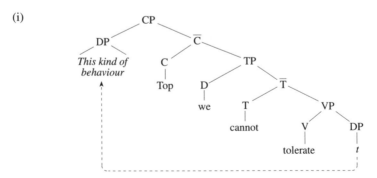

A second (similar but subtly different) possibility is to suppose that the topicalized expression moves into the specifier position within a **TopP** (= topic phrase) constituent headed by a null **Top** particle, as in (ii) below:

(ii)

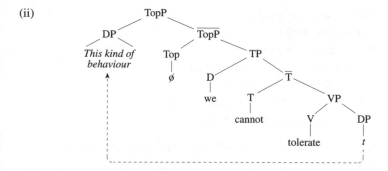

A third possibility (argued for by Jane Grimshaw, 1993a, 1993b) is to suppose that topicalization involves adjunction of the topicalized constituent to TP, thereby expanding TP into an extended TP constituent, as in (iii) below:

(iii)

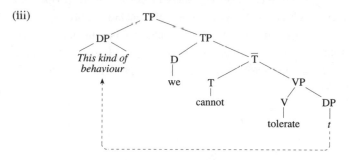

Topicalization would then involve an adjunction operation by which one maximal projection is adjoined to another: this would be the phrasal counterpart of the head-adjunction operation discussed in the previous chapter, in which one head (i.e. minimal projection) is adjoined to another. Adjunction of the topicalized constituent to TP results in the formation of a *split-segment category* – viz. a TP node which comprises two TP segments.

On the basis of sentences such as 1 alone, it is impossible to determine which is the optimal derivation for topicalization structures. (*You* take over at this point and say whether any of the sentences in 2–6 provides clues as to the nature of topicalization.)

Exercise IX

Discuss the derivation of the following sentences, accounting for the (un)grammaticality of each of the examples (note that % = 'grammatical in some varieties of English, but not in Standard English'):

1 He said nothing
2 Nothing did he say
3 Nobody said anything

4   Nothing did anyone say
5   Nobody said nothing
6   *Nothing did nobody say
7   I realize that nobody could do anything
8   I realize that nothing could anyone do
9   Nothing did he think would happen to her
10   %Nothing did he think could he do

Present arguments in support of your analysis, and explain the (un)grammaticality of each of the examples.

Helpful hints

Expressions such as *nobody* and *nothing* incorporate the negative operator *no*, and thus might be said to be negative operator expressions. Consider possible similarities and differences between the syntax of negative and interrogative operators. In considering the landing-site for preposed negative operators, bear in mind two possibilities: firstly, that preposed negative operators move to spec-CP; and secondly, that they move to the specifier position in a different kind of projection (e.g. a NEGP headed by a strong NEG affix).

8

A movement

8.1 Overview

In this chapter, we take a close look at the syntax of *subjects*. So far, we have assumed that subjects occupy the specifier position within TP and remain *in situ* (except where the subject is an interrogative operator which undergoes operator movement, e.g. in sentences like ***Who*** *did he say was coming?*). However, in this chapter we argue that subjects originate internally within VP, and subsequently move to spec-TP for checking purposes (an assumption known as the **VP-internal subject hypothesis**). We look at the syntax of so-called **raising predicates** like *seem*, and examine how (and why) they differ from **control predicates** like *try*. In addition, we look at the syntax of subjects in **passive sentences**. Finally, we look at the nature of the **A movement** operation by which subjects are raised up (in a successive cyclic fashion) into the spec-TP position which they occupy in the superficial syntactic structure of the sentence.

8.2 VP-internal subject hypothesis

We begin by looking at the structure of *expletive* sentences such as (1) below:

(1) (a)   *There* is nobody living **there**

(b)   *There* is someone knocking at the door

(c)   *There* are several patients waiting to see the doctor

Sentence (1a) contains two different occurrences of *there*. The second (bold-printed) ***there*** is a locative pronoun paraphraseable as 'in that place', and contains the diphthong /eə/; the first (italicized) *there* is an *expletive* (i.e. *dummy* or *pleonastic*) constituent which contains the unstressed vowel /ə/ and does not have a locative interpretation (i.e. it is not paraphrascable as 'in that place'), but rather has no intrinsic reference (as we see from the fact that its reference can't be questioned – hence the ungrammaticality of **Where is nobody living there?*). Expletive *there* seems to have the categorial status of a pronominal determiner, since (like other pronominal determiners – e.g. personal pronouns such as *he/she/it/they*) it can occur in sentence *tags*, as we see from examples like those in (2) below (where the part of the sentence following the comma is the *tag*):

(2) (a) Don Quickshot has been arrested, has *he*?

 (b) Peggy Prim buys her clothes at Marks and Spencer, does *she*?

 (c) Randy Rabbit is a regular at Benny's Bunny Bar, is *he*?

 (d) Bill and Ben are a happily unmarried couple, aren't *they*?

 (e) It always rains in Manchester, doesn't *it*?

 (f) There's nobody living there, is *there*?

 (g) There's someone knocking at the door, isn't *there*?

 (h) There are several patients waiting to see the doctor, are *there*?

It seems clear that the pronoun *there* in sentences such as (1) occupies the specifier position within TP. Some evidence in support of this claim comes from the fact that the auxiliary *is/are* can be moved in front of it (into COMP) in yes–no question structures such as (3) below:

(3) (a) **Is** *there* nobody living there?

 (b) **Is** *there* someone knocking at the door?

 (c) **Are** *there* several patients waiting to see the doctor?

where *is/are* originates in the head T position of TP and moves across expletive *there* (which occupies the specifier position in TP) into the head C position of CP. Given that auxiliary inversion typically moves an auxiliary across a subject in spec-TP, the fact that the auxiliary *is* moves across the expletive pronoun *there* in getting from its position in (1) into its position in (3) suggests that *there* must be in spec-TP.

Moreover, given that auxiliaries select a VP complement, it seems likely that the complement of the auxiliary *is/were* in (1) is a verb phrase. If this is so, then (1b) will be a TP with the simplified structure (4) below. (Here and throughout the rest of this chapter, we simplify tree diagrams by not showing the internal structure of T – e.g. we don't show the abstract present-tense affix which *is* merges with in (4) below.)

(4)

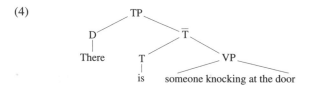

An analysis such as (4) would enable us to account for the fact that the verb *knocking* surfaces in the +*ing* form, and not (for example) in the infinitive form *knock*: given the structure in (4), we should expect that the head T constituent (= *is*) of TP will determine the morphological form of the head V constituent (= *knocking*) of the complement VP: since the progressive auxiliary *be* selects a complement headed by a verb in the +*ing* form, the fact that *knocking* is in the +*ing* form can be accounted for straightforwardly.

But what is the internal structure of the VP constituent in (4)? It seems clear that the V *knocking* is the head of the VP, and that *at the door* is its complement. But what is the role of the pronoun *someone* (which is sometimes referred to as the **associate** of expletive *there*)? A natural suggestion to make is that *someone* is the subject of *knocking at the door*; if we assume that the canonical position for the subject of a particular constituent is the specifier position within the relevant projection, we might suggest that the expletive associate *someone* in (4) occupies **spec-VP** (i.e. the specifier position within VP). If so, (4) will have the simplified structure (5) below:

(5)

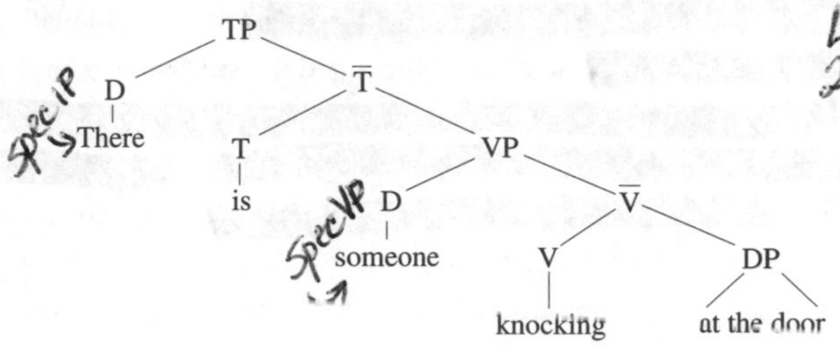

[Tree diagram: TP branches into D (*There*, labelled spec-TP) and T̄. T̄ branches into T (*is*) and VP. VP branches into D (*someone*, labelled spec-VP) and V̄. V̄ branches into V (*knocking*) and DP (*at the door*).*]*

[Handwritten margin note: "Looks like we have 2 subjects."]

What (5) claims is that the head V constituent (= *knocking*) of the VP merges with its PP complement (= *at the door*) to form a verbal expression which is conventionally termed a $\bar{V}$ (= V' = **V-bar**, in each case pronounced *vee-bar*), and the resulting V-bar constituent *knocking at the door* is then predicated of the pronominal quantifier/determiner *someone*, so forming the overall VP *someone knocking at the door*.

An interesting variant of a sentence like (1b) is the type of sentence illustrated in (6) below:

(6)   Someone is knocking at the door

[Handwritten note: "knocking merges w/ someone, that VP merges with T which has a spec TP, someone move up to fill spec TP slot. A trace is left."]

Here, *someone* is clearly the subject of the auxiliary *is*, and hence would appear to be positioned in spec-TP. And yet, in our earlier structure (5), *someone* was instead the subject of *knocking*, and occupied the specifier position in VP. The obvious question to ask is how we can account for the fact that subjects like *someone* are in spec-VP in expletive structures like (5), but in spec-TP in nonexpletive structures like (6). In this connection, recall our suggestion in chapters 6 and 7 that constituents can *move* from a lower to a higher position within the sentence containing them (e.g. auxiliaries can move from T to C, and operator expressions can move e.g. from VP-complement position to CP-specifier position). This opens up the possibility of a movement account of the dual position of *someone* in sentences like (1b) and (6). More specifically, let us suppose that *someone* originates in spec-VP and remains *in situ* in expletive structures such as (5), but is *raised* into spec-TP in nonexpletive structures such as (6). If this is so (and if we assume that a moved subject leaves behind a trace in the position out of which it moves), then (6) will be derived as in (7) below:

(7)

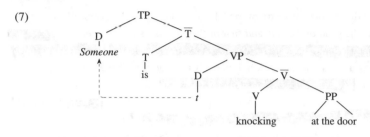

Since the movement operation which applies in (7) has the effect of raising *someone* from being the subject of VP to becoming the subject of TP, it is traditionally referred to as **subject-to-subject raising** (usually abbreviated to **subject raising**, or more simply **raising**). The more general claim underlying the analysis in (7) (known as the **VP-internal subject hypothesis**) is that subjects originate in spec-VP, and are subsequently raised into spec-TP in all but a few constructions – e.g. not in expletive structures like (5) above in which the spec-TP position is filled by a *dummy* or *expletive* constituent. Substantial empirical evidence in support of the hypothesis from a variety of languages is presented in papers by Kitagawa 1986, Speas 1986, Contreras 1987, Zagona 1987, Kuroda 1988, Sportiche 1988, Rosen 1990, Ernst 1991, Koopman and Sportiche 1991, Woolford 1991, Burton and Grimshaw 1992, Guilfoyle, Hung and Travis 1992, McNally 1992, and Huang 1993; in the next few sections, we review a tiny fragment of the relevant evidence.

8.3   Evidence that subjects originate in spec-VP

An interesting piece of evidence in support of the VP-internal subject hypothesis comes from cliticization facts. As we saw in relation to our earlier discussion of contracted forms like *they've* and *wanna*, cliticization (e.g. of *have* onto *they*, or of *to* onto *want*) is blocked by the presence of an intervening empty category. In the light of this, consider the fact that *to* can cliticize onto *want* (forming *wanta/wanna*) in sentences such as (8) below:

(8) (a)   We *want to* help you

     (b)   We *wanna* help you

We argued in chapters 4 and 5 that apparently subjectless infinitive complements (like *to help you* in (8a) above) have a null-case PRO subject in spec-TP. If this were so, (8a) would have the simplified structure (9) below:

(9)

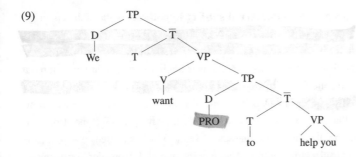

But then we should expect that the intervening empty category PRO would prevent *to* from cliticizing onto *want*, thereby wrongly predicting that (8b) is ungrammatical. What's gone wrong here? Baltin (1995, p. 244) suggests that the VP-internal subject hypothesis provides us with an answer. If we assume that PRO subjects originate (and remain) in spec-VP, then (8a) will no longer have the structure (9) above, but rather that in (10) below.

(10)

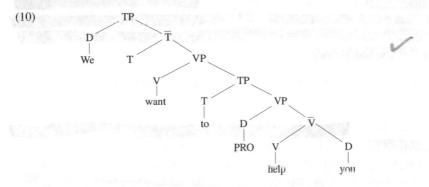

Since there is no (overt or covert) category intervening between *want* and *to* in (10), we correctly predict that *to* can cliticize onto *want*, forming (8b) *We wanna help you*. But note that a crucial premise in the argument is that PRO is positioned in spec-VP, not in spec-IP. (Of course, Baltin's analysis raises questions about how the null case carried by PRO is checked: if it is checked by *to* rather than by *help*, we are going to have to say that the case of PRO is checked from outside its containing VP by infinitival *to*, in much the same way as, in exceptional case-marking structures like *We expect **him** to resign*, the case of *him* is checked from outside its containing phrase by the verb *expect*. We return to this issue in §8.5 below.)

The core assumption of the **VP-internal subject hypothesis** is that subjects originate in spec-VP: in control structures like (10) and in expletive structures like (5), the subject remains in spec-VP; but in other structures, the subject raises from spec-VP into spec-TP. Given that a moved constituent leaves behind a trace in any position out of which it moves, it follows that subjects which move from spec-VP to spec-TP will leave behind a trace in the spec-VP position out of which they move. Empirical motivation for positing that moved subjects leave behind traces in spec-VP comes from evidence which is essentially similar in character to that which we used to support the postulation of a PRO subject in *control* structures in chapter 4. Consider, for example, how we account for the syntax of the italicized reflexive pronouns contained within the bracketed verb phrases in the sentences below:

(11) (a) He certainly has [compromised *himself/*themselves*]

  (b) [Compromised *himself/*themselves*], he certainly has

Reflexives generally require a *local* c-commanding antecedent within the phrase containing them. This being so, it follows that the reflexives in (11) must have an antecedent within the bracketed verb phrase containing them. This will obviously be the case if we assume that a sentence such as (11a) is derived in the manner indicated informally in (12) below:

(12) [$_{TP}$ *He* certainly [$_T$ has] [$_{VP}$ *t* [$_V$ compromised] himself]]

The derivation in (12) claims that the subject *he* originates in spec-VP as the subject of *compromised*, and is then raised into spec-TP, where it becomes the subject of *has* – leaving a trace *t* behind in the spec-VP position which it vacates. The trace *t* of the moved subject *he* provides an appropriate phrase-internal antecedent for *himself* in (12), since both *himself* and the trace are immediate constituents of the bracketed VP, and since both are third person masculine singular (the trace carrying the same grammatical properties as its antecedent *he*). By contrast, *themselves* could not be used in place of *himself* in (12) because it would lack an antecedent within the bracketed VP (the trace *t* cannot be its antecedent since the trace is third person masculine singular, and *themselves* is third person plural). If we suppose (following Chomsky 1995b) that a trace is a *silent copy* of the relevant moved constituent, it follows that traces will have the same syntactic and semantic properties as their antecedents, and will differ from their antecedents only in that they have no overt phonetic form: this assumption accounts for the fact that the trace *t* in (12) has the same *third person masculine singular* features as its antecedent *he*.

We can derive the structure associated with (11b) if we prepose the VP complement following *has* in (12), and move it to the relevant position in front of the overall TP – as in (13) below (where __ marks the position out of which the bracketed preposed verb phrase moves, and *t* is the trace of *he*):

(13)   [*t* Compromised himself], *he* certainly has __

Since the subject of the preposed bracketed VP is the trace *t* of the moved (third person masculine singular) subject *he*, the subject trace inside the bracketed VP can only bind (i.e. serve as the antecedent of) the third person masculine singular reflexive *himself*; hence, replacing *himself* by the third person plural reflexive *themselves* in (13) leads to ungrammaticality.

We can construct essentially parallel arguments in support of the claim that apparently subjectless VPs contain a trace subject in spec-VP in relation to structures such as the following (where *t* denotes a trace of the italicized moved subject, and where __ denotes the position out of which the preposed verb phrase moves):

(14) (a)   *They* probably will [*t* become **millionaires/*a millionaire**]
     (b)   [*t* Become **millionaires/*a millionaire**], *they* probably will __
(15) (a)   *John* certainly has [*t* damaged **his/*my own** credibility]
     (b)   [*t* Damaged **his/*my own** credibility], *John* certainly has __
(16) (a)   *You* definitely mustn't [*t* lose **your/*his** cool]
     (b)   [*t* Lose **your/*his** cool], *you* definitely mustn't __
(17) (a)   *We/*I* never would [*t* hurt **each other**]
     (b)   [*t* Hurt **each other**], *we/*I* never would __
(18) (a)   *They/*He* really shouldn't [*t* live **together**]
     (b)   [*t* Live **together**], *they/*he* really shouldn't __

If we posit a trace subject occupying the specifier position within the bracketed VP, we can account for the fact that the predicate nominal in (14) has to be in the plural form *millionaires*, since it agrees with the trace subject *t* in spec-VP (which is plural because it is the trace of the moved plural subject *they*). In much the same way, we can posit that *his* in (15) agrees with the trace of *John*, and that *your* in (16) agrees with the trace of *you*. Similarly, we can claim that *each other* (which requires a local plural antecedent) is bound by the trace of *we* in (17), and that *together* (which similarly requires a local plural antecedent) is bound by the trace of *they* in (18). The logic of the argumentation should be clear: in each case we have an expression which requires a local antecedent, and which will only have a local antecedent if we assume that subjects originate in spec-VP and thence raise to spec-TP, leaving behind a trace in spec-VP which can bind the expression requiring a local antecedent.

A rather different kind of argument in support of the VP-internal subject hypothesis can be formulated in relation to the syntax of quantifiers (cf. Sportiche 1988). In sentences such as (19) below:

(19) (a)   **They** are *both* helping her
     (b)   **We** can *all* work harder
     (c)   **You** will *each* receive a present

the italicized quantifiers *both/all/each* are separated from the bold-printed subjects **they/we/you** which they quantify. In this use, they are referred to as *floating quantifiers* (or *stranded quantifiers*), for obvious reasons. How can we account for the fact that (for example) in (19a) *both* quantifies *they*, and yet the two clearly occupy different positions? The VP-internal subject hypothesis provides us with an answer. Let us suppose that the pronoun *they* in (19a) originates as the complement of *both* (in much the same way as *of them* seems to function as the complement of *both* in an expression such as *both of them*). Let's also assume that the relevant QP (quantifier phrase) *both they* (which has essentially the same interpretation as *both of them*) originates as the subject of the VP headed by *helping*, and that the pronoun *they* is subsequently raised up to become the subject of *are*, as in (20) below:

(20)

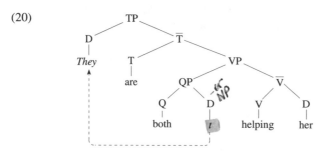

The quantifier *both* thereby ends up modifying the trace of the moved pronoun *they*. Movement of *they* leaves the quantifier *both* stranded within QP, separated from the pronoun *they* which it quantifies. The analysis in (20) correctly specifies that *both* superficially occupies an intermediate position between *are* and *helping* (the QP *both t* occupying spec-VP and so serving as the subject of *helping*).

Thus the assumption that subjects originate in spec-VP and raise to spec-TP provides us with an interesting account of how quantifiers come to be separated from the subject expressions which they quantify. A parallel separation argument can be formulated in relation to the syntax of *idioms*. We can define *idioms* as expressions (such as those italicized below) which have an idiosyncratic meaning that is not a purely componential function of the meaning of their individual parts:

(21) (a)   Let's have a couple of drinks to *break the ice*
    (b)   Be careful not to *upset the applecart*
    (c)   The president must *bite the bullet*
    (d)   We'll have to *grasp the nettle*
    (e)   He'll *hit the roof* when you tell him

There seems to be a constraint that only a string of words which forms a unitary *constituent* can be an idiom. Thus, while we find idioms like those in (21) which are of the form *verb + complement* (but where the subject isn't part of the idiom), we don't find idioms of the form *subject + verb* where the verb has a complement which isn't part of the idiom: this is because in *subject + verb + complement* structures, the verb and its complement form a unitary constituent (a *V-bar*), whereas the subject and the verb do not (and only unitary constituents can be idioms).

In the light of the constraint that an idiom is a string of words which forms a unitary constituent with an idiosyncratic interpretation, consider now more restrictive idioms such as the following:

(22) (a)   All hell broke loose

    (b)   The shit hit the fan

    (c)   The cat got his tongue

    (d)   The chickens came home to roost

In idioms like those in (22), not only is the choice of verb and complement fixed, but so too is the choice of subject. In such idioms, we can't replace the subject, verb or complement by near synonyms, so that sentences like (23) below are ungrammatical (on the intended idiomatic interpretation):

(23) (a)   *The whole inferno broke free

    (b)   *Camel dung was sucked into the air conditioning

    (c)   *A furry feline bit his lingual articulator

    (d)   *The hens returned to nest

Hence, since the choice of all three constituents (subject, verb and complement) in clauses like (22) is fixed, we might refer to such idioms as *clausal* idioms.

However, what is puzzling about clausal idioms like those in (22) is that auxiliaries can freely be inserted between the subject and verb; cf.

(24) (a)   All hell *will* break loose

    (b)   All hell *has* broken loose

    (c)   All hell *could have* broken loose

(25) (a)   The shit *might* hit the fan

    (b)   The shit *has* hit the fan

    (c)   The shit *must have* hit the fan

If (as suggested earlier) only a string of words which form a *unitary constituent* can constitute an idiom, how can we account for the fact that (for example) the idiom *all hell . . . break loose* is not a unitary constituent in any of the sentences in (24), since the subject *all hell* and the predicate *break loose* are separated by the auxiliaries *will/has/could have*? To put the question another way: how can we account for the fact that although the choice of subject, verb and complement is fixed, the choice of auxiliary is not?

A *movement* analysis for the subjects of auxiliaries provides a straightforward answer, if we suppose that clausal idioms like those in (22) are *VP idioms* which require a fixed choice of head, complement and specifier in the VP containing them. For instance, in the case of (22a), the relevant VP idiom requires the specific word *break* as its head verb, the specific adjective *loose* as its complement and the specific quantifier phrase *all hell* as its subject/specifier. We can then account for the fact that *all hell* surfaces in front of the auxiliary *will* in (24a) by positing that the QP *all hell* originates in spec-VP as the subject of the V-bar constituent *break loose*, and is then raised across the auxiliary *will* into spec-TP, where it becomes the subject of the T-bar constituent *will break loose* (by application of **raising**). Given these assumptions, (24a) will have the simplified derivation (26) below:

(26)

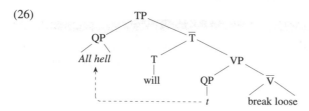

We can then say that (in the relevant idiom) *break loose* must be predicated of *all hell*, and that this condition will be met only if *all hell* originates in spec-VP as the subject of *break loose*. We can account for how the subject *all hell* comes to be separated from its predicate *break loose* by positing that subjects raise from spec-VP to spec-TP across an intervening auxiliary like *will*, so that the subject and predicate thereby come to be separated from each other.

8.4   Argument structure and theta-marking

Hitherto, the arguments which we have presented in support of the VP-internal subject hypothesis have been syntactic in nature. However, there is also strong semantic evidence in favour of the hypothesis, relating to **argument structure**. For those of you not familiar with this traditional term from predicate logic, let's briefly outline some of the relevant concepts.

Traditional work in logic maintains that **propositions** (which can be thought of as the semantic counterpart of simple clauses) comprise a **predicate** and a set of **arguments**. Simplifying somewhat, we can say that a predicate is an expression denoting (for example) an activity or event, and an argument is an expression denoting a participant in the relevant activity or event. For example, in sentences such as the following:

(27) (a)   [One of the prisoners] *died*
      (b)   [A member of the audience] *yawned*
      (c)   [Everybody] *laughed*

(28) (a)   [The police] *arrested* [the suspects]

     (b)   [John] *replied* [to her letter]

     (c)   [The pen] *rolled* [under the bed]

the italicized verbs are predicates, and the bracketed expressions represent their arguments; each of the verbs in (27) has a single argument, and so is said to function as a **one-place predicate** (in the use illustrated); each of the verbs in (28) has two arguments, and so is said to function as a **two-place predicate**. Using more familiar grammatical terminology, we can say that the arguments of a verb are its subject and complement. Since (according to the analysis we have assumed so far) the complements of verbs are positioned inside V-bar whereas their subjects are positioned outside V-bar (they originate in spec-VP and typically raise to spec-TP), complements are said to be **internal arguments** and subjects **external arguments**. Thus, in a sentence such as (28a) *The police arrested the suspects*, the DP *the suspects* is the complement and hence the internal argument of the predicate *arrested*, and the DP *the police* is the subject and hence the external argument of *arrested*. Using this terminology, we might say that the argument structure of the predicate *arrest* specifies that it is a two-place predicate which takes a DP as its internal argument and another DP as its external argument.

Not all of the expressions which are associated with a verb function as arguments of the verb; for example, in sentences like those in (29) below:

(29) (a)   [The police] *arrested* [the suspects] **on Saturday**

     (b)   [The police] *arrested* [the suspects] **in Beverly Hills**

     (c)   [The police] *arrested* [the suspects] **with minimum use of force**

it is clear that the bracketed DPs *the police* and *the suspects* are participants in the act of arrest, and so are arguments of the verb *arrested*. However, there's no sense in which we can say that the bold-printed prepositional phrases represent participants in the arrest. On the contrary, they simply serve to provide additional information about the event; thus, *on Saturday* specifies the day on which the arrest took place, *in Beverly Hills* specifies the place in which it took place and *with minimum use of force* specifies the manner in which the arrest was effected (e.g. the suspects were forced to lie face down in the mud and kicked into submission). Expressions such as those bold-printed in (29) are **adjuncts**.

However, simply saying that a verb like *arrest* takes two DP arguments (one as its subject, the other as its complement) fails to account for the fact that the two arguments play very different semantic roles in relation to the act of arrest – i.e. it fails to account for the fact that the policeman is the person who performs the act (and hence gets to verbally and physically abuse the suspect), and that the suspect is the person who suffers the consequences of the act (viz. being handcuffed, thrown into the back of a windowless vehicle and beaten up). Hence, any adequate account of argument structure should provide a proper description of the *semantic role* which each argument plays with respect to its predicate.

In research over the past three decades – beginning with the pioneering work of Gruber (1965), Fillmore (1968) and Jackendoff (1972) – linguists have attempted to devise a universal typology of the semantic roles played by arguments in relation to their predicates. In (30) below are listed some of the terms traditionally used to describe a range of different roles, and for each such role an informal gloss is given, together with an illustrative example (in which the italicized expression has the semantic role specified):

(30) THEME (or PATIENT) = entity undergoing the effect of some action
    (*Mary* fell over)
    AGENT/CAUSER = instigator of some action
    (*John* killed Harry)
    EXPERIENCER = entity experiencing some psychological state
    (*John* felt happy) *amuse, adore*
    RECIPIENT/POSSESSOR = entity receiving/possessing some entity
    (John got *Mary* a present)
    GOAL = entity towards which something moves
    (John went *home*)

We can illustrate how the terminology in (30) might be used to describe the semantic role fulfilled by arguments in terms of the following examples:

(31) (a) [The FBI] arrested [Larry Luckless]
    [AGENT]   [THEME]
  (b) [The suspect] received [a caution]
    [RECIPIENT]   [THEME]
  (c) [The audience] enjoyed [the play]
    [EXPERIENCER]   [THEME]
  (d) [The president] went [to Boston]
    [THEME]   [GOAL]

Given that – as we see from these examples – the THEME role is a central one, it has become customary over the past two decades to refer to the relevant semantic roles as **thematic roles**; and since the Greek letter θ (= *theta*) corresponds to *th* in English and the word *thematic* begins with *th*, it has also become standard practice to abbreviate the expression **thematic role** to θ-**role** (pronounced *theeta role* by some and *thayta-role* by others). Using this terminology, we can say (for example) that in (31a) *the FBI* is the AGENT argument of the predicate *arrested*, and that *Larry Luckless* is the THEME/PATIENT argument of *arrested*.

The thematic role played by a given argument in relation to its predicate determines the range of expressions which can fulfil the relevant argument function, as we see from examples such as (32) below (from Lakoff 1971, p. 332: **?** and **!** represent increasing degrees of pragmatic anomaly):

(32) (a) *My uncle* realizes that I'm a lousy cook

    (b) ?*My cat* realizes that I'm a lousy cook

    (c) ??*My goldfish* realizes that I'm a lousy cook

    (d) ?!*My pet amoeba* realizes that I'm a lousy cook

    (e) !*My frying-pan* realizes that I'm a lousy cook

The nature of the relevant restrictions depends on the semantic properties of the predicate on the one hand and on the semantic (= thematic) role played by the argument on the other. As sentences such as (32) illustrate, the EXPERIENCER argument (i.e. subject) of a cognitive predicate like *realize* has to be an expression denoting a *rational* entity (i.e. an entity capable of rational thought – hence e.g. not an expression denoting a politician).

A central theoretical question which arises is how theta-roles are assigned to arguments. It seems clear that in V-bar constituents of the form verb + complement, the thematic role of the complement is determined by the semantic properties of the verb. As examples like (31a–d) illustrate, the canonical (i.e. typical) θ-role associated with DP complements is that of THEME. However, the question of how subjects are assigned theta-roles is more complex. Marantz (1984, pp. 23ff.) and Chomsky (1986a, pp. 59–60) argue that although verbs directly assign theta-roles to their internal arguments (i.e. complements), it is not the verb but rather the whole V-bar constituent (i.e. *verb + complement* string) which determines the theta-role assigned to its external argument (i.e. subject). The evidence they adduce in support of this conclusion comes from sentences such as:

(33) (a) John threw a ball

    (b) John threw a fit

(34) (a) John broke the window

    (b) John broke his arm

Although the subject of the verb *threw* in both (33a) and (33b), *John* plays a different thematic role in the two sentences – that of AGENT in the case of *threw a ball*, but that of EXPERIENCER in *threw a fit*. Likewise, although the subject of the verb *broke* in both (34a) and (34b), *John* plays the role of AGENT in (34a) but that of EXPERIENCER on the most natural (accidental) interpretation of (34b) (though if he deliberately broke his own arm to get out of taking a syntax exam, *John* would have the role of AGENT). From examples such as these, Marantz and Chomsky conclude that the thematic role of the subject is not determined by the verb alone, but rather is compositionally determined by the whole verb+complement structure – i.e. by V-bar.

In a nutshell, what is being claimed is that a verb assigns a theta-role *directly* to its internal argument (i.e. complement), but only *indirectly* (= compositionally, i.e. as a compositional function of the semantic properties of the overall V-bar) to its external argument (= subject). To use the relevant technical terminology, we might say that verbs **directly θ-mark** their complements, but **indirectly θ-mark** their subjects.

A related observation here is that auxiliaries seem to play no part in determining the assignment of theta-roles to subjects. For example, in sentences such as:

(35) (a)   He *will* throw the ball/a fit

    (b)   He *was* throwing the ball/a fit

    (c)   He *had been* throwing the ball/a fit

    (d)   He *might have been* throwing the ball/a fit

the thematic role of the subject *he* is determined purely by the choice of V-bar constituent (i.e. whether it is *throw the ball* or *throw a fit*), and is not affected in any way by the choice of auxiliary. Clearly, any explanatory theory of **θ-marking** (i.e. θ-role assignment) should offer us a principled account of how thematic roles are assigned, and why some constituents (e.g. auxiliaries) play no part in this process.

One way of resolving the various puzzles surrounding θ-marking would be along the following lines. Since auxiliaries are functional categories and play no role in theta-marking, let us assume that theta-roles are assigned only by **lexical categories** (i.e. contentive categories), not by **functional categories**. More specifically, let's assume that θ-roles are assigned to arguments via the process of **merger with a lexical category**. Given these assumptions, a sentence such as (35a) *He will throw the ball* will be derived as follows.

The verb *throw* will be merged with the DP *the ball* (itself formed by merging *the* with *ball*) to form the V-bar *throw the ball*. As a corollary of this merger operation, the DP *the ball* is assigned the θ-role of THEME argument of *throw*. The V-bar *throw the ball* is in turn merged with pronominal determiner *he*; as a corollary of the merger operation, the subject *he* is assigned the role of AGENT argument of *throw the ball*. Thus, the relevant VP will have the simplified structure (36) below (where arrows indicate the assignment of thematic roles):

(36)

Subsequently, the VP in (36) is merged with a T constituent containing *will* so forming the T-bar *will throw the ball*. The subject *he* then moves to spec-TP, as in (37) below:

(37)

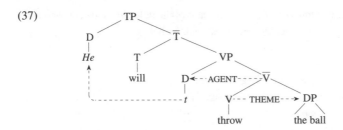

As noted earlier, the type of movement operation arrowed in (37) is traditionally known as **(subject-to-subject) raising**.

An important implication of our discussion here is that thematic considerations lend further support to the **VP-internal subject hypothesis**. The reason is that by positing that subjects originate internally within VP, we can arrive at a unitary and principled account of θ-marking, whereby *arguments are θ-marked by merger with a lexical (θ-assigning) category*, so that (for example) a complement is θ-marked by merger with a head V, and a subject is θ-marked by merger with a V-bar constituent. If subjects were directly generated in spec-TP, there would be no straightforward way of accounting for the fact that the thematic role of the subject is determined solely by V-bar, or for the fact that auxiliaries play no role in the θ-marking of subjects.

One final question which remains to be answered is this: if subjects originate in spec-VP, why do they subsequently raise to spec-TP, e.g. in structures such as (37) above? One answer might be: to satisfy Rothstein's (1995) **predication principle**, which requires that syntactic predicates (i.e. constituents such as V-bar and T-bar) should have subjects. Alternatively, we might look to **checking theory** to provide us with an answer. One checking account would be to suppose that subjects carry a strong nominative-case feature which can only be checked if the subject raises to spec-TP (e.g. *they/he* in (20) and (37) above carry a strong nominative-case head-feature which is checked by raising the pronoun to spec-TP): if PRO does not raise to spec-TP (as we argued in §8.3), we might assume that null case is a weak case (hence not checked by movement of PRO to spec-TP).

8.5 Case-checking via head adjunction and attraction

The assumption that subjects raise from spec-VP to spec-TP for reasons of **greed** (in order to check their strong case-features) raises the question of whether raising to spec-TP is the only way in which subjects can check their case-features. Chomsky (1995b) suggests three mechanisms by which features can be checked, namely (i) via a specifier–head relation, (ii) via adjunction of one head to another, and (iii) via attraction (i.e. by adjunction of a feature to a head). We have suggested in relation to (37) above that nominative case-features are canonically checked via a spec–head relation: but are there structures in English where case is checked via head–head adjunction? There may

329

indeed be. In this connection, consider how the case of the italicized subject pronouns is checked in *auxiliary contraction* structures such as those below:

(38) (a) *You've* upset her

    (b) I knew that *she'd* already gone home

    (c) *They'd* probably refuse if you asked them

    (d) *We'll* help you out

    (e) *I'm* working

Auxiliaries such as *have, had, would, will* and *am* have two unstressed forms: one comprises the reduced vowel schwa and a consonant, so that *have* reduces to /əv/, *would/had* to /əd/, *will* to /əl/ and *am* to /əm/ (I shall refer to these as *reduced* forms); the other is a nonvocalic form consisting of a single consonant segment, whereby *have* contracts down to /v/, *would/had* to /d/, *will* to /l/ and *am* to /m/ (I shall refer to these as *contracted* forms, since they involve complete loss of the vowel nucleus). Contracted forms (i.e. vowel-less forms which comprise only a single consonant) must attach to an immediately preceding word ending in a vocalic segment (i.e. a vowel or diphthong), for phonotactic reasons relating to syllable structure. Each of the italicized auxiliaries in (38) is a nonsyllabic contracted form, comprising only the single consonants /v, d, l, m/. (Note that for this and other reasons, the *'s* variant of *has* and *is* – which can immediately follow a word ending in a consonant as in *Tom's unhappy* – are excluded from our discussion of contracted auxiliary forms here; they are not subject to the same constraints on their use as the contracted auxiliary forms discussed in relation to (40) and (41) below.)

Returning now to our earlier discussion of case, consider how the case of the italicized nominative pronouns is checked in auxiliary contraction structures such as (38). The conventional answer is that case is checked by raising the subject pronoun to spec-TP, and that (for phonological reasons) the contracted auxiliary subsequently attaches to the pronoun in the PF component. However, an alternative (more economical) analysis would be the following. Let us suppose that contracted auxiliaries are affixal heads which are only legitimate PF objects if another head attaches to them. Let us further suppose that in structures such as (38), the italicized subject pronouns (by virtue of being heads) check their nominative case by adjoining directly to T. In concrete terms, this would mean that (38a) would be derived by raising the pronoun *you* out of spec-VP to adjoin directly to the auxiliary *'ve* in T as in (39) below (simplified by ignoring the possibility that *'ve* is itself adjoined to a tense affix):

(39)

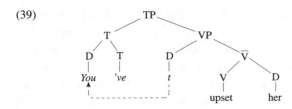

This analysis assumes that auxiliary contraction is an integral part of case-checking, and not simply the result of a PF attachment process. But what evidence is there that this is so?

Some evidence against the PF attachment view that contracted auxiliary forms simply attach to any immediately preceding word ending in a vowel or diphthong comes from the ungrammaticality of structures such as the following (*'ve* here represents the contracted form /v/, and not the reduced form /əv/):

(40) (a)   *The chairman may've gone home
  (b)   *It would have been a pity to've given up syntax
  (c)   *How many students would you say've failed syntax?
  (d)   *They now've found out the truth
  (e)   *She wouldn't let me've gone there on my own
  (f)   *Should we've helped him?

As we see from (40a–d), the contracted form /v/ cannot attach to a preceding auxiliary, infinitive particle, verb or adverb ending in a vowel or diphthong; nor can it attach to the pronouns *me/we* in (40e–f). If we assume that auxiliary contraction is only possible as part of a *checking via head-adjunction* process which (in structures like (39) above) is designed to check the case-feature of *you* and the agreement-features of *have*, the data in (40) are relatively straightforward to account for: in (40a–d) *have* contracts onto a non-nominal constituent which cannot in principle check the case/agreement properties of *have*: and in (40e–f), *have* contracts onto a pronoun (*me/we*) which has its own case/agreement properties, but which is not checked by *have* (the case of *me* is checked by *let*, that of *we* by *should*).

The *checking* analysis of auxiliary contraction also provides us with a principled account of the ungrammaticality of contraction in sentences such as the following:

(41) (a)   *John and you've got a lot in common
  (b)   *The Masai've been driven out of their homelands
  (c)   *Di'd like to be an ambassador for Britain

(Note that the asterisk here indicates that the contracted forms /v/ and /d/ are ungrammatical; the weak forms /əv/ and /əd/ are grammatical, but this is obviously of no relevance to our discussion of the syntax of contraction.) If auxiliary contraction involves checking via head-adjunction, it is clear why it is blocked in (41): structures like *John and you* and *the Masai* are clearly phrases (i.e. full DPs) and not heads, and hence cannot undergo adjunction to T, but rather must move to a phrasal position in spec-TP (thereby blocking contraction, which is only possible in structures where one head is adjoined to another for checking purposes). Similarly, if (as in §4.7) we argue that an expression like *Di* is a DP headed by a null determiner, it follows that *Di* is also phrasal and so cannot be adjoined to T (with the result that *Di* cannot serve as the subject of the contracted form *'d* of *would*).

The analysis of auxiliary contraction as a head-adjunction checking operation might be extended to cover contrasts such as the following:

(42) (a)   Who've they chosen?

    (b)   *Which one of you've they chosen?

Have can be reduced to /əv/, but not contracted to /v/ in (42b).) A possibility which we did not consider in the previous chapter is that rather than being moved to spec-CP, wh-pronouns like *who* in structures like (42a) (where C contains a contracted auxiliary) actually adjoin to the C node which contains the question particle Q, as shown informally in (43) below (where the middle trace is the trace of *they*):

(43)

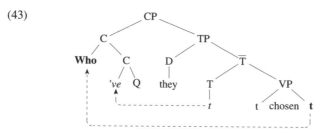

Adjunction of *who* to the C node containing Q here is driven by the need to check the [wh] feature of Q. The wh-adjunction analysis in (43) would predict that inverted *have* can only contract down to /v/ when it has a wh-head ending in a vowel or diphthong adjoined to it for checking purposes. This means that contraction will be blocked where the wh-constituent is a full DP such as *which one of you?* (since phrases cannot adjoin to heads); and this is indeed the case, as we see from the ungrammaticality of (42b) above.

If the analysis suggested above is along the right lines, it follows that the case properties of subjects can be checked either via a spec–head relation or by a head–head (adjunction) relation. But are there also structures in which the case properties of subjects are checked by *attraction* (i.e. adjunction of a feature to a higher head)? There are three types of subject for which this is a plausible assumption. One is the null-case subject PRO. As we noted in §8.3 above, if we follow Baltin (1995, p. 244) in positing that PRO remains in spec-VP in sentences such as:

(44)   I want [$_{TP}$ to [$_{VP}$ PRO be free]]

(so that PRO does not block cliticization of *to* onto *want* in *I wanna be free*), we have to assume that PRO does not check its case by raising to spec-TP, but rather by *attraction* (i.e. by percolation of the relevant null case-feature from the PRO subject in spec-VP to the infinitive particle *to* which heads TP). A natural inference would be that the null case carried by PRO is associated with a *weak* case-feature (which is therefore checked by attraction), whereas (for example) *nominative* case is associated with a *strong* case-feature which has to be checked by movement of a nominative DP to spec-TP (or by adjunction of a nominative pronoun to an affixal T).

A second type of construction in which the case (and indeed agreement) properties of subjects would seem to be checked by attraction are existential structures with expletive *there* subjects. In this connection, consider contrasts such as:

(45) (a)   There are *students* waiting for you
     (b)   *Students* are waiting for you
(46) (a)   *The students* are waiting for you
     (b)   *There are *the students* waiting for you

Such examples would seem to suggest that when the subject of *waiting for you* is an indefinite nominal like *students*, the subject remains in spec-VP as the subject of *waiting*, and the expletive pronoun *there* is used to fill spec-TP; but when the subject is a definite nominal like *the students*, it cannot remain in spec-VP but rather must raise into spec-TP. How can we account for this *definiteness effect*?

One possibility (adapting ideas suggested by Belletti 1988 and Lasnik 1992, 1995) is that the indefinite nominal *students* carries a different case from the definite nominal *the students*. Let's assume that *the students* carries nominative case, and so must raise to spec-TP to check its strong nominative case-feature (hence the grammaticality of (46a) and the ungrammaticality of (46b)). But let's also assume that the indefinite nominal *students* in (45) carries *partitive* case (as indefinite nominals do in languages like Finnish which have a morphologically distinct partitive case), and that partitive case is a *weak* case which is checked by *attraction* (so that the relevant partitive case-feature percolates up from the indefinite nominal *students* in spec-VP to the auxiliary *are*). If the agreement-features of *students* also percolate up to T in the same way, we can then account for the fact that *are* in (45a) agrees with the **associate** of expletive *there* – i.e. with *students*. Moreover, if we assume (following Groat 1995) that expletive *there* is a defective pronoun which carries case-features but not (number/person/gender) agreement-features, we can say that *there* in (45a) carries nominative case and is inserted in spec-TP in order to satisfy the strong nominative-case specifier-feature carried by a finite T-node. Finally, if only a handful of verbs like *be* can check partitive case (as argued by Lasnik 1992 and Bošković 1995), we can account for the ungrammaticality of sentences such as:

(47) (a)   *There had [*students* waited for you]

    (b)   *There will [*students* wait for you]

    (c)   *There might [*students* wait for you]

Sentences like (47) would then be ungrammatical because *be* is the only auxiliary which can check partitive case. (An alternative account modelled on Chomsky 1995b is that the expletive associate *students* carries a weak *nominative* case-feature which is checked by attraction, and that *there* is inserted in spec-TP to satisfy the strong [D] specifier-feature of T – i.e. to satisfy the need for T to have a D(P) specifier; this in turn may be a consequence of the **predication principle** posited by Rothstein 1995, requiring syntactic predicates like V-bar and T-bar to have syntactic subjects.) Numerous questions of detail and potential problems arise, but we shall not attempt to delve into these here. (For a technical discussion of expletive structures, see Authier 1991, Lasnik 1992, 1995, Chomsky 1995b, Groat 1995, Rothstein 1995 and Vikner 1995.)

A third type of construction in which the case properties of subjects may be checked by attraction are ECM structures such as:

(48) (a)   They expect [him to cooperate]

    (b)   They are anxious for [him to cooperate]

Since we argued in §5.8 that the objective case carried by the subject (*him*) of the [bracketed] infinitive complement in such structures is checked by the immediately preceding transitive head (*expect/for*), it would seem reasonable to suppose that here too the case of the infinitive subject is checked by attraction (the objective case head-feature of *him* being attracted to the immediately preceding transitive head *expect/for*).

8.6   Raising predicates

Thus far, we have argued that subjects originate in a θ-marked specifier position within VP, and typically move into a case-marked specifier position within TP by application of **raising**. In this section, we turn to look at a further instance of **raising**. To get our discussion onto a concrete footing, consider the alternations illustrated below:

(49) (a)   It **seems** [that *he* understands her]

    (b)   *He* **seems** [to understand her]

(50) (a)   It would **appear** [that *they* are lying]

    (b)   *They* would **appear** [to be lying]

(51) (a)   It **happened** [that *she* came across an old love-letter]

    (b)   *She* **happened** [to come across an old love-letter]

(52) (a)   It **turned out** [that *Mary* was right]

    (b)   *Mary* **turned out** [to be right]

The bold-printed verbs in these examples have a *that*-clause complement in the (a) examples, and an infinitive complement in the (b) examples. But what is puzzling about sentences like (49–52) is that the italicized expression which functions as the subject of the bracketed complement clause in the (a) examples surfaces as the subject of the matrix clause (i.e. the clause containing the complement clause) in the (b) examples: for example, *he* is the subject of *understands* in (49a), but the subject of *seems* in (49b). Moreover, the bracketed infinitive complements in the (b) examples appear to have no subject.

So, sentences like (49–52) raise two related questions: how does the complement-clause subject in the (a) examples come to be the matrix-clause subject in the (b) examples, and how does the complement clause in the (b) examples end up seemingly subjectless? A unitary answer to both questions is to suppose that the italicized nominal originates as the subject of the complement clause and is then raised up to become the matrix-clause subject by application of **(subject-to-subject) raising**, leaving behind an empty category trace as the subject of the complement clause. In other words, *he* in a sentence like (49b) originates as the subject of *understands*, but is subsequently raised up to become the subject of *seems*. If this is so, an obvious question to ask is *how* the subject comes to be raised.

In this connection, consider the following set of sentences:

(53) (a)   The men do *all* seem to understand the situation
     (b)   ?The men do seem *all* to understand the situation
     (c)   ??The men do seem to *all* understand the situation

Given our claim in §8.3 that floating quantifiers modify the traces of moved subjects, the fact that the quantifier phrase headed by *all* in (53a–c) can serve as the subject of *understand the situation*, or *to understand the situation*, or *seem to understand the situation* suggests that the subject DP *the men* is raised in a successive cyclic fashion. In other words, in a sentence such as:

(54)   *The men* do seem to understand the situation

the italicized subject DP *the men* originates as the subject of *understand*, then becomes the subject of *to*, then becomes the subject of *seem*, and finally becomes the subject of *do*. In case that was too fast for you, let's look at a slow-motion replay of what's going on here.

The verb *understand* merges with its DP complement *the situation* to form the V-bar *understand the situation*; this in turn merges with the DP *the men* to form the VP (55) below:

(55)
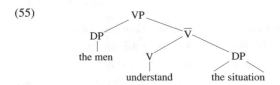

A movement

The VP (55) then merges with the infinitive particle *to* to form a T-bar; the DP *the men* is then raised to become the subject of this T-bar, as in (56) below:

(56)

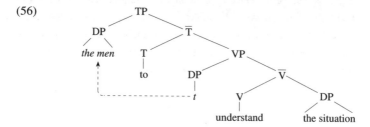

The resulting TP (56) in turn merges with the verb *seem* to form a V-bar; the DP *the men* raises to become the subject of this V-bar, as in (57) below:

(57)

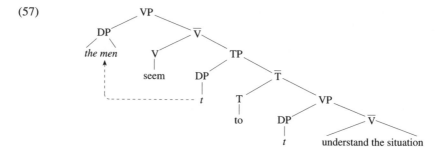

The VP thereby formed then merges with the auxiliary *do* to form a T-bar; the DP *the men* then raises to become the subject of this T-bar, as in (58) below:

(58)

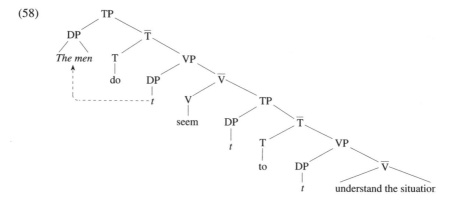

and (58) is the structure associated with (54) *The men do seem to understand the situation*. What (58) claims is that the DP *the men* originates as the subject of *understand the situation*, then raises in a successive cyclic fashion to become first the subject of *to understand the situation*, then the subject of *seem to understand the situation*, and

336

finally the subject of *do seem to understand the situation*. In each case, the movement operation which applies is **(subject-to-subject) raising**; assuming that each separate application of **raising** leaves behind a separate trace, there will be three (italicized) traces of the moved subject *the men* in (58) – one serving as the subject of *understand the situation*, another as the subject of *to understand the situation*, and the third as the subject of *seem to understand the situation*. If we further assume (as in §8.3) that floating quantifiers modify traces of moved subjects, we can account for sentences like those in (53) by supposing (in relation to (58) above) that *all* modifies the rightmost trace of *the men* in (53c) *The men do seem to **all** understand the situation*, the middle trace in (53b) *The men do seem **all** to understand the situation*, and the leftmost trace in (53a) *The men do **all** seem to understand the situation*. (What remains to be accounted for is why (53a) is better than (53b), and (53b) better than (53c). Perhaps floating quantifiers become more awkward the further away they are from the expression they quantify; perhaps they are only fully grammatical as the specifier of the complement of a finite T; and perhaps the awkwardness of (53c) is in part attributable to violation of the traditional prohibition against *split-infinitive* structures in which *to* is separated from its dependent verb. However, we shall not pursue these possibilities any further here.)

8.7 Differences between raising and control predicates

The conclusion which our discussion in the previous section leads us to is that **raising predicates** like *seem* take an infinitive complement with a trace subject (since the subject of *seem* serves as the subject of the infinitive complement prior to being raised up to become the subject of *seem*). In this respect, raising verbs like *seem* clearly have a very different syntax from **control predicates** like *try* which take an infinitive complement with a PRO subject, as in (59) below:

(59)   She will try [to PRO help him]

where PRO has a controller (= *she*) in the *will try* clause. An important question to ask, therefore, is how we can tell whether a given verb which selects an apparently subject-less infinitive complement is a raising predicate or a control predicate, and how we can explain the differences between the two classes of predicate.

One difference between the two is that raising verbs like *seem* allow a *dummy* subject like expletive *there*, whereas control verbs like *try* do not: cf.

(60) (a)   *There* **seemed/*tried** to be someone living there
     (b)   *There* **seemed/*tried** to be no milk left in the fridge
     (c)   *There* **seemed/*tried** to be little hope of finding them alive

The derivation of the *seem*-sentences in (60) seems straightforward: *there* originates as the subject of *be*, and is then raised in a successive cyclic fashion to become first the subject of *to*, then the subject of *seem* and finally the subject of the abstract T constituent preceding *seem*. More puzzling is the question of why a control verb like *try* doesn't allow expletive *there* as its subject – e.g. why we can't have a structure such as (61) below in which *there* is the controller of PRO:

(61)   **There* tried to PRO be a strike

One reason is that PRO is a referential pronoun which takes its reference from its controller; hence, the controller of PRO must be a referential expression. But since expletive *there* is a nonreferential pronoun (as we see from the fact that we can't question its reference – cf. **Where** *is someone living there?*), it cannot serve as the controller of PRO, and hence cannot serve as the subject of a control predicate like *try* which selects an infinitive complement with a PRO subject. From this, it follows that the subject of a control predicate like *try* must always be a referential expression.

A second reason why structures like (61) are ill formed relates to *thematic* considerations. It is a thematic property of the verb *try* that it assigns the θ-role AGENT to its subject: hence, it requires as its subject an expression denoting a rational being. Since *there* is a nonreferential dummy pronoun, the requirement for *try* to have an AGENT subject is clearly not met in sentences like (60–1) where *try* has expletive *there* as its subject. Conversely, the fact that *seem* allows expletive *there* as its subject in sentences like (60) suggests that it does not θ-mark its subject (e.g. it does not require an AGENT or EXPERIENCER subject), and hence allows a nonreferential subject like expletive *there*.

Our assumption that *try* θ-marks its subject whereas *seem* does not accounts for a further difference between the two. By virtue of requiring an AGENT subject, the verb *try* can only have as its subject an expression denoting an entity capable of rational thought, as we see from examples such as the following (where **?** and **!** indicate increasing degrees of anomaly):

(62) (a)   *John* tried to understand the problem
     (b)   ?*My goldfish* tried to escape
     (c)   ??*My pet amoeba* is trying to reproduce
     (d)   ?!*Your kettle* is trying to boil over
     (e)   !*Your theory* is trying to be foolproof

By contrast, the verb *seem* (by virtue of the fact that it doesn't θ-mark its subject) imposes no such restrictions on its choice of subject, as we can see by comparing (62) above with (63) below:

(63) (a)   *John* seemed to understand the problem
     (b)   *My goldfish* seems to have escaped
     (c)   *My pet amoeba* seems to be reproducing
     (d)   *Your kettle* seems to be boiling over
     (e)   *Your theory* seems to be foolproof

We noted in relation to the examples in (32) above that verbs which θ-mark their subjects impose restrictions on their choice of subject: hence, the fact that *try* constrains its choice of subject in (62) whereas *seem* imposes no restrictions on its choice of subject in (63) suggests that *try* θ-marks its subject whereas *seem* does not.

What our discussion here suggests is that the essential difference between control and raising predicates is that control predicates (like *try*) θ-mark their subjects, whereas raising predicates (like *seem*) do not. This core thematic difference between the two can be argued to determine why *seem* can function as a raising predicate but not as a control predicate, and conversely why *try* can function as a control predicate but not as a raising predicate. A crucial premise of the argumentation is that the way in which θ-roles are assigned is constrained by the following UG principle (called the θ-**criterion** because it is a criterion which an LF representation must meet in order to be well formed):

(64)   θ-CRITERION

Each argument bears one and only one θ-role, and each θ-role is assigned to one and only one argument. (Chomsky 1981, p. 36)

We can illustrate how this constraint works in terms of contrasts such as the following:

(65) (a)   Percy Peabrain admires himself
     (b)   *Percy Peabrain admires

In (65a), *Percy Peabrain* is the EXPERIENCER argument of *admire* and *himself* the THEME argument; thus, each separate θ-role is associated with a separate argument expression (and conversely), so the θ-**criterion** is satisfied. But what goes wrong in (65b)? One possibility is that *Percy Peabrain* is assigned the role of EXPERIENCER argument of *admire*, but that the THEME role associated with *admire* is unassigned: however, this would violate the θ-**criterion** requirement that each θ-role associated with a predicate must be assigned to some argument. An alternative possibility is that both the EXPERIENCER and THEME roles of *admire* are assigned to *Percy Peabrain*, thereby wrongly predicting that (65b) can have the same interpretation as (65a): however, this is ruled out by the θ-**criterion** requirement that each argument can carry only a single θ-role.

Consider now the role of the θ-**criterion** in determining that verbs (like *try*) which θ-mark their subjects can serve as control (but not raising) predicates, whereas conversely verbs (like *seem*) which don't θ-mark their subjects can serve as raising (but not control) predicates. More concretely, consider how we derive sentence pairs such as the following:

(66) (a)   He does seem to enjoy syntax
     (b)   He does try to enjoy syntax

If *seem* is a raising predicate, *he* will originate as the subject of *enjoy syntax* in (66a) and be assigned an appropriate θ-role (that of EXPERIENCER argument of *enjoy*).

339

Subsequently, *he* will be raised up (in successive cyclic fashion) to become first the subject of *to enjoy syntax*, then the subject of *seem to enjoy syntax* and finally the subject of *does seem to enjoy syntax* – as represented in simplified form in (67) below:

(67)   [$_{TP}$ *He* does [$_{VP}$ *t* seem [$_{TP}$ *t* to [$_{VP}$ *t* enjoy syntax]]]]

Given the assumption that auxiliaries, infinitival *to* and raising predicates like *seem* do not θ-mark their subjects, the only θ-role assigned to the pronoun *he* will be that of EXPERIENCER argument of *enjoy* (thereby satisfying the **θ-criterion** requirement that 'Each argument bears one and only one θ-role'). We might assume that *he* has to raise to become the subject of *does* for reasons of **greed** (i.e. to check its nominative case), and that it has to raise in a successive cyclic fashion in order to satisfy the **shortest movement principle**. But now consider what would happen if we tried to use *seem* as a control predicate. The pronoun *he* would originate as the subject of *seem* (raising to become subject of *does*), and would serve as the controller of the *PRO* subject of *enjoy syntax*, as in (68) below:

(68)   [$_{IP}$ *He* does [$_{VP}$ *t* seem [$_{IP}$ to [$_{VP}$ *PRO* enjoy syntax]]]]

The complement-clause subject PRO would be assigned the θ-role of EXPERIENCER argument of *enjoy syntax*. However, the pronoun *he* would be assigned no θ-role at all, since it originates as the subject of the raising verb *seem* and then raises to become the subject of *does* (and neither raising verbs nor auxiliaries θ-mark their subjects). Thus, a derivation such as (68) would violate the **θ-criterion** requirement that 'Each argument bears one and only one θ-role', and hence crash at LF.

Consider now the syntax of (66b) *He does try to enjoy syntax*. If we suppose that *try* is a *control* predicate, the pronoun *he* will originate as the subject of *try* (subsequently raising to become subject of *does*) and will control the *PRO* subject of *enjoy syntax*, as in (69) below:

(69)   [$_{TP}$ *He* does [$_{VP}$ *t* try [$_{TP}$ to [$_{VP}$ *PRO* enjoy syntax]]]]

The null pronoun PRO will be assigned the θ-role of EXPERIENCER argument of *enjoy*, and the nominative pronoun *he* will be assigned the θ-role of AGENT argument of *try* (by virtue of originating as the subject of *try*). Since PRO and *he* are each assigned a θ-role of their own, the **θ-criterion** is satisfied.

However, the picture is very different if we use *try* as a raising predicate, with *he* originating as the subject of *enjoy syntax* and then being raised up successive-cyclically to become subject of *to enjoy syntax*, *try to enjoy syntax* and *does try to enjoy syntax*, as in (70) below:

(70)   [TP *He* does [VP *t* try [TP *t* to [VP *t* enjoy syntax]]]]

The problem here is that *he* ends up with two different θ-roles, viz. as EXPERIENCER argument of *enjoy* (at the stage of derivation where it is subject of *enjoy syntax*) and AGENT argument of *try* (at the point where it becomes subject of *try to enjoy syntax*). This leads to obvious violation of the θ-**criterion** requirement that 'Each argument bears one and only one θ-role.'

8.8 Passivization

Having looked briefly at the syntax of *raising* predicates (and how they differ from *control* predicates), we now turn to look at the syntax of **passive predicates**. Traditional grammarians maintain that the bold-printed verbs in sentences such as the (a) examples below are in the **active voice**, whereas the italicized verbs in the corresponding (b) sentences are in the **passive voice**:

(71) (a)   Hundreds of passers-by **saw** the attack
     (b)   The attack was *seen* by hundreds of passers-by
(72) (a)   Lex Luthor **stole** the kryptonite
     (b)   The kryptonite was *stolen* by Lex Luthor
(73) (a)   They **took** everything
     (b)   Everything was *taken*

There are four main properties which differentiate passive sentences from their active counterparts – as the examples in (71–3) illustrate. One is that passive (though not active) sentences generally require the auxiliary *be*. Another is that the lexical verb in passive sentences is in the *n*-participle form (cf. *seen/stolen/taken*), known in this use as the *passive participle* form. A third is that passive sentences may (though need not) contain a *by*-phrase in which the complement of *by* seems to play essentially the same thematic role as the subject in the corresponding active sentence: for example, *hundreds of passers-by* in the active structure (71a) serves as the subject of *saw the attack*, whereas in the passive structure (71b) it serves as the complement of the preposition *by* (though in both cases seems to have the role of EXPERIENCER). The fourth difference is that the expression which serves as the *complement* of an active verb surfaces as the *subject* in the corresponding passive construction: for example, *the attack* is the complement of *saw* in the active structure (71a), but is the subject of *was seen by hundreds of passers-*

by in the passive structure (71b). Here, we focus on the syntax of the subjects of passive sentences (setting aside the derivation of *by*-phrases).

Evidence that passive subjects do indeed play the same thematic role as active complements comes from the fact that the two are subject to the same restrictions on the choice of expression which can fulfil the relevant argument function, as we see from sentences such as the following (where **?**, **?!** and **!** mark increasing degrees of pragmatic anomaly):

(74) (a)   *The students/?The camels/?!The flowers/!The ideas* were arrested

    (b)   They arrested *the students/?the camels/?!the flowers/!the ideas*

How can we account for this fact? If we assume that principles of UG correlate thematic structure with syntactic structure in a *uniform* fashion, then it follows that two arguments which fulfil the same thematic function with respect to a given type of predicate must occupy the same underlying position in the syntax. The assumption that there is a uniform mapping between thematic structure and syntactic structure is embodied in the **uniform theta assignment hypothesis/UTAH** argued for at length in Baker 1988. If we adopt UTAH, it follows that passive subjects must originate in the same position as active complements. Since the passive subject *the students* in (74a) *The students were arrested* bears that THEME/PATIENT role which is normally assigned to the complement of *arrest* (so that the students are the ones taken away for questioning), a natural suggestion to make is that *the students* originates as the complement of the verb *arrested*. But if this is so, how does *the students* come to be subject of the auxiliary *were*?

The answer we shall suggest here is that the DP *the students* is raised in a successive cyclic fashion to become first the subject of the passive participle *arrested* and then the subject of the auxiliary *were* – as in (75) below:

(75)

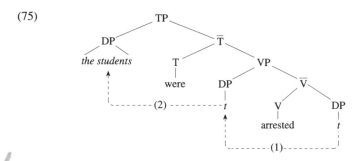

Thus, *the students* originates as the complement of *arrested*, then undergoes **passivization** (i.e. movement from being complement of the passive participle *arrested* to becoming its subject), and finally undergoes **raising** (i.e. movement from being subject of *arrested* to becoming subject of *were*).

342

Some evidence in support of the assumption that *the students* becomes the subject of the passive participle *arrested* before becoming subject of the auxiliary *were* comes from facts relating to floating quantifiers in sentences such as:

(76) The students were *all* arrested

If we assume (as in §8.3 above) that a floating quantifier modifies the trace of a moved subject, we can say that the quantifier *all* in (76) modifies the trace in spec-VP of the moved DP *the students* in (75).

Additional evidence in support of the claim that passivized arguments first become the subject of the passive participle before moving on to become the subject of the passive auxiliary comes from expletive structures such as:

(77) There were *several students* arrested

The quantifier phrase *several students* in (77) originates as the complement of the verb *arrested*. But where does it end up? Since it is positioned immediately in front of the passive participle *arrested*, it seems likely that it moves into (and remains in) spec-VP, and hence serves as the subject of *arrested*; this would mean that (77) has the (simplified) derivation (78) below:

(78)

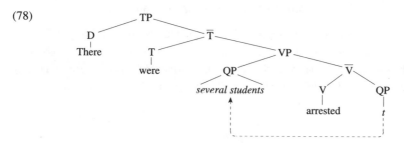

We might suppose that the person/number-features of *several students* are attracted to *were*, so that *were* agrees with *several students*.

Thus far, the simple instances of passivization which we have looked at have involved movement from complement to subject position. However, in passive structures such as (79) below:

(79) (a) *He* is thought [to admire her]
  (b) *Several prisoners* are believed [to have escaped]
  (c) *They* were alleged [to have lied under oath]
  (d) *He* is rumoured [to be writing a new syntax book]
  (e) *Rock around the Clock* is considered [to be a classic]

passivization seems to have the effect of raising the italicized expression out of subject position in the bracketed complement clause into subject position within the main clause. In other words, passivization in structures such as (79) appears to involve movement from one subject position to another. What lends empirical support to the claim that structures like (79) involve passivization of the subject of an infinitive complement is the fact that subject expressions which are part of VP idioms can be passivized in such structures – as we see from the grammaticality of examples such as (80) below:

(80) (a)　*The jig* is thought to *be up*

　　　(b)　*All hell* is believed to have *broken loose*

　　　(c)　*The chips* were said to *be down*

　　　(d)　*The fur* was alleged to be *flying*

Let's try and work out what's going on here, by looking at how (79a) *He is thought to admire her* is derived.

　　The passivized pronoun *he* originates as the subject of *admire her*. Some empirical evidence in support of this claim comes from the fact that the restrictions imposed on the choice of subject in (79a) above mirror those found in a simple sentence such as *He admires her*, as we see from (81) below:

(81) (a)　*He/?His goldfish/?!His piano/!His theory* is thought to admire her

　　　(b)　*He/?His goldfish/?!His piano/!His theory* admires her

Thus, it seems reasonable to suppose that the pronoun *he* in (79a) originates as the subject of *admire her* and is then raised up (in a successive cyclic fashion) to become first the subject of *to admire her* then the subject of *thought to admire her*, and finally the subject of *is thought to admire her*. This being so, (79a) will be derived in the manner indicated in (82) below:

(82)

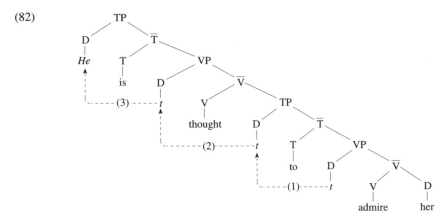

Step (1) in the derivation involves raising *he* to become the subject of the TP headed by infinitival *to*; step (2) involves passivizing *he*, i.e. moving it into a position where it becomes the subject of the VP headed by the passive participle *thought*; step (3) involves raising *he* to become the subject of the TP headed by the auxiliary *is*.

Although in describing the travels of the subject in (82), we used the terms **raising** and **passivization** as if they denoted different processes, closer reflection suggests that there is no meaningful distinction between the two. In relation to our earlier discussion of structures such as (75) above, we implicitly thought of raising as movement from one subject position to another and passivization as movement from complement to subject position. But the fact that passivization in structures such as (82) involves subject-to-subject movement undermines this distinction. In reality, passivization and raising are different manifestations of a single argument-movement operation (conventionally termed **A movement**) which has the effect of moving a constituent from one argument position into another (more specifically, from a subject or complement position into a subject position). Extending this terminology in a conventional way, we might say that operations which move maximal projections into a nonsubject position are instances of $\overline{\text{A}}$ **movement** (where the bar here is a negation operator, so that A-bar movement is movement to a nonargument position): so, for example, **operator movement** is one type of A-bar movement operation, since it moves wh-operators into spec-CP (and spec-CP is a nonargument position by virtue of the fact that nonarguments like *whether* or *why* can occupy spec-CP).

8.9 Explanation

Since the ultimate goal of any theory is to *explain* the phenomena which fall within its domain, an important question for us to ask is *why* arguments should undergo A movement in the way that they do (e.g. why *he* should move from being the subject of *admire* to becoming the subject of *is* in (82) above). The most principled answer which we can give to this question is that the syntax of A movement is entirely determined by principles of UG. Let's look at some of the principles which are involved.

Consider first the question of why A movement should involve movement from a *lower* to a *higher* position in structures such as (56–8), (75), (78) and (82). This follows from principles of **trace theory** (cf. §6.3) which require that a moved constituent leave behind a trace which must be bound by its antecedent, and from the **c-command condition on binding** (cf. §3.9) which requires a bound constituent to be c-commanded by its binder (i.e. its antecedent). This latter condition is satisfied e.g. in (82) by virtue of the fact that the trace subject of *admire* is c-commanded and bound by the trace subject of *to*, which in turn is c-commanded/bound by the trace subject of *thought*, which in turn is c-commanded/bound by the *he* subject of *is*.

Now let's look at the question of why A movement should involve movement to a higher *specifier* position, never to a higher complement position (e.g. the DP *the students* in (75) moves first to become subject and specifier of *arrested* and then to become subject/specifier of *were*). The answer is that within the theory assumed here, a complement position can only be created by **merger** with a head (not by **movement**), whereas a specifier position can be created either by **merger** or by **movement**.

A third aspect of the syntax of A movement which we need to explain is why it should apply in a successive cyclic fashion: e.g. why should *he* in (82) first become subject of *to admire her* and then subject of *thought to admire her* before finally becoming subject of *is thought to admire her*? Again, the answer comes from principles of UG: for example, the **shortest movement principle** requires that each application of A movement should move the relevant constituent into the *next highest subject position* in its containing structure. Alternatively, it may be that Rothstein's (1995) **predication principle** (requiring syntactic predicates to have a subject) will ensure successive cyclicity, if we assume that V-bar and T-bar are syntactic predicates (and hence require a subject at some stage of derivation).

A further principle which constrains the operation of A movement is the **θ-criterion** (64). This plays an important role not only in the syntax of raising (as we saw earlier), but also in the syntax of passivization. In this connection, consider how we account for why the complement of a passive verb can be passivized, but not the complement of an active verb – e.g. why *the jewels* can become the subject of the passive sentence (83a) below, but not the subject of its active counterpart (83b):

(83) (a)　　*The jewels* were stolen

　　　(b)　　**The jewels* stole (intended as synonymous with 83a)

The derivation of (83b) on its intended interpretation would be as follows. The DP *the jewels* originates as the complement of the verb *stole*, and is then raised in successive cyclic fashion to become first the subject of *stole* and then the subject of the abstract T constituent heading TP, as in (84) below:

(84)

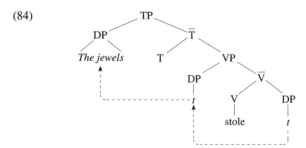

Why is the resulting sentence (83b) ungrammatical on the intended interpretation on which it is synonymous with (83a)? The answer should be obvious enough. The verb *steal* is a two-place predicate which (in active uses) requires an AGENT subject and a THEME complement. By virtue of originating as the complement of *stole*, the DP *the jewels* is assigned the θ-role of THEME argument of *stole*; but by virtue of moving into spec-VP and becoming the subject of *stole*, *the jewels* is also assigned the θ-role of AGENT argument of *stole*. However, since the θ-criterion specifies that no argument can carry more than one θ-role, the resulting derivation is correctly ruled out as ungrammatical. In other words, the θ-criterion correctly predicts that active verbs don't allow passivization.

But now consider the derivation of the corresponding passive sentence (83a) *The jewels were stolen*. If we assume that the DP *the jewels* originates as the THEME complement of *stolen* and is then raised up successive-cyclically to become first the subject of the passive participle *stolen* and then the subject of the auxiliary *were*, (83a) will have the derivation (85) below:

(85)

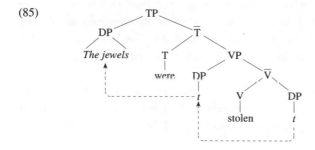

At first sight, it might seem as if the derivation (85) violates the θ-**criterion**, by virtue of the fact that the DP *the jewels* goes from being THEME complement of *stolen* to becoming AGENT subject of *stolen* (before eventually becoming subject of *were*). However, let us suppose (following Chomsky 1981, pp. 124–7) that passive participles θ-mark their complements but not their subjects: to use a traditional metaphor, we might say that the passive participle suffix +*n* **absorbs** the subject θ-role, thereby **dethematizing** the passive subject position (i.e. removing the ability of the passive participle to θ-mark its subject). If passive participles don't θ-mark their subjects, it follows that the θ-criterion will not prevent the DP *the jewels* from moving through spec-VP into spec-TP as in (85) above: the only θ-role which *the jewels* receives is that of THEME argument of *stolen*. (For a more detailed discussion of the thematic properties of passive verbs, see Roberts 1986, and Baker, Johnson and Roberts 1989.)

Thus, we see that passivization is made possible by the fact that passive participles do not θ-mark their subjects. However, an important question for us to ask is why it isn't just possible but rather *necessary* for a passivized argument to move. One answer is provided by the principle of **greed** – i.e. by the need for constituents to selfishly satisfy their own morphological requirements. We might suppose that (pro)nominal arguments have intrinsic case properties (e.g. *he* is nominative and *him* objective) which have to be *checked* in the course of a derivation (and this will only be possible if e.g. a nominative pronoun occupies a nominative position at some stage in the course of a derivation). Let us make the traditional assumption that passive participles are inherently *intransitive*: if this is so, then we can provide a straightforward account of why transitive verbs allow objective complements when used actively, but not passively – cf. contrasts such as:

(86) (a)   They saw *him*
     (b)   *It was seen *him*

The objective case carried by *him* can be checked when *him* is used as the complement of the active verb *saw* (since this is transitive), but not when used as the complement of the passive participle *seen* (since passive participles are intransitive). To use our earlier **absorption** metaphor, we might say that the passive participle +*n* inflection on *seen* absorbs the ability of a transitive verb like *see* to check objective case, and thereby **detransitivizes** the verb. Since the case-features carried by *him* cannot be checked in (86b), the resulting derivation crashes, so that such *impersonal passive* structures are ungrammatical in English.

But now suppose that in place of the objective pronoun *him*, we use the nominative pronoun *he*. We cannot use *he* as the complement of a passive participle like *seen*, as we see from the fact that impersonal passives such as (87) below are ungrammatical:

(87)   *It was seen *he*

The reason why (87) is ungrammatical is that a nominative pronoun cannot check its case if used as the complement of a passive participle like *seen*. But now suppose that *he* undergoes passivization, becoming first the subject of *seen* and then the subject of *was* – as in (88) below:

(88)

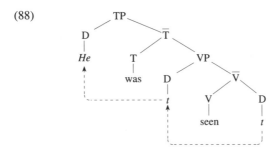

Since (as a result of two applications of **A movement**) *he* comes to occupy a nominative position (as the subject and specifier of the finite auxiliary *was*) in (88), its nominative case can be checked. The resulting sentence is therefore fully grammatical.

On this account, **greed** triggers passivization (i.e. the requirement for *he* to move into a position where it can check its nominative case-feature). One consequence of the greed analysis is that a constituent will move no further than it needs to in order to satisfy its morphological requirements. In this connection, consider how we account for contrasts such as the following:

(89) (a)   *He* is said [to have lied to Parliament]

     (b)   **He* is said [has lied to Parliament]

How come we can passivize the subject of an infinitive clause like that bracketed in (89a), but not the subject of a finite clause like that bracketed in (89b)? **Greed** provides us with the answer. If the subject *he* does not passivize but remains *in situ* within the bracketed clause, the result will be:

(90) (a)   *It is said [*he* to have lied to Parliament]

     (b)   It is said [*he* has lied to Parliament]

The pronoun *he* cannot remain *in situ* in (90a), since if it does it will be unable to check its nominative case-feature; hence, morphological (case-checking) requirements force it to passivize, and move into the nominative position it occupies in (89a). But the converse is the case in (90b): here *he* already occupies a nominative position (as subject of the finite auxiliary *has*), so that its nominative case-feature can be checked (and erased) *in situ*; hence, *he* in (90b) need not (and therefore, by the **economy principle**, *cannot*) move into another nominative position, so accounting for the ungrammaticality of passivization in (89b).

8.10   Summary

In this chapter, we have been concerned with the syntax of subjects. In §8.2 we looked at the syntax of expletive sentences such as *There is someone waiting for you*, and argued that the expletive pronoun *there* serves as the specifier of the TP headed by *is*, and that *someone* is the specifier of the VP headed by *waiting*. We then went on to compare this kind of structure with its nonexpletive counterpart *Someone is waiting for you*, suggesting that we could achieve a unitary account of both types of structure if we posited that *someone* originates in spec-VP in both cases, and remains *in situ* in the expletive structure (where spec-TP is filled by *there*), but raises to spec-TP in the corresponding nonexpletive structure. We noted that the assumption that subjects originate internally within VP is known as the **VP-internal subject hypothesis**. In §8.3 we presented a range of empirical evidence in support of the hypothesis, from data relating (for example) to the syntax of PRO, reflexives, floating quantifiers and idioms. In §8.4 we argued that the VP-internal subject hypothesis enables us to develop a principled theory of θ-**marking**, in which arguments are assigned a θ-role by *merger* with a lexical category: hence, the complement of a verb is θ-marked directly by the verb, and its subject is θ-marked by V-bar. We suggested that nominative subjects raise to spec-TP in order to check their (strong) case-feature. In §8.5 we argued that nominative pronouns can check their case by adjoining to a T constituent which contains an affixal (i.e. contracted) auxiliary, e.g. in sentences like *We'll help you out*. We suggested that the null case carried by PRO is checked by *attraction* to a nonfinite T constituent (containing e.g. infinitival *to*), and that the (partitive?) case of expletive associates (like *someone* in *There is someone waiting for you*) may be checked by attraction to the verb *be*. We also suggested that the objective case carried by the subject of an ECM infinitive complement may be checked by attraction to a matrix transitive head (e.g. the objective case-feature carried by *him* in *They expect him to win* is attracted to *expect*). In §8.6 we went on to argue that a handful of nonauxiliary verbs (like *seem*) resemble auxiliaries in that they do not θ-mark their subjects; in consequence, such verbs (traditionally known as **raising predicates**) allow the subject of an embedded complement to be raised up to become the subject of the raising verb. In §8.7 we contrasted **raising** predicates with **control** predicates, noting that *control* predicates θ-mark their subjects and take a complement clause with a PRO subject which is θ-marked by the predicate in the complement. We looked at syntactic differences between the two types of predicate, noting (for example) that raising predicates like *seem* allow an expletive *there* subject whereas control predicates like *try* don't. In §8.8 we examined the syntax of passivized arguments, claiming that (in simple cases) they originate as complements of passive participles and are raised up (in a successive cyclic fashion) to become first the subject of the passive participle, and then the subject of the passive auxiliary *be*. We argued that passive participles have two distinctive characteristics which differentiate them from the corresponding active verb forms – namely that they do not θ-mark their subject, and do not check the case of their complements. We noted that in infinitival passives such as *He is thought to admire her*, the passive subject *he* originates as the subject of the verb *admire* in the infinitive complement, and is raised up (by successive movement operations) to become first subject of *to*, then subject of *thought* and finally subject of *is*. We argued that raising and passivization are two different manifestations of a single **A movement** operation whereby an argument moves from a subject or complement position into a higher subject position. In §8.9 we argued that the operation of **A movement** is constrained by a number of UG principles, including the **c-command condition on binding**, the **shortest movement principle**, the θ-**criterion** and the **principle of greed**.

Workbook section

Exercise I (§§8.2–8.4)

Discuss the derivation of the following sentences, paying particular attention to the syntax of subjects:

1 They must have followed her
2 She has become an actress
3 The cat has got his tongue
4 They are living together
5 He loves you
6 There are people dying of hunger
7 Was there anyone helping you?
8 Could he have been blackmailing her?
9 What could they have done?
10 They want to fire the chairman

Model answer for 1

Given the assumptions made in the text, 1 will be derived as follows. The
verb *followed* is merged with the pronominal determiner *her* and assigns the θ-role
THEME to its complement; *followed* (by virtue of being a transitive verb) also checks the
objective case of *her*. The resulting V-bar *followed her* merges with (and thereby
assigns the θ-role AGENT to) its subject *they*, so forming the VP (i) below (simplified
inter alia by not showing case-features or θ-roles):

(i)

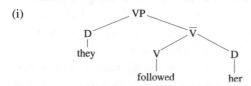

The resulting VP is merged with the perfective auxiliary *have*; the pronoun *they* raises
from being subject of *followed* in (i) above to becoming subject of *have* in (ii) below:

(ii)

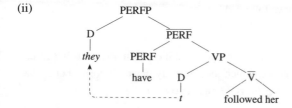

Finally, the PERFP in (ii) is merged with a T constituent which is itself formed by merging the modal *must* with a present-tense affix, and the subject *they* raises up to spec-TP to check its nominative case, as in (iii) below:

(iii)

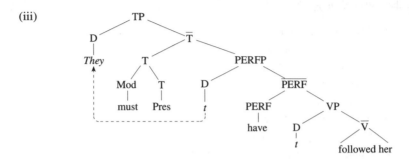

Everything about the syntax of the subject *they* follows from UG principles. *They* must originate in spec-VP in order to receive its AGENT θ-role (from the V-bar *followed her*) and thereby satisfy the θ-**criterion** (which requires that every argument be assigned a θ-role). It moves to spec-TP for reasons of **greed**, in order to check its strong nominative case-feature. The requirement for *they* to move in a successive cyclic fashion (becoming subject of *have* before becoming the subject of *must*) is imposed by the **shortest movement principle**, which requires that an argument which undergoes **raising** should move into the nearest subject position above it. Alternatively, we might suppose that *they* has to become the specifier of *have* (before becoming the specifier of *must*) because verbs and auxiliaries require a subject: this might either be for checking purposes (e.g. verbs and auxiliaries have some strong specifier feature which they need to check), or to satisfy some constraint such as Rothstein's (1995) **predication princi-ple** (which requires that syntactic predicates should have subjects).

Given the assumption that floating quantifiers can modify traces of moved con-stituents, an obvious prediction made by the successive cyclic analysis is that each of the two traces of *they* in (iii) can be modified by a floating quantifier like *all/both*. In the event, this prediction is correct: cf.

(iv) (a)   They must both have followed her
     (b)   ?They must have both followed her

For reasons which are not entirely clear, floating quantifiers seem to give better results the nearer they are to the expression which they quantify: hence (iv)(a) is better than (iv)(b) because *both* is closer to *they* in (iv)(a) than in (iv)(b).

Exercise II (§8.3)

Discuss the syntax of the quantifiers *both/all* in the following sentences:

1a Both the men were cheating at cards
 b The men were both cheating at cards
2a They were both cheating at cards
 b *Both they were cheating at cards
3a They had all been cheating at cards
 b ?*They had been all cheating at cards
4a He has eaten all of them
 b He has eaten all of the chocolates
5a *He has eaten all them
 b He has eaten all the chocolates
6a He has eaten them all
 b *He has eaten the chocolates all

Helpful hints

Make the following set of assumptions. Quantifiers like *all* or *both* have a variety of uses. They can function as the specifier of a DP headed by a determiner like *the*; but they cannot function as the specifier of a personal pronoun like *them* because personal pronouns are normally unprojectable and so allow neither specifier nor complement. Quantifiers like *all/both* can also function as heads taking a complement, but in this use are intransitive and so cannot directly assign case to their complement: this means that the complement must either be introduced by a *dummy* transitive preposition like *of*, or must move to a case position. Consider the possibility that in 6a the phrase *them all* is a QP headed by *all*, and that the pronoun *them* originates as the complement of *all*, and then adjoins to the left of the quantifier. Why might it be that the pronoun moves in this way – and why can't a DP like *the chocolates* move in much the same way?

Model answer for 1

In the light of the suggestions made above, we might assume that in 1a *both the men* is a DP in which *both* is the specifier of the D-bar *the men*, as in (i) below:

(i)

353

Given the VP-internal subject hypothesis, the DP *both the men* will originate in spec-VP as the subject of *cheating*, and will then raise into spec-TP to become the subject of *were*, as in (ii) below (to simplify exposition, we ignore the past-tense affix merged with *were*):

(ii)

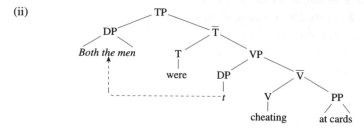

The DP *both the men* originates in spec-VP, where it receives its AGENT θ-role by merger with the V-bar *cheating at cards*: it raises to spec-TP for reasons of **greed**, to check the strong nominative case-features which it carries.

At first sight, it might seem plausible to derive 1b in essentially the same way, and to argue that *both the men* has the structure (i) and originates in spec-VP, with *the men* being preposed on its own, leaving the quantifier *both* stranded in spec-VP, as in (iii) below:

(iii)

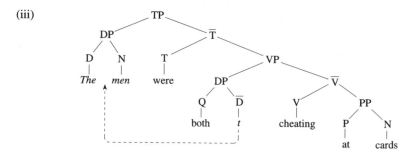

However, any movement such as that arrowed in (iii) would violate the **chain uniformity principle**, since the constituent at the head of the chain would be a maximal projection (viz. the DP *the men*), whereas the trace at the foot of the chain would be nonmaximal (since it is a D-bar which is nonmaximal because it projects into a larger DP containing *both*).

An alternative possibility is to suppose that in 1b, the phrase *both the men* which originates as the subject of *cheating* has the structure (iv) below:

(iv)

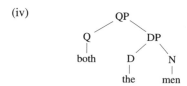

If we assume that *both* is intransitive, it follows that the DP *the men* occupies a caseless position in (iv), and so must move to a case position in order to check its case. It therefore moves into spec-TP (which is a nominative position), as in (v) below:

(v)

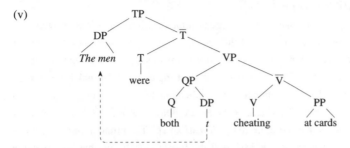

In this position, the DP can check its case and agreement properties against the specifier properties of *were* (which requires a plural or second person nominative subject). The resulting chain *the men . . . t* is uniform, since both the DP *the men* at the head of the chain and its trace *t* at the foot are maximal (DP) projections. Movement of the DP *the men* is motivated by **greed** – i.e. the need to move *the men* into a case position (= a position where it can check its nominative case). An interesting problem not discussed here relates to the question of what case (if any) the floating quantifier *both* carries in (v), and how it is checked.

Exercise III (§§8.2–8.4)

Discuss the derivation of the following Early Modern English (EME) sentences (taken from various plays by Shakespeare), highlighting points of particular interest.

1. Thee will I love (Antipholus, *Comedy of Errors*, III.iv)
2. These foils have all a length? (= 'These foils are all the same length?', Hamlet, *Hamlet*, V.ii)
3. They'll none have her (= 'None of them will have her', Lafeu, *All's Well That Ends Well*, II.iii)
4. Answer made it none (= 'It gave no answer', Horatio, *Hamlet*, I.ii)
5. He loves not you (Lysander, *Midsummer Night's Dream*, III.ii)
6. Knows he not thy voice? (First Lord, *All's Well That Ends Well*, IV.i)
7. What hast thou done? (Oberon, *Midsummer Night's Dream*, II.ii)
8. Whom overcame he? (Boyet, *Love's Labour's Lost*, IV.i)
9. Who knows not that? (Curtis, *Taming of the Shrew*, IV.i)
10. Fear you not him! (Tranio, *Taming of the Shrew*, IV.iv)

Helpful hints
See those for exercise V, chapter 7.

Model answer for 1

The pronoun *thee* in 1 undergoes *topicalization* – i.e. it is moved to a more prominent position at the front of the sentence in order to mark it as the topic of the sentence. One way of handling this phenomenon is to suppose that topic clauses in EME are CPs headed by a C containing an abstract topic affix **Top** which has strong head-features and a **[Top]** specifier-feature (indicating that it requires a topicalized constituent as its specifier). The strong (affixal) head-feature of *Top* is satisfied by moving the auxiliary *will* from T to adjoin to the *Top* affix in C. The pronoun *thee* originates in VP-complement position, and is assigned the θ-role THEME (and has its objective case checked) when merged with the verb *love*: since it is the topic of the sentence, we might assume that it also carries a [Top] head-feature; movement of *thee* to spec-CP will check (and erase) the [Top] specifier-feature of C. If we also assume (as in the text) that subjects originate in spec-VP and raise to spec-TP, 1 will have the (simplified) derivation (i) below:

(i)

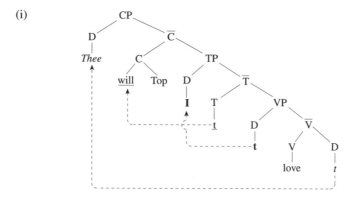

The subject *I* originates in spec-VP, where it is assigned the θ-role EXPERIENCER by merger with the V-bar *love thee* (thereby satisfying the **θ-criterion**), and from there raises to spec-TP in order to check its strong nominative case-feature. All three movements satisfy the **shortest movement principle**: thus, the auxiliary *will* moves into the next-highest head position in moving from T to C; the subject *I* moves out of spec-VP into the next-highest subject position, viz spec-TP; and the topic *thee* moves into the next-highest A-bar (i.e. nonsubject) specifier position, viz. spec-CP.

Exercise IV (§§8.2–8.4)

Discuss the syntax of the following child sentences produced by a young girl called Iris at around three years of age, concentrating particularly on the morphosyntax of subjects. (The adult counterpart of the relevant utterances is given in parentheses, where this is different from the child's utterance.)

  1   I might see Pauline
  2   I saw a rabbit
  3   We are going to the shops
  4   We want him
  5   Me want see outside (= 'I want to see outside')
  6   No me got him (= 'I don't have him')
  7   No Fraser play with me (= 'Fraser doesn't play with me')
  8   Want go in the car (= 'I want to go in the car')
  9   Want to go to bed? (= 'Do you want to go to bed?')
10   Where candle go? (= 'Where does the candle go?')

Model answer for 5

It has been claimed in the relevant acquisition literature (cf. Radford 1990 and Vainikka 1994) that objective subjects produced by young children are in spec-VP, whereas nominative subjects are in spec-TP. If this is so, then the objective subject *me* in 5 will occupy the specifier position within the VP headed by *want*. If we assume that child clauses (like their adult counterparts) are TPs, 5 will have a structure along the lines of (i) below (where ø is a null infinitive particle):

(i)

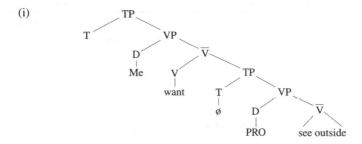

The analysis in (i) assumes *continuity* between the structure of clauses in adult and child grammars, since both are assumed to have the status of TPs. We might suppose that the null case carried by PRO is checked by attraction to the null infinitive particle ø. But how is the case of *me* checked? One possibility is that it is checked by attraction to T (which may carry no tense in this use and so be nonfinite). Another is that the case of *me* is not checked at all, and that objective case is the **default** case form in English (i.e. the one case which does not need to be checked). A *default* analysis of objective case might account for why in (adult) dialogues such as:

(ii)   SPEAKER A: Who failed syntax?
             SPEAKER B: *Me*

speaker B's utterance (in spite of being interpreted as an elliptical form of *I failed syntax*) carries objective case in a position where it is the only word in the sentence, so there is no other item to check its case. Default case would be carried by a (pro)nominal argument which occupies a position where it is unable to check any other case.

A radically minimalist analysis of child sentences like 5 (proposed in Radford 1990) would be to suppose that since they contain no evidence of tense-marking or infinitival *to*, the relevant clauses are simply VPs, so that 5 has the structure (iii) below:

(iii)

We might then suppose that case in children's earliest clause structures is checked (or assigned) by merger, and that a subject which merges with a nonfinite (tenseless) V-bar is thereby assigned either objective or null case. (Of course, we could alternatively claim that the subject *me* in (iii) is assigned objective case by default.)

Helpful hints

Since it is clear that sentences like 1 (by virtue of containing the finite auxiliary *might*) are TPs, the overall issue which arises in relation to the sentences in this exercise is whether (at the relevant stage of development) all Iris's clauses are TPs, or whether some are TPs and others are VPs – or whether we simply can't tell. Assume in relation to 6 and 7 that *no* is a negative particle occupying the head NEG position of a NEGP which has a VP complement.

Exercise V (§8.5)

Discuss the syntax of the following sentences. (The judgments given below in relation to the apostrophized auxiliaries relate to their use as contracted forms which comprise a single consonant segment and no vowel.)

1 They've eaten it
2 Who'd been helping her?
3 Who've they been helping?
4 Where've you been?
5 *Could they've made a mistake?
6 *Dave may've gone to a rave
7 *He would like to've met her
8 *The guy'd lied to her
9 *He wouldn't let you've done it

10 *Which students would you say've benefited from the course?

11 Who do you think's upsetting her?

12 I certainly am enjoying it

13 There's nobody waiting for you

14 They'd expected him to apologize to her

Helpful hints

Bear in mind that the *'s* variant of *is/has* may have a different status from contracted auxiliary forms like *'ve* and *'d* – e.g. *'s* may be a PF affix.

Model answer for 1

In the text, we suggested that subjects originate in spec-VP, and that nominative pronouns can check their case by adjoining to a T constituent containing a contracted auxiliary. If this is so, sentence 1 will have the derivation (i) below (simplified by ignoring the tense affix which *'ve* merges with):

(i)

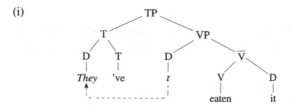

Thus, the pronoun *they* originates in spec-VP as the AGENT argument (and subject) of *eaten it*, and checks its nominative case by adjoining to the T constituent containing the contracted (affixal) auxiliary form *'ve*. On this view, auxiliary contraction is an integral part of case-checking, and not (except in the case of the *'s* forms mentioned in the **helpful hints**) the result of a PF attachment process. Evidence against the PF attachment analysis of contracted auxiliaries is presented in the main text, in relation to sentences such as (40–1).

Exercise VI (§§8.6–8.7)

Say whether the italicized verbs as used in the type of construction illustrated in the examples below function as **raising** and/or **control** predicates, and discuss the derivation of each sentence, giving arguments in support of your answer.

1 Power *tends* to corrupt people

2 John has *decided* to quit his job

3 We *came* to understand her point of view

4 You *have* to listen to me

5 They *failed* to achieve their objectives

6   You *appear* to have misunderstood me

7   He *refused* to sign the petition

8   He's *beginning* to irritate me

9   They *attempted* to pervert the course of justice

10   I *happened* to be passing your house

11   He is *going* to quit his job

12   He *stands* to lose a fortune

13   Dork *promises* to be a good student

14   He *needs* to have a shave

15   They *managed* to open the door

16   We *intend* to look into it

17   The weather is *threatening* to ruin our holiday

18   We are *hoping* to get a visa

19   She has *chosen* to ignore him

20   They are *planning* to visit their family

Model answer for 1

There are a number of reasons for suggesting that *tend* functions as a raising predicate when it takes an infinitive complement. For one thing, it allows a nonthematic subject like expletive *there*: cf.

(i)   *There* tends to be a lot of confusion about syntax

It also seems to impose no restrictions on its choice of subject: cf.

(ii) (a)   *Larry Loudmouth* tends to exaggerate

     (b)   *My goldfish* tends to eat too much

     (c)   *My pet amoeba* tends to reproduce in the evenings

     (d)   *My kettle* tends to boil over

     (e)   *My theory* tends to confuse people

The fact that *tend* can have a nonreferential subject like expletive *there* and imposes no restrictions on the type of referential subject it allows is consistent with the assumption that it does not θ-mark its subject, and hence can function as a raising predicate (for the reasons set out in the text in relation to *seem*).

A further piece of evidence (not noted in the text) in support of the same conclusion comes from the fact that *tend* can have an idiomatic subject: cf.

(iii) (a)   *All hell* tends to break loose

      (b)   *The shit* tends to hit the fan

      (c)   *The chickens* tend to come home to roost

Given that *all hell* can serve only as the subject of *break loose* in the relevant idiom, it is clear that we could not analyse *tend* as a control predicate in (iii)(a) and claim that *all hell* originates as the subject of *tends* and PRO as the subject of *break loose*, since this would violate the requirement that *all hell* can occur only as the subject of *break loose* (in the relevant idiom). By contrast, if *tend* is a raising predicate, we can claim that *all hell* originates as the subject of *break loose* and then raises up in a successive cyclic fashion to become first the subject of *to break loose*, then the subject of *tends to break loose* and finally the subject of the abstract T constituent preceding *tends*.

Given the assumption that *tend* is a raising predicate, sentence 1 will have the simplified derivation (iv) below:

(iv)   [TP *Power* T [VP *t* [V tends] [TP *t* [T to] [VP *t* [V corrupt] people]]]]

That is, *power* will originate as the subject of *corrupt people*, and will then be raised (in a successive cyclic fashion) first to become the subject of *to corrupt people*, then to become the subject of *tends to corrupt people*, and finally to become the subject of the abstract T constituent which heads the overall TP. The relevant derivation satisfies the θ-**criterion** by virtue of the fact that *power* is assigned only a single θ-role (by the V-bar *corrupt people*); it also satisfies the **shortest movement principle** because movement applies in a successive cyclic fashion; and it satisfies the principle of **greed** in that the subject moves only the minimal distance required in order to get into a position (as the specifier of the T constituent in the main clause) where it can check its nominative case (the *present-tense* head-features and *third person nominative singular* specifier-features of *tends* are attracted to the main-clause T constituent).

Exercise VII (§§8.6–8.7)
Discuss the syntax of **raising** in the following sentences:

1a It seems he hates syntax
 b *He seems hates syntax
 c *Syntax seems he hates
2a *It seems people to hate syntax
 b People seem to hate syntax
 c *Syntax seems people to hate
3a It would be unforgiveable for you to fail syntax
 b *You would be unforgiveable for to fail syntax
 c *Syntax would be unforgiveable for you to fail
4a It seems it was expected for you to win the race
 b *You seem it was expected (for) to win the race
 c *The race seems it was expected (for) you to win

Model answer for 1

Sentence 1a could be argued to have the simplified derivation (i) below:

(i)

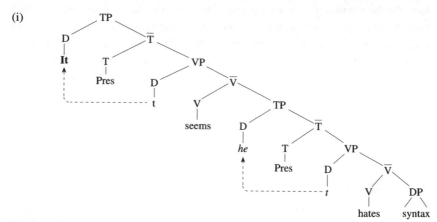

The pronoun *he* originates in spec-VP and raises to spec-TP; the tense- and agreement-features of the finite verb *hates* are attracted to T. In consequence, the case- and agreement-features of *he* and *hates* can be checked, and also the strong specifier-feature of T. In a similar fashion, we might suppose that the impersonal *it* subject of the overall sentence originates in spec-VP and raises to spec-TP (at any rate, if we assume that in consequence of Rothstein's **predication principle**, syntactic predicates like T-bar and V-bar require a subject).

Sentence 1b is generated by allowing *he* to raise further, first to become the subject of *seems*, and then the subject of the T constituent above *seems*, as in (ii) below:

(ii)

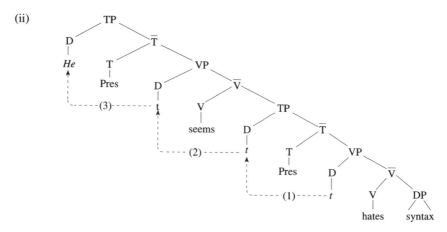

However, the illicit movements (2) and (3) are blocked by the principle of **greed**: since the pronoun *he* has its nominative case-feature checked and erased in the lower spec-

TP position (after movement (1) has taken place), the principle of greed dictates that it cannot move any further; in particular, it cannot move to the higher spec-TP position, since if it does so it cannot satisfy the requirement for the finite T constituent heading the overall sentence to have a nominative subject, because the nominative case-feature of *he* has already been checked and erased.

Sentence 1c is derived by moving the DP *syntax* (which is headed by a null determiner) to become the subject of the overall sentence; it may be that it first becomes the subject of *seems* and then the subject of the T constituent above *seems*, as in (iii) below:

(iii)

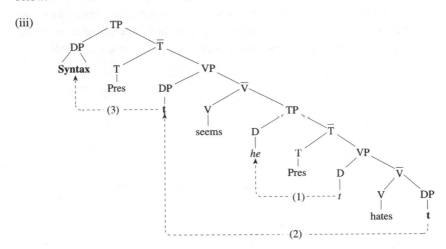

However, such a derivation violates at least two UG principles. One is the principle of **greed**, which *inter alia* forbids movement from one case position to another: since the DP *syntax* can check its case by remaining *in situ* (since it is the complement of the transitive verb *hates*), it cannot undergo movement to a further case position – e.g. to the nominative root specifier position at the top of the tree. A second principle which is violated in (iii) is the principle of **shortest movement**, which is violated because *syntax* does not move into the nearest subject position above the position in which it originates (the next-highest subject position would be subject/specifier position in the VP headed by *hates* – a position which is occupied by the trace of *he*).

Exercise VIII (§§8.8–8.9)

Discuss the derivation of the following passive sentences:

1 She may get arrested
2 They don't seem to have been consulted
3 We would all like to be promoted
4 The prisoners were thought to be planning to escape from jail

5 What was he alleged to have done?
6 Nobody was meant to get hurt
7 Who is believed to have attempted to bribe the judge?
8 He is thought to have tried to get arrested
9 Justice must be seen to be done
10 *He was alleged had cheated at syntax

Model answer for 1

The pronoun *she* here is the PATIENT argument of *arrested* (i.e. represents the person taken away for questioning), and so originates as the complement of *arrested*. It is then raised in successive cyclic fashion to become first the subject of *arrested*, then the subject of *get arrested* and finally the subject of *may get arrested*, as in (i) below:

(i)

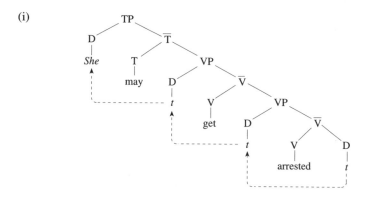

The derivation in (i) satisfies the **c-command condition on binding** by virtue of the fact that the rightmost trace is c-commanded (and bound) by the middle trace, which in turn is c-commanded (and bound) by the leftmost trace, which itself is c-commanded (and bound) by the moved pronoun *she*. The derivation (i) also satisfies the **shortest movement principle** by virtue of the fact that each movement of *she* takes it into the next-highest subject position in the structure. The **principle of greed** is also satisfied, since *she* moves from (and through) a series of positions in which it can't check its nominative case, into its ultimate position as subject of *may* (where it can check its case against the *nominative* specifier-feature of *may*). Since the resulting sentence 1 is grammatical, it follows that the derivation (i) must also satisfy the **θ-criterion**. This means that neither *arrested* nor *get* nor *may* θ-marks its subject: *arrested* because it is a passive participle (and passive participles have dethematized subjects), *get* because it is a raising predicate in this use (and raising predicates don't θ-mark their subjects), and *may* because it is an auxiliary (and functional categories aren't θ-markers). Thus, the only θ-role which *she* is assigned is that of PATIENT argument of *arrested* (thereby satisfying the θ-criterion requirement that each argument is assigned one and only one θ-role).

Exercise IX (§§8.8–8.9)

Discuss the syntax of the following passive sentences:

1a They were arrested
 b They may get arrested
 c They are thought to have been arrested
 d Nobody expected them to be arrested

2a It was thought the prisoners had escaped from jail
 b *It was thought the prisoners to have escaped from jail
 c The prisoners were thought to have escaped from jail
 d *The prisoners were thought had escaped from jail

3a It hadn't been intended for anyone to get hurt
 b *Nobody had been intended for to get hurt
 c *It hadn't been intended anyone to get hurt
 d Nobody had been intended to get hurt

4a He seems to have been arrested
 b He wants to be arrested
 c He seems to want to be arrested
 d He is thought to have tried to get arrested

5a What was he alleged to have done?
 b What was alleged to have happened to him?
 c Who is believed to have attempted to bribe the judge?
 d *Who was it believed to have bribed the jury?

6a There have been several incidents reported
 b *There have several incidents been reported

7a There were several students being detained
 b *There were being several students detained

In addition, comment on the syntax of the following *real-life* passive sentences:

8a 'The word has tried to be defined in terms of a phonetic matrix'
 b 'Dialects are often attempted to be suppressed'
 c 'When bottles and bricks are started to be thrown, things are getting serious'
 d 'Some journalists have been attempted to be attacked'
 e 'That's hoping to be happened'

(Examples 8a–b are from student exam papers; example 8c was produced by the deputy commissioner of police for south-west London in a BBC radio interview; examples 8d–e were produced by BBC radio reporters – complaints about falling standards should be addressed directly to the Director General of the BBC, Bush House, London.) Discuss the derivation of the relevant sentences and say what's odd about (the people who produced) them.

Model answers for 1a–b

Sentence 1a is discussed in the text, where it is argued that it has the derivation (i) below:

(i)

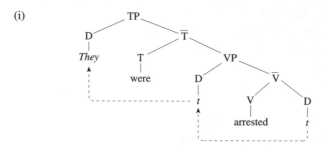

At first sight, it might seem as if 1b can be derived in the same way. However, there is an important difference between *be* and *get* – namely that *be* is an auxiliary, whereas *get* is a nonauxiliary verb – as we see from the fact that *be* can undergo auxiliary inversion whereas *get* cannot: cf.

(ii) (a)   *Were* they arrested?

(b)   **Got* they arrested?

Accordingly, it would seem likely that 1b has the more complex derivation (iii) below:

(iii)

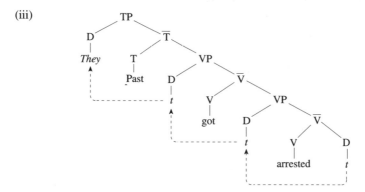

It follows that the auxiliary *were* in (i) can undergo inversion because it is positioned in T, but the verb *got* in (iii) can't undergo inversion because it is positioned in V. What lends plausibility to the assumption that the passivized subject *they* becomes subject of the passive participle before becoming subject of *get* is the existence of sentences such as:

(iv)   Careless talk can get *you* arrested

where the passivized pronoun *you* appears to be the subject of the passive participle *arrested*.

9

VP shells

9.1 Overview

In this chapter, we take a close look at the internal constituent structure of verb phrases. We shall argue that VPs have a complex structure, comprising an inner **VP** core and an outer **vp** shell, and that some (e.g. AGENT) arguments originate within the outer vp shell, while other (e.g. THEME) arguments originate within the inner VP core.

9.2 Ergative predicates

Thus far, the verb phrase structures we have looked at have generally contained verbs with a single complement. Such verbs can easily be accommodated within the binary-branching framework adopted here, since all we need say is that a verb merges with its complement to form a (binary-branching) V-bar constituent. However, a particular problem for the binary-branching framework adopted here is posed by three-place predicates like those italicized in (1) below which have two [bracketed] complements:

(1) (a)   We *rolled* [the ball] [down the hill]
    (b)   He *filled* [the bath] [with water]
    (c)   He *broke* [the vase] [into pieces]

If we make the conventional assumption that complements are sisters to heads, it follows that the V-bar constituent headed by *rolled* in (1a) will have the structure (2) below:

(2)

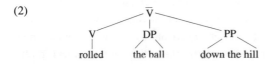

However, a structure such as (2) is problematic within the framework adopted here. After all, it is a *ternary-branching* structure ($\bar{V}$ branches out into three separate constituents, namely the V *rolled*, the DP *the ball* and the PP *down the hill*), and this poses an obvious problem within a framework which assumes that the merger operation which forms phrases is an inherently binary operation which can only combine constituents in a *pairwise* fashion. Moreover, a ternary-branching structure such as (2) would wrongly predict that the string following the verb *rolled* does not form a constituent, and so cannot be coordinated with another similar string (given the traditional assumption that only constituents can be conjoined); yet this prediction is falsified by sentences such as:

(3)   He rolled *the ball down the hill* and **the acorn up the mountain**

How can we overcome these problems?

   One way would be to suppose that the string *the ball down the hill* in (3) is a clausal constituent of some kind, in which *the ball* functions as the subject of the clause, and *down the hill* functions as the complement of the clause. Such an analysis is by no means implausible, since many three-place predicates like *roll* can also be used as two-place predicates in which the DP which immediately follows the verb in the three-place structure functions as the subject in the two-place structure – as we see from sentence pairs such as the following:

(4) (a)   We **rolled** *the ball* down the hill
    (b)   *The ball* **rolled** down the hill
(5) (a)   He **filled** *the bath* with water
    (b)   *The bath* **filled** with water
(6) (a)   He **broke** *the vase* into pieces
    (b)   *The vase* **broke** into pieces
(7) (a)   They **withdrew** *the troops* from the occupied territories
    (b)   *The troops* **withdrew** from the occupied territories
(8) (a)   They **moved** *the headquarters* to Brooklyn
    (b)   *The headquarters* **moved** to Brooklyn
(9) (a)   They **closed** *the store* down
    (b)   *The store* **closed** down

(Verbs which can be used in this way either as three-place or as two-place predicates are sometimes referred to as **ergative predicates**.) Moreover, the italicized DP seems to play the same thematic role with respect to the bold-printed verb in each pair of examples: for example, *the ball* is the THEME argument of *roll* (i.e. the entity which undergoes a rolling motion) both in (4a) *We rolled the ball down the hill* and in (4b) *The ball rolled down the hill*. Evidence in support of the claim that *the ball* plays the same semantic role in both sentences comes from the fact that the italicized argument is subject to the same restrictions on the choice of expression which can fulfil the relevant argument function in each type of sentence: cf.

368

(10) (a) *The ball/the rock/!the theory/!sincerity* rolled down the hill

(b) John rolled *the ball/the rock/!the theory/!sincerity* down the hill

If we assume that principles of UG correlate thematic structure with syntactic structure in a *uniform* fashion (in accordance with Baker's 1988 **uniform theta assignment hypothesis/UTAH**), then it follows that two arguments which fulfil the same thematic function with respect to a given predicate must occupy the same underlying position in the syntax.

An analysis within the spirit of UTAH would be to assume that since *the ball* is clearly the subject of *roll* in (4b) *The ball rolled down the hill*, then it must also be the case that *the ball* originates as the subject of *roll* in (4a) *We rolled the ball down the hill*. But if this is so, how come *the ball* is positioned *after* the verb *rolled* in (4b), when subjects are normally positioned *before* their verbs? A natural answer to this question within the framework we are adopting here is to suppose that the verb *moves* from its original (post-subject) position after *the ball* into a higher verb position to the left of *the ball*. More specifically, adapting ideas put forward by Larson (1988, 1990), Hale and Keyser (1991, 1993, 1994) and Chomsky (1995b), let's suppose that the (b) examples in sentences like (4–9) are simple VPs, but that the (a) examples are complex double-VP structures which comprise an outer vp **shell** with an inner VP core embedded within it.

More concretely, let's make the following assumptions. In (4b) *The ball rolled down the hill*, the V *rolled* is merged with its PP complement *down the hill* to form the V-bar *rolled down the hill*; this is then merged with the DP *the ball* to form a VP with the structure (11) below:

(11)

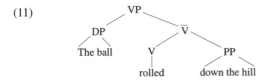

In the case of (4b), the resulting VP will then be merged with a null tense affix to form a T-bar constituent; the subject *the ball* will then be raised to spec-TP (by **A movement**), as in (12) below (simplified e.g. by ignoring attraction of the tense/agreement-features of *rolled* to T):

(12)

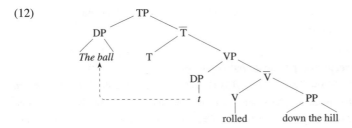

369

But what of (4a) *We rolled the ball down the hill*?

Let's suppose that once the VP structure (11) has been formed, it is then merged with an abstract causative **light verb** ø – i.e. a null verb with much the same causative interpretation as a verb like *make* (so that *We rolled the ball down the hill* has a similar interpretation to *We made the ball roll down the hill*). Let's also suppose that this causative light verb is affixal in nature (and so a strong head), and that the verb *rolled* raises to adjoin to it (producing a structure which can be paraphrased literally as 'We *made + roll* the ball down the hill'). The resulting v-bar structure is then merged with the subject *we* (which is assigned the θ-role of AGENT by the causative light verb), to form the complex vp (13) below (lower-case letters are used to denote the light verb and its projections):

(13)

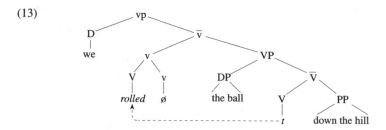

Subsequently, the vp in (13) merges with an abstract tense affix to form a T-bar, and the subject *we* raises into spec-TP to check its nominative case, as in (14) below:

(14)

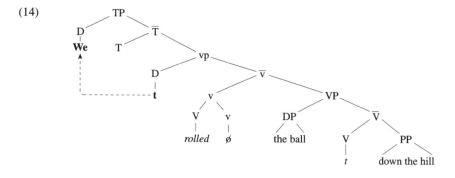

The objective case carried by the DP *the ball* is checked by the transitive verb *rolled* (or perhaps by the light verb ø).

9.3 Adverbs and prepositional particles

The VP shell analysis in (14) provides a straightforward account for an otherwise puzzling aspect of the syntax of sentences like (4a) – namely the fact that adverbs like *gently* can be positioned either before *rolled* or after *the ball*, as we see from:

(15) (a)   We *gently* rolled the ball down the hill

(b)   We rolled the ball *gently* down the hill

Let us make the traditional assumption that adverbs like *gently* merge with intermediate verbal projections like V-bar and v-bar. Let's also assume that such adverbs are **adjuncts** which have the property that when they merge with a given category, they form an expanded category of the same type (so that an adverb merged with V-bar forms an expanded V-bar, and an adverb merged with v-bar forms an expanded v-bar). Given these assumptions and the light-verb analysis in (14), we could then propose the following derivations for (15a–b).

In (15a), the verb *rolled* merges with the PP *down the hill* to form the V-bar *rolled down the hill*, and this V-bar in turn merges with the DP *the ball* to form the VP *the ball rolled down the hill*, as in (11) above. This VP then merges with a causative light verb ø to which the verb *rolled* adjoins, forming the v-bar *rolled the ball down the hill*. The resulting v-bar merges with the adverb *gently* to form the expanded v-bar *gently rolled the ball down the hill*; and this v-bar in turn merges with the subject *we* to form the vp *we gently rolled the ball down the hill*. The vp thereby formed merges with an abstract tense affix, forming a T-bar; the subject *we* raises to spec-TP forming the TP (15a) *We gently rolled the ball down the hill*. Thus (15a) has the derivation (16) below:

(16)

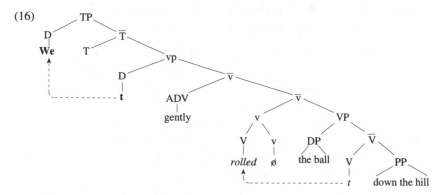

Now consider how (15b) *We rolled the ball gently down the hill* is derived. As before, the verb *rolled* merges with the PP *down the hill*, forming the V-bar *rolled down the hill*. The adverb *gently* then merges with this V-bar to form the expanded V-bar *gently rolled down the hill*. This V-bar in turn merges with the DP *the ball* to form the VP *the ball gently rolled down the hill*. The resulting VP is merged with a causative light verb ø to which the verb *rolled* adjoins, so forming the v-bar *rolled the ball gently down the hill*. This v-bar is then merged with the subject *we* to form the vp *we rolled the ball gently down the hill*. The vp thereby formed merges with an abstract tense affix, forming a T-bar; the subject *we* raises to spec-TP forming the TP (15b) *We rolled the ball gently down the hill*, which has the derivation (17) below:

VP shells

(17)

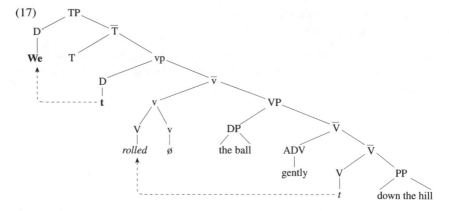

The different positions occupied by the adverb *gently* in (16) and (17) reflect a subtle meaning difference between (15a) and (15b): (15a) means that the action which initiated the rolling motion was gentle, whereas (15b) means that the rolling motion itself was gentle.

A light-verb analysis such as that sketched above also offers us an interesting account of adverb position in sentences like:

(18) (a)   He had *deliberately* rolled the ball *gently* down the hill
       (b)   *He had *gently* rolled the ball *deliberately* down the hill

It seems reasonable to suppose that *deliberately* (by virtue of its meaning) can only be an adjunct to a projection of an *agentive* verb (i.e. a verb whose specifier has the thematic role of AGENT). If we suppose (as earlier) that the light verb ø is a causative verb with an agentive subject, the contrast in (18) can be accounted for straightforwardly: in (18a) *deliberately* is contained within a vp headed by the agentive causative light verb ø; but in (18b) it is contained within a VP headed by the nonagentive verb *roll* (*roll* is a nonagentive verb because its specifier has the θ-role THEME, not AGENT). We can then say that adverbs like *deliberately* are strictly vp adverbs.

This in turn might lead us to expect to find a corresponding class of VP adverbs. In this connection, consider the following contrasts (adapted from Bowers 1993, p. 609):

(19) (a)   Mary jumped the horse *perfectly* over the last fence
       (b)   *Mary *perfectly* jumped the horse over the last fence

Given the assumptions made here, the derivation of (19a) would be parallel to that in (17), while the derivation of (19b) would be parallel to that in (16). If we assume that *perfectly* (in the relevant use) can function only as a VP-adverb, the contrast between (19a) and (19b) can be accounted for straightforwardly: in (19a), *perfectly* is merged with a V-bar (consistent with its status as a VP adverb), whereas in (19b) it is merged with a v-bar (in violation of the requirement that it can only serve as a VP adverb).

372

We can formulate a similar type of argument in support of the VP-shell analysis in relation to the dual position occupied by the prepositional particle *down* in sentence pairs such as:

(20) (a)   They may close the store down
     (b)   They may close down the store

We might suppose that (20a) is derived as follows. The DP *the store* originates as the subject of *close down* as in (21) below:

(21)

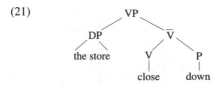

The VP in (21) is then merged with a causative light verb ø (whose AGENT subject is *they*), and the verb *close* adjoins to the light verb as in (22) below:

(22)

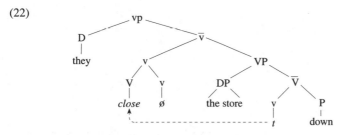

The vp in (22) then merges with a T constituent containing *may* (and an abstract tense affix, though this is a detail which we overlook below); the pronoun *they* raises to spec-TP to become the subject of *may* as in (23) below:

(23)

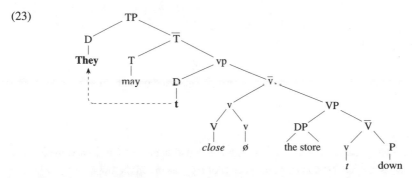

And (23) is the structure associated with (20a) *They may close the store down*.

Now consider how we derive (20b) *They may close down the store*. Let's suppose that *close* merges with *down* to form the V-bar (24) below:

(24)

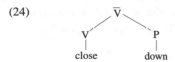

Let's further suppose that the particle *down* (optionally) adjoins to the verb *close*, forming the complex verb *close down*, as in (25) below:

(25)

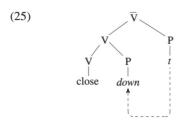

The resulting V-bar merges with its DP subject *the store* to form the VP (26) below:

(26)

The VP in (26) is then merged with a causative light verb ø whose AGENT subject is *they*; the complex verb *close down* adjoins to this light verb, as in (27) below:

(27)

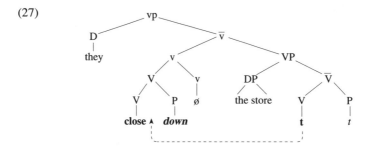

Subsequently, the vp in (27) merges with a T constituent containing *may*; the subject *they* raises to spec-TP to become the subject of *may*, as in (28) below:

(28)

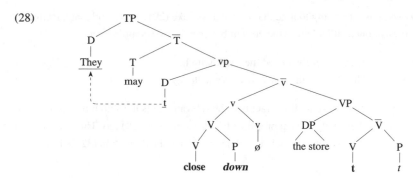

And (28) is the structure of (20b) *They may close down the store*. Thus, we see that a VP shell analysis enables us to provide a principled account of the two positions which can be occupied by prepositional particles in sentences such as (20a–b).

As we have seen, the *VP shell* analysis outlined here provides an interesting solution to the problems posed by three-place ergative predicates which appear to take two complements. However, the problems posed by predicates which take two complements arise not only with transitive verbs (like those in (4–9) above) which have intransitive counterparts, but also with verbs such as those italicized in (29) below (the complements of the verbs are bracketed):

(29) (a)   They *loaded* [the truck] [with hay]

    (b)   He *gave* [no explanation] [to his friends]

    (c)   They *took* [everything] [from her]

    (d)   Nobody can *blame* [you] [for the accident]

    (e)   He *assured* [her] [of his good intentions]

    (f)   He *handed* [the documents] [over]

    (g)   They *brought* [the suspects] [in]

Verbs like those in (29) cannot be used intransitively, as we see from the ungrammaticality of sentences such as (30) below:

(30) (a)   *The truck loaded with hay

    (b)   *No explanation gave to his friends

    (c)   *Everything took from her

    (d)   *You can blame for the accident

    (e)   *She assured of his good intentions

    (f)   *The documents handed over

    (g)   *The suspects brought in

However, it is interesting to note that in structures like (29) too we find that VP adverbs can be positioned either before the verb or between its two complements: cf.

(31) (a)   They *carefully* loaded the truck with hay
     (b)   They loaded the truck *carefully* with hay

This suggests that (in spite of the fact that the relevant verbs have no intransitive counterpart) a VP shell analysis is appropriate for structures like (29) too. This would mean (for example) that a sentence such as (29a) would have the derivation (32) below:

(32)

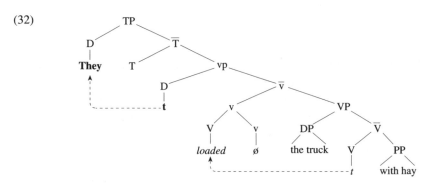

We could then say that the adverb *carefully* adjoins to v-bar in (31a), and to V-bar in (31b). If we suppose that verbs like *load* are essentially affixal in nature (and so must adjoin to the agentive light verb ø) we can account for the ungrammaticality of intransitive structures such as (30a) **The truck loaded with hay*. Alternatively, we might conjecture that *load* is an obligatorily transitive verb (and so has to check objective case), and hence can only occur in structures like (32) where it is raised into a position where it can check the objective case of the immediately following DP *the truck*. A third possibility would be to posit that verbs like *load* carry a strong causative feature [+caus] which has to be checked by adjunction to an abstract causative light verb.

   Moreover, sentences like (29f–g) show the same dual position of prepositional particles as sentences such as (20): cf.

(33) (a)   He handed the documents *over*
     (b)   He handed *over* the documents
(34) (a)   They brought the suspects *in*
     (b)   They brought *in* the suspects

This suggests that they should be given essentially the same kind of VP shell analysis as sentences like (20a–b).

9.4 Ditransitive and resultative predicates

We can extend the *VP shell* analysis still further, to take in *ditransitive predicates* (i.e. verbs which take two DP objects) such as those italicized in (35) below:

(35) (a) They will *get* [the teacher] [a present]

  (b) Could you *pass* [me] [the salt]?

  (c) James Bond *showed* [her] [his credentials]

Since complement DPs are referred to as **objects** in traditional grammar, structures like (35) are said to be instances of the **double-object construction**. (The first bracketed DP in each case is said to be the **indirect object** of the italicized verb and the second its **direct object**.) More specifically, we might suggest that (35a) is derived in the following manner. The verb *get* merges with the DP *a present* (assigning it the θ-role RECIPIENT) to form the V-bar (36) below:

(36)

```
        V̄
      /    \
     V      DP
     |     /  \
    get   a present
```

This in turn merges with the DP *the teacher* (which is assigned the θ-role RECIPIENT) to form the VP (37) below:

(37)

```
            VP
          /    \
        DP       V̄
       /  \     /  \
  the teacher  V    DP
              |    /  \
             get  a present
```

The resulting VP (37) merges with the abstract causative light verb ø (whose AGENT subject is *they*), and the verb *get* adjoins to this light verb as in (38) below:

(38)

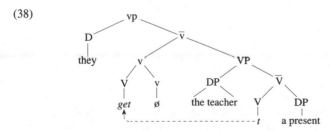

The vp thereby formed then merges with a T constituent containing *will*, and the subject *they* raises to spec-TP to become the subject of *will*, as in (39) below:

(39)

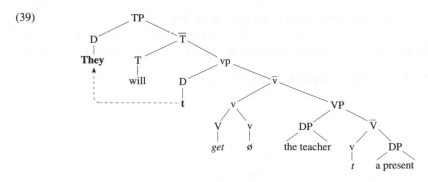

And (39) is the structure associated with sentence (35a) *They will get the teacher a present*. (For a range of alternative analyses of the *double-object* construction, see Larson 1988, 1990, Johnson 1991, Bowers 1993 and Pesetsky 1995.)

The *VP shell* analysis outlined above can further be extended to so-called **resultative** predicates like those italicized below:

(40) (a)   The acid *turned* [the litmus paper] [red]
    (b)   They *painted* [the house] [pink]

(The verb *paint* as used in structures like (40b) is called a resultative predicate because the result of the painting process in that the house becomes pink.) Resultative predicates pose much the same problem as the three-place predicates which we looked at earlier – namely that the resultative verb in each case appears to have two complements, and thus poses a potential problem for a binary-branching framework. However (as we shall see), we can overcome these problems if we adopt a light-verb analysis of resultatives.

More concretely, we might suppose that (40a) is derived as follows. The verb *turned* originates in the head V position of VP, with the DP *the litmus paper* as its subject and the adjective *red* as its complement, as in (41) below:

(41)

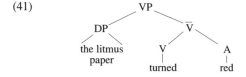

The VP in (41) then merges with the causative light verb ø (whose subject is the DP *the acid*), and the verb *turned* raises to adjoin to ø as in (42) below:

(42)

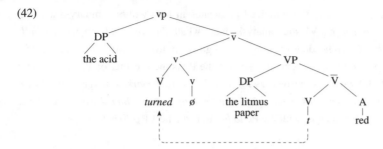

Subsequently, the vp in (42) merges with an abstract tense affix, and the DP *the acid* raises to spec-TP, so deriving (40a) *The acid turned the litmus paper red.* (For very different analyses of resultative sentences like (40), see Carrier and Randall 1992 and Keyser and Roeper 1992.)

9.5 Three-place predicates with clausal complements

A further class of predicates which pose potential problems for a binary-branching framework are three-place predicates with a clausal complement. For example, there are a number of verbs (like those italicized below) which take [bracketed] PP and CP complements:

(43) (a)   He had *remarked* [to her] [that Senator Scumme-Bagge was a fraud]

(b)   She *suggested* [to him] [that they should try safe syntax]

(c)   I *concluded* [from his tight fist] [that Dougal Frugal was Scots]

(d)   He *learned* [from Superman] [that Lois Lane was a pain]

(e)   He *agreed* [with her] [that Senator Doleful was soulful]

If we make the traditional assumption that the two bracketed expressions in each example in (43) are complements of the italicized verbs and that complements are sisters to their heads, the V-bar headed by *remarked* in (43a) will have a structure along the lines of (44) below:

(44)

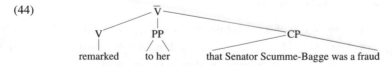

But the problem with (44) is that V-bar is a ternary-branching category (since it has three immediate constituents, namely V, PP and CP); hence, the traditional analysis in (44) is incompatible with our key assumption that syntax is binary-branching.

VP shells

One way of analysing the italicized predicates in (43) within a binary-branching framework is to adopt a VP shell analysis under which the preverbal subject (*he/she/I*) is the subject of a vp headed by an agentive light verb, the CP is the complement of a VP headed by the italicized lexical verb, and the PP is the specifier of VP. This would mean that (43a) would be derived as follows. The verb *remarked* merges with its CP complement to form the V-bar *remarked that Senator Scumme-Bagge was a fraud*; the resulting V-bar then merges with the PP *to her* to form the VP (45) below:

(45)

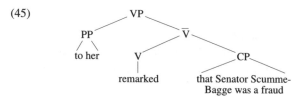

The VP in (45) then merges with an agentive light verb whose subject is *he*; the verb *remarked* adjoins to the light verb as in (46) below:

(46)

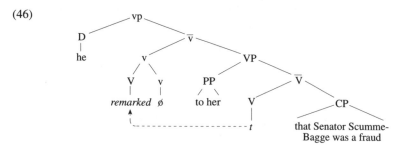

Subsequently, the vp in (46) merges with a T constituent containing the auxiliary *had*, and *he* raises to spec-TP to become the subject of *had*, so deriving (43a) *He had remarked to her that Senator Scumme-Bagge was a fraud*.

We might propose a similar derivation for structures like those below which have so-called 'impersonal *it*' as their subject:

(47) (a)   It seems [to me] [that Cindy Suquet was taking him for a ride]
      (b)   It occurs [to me] [that your analysis needs more light verbs]
      (c)   It appears [to me] [that there is evidence of a cover-up]

The main difference from (46) would be that the subject of the light verb in (47) would be impersonal *it* rather than an AGENT argument like *he* in (46).

A second class of three-place predicates with clausal complements are verbs like those italicized below, which take bracketed D(P) and CP complements:

(48) (a)   You must *satisfy* [the jury] [that you are innocent]
      (b)   She *reminded* [him] [that the FBI were tailing him]

(c)   He *assured* [her] [that he was only firing blanks]

(d)   They *told* [us] [that President Klingon liked Whitewater Whiskey]

(e)   He *convinced* [me] [that Snow White was not a nanophile]

(f)   I *warned* [her] [that she should handle Bert Squirt with kid gloves]

Once again, if we make the traditional assumption that complements are sisters to their heads, the V-bar headed by *satisfy* in (48a) will be analysed as in (49) below:

(49)

But since V-bar in (49) is a ternary-branching constituent, an analysis like (49) is incompatible with the binary-branching framework adopted here.

However, we might propose a binary-branching analysis for structures like (48) which is similar to our earlier analysis of ditransitive predicates in sentences like (35) above. This would mean that (48a) would be derived by merging the verb *satisfy* with its CP complement to form the V-bar *satisfy that you are innocent*; this V-bar would then be merged with the DP *the jury* to form the VP (50) below:

(50)

The VP in (50) would then merge with a causative light verb whose subject is *you*, with the verb *satisfy* raising to adjoin to the light verb as in (51) below:

(51)

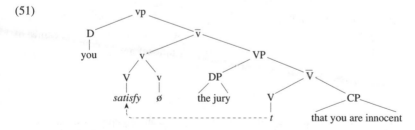

The resulting vp would then merge with a T constituent containing the modal auxiliary *must*, and the subject *you* would raise to spec-TP to become the subject of *must*, so deriving (48a) *You must satisfy the jury that you are innocent*. We might propose a similar derivation for impersonal sentences like (52) below:

(52)   It *strikes* [me] [that syntax really screws you up]

save that the subject of the light verb in (52) is impersonal *it* rather than an AGENT argument like *you* in (51).

9.6   Object-control predicates

In the previous section, we looked at the syntax of three-place predicates which take a finite *that*-clause as their complement. However, we also find three-place predicates which take an infinitival complement, like the verbs italicized below:

(53) (a)   What *decided* [you] [to take syntax]?

   (b)   She *persuaded* [me] [to try phoneme-free phonology]

   (c)   They *asked* [the president] [to fire Senator Scroople]

   (d)   He *told* [me] [to keep a low profile]

   (e)   The FBI *advised* [us] [to bug Macdonalds]

   (f)   Someone should *remind* [him] [to activate his memory-bank]

Each of the verbs in (53) takes a D(P) object and an infinitive complement with a PRO subject: thus, (53a) has the fuller structure (54) below:

(54)   What decided [you] [to PRO take syntax]?

Since in each of the sentences in (53) the PRO subject of the infinitive is controlled by the D(P) object of the italicized verb, the relevant predicates (in this kind of use) are known as **object-control predicates**.

   Some evidence in support of positing that the verb *decide* in sentences like (53a) is indeed a three-place object-control predicate, and that *you* is the object of *decided* (rather than the subject of *to take syntax*) comes from the fact that (53a) can be paraphrased (for some speakers, albeit rather awkwardly) as in (55) below:

(55)   What decided *you* [that **you** should take syntax]?

where the first *you* corresponds to the object *you* in (54) and the second **you** corresponds to PRO in (54). Moreover, the verb *decide* imposes restrictions on the choice of argument expression following it (which must be a rational entity – not an irrational entity like *the exam*):

(56)   *What decided *the exam* to be difficult?

Furthermore, the expression following *decide* cannot be an expletive pronoun such as *there*:

(57)   *What decided *there* to be an election?

The obvious conclusion to draw from facts such as these is that the (pro)nominal following *decide* is an (object) argument of *decide* in sentences such as (53a), and serves as the controller of a PRO subject in the following *to*-infinitive.

This means that *decide* has two complements in structures such as (54) – the pronoun *you* and the infinitive *to take syntax*. If we make the traditional assumption that complements are sisters to the verb which θ-marks them, this would seem to lead us to the conclusion that the V-bar headed by *decided* in (54) has the structure (58) below:

(58)

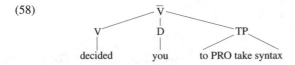

However, a ternary-branching structure such as (58) is incompatible with the core assumption made here that the merger operation by which phrases are formed is intrinsically binary. One way of overcoming this problem is to suppose that (53a) has a structure more akin to that of:

(59)   What made you decide to take syntax?

More specifically, we might suppose that (53a) is derived as follows. The verb *decided* merges with the infinitival TP *to PRO take syntax*, so forming a V-bar which in turn merges with the pronoun *you* to form the VP (60) below:

(60)

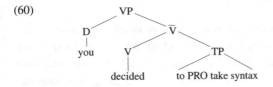

The resulting VP then merges with an abstract causative light verb ø (a null counterpart of *made* in (59) above) whose subject is *what*; the verb *decide* adjoins to the light verb ø, as in (61) below:

(61)

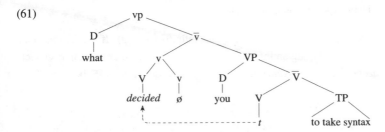

(a structure paraphraseable as 'What made + decide you to take syntax?'). The objective case carried by the pronoun *you* is checked by the immediately preceding transitive light verb ø (or by the verb *decided*, which is transitive in this use). The resulting vp is then merged with an abstract T constituent, and the pronoun *what* raises to spec-TP to check its nominative case, as in (62) below:

(62)

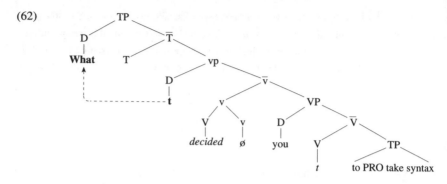

The light-verb analysis in (62) offers two main advantages over the traditional analysis in (58). Firstly, (62) is consistent with the view that the merger operation by which phrases are formed is binary; and secondly, (62) enables us to attain a more unitary theory of control under which the controller of PRO is always a *subject*, never an *object* (since PRO in (62) is controlled by *you*, and *you* is the subject of the VP headed by the verb *decided*). This second result is a welcome one, since the verb *decide* clearly functions as a subject-control verb in structures such as:

(63)   He decided to PRO take syntax

where the PRO subject of *take syntax* is controlled by the *he* subject of *decided*.

Object-control verbs like *decide* in sentences like (53a) *What decided you to take syntax?* occur in structures in which they are followed by an objective argument and a *to*-infinitive: using traditional grammatical terminology, we might say that verbs like *decide* allow an *accusative and infinitive* string after them (the traditional term *accusative* denotes objective case). In this respect, they resemble ECM (exceptional case-marking) infinitive structures like (64) below:

(64)   They expected me to take syntax

(where *me to take syntax* is an accusative and infinitive string). If we assume that *expect* is an ECM verb taking an infinitival TP complement with an objective subject, the V-bar *expected me to take syntax* in (64) will have the derivation (65) below:

(65)

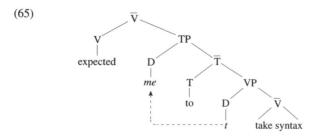

with *me* originating in spec-VP as the subject of *take syntax*, and raising to spec-TP in order to get into a position where it can have its objective case checked by the immediately preceding transitive verb *expected*. Since some *accusative and infinitive* verbs (e.g. *decide*) are object-control predicates and others (e.g. *expect*) are ECM predicates, an obvious question to ask is how we determine whether a given verb which allows the accusative and infinitive construction is a control predicate or an ECM predicate.

Work in the 1960s (e.g. Chomsky 1965 and Rosenbaum 1967) uncovered numerous differences between ECM predicates like *expect* and object-control predicates like *persuade* (the verb *persuade* was argued to be a typical object-control predicate). For one thing, the two have different semantic properties: in structures like *persuade someone to . . .* , *someone* is an argument of *persuade*, whereas in *expect someone to . . .* , *someone* is not an argument of *expect*, as we can see from the two different finite-clause paraphrases for the relevant structures given in (66) and (67) below:

(66) (a)   He persuaded *me* to take syntax
     (b)   He persuaded *me* [that I should take syntax]
(67) (a)   He expected *me* to take syntax
     (b)   He expected [that *I* would take syntax]

The fact that *me* in (66a) is an argument of *persuade* is suggested by the fact that its italicized counterpart *me* in (66b) is positioned outside the bracketed *that*-clause. Conversely, the fact that *me* in (67a) is the subject of the infinitive *to take syntax* is suggested by the fact that its italicized counterpart *I* in (67b) is positioned inside the bracketed *that*-clause, and carries the nominative case typical of the subject of a finite clause.

Further evidence that the nominal following *persuade* is an argument of *persuade* (whereas that following *expect* is not an argument of *expect*) comes from the fact that the verb *persuade* imposes restrictions on the choice of nominal following it (requiring it to be a rational entity, not an irrational entity like *the exam*), whereas the verb *expect* does not: cf.

(68)   He expected/*persuaded *the exam* to be difficult

Similarly, *expect* (but not *persuade*) can be immediately followed by an idiomatic subject (i.e. by a subject which is part of a clausal idiom): cf.

(69) (a)   They expected/*persuaded *the fur* to fly
     (b)   They expected/*persuaded *the chickens* to come home to roost
     (c)   They expected/*persuaded *the shit* to hit the fan

Likewise, *expect* (but not *persuade*) can be followed by expletive *there*: cf.

(70)   He expected/*persuaded *there* to be someone waiting for him

The relevant differences follow from the assumption that *expect* is an ECM predicate, whereas *persuade* is an object control predicate: the nominal following *persuade* is an EXPERIENCER argument of *persuade*, and so must be a rational entity (hence cannot e.g. be an irrational entity like *the exam* or a dummy pronoun like *there*); but the nominal following *expect* is not an argument of *expect*, and so is not constrained by *expect*.

Given the assumption that *persuade* is an object-control predicate in sentences like (66a), we might propose to analyse it in essentially the same way as we earlier analysed the verb *decide* in (62) above. This would mean that the nominal expression following *persuade* would originate as the subject of *persuade*, and the verb *persuade* would itself originate as the complement of an agentive light verb ø with a causative sense (so that (66a) *He persuaded me to take syntax* would be analysed as being similar in certain respects to *He made me decide to take syntax*). On this view, *persuade* would merge with its infinitival TP complement to form a V-bar, and the resulting V-bar would then merge with its EXPERIENCER subject *me* to form the structure (71) below (where *persuade* has much the same sense as *decide*):

(71)

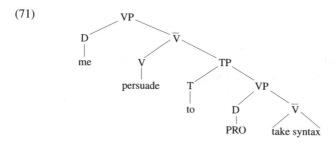

Some evidence in favour of analysing *me* as an EXPERIENCER subject comes from the fact that it can be associated with the adverb *personally*, e.g. in sentences such as:

(72)   *Personally*, nothing could persuade *me* to take syntax

Fillmore (1972, p. 10) suggested that *personally* is typically associated with EXPERIENCER subjects, and this suggestion would appear to be borne out by the contrast in (73) below:

(73) (a)   *Personally*, I hated him
     (b)   **Personally*, I killed him*

where *personally* can be associated with *I* in the first sentence but not the second – and this would seem to correlate with the fact that *I* is an EXPERIENCER subject in (73a), but an AGENT subject in (73b). Thus, the fact that *personally* can be construed with *me* in (72) lends empirical support to the analysis of *me* as the EXPERIENCER subject of *persuade* in (71).

386

The VP in (71) is subsequently merged with the agentive light verb ø, and *persuade* adjoins to the light verb, so forming a v-bar which itself merges with its AGENT subject *he*, as in (74) below:

(74)

The agentive light verb ø assigns the θ-role AGENT to its subject *he*; the objective case carried by *me* is checked by the immediately preceding transitive verb *persuaded* (or, perhaps, by the light verb to which it adjoins). Subsequently, the vp in (74) merges with an abstract tense affix, so forming a T-bar; the subject *he* then raises to spec-TP to check its nominative case. (See Larson 1991 and Bowers 1993 for a similar analysis of object-control verbs like *persuade*.)

Some supporting empirical evidence in favour of the light-verb analysis in (74) comes from the fact that an adverb like *eventually* can be positioned either before *persuaded* or after *me*: cf.

(75) (a)   He *eventually* persuaded me to take syntax
     (b)   He persuaded me *eventually* to take syntax

If we assume that adverbs like *eventually* adjoin to intermediate verbal projections, we can then say (in terms of the analysis in (74) above) that *eventually* is adjoined to v-bar in (75a), and to V-bar in (75b).

The light-verb analysis of *persuade* outlined in (74) above assumes that *persuade* has essentially the same syntax as *decide* in (72) above. Yet there is one important respect in which the two differ – as we see from the contrast in (76) below:

(76) (a)   I decided to take syntax
     (b)   *I persuaded to take syntax

How can we account for this difference? One possibility is to assume that *persuade* is an inherently affixal (or causative) verb which can therefore only be used in structures like (74) which contain a causative light verb; another is to make the traditional assumption that *persuade* (in active uses) is an obligatorily transitive verb, and hence can only occur in structures like (74) (where it can check the objective case of the immediately following objective pronoun *me*).

9.7 Monotransitive predicates

Thus far, we have considered how to deal with three-place predicates. However, many three-place predicates can also function as two-place predicates (i.e. as predicates which have a direct but no indirect object), as we see from the examples below:

(77) (a)   He **read** *me* the letter

(b)   He **read** the letter

(78) (a)   He **bought** *me* a new car

(b)   He **bought** a new car

(79) (a)   He **sold** *me* a painting

(b)   He **sold** a painting

(80) (a)   The waiter **brought** *me* a bottle of champagne

(b)   The waiter **brought** a bottle of champagne

(81) (a)   He **ordered** *me* a taxi

(b)   He **ordered** a taxi

(82) (a)   He **played** *me* the tape

(b)   He **played** the tape

(83) (a)   Could you **pass** *me* the salt?

(b)   Could you **pass** the salt?

(84) (a)   He **found** *me* a replacement

(b)   He **found** a replacement

(85) (a)   He **sent** *me* a card

(b)   He **sent** a card

In the (a) examples in (77–85), the bold-printed verb has both an (italicized) indirect object (= *me*) and a direct object (= the DP following *me*), and thus serves as a *ditransitive* predicate; but in the corresponding (b) examples, the verb has a direct object but no indirect object, and thus serves as a *monotransitive* predicate (i.e. a predicate which has only one object). How are we to analyse monotransitive predicates?

To make our discussion more concrete, consider how we derive a sentence such as (85b) *He sent a card*. If we adopt the **uniform theta assignment hypothesis**, we clearly want to arrive at an analysis of (85b) which maximizes structural symmetry with (85a) *He sent me a card*. So, let's first consider how we might analyse (85a). Given our earlier analysis of ditransitive verbs in §9.4, (85a) will be derived as follows. The verb *sent* merges with its THEME argument *a card* to form the V-bar *sent a card*; this V-bar in turn merges with its RECIPIENT argument *me* to form the VP (86) below:

(86)

The VP in (86) then merges with an abstract agentive light verb whose AGENT subject is *he*, and the verb *sent* adjoins to the light verb as in (87) below:

(87)

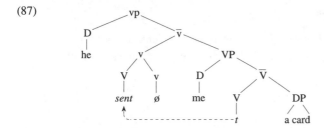

The case of the indirect object *me* is checked by the immediately preceding transitive verb *sent* (or by the agentive light verb ø), and the case of *he* is checked by raising *he* to spec-TP.

Now consider how we derive the corresponding monotransitive structure (85b) *He sent a card.* Since the DP *a card* plays the same thematic role of THEME argument and complement of *sent* as in (85a) *He sent me a card*, let's assume (in conformity with the **uniform theta assignment hypothesis/UTAH**) that it again serves as the complement of *sent*; but since there is no overt RECIPIENT argument in (85b), let's also assume that the VP headed by *sent* simply comprises the verb *sent* and its THEME argument *a card*, as in (88) below:

(88)

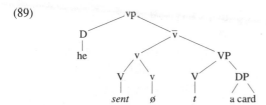

(An alternative possibility would be to assume that there is an implicit RECIPIENT argument in (88), represented by an empty category of some kind.) Since *he* is an AGENT argument in (85b) *He sent a card*, and since we have analysed AGENT arguments as specifiers of an agentive light verb, let's assume that the VP in (88) merges with an agentive light verb whose AGENT subject is *he*, and the verb *sent* adjoins to the light verb as in (89) below:

(89)

The following tree is drawn for (89):

vp
├── D
│   └── he
└── v̄
    ├── v
    │   ├── V — sent
    │   └── v — ø
    └── VP
        ├── V — t
        └── DP — a card

Subsequently, *he* raises to spec-TP to check its nominative case. An analysis such as (89) would provide us with a straightforward account of the syntax of monotransitive predicates with AGENT subjects and THEME complements.

We might extend the account to monotransitive predicates which have no ditransitive counterpart, e.g. verbs like *hit* in:

(90)   She hit him

This would mean that *him* would originate as the complement of a VP headed by *hit*, and *she* as the subject of an agentive light verb to which *hit* adjoins, as in (91) below:

(91)

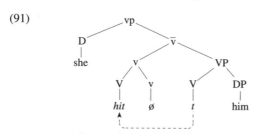

(Subsequently *he* raises to spec-TP for case-checking.) The agentive light verb ø has a performative sense, so that (91) can be paraphrased as 'She performed the act of hitting him.' It may be that the (italicized) verb *do* found in so-called *pseudo-cleft* sentences such as:

(92) (a)   What she *did* was hit him
     (b)   What I should have *done* was hit him

is an overt reflex of the kind of abstract agentive light verb found in (91). (A very different analysis of the complements of monotransitive verbs as VP-specifiers is offered in Stroik 1990 and Bowers 1993.)

9.8   Unergative predicates

As we see from the previous section, typical transitive verbs such as *hit* have an AGENT subject and a THEME object. A rather different kind of predicate are verbs such as those italicized below which have an AGENT subject but which seem to have no complement:

(93) (a) He may *protest*   (b) He *complained*
     (c) They are *lunching*   (d) Let's *party!*
     (e) Don't *fuss!*   (f) Why not *guess?*
     (g) He was *lying*   (h) He *overdosed*
     (i) He was *fishing*   (j) We were *golfing*

Verbs like those italicized in (93) which have AGENT subjects but no direct object complement are referred to in the relevant technical literature as **unergative predicates**. Some of these verbs also allow *to*-phrase PP complements, as we see from structures such as (94) below:

390

(94) (a)   He may *lie* to you

    (b)   He *complained* to the press council

    (c)   He *protested* to the prime minister

In accordance with the **uniform theta assignment hypothesis**, we might assume that the *to*-phrase in structures like (94) has the same syntax as the *to*-phrase in structures like (45) above, and thus serves as the specifier of a VP headed by a lexical verb. However, this assumption poses something of a problem, in that the verbs in (94) have no complement; hence, the inner VP core of a sentence like (94a) would appear to have a structure along the lines of (95) below:

(95)

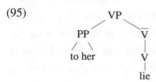

But the problem posed by (95) is that it is not a binary-branching structure, since V-bar is a unary-branching constituent (its sole immediate constituent being the V *lie*). Thus, sentences like (94) pose a further potential problem for our binary-branching framework. How can we overcome this problem?

A clue comes from the fact that unergative verbs like those in (93) generally have verb + noun paraphrases: cf.

(96) (a)   He may *make a protest*   (b)   He *made a complaint*

    (c)   They are *having lunch*   (d)   Let's *have a party*!

    (e)   Don't *make a fuss*!   (f)   Why not *make a guess*?

    (g)   He was *telling lies*   (h)   He *took an overdose*

    (i)   He was *catching fish*   (j)   We were *playing golf*

This might lead us to follow Baker 1988 and Hale and Keyser 1993 in positing that unergative verbs like those in (93) are *denominal* predicates (i.e. verbs derived from nouns) which are formed by incorporation of a noun complement into a verb. This would mean (for example) that the verb *lie* in a sentence such as (94a) *He may lie to you* is an implicitly transitive verb, formed by merging the noun *lie* with an abstract verb Ø (with much the same sense as 'tell') as in (97a) below, and then incorporating the noun into (i.e. adjoining it to) the verb as in (97b), so forming the lexical verb *lie*:

(97) (a)   (b)

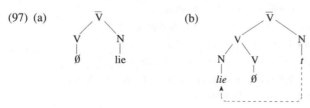

The resulting V-bar in (97b) is then merged with the PP *to you*, forming the VP in (98) below:

(98)

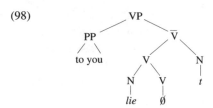

(It goes without saying that if we take the abstract verb ∅ to be a light verb, it will project into v̄ and vp rather than V̄ and VP; however, if categories are sets of features, the labels they carry are little more than labels of convenience, so little hangs on this essentially notational issue.) The VP in (98) in turn merges with an agentive light verb ø whose subject is *he*, and the verb *lie* raises to adjoin to the light verb as in (99) below:

(99)

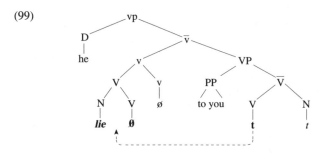

Subsequently, the vp in (99) merges with a T constituent containing the auxiliary *may*, and *he* raises to spec-TP to become the subject of *may*, so deriving (94a) *He may lie to you*. The crucial assumption underlying the analysis in (99) is that verbs like *lie* are implicitly transitive.

9.9 Unaccusative predicates

We now turn to look at the syntax of an interesting class of verbs which have become known in recent work as **unaccusative predicates**. In this connection, consider the syntax of the italicized arguments in unaccusative structures such as the following:

(100) (a) There arose *an unfortunate misunderstanding*
    (b) There came *a cry of anguish* from inside the house
    (c) There appeared *a ghostly face* at the window
    (d) There could have occurred *a diplomatic incident*
    (e) In front of the house, there stands *a statue of General Ghouly*
    (f) There have arisen *several problems*

In some respects, the italicized arguments seem to behave like complements – for example, they occupy the postverbal position canonically associated with complements. However, in other ways, they seem to behave like subjects: for instance, the italicized argument agrees with the verb preceding it, as we see (for example) from the fact that *stands* in (100e) is a singular form which agrees with the singular nominal *a statue of General Ghouly*, so that we require the plural form *stand* if we are unfortunate enough to have *several statues of General Ghouly*. Moreover, the postverbal argument arguably carries the *nominative* case associated with subjects, not the objective/accusative case associated with complements. This is clearer in languages where nouns carry overt case-marking (cf. Vikner 1995), but is also suggested by (somewhat archaic) structures such as:

(101)   There (but for the grace of God) go *I*

(It should be noted, however, that Belletti 1988 suggests that unaccusative subjects carry *partitive* case.)

Only certain types of verb seem to allow postverbal subjects, as we see from the fact that structures such as those in (102) below are ungrammatical:

(102) (a)   *When the British Rail snail arrived five hours late, there *complained* many passengers
     (b)   *In the dentist's surgery, there *groaned* a toothless patient
     (c)   *Every time General Wynott Nukem goes past, there *salutes* a guard at the gate
     (d)   *There *waved* Wee Willie Widget at the window
     (e)   *There has *apologized* Major Muddle for his minor indiscretions

We might refer to verbs like those in (100) which can have postverbal subjects as **unaccusative predicates**. By contrast, verbs with AGENT subjects but no overt object like those in (102) are known as **unergative predicates** (as noted in §9.8).

In addition to the contrast illustrated in (100/102) above, there are a number of other important syntactic differences between unaccusative verbs and other types of verb (e.g. unergative verbs or transitive verbs). For example, Alison Henry (1995) notes that in one dialect of Belfast English (which she refers to as *dialect A*) unaccusative verbs can be used with (italicized) postverbal subjects in imperative structures like (103) below:

(103) (a)   Be going *you* out of the door when he arrives!
     (b)   Leave *you* now!
     (c)   Arrive *you* before 6 o'clock!

By contrast, other (unergative or transitive) verbs don't allow postverbal imperative subjects, so that imperatives such as (104) below are ungrammatical in the relevant dialect:

(104) (a)   *Read *you* that book!

(b)   *Eat *you* up!

(c)   *Always laugh *you* at his jokes!

There are also developmental differences between unaccusative verbs and others. Amy Pierce (1992) observes that although children around two years of age correctly position subjects in front of transitive or unergative verbs, they sometimes position subjects *after* unaccusative verbs like *come*, *go* and *fall* – as we see from examples such as the following (the information in parentheses indicates the names and ages in years;months of the children producing the relevant utterances):

(105) (a)   Go *truck* (Mackie 2;2)

(b)   Allgone *big stick*. Allgone *rock*. Allgone *stone*. Allgone *bee* (Jonathan 1;11–2;0)

(c)   (Here) come *Eve*. All gone *grape juice*. Come *Fraser* (Eve 1;7–1;8)

(d)   Fall *the cradle* (Peter 2;2)

(e)   Going *(re)corder*. Going *it*. Allgone *sun* (Naomi 1;10–1;11)

(f)   Go *Foster* in town (April 2;9)

(g)   Come *Mommy*. Come *airplane*. Here come *tickle*. Come *Cromer*? (Adam 2;3–2;5)

(Young children often seem to use *allgone* as a variant of *gone*.) Why should it be that they position unaccusative arguments postverbally? If we assume that the nature of children's initial grammars is determined by UG principles, it may be that children assume that in consequence of the **uniform theta assignment hypothesis/UTAH**, THEME arguments are projected as complements – hence they are positioned postverbally.

Additional evidence for positing that unaccusative verbs are syntactically distinct from other verbs comes from *auxiliary selection* facts in relation to earlier stages of English when there were two perfective auxiliaries, *have* and *be*, each taking a complement headed by a specific kind of verb. The sentences in (106) below (taken from various plays by Shakespeare) give examples of verbs which could be used with the perfective auxiliary *be* in Early Modern English:

(106) (a)   Mistress Page is *come* with me (Mrs Ford, *Merry Wives of Windsor*, V.v)

(b)   Is the duke *gone*? Then is your cause *gone* too (Duke, *Measure for Measure*, V.i)

(c)   How chance thou art *returned* so soon? (Antipholus, *Comedy of Errors*, I.ii)

(d)   I am *arriv'd* for fruitful Lombardy (Lucentio, *Taming of the Shrew*, I.i)

(e)   You shall hear I am *run* away (Countess, *All's Well That Ends Well*, III.ii)

(f)   The heedful slave is *wandered* forth (Antipholus, *Comedy of Errors*, II.i)

(g)   Don Pedro is *approached* (Messenger, *Much Ado About Nothing*, I.i)

(h)   Did he not say my brother was *fled*? (Don Pedro, *Much Ado About Nothing*, V.i)

(i)   Thou told'st me they were *stol'n* into this wood (Demetrius, *Midsummer Night's Dream*, II.i)

(j)   She is *fallen* into a pit of ink (Leonato, *Much Ado About Nothing*, IV.i)

(k)   And now is he *become* a man (Margaret, *Much Ado About Nothing*, III.iv)

(l)   Why are you *grown* so rude? (Hermia, *Midsummer Night's Dream*, III.ii)

We find a similar contrast with the counterparts of perfective *have/be* in a number of other languages – e.g. Italian and French (cf. Burzio 1986), Sardinian (cf. Jones 1994), German and Dutch (cf. Haegeman 1994) and Danish (cf. Spencer 1991).

A further difference between unaccusative predicates and others relates to the adjectival use of their perfective participle forms. As the examples below indicate, perfective participle (+*n*/+*d*) forms of unaccusative verbs can be used adjectivally (to modify a noun), e.g. in sentences such as:

(107) (a)   The train *arrived* at platform 4 is the 8.28 for London Euston

       (b)   They arrested a business man recently *returned* from Thailand

       (c)   Several facts recently *come* to light point to his guilt

       (d)   A number of objects *gone* from the church were found in his room

       (e)   OJ is something of a *fallen* hero

By contrast, participle forms of transitive or unergative verbs cannot be used in the same way, as we see from the ungrammaticality of examples like (108) below:

(108) (a)   *The man *committed* suicide was a neighbour of mine

       (b)   *The thief *stolen* the jewels was never captured

       (c)   *The man *overdosed* was Joe Doe

       (d)   *The *yawned* student eventually fell asleep in class

In this respect, unaccusative verbs resemble passive participles, which can also be used adjectivally (cf. *a **changed** man, a **battered** wife, a woman **arrested** for shoplifting*, etc.).

We thus have a considerable body of empirical evidence that unaccusative subjects behave like complements in certain respects. (Supporting evidence is available from other languages: cf. e.g. Burzio 1986 on the syntax of *ne* 'of it/of them' in Italian, and Contreras 1986 on bare nominals in Spanish.) We might therefore suppose (following Burzio 1986) that unaccusative structures with postverbal arguments involve leaving the relevant argument *in situ* in VP-complement position. Thus, we might posit that in unaccusative expletive structures such as (100) above, in Belfast English unaccusative imperatives such as (103) above and in Child English unaccusative declaratives/

interrogatives such as (105) above, the italicized argument remains *in situ* in VP-complement position. On this view, a sentence such as (100f) *There have arisen several problems* would have a derivation along the lines of (109) below (in which *several problems* is analysed as the complement of *arisen*):

(109)

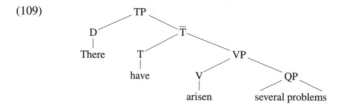

However, analysing unaccusative subjects as underlying complements poses a number of problems. One of these concerns how to handle the agreement between *have* and *several problems* in (109). If postverbal unaccusative arguments are *in situ* complements (and so *several problems* in (109) is in VP-complement position), how do we account for agreement between the auxiliary *have* and the supposed complement *several problems* in (109), given that English is not a language in which verbs agree with complements?

A second problem with the complement analysis concerns how to deal with two-place unaccusative predicates – i.e. unaccusative verbs which take two arguments. In this connection, consider unaccusative imperative structures such as the following in (dialect A of) Belfast English:

(110) (a) Go you to school!
    (b) Run youse to the telephone!
    (c) Walk you into the garden!

If (as suggested in Henry 1995) postverbal arguments of unaccusative predicates are *in situ* complements, this means that each of the verbs in (110) must have two complements. But if we make the traditional assumption that complements are sisters of a head, this means (for example) that if both *you* and *to school* are complements of the verb *go* in (110a), they must be sisters of *go*, and hence the VP headed by *go* must have the (simplified) structure (111) below:

(111)

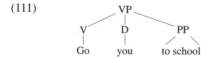

However, a ternary-branching structure such as (111) is obviously incompatible with a framework such as that used here which assumes that the merger operation by which phrases are formed is inherently binary.

The problem posed by unaccusative verbs with two 'complements' is essentially the same as that posed by three-place predicates which take two complements. In our earlier discussion of three-place predicates, we suggested that AGENT arguments originate in spec-vp (as the subject of an agentive light verb), but that other arguments originate within VP. It is clear that unaccusative verbs don't take AGENT arguments, as we can see from the fact (noted by Ritter and Rosen 1993, pp. 526–7) that they cannot be used as the complement of causative *have*: cf. their examples:

(112) (a) *Ralph had Sheila die

  (b) *Ralph had his goldfish die

  (c) *Ralph had Sheila fall down

  (d) *Ralph had the plants grow

  (e) *The warm sunshine had the plants grow

  (f) *Ralph had the walls crack

  (g) *Ralph had his student go crazy

If we suppose that causative *have* requires a complement whose subject has volitional control (e.g. is an AGENT), then a natural conclusion to draw is that unaccusative verbs have no AGENT argument.

So, if unaccusative arguments are nonagentive, and nonagentive arguments originate in VP, the obvious inference to draw is that the two arguments of two-place unaccusative predicates must both originate within VP, one as the complement of VP, the other as the specifier of VP. Given this assumption, the inner VP *core* of a Belfast English unaccusative imperative structure such as (110a) *Go you to school!* will not be (111) above, but rather (113) below:

(113)

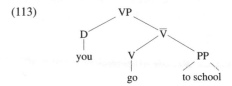

But the obvious problem posed by a structure like (113) is that it provides us with no way of accounting for the fact that unaccusative subjects surface postverbally in structures such as (110) above. How can we overcome this problem?

One suggestion might be the following. Let us suppose that unaccusative VPs like (113) (i.e. VPs headed by an unaccusative verb) are embedded as the complement of an outer vp shell headed by a strong v, and that the unaccusative verb raises to v in the manner indicated by the arrow in (114) below:

(114)

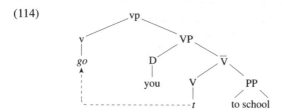

(It may be that *v* is strong because it contains an affixal eventive light verb – i.e. a light verb denoting an event – which has much the same sense as *happen*.) If we assume (as Alison Henry argues) that subjects remain *in situ* in imperatives in dialect A of Belfast English, the postverbal position of unaccusative subjects in sentences such as (110) can be accounted for straightforwardly. And the *vp shell* analysis is consistent with the assumption that the merger operation by which phrases are formed is intrinsically binary.

Moreover, the *vp shell* analysis in (114) enables us to provide an interesting account of the position of VP adverbs like *quickly* in unaccusative imperatives (in dialect A of Belfast English) such as:

(115)   Go you quickly to school!

If we suppose that VP adverbs like *quickly* are adjuncts which merge with an intermediate verbal projection (i.e. a single-bar projection comprising a verb and its complement), we can say that *quickly* in (115) is adjoined to the V-bar *go to school* in (113). What remains to be accounted for (in relation to the syntax of imperative subjects in dialect A of Belfast English) is the fact that subjects of transitive and unergative verbs occur in *preverbal* (not postverbal) position: cf.

(116) (a)   You read that book!   (b)   *Read you that book!
       (b)   You protest!   (b)   *Protest you!

Why should this be? If we assume (as in §9.7) that monotransitive verbs with AGENT subjects originate as the head of a VP complement of an agentive light verb ø, an imperative such as (116a) will contain a vp derived as in (117) below:

(117)

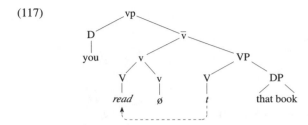

The AGENT subject *you* will originate in spec-vp, as the subject of the agentive light verb ø. Even after the verb *read* adjoins to the light verb ø, the subject *you* will still be preverbal.

Given these assumptions, we could then say that the difference between unaccusative subjects and transitive/unergative subjects is that unaccusative subjects originate in spec-VP (as the subject of a lexical verb), whereas transitive/unergative subjects originate in spec-vp (as the subject of an agentive light verb). If we assume that unaccusative structures contain an outer vp shell headed by a strong v (e.g. an eventive light verb) and an inner VP core headed by a lexical verb, and that the lexical verb raises from V to v, the postverbal position of unaccusative subjects can be accounted for by positing that the subject remains *in situ* in such structures.

The light verb analysis sketched here also offers us a way of accounting for the fact that in Early Modern English, the perfective auxiliary used with unaccusative verbs was *be* (as we see from the examples in (106) above), whereas that used with transitive and unergative verbs was *have*. We could account for this by positing that the perfective auxiliary *have* in EME selected a vp complement headed by an agentive light verb with a thematic subject (much as causative *have* does in present-day English: cf. our discussion of (112) above), whereas the perfective auxiliary *be* in EME selected a complement headed by an eventive light verb which lacked a thematic subject. This distinction has been lost in Modern English, with perfective *have* being used with either type of vp complement (though sentences such as *They are gone* are a last vestige of the earlier use of *be* as a perfective auxiliary).

The analysis of unaccusative verbs outlined here also enables us to account for expletive unaccusative structures such as the following:

(118)   There came a cry of anguish from inside the house

We might suppose that *a cry of anguish* in (118) is in spec-VP, that *came* originates in V and raises to v, and that *there* originates in the nonthematic spec-vp position and from there raises to spec-TP, as in (119) below:

VP shells

(119)

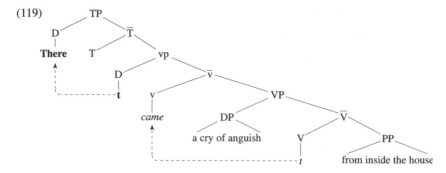

Such a derivation would satisfy Rothstein's (1995) **predication principle** (which requires that syntactic predicates like v-bar, V-bar and T-bar should have subjects) by virtue of the fact that VP has the subject *a cry of anguish*, vp has a trace of *there* as its subject and TP has *there* as its subject. We might suppose that the case/agreement properties of the subject *a cry of anguish* and the agreement properties of the verb *came* are attracted to T, and there checked (so that *came* is singular because its subject is singular). This would allow us to account for the fact that the unaccusative verb agrees with its postverbal argument, as we see from sentences such as:

(120) (a)   Every so often, there *comes/*come* a cry of anguish from inside the house
       (b)   Every so often, there *come/*comes* cries of anguish from inside the house

For alternative analyses of expletive structures, see Authier 1991, Lasnik 1992, 1995, Chomsky 1995b, Groat 1995, Rothstein 1995 and Vikner 1995.

Alongside expletive unaccusative structures such as (118) we also find nonexpletive structures such as:

(121)   A cry of anguish came from inside the house

In this type of sentence, the need for T to have a subject is satisfied not by the use of expletive *there* but rather by raising the subject *a cry of anguish* from spec-VP through spec-vp into spec-TP, as in (122) below:

(122)

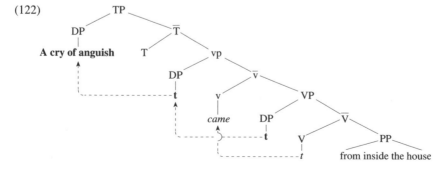

Thus, the subject *a cry of anguish* remains *in situ* in expletive structures such as (119), but raises to spec-TP in structures such as (122).

9.10 Summary

We began this chapter in §9.2 by looking at the syntax of ergative verbs like *roll* which can be used both transitively and intransitively. We suggested that in intransitive structures like *The ball rolled down the hill*, the THEME argument of *roll* (= the DP *the ball*) originates as the subject/specifier of a VP headed by the lexical verb *roll*, and then raises up into spec-TP for case-checking purposes. We noted that in transitive structures such as *We rolled the ball down the hill*, the verb *roll* appears to have two complements (namely the DP *the ball* and the PP *down the hill*), and that this poses problems for the assumption that syntactic structures are binary-branching. We suggested that these problems could be solved if we assume that *the ball* (in transitive structures like *We rolled the ball down the hill*) originates as the subject/specifier of a VP headed by the lexical verb *roll*, and that this VP serves as the complement of a null causative light verb ∅ which has an AGENT subject (*we*), with the verb *roll* raising to adjoin to the light verb (deriving a structure paraphraseable as 'We made + roll the ball down the hill'). We noted that such an analysis would be compatible with Baker's **uniformity of theta assignment hypothesis**, since both in transitive structures like *We rolled the ball down the hill* and in intransitive structures like *The ball rolled down the hill* the THEME argument (*the ball*) would originate as the subject and specifier of a VP headed by the lexical verb *roll*. In §9.3 we argued that the light-verb analysis would also enable us to provide a straightforward account of the dual position occupied by the adverb *gently* in sentences such as *We gently rolled the ball down the hill* and *We rolled the ball gently down the hill*, with *gently* modifying either a V-bar headed by a lexical verb, or a v-bar headed by a light verb. We also suggested that a light-verb analysis would provide a principled account of the dual position occupied by the prepositional particle *down* in sentences such as *They closed the store down* and *They closed down the store*, if we assumed that either the simple verb *closed* or the complex verb *closed down* could adjoin to an abstract causative light verb. In §9.4 we looked at the syntax of ditransitive verbs like *get* as they are used in double-object constructions such as *They will get the teacher a present*. We suggested that *the teacher* originates as the subject of a VP headed by *get* (precisely as in *The teacher got a present*), and that the resulting VP serves as the complement of a causative light verb with an AGENT subject (*they*), with the verb *get* raising to adjoin to the causative light verb, and the subject (*we*) of the light verb raising to become the subject of *will* (so deriving *They will get the teacher a present*). We then examined the syntax of resultative structures such as *The acid turned the litmus paper red*. We argued that the DP *the litmus paper* originates as the subject of the V-bar *turned red*, and that the resulting VP *the litmus paper turned red* merges with a causative light verb ∅ (whose subject is *the acid*), with the verb *turned* adjoining to the causative light verb, so deriving a structure which can be para-phrased as 'The acid made + turn the litmus paper red.' (The DP *the acid* subsequently raises to spec-TP.) In §9.5 we discussed the syntax of three-place predicates which have a clausal complement. We argued that in a sentence like *He had remarked to her that Senator Scumme-Bagge was a fraud* the *that*-clause serves as the complement of a VP headed by the lexical verb *remarked*, and the *to*-phrase serves as its specifier; we hypothesized that the VP serves as the complement of an agentive light verb whose subject is *he*, and that the verb *remarked* adjoins to this light verb thereby forming a structure which can loosely be paraphrased as 'He made + remark to her that Senator Scumme-Bagge was a fraud.' Subsequently, the pronoun *he* raises to spec-TP to become the subject of the auxiliary *had*, so deriving *He had remarked to her that Senator Scumme-Bagge was a fraud*. We suggested a similar derivation for sentences such as *You must satisfy the jury that you are innocent*, in which the *that*-clause serves as the complement of a VP headed by the lexical verb *satisfy*, and the DP *the jury* serves as its specifier, with the subject *you* originating as the subject of an agentive light verb (to which *satisfy* adjoins), and then being raised up to become the subject of the auxiliary *must*. In §9.6 we examined the syntax of object-control structures such as *What decided you to take syntax?*, noting that under the traditional analysis the verb *decided* has two complements, the object pronoun *you* and the infinitive complement *to take syntax*. We proposed an alternative analysis under which *you* originates as the subject of *decided to take syntax*, and the resulting VP *you decided to take syntax* serves as the complement of a causative light verb ø whose subject is *what*, with *decided* adjoining to the light verb (and *what* raising to spec-TP) to derive *What decided you to take syntax?* We went on to examine differences between object-control predicates like *persuade* and ECM (exceptional case-marking) predicates like *expect*, noting that they differ in the type of *that*-clause paraphrase they allow (*He persuaded me to take syntax* is paraphraseable as 'He persuaded me that I should take syntax', whereas *He expected me to take syntax* is paraphraseable as 'He expected that I would take syntax'), in whether they constrain the choice of DP following *persuade/expect* (cf. *He expected/*persuaded the exam to be difficult*), and in whether they permit an expletive + infinitive structure (cf. *He expected/*persuaded there to be someone wait-ing for him*). In §9.7 we outlined an analysis of monotransitive verbs (like *sent* in *He sent a card*) in which the THEME argument (*a card*) originates as the complement of a VP headed by a lexical verb (*sent*), and the subject (*he*) originates as the AGENT argu-ment (and specifier) of a vp headed by an agentive light verb. In §9.8 we suggested that unergative verbs like *lie* are derived via incorporation of a noun into an abstract verb. In §9.9 we turned to look at a special class of intransitive verbs called *unaccusative* predicates (like *come, go, occur, arise, appear*, etc.). We noted that the subjects of such verbs behave in certain respects like complements: for example, they are positioned after the verb in expletive structures (cf. *There arose **an unfortunate misunderstand-***

ing), and in imperative structures in dialect A of Belfast English (cf. *Leave **you** now!*). We outlined the traditional analysis of unaccusative structures, under which the 'subject' originates as the complement of the unaccusative verb, and remains *in situ* in expletive structures such as *There will come **a time when you are sorry***. We noted, however, that such an analysis faces obvious problems in relation to unaccusative predicates which have two arguments (e.g. *go* in *John went to school*), since the complement analysis would require us to suppose that such verbs have two complements (i.e. *John* and *to school* in the case of *John went to school*) – an assumption which is incompatible with our hypothesis that constituent structure is binary-branching. We therefore outlined an alternative light-verb analysis of unaccusative predicates under which unaccusative verbs and their arguments originate within a VP which is embedded as the complement of an eventive light verb (with much the same sense as 'happen'), and the unaccusative verb raises up to adjoin to the light verb (thereby moving into a position where it precedes the subject in spec-VP). We noted that such an analysis would provide an account of the fact that unaccusative verbs are positioned in front of both their arguments e.g. in Belfast English imperatives such as *Go you to school!* (if we assume, following Alison Henry, that imperative subjects remain *in situ* in the relevant variety of Belfast English).

Workbook section
Exercise I (§§9.2–9.5)
Discuss the derivation of the following sentences, saying why each derivation crashes or converges:

1a It kept warm
  b She kept it warm
2a I'm going crazy
  b You're driving me crazy
3a He deliberately spilled the milk over the floor
  b *The milk deliberately spilled over the floor
4a He carefully reversed the car into the garage
  b He reversed the car carefully into the garage
5a He drives the car well round bends
  b *He well drives the car round bends
6a The building blew up
  b They blew the building up
7a Taxes went up
  b They put up taxes
8a He turned the key slowly round
  b He slowly turned round the key

9a   What did she give you?
  b   He may ask you what she gave you
10a   He informed her that the rent would increase
  b   He explained to her that he would increase the rent

Model answer for 1

Sentence 1a might be derived as follows. The verb *kept* merges with the adjective *warm* to form the V-bar *kept warm*; this in turn merges with the pronoun *it* to form the VP (i) below:

(i)

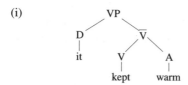

The resulting VP merges with a tense affix T to form a T-bar; the subject *it* then raises to spec-TP to check its nominative case, as in (ii) below:

(ii)

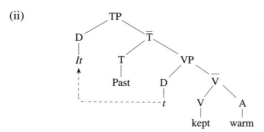

The subject *it* carries nominative case by virtue of being the subject of a finite T constituent.

Sentence 1b has the following derivation. As before, the verb *kept* merges with the adjective *warm* to form the V-bar *kept warm*; the subject *it* merges with V-bar to form the VP (i) above. The resulting VP then merges with a causative light verb ø with an AGENT subject (*she*), and the verb *kept* adjoins to the light verb, as in (iii) below:

(iii)

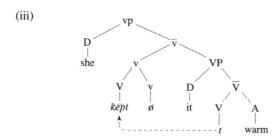

The objective case of *it* is checked by the immediately preceding transitive light verb ø (or by the verb *kept*, which is transitive in this use). The vp in (iii) then merges with an abstract tense constituent to form a T-bar, and the pronoun *she* raises to spec-TP to check its nominative case, as in (iv) below:

(iv)

An analysis such as that outlined here is consistent with the **uniform theta assignment hypothesis** in that in both 1a and 1b the THEME argument of *kept* (= *it*) originates as the subject/specifier of a VP headed by the lexical verb *kept*.

Exercise II (§9.6)

Discuss the syntax of the following infinitive structures:

1   She wanted you to read it
2   They can't force you to sign a confession
3   They had reported him to be absent
4   He may ask you to apologize to her
5   He would like me to help him
6   She reminded me to lock the door
7   They consider him to have misled them
8   They may require you to take a test
9   We never intended anyone to get hurt
10   Nobody can compel you to say anything
11   We'd prefer you to stay at home
12   You aren't obliged to say anything
13   He was believed to have stolen them
14   He was forbidden to say anything
15   Gentlemen are requested to wear ties
16   Can you help me unload the car?
17   You should let him pay for it
18   I've never known anyone fail syntax

19 Nothing will make me change my mind

20 We had ten students refuse to take the exam

Model answer for 1

The issue which arises in relation to sentence 1 is whether *want* is an ECM predicate or a control predicate. There are several reasons for preferring an ECM analysis of *want*. For one thing, 1 can be paraphrased (in some varieties of English) by a *that*-clause structure in which the pronoun *you* is clearly the subject of the *that*-clause: cf.

(i)   %She wanted that *you* should read it

Moreover, if we have an adverb like *desperately* following *want*, we can use the complementizer *for*, and the pronoun *you* follows *for* (and thus is clearly the subject of the [bracketed] complement clause introduced by *for*, not the object of *want*): cf.

(ii)   She wanted desperately [for *you* to read it]

Moreover, *want* appears to impose no restrictions on the choice of objective expression following it, as we see from sentences such as:

(iii) (a)   She wanted *her uncle* to shave his beard off

(b)   She wanted *her goldfish* to swim faster

(c)   She wanted *her pet amoeba* to reproduce

(d)   She wanted *the kettle* to boil

(e)   She wanted *her theory* to be foolproof

The postverbal expression can even be an idiomatic subject: cf:

(iv) (a)   She wanted *the fur* to fly

(b)   She didn't want *the cat* to get his tongue

or indeed expletive *there*: cf.

(v)   Everyone wants *there* to be peace in Ruritania

Since control verbs impose restrictions on the choice of postverbal expression following them (but ECM verbs do not), it seems likely that *want* is an ECM verb.

If this is so, sentence 1 will be derived as follows (if we ignore the later discussion of monotransitive verbs in §9.7). The pronoun *you* originates as the subject of *read it*, as in (vi) below:

(vi)

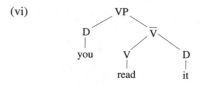

The VP in (vi) merges with a T constituent containing infinitival *to* (perhaps adjoined to an abstract tense affix, though this is a point of detail which we overlook here); the pronoun *you* raises to spec-TP as in (vii) below:

(vii)

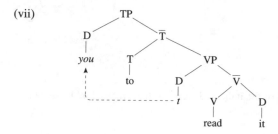

The TP in (vii) is merged with the verb *wanted*, forming a V-bar which is further projected into the VP in (viii) below by merger with the subject *she*:

(viii)

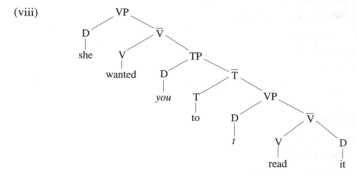

The objective case carried by *you* is checked by the immediately preceding transitive verb *wanted*. Subsequently, the VP in (viii) merges with an abstract T constituent, and the subject *she* raises to spec-TP to check its nominative case, as in (ix) below:

VP shells

(ix)

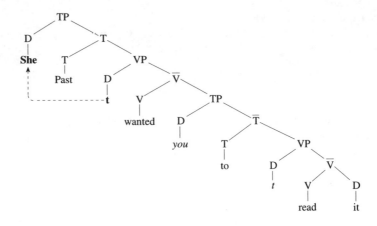

Exercise III (§§9.7–9.8)

Discuss the syntax of the italicized verbs as they are used in the sentences below:

1 It would *surprise* me
2 He *sold* the television
3 She *received* a letter
4 The rhino may *charge*
5 He wants her to *slave* for him
6 She may *fear* him
7 They could *fine* him
8 He should *shave*
9 He might *appeal* to the Supreme Court
10 They *disgust* me
11 It could *snow*
12 You can't *fool* me
13 She should *kick* him
14 He can *cash* the cheque
15 They should *fire* him
16 They may *jail* him
17 It will *anger* him
18 The government should *tax* the opposition
19 I *pity* you
20 He could *poison* the wine

Note that there are a number of different predicate types represented above; different analyses will be appropriate for different types of predicate. Which examples are the most problematic, and why?

Model answer for 1

As noted in relation to (73) in the main text, the adverb *personally* can be associated with an EXPERIENCER (but not e.g. an AGENT) subject. In the light of this observation, it is interesting to note that *me* in 1 can be modified by *personally*: cf.

(i)   Personally, it would surprise me

If *personally* modifies EXPERIENCER subjects, this suggests that *me* must originate as the subject of the verb *surprise*. But if subjects are specifiers which merge with a V-bar constituent, it follows that the verb *surprise* must be a V-bar constituent with a 'hidden' complement of some kind. How can this be? One possibility is that the verb *surprise* is derived by incorporating the noun *surprise* into an abstract experiential verb ∅, and so in effect has much the same meaning as 'experience a feeling of surprise'. If this is so, then 1 has a derivation which is similar in certain respects to that of *It would make me feel surprise*.

If we follow this line of reasoning, 1 will be derived as follows. The experiential verb ∅ is merged with the noun *surprise* to form the V-bar (ii) below (which has much the same meaning as 'experience surprise'):

(ii)

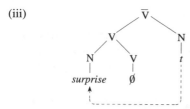

(Of course, if we treat ∅ as a light verb, it will have the status of v rather than V, and will project into v̄ rather than V̄; however, since category labels are abbreviations for sets of grammatical features, little of any consequence hangs on the category labels we use here.) The noun *surprise* is then incorporated into (i.e. adjoined to the left of) the affixal verb ∅ as in (iii) below:

(iii)

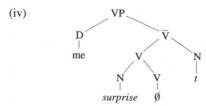

The resulting V-bar is then merged with the subject *me* as in (iv) below, and the subject is indirectly assigned the θ-role of EXPERIENCER by the experiential verb ∅:

(iv)

The VP thereby formed is then merged with a causative light verb ø (whose subject is *it*), and the (complex) verb *surprise+ø* is then adjoined to the higher (causative) light verb as in (v) below:

(v)

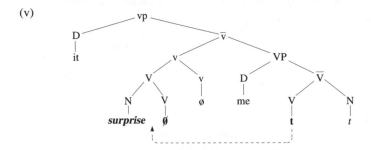

The vp in (v) is then merged with a T constituent containing the auxiliary *would* (and a past-tense affix, which we ignore below), and the subject *it* raises to spec-TP to check its nominative case, as in (vi) below:

(vi)

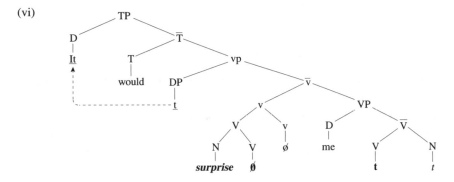

The nominative case carried by the pronoun *it* is checked by the tense morpheme T, and the objective case carried by *me* is checked by the transitive agentive light verb ø. (Note that an issue not addressed above is how we account for the fact that the verb *surprise* as used in 1 is an infinitive form.)

Exercise IV (§9.8)

Discuss the syntax of the italicized verbs as they are used in the sentences below:

1. It can *blind* you
2. The sky will *clear*
3. Alcohol can *dull* the brain
4. He can *save* her from destitution

5 You should *empty* the bottle of its contents

6 He may *absent* himself from the class

7 She could *faint*

8 The gap will *narrow*

9 You could *lower* the ceiling

10 The cheese will *mature*

Model answer for 1

In §9.8 in the text, we discussed the syntax of denominal verbs (i.e. verbs derived from nouns), but did not discuss the syntax of deadjectival verbs (i.e. verbs derived from adjectives). However, if denominal verbs are formed by incorporating a noun complement into a verb, we might suppose that deadjectival verbs are similarly formed by incorporating an adjective complement into a verb. Since the expression *blind you* can be paraphrased as 'make you become blind', we might suggest that 1 is derived as follows.

The adjective *blind* originates as the complement of an abstract inchoative verb Ø which has much the same sense as *become*, as in (i) below. (An inchoative verb is one which indicates the beginning of a state or action: hence *become* is an inchoative verb since it is paraphraseable as 'begin to be'.)

(i)

(Of course, if we analyse Ø as an inchoative light verb, it will carry the label v rather than V, and project into v-bar rather than V-bar.) The adjective *blind* then incorporates into (i.e. adjoins to) the abstract inchoative verb Ø, and *you* merges with $\overline{V}$ as in (ii) below:

(ii)

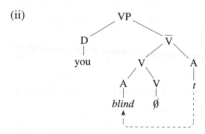

(a structure paraphraseable as 'you become blind'). The VP in (ii) is then merged with a causative light verb ø whose subject *it* has the thematic role of CAUSER; the deadjectival verb *blind*+Ø then adjoins to the causative light-verb, as in (iii) below:

411

VP shells

(iii)

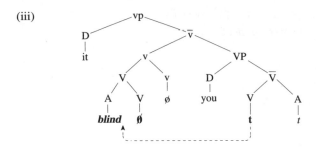

(where the verb *blind* is paraphraseable as 'make become blind'). The vp in (iii) then merges with a T constituent containing the modal auxiliary *can*, and the subject *it* raises to spec-TP to become the subject of *can*, as in (iv) below:

(iv)

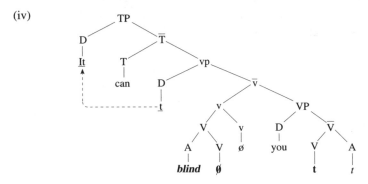

The nominative case carried by *it* is checked by T, and the objective case carried by *you* is checked by the immediately preceding transitive causative light verb ø.

Exercise V (§9.8)
Discuss the syntax of verbs formed with the suffixes listed below:

+*ize* (e.g. apologize, colonize, commercialize, computerize, criminal-
ize, fertilize, glamorize, legalize, liquidize, magnetize, moisturize,
pressurize, randomize, vaporize)

+*ify* (e.g. beautify, clarify, classify, codify, electrify, glorify, horrify,
modify, mummify, mystify, nullify, purify, solidify, terrify)

+*en* (e.g. broaden, frighten, harden, hasten, hearten, heighten, lengthen,
liken, loosen, sicken, strengthen, thicken)

Which verbs are problematic to derive and why?

Model answer for apologize
The verb *apologize* can be used with a *to*-phrase complement, as in (i)
below:

412

(i)   He should apologize to her

It cannot, however, be used with a direct object DP, as we see from the ungrammaticality of (ii) below:

(ii)   *He should apologize *many things* to her

One reason why *apologize* cannot be used with a direct object DP may be that it is itself a denominal verb, formed by incorporating the noun object *apology* into the suffixal verb *+ize*. If we assume (as in (45) in the main text) that the *to*-phrase in (i) is the specifier of the VP headed by *apologize*, sentence (i) will be derived as follows.

The suffixal verb *+ize* is merged with the noun *apology*, forming the V-bar in (iii) below (paraphraseable as 'offer an apology')

(iii)

```
        V
      /   \
    V       N
    |       |
  +ize    apology
```

The noun *apology* incorporates into (i.e. is adjoined to) the suffixal verb *+ize*, and in so doing loses its final *y*, as in (iv) below:

(iv)

```
              V
           /     \
        V          N
      /   \        |
    N      V       t
    |      |
  apolog  ize
```

The PP *to her* merges with the resulting V-bar, as in (v) below:

(v)

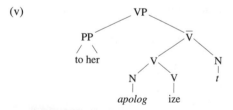

The VP in (v) merges with an agentive light verb ø, whose subject is *he*; the verb *apologize* raises to adjoin to this light verb as in (vi) below:

(vi)

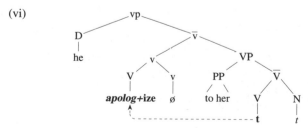

The vp in (vi) then merges with a T constituent containing the modal auxiliary *should*, and *he* raises to spec-TP to become the subject of *should* as in (vii) below:

(vii)

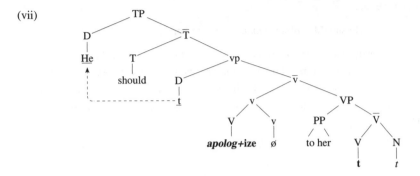

(To simplify exposition, we ignore the possibility that T also contains an abstract past-tense morpheme; we also leave aside the question of how we account for the fact that *apologize* as used here is an infinitive form.)

> *Model answer for* horrify
> One use of the verb *horrify* is illustrated in (viii) below:

(viii)   It will horrify you

The expression *horrify you* is paraphraseable as 'make you feel horror', so that *horrify* can plausibly be taken to be a denominal verb. One way of deriving (viii) is to suppose that the suffixal verb *+ify* is used as a causative experiential verb (i.e. a verb paraphraseable as 'cause to experience') which merges with the noun *horror* to form the V-bar (ix) below:

(ix)

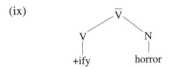

The noun *horror* then incorporates into the verb *+ify* (in the process losing its final *or* segments), as in (x) below:

(x)

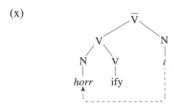

The V-bar in (xi) merges with its EXPERIENCER subject *you*, so forming the VP (xi) below:

(xi)

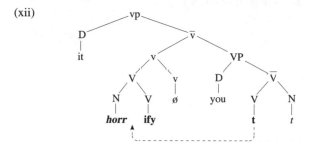

This VP in turn merges with an abstract causative light verb ø whose subject *it* has the thematic role of CAUSER, and the verb *horrify* raises to adjoin to the light verb as in (xii) below:

(xii)

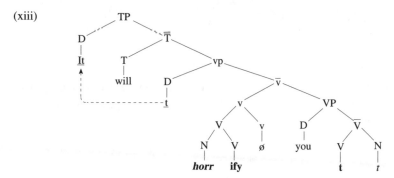

Finally, the vp in (xii) merges with a T constituent containing the modal auxiliary *will*, and the pronoun *it* raises to spec-TP to become the subject of *will* as in (xiii) below:

(xiii)

The nominative case carried by *it* is checked by the T constituent containing (an abstract tense morpheme and) the auxiliary *will*, and the objective case carried by *you* is checked by the transitive light verb ø.

>   *Model answer for* thicken
>   One use of the verb *thicken* is illustrated in (xiv) below:

(xiv)   The soup may thicken

415

VP shells

Since *thicken* (in this use) is paraphraseable as 'become thick', we might suppose that
+*en* functions as a suffixal *inchoative* verb (i.e. a verb which indicates the beginning of
a state or action) paraphraseable as 'begin to be', 'come to be' or 'become'. This would
mean that (xiv) is derived as follows. The inchoative verb +*en* originates in the head V
position of VP, and merges with the adjective *thick* as in (xv) below:

(xv)

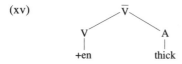

The resulting V-bar is paraphraseable as 'become thick'. The adjective *thick* then
adjoins to the affixal verb +*en*, as in (xvi) below:

(xvi)

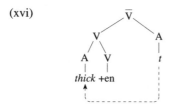

The V-bar in (xvi) merges with the DP *the soup*, so forming the VP (xvii) below:

(xvii)

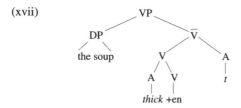

The resulting VP then merges with a T constituent containing *will* (and an abstract
tense affix, which we ignore below); the DP *the soup* raises to spec-TP to become the
subject of *may* as in (xviii) below:

(xviii)

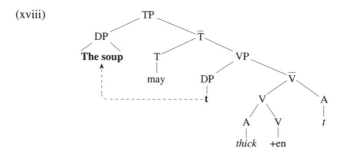

The resulting structure is paraphraseable as 'The soup may become thick.'

416

One salient feature of the three model answers sketched out above is the assumption that the suffixes *+ize*, *+ify* and *+en* originate as independent items from the nouns or adjectives which incorporate into them (e.g. *horrify* is treated as composed of two separate words, a noun *horr(or)* and a verb *+ify*). An alternative possibility would be to treat a word like *horrify* as a unitary lexical item (i.e. as a single word) which originates as an A, then raises to adjoin to a null experiential verb and subsequently raises to adjoin to a null causative light verb. The other two model answers presented here could be revised along similar lines.

Exercise VI (§9.9)

Discuss the derivation of the following sentences, saying why each derivation crashes or converges. (The sentences in 3 are from dialect A of Belfast English; those in 4 were produced by two-year-old children; those in 5 are from plays by Shakespeare.)

1a Down came the rain
 b The rain came down
2a There arose several problems
 b *There complained several passengers
3a Run youse to the telephone! (dialect A of Belfast English)
 b *Protest you! (dialect A of Belfast English)
4a Go Foster in town (April 2;9)
 b Here come tickle (Adam 2;4)
5a My master is grown quarrelsome (Grumio, *Taming of the Shrew*, I.ii)
 b That letter hath she delivered (Speed, *Two Gentlemen of Verona*, II.i)

Model answer for 1a

The verb *come* behaves like a typical unaccusative predicate in numerous respects. For one thing, it can occur in expletive structures such as:

(i)   There will come a day when you are sorry

In addition, its perfective participle form can be used adjectivally, as in:

(ii)   Several facts recently come to light point to his guilt

Moreover, it allows a postverbal subject in dialect A of Belfast English, e.g. in sentences such as:

(iii)   Come you here!

And in Shakespearean English, we find it used with the auxiliary *be*: cf.

(iv)   The time is come even now (Duke, *Measure for Measure*, IV.i)

Given the status of *come* as an unaccusative predicate, 1a can be derived as follows. The verb *came* merges with the prepositional particle *down* to form the V-bar *came down*; this in turn merges with the DP *the rain* to form the VP (v) below:

(v)

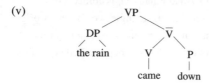

The VP in (v) then merges with an abstract eventive light verb ∅; the verb *came* raises to adjoin to the light verb, as in (vi) below:

(vi)

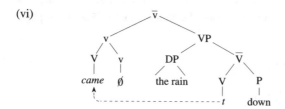

The prepositional particle *down* then moves into the vacant (nonthematic) spec-vp position (perhaps to satisfy a requirement that vp have a specifier) as in (vii) below:

(vii)

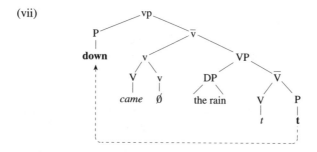

Subsequently, the vp in (vii) merges with an abstract tense morpheme, and the prepositional particle *down* moves from spec-vp into spec-TP as in (viii) below, thereby satisfying the requirement for spec-TP to be filled:

(viii)

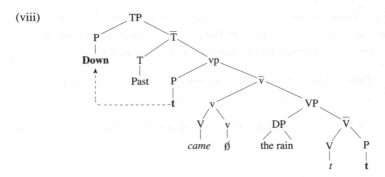

Although the prepositional particle *down* occupies spec-TP, it is clearly not the subject of the overall clause. For one thing, it does not permit *subject–auxiliary inversion*, as we see from the ungrammaticality of (ix) below:

(ix)   *Did down come the rain?

Moreover, if we replace the agreementless past-tense form *came* by an agreement-inflected present-tense form, we find that it is the DP *the rain* which agrees with the verb (and which must therefore be the subject of the verb): cf.

(x) (a)   Down *comes/*come* the rain
     (b)   Down *come/*comes* the rains

From this, we can conclude that there is no specific requirement for TP (or vp) to have a *subject*, but merely a requirement for TP (and vp) to have a *specifier*. The **shortest movement principle** will determine that the constituent which moves into spec-TP is that which occupies spec-vp. With agentive verbs, spec-vp is always occupied by a the-matic (AGENT) subject, and so it is this subject which moves into spec-TP; but with unaccusative verbs, spec-vp is a θ-bar position and so can be filled by a nonthematic element like expletive *there* or (as in this case) a preposed prepositional particle.

Needless to say, there are numerous questions of detail which remain to be worked out in relation to the derivation in (viii). One relates to the case carried by the DP subject *the rain*: does it carry partitive case (checked by the immediately preceding unaccusative verb *came*), or nominative case (checked by attraction of the relevant case-feature to T)?

Another relates to whether the preposed prepositional particle *down* actually ends up in spec-TP (as claimed above), or in spec-CP. The fact that sentence 1a can itself serve as the complement of a complementizer like *that*, e.g. in a sentence such as:

(xi)   He was upset to find *that* [down came the rain], washing away the seeds he had just planted

makes it less likely that *down* occupies spec-CP, and more likely that it occupies spec-TP.

Exercise VII (§§9.2–9.9)

Melissa Bowerman (1995) reports the following errors produced by children in the way they use verbs (the initials represent the children's names, and the figures indicate their ages in years;months; informal glosses in adult English are provided where appropriate):

1   She came it over there (C 3;4 = 'took it over there')
2   Singing goes it faster (C 5;0 = 'makes it go faster')
3   Let's stay this open (C 2;4 = 'keep this open')
4   Salt clings it together (C 12;3 = 'makes it cling')
5   Will you climb me up there? (E 3;3 = 'help me climb')
6   That will water my eyes (E 3;9 = 'make my eyes water')
7   Can I glow him? (E 4;3 = 'make him glow')
8   I meant to be it like this (C 5:5 = 'have it be')
9   I want to watch you this book (C 4;3 = 'show you')
10   Bert knocked down (C 2;11 = 'fell down')
11   It blowed up (C 2;3 = 'The beach ball inflated')
12   It stirs around (E 3:11 = 'The ice tea swirls around')

Discuss the derivation of the relevant sentences, and the nature of the errors made by the children.

Model answer for 1

One way in which we might analyse 1 is as follows. Let us suppose that the verb *came* initially projects into the VP (i) below (with *it* as the subject of *came*, and *over there* as its complement):

(i)

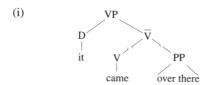

Let's further assume that the VP in (i) is merged with a strong causative light verb ø (whose AGENT subject is *she*), and that *came* raises to adjoin to ø as in (ii) below:

(ii)

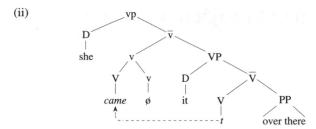

Subsequently, the subject *she* raises to spec-TP in order to check its nominative case, as in (iii) below:

(iii)

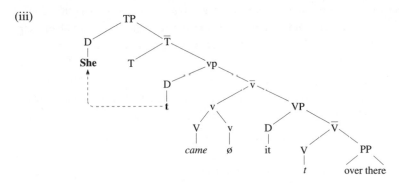

However, since the corresponding sentence *She came it over there* is ungrammatical in adult English (instead, we say *She took it over there*), an important question to ask is 'What's wrong with sentences like 1 in adult English?'

One minor error in 1 relates to the use of the locative adverb *there* in place of *here*. (Generally, we use *here* with the verb *come* and *there* with the verb *go*: cf. *Come here! Go there!*) However, the error which is our main concern here is employing the motion verb *come* in a causative use. Why can't *come* be used causatively in adult English (so deriving sentences like **Come it here!*)? One answer might be that *come* is a nonaffixal verb, and hence cannot be adjoined to a causative light verb like ø: an alternative possibility would be to suppose that *come* lacks the causative feature which would enable it to be adjoined to a causative light verb; a third (more traditional analysis) is to say that *come* is intransitive (and so could not check the objective case of *it* if used in causative structures such as (iii) above). On the first view, the child's error lies in not having learned which verbs are (and which aren't) affixal stems; on the second, it lies in not having identified which verbs do (or don't) carry the relevant causative feature; on the third, it lies in not having identified which verbs are transitive (and so carry an uninterpretable objective case-feature which needs to be checked) and which are intransitive.

421

10

Agreement projections

[handwritten annotations: morphology; Takes Infl and breaks it up. Trying to build into the syntax a way to talk to morphology; LF – syntax related to semantics; PF – to phonology]

10.1 Overview

In this chapter, we take a closer look at the internal structure of clauses, examining the range of projections which they contain. We shall argue that clauses have a much more richly articulated constituent structure than we have hitherto supposed, and that they contain subject and object **agreement projections**.

10.2 Subject agreement projections

Let's begin our discussion of clause structure by looking at the syntax of the adverb *probably* and the quantifier *all* in the following sentence:

(1)   They have *probably* **all** given up smoking

At first sight, (1) seems relatively unproblematic. After all, we might suppose that *all* is a floating quantifier stranded in spec-vp (by movement of *they* into spec-TP), and *probably* is an adverb adjoined to vp, so that (1) has the simplified derivation (2) below. (Throughout this chapter, the internal structure of complex heads is sometimes simplified by omitting the category label of one or more of the heads, where this is self-evident: hence *have* is not labelled PERF here.)

(2)

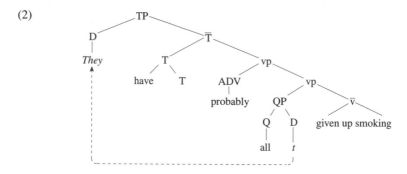

Of course, the analysis in (2) requires us to posit that adverbs like *probably* adjoin to maximal projections rather than (as assumed in earlier chapters) to intermediate projections. However, there are theoretical reasons for supposing that this is a plausible assumption.

The relevant considerations relate to the traditional assumption that languages contain movement rules which **adjoin** one constituent to another (for obvious reasons, the relevant type of movement operation is referred to as **adjunction**). For example, a traditional way of handling the relation between sentence pairs such as (3a–b) below:

(3) (a)   They have not understood anything

    (b)   They haven't understood anything

is to suppose that in (3b) the word *not* (in the guise of its contracted form *n't*) adjoins to the auxiliary *have*, so forming *haven't* (which behaves like a single word e.g. in respect of undergoing inversion in sentences like *Haven't they understood anything?*). Similarly, one way of describing what happens when the italicized phrase *such behaviour* is preposed (in order to focus it in some way) in a sentence pair such as:

(4) (a)   You must know that we cannot tolerate *such behaviour*

    (b)   You must know that *such behaviour* we cannot tolerate

is to say that the DP *such behaviour* adjoins to the TP headed by *cannot* (cf. Grimshaw 1993a). We might then conclude (as Chomsky does in his *Barriers* monograph, 1986b) that the only type of adjunction operations which can result from movement are adjunction of one head to another or of one maximal projection to another. It would therefore seem natural to suppose that the same is true of the merger operations which attach adverbial adjuncts to the expressions they modify: and this in turn would rule out the possibility of merging an adverb with an intermediate projection, but would allow for structures like (2) in which *probably* (which is itself a maximal projection in (2) above) is an adjunct to the maximal projection vp.

However, the analysis in (2) proves to be descriptively inadequate for a number of reasons. For one thing, it assumes that adverbs like *probably* can serve as vp-adjuncts. Yet if this were so, we'd expect that *probably* could be positioned before or after another vp-adjunct like *completely*, given the traditional assumption that adjuncts of the same kind can be freely ordered with respect to one another. However, this is not so, as we see from sentences such as:

(5) (a)   They have *probably* **completely** given up smoking

    (b)   *They have **completely** *probably* given up smoking

The fact that *probably* must be positioned to the left of the vp-adverb *completely* suggests that it is a different kind of adverb altogether. More concretely, it seems plausible to posit that *probably* is a TP-adverb – i.e. an adverb which merges with a TP to form an extended TP. But, of course, if *probably* is not a vp-adverb, the analysis in (2) cannot be right.

Further support for the claim that *probably* is not a vp-adverb comes from sentences like (6) below:

(6)　　　　They have probably not given up smoking

Given the traditional assumption that the NEGP constituent containing *not* is positioned between TP and vp, it follows that *probably* cannot be adjoined to vp in sentences like (6).

The problems are compounded when we come to consider how to deal with sentences such as:

(7)　　　　They *probably* **all** have given up smoking

It is less than obvious how we might deal with sentences like (7) if we continue to assume that auxiliaries like *have* are generated in T (merged with a tense morpheme), and that floating quantifiers are stranded in subject QPs: after all, how can *they* and the QP containing *all* both be subjects of the same auxiliary *have*?

Given the conventional assumption that each auxiliary permits only one subject, the answer is that they can't. So, an alternative possibility which we might pursue is that there are in fact two different functional projections between CP and vp, with *they* serving as the subject of one of them, and the QP containing the stranded quantifier *all* as the subject of the other (a claim which amounts to positing that there are two different auxiliary positions in clauses). Since auxiliaries like *have/be* typically inflect for *tense* and *agreement*, and since we have already suggested that *tense* heads its own projection into a tense phrase (TP), an obvious suggestion to make (following Pollock 1989, Belletti 1990 and Chomsky 1993) is that finite clauses also contain an abstract **agreement** morpheme which projects into an **agreement phrase**. Let us also suppose (following Belletti and Chomsky) that the relevant agreement head occupies a higher position than T, and that auxiliaries are generated in T and from there can raise to adjoin to the separate agreement head, and that subjects raise from spec-vp to the specifier position in the agreement phrase, to check their case and agreement features. Since the agreement relation in question involves subjects, it has become conventional in the relevant literature to denote the relevant subject agreement constituent as **AgrS** (and to its maximal projection as **AgrSP**). If we go down this road, our earlier INFL head will in effect be split into two different heads – a T head and an AgrS head: hence, for obvious reasons, this assumption has become known as the **split-INFL hypothesis**.

Within the *split-INFL* framework, a sentence such as (1) *They have probably all given up smoking* might be derived as follows. The QP *all they* originates in spec-vp (as the subject of *given up smoking*), and from there raises up into spec-TP; the adverb *probably* merges with TP to form an extended TP, as in (8) below:

(8)

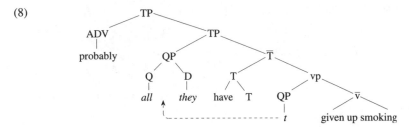

TP is then merged with an AgrS (= subject agreement) head which projects into AgrSP (= subject agreement phrase); the pronoun *they* raises to spec-AgrSP (i.e. into the specifier position within the subject agreement phrase) to check its nominative case, and the auxiliary *have* raises from T to adjoin to AgrS (thereby enabling it to check its agreement properties) as in (9) below (where the righthand trace is left behind by movement of the QP *all they* from spec-vp to spec-TP):

(9)

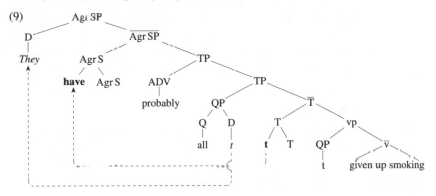

Since there are two functional projections above vp in (9) (AgrSP and TP), it follows that there are two different subject positions outside vp, one of which (= spec-AgrSP) houses the subject pronoun *they*, and the other of which (= spec-TP) houses the QP containing the stranded quantifier *all*.

We might propose to derive (7) *They probably all have given up smoking* in essentially the same way, except that the auxiliary *have* remains in the head T position of TP, and does not adjoin to AgrS. If this is so, (7) will have the (simplified) derivation (10) below (where the righthand trace is left behind by movement of the QP *all they* from spec-vp to spec-TP):

425

(10)

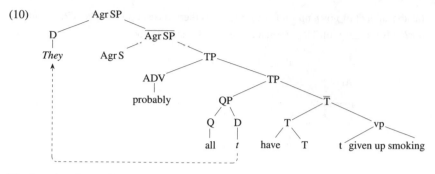

The fact that the auxiliary *have* is positioned after the TP-adverb *probably* in (10) but before it in (9) would suggest that *have* occupies the head T position of TP in (10), and moves from there to occupy the head AgrS position of AgrSP in (9) (as argued by Koizumi 1995, p. 41). We might follow Bošković (1995, p. 22) in supposing that finite auxiliaries in English can have either strong or weak agreement-features, and raise to AgrS when they have strong agreement-features, but remain in T when they have weak agreement-features. If we assume that AgrS has strong specifier-features in English, it follows that subjects will always raise to spec-AgrSP to check their case- and agreement-features.

A further argument in support of the *split-INFL* analysis comes from facts relating to the relative **scope** of adverbs and modal auxiliaries. Ernst (1991, p. 754) notes that in a sentence such as:

(11)   Gary can apparently lift 100 pounds

the adverb *apparently* has scope over the modal *can*, as we see from the fact that (11) can be paraphrased as 'It is apparent that Gary can lift 100 pounds.' If we make the traditional assumption that scope relations are defined in terms of the relation *c-command* (so that X has scope over Y only if X c-commands Y), it is difficult to account for the fact that *can* falls within the scope of *apparently* in (11), since *apparently* does not c-command *can*. How can we resolve this problem? One answer is to suppose that *can* originates in T and from there raises to AgrS across the TP adverb *apparently*, as in (12) below (where each italicized *t* denotes a trace of the moved subject *he*):

(12)

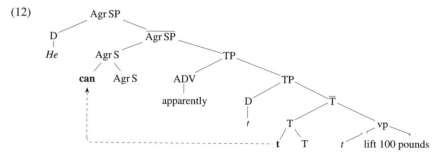

If we follow Ernst (1991, p. 753) in positing that scope is determined by the following **scope principle** (the term *operator* here is used to denote a constituent with scope properties):

(13)   An operator A has scope over an operator B in case A c-commands a member of the chain containing B.

then we can say that *apparently* has scope over *can* in (12) by virtue of the fact that *apparently* c-commands the trace of *can* which occupies the head T position of TP.

10.3 Evidence from other varieties of English

Thus far, the evidence we have adduced in support of an AgrSP/TP analysis of clauses has come from data relating to Modern Standard English. However, additional evidence comes from other varieties of English. One such piece of evidence relates to a phenomenon sometimes referred to as **scrambling**. As the Shakespearean examples below illustrate, in Early Modern English the complement of a verb could be *scrambled* – i.e. moved out of its underlying position as a complement of the verb into some position higher up in the clause (in the examples below, the scrambled constituent is italicized):

(14) (a)   *Thy physic* I will try (King, *All's Well That Ends Well*, II.i)

(b)   She may *more suitors* have (Tranio, *The Taming of the Shrew*, I.ii)

(c)   The king *your mote* did see (Boyet, *Love's Labour's Lost*, IV.i)

Scrambling is traditionally analysed as involving adjunction of the moved constituent to a maximal projection higher up in the structure. Sentences such as (14a) and (14b) can be dealt with straightforwardly within the traditional IP/VP analysis of clauses if we assume that *thy physic* is adjoined to the left of the IP headed by *will* in (14a), and that *more suitors* is adjoined to the left of the VP headed by *have* in (14b). But this leaves us with the question of where *your mote* is positioned in (14c). Under the traditional IP/VP analysis, there is no obvious answer to this question: if we assume that maximal projections can only adjoin to other maximal projections (as argued e.g. in Chomsky 1986b), we can't say that *your mote* in (14c) is adjoined to an I-bar headed by *did*, since I-bar is an intermediate projection, not a maximal projection. However, the split-INFL analysis provides us with a natural answer. If we suppose that *did* in (14c) occupies the head T position of TP, we can then say that the scrambled complement *your mote* is adjoined to TP, while the subject *the king* occupies spec-AgrSP. More specifically, we might suggest that (14c) is derived as in (15) below:

(15)

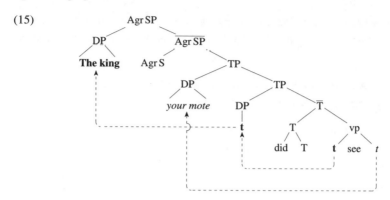

Of course, given the assumption that scrambling in (15) involves adjunction of the scrambled DP to TP, we might propose to analyse (14b) in a parallel fashion, with the auxiliary *may* moving from T to AgrS (hence preceding the scrambled nominal *more suitors*).

Alison Henry (1995) presents an interesting argument from the syntax of Belfast English (BE) in support of the AgrSP/TP analysis of clause structure presented above. She notes that in BE, we find sentences such as (16) below in which (what appears to be) a singular verb form is used with a plural objective subject:

(16) (a) *Themuns* **is** annoying youse (*themuns* = 'them ones')
  (b) *Usuns* **was** late (*usuns* = 'us ones')
  (c) *Us students* **doesn't** have much money
  (d) *Them* **is** no good
  (e) *Me and you* **is** supposed to help ourselves
  (f) *Him and me* **goes** there every week

She argues that the +*s* inflection on verb forms like *is/was/has/does/goes* in BE structures like (16) marks present tense (as indeed is the case in many other varieties of English – e.g. in South-Western British English, where we find paradigms such as *I/we/you/he/she/they* **hates** *syntax*), and that consequently there is no morphological marking of agreement in structures like (16). She notes that absence of agreement-marking correlates with the assignment of objective case to the subject of the verb. (Where a nominative subject is used, the verb must obligatorily agree with the subject, as in *They* **are/*is** *working hard.*) She also notes that agreementless finite verb forms like those in (16) cannot undergo auxiliary inversion – as we see from the ungrammaticality of questions such as:

(17) (a) **Is themuns annoying youse?*
  (b) **Is us students entitled to free condoms?*
  (c) **Is you and me supposed to help ourselves?*

428

(By contrast, sentences with nominative subjects and agreement-inflected verbs do indeed allow inversion – cf. *Are they going to the disco?*) How can we account for the fact that agreementless finite verbs and auxiliaries have objective subjects and don't allow inversion?

Henry argues that the absence of agreement-marking in finite clauses like (16) means that AgrS in such clauses has weak head-features, and so does not allow movement of an auxiliary from T to AgrS. She conjectures that (again in consequence of the absence of subject agreement) AgrS also has weak specifier-features, and so does not trigger raising of the subject to spec-AgrSP. In consequence, agreementless finite auxiliaries remain in T, and their subjects raise only as far as spec-TP, where they check objective case by default (i.e. because the subject needs to be case-checked but is unable to raise to spec-AgrSP to check nominative case, the subject checks objective case in spec-TP as a last resort). On this view, a sentence such as (16a) *Themuns is annoying youse* will contain the TP (18) below (*t* is the trace left behind by movement of the subject *themuns* from spec-vp to spec-TP):

(18)

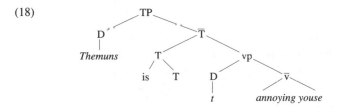

Consider now why the interrogative counterpart (17a) **Is themuns annoying youse?* is ungrammatical. If we suppose that questions are CP/AgrSP/TP/vp/VP structures and involve adjunction of an auxiliary to an abstract Q morpheme in the head C position of CP, there are two ways in which we might seek to move the auxiliary *is* from T to C (to adjoin to Q). One is in two short steps, adjoining *is* first to AgrS (as in movement (1) below) and then to Q (as in movement (2) below):

(19)

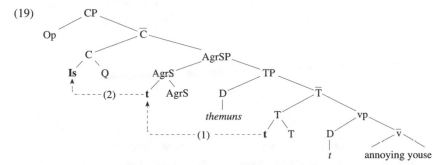

(As before, the italicized *t* is the trace of the subject *themuns* which moves from spec-vp to spec-TP; *Op* is the abstract yes–no question operator which we posited in §7.8.)

However, the successive cyclic derivation in (19) is ruled out by virtue of the fact that AgrS is weak in agreementless finite clauses, so step (1) of the derivation violates the principle of **greed** (which licenses movement only as a way of checking strong features).

A second way in which we might seek to derive questions like (17a) is to move *is* directly from T to adjoin to Q, as in (20) below:

(20)

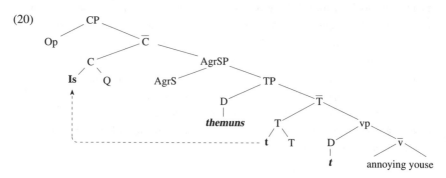

However, the problem posed by the arrowed movement of *is* directly from T to C is that it violates the **shortest movement principle**, because *is* does not adjoin to the next-highest head (which would be AgrS), but rather to the next-highest-but-one head (i.e. to Q). Since we cannot derive (17a) either by a single long movement of *is* from T to C, or by two successive short movements of *is* from T to AgrS to C, our grammar correctly specifies that sentences such as (17a) are ungrammatical. But note that a central pillar of the argumentation is the assumption that all finite clauses contain an AgrSP projection in addition to (and on top of) a TP projection.

Our discussion here has interesting implications for our earlier discussion of checking in chapter 5, where we assumed that modals like *can* in Modern Standard English (MSE) have no person/number agreement-features. There are two important points to bear in mind about MSE here – namely (i) that modals have nominative subjects and (ii) that they undergo inversion in questions, as we see from examples like (21) below:

(21) (a)   *He* can swim
     (b)   *Can* you swim?

If we suppose that only items which carry agreement properties license nominative subjects, and can raise to AgrS (and thence to C in inversion structures), it follows that we must assume that modals like *can* have covert agreement properties in MSE. If (like auxiliaries in Belfast English) they were agreementless forms, we should (wrongly) predict that they don't allow nominative subjects, and can't undergo inversion. (Recall that Bošković 1995 assumes that finite auxiliaries in MSE may have either strong or weak agreement-features, and so can either stay in T or move to AgrS.) Rather than say

430

that modals like *can* have no (person/number) agreement properties, we might there-fore conclude that they have the *variable* agreement properties [αPerson, αNumber], and that these variable person/number-features can be checked by a first, second or third person subject which is singular or plural in number. (See Rooryck 1994 for dis-cussion of the use of feature variables in syntax and phonology.)

10.4 Object agreement projections

Just as recent work has argued in favour of splitting IP into two different projections (introducing a new subject agreement projection), so too it has been argued that VP should similarly be split into a number of different projections, including one headed by an **object agreement** constituent (designated as **AgrO**). Although there are a number of variants of this proposal in the relevant literature, the one which we shall outline here assumes that the object agreement phrase (= **AgrOP**) is positioned between vp and VP: for obvious reasons, this has come to be known as the **split-VP hypothesis** (cf. Bobaljik 1995, Carnie 1995, Harley 1995 and Koizumi 1995). The core assumption underlying the analysis is that just as nominative DPs raise to spec-AgrSP in order to check their nominative case- and subject agreement-features under spec–head agreement with AgrS, so too objective DPs raise to spec-AgrOP in order to check their objective case-feature and (in languages in which verbs inflect for agree-ment with their objects) their object agreement-features under spec–head agreement with AgrO. From a theoretical perspective, the obvious advantage that such an analysis offers is that it enables us to provide a unified account of case- and agreement-checking, in which all case- and agreement-features are checked under a spec–head relation between a functional head and its specifier. Let's begin by looking at some of the evidence in support of positing object agreement projections.

One piece of evidence in support of the assumption that objective DPs move in order to check their case comes from systematic differences between the position of CP com-plements and DP complements, illustrated by the examples below:

(22) (a)　　He reported to the police *that there had been a robbery*
　　 (b)　　He reported **the robbery** to the police
(23) (a)　　He admitted to her *that he was guilty*
　　 (b)　　He admitted **his guilt** to her
(24) (a)　　He announced *to the press* that he was retiring
　　 (b)　　He announced **his retirement** to the press
(25) (a)　　He mentioned to his boss *that the miners were on strike*
　　 (b)　　He mentioned **the strike** to his boss
(26) (a)　　He recommended to her *that she should consult Cy Coe*
　　 (b)　　He recommended **an analyst** to her
(27) (a)　　He whispered to her *that he loved her*
　　 (b)　　He whispered **sweet nothings** to her

It seems reasonable to suppose that *that*-clause complements don't carry objective case: after all, they can't occur as the complements of transitive prepositions like those bold-printed in the examples below:

(28) (a)   *I was sure **of** *that she'd come*

   (b)   *Concern was expressed **about** *that he had lied*

   (c)   *There isn't time **for** *that we have a meal*

If *that*-clause complements don't carry case, it seems reasonable to assume that they don't move for case-checking purposes, but rather remain *in situ*. This being so, consider how we account for the clause-final position of the *that*-clause in a sentence such as (22a) *He reported to the police that there had been a robbery*.

Given the VP shell analysis outlined in the previous chapter, (22a) will be derived as follows. The verb *reported* merges with its THEME argument (the CP *that there had been a robbery*) to form a V-bar; the resulting V-bar *reported that there had been a robbery* merges with its RECIPIENT argument (the PP *to the police*) to form the VP (29) below:

(29)

The VP in (29) then merges with a performative light verb ø whose AGENT subject is *he*, and the verb *reported* adjoins to the light verb as in (30) below:

(30)

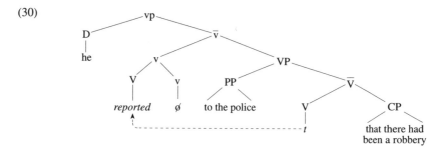

Subsequently, the subject *he* raises through spec-TP to spec-AgrSP to check its nominative case. A crucial assumption underlying the derivation in (30) is that the CP *that there had been a robbery* remains *in situ* throughout.

If we adopt the **uniform theta assignment hypothesis**, it follows that the DP complement *the robbery* in (22b) *He reported the robbery to the police* must originate in the same position as the CP complement *that there had been a robbery* in (30), since the relevant DP and CP constituents play the same thematic role as the THEME argument of *reported*. But since the DP *the robbery* ends up in a position between the verb *reported* and the PP *to the police*, it must subsequently move to some higher position between the vp containing the verb *reported* in (30) and the VP containing the PP *to the police*. By hypothesis, the higher position which *the robbery* moves to is the specifier position within an AgrOP projection positioned between vp and VP. If this is so, (22b) will have the following derivation.

The verb *reported* merges with its DP complement *the robbery* to form a V-bar; the resulting V-bar *reported the robbery* then merges with the PP *to the police* to form the VP below:

(31)

The resulting VP merges with an AgrO constituent to form an AgrO-bar projection, with the verb *reported* adjoining to AgrO; the DP *the robbery* raises to become the specifier of AgrO-bar, so forming the AgrOP (32) below:

(32)

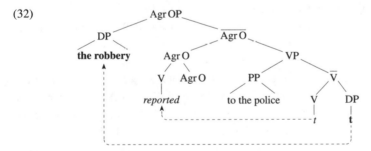

Since the DP *the robbery* and the AgrO constituent containing the transitive verb *reported* are in a spec–head relation in (32), the objective case-feature carried by each can be checked against that of the other, and erased. Subsequently, the AgrOP constituent in (32) merges with a performative light verb ø (whose AGENT subject is *he*) and the verb *reported* adjoins to this light verb as in (33) below:

(33)

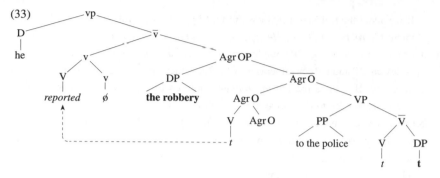

(An alternative possibility is that AgrO is pied-piped along with the verb, so that the whole V+AgrO constituent adjoins to the light verb ø, rather than just the V *reported*.) Subsequently, the subject *he* raises through spec-TP to spec-AgrSP to check its nominative case.

An analysis along the lines sketched out above has both empirical and theoretical merits. From an empirical point of view, its main merit is that it accounts for why DP objects are postverbal, whereas CP complements are clause-final – i.e. it accounts for the word-order contrasts illustrated in (22–7) above. On the analysis presented here, this follows from the fact that DP complements carry objective case and hence have to raise to spec-AgrOP for case-checking; by contrast, CP complements are caseless and so need not (and therefore, by the **economy principle,** cannot) raise to spec-AgrOP. (We might also assume that the **economy principle** determines that clauses which have no DP object do not contain an AgrOP projection at all – as indeed we tacitly assumed earlier in relation to the derivation sketched out in (30) above.)

From a theoretical point of view, the main merit of the AgrOP analysis in (33) is that it enables us to arrive at a more unitary theory of checking. Until now, we had assumed that three main types of relation were involved in checking, viz. a relation between a head and another head which is adjoined to it, a relation between a head and its specifier, or a relation between a head and its complement. This led to obvious asymmetries, in that (for example) checking the case of a nominative DP involved a specifier–head relation, whereas checking the case of an objective DP involved a head–complement relation (or, in ECM structures, a relation between a matrix head and a complement specifier). But suppose we now eliminate the possibility that head–complement relations are involved in checking, and argue instead that a head can only check its features against those of its specifier, or against those of another head (or feature) which is adjoined to it. If we further suppose that nominative and objective DPs in English carry strong case-features, it follows that the only way in which an objective DP can check its case-feature is by raising into a position in which it can enter into a spec–head relation with a transitive verb: the required spec–head configuration will obviously come about if the object raises to spec-AgrOP and the transitive verb raises to AgrO (perhaps with the case-features of the verb and the object both being copied onto AgrO in order to be checked, as suggested by Koizumi 1995, p. 40).

We can formulate a different kind of argument in support of the claim that DP objects move to spec-AgrOP for case-checking purposes in relation to the position of *adverbs*. In this connection, consider how we account for the following contrasts:

(34) (a)   He plays chess well
    (b)   *He plays well chess
    (c)   *He well plays chess

If we make the traditional assumption that *well* is a VP-adverb, and if we further assume (as we did in relation to our discussion of *probably* in (9) and (10) above) that adverbs merge with maximal projections, (34a) will be derived as follows. The verb *plays* originates in the head V of VP, and merges with its complement *chess* (which is a DP headed by a null determiner Ø) to form the VP *plays chess*; the adverb *well* merges with this VP, so deriving the extended VP in (35) below:

(35)
```
              VP
           /      \
        ADV        VP
         |        /   \
        well     V      DP
                 |     /   \
               plays  Ø    chess
```

The VP in (35) is then merged with an AgrO morpheme (which projects into AgrOP); the verb *plays* adjoins to AgrO, and the DP Ø *chess* raises to spec-AgrOP as in (36) below:

(36)
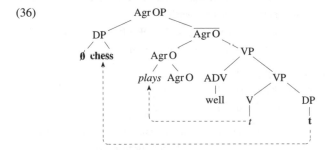

The objective case-feature carried by the DP Ø *chess* (cf. *He plays lots of games, and plays **them** well*) is checked at this point, since the DP Ø *chess* is in a spec–head relation with the transitive verb *plays* (by virtue of the fact that *plays* is in AgrO, and Ø *chess* is in spec-AgrOP: Koizumi 1995, p. 40, suggests that checking involves copying the objective case-feature of both the verb and its specifier onto AgrO, and erasing both if they match).

The AgrOP constituent in (36) is then merged with a performative light verb ø whose subject is *he*; the verb *plays* adjoins to the light verb, as below:

(37)

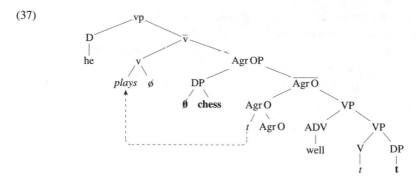

The pronoun *he* then raises through spec-TP to spec-AgrSP, so deriving (34a) *He plays chess well*. The assumption that both verbs and objective DPs raise across VP-adverbs correctly predicts that sentences like (34b–c) are ungrammatical.

An analysis along the lines sketched out above accounts for the fact that verbs in English are immediately adjacent to their objects (as illustrated in (34) above) and cannot be separated from them by intervening adverbials. On this account, the only way in which a transitive verb could be separated from its object would be for an adverb to be adjoined to AgrOP. But if we make the traditional assumption that adverbs modify projections whose heads have specific semantic content, it follows that we can have adverbs adjoined to projections of V, v or T (since V contains a lexical verb with its own semantic properties, v contains an abstract light verb which has a specific – e.g. causative or performative – sense and T has temporal properties), but that we can't adjoin adverbs to projections of agreement heads, since these have a purely formal function (viz. that of checking case/agreement properties).

The assumption that objective DPs raise to spec-AgrOP offers us an interesting account of the syntax of particles like *out* in sentences such as the following:

(38) (a)   He poured the whisky slowly out
     (b)   He poured the whisky out slowly
     (c)   He poured out the whisky slowly

If we make the traditional assumption that *slowly* functions as a VP-adverb, and if we further assume (as in (9) and (10) above) that adverbs adjoin to maximal projections, we can derive (38a) as follows. The verb *poured* originates as the head V of VP and projects into the structure (39) below:

(39)

The VP in (39) is then merged with an AgrO constituent; the verb *poured* adjoins to AgrO, and its DP specifier *the whisky* raises to spec-AgrOP: cf.

(40)

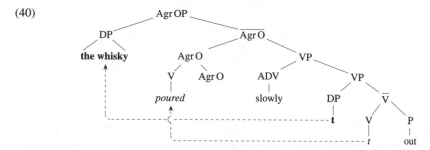

The objective case-features carried by the DP *the whisky* (cf. *He poured **them** slowly out*) and by the verb *poured* (which is transitive as used in (38) above, though is intransitive in other uses) are checked at this point; by hypothesis, objective-case checking involves a spec–head relation between an AgrO containing a transitive verb and an objective DP in spec-AgrOP (here, between an AgrO containing the transitive verb *poured* and its DP specifier *the whisky*).

The next stage of derivation is for AgrOP to be merged with an abstract performative light verb ø whose AGENT subject is *he*; since ø is a strong head, the verb *poured* adjoins to it, as in (41) below:

(41)

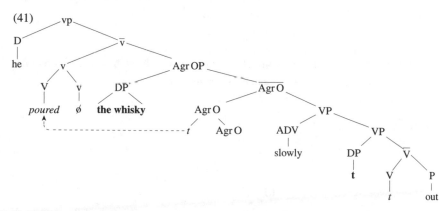

Subsequently, the subject pronoun *he* raises to spec-TP and from there to spec-AgrSP to check its case and agreement properties, so deriving (38a) *He poured the whisky slowly out*.

Now consider how we derive (38b) *He poured the whisky out slowly*. Let us suppose that (as before) the verb *pour* projects into a VP of the form (39) above. But let's also suppose that the particle *out* incorporates into the verb *poured* as in (42) below, so forming the complex verb *poured out*:

(42)

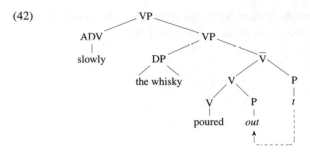

Let's further suppose that the whole complex verb *poured out* adjoins to AgrO (and that the DP *the whisky* raises to spec-AgrOP to check its objective case-feature) as in (43) below (where the rightmost trace is the trace of the particle *out* which has incorporated into the verb):

(43)

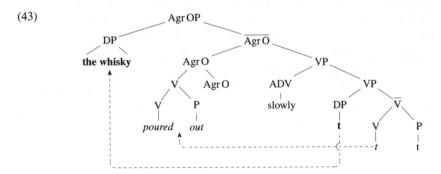

AgrOP then merges with the performative light verb ø; if the verb *poured* excorporates out of the V complex *poured out* and raises on its own to adjoin to ø, the result will be (44) below:

(44)

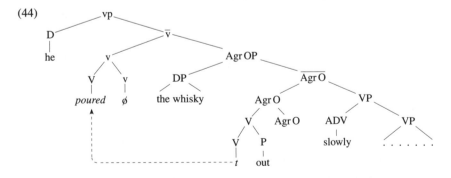

The pronoun *he* then raises through spec-TP to spec AgrSP, so deriving (38b) *He poured the whisky out slowly*.

438

But now suppose that instead of the simple verb *poured* adjoining to the light verb ø on its own in (44), the prepositional particle *out* is pied-piped along with it, so that the whole verbal complex *poured out* adjoins to ø. The result will be (45) below:

(45)

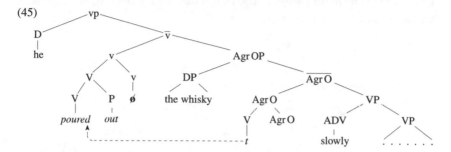

The pronoun *he* then raises through spec-TP into spec-AgrSP, thereby deriving (38c) *He poured out the whisky slowly*. Thus, our assumption that (in transitive structures) objective DPs move to spec-AgrOP and verbs move through AgrO to adjoin to v (and can strand a particle in AgrO) provides an interesting account of the syntax of verb + particle structures like (38).

10.5 Exceptional case-marking

The AgrOP analysis also turns out to provide us with a solution to a puzzling problem which arises in relation to how we analyse ECM (= exceptional case-marking) structures such as the following, involving a [bracketed] infinitive complement with an objective subject:

(46) (a)   The DA *proved* [the witness **conclusively** to have lied] (adapted from Bowers 1993, p. 632)

(b)   I *suspect* [him **strongly** to be a liar] (Authier 1991, p. 729)

(c)   I've *believed* [Gary **for a long time now** to be a fool] (Kayne 1984, p. 114)

(d)   I have *found* [Bob **recently** to be morose] (Postal 1974, p. 146)

In sentences such as these, the bold-printed adverbial/prepositional expression is positioned *inside* the bracketed infinitive complement, and yet is construed as modifying an (italicized) verb which lies *outside* the bracketed complement clause. How can we account for this seeming paradox? To make our discussion more concrete, let's consider how we might derive (46a).

If we assume that an adverb such as *conclusively* is a VP adverb (more specifically, a VP adjunct) and that *proved* originates in the head V position of VP, the obvious problem we are left with is accounting for how both the verb *proved* and the DP *the witness* end up in front of the adverb *conclusively*. One answer might be the following. Let's suppose that the verb *prove* merges with the infinitive phrase *the witness to have lied* to form the VP *proved the witness to have lied*, and that the adverb *conclusively* adjoins to this VP to form the VP (47) below. (Here I am assuming, as in relation to examples such as (9) and (10) above, that adverbs adjoin to maximal projections; for familiarity, I have labelled infinitive phrases as IPs, though they are arguably AgrSPs with much the same internal structure as finite clauses.)

(47)

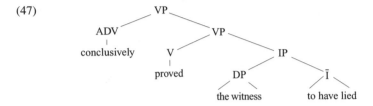

Let's further suppose that the VP in (47) then merges with an AgrO constituent to which the verb *proved* adjoins, and that the DP *the witness* raises to spec-AgrOP, as in (48) below. (Here and elsewhere, in accordance with the convention noted at the beginning of the chapter, I simplify the internal structure of complex head-adjunction structures by omitting the category labels of some of the heads, where these are self-evident; hence *proved* is not labelled V.)

(48)

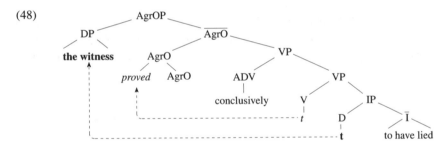

The objective case-features carried by *the witness* (cf. *The DA proved **him** conclusively to have lied*) and by the transitive verb *proved* are checked at this point, via a spec–head relation between the verb *proved* in AgrO and its specifier *the witness* in spec-AgrOP.

The AgrOP in (48) is subsequently merged with an abstract performative light verb ø whose AGENT subject/specifier is the nominative DP *the DA*: because ø is a strong head, the verb *proved* raises to adjoin to it, as in (49) below. (The subject *the DA* subsequently raises from spec-vp through spec-TP into spec-AgrSP, but we do not show these later stages of derivation here.)

(49)

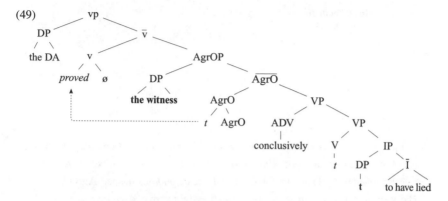

As a result of movement of the DP *the witness* to spec-AgrOP and of the verb *proved* to the head v position of vp, both end up positioned in front of the adverb *conclusively* – precisely as we find in (46a). Thus, in effect what happens in ECM structures is that the subject of the infinitive raises up to become the object of the main-clause verb (as was suggested in an earlier framework by Paul Postal in his 1974 book *On Raising*).

Bošković (1995, p. 176) argues that an AgrOP analysis provides a straightforward account of the syntax of floating quantifiers in ECM structures such as (50) below:

(50)   The DA proved the defendants all to be lying

We might derive (50) as follows. Let's assume that (at some point in the derivation), the verb *proved* is merged with an infinitive phrase (= IP) complement whose subject is the QP *all the defendants*, as in (51) below:

(51)

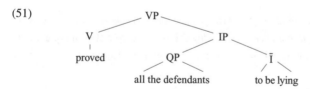

The VP in (51) is then merged with AgrO, the verb *proved* adjoins to AgrO and the DP *the defendants* moves to spec-AgrOP as in (52) below, stranding the quantifier *all* in spec-IP:

(52)

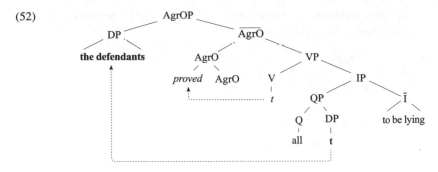

The objective case carried by *the defendants* (cf. *The DA proved **them** all to be lying*) is checked at this point; case-checking involves a spec–head relation between the transitive verb *proved* in AgrO and the objective DP *the defendants* in spec-AgrOP.

The V *proved* then adjoins to the performative light verb ø, deriving:

(53)

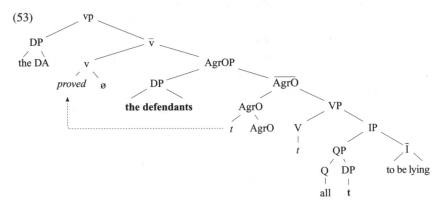

The subject *the DA* subsequently raises through spec-TP into spec-AgrSP, so deriving (50) *The DA proved the defendants all to be lying*. Thus, facts from floating quantifiers lend further support to the claim that the objective infinitive subject in ECM structures raises overtly to spec-AgrOP.

The raising analysis of ECM structures, taken together with our earlier analysis of verb + particle structures, enables us to provide a principled account of the syntax of ECM particle structures such as the following:

(54) (a)   The DA made out the defendants to be lying
     (b)   The DA made the defendants out to be lying

Let's suppose that *made out* is (at some stage of derivation) a complex verb in which the particle *out* is adjoined to the verb *made*. (This does not preclude the possibility that *out* may originate as an independent head, and incorporate into the verb *made*.)

442

Let's also suppose that the complex verb *made out* merges with the infinitive complement *the defendants to be lying* to form the VP (55) below:

(55)

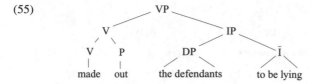

The VP in (55) is then merged with AgrO; the DP *the defendants* raises to spec-AgrOP,
and the complex V *made out* raises to adjoin to AgrO, as in (56) below:

(56)

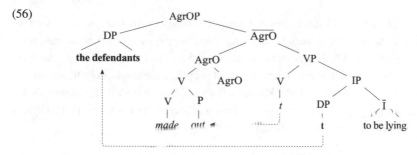

Both movements are motivated by **greed** – i.e. by the need for the objective case carried by *the defendants* to be checked in a spec–head relation within AgrOP.

AgrOP is then merged with an abstract light verb ø whose subject is *the DA*.
Because ø is a verbal affix, a V constituent must adjoin to it. However, there are two V
constituents contained within AgrO in (56): one is the simple verb *made*, the other is
the complex verb *made out*. If the complex V *made out* adjoins to the light verb ø, the
result will be (57) below:

(57)

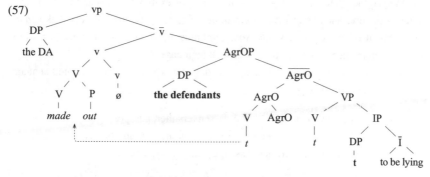

The DA subsequently raises from spec-vp through spec-TP to spec-AgrSP, so deriving
the structure associated with (54a) *The DA made out the defendants to be lying*.

But now suppose that instead of adjoining the complex V *made out* to the light verb,
we adjoin the simple V *made*, as in (58) below:

(58)

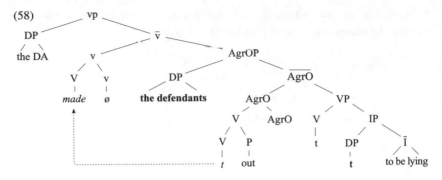

Here, the verb *made* has excorporated out of the complex verb *made out*, so leaving the particle *out* stranded between *the defendants* and *to be lying*. *The DA* raises from spec-vp through spec-TP to spec-AgrSP, so deriving (54b) *The DA made the defendants out to be lying*. (For further arguments that ECM subjects raise to spec-AgrOP, see Authier 1991, Johnson 1991, Ura 1993, Koizumi 1995 and Bošković 1995; for further discussion of the syntax of particle constructions, see Kayne 1984, Guéron 1990, Johnson 1991 and the references cited there.)

10.6 Indirect object agreement projections

Thus far, we have argued that nominative DPs raise to spec-AgrSP in order to check their nominative-case head-feature, and similarly that objective DPs raise to spec-AgrOP in order to check their objective-case head-feature. An interesting extension of this analysis might be to suppose that *all* DPs in English have to check their case by moving to the specifier position within an agreement projection of some kind. As we shall see, this unifying assumption has far-reaching consequences for how we analyse the syntax of a range of structures. For example, it means that in double-object structures such as *give someone something*, not only direct objects (like *something*) but also indirect objects (like *someone*) must move to a higher specifier position within an agreement phrase in order to check their case.

To see what this means in practice, consider how we might derive related sentence pairs such as the following:

(59) (a)   The crew handed back the passengers their passports

(b)   The crew handed the passengers back their passports

(c)   The crew handed the passengers their passports back

Let's suppose that at an intermediate stage of derivation, *handed back* is a complex verb (perhaps formed by merging *handed* with *back*, or by movement of *back* from some lower position to adjoin to *handed*) which projects into the VP (60) below:

(60)

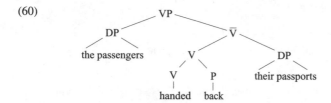

The direct object DP *their passports* in (60) has the θ-role THEME, and the indirect object DP *the passengers* has the θ-role of RECIPIENT. We can assume that the case carried by internal arguments such as these is determined by their thematic function, and that *dative* is the case canonically associated with RECIPIENT DPs, and *objective* the case canonically associated with THEME DPs. In languages like German or Romanian which have a relatively rich nominal morphology, dative and objective DPs are morphologically distinct; but in languages like English which have an impoverished nominal morphology, the two have the same morphological form (e.g. *them* is an objective pronoun in *I gave **them** to Mary* and a dative pronoun in *I gave **them** a present*).

The VP in (60) merges with AgrO, and the complex verb *handed back* adjoins to AgrO and the objective DP *their passports* raises to spec-AgrOP as in (61) below:

(61)

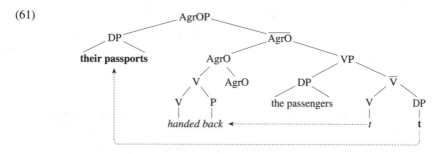

The objective case of the DP *their passports* in spec-AgrOP can then be checked under a spec–head relation with the ditransitive verb *handed (back)* in AgrO (which, by virtue of being ditransitive, can check both objective and dative case).

Subsequently, AgrOP in (61) is merged with an indirect object agreement morpheme (here symbolized as **AgrIO**); the complex verb *handed back* adjoins to AgrIO, and the dative DP *the passengers* raises to spec-AgrIOP as in (62) below:

(62)

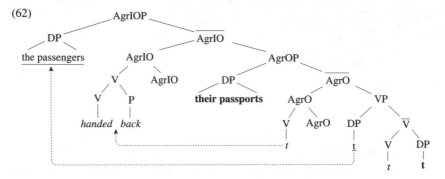

The dative case carried by the DP *the passengers* in spec-AgrIOP is then checked under a spec–head relation with the ditransitive verb *handed* (*back*) adjoined to AgrIO.

Finally, the complex verb *handed back* raises to adjoin to a performative light verb ø which heads vp (and whose AGENT subject is the nominative DP *the crew*), so forming the vp (63) below:

(63)

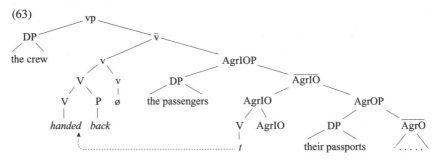

The DP *the crew* then raises through spec-TP into spec-AgrSP to check its nominative case, so deriving (59a) *The crew handed back the passengers their passports*.

Now consider how we derive (59b) *The crew handed the passengers back their passports*. Assume that the derivation proceeds essentially as for (59a), until we reach the stage of derivation represented in (62) above. At that point, the verb *handed* excorporates out of AgrIO and adjoins to the light verb ø on its own, as in (64) below:

(64)

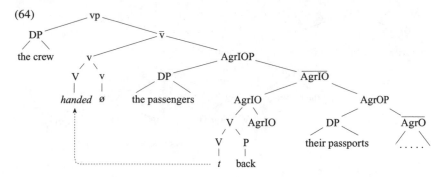

The result will be that the particle *back* is stranded in AgrIO, between the indirect object *the passengers* and the direct object *their passports*. Raising the DP *the crew* through spec-TP to spec-AgrSP will then derive (59b) *The crew handed the passengers back their passports*.

Finally, consider how we derive (59c) *The crew handed the passengers their passports back*. Let's assume that the derivation proceeds as for (59a) until we reach the stage represented in (61) above. At that point, the verb *handed* excorporates out of AgrO and adjoins to AgrIO on its own, with the indirect object *the passengers* raising to spec-AgrIOP to check its case, as in (65) below:

(65)

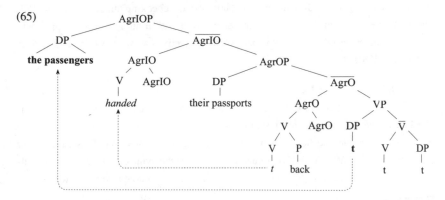

Subsequently, the verb *handed* adjoins to the strong light verb ø heading vp, as in (66) below:

(66)

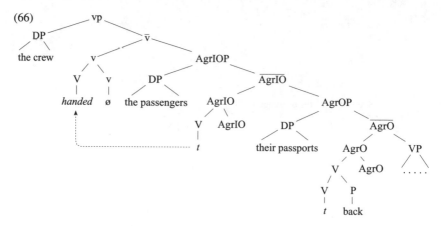

The DP *the crew* then raises through spec-TP to spec-AgrSP, thereby deriving (59c) *The crew handed the passengers their passports back.*

So, we see that the assumption that indirect object DPs raise to spec-AgrIOP in order to check their dative case (taken together with the assumption that when the verb in a *verb + particle* complex raises, the particle can either be pied-piped along with the verb or stranded) provides us with a principled account of the syntax of double-object particle structures such as (59a–c) above. From a theoretical standpoint, the assumption that dative DPs raise to spec-AgrIOP to check their case offers the obvious advantage of providing us with a unitary account of case-checking under which all DPs check their case by raising to the specifier position within an appropriate agreement phrase (nominative DPs raising to spec-AgrSP, objectives to spec-AgrOP and datives to spec-AgrIOP).

10.7 Genitive DPs

The assumption that the case of nominative, objective and dative DPs is checked by raising the relevant DP to the specifier position within a higher functional projection raises the question of how we deal with genitive DPs – i.e. DPs which carry the genitive-case suffix *'s*. In this connection, consider the syntax of the bracketed **genitive gerund** constituent in (67) below. (We use this term to denote a structure which contains a gerund verb form in +*ing* which has a DP subject carrying the genitive suffix *'s*.)

(67)   [*The UN's withdrawing troops from Utopia*] caused consternation

Genitive gerund structures like that bracketed in (67) have the twin properties that they occupy typical DP positions (and hence can function as the complement of a preposition, for example), yet clearly contain a vp structure internally within them. One way of accounting for the dual DP/vp status of gerunds is to suppose that they are DPs headed by a null determiner which has a vp complement, and that the subject of the gerund (viz. the genitive nominal *the UN's*) moves from spec-vp to spec-DP as in (68) below:

(68)

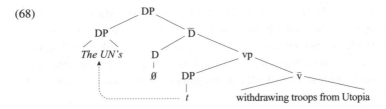

(A variant of this analysis is to suppose that *'s* originates as the head D of DP, and subsequently attaches to the DP *the UN*.) An analysis such as (68) would lead us to expect that the vp *withdrawing troops from Utopia* can be modified by an adverb – and this expectation is borne out by sentences such as:

(69)   [*The UN's **unexpectedly** withdrawing troops from Utopia*] caused
         consternation

If we make the traditional assumption that the DP *the UN's* carries genitive case in (67/69), we can maintain that movement of the subject DP *the UN's* from spec-vp to spec-DP is motivated by **greed** – i.e. by the need to check the genitive case carried by *the UN's*. More generally, we can maintain that DPs check their case properties by moving into the specifier position within an appropriate functional projection. If (as Abney 1987 argues) the head D in DPs with a genitive specifier has abstract agreement properties (and so is in effect an abstract *Agr* head), we can maintain the even stronger position that case-checking always involves an (overt or covert) agreement relation between an agreement head and its specifier. There is much more to be said about genitive case-marking, but we shall not pursue the relevant issues here. The main issue from our point of view is that there is no reason to think that genitive DPs provide any challenge to the claim that DPs are case-checked by raising to the specifier position within an appropriate functional projection.

10.8   *For*-infinitives and prepositional objects

A rather different challenge to the theory of case-checking outlined in this chapter is posed by the subjects of *for*-infinitive complements like that bracketed below:

(70)   She is keen [for *him* to succeed]

At the end of §8.5, we suggested that the objective case of the (italicized) infinitive subject in such structures is checked by *attraction*, the objective case-feature carried by *him* percolating up to the c-commanding transitive complementizer *for*. However, any such analysis is inconsistent with the view expressed in this chapter that objective DPs in English carry a strong case-feature, and raise to spec-AgrOP in order to check their case. One way of overcoming this problem would be to treat structures like (70) in a way which is more directly comparable to the way that we earlier treated subjects in

449

ECM structures like *We believe **him** to be innocent*. One possibility which we might explore along these lines would be to propose a *split-CP* analysis of complementizer phrases parallel to the *split-VP* analysis of verb phrases outlined in the text. This might mean (for example) that CP serves as the complement of an AgrOP constituent, with the complementizer adjoining to AgrO and the infinitive subject raising to spec-AgrOP as in (71) below:

(71)

We could then hypothesize that checking the case of the infinitive subject involves a spec–head relation between the transitive preposition *for* in AgrO and the objective pronoun *him* in spec-CP. The complementizer *for* would subsequently raise to adjoin to the (strong) head **c** constituent of a superordinate **cp** as in (72) below:

(72)

Such an analysis (although involving considerable abstraction) would enable us to posit that objective infinitive subjects always raise to spec-AgrOP in order to check their case.

The *split-CP* hypothesis might be argued to gain plausibility from complement-clause structures such as that bracketed in (73) below:

(73)   I can assure you [that never again will I take a syntax course]

Given the assumption made in chapter 6 that inverted auxiliaries adjoin to a null COMP, a sentence such as (73) is problematic in that it contains the overt complementizer *that* in addition to the inverted auxiliary *will*: moreover, since the two are separated by the adverbial phrase *never again*, it is clearly implausible to claim that *will* has adjoined to the complementizer node containing *that*. So, how are we to analyse such sentences? The *split-CP* hypothesis offers us one possible answer: perhaps the auxiliary adjoins to the head C of CP (with the negative adverbial *never again* occupying spec-CP) and the complementizer *that* merges with the head c constituent of a higher cp projection, as in (74) below:

(74)

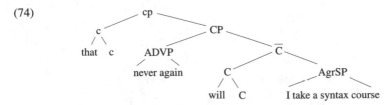

(It goes without saying that (74) is simplified in a number of respects, e.g. by omitting traces of moved constituents.) What is less than immediately self-evident, however, is the extent to which relatively plausible structures like (74) justify postulating rather more abstract structures like (72).

Returning now to the problems posed by the assumption that all DPs check their case by raising to the specifier position within an agreement projection, further potential problems are posed by prepositional objects (i.e. objective (pro)nominals which serve as the complements of prepositions) such as *me* in structures like *with me*. If we are to maintain that all objective D(P)s in English check their case by raising to spec-AgrOP, we have to propose a parallel *split-PP* analysis for prepositional phrases. This would mean that a PP like *with me* would be derived as follows. The preposition *with* merges with the pronoun *me* to form the PP *with me*. The resulting PP merges with an AgrO constituent; the preposition *with* adjoins to AgrO and its complement *me* raises to spec-AgrOP (in order to check its objective case in a spec–head relation with the transitive preposition *with*) as in (75) below:

(75)

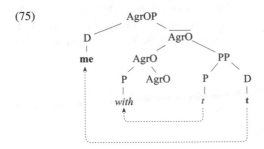

The intermediate stage of derivation in (75) may provide us with a clue to the structure of interrogative phrases such as that italicized in (76) below:

(76)   I know he's going out with someone, but I'm not sure *who with*

where the complement *who* precedes the preposition *with*; it might also give us some insight into the syntax of postpositional structures like Latin *mecum* (literally 'me + with').

Subsequently, AgrOP merges with a **light preposition** ø, and the preposition *with* raises to adjoin to the light preposition as in (77) below:

(77)

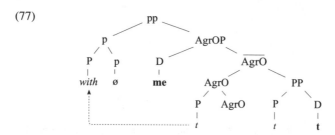

The assumption in (75/77) that the preposition originates in P and raises to p may provide us with an insight into the structure of Spanish PPs such as *conmigo* 'with me' (which is paraphraseable as 'with + me + with').

We might extend the analysis still further to account for compound prepositional phrases such as those italicized below (% indicates a structure found only in some varieties of English):

(78) (a)　She fell *out of the window*

　　(b)　%The handle came *off of the door*

　　(c)　She wouldn't go out *because of him*

We could derive a structure such as *out of the window* as follows. Let's suppose that *out* (in this use) is an intransitive preposition which merges with the DP *the window* to form the PP *out the window*. This in turn merges with an AgrO containing the dummy transitive preposition *of*; *out* adjoins to the AgrO constituent containing *of* and *him* raises to spec-AgrOP as in (79) below. (It may be that *of* is a preposition which itself merges with an abstract AgrO constituent, but this is a question of detail which we shall not pursue here.)

(79)

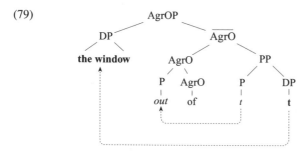

The objective case of the DP *the window* (cf. *She fell out of them*) is checked via the spec–head relation it enters into with the dummy transitive preposition *of* in AgrO. AgrOP then merges with a light preposition ∅ to which the compound preposition *out of* adjoins, as in (80) below:

(80)

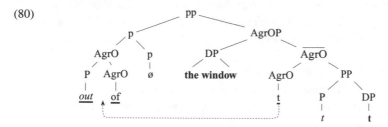

The analysis in (80) enables us to provide a straightforward account of the syntax of the italicized preposed operator phrases in sentences such as:

(81) (a)   *Which window* did she fall out of?

    (b)   *Out of which window* did she fall?

    (c)   **Of which window* did she fall out?

In the (informal-style) sentence (81a), the DP *which window* has been preposed: in the (formal-style) sentence (81b), the pp *out of which window* has been preposed; in the ungrammatical (81c) the nonconstituent string *of which window* has been preposed (and we know that only unitary constituents can be preposed). One question of detail which remains to be resolved is why *out* cannot be adjoined to the light preposition ∅ in (80) without *of*; perhaps this is because the one cliticizes onto the other, or perhaps it is because *of* (by virtue of being a preposition) must adjoin to the light preposition ∅. At any rate, the split-PP analysis of compound prepositions sketched out above seems preferable to the traditional analysis of dummy *of* as a *genitive*-case particle, since what has always remained a mystery under the genitive analysis is why *of* takes an objective complement (cf. *The windows were open and she fell out of them*). The analysis of dummy *of* as a prepositional AgrO constituent (or a transitive preposition merged with an AgrO constituent) can be extended to adjectival structures such as *fond of him* and nominal structures such as *loss of income* in ways which we shall not explore here.

In more general terms, what our discussion here illustrates is that a uniform *spec–head agreement* theory of case-checking (under which all case-marked DPs check their case by raising to the specifier position within a higher agreement phrase) can only be bought at the price of considerable abstraction – e.g. positing split cp/CP and pp/PP projections, positing a different type of AgrP projection for each different type of DP (e.g. for subjects, direct objects and indirect objects), positing syntactically distinct cases which are not morphologically distinct in English (e.g. dative and objective) – and so on. If we reject the level of abstraction involved and return to the more traditional position that the case of some constituents (e.g. subjects) is checked via spec–head agreement whereas the case of others (e.g. objects of prepositions) is checked via attraction, the price we pay is that we end up with a nonunitary theory of case-checking. The alternatives are clear – though for the moment we don't have sufficient empirical evidence to make a principled choice between them: this will have to await the outcome of future research.

10.9   Passives and unaccusatives reconsidered

Our assumption that DP objects raise to the specifier position within an appropriate AgrP projection raises interesting questions about the syntax of active–passive sentence pairs such as:

(82) (a)   The president signed the agreements
     (b)   The agreements were signed by the president

In the active sentence (82a), the DP *the agreements* is the complement of the verb *signed*, and raises to spec-AgrOP in order to check its objective case (cf. *The president signed **them***). But in (82b) the same DP raises to spec-AgrSP in order to check its nominative case (cf. ***They** were signed by the president*). A question we might ask is whether the DP *the agreements* in the passive sentence (82b) moves through spec-AgrOP before moving into spec-AgrSP, or whether (on the contrary) passive sentences contain no AgrOP projection at all.

An interesting argument that passivized complements move through spec-AgrOP on their way to spec-AgrSP is provided by Kayne (1989); he notes that passive participles in French agree with their superficial subjects, e.g. in sentences such as the following (FS = feminine singular):

(83)   **La décision**   a   été   *prise*   par   le   sénat
              The decision-FS has been taken-FS by   the senate

If we suppose that the DP *la décision* moves to spec-AgrOP before moving into spec-AgrSP, (83) will involve an intermediate stage of derivation at which *la décision* has moved into spec-AgrOP and the participle *prise* has adjoined to AgrO, as in (84) below (we ignore *par le sénat* 'by the senate' here):

(84)

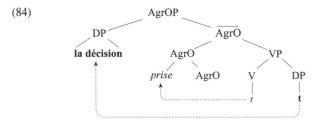

Since the DP *la décision* and the passive participle *prise* will then be in a spec–head agreement relation, we can account for the fact that the two agree in number and gender (as a reflex of spec–head agreement).

Interestingly, we find a similar pattern of agreement with perfective participles of unaccusative (though not transitive or unergative) verbs in French, as can be seen from the example below (FP = feminine plural):

(85)   **Les écolières**   sont *parties*   en Belgique
         the schoolgirls-FP are departed-FP in Belgium
         'The schoolgirls have gone off to Belgium'

In this connection, it is instructive to recall the observation by Luigi Burzio (1986) that unaccusative subjects seem to share many properties in common with objects. One way of accounting for this would be to suppose that (at an intermediate stage of derivation) unaccusative subjects raise to spec-AgrOP, so that the derivation of (85) would involve the intermediate stage represented in (86) below (if we suppose that THEME arguments are canonically projected as complements, and hence the subject of the sentence originates as the complement of the unaccusative verb):

(86)

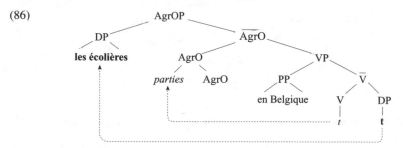

We could then say that the agreement between the DP *les écolières* 'the schoolgirls' and the unaccusative participle *parties* 'departed' is a reflex of a spec–head agreement relation within AgrOP. If we were to extend this analysis to unaccusative verbs in English, we could further say that in sentences such as:

(87)   From inside the pub were coming *hoots of derision*

the italicized nominal is in spec-AgrOP.

The possibility that unaccusative subjects may raise to spec-AgrOP offers us an interesting account of the syntax of unaccusative imperative structures such as (88) below in dialect A of Belfast English:

(88)   Go you to school!

In our treatment of such structures in §9.9, we hypothesized that *you* originates as the specifier of a VP headed by *go*, and *to school* as its complement, and that *you* remains *in situ* in spec-VP, while the verb *go* raises to adjoin to v. However, this assumption is at variance with the analysis of structures like (31) adopted in this chapter, under which internal D(P) arguments are canonically projected as complements, and PP arguments as specifiers. An analysis of unaccusative imperatives like (88) more in keeping with the assumptions made in this chapter would be the following. The verb *go* merges with its pronoun complement *you* to form the V-bar *go you*; the resulting V-bar then merges with its PP specifier *to school* to form the VP (89) below:

(89)

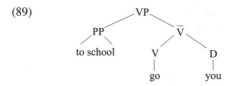

VP then merges with an AgrO constituent; the verb *go* adjoins to AgrO and the complement *you* raises to spec-AgrOP, as in (90) below:

(90)

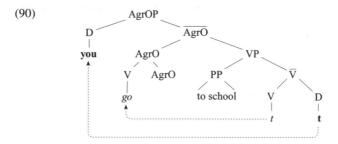

AgrOP then merges with an abstract light verb, to which the verb *go* adjoins, as in (91) below:

(91)

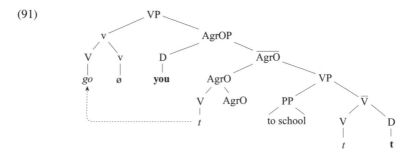

If we assume that the subject and verb subsequently remain in the positions they occupy in (91), we can account for the fact that the verb precedes the subject in unaccusative imperatives (though the converse word order holds e.g. in transitive imperatives, since transitive subjects originate in spec-vp). An analysis such as (91) in effect incorporates Burzio's intuition that unaccusative subjects are like complements in respect of their syntax. Of course, questions of detail remain to be worked out – e.g. 'What case does the subject *you* carry, and how is it checked?' If *you* carries partitive case, it may well be that this is checked via a spec–head relation between the verb *come* in AgrO and the pronoun *you* in spec-AgrOP.

In much the same way as we might argue that postverbal unaccusative subjects are in spec-AgrOP, so too we might argue that the italicized postverbal subject in a passive structure such as (92) below

(92)   Below are listed *the names of students who failed syntax*

(in which the italicized argument follows the passive participle *listed*) is a further instance of a complement DP raising to spec-AgrOP and then remaining there (with the verb raising above it to adjoin to v). As should be self-evident, numerous questions are left unanswered by such an analysis (e.g. what case does the italicized postverbal nominal carry and how is it checked; and how do we account for agreement between the postverbal nominal and the plural auxiliary *are/were*?).

If passivized arguments raise to spec-AgrOP in French structures like (83–4) and in English sentences such as (92), the most general conclusion we can arrive at is that passivized arguments raise through spec-AgrOP on their way to spec-AgrSP. However, if we assume that all movement is motivated by **greed**, this raises the question of why passivized objects should move into spec-AgrOP in English. An interesting answer is suggested by French passives such as (83–4), where the passive participle adjoins to AgrO and the object moves to spec-AgrOP in order to check that the passive participle agrees with its object. Just as a French passive participle like *prise* 'taken' carries an object agreement suffix (marked by the final +*e* in the spelling), so too we might suppose that the suffix +*n* (and its variants +*d*/+*t*) carried by passive participles like *seen/heard/sent* etc. in English is also an object-agreement inflection (one which has variable agreement properties, and hence can agree with an object carrying any set of person/number/gender-features – in much the same way as an auxiliary like *can* has variable subject agreement properties). It would then follow that the object agreement properties of passive participles can only be checked if the passive participle adjoins to AgrO and its complement moves into spec-AgrOP. This in turn correctly predicts that only transitive verbs can passivize, since only if a verb has an object which can move into spec-AgrOP can the object agreement properties of the passive participle be checked.

If our reasoning here is along the right lines, it follows that verbs raise to AgrO and their objects to spec-AgrOP either to check agreement or to check case. Active transitive verbs and their objects in English raise to appropriate positions within AgrOP in order to check the case of the object (but do not check agreement, since active verbs carry no object agreement inflections in English); passive verbs and their objects raise to appropriate positions within AgrOP in order to check the agreement properties of the passive participle, but do not check the case of the object (with the result that the passivized DP has to raise to spec-AgrSP in order to check nominative case). In other words, active transitive verbs in English check the case properties (but not the agreement properties) of their DP complements, whereas passive participles check the agreement properties (but not the case properties) of their DP complements. It would seem that (for languages like English), the following generalization (relating to the case and agreement properties of verbs and their objects) holds:

(93)   A verb doesn't case-check an object DP it agrees with, and doesn't agree
         with an object DP which it case-checks.

While I shall not be concerned here with the question of the extent to which (93) holds cross-linguistically, it is interesting to note that data from Ukrainian (reported in Sobin 1985) seem to lend some support to (93). Ukrainian has two passive constructions: in one, the passivized argument carries nominative case, and the passive verb form agrees with it in gender and number (i.e. the verb is agreeing with, but not case-checking, its object): in the other (so-called 'impersonal passive') structure, the passivized argument carries objective case, but the passive verb form does not agree with it (i.e. the verb is case-checking, but not agreeing with, its object).

Consider what all of this means for the derivation of a passive sentence such as:

(94)   The jewels have been stolen

The DP *the jewels* originates as the complement of a VP headed by *stolen*, as in (95) below:

(95)
```
            VP
          /    \
        V        DP
        |       /   \
      stolen   the jewels
```

The VP in (95) is then merged with AgrO; the passive participle *stolen* adjoins to AgrO and the DP *the jewels* raises to spec-AgrOP as in (96) below:

(96)

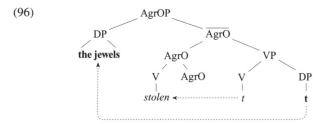

At this point, the participle *stolen* is checked for agreement with its specifier *the jewels*: since *stolen* has variable agreement properties (i.e. it can agree with any object DP), this requirement is satisfied in (96). However, the case properties of *the jewels* are not checked at this point, given the generalization (93). Subsequently, the passive participle *stolen* raises up to adjoin to the strong light verb heading vp as in (97) below:

(97)

The DP *the jewels* is then raised up in a successive cyclic fashion to become first the subject of vp, then the subject of the PROGP headed by *been*, then the subject of TP and then the subject of the AgrSP headed by *have* (checking its nominative case in spec-AgrSP). If such an analysis of passives can be maintained, it follows that the 'object' of both an active and a passive verb will raise to spec-AgrOP, in active sentences for case-checking purposes, and in passive sentences for agreement-checking purposes. Needless to say, numerous details of the syntax of passive sentences remain to be worked out (particularly the syntax of *by*-phrase agents and the syntax of the implicit agent arguments in *by*-less passives), but the motivation for assuming that passivized objects move to spec-AgrOP at an intermediate stage of derivation should be clear.

10.10 Summary

In this chapter, we have argued that clauses contain three different types of agreement phrase. We began by outlining the *split-INFL hypothesis* in §10.2, arguing that we need to posit the existence of a subject agreement phrase (AgrSP) in addition to a tense phrase (TP) in order to account for the fact that adverbs like *probably* and floating quantifiers like *all* can be positioned either before or after a finite auxiliary. We noted that the *split-INFL* analysis would also enable us to account for the fact that an adverb positioned after an auxiliary can have scope over the auxiliary, e.g. in a sentence such as *Gary can apparently lift 100 pounds*. In §10.3 we saw that the split-INFL analysis would provide a straightforward account of *scrambling* in Early Modern English, and would enable us to say that in sentences like *The king your mote did see*, the DP *your mote* has adjoined to TP, while the subject *the king* is in spec-AgrSP. In addition, we noted Alison Henry's arguments that the split-INFL analysis enables us to provide an insightful description of the syntax of the case and agreement properties of subjects and auxiliaries in Belfast English, under which nominative subjects are in spec-AgrSP, and any auxiliary which checks the agreement properties of the subject is in AgrS (and so can move to C in questions), whereas objective subjects are in spec-TP

459

and any associated auxiliary is in T, and (by virtue of lacking agreement properties) can't move through AgrS to C in questions.

In §10.4 we outlined the *split-VP hypothesis*, under which clauses headed by transitive verbs contain an object agreement phrase (AgrOP) positioned between vp and VP: we argued that a direct object DP raises to spec-AgrOP and its associated verb adjoins to AgrO in order to check objective case (the verb subsequently raising still further to adjoin to v). We noted that such an analysis would provide a principled account of why object DPs occupy a different position from object CPs (e.g. in sentences such as *He reported to the police that there had been a robbery* and *He reported the robbery to the police*), why DP objects are positioned in front of VP adverbs (e.g. in sentences such as *He plays chess well*), and why prepositional particles can occupy three different positions in sentences such as *He poured the whisky slowly out/He poured the whisky out slowly/He poured out the whisky slowly*. In §10.5 we argued that the *split-VP hypothesis* provides an interesting account of a range of aspects of the syntax of ECM structures, including the position of the adverb *conclusively* in sentences such as *The DA proved the witness **conclusively** to have lied*, the position of the quantifier *all* in sentences like *The DA proved the defendants **all** to be lying*, and the position of the particle *out* in sentences such as *The DA made the defendants **out** to be lying*.

In §10.6 we argued that indirect object DPs carry dative case, and check their case by raising to the specifier position within an indirect object agreement projection (AgrIOP) which is positioned immediately above AgrOP (with the verb raising to adjoin first to AgrO, then to AgrIO and finally to v). We saw that such an analysis would allow us to claim that in sentences such as *The crew handed the passengers back their passports*, the particle *back* has been stranded in AgrIO. More generally, we concluded that an analysis in which a nominative DP checks its case by raising to spec-AgrS, an objective DP by raising to spec-AgrOP, and a dative DP by raising to spec-AgrIOP would enable us to maintain the position that case-checking in English canonically involves a spec–head relation between a functional (agreement) head and its specifier. In §10.7 we briefly looked at how such an analysis might be extended to handle DPs which carry the genitive case-suffix *'s*; and in §10.8 we suggested a split-CP analysis of *for*-infinitive structures, and a split-PP analysis of transitive prepositional phrases.

Finally, in §10.9 we went on to consider whether passivized direct object DPs move through spec-AgrOP on their way to spec-AgrSP. We saw that there was some evidence in support of this suggestion from the fact that passive participles agree with their (underlying) objects in French. And we noted that if the passive participle suffix +*n* is taken to be an agreement marker in English, we could claim that in passive sentences such as *The jewels have been stolen* the passivized object DP *the jewels* moves into spec-AgrOP at an intermediate stage of derivation (to check agreement with the passive participle *stolen*), before moving on to check its nominative case-feature in spec-AgrSP. We also suggested that unaccusative subjects might also move into spec-AgrOP at an intermediate stage of derivation.

It need scarcely be pointed out that the analyses we have presented in this chapter are not fully worked out (and doubtless flawed) in a number of respects. The reason is simple: the ideas explored in this chapter (inspired by Chomsky's *minimalist program* in the 1990s) are part of an ongoing research programme which is leading different researchers in different directions. Many important questions of detail and principle remain unresolved for the present. For example, there is disagreement on whether *all* objective DPs (or *some*, or *none*) in English check their case by raising overtly to spec-AgrOP. Koizumi (1995) maintains that all objective DPs check their case in this way (though does not discuss CPs or PPs with a transitive head): Bošković (1995) maintains that while it is plausible to analyse objective subjects in ECM structures as raising to spec-AgrOP in English, it is not plausible to extend the raising-to-spec-AgrOP analysis to other direct (or indirect) object DPs. Bobaljik (1995) goes even further and rejects the claim that any objective DPs raise to spec-AgrOP in English, preferring to maintain that objective case-checking canonically involves a head–complement relation (much as we assumed in chapter 5). It might seem ironic that linguists can't agree about the syntax of agreement; but it should be emphasized that work in this domain is only in its infancy, and the first step in understanding any problem is to identify the nature of the problem, to outline possible solutions, and to be aware of the hidden costs associated with such solutions.

While it is true that there are a wide range of alternative analyses of particular structures (e.g. passives or double-object constructions) found in the contemporary linguistic literature, it is equally true that a considerable amount of the relevant research work presupposes some variant of the richly articulated AgrSP/TP/vp/AgrIOP/AgrOP/VP clause structure that we have argued for in this chapter – and in particular, assumes the existence of subject agreement and object agreement projections (and perhaps also indirect object agreement projections); and indeed, some work goes still further and posits the existence of **aspect phrase**, **voice phrase** and **modal phrase** projections as well (cf. e.g. Ouhalla 1991 and Cinque 1995). Moreover, even work which questions the empirical and theoretical motivation for positing agreement projections (e.g. Bobaljik 1995 and Chomsky 1995b) presupposes familiarity with work on the syntax of AgrP constituents. So, for both AgrOphiles and AgrOphobes alike, the syntax of agreement remains at the very heart of contemporary debates about the nature of syntactic structure.

Workbook section

(Note that some of the exercises below are rather more challenging than those in previous chapters, and invite you to consider alternatives to the analyses suggested in the main text.)

Exercise I (§10.2)

Discuss the syntax of the adverbs and floating quantifiers in the following sentences, saying which of the sentences pose problems for the analysis proposed in the text (and why), and suggesting alternative analyses.

1a   They have all apparently given up smoking
 b   They all apparently have given up smoking
2a   They apparently have all given up smoking
 b   They all have apparently given up smoking
3a   They will probably subsequently all give up smoking
 b   They will probably all subsequently give up smoking
4a   They have definitely all completely given up smoking
 b   *They have definitely completely all given up smoking
5a   They were probably not all paying attention
 b   They were probably all not paying attention

Model answer for 1a

The adverb *apparently* seems to be a TP adverb, in that it can not only follow a finite auxiliary like *have* as in 1a, but also precede it as in 1b. Moreover, *apparently* precedes a vp adverb like *completely*: cf.

(i)   They have apparently completely given up smoking

If we assume that *apparently* is a TP adverb, and that adverbs adjoin to maximal projections, *apparently* will originate as an adjunct to the TP in which *have* originates, as shown informally in (ii) below (where **SP** = AgrSP and **S** = AgrS):

(ii)   [$_{SP}$ *They* [$_S$ **have**] [$_{TP}$ apparently [$_{TP}$ *t* [$_T$ **t**] [$_{vp}$ *t* given up smoking]]]]

On this view, *have* would originate in T and adjoin to AgrS, and *they* would originate in spec-vp and move through spec-TP into spec-AgrSP; *apparently* would adjoin to TP to form a split-segment TP category.

The problem with the analysis in (ii), however, is that it provides no account of the position of the floating quantifier *all* in 1a. If floating quantifiers are stranded internally within subject QPs, we'd expect the quantifier *all* to be stranded within the QP subject of TP, to the right of the TP adjunct *apparently* – as in:

(iii)   They have apparently all given up smoking

Of course, (iii) is perfectly grammatical – but so is 1a, and the crucial point is that analysis (ii) provides no way of accounting for the grammaticality of 1a.

In order to account for the grammaticality of 1a, we need to modify one (or more) of the assumptions implicit in analysis (ii). These assumptions are spelled out in (iv) below:

(iv) (a) Finite auxiliaries originate in T and optionally adjoin to AgrS.

(b) Adverbs are adjuncts to maximal projections like TP, vp, VP, etc.

(c) Floating quantifiers are stranded by movement out of subject QPs.

(d) Each head licenses only one specifier.

One way of handling 1a is to reject assumption (iv)(a), while retaining the other assumptions in (iv). We might suppose, for example, that the perfective auxiliary *have* originates as the head **Aux**(iliary) constituent of an **AuxP** (= auxiliary phrase) projection which is positioned between TP and VP (with *have* raising to adjoin first to T and then to AgrS), and that *apparently* is an adjunct to AuxP, as shown informally in the partial structure (v) below:

(v) $[_{SP}$ *They* $[_S$ **have**$]$ $[_{TP}$ $[_{QP}$ all $t]$ $[_T$ t$]$ $[_{AuxP}$ apparently $[_{AuxP}$ t $[_{Aux}$ t$]$ $[_{vp}$ $\cdots$ $]]]]]$

This would mean that the QP *all they* originates in spec-vp, and then raises through spec-AuxP into spec-TP; subsequently, the pronoun *they* raises to spec-AgrSP, stranding the quantifier *all* inside a QP in spec-TP; the adverb *apparently* is an adjunct to AuxP. Such an analysis would correctly predict that a further adverb can be adjoined to TP, as in (vi) below·

(vi) They have *now* all apparently given up smoking

The core assumption underlying the analysis is that there are *three* different (auxiliary-like) functional projections between CP and vp, so that INFL would be split up into *three* distinct heads.

We reach a similar conclusion if we reject assumption (iv)(b) in favour of the suggestion in Cinque (1995) that adverbs are not adjuncts, but rather are *specifiers* – and that each different type of adverb serves as the specifier of a different kind of head. If (as Cinque assumes) QPs containing floating quantifiers are also specifiers, we might arrive at an analysis of 1a along the lines of (vii) below:

(vii) $[_{SP}$ *They* $[_S$ **have**$]$ $[_{TP}$ $[_{QP}$ all $t]$ $[_T$ t$]$ $[_{AuxP}$ apparently $[_{Aux}$ t$]$ $[_{vp}$ $\cdots$ $]]]]$

A variant of Cinque's analysis would be to reject assumption (iv)(d) and assume instead that DP/QP subjects and adverbs are different kinds of specifier, and that a given head may license more than one kind of specifier (as argued by Koizumi 1995 and Chomsky 1995b). We could then suggest that the QP containing the floating quantifier *all* and the adverb *apparently* are two different specifiers for T in 1a, with *have* originating in T and then adjoining to AgrS, as in (viii) below:

(viii) $[_{SP}$ *They* $[_S$ **have**$]$ $[_{TP}$ $[_{QP}$ all $t]$ $[_{\bar{T}}$ apparently $[_{\bar{T}}$ $[_T$ t$]$ $[_{vp}$ $\cdots$ $]]]]]$

Following the system of category labels adopted by Chomsky (1995b, p. 356), we might suppose that *apparently* is a specifier for T-bar (expanding T-bar into an extended T-bar), and that the QP containing *all* is a specifier for TP (expanding T-bar into TP). An analysis along the lines of (viii) would enable us to avoid splitting INFL into three different heads, since we would no longer need to posit an AuxP projection in sentences like 1a. Of course, it might be argued that the analysis in (viii) amounts to returning to our assumption in earlier chapters that adverbial adjuncts can adjoin to intermediate projections (especially if we follow Kayne 1994 in maintaining that specifiers are adjuncts).

Yet a further possibility would be to abandon Sportiche's assumption (iv)(c) that floating quantifiers are stranded via movement of D(P)s out of subject positions, and instead to assume (as in Bowers 1993 and Baltin 1995) that floating quantifiers are directly generated as adjuncts (rather like adverbs). After all, given that we saw in §7.4 that subjects are islands (i.e. no constituent can generally be extracted out of a subject), it might seem implausible to suppose that a pronoun like *they* can 'escape' out of a subject QP, in violation of the **condition on extraction domains**. More specifically, if (like Bowers) we suppose that floating quantifiers are merged with maximal clausal projections, both *all* and *apparently* in 1a would be adjuncts merged with TP, and hence (if we make the traditional assumption that multiple adjuncts of the same kind can be freely ordered with respect to each other) we should expect both structures in (ix)(a–b) to be possible (where **t** is the trace of **have** and *t* is the trace of *they*):

(ix) (a) $[_{SP}$ *They* $[_S$ **have**$]$ $[_{TP}$ all $[_{TP}$ apparently $[_{TP}$ *t* $[_T$ **t**$]$ $[_{vp}$ $\cdots$ $]]]]]$

   (b) $[_{SP}$ *They* $[_S$ **have**$]$ $[_{TP}$ apparently $[_{TP}$ all $[_{TP}$ *t* $[_T$ **t**$]$ $[_{vp}$ $\cdots$ $]]]]]$

Of course, if (like Baltin) we assume that floating quantifiers can merge with intermediate projections, additional possibilities arise. But I'll leave you to ponder over these (and the problems posed by the other examples in the exercise) for yourself.

Exercise II (§10.4)

Discuss the derivation of the following sentences, saying which sentences prove problematic for the analysis proposed in the text (and why), and considering alternative possibilities:

  1a He explained the problem carefully to her
   b He carefully explained the problem to her
   c He explained the problem to her carefully
   d *He explained carefully the problem to her
  2a He explained carefully to her that he had a problem
   b He explained to her carefully that he had a problem

   c   He carefully explained to her that he had a problem

   d   *He explained to her that he had a problem carefully

3a   She found out the truth later

   b   She found the truth out later

   c   She later found out the truth

   d   *She found the truth later out

4a   She found out later that he was married

   b   *She found that he was married out later

   c   She later found out that he was married

   d   *She found later out that he was married

5a   It turned out later that the witness had lied

   b   It later turned out that the witness had lied

   c   *It turned later that the witness had lied out

   d   *It turned later out that the witness had lied

6a   He put his hands up slowly

   b   He put his hands slowly up

   c   He put up his hands slowly

   d   He slowly put his hands up

7a   The CIA handed the tapes over secretly to the FBI

   b   The CIA handed over the tapes secretly to the FBI

   c   The CIA secretly handed the tapes over to the FBI

   d   *The CIA secretly handed the tapes to the FBI over

Model answer for 1

Given the assumptions made in the text, the DP *the problem* in 1a will originate as the complement (and the PP *to her* as the specifier) of the VP headed by *explained*, and the adverb *carefully* as a VP adjunct: cf.

(i)

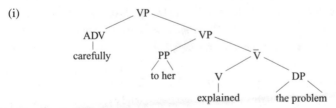

The VP in (i) will merge with an AgrO constituent; the verb *explained* will adjoin to AgrO, and the DP *the problem* will raise to spec-AgrOP (to check its objective case-feature), as in (ii) below:

(ii)

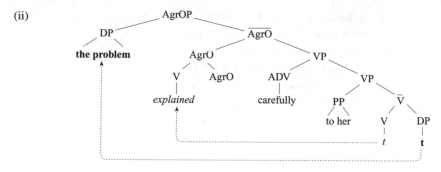

AgrOP then merges with a performative light verb ø whose subject is *he*, and the verb *explained* adjoins to the light verb as in (iii) below:

(iii)

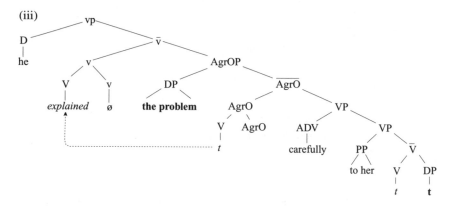

(Alternatively, we might assume that AgrO is pied-piped along with the moved verb *explained*.) The subject *he* subsequently raises through spec-TP to spec-AgrSP to check its nominative case, so deriving 1a *He explained the problem carefully to her*.

It seems likely that the derivation of 1b *He carefully explained the problem to her* is similar in most respects, save that the adverb *carefully* is an adjunct to vp rather than VP.

More problematic is the derivation of 1c *He explained the problem to her carefully*. Given what we have said so far in this model answer, we should expect *carefully* to end up either to the immediate left of *to her* as in 1a, or to the immediate left of *explained* as in 1b. How come it ends up at the end of the overall clause? One (traditional) possibility would be to suppose that (at least some) adjuncts can be positioned either to the left or to the right of the constituent they merge with. Reasoning along these lines, we might suppose that the VP headed by *explained* could either have the adverb *carefully* positioned *initially* (as the first constituent of the VP) as in (i) above, or *finally* (as the last constituent of VP) as in (iv) below:

(iv)

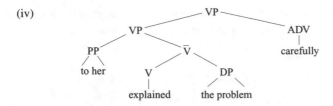

The remaining stages of derivation would then be as outlined above for sentence 1a, and the result would be a structure in which *carefully* occupies the final position in the sentence, precisely as we find in 1c *He explained the problem to her carefully*.

One potential problem posed by the analysis in (iv) is that it allows for the possibility that an adverb can be positioned either before or after the constituent it modifies. However, English is a language in which modifiers generally precede the expressions they modify (e.g. the modifying adjective *safe* precedes the noun *syntax* in an expression such as *safe syntax*), so we might want to exclude any possibility of generating the modifying adverb *carefully* in a position where it follows the VP it modifies in (iv). In other words, all things being equal, we would prefer a derivation in which the adverb *carefully* is generated in a position where it precedes the VP it modifies.

One way of attaining this goal would be to propose an even more complex model of clause structure in which each separate argument of a verb is contained within a separate projection, and in which each projection can be modified by an appropriate kind of adverb. Given this possibility, we could derive 1c as follows. The verb *explained* merges with its DP complement *the problem* to form a VP to which the adverb *carefully* adjoins, as in (v) below:

(v)

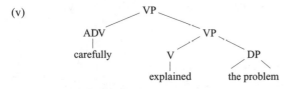

(Note that *carefully* is positioned to the left of the VP *explained the problem* which it modifies.) The resulting VP merges with a VP headed by a light verb ø whose specifier is the PP *to her*, and the verb *explained* adjoins to this light verb as in (vi) below:

(vi)

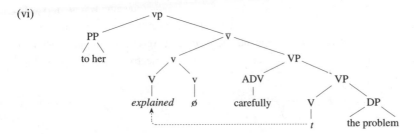

467

The vp in (vi) then merges with an AgrO constituent; the verb *explained* adjoins to AgrO, and the DP *the problem* moves to spec-AgrOP as in (vii) below:

(vii)

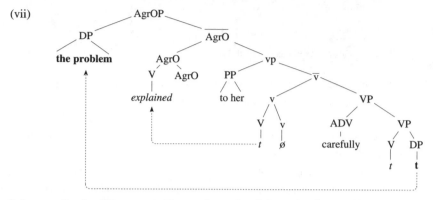

Subsequently, AgrOP merges with a performative light verb whose subject is *he*, and the verb *explained* raises to adjoin to the light verb as in (viii) below:

(viii)

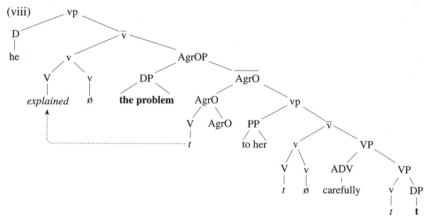

The subject *he* then raises through spec-TP into spec-AgrSP to check its nominative case, so deriving 1c *He explained the problem to her carefully*.

The ungrammaticality of 1d **He explained carefully the problem to her* can be accounted for rather more straightforwardly. As we can see from (viii) above, the only way of deriving this sentence would be by merging the adverbial adjunct *carefully* with AgrOP; but given the constraint noted in the text that adverbs can only modify projections which have clear semantic content, and given that AgrO is a morpheme with no intrinsic semantic content (its sole function is to check objective case), this possibility is ruled out.

Exercise III (§10.5)

Discuss the syntax of the following complement-clause structures (example 4a is from Bowers 1993, p. 632):

1a   She wanted desperately for them to start a family
 b   *She wanted for them desperately to start a family
 c   She wanted them desperately to start a family
2a   The DA made the witnesses out convincingly to have lied
 b   The DA made them out all to have lied
 c   *The DA made that the witnesses had lied out
3a   He gave the press to understand that he would make a statement
 b   The secret police made the prisoners forcibly sign confessions
 c   I wouldn't let him ever drive my car
4a   We proved Smith conclusively to the authorities to be the thief
 b   We proved conclusively to the authorities that Smith was the thief
 c   *We proved conclusively that Smith was the thief to the authorities

(Note that in 1, the adverb *desperately* is intended to be construed as modifying a projection of *wanted*, and in 3c *ever* is intended to be construed as modifying a projection of *let*.)

Model answer for 1

The derivation of 1a seems relatively straightforward: it involves projecting *want* into the VP (i) below:

(i)

and then raising *want* to adjoin to a superordinate light verb as in (ii) below:

(ii)

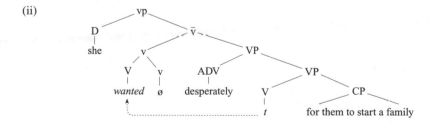

Raising the subject *she* through spec-TP into spec-AgrSP to check its nominative case will derive 1a *She wanted desperately for them to start a family.* (We shall not be concerned here with the internal syntax of the CP *for them to start a family*; for one suggestion, see the discussion of *for*-infinitives in §10.8.) Since the adverb *desperately* is an adjunct to the VP originally headed by *wanted*, it follows that it cannot be positioned internally within CP – hence the ungrammaticality of 1b **She wanted for them desperately to start a family.*

More interesting is the sentence in 1c. For almost three decades (in work dating from Bresnan 1972 to Bošković 1995) it has been argued that objective-subject infinitive complements of *want*-class verbs are CPs headed by a null complementizer, while those of *believe*-class verbs are simple IPs. However, the CP analysis provides no account of the fact that *desperately* can be positioned between *them* and *to* in 1c, since this is not possible in the clearcut CP structure 1a. Hence, it would seem more plausible to treat the infinitive complement of *wanted* in 1c as an IP. We could then say that *wanted* originates as the head V of the VP in (iii) below:

(iii)

The transitive verb *wanted* subsequently adjoins to AgrO and the pronoun *them* moves to spec-AgrOP to check its objective case, as in (iv) below:

(iv)

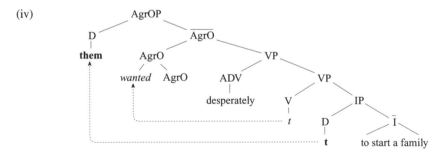

The verb *wanted* then raises to adjoin to the strong light verb ø occupying the head v position of vp as in (v) below:

(v)

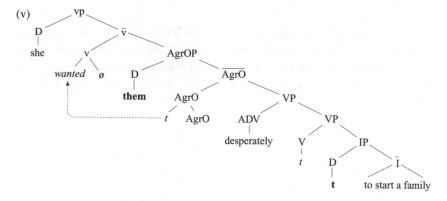

Finally, *she* raises through spec-TP into spec-AgrSP for case-checking.

Exercise IV (§10.6)

Discuss the syntax of the following sentences, saying which sentences prove problematic to derive, and why:

1a The FBI handed the CIA the tapes
 b *The FBI handed the tapes the CIA
 c The FBI handed the tapes to the CIA
2a The FBI handed the CIA the tapes secretly
 b *The FBI handed the CIA secretly the tapes
 c *The FBI handed secretly the CIA the tapes
3a The FBI handed the CIA the tapes back
 b The FBI handed the CIA back the tapes
 c The FBI handed back the CIA the tapes
4a The FBI handed the tapes over to the CIA
 b The FBI handed over the tapes to the CIA
 c *The FBI handed the tapes to the CIA over
5a *The FBI handed the CIA the tapes over
 b *The FBI handed the CIA over the tapes
 c *The FBI handed over the CIA the tapes
6a Which tapes did the FBI hand the CIA?
 b Which agency did the FBI hand the tapes to?
 c *Which agency did the FBI hand the tapes?

Model answer for 1

Given the assumption in the text that THEME arguments are canonically projected as complements, the DP *the tapes* in 1a will originate as the THEME complement of *handed*; and given the assumption that RECIPIENT arguments are canonically projected as specifiers, the DP *the CIA* will originate as the specifier of *handed*, as in (i) below:

(i)
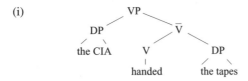

The VP in (i) will then merge with an AgrO constituent, the V *handed* will adjoin to AgrO and the DP *the tapes* will raise to spec-AgrOP to check its objective case, as in (ii) below:

(ii)
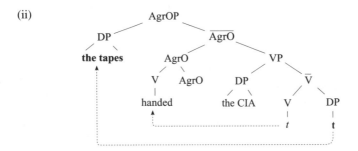

AgrOP merges with an AgrIO constituent, the V *handed* adjoins to AgrIO and the DP *the CIA* raises to spec-AgrIOP in order to check its dative case, as in (iii) below:

(iii)
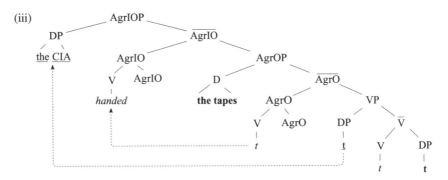

AgrIOP then merges with an agentive light verb (whose AGENT subject is *the FBI*), and the V *handed* adjoins to the performative verb, as in (iv) below:

472

(iv)

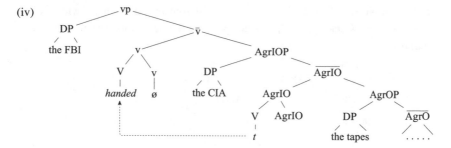

Subsequently, the DP *the FBI* raises through spec-TP into spec-AgrSP to check its nominative case, so deriving the structure associated with sentence 1a *The FBI handed the CIA the tapes*.

Consider now why the corresponding sentence 1b **The FBI handed the tapes the CIA* is ungrammatical. Here, the objective THEME argument *the tapes* is positioned in front of the dative RECIPIENT argument *the CIA*. There are a number of suggestions we can make about why the derivation of 1b crashes. One might be that case is misassigned, with the RECIPIENT DP *the CIA* being wrongly assigned objective case (so raising to spec-AgrOP), and the THEME DP *the tapes* being wrongly assigned dative case (so raising to spec-AgrIOP, and ending up in front of *the CIA*): however, this possibility would be ruled out if we assume that UG principles specify that objective is the case canonically associated with THEME arguments, and dative with RECIPIENT arguments. An alternative possibility is that case is correctly assigned, but AgrOP is generated above AgrIOP (so that the objective DP *the tapes* raises to a higher position than the dative DP *the CIA*). After all, nothing in what we have said in the text guarantees that AgrIOP will be generated above AgrOP: we have simply *stipulated* this in our description thus far. And indeed, ordering AgrOP above AgrIOP might be appropriate for those (%) varieties of English in which direct objects can precede indirect objects, e.g. in sentences such as:

(v)   %Give *it* **me**!

We might derive sentence 1c *The FBI handed the tapes to the CIA* as follows. If we assume (as in the text) that THEME arguments are canonically projected as complements and RECIPIENT arguments as specifiers, the THEME DP *the tapes* will originate as the complement of *handed*, and the RECIPIENT PP *to the CIA* as the specifier of *handed*, as in (vi) below:

(vi)

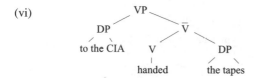

The VP in (vi) will then merge with an AgrO constituent, the V *handed* will adjoin to AgrO and the DP *the tapes* will raise to spec-AgrOP to check its objective case, as in (vii) below:

(vii)

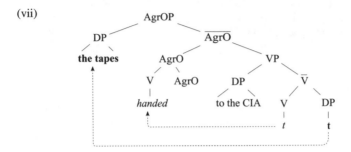

AgrOP then merges with an agentive light verb whose AGENT subject is *the FBI*; the verb *hand* adjoins to the light verb as in (viii) below:

(viii)

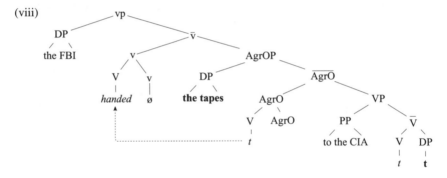

Subsequently, the DP *the FBI* raises through spec-TP into spec-AgrSP to check its nominative case, so deriving the structure associated with sentence 1c *The FBI handed the tapes to the CIA*.

Exercise V (§10.8)

Discuss the derivation of the infinitive structures in the sentences below (the Belfast English examples in 1 are from Henry 1995, and the Jamaican Creole examples in 2 from Bailey 1966):

1a	I wanted Jimmy for to come with me (Belfast English)
b	*I wanted for Jimmy to come with me (Belfast English)
c	I want for to meet them (Belfast English)
2a	Mi miin se yu fi go (Jamaican Creole)
	Me mean say you for go
	'I mean that you should go'

b	Mi waan yu fi sel i (Jamaican Creole)
	Me want you for sell it
	'I want you to sell it'
c	Im waan fi haid dem (Jamaican Creole)
	Him want for hide them
	'He wants to hide them'
3a	We are expecting them not to deny the allegations
b	We are expecting them strenuously to deny the allegations
c	We are expecting them to both strenuously deny the allegations

Helpful hints

The Jamaican Creole word *se* (although cognate with the English verb *say*) is generally taken to have the status of a declarative complementizer (rather like English *that*). Pronouns in Jamaican Creole are not overtly inflected for case.

Model answer for 1a

One way of dealing with this type of structure would be to suppose that *for* is an intransitive complementizer in Belfast English (BE), and that only transitive complementizers project into a cp/CP structure. On this view, the complementizer *for* would merge with the infinitive complement *Jimmy to come with me* (whose derivation we shall not be concerned with here), so forming the CP (i) below (where we assume that *Jimmy* is a DP headed by a null determiner, and we use IP as a label of convenience for the infinitive clause *Jimmy to come with me*):

(i)

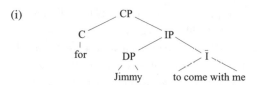

The CP in (i) would then merge with a V headed by the verb *wanted*, so forming the VP (ii) below:

(ii)

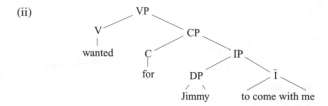

If we suppose that *want* (in this use) is a transitive verb, the VP in (ii) will merge with an AgrO constituent to which *wanted* adjoins, with the DP *Jimmy* raising to spec-AgrOP in order to check its objective case, as in (iii) below:

(iii)

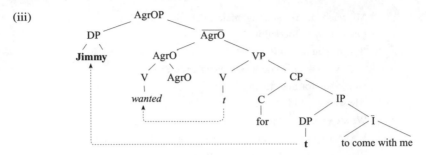

AgrOP then merges with an experiential light verb ø (whose subject is the EXPERIENCER argument *I*), and the verb *wanted* adjoins to the light verb as in (iv) below:

(iv)

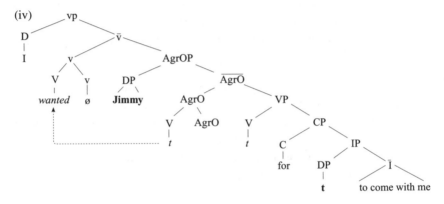

Subsequently, the subject *I* raises through spec-TP to spec-AgrSP to check its nominative case, so deriving the structure associated with sentence 1a *I wanted Jimmy for to come with me*. A crucial assumption underlying the derivation sketched out above is that complementizers like *for* project into the minimal structure needed to satisfy grammatical and lexical requirements: hence, since *for* is not transitive in this use, there is no need to project a cp/AgrOP structure on top of the CP headed by *for*.

Exercise VI (§10.9)

Discuss the derivation of the following passive sentences:

1a   The FBI were given the tapes back
 b   The FBI were given back the tapes
2a   The tapes were given back to the FBI
 b   *The tapes were given back the FBI

3a   The students were probably not all treated equally

 b   Were the students ever all treated equally?

4a   The FBI had their best agents all secretly sent to Ruritania

 b   The FBI had their agents all secretly sent a coded message

5a   The FBI had the tapes all sent back secretly to the CIA

 b   The FBI had the CIA agents all sent copies of the suicide manual

6a   The tapes were apparently later all sent back anonymously to the FBI

 b   The FBI was apparently later sent all the tapes back anonymously

7a   The witnesses were all subsequently made out to have lied

 b   The witnesses were subsequently all proved convincingly to have lied

Model answer for 1a

Let's assume that at some stage of derivation, *given back* is a complex verb which projects into the VP (i) below (in which the DP *the FBI* has the θ-role RECIPIENT, and the DP *the tapes* has the θ-role THEME):

(i)

The VP in (i) then merges with AgrO; the transitive V *given* raises to AgrO, and the DP *the tapes* raises to spec-AgrOP to check its objective case (cf. *The FBI were given **them** back*), as in (ii) below:

(ii)

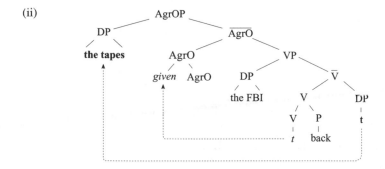

AgrOP in (ii) is then merged with AgrIO: the verb *given* adjoins to AgrIO and its indirect object *the FBI* raises to spec-AgrIOP, as in (iii) below:

(iii)

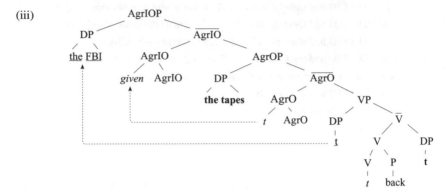

At this point, the (variable) agreement properties of the passive participle *given* are checked against those of its specifier *the FBI*; this in turn means that the case of *the FBI* cannot be checked (since verbs do not case-check object DPs with which they enter into an agreement-checking relation in English). Subsequently, the verb *given* adjoins to the head v of vp, as in (iv) below:

(iv)

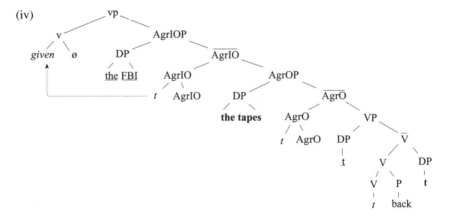

The indirect object DP then 'passivizes' – i.e. it moves in a successive cyclic fashion into spec-AgrSP, where it checks its nominative case. Whether or not it moves into spec-vp prior to moving into spec-TP and thence to spec-AgrSP is a matter for you to determine empirically – on the basis of the potential evidence provided by some of the example sentences in this exercise.

Exercise VII

As the examples below illustrate, there is evidence from verb + particle structures that weak object pronouns behave differently from other objective nominals – i.e. from contrastively stressed objective pronouns and from ordinary nominals like *Mary*, *the president*, etc. On the basis of the examples below, say which of the various analyses of weak pronouns proposed in the *model answer* provides the most adequate characterization of the syntax of weak object pronouns:

1a   He turned the lights off
  b   He turned them off
  c   He turned off the lights
  d   *He turned off them
2a   The DA made the defendants out to be lying
  b   The DA made out the defendants to be lying
  c   The DA made them out to be lying
  d   *The DA made out them to be lying
3a   They handed back the suspect his passport
  b   *They handed back the suspect it
  c   *They handed back him his passport
  d   *They handed back him it
4a   They handed the suspect back his passport
  b   *They handed the suspect back it
  c   They handed him back his passport
  d   *They handed him back it
5a   They handed the suspect his passport back
  b   *They handed the suspect it back
  c   They handed him his passport back
  d   They handed him it back

(Note that the adjective *weak* here is used to refer to the phonetic properties of pronouns, indicating lack of stress and possible reduction in the form of the pronoun e.g. from *them* to *'em*, and is not to be confused with the very different use of the word *weak* in checking theory.)

Model answer for 1b and 1d

The data in 1 would seem to suggest that there is a constraint against positioning a particle between a weak object pronoun and the verb with which it is associated: so, where the pronoun and verb are immediately adjacent, the resulting sentence is grammatical, as in 1b *He turned them off*; but where the pronoun and verb are separated by the particle, the sentence is ungrammatical, as in 1d **He turned off them*. But the question we have to ask is *why* the pronoun should have to be immediately adjacent to the verb.

One answer might be (as suggested by Postal 1974, p. 102) that weak object pronouns are phonetic clitics. We might interpret this as meaning that they must cliticize to an appropriate host in the PF component: if we suppose that verbs can host clitics but particles can't, and that the presence of an intervening constituent between a clitic and its host blocks cliticization, the behaviour of the pronouns in 1 can be accounted for. However, such an analysis begs two very important questions, namely 'Why are verbs so hospitable and particles so inhospitable?' and 'What is the precise nature of PF cliticization?'

One way of accounting for why weak pronouns attach to verbs rather than particles would be to correlate this with the fact that it is the verb which case-checks the pronoun, not the particle. Since pronouns attach to the verb which case-checks them, it would seem natural to suppose that attachment is an integral part of the case-checking process (and hence is a syntactic rather than a purely phonetic phenomenon). Bearing in mind that a head can check its features by adjoining to another (functional) head and that pronouns (by virtue of being D constituents) are heads, we might suggest that weak pronouns check their case by adjoining directly to the relevant agreement head. Such an analysis seems plausible for (say) weak subject pronouns in French like *je* 'I', *tu* 'you', *il* 'he', etc. which arguably adjoin directly to the same functional head as finite verbs in French (perhaps AgrS), and hence cannot be separated from their dependent verbs by intervening adverbs etc. We might therefore extend it to weak object pronouns in English, and argue that they check their case by adjoining directly to AgrO. (Of course, the verb which case-checks any such pronoun will also have to adjoin to AgrO.) This would mean that objective DPs and weak objective pronouns check their case in different ways: objective DPs by raising to spec-AgrOP, and weak objective pronouns by adjoining to AgrO.

Given this assumption, 1b might be derived as follows. The verb *turn* projects into a VP of the form:

(i)

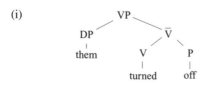

VP is then merged with AgrO; both the transitive verb *turned* and the objective pronoun *them* adjoin to AgrO, as in (ii) below:

(ii)

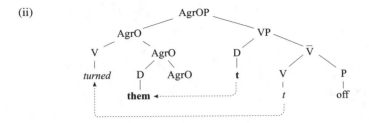

Since the verb *turned* and the objective pronoun *them* are both adjoined to AgrO at this point, their objective case properties can be checked (via a head–head relation).

Subsequently, the verb *turn* raises up to adjoin to the strong light verb ø which heads vp, as in (iii) below:

(iii)

(An alternative possibility is that the whole AgrO constituent is adjoined to ø, so that the pronoun is pied-piped along with the verb *turned* and adjoined to ø, perhaps because a weak pronoun cannot be separated from a verb which case-checks it.) Subsequently, *he* raises through spec-TP into spec-AgrSP, so deriving 1b *He turned them off*.

What remains to be accounted for is the ungrammaticality of 1d **He turned off them*. Here, we might conjecture that the particle *off* adjoins to the verb *turned* as in (iv) below:

(iv)

Both the pronoun *them* and the complex verb *turned off* then adjoin to AgrO, as in (v) below (where the righthand trace is the trace of the particle *off* which has incorporated into the verb):

481

(v)

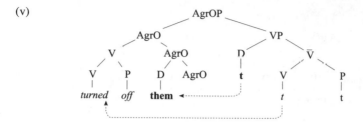

The verb *turned* then excorporates out of AgrO, adjoining to the strong light verb ø heading vp, as in (vi) below:

(vi)

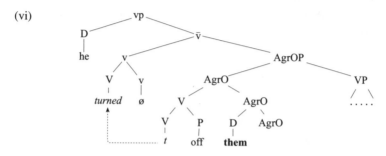

(Alternatively, it might be that the complex verb *turned off* or even the whole AgrO constituent *turned off them* is adjoined to ø.) The subject *he* then raises through spec-TP into spec-AgrSP, so deriving 1d **He turned off them*. However, the fact that the resulting sentence 1d is ungrammatical means that one or more steps in the derivation (iv/v/vi) must be impermissible. But which?

A likely candidate is step (v). We might rule out (v) by a constraint to the effect that a verb cannot be part of a head which has more than one other overt constituent adjoined to it: this would rule out (v) because AgrO contains not only the verb *turned* but also the particle *off* and the pronoun *them*. However, the *one-on-one* constraint seems arbitrary, and clearly has no explanatory force whatever; moreover, passives such as:

(vii) (a)   These regulations should be **done** *away with*

(b)   His unruly behaviour can't be **put** *up with* any longer

arguably involve incorporation of two (italicized) particles into a single (bold-printed) verb, and if so falsify the *one-on-one* constraint.

A variant of the constraint, however, would be to suppose that a verb cannot be part of a head which has *more than one different kind of head* adjoined to it: we could then say that what's wrong with (v) is that AgrO contains both a pronoun and a particle, and these are different kinds of head. Once again, however, such a constraint seems to lack explanatory force (why should things be that way?); and passives such as:

482

(viii) (a)   She was **taken** *advantage of*

    (b)   It must be **got** *rid of*

would seem to falsify it, if we make the traditional assumption that (for example) in (viii)(a) the noun *advantage* and the preposition *of* (which are clearly different kinds of head) are both adjoined to the verb *taken*.

A third way of ruling out (v) would be in terms of a structural constraint to the effect that a verb can only case-check an incorporated pronoun which it head-commands. We can define the term *head-command* as follows:

(ix)   X head-commands Y if the head immediately dominating X dominates Y, and X does not dominate Y.

The AgrO complex in (v) has the structure (x) below:

(x)

The head which immediately dominates the V *turned* here is the bracketed [V] node, and since this does not dominate the D-node containing *them*, the verb *turned* cannot check the objective case of the pronoun *them*. Since case-features are uninterpretable at LF, the relevant derivation crashes at LF. Of course, the weakness of this account is that we have given no independent motivation for the *head-command condition* (though command constraints of various kinds seem to be required elsewhere in the grammar – e.g. in relation to the syntax of scope). (*You* take over at this point, and discuss the syntax of the pronouns in the remaining examples. Try and establish whether some form of case-checking account can be made to work for more complex examples, or whether we have to fall back on a PF cliticization account. Be warned that this is a difficult exercise which you need to think through very carefully, taking a range of alternative possibilities into account.)

Exercise VIII

The sentences below illustrate a phenomenon which is sometimes referred to as **pronoun shift** which affects (phonetically) weak object pronouns (the relevant weak pronouns are italicized in the examples below). The examples in (1–3) are imperative structures found in what Alison Henry (1995) terms 'dialect B' of Belfast English (here abbreviated to *BEB*), while those in (4–5) are from Early Modern English (= *EME*) and come from various plays by Shakespeare:

    1a   Read you *it* always to me!

     b   Read *it* always you to me!

    c   *Read *it* you always to me!

    d   *Read always *it* you to me!

    e   *Read you always *it* to me!

    f   *Read the book always you to me

    g   Read you always the book to me!

  2a   Tell you *them* always the truth!

    b   Tell *them* always you the truth!

    c   *Tell *them* you always the truth

  3a   Give you *them* it always!

    b   Give *them* it always you!

    c   *Give *them* you it always!

    d   *Give *it* them always you!

  4a   I fear *thee* not (Leonato, *Much Ado About Nothing*, V.i)

    b   The musician likes *me* not (Julia, *Two Gentlemen of Verona*, IV.ii)

    c   Anne loves *him* not (Quickly, *Merry Wives of Windsor*, I.iv)

  5a   Give *me* not the boots! (Proteus, *Two Gentlemen of Verona*, I.i)

    b   Wrong *me* not! (Bianca, *Taming of the Shrew*, II.i)

    c   Do *him* not that wrong! (Julia, *Two Gentlemen of Verona*, II.vii)

(I am grateful to Alison Henry for providing examples 1c and 3a–d; the other examples in 1 and 2 are from Henry 1995.) Discuss the syntax of weak object pronouns in these two varieties of English.

Helpful hints

Make the following assumptions about BEB (adapted from Henry 1995): (i) imperative verbs in BEB adjoin to an **Imp** morpheme in C in order to check their imperative morphology; (ii) *always* in the relevant sentences is adjoined to the left of vp; (iii) subjects either remain *in situ* (in spec-vp) or raise to spec-AgrSP; (iv) imperative clauses contain no TP projection, since imperative verbs have no tense inflections to check; (v) AgrIOP and AgrOP are positioned between AgrSP and vp; (vi) only weak direct and indirect object pronouns check their case by raising overtly to an appropriate position within AgrOP/AgrIOP; other direct and indirect object D(P)s remain *in situ* within VP.

Model answer for 1a

Given the assumptions made in the *helpful hints* (which are transparently very different from those made in the text), 1a might be derived as follows. Let us suppose that the verb *read* originates as the head V of VP and subsequently adjoins to an agentive light verb heading vp as in (i) below:

(i)

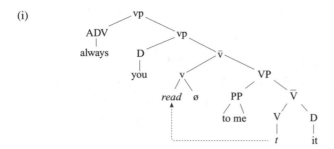

Let's also suppose (contrary to what was assumed in the text) that AgrOP is positioned above vp. Henry (1995, p. 75) suggests that weak object pronouns move to spec-AgrOP to check their case; however, this seems unlikely, since it would mean that AgrO has strong specifier-features, and we would therefore expect that strong (e.g. contrastively stressed) object pronouns and objective DPs like *the book* would also raise in the same way – yet this is not the case, as we see from the ungrammaticality of 1f. Since only weak object pronouns can raise, and weak elements are arguably affixal in nature, it seems more likely that weak object pronouns adjoin to AgrO (together with the verb), as in (ii) below:

(ii)

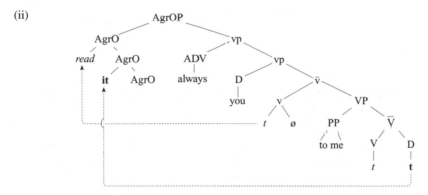

The objective case-features carried by the pronoun *it* and the transitive verb *read* can then be checked and erased (checking here involving a relation between two constituents adjoined to the same functional head, AgrO). Subsequently, the verb *read* excorporates out of AgrO and adjoins to AgrS (recall that Henry argues that imperatives contain no TP projection); in addition, the subject *you* raises to spec-AgrSP (where the case and agreement properties of *you* are checked against those of the imperative verb *read*: note that imperative verbs license only a restricted choice of subject – cf. **Read we/he the book!*), as in (iii) below:

(iii)

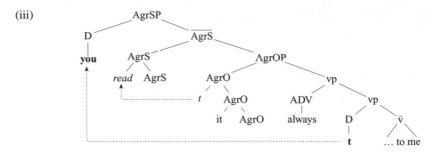

Finally, the verb *read* raises to adjoin to the strong Imp morpheme in C, as in (iv) below:

(iv)

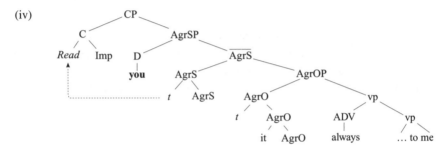

The analysis presented here is in effect a hybrid, grafting the vp/VP analysis of clause structure outlined in chapter 9 onto Henry's assumptions that AgrOP is positioned outside the projection in which subjects originate (in our terms, vp), and that only weak pronouns raise to a position within AgrOP.

This exercise serves to illustrate the diversity of views in current work on what kinds of objects check their case by raising to an appropriate position in AgrOP (only weak pronouns in specific varieties of English, or all objective D(P)s in all varieties?), and where AgrOP is positioned (above or below vp?). Anyone who wants to maintain that (in BEB and EME) all direct and indirect object DPs raise to the specifier position within an appropriate agreement phrase which is positioned below vp will clearly have to maintain that weak object pronouns in BEB and EME raise to adjoin to some higher functional head *F* positioned somewhere above vp: in this connection, it is interesting to note Uriagereka's (1995) claim that, in Spanish, weak object pronouns raise out of vp to adjoin to a higher functional head *F* which heads a separate *FP* projection. Of course, given the assumption that constituents only move to check grammatical features, we would then have to ask what kind of feature is checked by adjoining weak pronouns to F. (Not case, on this account, since this would already have been checked in AgrOP; perhaps some discourse feature, relating to the fact that weak pronouns – like topics – typically represent *old* information which is familiar from the discourse.)

Exercise IX

Discuss the syntax of the Early Modern English sentences below (from various plays by Shakespeare). Which sentences prove problematic to derive, and why?

1   Hast stole it from her? (Iago, *Othello*, III.iii)
2   I sat me down (Hamlet, *Hamlet*, I.i)
3   Go we to the king! (Polonius, *Hamlet*, II.i)
4   What do you promise me? (Helena, *All's Well That Ends Well*, II.i)
5   This will I tell my master (Ariel, *The Tempest*, III.ii)
6   I profess me thy friend (Iago, *Othello*, I.iii)
7   Call you this gamut? (Bianca, *Taming of the Shrew*, III.i)
8   We may soon our satisfaction have (Angelo, *Measure for Measure*, I.i)
9   I might not this believe (Horatio, *Hamlet*, I.i)
10   Thou hast thy father much offended (Gertrude, *Hamlet*, III.iv)
11   I your commission will forthwith dispatch (Claudius, *Hamlet*, III.iii)
12   I'll get me one (Duke, *Two Gentlemen of Verona*, III.i)
13   He would have given it you (Lucetta, *Two Gentlemen of Verona*, I.ii)
14   The common executioner falls not the axe upon the humbled neck (Rosalind, *As You Like It*, III.v)
15   Your ships are stay'd at Venice (Tranio, *Taming of the Shrew*, IV.ii)
16   What will be said? (Baptista, *Taming of the Shrew*, III.ii)
17   Were you not sent for? (Hamlet, *Hamlet*, II.ii)
18   They were given me by Claudius (Messenger, *Hamlet*, IV.vii)
19   . . . to let them know both what we mean to do (Claudius, *Hamlet*, IV.i)
20   They smack of honour both (Duncan, *Macbeth*, I.iii)

Model answer for 1

Given the assumptions made in the text, sentence 1 could be derived as follows. The verb *stole* merges with its pronoun complement *it* to form the V-bar *stole it*; V-bar in turn merges with the PP *from her* to form the VP (i) below:

(i)

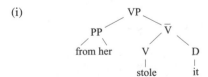

VP then merges with an AgrO constituent; the transitive V *stole* adjoins to AgrO and the D *it* raises to spec-VP to check its objective case as in (ii) below:

(ii)

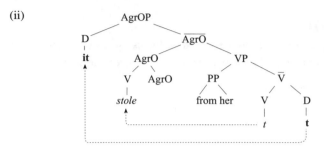

AgrOP then merges with a light verb which has a null (second person singular) *pro* subject, and the V *stole* adjoins to the light verb as in (iii) below:

(iii)

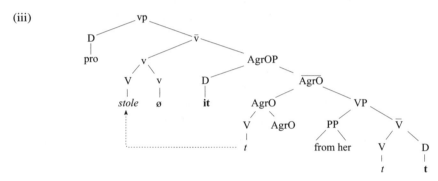

The vp constituent in (iii) then merges with a T constituent containing the perfective auxiliary *hast*, and *pro* raises to spec-TP to check its nominative case (and to check that *hast* agrees with it), as in the simplified structure (iv) below:

(iv)

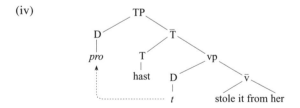

TP then merges with a C constituent containing a question particle *Q* which has a yes–no question operator *Op* as its specifier; *hast* adjoins to Q as in (v) below:

(v)

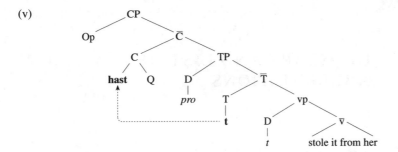

And (v) is a simplified representation of the structure of sentence 1 *Hast stole it from her?*

GLOSSARY AND LIST OF ABBREVIATIONS

(Abbreviations used here are: *ch.* = chapter; *ex.* = exercise; *§6.2* = chapter 6, section 2; bold-printed terms within glosses denote technical terms, and generally cross-refer to related entries elsewhere in the glossary.)

A   See **adjective**.

A-bar movement   An *A-bar movement* operation is one which moves a maximal projection into an *A-bar position* (i.e. a nonargument position, or more specifically, a position which can be occupied by expressions which are not arguments). So, **operator movement, scrambling** and the kind of **adjunction** operation whereby *this kind of behaviour* is adjoined to the clause containing it in a sentence such as ***This kind of behaviour*** *we cannot tolerate* are all specific types of A-bar movement operation.

Absorption   A passive participle is said to *absorb* the theta-role which a verb would otherwise assign to its subject (thereby dethematizing the subject) and to *absorb* the objective case which a transitive verb would otherwise assign to its object (thereby detransitivizing the verb, so that passive participles are intransitive). See §8.9.

Acceptability   Native speakers have the ability to judge sentences to be acceptable or unacceptable. However, the fact that a sentence is regarded as unacceptable doesn't mean that it is necessarily ungrammatical (i.e. syntactically ill formed), since (for example) a sentence might be regarded as unacceptable because it is semantically incoherent, stylistically incongruous, pragmatically infelicitous, etc. See ch. 1, ex. VII.

Accusative   See **case**.

Acquisition   The study of the way in which children acquire their first language (i.e. their mother tongue) – referred to more precisely as *L1 acquisition*, to differentiate it from *L2 acquisition*, the acquisition of a second language (i.e. a language which is not one's mother tongue).

Active   A contrast is traditionally drawn between sentence pairs such as (i) and (ii) below:

(i)   The thieves stole the jewels
(ii)   The jewels were stolen by the thieves

Example (i) is said to be an *active* clause (or sentence), and (ii) to be its *passive* counterpart; similarly, the verb *stole* is said to be an *active* verb (or a verb in the *active voice*) in (i), whereas the verb *stolen* is said to be a *passive* verb (or a verb in the *passive voice* – more specifically, a *passive participle*) in (ii); likewise, the auxiliary *were* in (ii) is said to be a *passive auxiliary*.

Adequacy, criteria of   These are the criteria which an adequate grammar or linguistic theory must meet. See §1.3.

Adjacency condition   A condition requiring that two expressions must be immediately adjacent (i.e. one must immediately follow the other) in order for some operation to apply. For example, *to* can only contract onto *want* (forming *wanna*) if the two are immediately adjacent.

Adjective   A category of word which often denotes states (e.g. *happy*, *sad*), which typically has an adverb counterpart in *+ly* (cf. *sad/sadly*), which typically has comparative/superlative forms in *+er/+est* (cf. *sadder/saddest*), which can often take the prefix *+un* (cf. *unhappy*), and which can often form a noun by the addition of *+ness* (cf. *sadness*). See §§2.2 and 2.3.

Adjoin   See **adjunction**.

Adjunct   One way in which this term is used is to denote an optional constituent typically used to specify e.g. the time, location or manner in which an event takes place (e.g. *in the pub* is an adjunct in a sentence such as *We had a drink in the pub*). Another way in which it is used is to denote a constituent which has been *adjoined* to another to form an extended constituent. (See **adjunction**.)

Adjunction   A process by which one word is adjoined (= attached) to another to form a larger word, or one phrase is adjoined to another phrase to form a larger phrase. For example, we might say that in a sentence such as *He shouldn't go*, *not* (in the guise of its contracted form *n't*) has been adjoined to the auxiliary *should* to form the negative auxiliary *shouldn't*. Likewise, in a sentence such as *You know that such behaviour we cannot tolerate*, we might argue that *such behaviour* has been adjoined to the *we*-clause. See §10.2.

Adposition   A cover term for *preposition* and *postposition*. For example, the English word *in* is a preposition since it is positioned before its complement (cf. *in Tokyo*), whereas its Japanese counterpart *ni* is a postposition because it is positioned after its complement (cf. *Tokyo ni*). Both words are adpositions.

ADV/Adverb   A category of word which typically indicates manner (e.g. *wait **patiently***) or degree (e.g. ***exceedingly** patient*). In English, most (but not all) adverbs end in *+ly* (cf. *quickly* – but also *almost*). See §2.2 and 2.3.

Adverbializing suffix   A derivational suffix which converts another class of word into an adverb. For example *+ly* is an adverbializing **suffix** which converts an adjective like *sad* into the corresponding adverb *sadly*.

Affective   An affective constituent is a (negative, interrogative or conditional) expression which can have a **polarity expression** like (partitive) *any* in its scope. So, for example, interrogative *whether* is an affective constituent as we see from the fact that a *whether*-clause can contain partitive *any* in a sentence such as *He asked me whether I had any news about Jim*.

Affix   A grammatical morpheme which cannot stand on its own as an independent word, but which must be attached to an item of an appropriate kind. An affix which attaches to the beginning of a word (e.g. *un+* in *unhappy*) is called a *prefix*: an affix which attaches to the end of a word (e.g. *+s* in *chases*) is called a *suffix*.

AGENT   A term used to describe the semantic (= thematic) role which a particular type of **argument** plays in a given sentence. It typically denotes a person who deliberately causes some state of affairs to come about – hence e.g. *John* plays the thematic role of an AGENT in a sentence such as *John smashed the bottle*. The terms ACTOR and CAUSER are sometimes used in a similar sense. See §8.4.

Agreement   Two words (or expressions) are said to *agree* in respect of some grammatical feature(s) if they have the same value for the relevant feature(s): so, in a sentence such as *He smokes*, the verb *smokes* is said to agree with its subject *he* because both are third person singular expressions. See also **AgrS, AgrO, AgrIO**.

AgrIO/$\overline{\text{AgrIO}}$/AgrIO-bar/AgrIOP   *AgrIO* is an indirect object agreement constituent which has an intermediate projection into $\overline{\text{AgrIO}}$/AgrIO-bar, and a maximal projection into *AgrIOP*, an indirect object agreement phrase. See §10.6.

AgrO/$\overline{\text{AgrO}}$/AgrO-bar/AgrOP   *AgrO* is an object agreement constituent which has an intermediate projection into $\overline{\text{AgrO}}$/AgrO-bar, and a maximal projection into *AgrOP*, an object-agreement phrase. See §10.4.

AgrS/$\overline{\text{AgrS}}$/AgrS-bar/AgrSP   *AgrS* is a subject agreement constituent which has an intermediate projection into $\overline{\text{AgrS}}$/AgrS-bar, and a maximal projection into *AgrSP*, a subject agreement phrase. See §10.2.

A head/$\overline{\text{A}}$ -head   An A head is the kind of head which can only have an argument as its specifier; an A-bar head is the kind of head which can have a nonargument as its specifier. See §6.6.

Algorithm   A term borrowed from mathematics to denote an explicit set of instructions which specify in precise detail the exact sequence of steps which you have to go through in order to perform some operation.

Allomorphs   Variant phonetic forms of a single morpheme. For example, the noun plural morpheme *+(e)s* in English has the three allomorphs /s/ (e.g. in *cats*), /z/ (e.g. in *dogs*) and /ɪz/ (e.g. in *horses*).

Altruism   See **enlightened self-interest**.

Ambiguous   An expression is *ambiguous* if it has more than one **interpretation**. For example, a sentence such as *He loves her more than you* is ambiguous by virtue of the fact that it has two interpretations, one paraphraseable as 'He loves her more than he loves you', the other as 'He loves her more than you love her.'

A-movement   Movement from one **A position** to another (typically, from a subject or complement position into another subject position). See ch. 8.

Anaphor(a)   An *anaphor* is an expression (like *himself*) which cannot have independent reference, but which must take its reference from an **antecedent** (i.e. expression which it refers to) within the same phrase or sentence. Hence, while we can say *John is deluding himself* (where *himself* refers back to *John*), we cannot say

Himself is waiting, since the anaphor *himself* here has no antecedent. *Anaphora* is the phenomenon whereby an anaphor refers back to an antecedent.

Animate
A term used to describe the property of denoting a living being (e.g. a human being or animal); the corresponding term **inanimate** is used in relation to an expression which denotes lifeless entities. For example, the pronoun *he* is often said to be animate in **gender**, and the pronoun *it* to be inanimate, since *he* can refer to a male human being or male animal, whereas *it* is typically used to refer to a thing.

Antecedent
An expression which is referred to by a pronoun or anaphor of some kind. For example, in *John cut himself shaving*, *John* is the antecedent of the **anaphor** *himself*, since *himself* refers back to *John*. In a sentence such as *He is someone whom we respect*, the antecedent of the pronoun *whom* is *someone*.

Antonym
A term used to denote an expression which has the opposite meaning to another expression: e.g. *tall* is the antonym of *short* (and conversely) – hence *tall* and *short* are antonyms.

AP
Adjectival phrase – i.e. a phrase headed by an adjective – e.g. *fond of chocolate, keen on sport, good at syntax*, etc.

A position
A position which can be occupied by an argument, but not by a nonargument expression (e.g. not by an **adjunct**) – e.g. a **subject** position, or a position as the **complement** of a verb, adjective or noun. See ch. 8.

Arbitrary
When we say that an expression has *arbitrary reference*, we mean that it can denote an unspecified set of individuals, and hence have much the same meaning as English *one/people*, French *on*, German *Man*, etc. In a sentence such as *It is difficult [to learn Japanese]*, the bracketed clause is said to have an abstract pronoun subject **PRO** which has arbitrary reference, so that the sentence is paraphraseable as 'It's difficult for *people* to learn Japanese.' See §4.2.

Argument
This is a term borrowed by linguists from philosophy (more specifically, from predicate calculus) to describe the role played by particular types of expression in the semantic structure of sentences. In a sentence such as *John hit Fred*, the overall sentence is said to be a *proposition* (a term used to describe the semantic content of a clause), and to consist of the predicate *hit* and its two arguments *John* and *Fred*. The two *arguments* represent the two participants in the act of hitting, and the *predicate* is the expression (in this case the verb *hit*) which describes the activity in which they are engaged. By extension, in a sentence such as *John says he hates syntax* the predicate is the verb *says*, and its two arguments are *John* and the clause *he hates syntax*; the second argument *he hates syntax* is in turn a proposition whose predicate is *hates*, and whose two arguments are *he* and *syntax*. Since the complement of a verb is positioned internally within V-bar (in terms of the analysis in ch. 8) whereas the subject of a verb is positioned outside V-bar, complements are also referred to as *internal arguments*, and subjects as *external arguments*. Expressions which do not function as arguments are *nonarguments*. The *argument structure* of a predicate provides a description of the set of arguments associated with the predicate, and the **thematic role** which each fulfils in relation to the predicate. See §8.4.

Article   A term used in traditional grammar to describe a particular subclass of determiners: the determiner *the* is sometimes called the *definite article*, and the determiner *a* the *indefinite article*.

Aspect   A term typically used to denote the duration of the activity described by a verb (e.g. whether the activity is ongoing or completed). In sentences such as:

(i)   He has taken the medicine
(ii) He is taking the medicine

the auxiliary *has* is said to be an auxiliary which marks *perfective aspect*, in that it marks the perfection (in the sense of 'completion' or 'termination') of the activity of taking the medicine; for analogous reasons, *taken* is said to be a perfective (participle) verb form in (i) (though is referred to in traditional grammars as a *past participle*). Similarly, *is* is said to be an auxiliary which marks *imperfective* or *progressive aspect* in (ii), because it relates to an activity which is not yet perfected (i.e. 'completed') and hence which is ongoing or in progress (for this reason, *is* in (ii) is also referred to as a *progressive* or *imperfective* auxiliary); in the same way, the verb *taking* in (ii) is said to be the *imperfective* or *progressive* (participle) form of the verb (though is known in traditional grammars as a *present participle*).

Aspectual auxiliaries   Auxiliaries which mark **aspect** – e.g. perfective *have* and progressive *be*. See **aspect**.

Associate   An expression which represents the thematic subject in an **expletive** construction, and which is associated with the expletive subject *there*: e.g. *someone* in *There's someone waiting for you.*

Attraction   An operation by which features carried by one constituent percolate up to (and are inherited by) another. See §6.5.

Attributive adjectives   These are adjectives which are used to modify a following noun expression – e.g. *red* in *John has a red Ferrari*, where *red* attributes the property of being red to the noun *Ferrari*. Attributive adjectives contrast with *predicative adjectives*, which are adjectives used in structures such as *The house was red*, *They painted the house red*, etc. (where the property of being red is said to be predicated of the expression *the house*).

AUX/Auxiliary   A term used to describe items such as *will/would/can/could/shall/should/may/might/must/ought* and some uses of *have/be/do/need/dare*. Such items differ from typical lexical verbs e.g. in that they undergo **inversion** (cf. *Can I help you?*). See §2.5.

Auxiliary inversion   See **inversion**.

Auxiliary phrase   A phrase/clause/sentence headed by an auxiliary. For example, a sentence such as *He will help* is an auxiliary phrase headed by the modal auxiliary *will* (hence also a modal phrase, or *will*-phrase).

Auxiliary selection   This term relates to the type of verb which a given auxiliary selects as its complement: e.g. in many languages (the counterpart of) *be* when used as a perfective auxiliary selects only a complement headed by an **unaccusative** verb (like *come*, *go*, etc.), whereas (the counterpart of) *have* selects a complement headed by other types of verb. See §9.9.

Baa Baa Black Sheep variety   A variety of English which allows the verb *have* (in its possessive use, where it has much the same meaning as *possess*) to be used as an auxiliary, and hence to undergo inversion in sentences like *Have you any wool?* (the second line from a well-known nursery rhyme called *Baa Baa Black Sheep*).

-bar   An *X-bar*/$\overline{X}$ constituent is an intermediate projection of some head X – i.e. a projection which is larger than X but smaller than XP (see **projection**). In another use of the term (in which the *-bar* suffix has much the same function as the prefix *non-*), an *A-bar*/$\overline{A}$ *position* is a nonargument position. See **argument**.

Bare   A *bare infinitive* clause is a clause which contains a verb in the infinitive form, but does not contain the infinitive particle *to* – e.g. the bracketed clause in *He won't let* [*me help him*]. A *bare noun* is a noun used without any determiner to modify it (e.g. *fish* in *Fish is smelly*). *Bare phrase structure* is a system of representing syntactic structure in terms of unlabelled tree diagrams (i.e. tree diagrams in which **nodes** do not carry category labels).

Base form   The *base form* of a verb is the simplest, uninflected form of the verb (the form under which the relevant verb would be listed in an English dictionary) – hence forms like *go/be/have/see/want/love* are the base forms of the relevant verbs.

Binarity principle   A principle of Universal Grammar specifying that all nonterminal nodes in tree diagrams are binary-branching. See §3.5.

Binary   A term relating to a *two-valued* property or relation. For example, *number* is a binary property in English, in that we have a two-way contrast between singular forms like *cat* and plural forms like *cats*. It is widely assumed that parameters have binary settings, that features have binary values, and that all branching in syntactic structure is binary.

Binary-branching   A tree diagram in which every nonterminal **node** (i.e. every node not at the very bottom of the tree) branches down into two other nodes is *binary-branching*.

Bind/Binder   To say that one constituent *x* binds (or serves as the binder for) another constituent *y* (and conversely that *y* is bound by *x*) is to say that *x* determines the semantic (and grammatical) properties of *y*. For example, in *John wants to PRO leave*, *John* binds (and is the binder for) **PRO**, and PRO is bound by *John*.

Bound   In one use of this term, a *bound* form is one which cannot stand alone and be used as an independent word, but rather must be attached to some other morpheme (e.g. negative *n't*, which has to attach to some auxiliary such as *could*). In a completely different use of the term, a *bound* constituent is one which has a *binder* (i.e. antecedent) within the structure containing it (see **bind**).

Bracketing   A technique for representing the categorial status of an expression, whereby the expression is enclosed in square brackets, and the lefthand bracket is labelled with an appropriate category symbol – e.g. [$_D$ the]. See §2.7.

Branch   A term used to represent a solid line linking a pair of nodes in a tree diagram, marking a **mother/daughter** relation between them.

C/C̄/C-bar/CP   C represents the category of *complementizer*; C̄/C-bar is an intermediate
projection headed by C; and CP ('complementizer phrase') is a maximal projection headed by C. See **complementizer** and **projection**.

Canonical   A term paraphraseable as 'usual', 'typical' or 'normal', as in 'The canonical
word order in English is specifier + head + complement.'

Case   The different *case* forms of a pronoun are the different forms which the pronoun
has in different sentence positions. It is traditionally said that English has three
cases – *nominative*, *objective/accusative* and *genitive*. *Personal pronouns* typically inflect overtly for all three cases, whereas noun expressions inflect only for
genitive case. The different case forms of typical pronouns and nouns are given
below:

nominative	I	we	you	he	she	it	they	who	John
objective	me	us	you	him	her	it	them	who(m)	John
genitive	my	our	your	his	her	its	their	whose	John's

One problem posed by this (traditional) classification relates to the fact that so-
called 'genitive' pronouns like *my/your/their* etc. have the variant forms
mine/yours/theirs – and it is not obvious why such items should have two different genitive case forms. An alternative analysis of items like these is to say that
they are not genitive pronouns but rather are determiners, which have the form
my/your/their when used prenominally, and the form *mine/yours/theirs* when
used pronominally. Similarly, some linguists have claimed that the so-called genitive *'s* inflection is actually a determiner rather than a case inflection, so that an
expression such as *John's father* is a determiner phrase whose head determiner is
's, whose specifier is *John* and whose complement is *father*: if so, then this raises
the possibility that English simply has no genitive case at all. However, it has
been suggested by others that *of* serves as a genitive case marker (perhaps
belonging to the category **K** of **case particle**) in expressions such as *fond of
whisky*, *loss of face*, etc. (since in languages with richer case morphology than
English, the relevant *of*-phrases correspond to a nominal which is morphologically marked for genitive case: see ch. 2, ex. VI). In chapter 10, we suggest that
indirect objects in English (e.g. *him* in *I gave him some*) carry *dative case*, even
though dative forms are not morphologically distinct from objective forms. In
some works (e.g. Chomsky 1980) it is claimed that transitive verbs assign **objective** case to their complements, whereas transitive prepositions assign **oblique**
case to their complements (although the two cases are not morphologically distinct in English): under this analysis, *him* in *Fetch him!* would carry objective
case, whereas *him* in *Fetch one for him* would carry oblique case. Belletti (1988)
suggests that in sentences like *There could have been an accident*, the expression
an accident carries partitive case (Finnish has overt marking of partitive case
forms). In Chomsky and Lasnik 1995, it is suggested that the null subject **PRO**
found in (control) infinitive constructions carries **null case**.

Caseless   A caseless constituent is one which has no case properties (i.e. which neither carries a case of its own nor checks the case of another constituent). A caseless position is a position in which no case can be checked (hence which cannot be occupied by a constituent carrying case).

Case particle   See **case**.

Case position   A position in which some case is checked.

Categorization   Assigning an expression to a (grammatical) **category**.

Category   A term used to denote a set of expressions which share a common set of linguistic properties. In syntax, the term is used for expressions which share a common set of *grammatical* (i.e. morphological/syntactic) properties. For example, *boy* and *girl* belong to the (grammatical) category **noun** because they both inflect for plural number (cf. *boys/girls*), and can both terminate a sentence such as *The police haven't yet found the missing __*. See ch. 2.

Causative verb   A verb which has much the same sense as 'cause'. For example, the verb *have* in sentences such as *He had them expelled* or *He had them review the case* could be said to be causative in sense (hence to be a causative verb).

C-command   A structural relation between two categories. To say that one category *X* c-commands another category *Y* is (informally) to say that *X* is no lower than *Y* in the structure (i.e. either *X* is higher up in the structure than *Y*, or the two are at the same height). If you think of *X* and *Y* as different stations in a train network, we can say that *X* c-commands *Y* if you can get from *X* to *Y* by taking a northbound train from *X*, getting off at the first stop, and then taking a southbound train to *Y* (on a different line). More formally, *X* c-commands *Y* if the **mother** of *X* dominates *Y*, and *X* and *Y* are **disconnected** (i.e. $X \neq Y$, and neither dominates the other). The **c-command condition on binding** is a condition to the effect that a bound constituent (e.g. a reflexive **anaphor** like *himself* or the **trace** of a moved constituent) must be c-commanded by its **antecedent** (i.e. by the expression which binds it). This amounts to claiming that the antecedent must be higher up in the structure than the anaphor/trace which it binds. See §3.9.

CED   See **condition on extraction domains**.

Chain   A set of one or more constituents comprising an expression and any traces associated with it.

Chain uniformity principle/condition   A principle of Universal Grammar requiring that a **chain** should be uniform with regard to its phrase structure status. See §7.4.

Checked/Checker   In a sentence such as *He has left*, the auxiliary *has* checks the nominative case-feature carried by *he*: accordingly, *has* is said to be the checker (for the relevant nominative case-feature), and *he* the checked.

Checking (domain/theory)   In Chomsky's *checking theory*, words carry grammatical features which have to be *checked* in the course of a derivation. For example, a nominative pronoun like *I* must have its nominative **case** checked, which means that it must occupy a nominative position (as the subject of the kind of constituent which allows a nominative subject, e.g. a finite auxiliary) at some point in the derivation. When a feature has been checked, it is erased if it is uninterpretable (i.e. if it is a purely formal feature with no semantic content). Any uninterpretable

497

features which remain unchecked (and hence which have not been erased) at the level of logical form will cause the derivation to *crash* (i.e. to be ungrammatical). See ch. 5. For *checking domain*, see **domain**.

Clause   A clause is defined in traditional grammar as an expression which contains a **subject** and a **predicate**, and which may contain other types of expression as well (e.g. a complement and an adjunct). In most cases, the predicate in a clause is a lexical (= nonauxiliary) verb, so that there will be as many different clauses in a sentence as there are different lexical verbs. For example, in a sentence such as *She may think that you are cheating on her*, there are two lexical verbs (*think* and *cheating*), and hence two clauses. The *cheating*-clause is *that you are cheating on her*, and the *think*-clause is *She may think that you are cheating on her*, so that the *cheating*-clause is one of the **constituents** of the *think*-clause. More specifically, the *cheating*-clause is the **complement** of the *think*-clause, and so is said to function as a **complement clause** in this type of sentence.

Clitic(ization)   The term *clitic* denotes an item which resembles a word but which has the property that it must cliticize (i.e. attach itself) to another word. For example, we could say that the contracted negative particle *n't* is a clitic which attaches itself to a finite auxiliary verb, so giving rise to forms like *isn't, shouldn't, mightn't*, etc. Likewise, we might say that *'ve* is a clitic form of *have* which attaches itself to (for example) a pronoun ending in a vowel or diphthong, so giving rise to forms like *we've, you've, they've*, etc.

Cognition/Cognitive   (Relating to) the study of human knowledge.

Common Noun   In traditional grammar, *common nouns* are contrasted with **proper nouns**. Proper nouns are names of individual people (e.g. *Chomsky*), places (e.g. *Colchester, Essex, England*), dates (e.g. *Tuesday, February, Easter*), magazines (e.g. *Cosmopolitan*), etc., whereas common nouns (e.g. *boy, table, syntax*, etc.) are nouns denoting general (nonindividual) entities. Proper nouns have the semantic property of having unique reference, and the syntactic property that they generally can't be modified by a determiner (cf. **the London*).

COMP   See **complementizer**.

Comparative   The comparative form of an adjective or adverb is the *+er* form used when comparing two individuals or properties: cf. *John is taller than Mary*, where *taller* is the comparative form of *tall*.

Competence   A term used to represent fluent native speakers' knowledge of the grammar of their mother tongue(s). See ch. 1.

Complement   This is a term used to denote a specific grammatical function (in the same way that the term **subject** denotes a specific grammatical function). A complement is an expression which combines with a **head** word to project the head into a larger structure of essentially the same kind. In *close the door*, *the door* is the complement of *close*; in *after dinner*, *dinner* is the complement of *after*; in *good at physics*, *at physics* is the complement of *good*; in *loss of face*, *of face* is the complement of *loss*. As these examples illustrate, complements typically follow their heads in English. The choice of complement (and the morphological form of the complement) is determined by properties of the head: for example, an auxiliary such as *will* requires as its complement an expression headed by a verb in the infinitive form (cf. *He will go/*going/*gone home*). Moreover, complements bear a close semantic relation to their heads (e.g. in *kill him*, *him* is the complement of the verb *kill* and plays the **thematic role** of PATIENT argument of the verb *kill*). Thus, a complement has a close morphological, syntactic and semantic relation to its head. A *complement clause* is a clause which is used as the complement of some other word (typically as the complement of a verb, adjective or noun). Thus, in a sentence such as *He never expected that she would come*, the clause *that she would come* serves as the complement of the verb *expected*, and so is a complement clause. *Complement-features* are features that specify the kind of complement which a given head can have (see ch. 3). On *complement selection*, see **selection**.

Complementizer   This term is used in two ways. On the one hand, it denotes a particular category of clause-introducing word such as *that/if/for*, as used in sentences such as *I think **that** you should apologize*, *I doubt **if** she realizes*, *They're keen **for** you to show up*. On the other hand, it is also used to denote the presubject position in clauses ('the complementizer position') which is typically occupied by a complementizer like *that/if/for*, but which can also be occupied by an inverted auxiliary in sentences such as ***Can** you help?*, where *can* is taken to occupy the complementizer position in the clause. In general, I use the term *complementizer* to denote the relevant category, and the abbreviated terms *COMP* and *C* to denote the associated position. A *complementizer phrase* (CP) is a phrase/clause headed by a complementizer (or by an auxiliary or verb moved into COMP). See §3.4 and §6.2.

Complex   A *complex sentence* is one which contains more than one clause; a *complex head* is one which contains more than one head.

Compound word   A word which is built up out of two (or more) other words – e.g. *man-eater*.

Conditional   A term used to represent a type of clause (typically introduced by *if* or *unless*) which lays down conditions – e.g. *If you don't behave, I'll bar you*, or *Unless you behave, I'll bar you*. In these examples, the clauses *if you don't behave* and *unless you behave* are conditional clauses.

Condition on extraction domains   A **constraint** proposed by Huang 1982 to the effect that complements are the only type of constituent which allow something to be extracted out of them. See §7.4.

Configurational   Positional – i.e. relating to the position occupied by one or more constituents in a tree diagram. For example, a *configurational* definition of a subject (for English) would be 'an argument which occupies the specifier position in **IP**'. This definition is configurational in the sense that it tells you what position within IP the subject occupies.

Conjoin   To join together two or more expressions, usually by a coordinating conjunction such as *and/or/but*. For example, in *naughty but nice*, *naughty* has been conjoined with *nice* (and conversely *nice* has been conjoined with *naughty*).

Conjunct   One of a set of expressions which have been **conjoined**. For example, in *rather* *tired but otherwise all right*, the two conjuncts (i.e. expressions which have been conjoined) are *rather tired* and *otherwise all right*.

Conjunction   A word which is used to join two or more expressions together. For example, in a sentence such as *John was tired but happy*, the word *but* serves the function of being a **coordinating conjunction** because it coordinates (i.e. joins together) the adjectives *tired* and *happy*. In *John felt angry and Mary felt bitter*, the conjunction *and* is used to coordinate the two clauses *John felt angry* and *Mary felt bitter*. In traditional grammar, **complementizers** like *that/for/if* are categorized as (one particular type of) *subordinating conjunction*.

Constituent   A structural unit – i.e. an expression which is one of the components out of which a phrase or sentence is built up. For example, the various constituents of a prepositional phrase (= PP) such as *straight into touch* (e.g. as a reply to *Where did the ball go?*) are the preposition *into*, the noun *touch*, the adverb *straight* and the intermediate projection (P-bar) *into touch*.

Constituent structure   The constituent structure (or *phrase structure*, or *syntactic structure*) of an expression is (a representation of) the set of constituents which the expression contains. Constituent structure is usually represented in terms of a **labelled bracketing** or a **tree diagram**.

Constrained   See **restrictive**.

Constraint   A principle of Universal Grammar which prohibits certain types of grammatical operation from applying to certain types of structure.

Content   This term is generally used to refer to the *semantic content* (i.e. meaning) of an expression. However, it can also be used in a more general way to refer to other linguistic properties of an expression: e.g. the expression *phonetic content* is used to refer to the phonetic form of an expression: hence, we might say that **PRO** is a pronoun which has no/null *phonetic content* (meaning that it is a *silent* pronoun with no audible form).

Contentives/content words   Words which have intrinsic descriptive content (as opposed to **functors**, i.e. words which serve essentially to mark particular grammatical functions). Nouns, verbs, adjectives and (most) prepositions are traditionally classified as contentives, while pronouns, auxiliaries, determiners, complementizers and particles of various kinds (e.g. infinitival *to*) are classified as **functors**. See §2.4.

Contracted form/Contraction   *Contraction* is a term used in §8.5 to indicate a process by which a word like *have* comes to be reduced to the contracted form /v/, and thereby loses its vowel nucleus (along with the consonant /h/). Compare **reduced form**.

Control(ler)/Control predicate   In infinitive structures with a **PRO** subject which has an antecedent, the antecedent is said to be the **controller** of PRO (or to **control** PRO), and conversely PRO is said to be controlled by its antecedent; and the relevant kind of structure is called a **control structure**. So, in a structure like *John decided to PRO quit*, *John* is the controller of PRO, and conversely PRO is controlled by *John*. The term **control predicate** denotes a word like *try* which takes an infinitive complement with a (controlled) PRO subject. Verbs like *try* which takes a complement containing a PRO subject controlled by the subject of *try* are called *subject-control predicates* (see §4.2): verbs like *persuade* in sentences like *I persuaded him to take syntax* which take an infinitive complement whose PRO subject is controlled by the object of the main verb (here, the *him* object of *persuade*) are called *object-control predicates* (see §9.6).

Convergence   A derivation *converges* if the resulting PF representation contains only phonetically interpretable features, and the associated LF representation contains only semantically interpretable features.

Coordinate/Coordination   A coordinate structure is a structure containing two or more expressions joined together by a coordinating **conjunction** such as *and/but/or/ nor* (e.g. *John and Mary* is a coordinate structure.). Coordination is the process by which two or more expressions are joined together by a coordinating conjunction.

Copula/Copular verb   A verb used to link a **subject** with a verbless **predicate**. The main copular verb in English is *be* (though verbs like *become, remain, stay*, etc. also have the same copular – i.e. linking – function). In sentences such as *They are lazy, They are fools* and *They are outside*, the verb *are* is said to be a copula in that it links the subject *they* to the adjective predicate *lazy*, or the noun predicate *fools*, or the prepositional predicate *outside*.

Coreferential   Two expressions are coreferential if they refer to the same entity. For example, in *John cut himself while shaving, himself* and *John* are cofererential in the sense that they refer to the same individual.

Countability   The countability properties of a noun determine whether the relevant item is a **count noun** or not.

Counterexample   An example which falsifies a particular hypothesis. For example, an auxiliary like *ought* would be a counterexample to any claim that auxiliaries in English never take an infinitive complement introduced by *to* (cf. *You ought to tell them*).

Count noun   A noun which can be counted. Hence, a noun such as *chair* is a count noun since we can say *one chair, two chairs, three chairs*, etc.; but a noun such as *furniture* is a **noncount noun** or **mass noun** since we cannot say **one furniture, *two furnitures, *three furnitures*, etc.

Covert   A covert expression is one which has no phonetic content (i.e. which is *empty* of phonetic content and so is inaudible). For example, in a structure such as *He may try [to PRO escape from prison]*, the bracketed clause has a *covert* (= null = empty = silent) subject pronoun PRO. A *covert feature* (or *property*) is one which has no overt morphological realization: for example, we might say that an invariable noun like *sheep* has covert (singular/plural) number properties, since (unlike *cat/cats*) the word *sheep* doesn't add *+s* in the plural (cf. *one sheep/two sheep*).

501

CP   Complementizer phrase (see **complementizer**).

Crash   A derivation is said to **crash** if one or more features carried by one or more constituents is uninterpretable at one of the two interface levels (phonetic form/logical form). For example, the derivation of a sentence like *Him will help* will crash at LF because the objective case-feature of the pronoun *him* remains unchecked (since finite auxiliaries don't allow objective subjects), and case-features are purely formal/grammatical features with no semantic content, and hence uninterpretable at the level of logical form. More generally, a derivation will crash if any purely formal features remain unchecked.

Cross-categorial properties   Properties which extend across categories, i.e. which are associated with more than one different category. See §2.9.

D/D̄/D-bar/DP   D represents the category of *determiner*; D̄/D-bar is an intermediate projection headed by D; and DP ('determiner phrase') is a maximal projection headed by D. See **determiner**, **determiner phrase** and **projection**.

+d   An affix used to form the past tense of a verb, so called because most regular verbs form their past tense by the addition of +(*e*)*d* in English (e.g. *showed*).

Dative   See **case**.

Daughter   A node carrying the category label X is the daughter of another node carrying the category label Y if Y is the next highest node up in the tree from X, and the two are connected by a branch (solid line).

Deadjectival   A *deadjectival verb* is one derived from an adjective: e.g. the verb *enrich* is deadjectival by virtue of the fact that it is formed by combining the prefix *en*+ with the adjective *rich*.

Declarative   A term used as a classification of the **illocutionary force** (i.e. semantic function) of a clause which is used to make a statement (e.g. *Syntax is fun*), as opposed to an **interrogative**, **exclamative** or **imperative** clause.

Default   A default value/interpretation is one which obtains if all else fails (i.e. if other conditions are not satisfied). For example, if we say that clauses are interpreted as declarative by default we mean they are interpreted as declarative unless they contain (for example) an interrogative, exclamative or imperative constituent of some kind.

Defective   A defective item is one which lacks certain inflected forms. For example, *beware* is an irregular verb in that it has no inflected +*ing* form (cf. **bewaring*).

Definite   Expressions containing determiners like *the*, *this*, *that*, etc. are said to have definite reference in that they refer to an entity which is assumed to be known to the addressee(s): e.g. in a sentence such as *I hated the syntax course*, the DP *the syntax course* refers to a specific syntax course whose identity is assumed to be known to the hearer/reader. In much the same way, personal pronouns like *he/she/it/they* etc. are said to have definite reference. By contrast, expressions containing a determiner like *a* have **indefinite reference**, in that (for example) if you say *I'm taking a syntax course*, you don't assume that the hearer/reader knows which syntax course you are taking. For *definite article*, see **article**.

Degemination   Reduction of a sequence of two identical consonants to a single consonant.

Degenerate   To say that the speech input which children receive is *degenerate* is to say that it is imperfect – i.e. that it contains **performance** errors. See §1.4.

Degree word   A term used for words like *so/such* (in expressions such as *so courageous* and *such courage*) which describe the extent of a given property (in this case, the property of courage/being courageous).

Demonstrative   This is a term used to refer to words like *this/that*, *these/those* and *here/there* which indicate a location relatively nearer to or further from the speaker (e.g. *this book* means 'the book relatively close to me' and *that book* means 'the book somewhat further away from me').

Denominal   A *denominal verb* is one which is derived from a noun. For example, the verb *rubbish* (as in *to rubbish a proposal*) is a denominal verb in the sense that it is a derivative of the noun *rubbish*.

Derivation   The derivation of a phrase or clause is the set of syntactic (e.g. merger and movement) operations used to form the relevant structure. The derivation of a word is the set of morphological operations used to form the word.

Derivational/Derivative   Derivational morphology is the study of the processes by which one type of word can be formed from another: for example, by adding the derivational suffix *+ness* to the adjective *sad* we can form the noun *sadness*, so that *+ness* is a derivational suffix, and the word *sadness* is a derivative of the adjective *sad*. See §2.2.

Derived structure   A structure which is derived (i.e. produced) by the application of one or more syntactic (merger or movement) operations.

Descriptive adequacy   A grammar of a particular language attains *descriptive adequacy* if it correctly specifies which strings of words do (and don't) form grammatical phrases and sentences in the language, and correctly describes the structure and interpretation of the relevant phrases and sentences. See §1.3.

Descriptive content   A noun like *car* could be said to have *descriptive content*, in that you can draw a picture of a typical car, but not a pronoun like *they* (you can't draw a picture of *they*). See §2.4.

Descriptive linguistics   The study of (aspects of) the grammars of particular languages.

DET/Determiner   A word like *a/the/this/that* which is typically used to modify a noun, but which has no descriptive content of its own. Most determiners can be used either prenominally (i.e. in front of a noun that they modify) or pronominally (i.e. used on their own without a following noun) – cf. the two uses of *that* in *I don't like that idea/I don't like that*. See §2.4.

Determiner phrase/DP   A phrase like *(such) a pity* which comprises a determiner *a*, a noun complement *pity* and an (optional) specifier *such*. In earlier work, a determiner + noun sequence would have been analysed as a **noun phrase** (= NP), with the determiner occupying the specifier position within NP.

Dethematize/Detransitivize   See **absorption**.

Dialect   A regional variety of a language.

Direct object   See **object**.

Direct theta-marking   See **theta-marking**.

Disconnected   Two nodes X and Y are disconnected if they are different nodes (i.e. if $X \neq Y$) and if neither **dominates** the other.

Discourse   Discourse factors are factors relating to the extrasentential setting in which an expression occurs (where extrasentential means 'outside the immediate sentence containing the relevant expression'). For example, to say that the reference of **PRO** is discourse-determined in a sentence such as *It would be wise to PRO prepare for the worst* means that PRO has no antecedent within the sentence immediately containing it, but rather refers to some individual(s) outside the sentence (in this case, the person being spoken to).

Distribution(al)   The *distribution* of an expression is the set of positions which it can occupy within an appropriate kind of phrase or sentence. Hence, a *distributional* property is a word-order property.

Ditransitive   A ditransitive verb is one which takes both a direct object and an indirect object – e.g. a verb like *tell* in a sentence such as *John told Mary nothing*, where *Mary* is the indirect object and *nothing* the direct object of *tell*. See **object** and **transitive**.

Domain   The domain of a particular grammatical operation is the (minimal) structure within which it operates. For example, we might say that the checking domain for nominative case or (subject–auxiliary) agreement in English is **IP**, since nominative case and subject agreement involve a relation between the head and specifier of **IP**. Thus, by saying that **IP** is the checking domain for nominative case and subject agreement, we mean that these are operations which apply internally within **IP**. Manzini (1994, p. 482) defines the **minimal domain** of a head X as including those constituents which are immediately contained by, but do not immediately contain, a projection of X (i.e. the specifier and complement of X, and any constituent adjoined to some projection of X).

Dominance/Dominate   Domination is a superiority relation between two categories (X and Y) in a tree structure. More specifically, X dominates Y if X occurs higher up in the tree than Y, and X is connected to Y by a continuous (unbroken) set of downward-sloping branches (the **branches** being represented by the solid lines connecting pairs of nodes in a tree diagram). See §3.6.

Do-**support**   This refers to the use of the **dummy** auxiliary *do* to form questions or negatives in sentences which would otherwise contain no auxiliary. Hence, an auxiliariless declarative sentence (= statement) such as *He hates syntax* has the negative counterpart *He doesn't hate syntax*, and the interrogative counterpart *Does he hate syntax?* So, we might say that *do*-support is required to form the negative or interrogative counterpart of an auxiliariless sentence such as *He hates syntax*.

Double-object construction   See **object**

DP   See **determiner phrase**.

DP hypothesis   The hypothesis that all **nominals** are D-projections, so that e.g. *the president* is a DP headed by *the*, *politicians* (in a sentence like *Politicians lie*) is a DP headed by a null determiner, and a pronoun like *they* (e.g. in *They lie*) is a **pronominal** determiner. See §4.7 and §4.8.

Dummy   A type of word which has no intrinsic semantic content, but which is used simply to satisfy a structural requirement that a certain position in a structure be filled. For example, the auxiliary *do* in a sentence such as *Does he like pasta?* is said to be a dummy, satisfying the need for COMP to be filled in questions. Likewise, the first occurrence of the pronoun *there* in a sentence like *There is nobody there* is a dummy (i.e. contentless) pronoun, since it cannot have its **reference** questioned (cf. **Where is someone there?*).

Early Modern English   The type of English found in the early seventeenth century (at around the time Shakespeare wrote most of his plays, between 1590 and 1620). In the text, all examples of Early Modern English are taken from various plays by Shakespeare. It should perhaps be noted that some linguists have suggested that Shakespeare's English is rather conservative, and hence reflects a slightly earlier stage of English.

Echo question   A type of sentence used to question something which someone else has just said (often with an air of incredulity), repeating all or most of what they have just said. For example, if I say *I've just met Nim Chimpsky* and you don't believe me (or don't know who I'm talking about), you could reply with an echo question such as *You've just met who?*

ECM   See **exceptional case-marking**.

Economy principle   A principle which requires that (all other things being equal) syntactic representations should contain as few constituents and syntactic derivations involve as few grammatical operations as possible.

Ellipsis/Elliptical   Ellipsis is a process by which an expression is omitted in order to avoid repetition. For example, in a sentence such as *I will do it if you will do it*, we can *ellipse* (i.e. omit) the second occurrence of *do it* to avoid repetition, and hence say *I will do it if you will*: the resulting sentence is an *elliptical* structure (i.e. a structure from which something has been omitted).

Embedded clause   An *embedded clause* is a clause which is positioned internally within some other phrase or clause. For example, in a sentence such as *He may suspect that I hid them*, the *hid*-clause (= *that I hid them*) is embedded within the *suspect* clause.

EME   See **Early Modern English**.

Empirical evidence   Evidence based on observed linguistic phenomena. In syntax, the term *empirical evidence* usually means 'evidence based on grammaticality judgments by native speakers'. For example, the fact that sentences like **Himself likes you* are judged ungrammatical by native speakers of Standard English provides us with empirical evidence that **anaphors** like *himself* can't be used without an appropriate **antecedent** (i.e. an expression which they refer back to).

Empty category   A category which is **covert** (i.e. which is silent or null and hence has no overt phonetic form). Empty categories include **traces**, the null pronouns **PRO** and **pro**, the null generic/partitive determiner $\emptyset$, etc. See ch. 4.

Endocentric   Headed: for example, an expression such as *fond of pasta* is an adjectival phrase whose head is the adjective *fond*; hence, the overall expression is *endocentric* (i.e. headed).

Enlightened self-interest   A principle of grammar suggested by Lasnik (1995) to the effect that constituents move in order to satisfy the morphological requirements of other constituents (e.g. auxiliaries undergo inversion in questions like *Can you help me?* because **COMP** contains a **Q** affix which needs a head to attach to). See §7.3.

Entry   A **lexical entry** is an entry for a particular word in a dictionary (and hence by extension refers to the set of information about the word given in the relevant dictionary entry).

Ergative   This term originally applied to languages like Basque in which the complement of a transitive verb and the subject of an intransitive verb are assigned the same case. However, by extension, it has come to be used to denote verbs like *break* which occur both in structures like *Someone broke the window* and in structures like *The window broke*, where *the window* seems to play the same **thematic role** in both types of sentences, in spite of being the complement of *broke* in one sentence and the subject of *broke* in the other. See §9.2.

Exceptional case-marking/ECM   Objective subjects of infinitive clauses (e.g. *him* in *I believe* [*him to be innocent*]) are said to carry exceptional objective case (for the simple reason that the case of the objective subject is checked by the preceding verb *believe*, and it is exceptional for the case of the subject of one clause to be checked by the verb in a higher clause). Verbs (like *believe*) which take an infinitive complement with an objective subject are said to be *ECM verbs*. See §§5.8 and 10.5.

Exclamative   A type of structure used to exclaim surprise, delight, annoyance, etc. In English syntax, the term is restricted largely to clauses beginning with wh-exclamative words like *what!* or *how!* – e.g. *What a fool I was! How blind I was!*

Excorporation   An operation by which a head which is adjoined to another head is detached from the head to which it is adjoined and moved elsewhere. See §6.9.

Existential   An *existential* sentence is one which relates to the existence of some entity. For example, a sentence such as *Is there any coffee left?* questions the existence of coffee. The word *any* here is similarly said to be an *existential quantifier* (as is *some* in a sentence like *There is some coffee in the pot*).

Experience   A child's *experience* relates to the speech input which the child receives (or, more generally, the speech activity which the child observes).

EXPERIENCER   A term used in the analysis of semantic/thematic roles to denote the entity which experiences some emotional or cognitive state – e.g *John* in *John felt unhappy*. See §8.4.

Experiential verb   A verb (like *feel*) which has an EXPERIENCER as its subject.

Explanatory adequacy   A linguistic theory meets the criterion of *explanatory adequacy* if it explains why grammars have the properties that they do, and how children come to acquire grammars in such a short period of time. See §1.3.

Expletive   A dummy constituent with no inherent semantic content such as the pronoun *there* in sentences like *There is almost no truth whatever in the rumour* (which is nonreferential and so cannot be questioned by *where?*).

Expression   This word is used in the text as an informal term meaning **string** (i.e. continuous sequence of one or more words).

Extended projection   In a 1991 paper, Jane Grimshaw suggested that IP and CP are extended projections of V, and that DP and PP are extended projections of N. See §4.8.

External argument   Subject (see **argument**).

Extraction   An operation by which one constituent is moved out of another. For example, in a structure such as *Who do you think* [*he saw* —-]? the pronoun *who* has been extracted out of the position marked —- in the bracketed clause, and moved to the front of the overall sentence. The *extraction site* for a moved constituent is the position out of which it is extracted/moved (marked by — in the example above).

F   This symbol is used as a category label to denote an abstract functional head of some kind (see §4.9). It is also used (in a different way) to represent the gender-feature [feminine].

Feature   A device used to describe a particular linguistic property (e.g. we might use a feature such as [Nom] to denote the nominative **case**-feature carried by pronouns such as *he*). By convention, features are normally enclosed in square brackets, and semantic features written in capital letters. The *head-features* of an item describe its intrinsic grammatical properties; the *complement-features* of an item determine the range of complements which it allows; the *specifier-features* of an item determine the range of specifiers which it allows (see §5.3). A *feature matrix* is a set of features describing the grammatical properties of some particular category or expression. The *feature specification* of a word is (a representation of) the set of features which characterize the idiosyncratic properties of the word. See also **strong features** and **weak features**.

Feminine   This term is used in discussion of grammatical **gender** to denote pronouns like *she/her/hers* which refer to female entities.

Finite   The term *finite verb/clause* denotes an auxiliary or nonauxiliary verb or clause which can have a subject with nominative **case** like *I/we/he/she/they*. Thus, if we compare the two bracketed clauses in:

(i)   What if [people annoy her]?

(ii)   Don't let [people annoy her]

we find that the bracketed clause and the verb *annoy* in (i) are finite because in place of the subject *people* we can have a nominative pronoun like *they*; by contrast, the bracketed clause and the verb *annoy* are nonfinite in (ii) because *people* cannot be replaced by a nominative pronoun like *they* (only by an objective pronoun like *them*): cf.

(iii)   What if [*they* annoy her]?

(iv)   *Don't let [*they* annoy her]

By contrast, a verb or clause which has a subject with objective or null case is *nonfinite*; hence the bracketed clauses and bold-printed verbs are nonfinite in the examples below:

        (v)   Don't let [*them* **annoy** you]

        (vi)   You should try [to *PRO* **stay** calm]

In general, finite verbs carry tense/agreement properties, whereas nonfinite verbs are tenseless and agreementless forms (i.e. forms which do not overtly inflect for tense/agreement – e.g. infinitive forms like *be*, and *+ing/+n* participle forms like *being/been* are nonfinite).

First person   See **person**.

Floating quantifier   A **quantifier** which does not immediately precede the expression which it quantifies. For example, in a sentence such as *The students have **all** passed their exams*, *all* quantifies (but is not positioned in front of) *the students*, so that *all* is a *floating* (or *stranded*) quantifier here. See §8.3.

Foot   The foot of a (movement) **chain** is the lowest/rightmost constituent in the chain.

Formal   In an expression such as *formal speech style*, the word *formal* denotes a very careful and stylized form of speech (as opposed to the kind of informal colloquial speech style used in a casual conversation in a bar): in an expression such as *formal features*, the word *formal* means 'grammatical' (i.e. **morphosyntactic**); in an expression such as *the formal properties of grammars*, the word *formal* means 'mathematical'.

Fragment   An utterance which is not a complete clause or sentence. So, a phrase such as *a new dress* used in reply to a question such as *What did you buy?* would be a sentence fragment. (By contrast, a complete sentence such as *I bought a new dress* would not be a sentence fragment.)

Free   A free form is a form which can serve as an independent word (unlike a **bound** form, which has to attach to some other word). For example, *not* is a free form whereas *n't* is a bound form.

Fronting   An informal term to denote a movement operation by which a given expression is moved to the front of some phrase or sentence.

Full interpretation   The *principle of full interpretation* specifies that the representation of an expression must contain all and only those features which are relevant to determining its interpretation at the relevant level: e.g. the **LF representation** for a given expression must contain all and only those semantic features which determine linguistic aspects of the meaning of the expression, and its **PF representation** must contain all and only those phonetic features which determine its pronunciation.

Function   Expressions such as **subject**, **specifier**, **complement**, **object**, **head** and **adjunct** are said to denote the **grammatical function** which a particular expression fulfils in a particular structure (which in turn relates to the position which it occupies and certain of its morphological properties – e.g. case and agreement properties).

Function word/Functional category/Functor   A word which has no **descriptive content** and which serves an essentially grammatical function is said to be a *function word* or *functor*. (By contrast, a word which has descriptive content is a *content word* or *contentive*.) A *functional category* is a category like **INFL, COMP, D, T, AgrS**, etc. whose members are functors (i.e. items with an essentially grammatical function) – and, by extension, a category which is a projection of a function word (e.g. I-bar, IP, C-bar, CP, D-bar, DP, T-bar, TP, $\overline{\text{AgrS}}$, AgrSP etc.). See §2.4.

Gapping A form of **ellipsis** in which a head word is omitted from one (or more) parallel structures, to avoid repetition. For example, the italicized second occurrence of *bought* can be *gapped* (i.e. omitted) in a sentence such as *John bought an apple and Mary bought a pear*, giving *John bought an apple, and Mary a pear*.

Gender A grammatical property whereby words are divided into different grammatical classes on the basis of inflectional properties which play a role in processes such as **agreement** or **anaphora**. In French, for example, nouns are intrinsically masculine or feminine in gender (e.g. *pommier* 'apple tree' is masculine, but *pomme* 'apple' is feminine), and determiners inflect for gender (as well as number), so that *un* 'a' is the masculine form of the determiner corresponding to English 'a', and *une* is its feminine form. Determiners in French have to agree in gender (and **number**) with the nouns they modify, hence we say *un pommier* 'an apple tree', but *une pomme* 'an apple'. In English, nouns no longer have inherent gender properties, and adjectives/determiners don't inflect for gender either. Only personal pronouns like *he/she/it* carry gender properties in Modern English, and these are traditionally said to carry masculine/feminine/neuter gender respectively (though the term *inanimate* is sometimes used in place of *neuter*).

Generate To say that a grammar *generates* a given type of structure is to say that it specifies how to form the relevant structure.

Generic To say that an expression like *eggs* in a sentence such as *Eggs are fattening* has a generic interpretation is to say that it is interpreted as meaning 'eggs in general'.

Genitive See **case**.

Gerund This refers to a particular use of +*ing* verb forms in which they can be used as subjects, or as complements of verbs or prepositions, and in which they can have a genitive subject like *my*. Thus *writing* is a gerund (verb form) in a sentence such as *She was annoyed at [my writing to her mother]*, since the bracketed gerund structure is used as the complement of the preposition *at*, and has a genitive subject *my*.

GOAL A term used in the analysis of semantic/thematic roles to denote the entity towards which something moves – e.g. *home* in *John went home*. See §8.4.

Gradable Words are gradable if they denote a concept or property which can exist in varying degrees. For example, *tall* is a gradable word since we can say (for example) *fairly/very/extremely tall*; by contrast, *dead* is an *ungradable* word, since it denotes an absolute property (hence we can't say **very dead*).

Grammar In traditional terms, the word grammar relates to the study of morphology and syntax. In a broader Chomskyan sense, grammar includes the study of phonology and structural aspects of semantics: i.e. a grammar of a language is a computational system which derives the phonetic form and logical form of phrases and sentences.

Grammatical An expression is grammatical if it contains no morphological or syntactic error. *Grammatical features* are (e.g. person, number, gender, case, etc.) features which play a role in grammatical operations (e.g. in the checking of agreement relations).

Greed   A principle of grammar (cf. Chomsky 1995b) which specifies that constituents move only in order to satisfy their own morphological requirements. See §6.5.

Have-**cliticization/-contraction**   An operation by which *have* (in the guise of its contracted variant /v/) attaches to an immediately preceding word ending in a vowel or diphthong, resulting in forms such as *I've, we've, they've*.

Head   This term has two main uses. The *head* (constituent) of a phrase is the key word which determines the properties of the phrase. So, in a phrase such as *fond of fast food*, the head of the phrase is the adjective *fond*, and consequently the phrase is an adjectival phrase (and hence can occupy typical positions occupied by adjectival expressions – e.g. as the complement of *is* in *He is fond of fast food*). In many cases, the term *head* is more or less equivalent to the term *word* (e.g. in sentences such as 'An objective pronoun can be used as the complement of a transitive *head*'). In a different use of the same word, the *head* of a movement **chain** is the leftmost constituent in the chain. On *head features*, see **features**.

Head-first/-last language   A *head-first language* is one in which heads are canonically (i.e. normally) positioned before their complements; a *head-last language* is one in which heads are canonically positioned after their complements. See §1.7.

Head movement   Movement of a word from one head position to another. See ch. 6. For particular examples of head-movement, see also **I movement** and **V movement**.

Head movement constraint   A constraint (proposed by Travis 1984) which amounts to the requirement that a moved head can only move into the head position in the next-highest phrase immediately containing it (in any single movement operation).

Head (position) parameter   The **parameter** which determines whether a language positions heads before or after their complements. See §1.7.

Heuristic   A diagnostic procedure, or test.

Homophonous   Two different expressions are homophonous if they have the same phonetic form (e.g. *we've* and *weave*).

Host   An expression to which a **clitic** attaches. For example, if we say that *n't* cliticizes onto *could* in forms like *couldn't*, we can say that *could* is the host onto which *n't* cliticizes.

I/Ī/I-bar/IP   I represents the category of *INFL/Inflection*; Ī/I-bar is an intermediate projection headed by I; and IP (inflection phrase) is a maximal projection headed by I. See **INFL** and **projection**.

Identify   To say that an inflection serves to *identify* an empty category is to say that the inflection determines the **interpretation** of the empty category. For example, we might say that the second person singular inflection +*st* identifies the implicit null subject **pro** as second person singular in a Shakespearean sentence such as *Hast **pro** any more of this?* (Trinculo, *The Tempest*, II.ii). See §6.5.

Idiom   A string of words which has an idiosyncratic meaning (e.g. *hit the roof* in the sense of 'get angry'). See §8.3.

I-language   Language viewed as a computational system internalized within the brain. See §1.2.

Illocutionary force   The *illocutionary force* of a sentence (or clause) describes the kind of speech act which it is used to perform (e.g. a sentence is **declarative** in force if used to make a statement, **interrogative** in force if used to ask a question, **imperative** in force if used to issue an order, **exclamative** in force if used to exclaim surprise, etc.). See Grice 1975.

Immediate constituent   The immediate constituents of a given phrase XP are those constituents which are contained within XP, but not within any other phrase which is itself contained within XP. In practice, the immediate constituents of XP are the head X of XP, the complement of X, the specifier of X and any adjunct attached to a projection of X.

I(-to-C) movement   Movement of a verb out of the head **I** position in **IP** into the head **C** position in **CP**. See §6.2, and **inversion**.

Imp   A symbol used to designate an (affixal) imperative morpheme which occupies the head C position of CP in an **imperative** sentence.

Imperative   A term used to classify a type of sentence used to issue an order (e.g. *Be quiet!*, *Don't say anything!*), and also to classify the type of verb form used in an imperative sentence (e.g. *be* is an imperative verb form in *Be quiet!*).

Imperfective   See **aspect**.

Impersonal   The pronoun *it* is said to be *impersonal* when it has no **thematic role** (and doesn't refer to any external entity outside the sentence), e.g. in sentences such as *It is rumoured that he is unhappy*, or *It is unlikely that he'll come back*.

Impoverished   See **rich**.

Inanimate   See **animate**.

Inchoative   An inchoative verb is one which marks the beginning of an action or state. For example, we might say that *become* is an inchoative verb in a sentence such as *He didn't become famous until he released his first album*, since it can be paraphrased as 'start to be'.

Indefinite   See **definite**.

Indicative   Indicative (auxiliary and nonauxiliary) verb forms are finite forms which are used (*inter alia*) in declarative and interrogative clauses (i.e. statements and questions). Thus, the bold-printed items are indicative forms in the following sentences: *He **is** teasing you*, ***Can** he speak French?*, *He **had** been smoking*, *He **loves** chocolate*, *He **hated** syntax*. An indicative clause is a clause which contains an indicative (auxiliary or nonauxiliary) verb. See **mood**.

Indices   Subscript letters attached to sets of constituents to indicate whether or not there is a **binding** relation between them. For example, in a structure such as *John$_i$ thinks that Harry$_j$ is deceiving himself$_j$*, the indices indicate that *himself* is bound by (i.e. interpreted as referring to) *Harry*, not by *John*.

Indirect object   See **object**.

Indirect question   An interrogative complement clause (i.e. an interrogative clause used as the complement of a word like *ask, unsure, question*, etc.) such as those bracketed in *I wonder [what he will do]* and *I don't know [if he will turn up]*.

Indirect theta-marking   See **theta-marking**.

Inf An informal abbreviation for the feature [infinitival].

Infinitive The *infinitive* form of a verb is the (uninflected) form which is used when the verb is the complement of a modal auxiliary like *can*, or of the infinitive particle *to*. Accordingly, the bold-printed verbs are infinitive forms in the following sentences: *He can **speak** French, He's trying to **learn** French*. An *infinitive clause* is a clause which contains a verb in the infinitive form. Hence, the bracketed clauses are infinitive clauses in the following examples: *He is trying* [*to help her*], *Why not let* [*him help her*]*?* (In both examples, *help* is an infinitive verb form.) Since clauses are analysed as phrases within the framework used here, the term *infinitive phrase* is used interchangeably with *infinitive clause*, to denote an IP projection headed by the infinitive particle *to* (or by the null counterpart of the infinitive particle *to* discussed in §4.5).

INFL/I A category devised by Chomsky whose members include finite auxiliaries (which are *INFL*ected for tense/agreement), and the *INF*initiva*L* particle *to*. See §2.5.

Inflection(al morphology) An *inflection* is an **affix** which marks grammatical properties such as number, person, tense, case. For example, English has four verb inflections – namely past tense +*d*, third person singular present tense +*s*, perfective/passive +*n* and imperfective/progressive +*ing*. By contrast, English has only one noun inflection, namely plural +*s*. The term *inflectional morphology* denotes the study of the grammar of inflections. The term *inflection* is also used (in a different sense) as the full label for the category **INFL**.

+*ing* An inflectional suffix which has two main roles. On the one hand, it can serve as a *progressive/imperfective suffix* which (when attached to a verb stem) produces a *progressive/imperfective participle* (e.g. in a sentence such as *He was **smoking*** (see **aspect**)). On the other hand, it can serve as a suffix used to derive the **gerund** form of a verb (e.g. in sentences like *She doesn't approve of my smoking a pipe*).

Initial grammar The earliest grammar of their native language developed by (one-year-old) children.

Innateness hypothesis The hypothesis that children have a biologically endowed innate **language faculty**. See §1.4.

In situ A constituent is said to remain *in situ* if it remains in place, and doesn't undergo movement.

Interface levels Levels at which the grammar interfaces (i.e. connects) with systems which lie outside the domain of grammar. PF (phonetic form) is the level at which the grammar interfaces with articulatory–perceptual systems, and LF (logical form) is the level at which it interfaces with conceptual–intentional systems.

Intermediate projection A constituent which is larger than a word, but smaller than a phrase. See §3.3, and **projection**.

Internal argument Complement. See **argument**.

Interpretable A feature is interpretable at the level of LF/logical form if it has semantic content: so, for example, a feature such as [plural] is interpretable at LF, but a phonetic feature like [nasal] is uninterpretable at LF, and so too are purely grammatical/formal features (e.g. case-features). See §5.2.

Interpretation   To say that an expression has a particular *interpretation* is to say that it expresses a particular set of semantic relations. So, for example, we might say that a sentence such as *He loves you more than Sam* has two different interpretations – one on which *Sam* has a subject interpretation and is implicitly understood as the **subject** of *loves you*, and a second on which *Sam* has an object interpretation and is implicitly understood as the **object** of *he loves*. The first interpretation can be paraphrased as 'He loves you more than Sam loves you', and the second as 'He loves you more than he loves Sam.'

Interrogative   An **interrogative** clause or sentence is one which is used to ask a question. For example, the overall sentence is interrogative in *Is it raining?*, and the bracketed **complement clause** is interrogative in *I wonder* [*if it is raining*].

Intransitive   See **transitive**.

Inversion   A term used to denote a movement process by which the relative order of two expressions is reversed. It is most frequently used in relation to the more specific operation by which an auxiliary (and, in earlier stages of English, nonauxiliary) verb comes to be positioned before its subject, e.g. in questions such as *Can you speak Swahili?*, where *can* is positioned in front of its subject *you*. See §6.2.

Inverted auxiliary/verb   An auxiliary/verb which is positioned in front of its subject (e.g. *will* in *Will I pass the syntax exam?*). See §6.2.

IP   Inflection phrase, i.e. a phrase/clause which is a projection of **INFL**. Thus, a sentence such as *It might rain* is an IP – more specifically, a projection of the INFL constituent *might*.

IP adverb   An adverb (like *certainly*) which is positioned internally within IP (i.e. which is adjoined to some projection of **INFL**).

Island   A structure which does not allow any constituent to be extracted from it (e.g. *and*-structures are islands – hence we can't say **John I admire Harry and*, moving *John* out of the *and*-structure *Harry and John*).

K   Case particle. See **case**.

Labelled bracketing   See **bracketing**.

Landing-site   The landing-site for a moved constituent is the position it ends up in after it has been moved (e.g. the specifier position within CP is the landing-site for a moved operator expression).

Language faculty   Chomsky has argued that human beings have an innate **language faculty** (i.e. brain module) which provides them with an algorithm (i.e. set of procedures or program) for developing a grammar of their native language(s). See §1.4.

Last resort principle   The principle that grammatical operations do not apply unless they have to as the only way of satisfying some grammatical requirement: for example, *do*-**support** is used in questions only as a last resort, i.e. if there is no other auxiliary in the structure which can undergo inversion. See §6.2.

Leaf   In tree diagrams, the term *leaf* refers to a word attached to a terminal node in a tree.

Learnability   A criterion of adequacy for linguistic theory. An adequate theory must explain how children come to learn the grammar of their native languages in such a short period of time, and hence must provide for grammars of languages which are easily learnable by children. See §1.3.

Least effort principle   See **economy principle**.

Level (of representation)   A level of representation (of the structure of a sentence) is a stage (in a **derivation**) at which representations comprise only features of a single type. There are two different levels of representation in a grammar, **LF** and **PF**. **LF/logical form** is the level at which representations include only semantic features; **PF/phonetic form** is the level at which representations include only phonetic features. By contrast, the grammatical structures produced by merger and movement operations do not constitute a separate level of representation, since they contain three different sets of features (phonetic, grammatical and semantic).

Lexical/Lexicon   The word *lexical* is used in a number of different ways. Since a **lexicon** is a dictionary (i.e. a list of all the words in a language and their idiosyncratic linguistic properties), the expression *lexical item* means 'word', the expression *lexical entry* means 'the entry in the dictionary for a particular word', the term *lexical property* means 'property associated with some individual word' and the term *lexical learning* means 'learning words and their idiosyncratic properties'. However, the word *lexical* is also used in a second sense, in which it is contrasted with **functional** (and hence means 'nonfunctional'). In this second sense, a *lexical category* is a category whose members are **contentives** (i.e. items with idiosyncratic descriptive content): hence, categories such as noun, verb, adjective or preposition are lexical categories in this sense. So, for example, the term *lexical verb* means 'nonauxiliary verb' (i.e. a verb like *go, find, hate, want*, etc.).

LF   Logical form. An LF representation (for an expression) is a representation of the logical form of the expression (see **representation**). The **LF component** of a grammar is the component which converts the syntactic structures produced by merger and movement operations into LF representations.

LF movement   A movement operation which applies in the **LF component**, and hence which does not affect the phonetic form of a given sentence.

License   To say that a head *licenses* a certain type of specifier/complement is to say that it can have such a specifier/complement. For example, a finite auxiliary licenses a nominative subject (but since this is the only type of subject licensed by a finite auxiliary, this in effect means that a finite auxiliary *must* have a nominative subject).

Light verb   An affixal verb (often with a causative sense like that of *make*) to which a noun, adjective or verb adjoins. For example, it might be claimed that the suffix *+en* in a verb like *sadden* is an affixal light verb which can combine with an adjective like *sad* to form the causative verb *sadden* (meaning 'make sad', 'cause to become sad'). This type of analysis could be extended to verbs like *roll* as they are used in sentences like *He rolled the ball down the hill*, where we could suggest that *roll* is used causatively (in the sense of 'make roll' or 'cause to roll'), and hence involves adjunction of the verb *roll* to an abstract light verb (i.e. to a null verbal counterpart of +*en*). See ch. 9.

Link   A constituent (or position) which is part of a movement **chain**.

Local   An operation is *local* only if it operates within a highly restricted domain (e.g. internally within a phrase, or across no more than one intervening phrasal boundary). For example, **agreement** typically involves a local relation between the head and specifier of a given type of phrase (e.g. in a sentence like *He has gone*, between the INFL constituent *has* and its specifier/subject *he*). Similarly, anaphors like *himself* typically require a local antecedent (i.e. an antecedent within the phrase containing them). A movement operation like **head movement** is local in the sense that a head can only move into the next-highest head position within the structure (and so can cross only one intervening phrase boundary containing it).

Locative   A locative expression is one which denotes place. So, for example, *there/where* are locative pronouns in sentences such as *Are you going there?* or *Where are you going?*

Main clause   See **root**.

Map   To say that one structure is *mapped* into another is to say that it is 'transformed' or 'converted' or 'changed' into the other structure by a grammatical operation of some kind.

Masculine   A term used in discussions of grammatical **gender** to denote pronouns like *he/him/his* which refer to male entities.

Mass noun   See **count noun**.

Matrix   In a sentence like *I think* [*you are right*], to say that the *think*-clause is the matrix clause for the bracketed **complement clause** is to say that it is the clause which immediately contains the bracketed clause (hence that the bracketed clause is **embedded** within the *think*-clause). For a different use of the term, see **feature (matrix)**.

Maximal projection   See **projection**.

Merger   An operation by which two categories are combined to form another category. See ch. 3.

Minimal domain   See **domain**.

Minimalism/Minimalist program   A theory of grammar (outlined in Chomsky 1995b) whose core assumption is that grammars should be described in terms of the minimal set of theoretical and descriptive apparatus necessary.

Minimal link condition/Minimality condition   A principle of grammar requiring that the links in movement chains should be as short as possible (hence that constituents should move from one position to another in the shortest possible steps). See also **shortest movement principle**.

Minimal projection   See **projection**.

MIT   The Massachusetts Institute of Technology (located in Cambridge, Massachusetts), where Chomsky has worked for the past four decades.

Mod(al)/Modality   A modal auxiliary is an auxiliary which expresses modality (i.e. a notion such as possibility, futurity or necessity). The set of modal auxiliaries in English is usually assumed to include *will/would/can/could/shall/should/may/might/must*, and perhaps *ought*, and *need/dare* when followed by a **bare** (*to*-less) infinitive complement.

Modifier/Modify   In an expression such as *tall men*, it is traditionally said that the adjective *tall* modifies (i.e. attributes some property to) or is a modifier of the noun *men*. Likewise, in a sentence such as *Eat slowly!*, the adverb *slowly* is said to modify the verb *eat* (in the sense that it describes the manner of eating).

ModP   A modal phrase – i.e. a phrase headed by a **modal** auxiliary.

Module   An individual autonomous component of a larger system. For example, a grammar might be said to contain a *case module* – i.e. a component which accounts for the case properties of relevant constituents.

Monotransitive   A *monotransitive* verb is one which takes a single **object** (as opposed to a **ditransitive verb**, which is a verb which takes two objects). For example the verb *said* in a sentence like *He said nothing* is monotransitive (its only object is *nothing*), whereas the verb *told* in *He told her nothing* is ditransitive in that it has two objects – *her* and *nothing*.

Mood   This is a term describing inflectional properties of finite verbs. (Auxiliary and nonauxiliary) verbs in English can be in the **indicative** mood, **subjunctive** mood or **imperative** mood. Examples of each type of mood are given by the bold-printed verb forms in the following: *He **hates*** (= indicative) *spaghetti*; *The court ordered that he **be*** (= subjunctive) *detained indefinitely*; ***Keep*** (= imperative) *quiet!* Occasionally, this term is extended to nonfinite forms of the verb (so that one can talk about a verb in the *infinitive mood* (i.e. in its infinitive form).

Morpheme   The smallest unit of grammatical structure. Thus, a plural noun such as *cats* comprises two morphemes, namely the stem *cat* and the plural suffix +*s*.

Morphology   The study of how **morphemes** are combined together to form words.

Morphosyntactic   A morphosyntactic property is a grammatical property, i.e. a property which is morphologically and syntactically conditioned. For instance, **case** is a morphosyntactic property, in that (for example) **personal pronouns** have different morphological forms and occupy different syntactic positions according to their case: e.g. the nominative form of the first person plural pronoun is *we* and its objective form is *us*; the two occupy different syntactic positions in that the nominative form occurs as the subject of a **finite** verb or auxiliary (cf. *we* in *We disagree*), whereas the objective form occurs as the complement of a **transitive** verb or preposition (cf. *us* in *He disagrees with us*).

Mother   A node *X* is the mother of another node *Y* if *X* is the next highest node up in the tree from *Y*, and the two are connected by a branch (solid line). See §3.6.

Movement   An operation by which a word, phrase or set of features is moved from one position in a structure to another. Types of movement operation include **attraction**, **head movement**, **A movement**, **A-bar movement** (including **operator movement**) and **adjunction**.

MSE   Modern Standard English.

516

Multiple wh-questions   Questions containing more than one wh-word. See §7.3.

Multiword speech   A stage in child language acquisition at which (one-year-old) children first begin combining words together into two- and three- (etc.) word utterances.

N/N̄/N-bar/NP   N represents the category of *noun*; N̄/N-bar is an intermediate projection headed by N; and NP (noun phrase) is a maximal projection headed by N. See **noun, noun phrase** and **projection**; see also ch. 4.

+*n*   The inflection used to form the perfective/passive participle form of a verb (see **aspect, active**). For example, *shown* is a perfective participle in *The referee has already shown him the yellow card once*, but is a passive participle in *He has already been shown the yellow card once*. The term *n-participle* refers to the perfective/passive participle form of a verb (for some verbs, this may end in +*d*/+*t*: cf. *He has **tried***, *She has **bought** one*).

Natural language   Human language; more specifically, a language acquired in a natural setting by human beings (hence, excluding e.g. computer languages, animal communication systems, etc.).

NEG/NEGP   A negative constituent which heads a projection into a NEGP (negative phrase): see §6.6.

Negation   A process or construction in which some proposition is said to be false. Negation involves the use of some negative item such as *not*, *n't*, *nobody*, *nothing*, *never*, etc. – though most discussions of negation tend to be about *not/n't*.

Negative evidence   In the context of discussions of child language acquisition, this term relates to evidence based on the nonoccurrence of certain structures in the child's speech input. See §1.9.

Negative particle   This informal term typically denotes *not/n't*.

Neuter   See **gender**.

Neutralization   When a morphological contrast (e.g. that between a singular noun like *cat* and a plural noun like *cats*) is not marked in some expression (e.g. the singular/plural noun form *sheep*), the contrast is said to have been *neutralized* (in the relevant item).

No-contentless-projections constraint   The informal name given in the text for a **constraint** proposed in Speas 1995 to the effect that projections cannot have heads and specifiers which lack content. This amounts to a requirement to the effect that either the head of a projection must have content, or its specifier must – or both of them.

Node   A term used to denote a point in a tree diagram which carries a category label.

Nom   An informal abbreviation for the case-feature [nominative]. See **case**.

Nominal   This is the adjective associated with **noun**, so that in principle a *nominal* or a *nominal constituent* is an expression headed by a noun. However, the term is often extended to mean 'expression which is a projection or **extended projection** of a noun or pronoun'. In current work, a phrase like *a supporter of monetarism* would be analysed as a **determiner phrase**, and hence is not a nominal, if by *nominal* we mean 'expression headed by a noun'. However, if we say that the **DP** (= determiner phrase) here is an extended projection of the noun *supporter*, we can none the less continue to say that it is a *nominal*. Further confusion is caused by the fact that in earlier work, what are now analysed as determiner phrases would then have been analysed as noun phrases.

Nominalization/Nominalizing affix   Nominalization is a process by which some other type of expression is converted into a **nominal** (i.e. noun expression). For example, *+ness* is a nominalizing affix in that if we suffix *+ness* to an adjective like *sad*, we form the noun *sadness*.

Nominative   See **case**.

Nonargument   See **argument**.

Nonauxiliary verb   A **lexical** verb (like *want*, *try*, *hate*, *smell*, *buy*, etc.) which requires *do*-support to form questions, negatives and tags.

Nonconstituent string/sequence   A string/sequence of words which do not together form a constituent.

Noncount noun   See **count noun**.

No-negative-evidence hypothesis   The hypothesis that children acquire their native language(s) on the basis of **positive evidence** alone, and do not make use of **negative evidence**. See §1.9.

Nonfinite   See **finite**.

Nonoperator question   A question which does not contain an interrogative operator. See §7.9.

Nonterminal   See **terminal node**.

Nonuniform chain   See **chain uniformity principle**.

Nonvocalic   Not containing a vowel or diphthong.

Noun   A category of word (whose members include items such as *boy/friend/thought/ sadness/computer*) which typically denotes an entity of some kind. See §2.2.

Noun phrase   A phrase whose **head** is a noun. Thus, the expression *lovers of opera* is a noun phrase, since its head is the noun *lovers*. In earlier work, determiners were thought to be the specifiers of noun phrases, so that an expression such as *a fan of Juventus* would have been analysed as a noun phrase (though in more recent work, it would be analysed as an expression headed by the determiner *a*, and hence as a **determiner phrase, DP**). See chs. 3 and 4.

NP   See **noun phrase**.

Null   See **covert**.

Null case   The case carried by **PRO** (see **case**).

Null operator   See **Op**.

Null subject   A subject which has grammatical/semantic properties but no overt phonetic form. More specifically, this term usually denotes the null **pro** subject found in finite declarative or interrogative clauses in languages like Italian or Early Modern English, and not the covert subject found in imperative clauses like *Shut the door!* or the covert **PRO** subject found in **control** structures like *The prisoners tried to PRO escape from jail*. Accordingly, a *null subject language* is a language which allows finite **declarative** or **interrogative** clauses to have a null *pro* subject. For example, Italian is a null subject language and so allows us to say *Sei* *simpatica* (literally 'Are nice', meaning '*You* are nice'); by contrast, English is not a null subject language, and so doesn't allow the subject to be omitted in this type of structure (hence *Are nice is ungrammatical in English). The null subject parameter is a dimension of variation between languages according to whether finite (declarative and interrogative) verbs allow null *pro* subjects or not.

Number   A term used to denote the contrast between **singular** and **plural** forms. In English, we find number contrasts in nouns (cf. *one dog*, *two dogs*), in some determiners (cf. *this book*, *these books*), in pronouns (cf. *he/they*) and in finite verbs (cf. *He smells*, *They smell*).

Obj   An informal abbreviation for the case-feature [objective]. See **case**.

Object   The **complement** of a **transitive** item (e.g. in *Help me!*, *me* is the object of the transitive verb *help*; and in *for me*, *me* is the object of the transitive preposition *for*). The term *object* is generally restricted to complements which carry objective case – i.e. to nominal or pronominal complements: hence, *nothing* would be the object (and complement) of *said* in *He said nothing*, but the *that*-clause would be the complement (but not the object) of *said* in *He said [that he was tired]* – though some traditional grammars extend the term object to cover clausal complements as well as (pro)nominal complements. In sentences such as *She gave him them*, the verb *give* is traditionally said to have two objects, namely *him* and *them*: the first object *him* (representing the recipient) is termed the *indirect object*, and the second object *them* (representing the gift) is termed the *direct object*; the relevant construction is known as the *double-object construction*. Where a verb has a single object (e.g. *nothing* in *He said nothing*), this is the *direct object* of the relevant verb.

Object-control predicate   See **control**.

Objective   See **case**.

Oblique   See **case**.

O movement   See **operator movement**.

One-place predicate   A **predicate** which has only one **argument** (e.g. *yawn* in *John yawned*, where *John* is the sole argument of the predicate *yawn*).

Op   A symbol used to denote the empty question operator found in yes–no questions like *Do you enjoy syntax?* It can be thought of as a counterpart of the question-mark used in the spelling system to indicate that a sentence is a question, or as the counterpart of *whether* in *I wonder whether you enjoy syntax*. See §7.8.

Operator   This term is used in syntax to denote (for example) interrogative and negative expressions which have the syntactic properties that they trigger auxiliary inversion (cf. **What** *have you done?*, **Nothing** *would I ever do to upset anyone*).

Operator movement   Movement of an operator expression into **spec-CP** (i.e. into the specifier position within **CP**). See ch. 7.

Orphaned   See **stranded**.

Overt   An expression is *overt* if it has phonetic content, but **covert** if it lacks phonetic content. Thus, *him* is an overt pronoun, but **PRO** is a covert (or *null*, or *empty* or *silent*) pronoun.

P   As a category label, it is an abbreviation of **preposition**; as a number feature, it is an abbreviation of [plural].

Parameter   A dimension of grammatical variation between different languages or different varieties of the same language (e.g. the **null subject parameter**, **head parameter**, **wh-parameter**). See §1.7.

Parameter-setting   The process by which children determine which setting of a parameter is appropriate for the native language they are acquiring. See §1.8.

Parametric variation   Variation from one language (variety) to another in respect of some particular **parameter(s)**. For example, there is parametric variation between English and Italian in respect of the **null subject parameter**, in that Italian is a *null subject language* whereas English is a *non-null subject language*. See §1.7.

Parsing   The grammatical analysis of phrases and sentences – most frequently used in connection with analysing their categorial status and their syntactic structure in terms of a **labelled bracketing** or **tree diagram**.

Participle   The **+*ing*** and **+*n*** forms of a verb (in certain uses) are traditionally said to be *participles*. More specifically, the +*ing* form (when not used as a **gerund**) is said to be an *imperfective/progressive/present participle* (e.g. in *He is **leaving***), whereas the +*n* form is said to function as a *perfective/past participle* in some uses (e.g. in *He has **stolen** them*) and as a *passive participle* in others (e.g. *They have been **stolen***). See **aspect**, **active**.

Particle   This is a pretheoretical term used to describe a range of items which are invariable in form, and which don't fit easily into traditional systems of grammatical categories. For example, infinitival *to* (cf. *Try **to** be nice*) is said to be an *infinitive particle*, and *not/n't* are said to be *negative particles*. The term is sometimes extended to include prepositions used without a complement (e.g. *up* in *Give **up!***).

Partitive   A partitive quantifier is a word like *some/any* which quantifies over part of the members of a given set (as in *Some people are lazy*). For a different use of the word in the expression *partitive case*, see **case**.

Passive   See **active**, **passivization**.

Passivization   A movement operation whereby the complement of a verb becomes its subject (cf. ***The jewels** were stolen*), or the subject of an infinitive complement of a passive participle becomes the subject of the passive auxiliary (cf. ***The ministers** were thought to have lied to Parliament*). See §8.8.

Past tense   See **tense**.

PATIENT   A particular **thematic role**, associated with an entity which suffers the consequences of some action. For example, in a sentence such as *John killed Harry*, *Harry* is the PATIENT **argument** of the verb *kill*.

Percolation   An operation (also known as **attraction**) by which a feature which is attached to one category comes to be attached to another category higher up in the structure. See §4.4.

PERF   Perfective auxiliary (e.g. *has* in *He has left*). See **aspect**.

Perfective   See **aspect**, **participle**.

Performance   A term which denotes observed language behaviour, e.g. the kind of things people actually say when they speak a language, and what meanings they assign to sentences produced by themselves or other people. Performance can be impaired by factors such as tiredness, drunkenness, etc. *Performance* is contrasted with **competence** (which denotes the fluent native speakers' knowledge of the grammar of their native language). See §1.2.

PERFP   A phrase headed by a perfective auxiliary.

Person   In traditional grammar, English is said to have three grammatical *persons*: a *first person* expression (e.g. *I/we*) is one whose reference includes the speaker(s); a *second person* expression (e.g. *you*) is one which excludes the speaker(s) but includes the addressee(s) (i.e. the person or people being spoken to); a *third person* expression (e.g. *he/she/it/they*) is one whose reference excludes both the speaker(s) and the addressee(s) – i.e. an expression which refers to someone or something other than the speaker(s) or addressee(s).

Personal pronouns   These are pronouns which carry inherent **person** properties – i.e. first person pronouns such as *I/we*, second person pronouns such as *you* and third person pronouns such as *he/she/it/they*.

PF (representation)   (A representation of the) phonetic form (of an expression). See **representation**. The **PF component** of a grammar is the component which converts the syntactic structures produced by merger and movement operations into PF representations. A PF clitic is a clitic which attaches to another item in the PF component (not in the syntax), so that the two form a single phonetic word, but not a single syntactic constituent. See §6.9, and ch. 6, ex. V.

PFI   The principle of full interpretation (see **full interpretation**).

PF movement   An operation which moves the phonetic features of a constituent but not its other (e.g. grammatical) features. See §6.9.

Phonetic representation   See **representation**.

Phonological features   Features used to describe sound properties. For example, the difference between nasal and oral sounds might be described in terms of the feature [nasal].

Phrase   The term *phrase* is used to denote an expression larger than a word which is a *maximal projection*: see **projection**. In traditional grammar, the term refers strictly to nonclausal expressions. (Hence, *reading a book* is a phrase, but *He is reading a book* is a clause, not a phrase.) However, in more recent work, clauses are analysed as types of phrases: e.g. *He will resign* is an auxiliary phrase (IP), and *That he will resign* is a complementizer phrase (CP).

Phrase-marker   A **tree diagram** used to represent the syntactic structure of a phrase or sentence. See §3.5.

Phrase structure   See **constituent structure**.

Pied-piping   A process by which a moved constituent (or set of features) drags one or more other constituents (or sets of features) along with it when it moves. For example, if we compare a sentence like *Who were you talking to?* with *To whom were you talking?*, we might say that in both cases the pronoun *who(m)* is moved to the front of the sentence, but that in the second sentence the preposition *to* is pied-piped along with *whom*. See §7.4.

Plural A plural expression is one which denotes more than one entity (e.g. *these cars* is a plural expression, whereas *this car* is a singular expression).

P-marker See **phrase-marker**.

Polarity expression A word or phrase (e.g. a word like *ever* or a phrase like *at all* or *care a damn*) which has an inherent **affective** polarity, and hence is restricted to occurring within the scope of an affective (e.g. negative, interrogative or conditional) constituent.

Polycategorial word A word which belongs to more than one category.

Positive evidence In discussions of child language acquisition, this expression denotes evidence based on the occurrence of certain types of structure in the child's **experience**. See §1.9.

Possessive A possessive structure is one which indicates possession: the term is most commonly used in relation to structures like *John's book* (where *'s* is said to be a possessive morpheme) or *his book* (where *his* is said to be a possessive pronoun or possessive determiner). The expression 'possessive *have*' relates to a particular use of the verb *have* to express possession (e.g. *John has a house on the Costa Brava*).

Postmodify To say that *nice* in an expression such as *someone nice* postmodifies *someone* is to say that *nice* **modifies** and follows *someone*.

Postposition A type of **adposition** which is the counterpart of a **preposition** in languages which position prepositions after their complements.

Postulate A postulate is a theoretical assumption or hypothesis; to postulate is to assume or hypothesize.

PP See **prepositional phrase**.

PPT See **principles-and-parameters theory**.

Pragmatics The study of the role played by nonlinguistic knowledge in our use of language.

Precede(nce) To say that one constituent *precedes* another is to say that it is positioned to its left (on the printed page) and that neither constituent **dominates** the other.

Preclausal A preclausal expression is one which is positioned in front of a clause.

Predicate On *predicate*, see **argument**. A *predicate nominal* is a nominal expression used as a predicate – e.g. the bold-printed expressions in *John is **a fool**, I consider them **fools*** (where the expressions *a fool/fools* are said to be predicated of *John/them*).

Predication The process by which a predicate is combined with a subject in order to form a proposition (see **argument**). For example, in a sentence such as *Boris likes vodka*, the property of liking vodka is said to be predicated of Boris.

Predication principle A principle suggested by Rothstein (1995) to the effect that a syntactic predicate (e.g. an I-bar or V-bar constituent) requires a subject.

Predicative An adjective which is used as a **predicate** is said to be predicative in the relevant use – e.g. the bold-printed adjectives in *John is **drunk**, I consider your behaviour **unforgiveable***. Likewise, the nominal *fools* is said to be used predicatively in sentences such as *They are **fools**, I consider them **fools***.

Prefix   See **affix**.

Premodify   To say that the adjective *tall* premodifies the noun *men* in the expression *tall men* is to say that *tall* precedes and **modifies** *men*.

Prenominal   A *prenominal* expression is one which is positioned in front of a nominal (i.e. a noun expression). For example, both *a* and *red* are prenominal in an expression such as *a red car*, because they precede the noun *car*.

Preposing   An informal term to indicate a movement operation by which a constituent is moved further to the left within a phrase or sentence.

Preposition   A preposition is an invariable word generally used to express location, manner, etc. – e.g. *at/in/on/under/by/with/from/against* etc. It is a characteristic property of most prepositions that they can be premodified by *straight/right*. Where a preposition has a nominal or pronominal complement, it is said to be **transitive**; where it has no complement, it is said to be **intransitive**. So, for example, the preposition *inside* is transitive in *There was nobody inside the house*, but intransitive in *There was nobody inside*. See §2.2 and §2.3.

Prepositional phrase   A phrase whose head is a preposition – e.g. *in town, on Sunday, to the market, for someone else*, etc.

Preposition-stranding   See **stranded**.

Prescriptive grammar   An approach to grammar (often found in traditional textbooks used to teach grammar in secondary schools) which seeks to prescribe (i.e. lay down) norms of linguistic behaviour (taken from the so-called standard language) for all speakers of a language. In such an approach, certain types of colloquial construction found in the spoken language (e.g. **split infinitives**) are stigmatized as alleged instances of 'bad grammar'.

Present   See **tense**.

Primary data   In discussions of language acquisition, this refers to the child's **experience** – i.e. to the speech input which the child receives.

Principles   Principles describe potentially universal properties of grammatical operations or structures: the terms *condition* and *constraint* are also used with much the same meaning. Potential principles of Universal Grammar include the **structure dependence principle**, the **head movement constraint**, the **shortest movement principle**, the **economy principle**, the principle of **greed**, the **principle of full interpretation**, etc.

Principles-and-parameters theory   A theory devised by Chomsky in work over the past two decades which maintains that universal properties of natural language grammars reflect the operation of a set of universal grammatical **principles**, and that grammatical differences between languages can be characterized in terms of a restricted set of **parameters**. See ch. 1.

PRO/pro   *PRO* designates a covert null-case pronoun (known informally as *big PRO*, because it is written in capital letters) which represents the understood subject of an infinitive complement of a **control** predicate, e.g. in a structure such as *John decided to PRO leave* (see §4.2 and §9.6). By contrast, *pro* is a covert nominative-case pronoun (known informally as *little pro*, because it is written in lower-case letters) which represents the understood subject of a finite clause in (for example) a Shakespearean sentence such as *Wilt come?* (= 'Will [you] come?', Stephano, *The Tempest*, III.ii; see §6.5).

Proconstituent See **proform**.

Productive A process is **productive** if it applies to all (or at any rate, virtually all) of the expressions of a given type. A process has limited productivity if it applies only to some expressions of a given type, not others (i.e. if there are a number of unexplained exceptions).

Proform A proform is an expression (typically a word) which has no specific content of its own, but which derives its content from its **antecedent**. In a sentence such as *John knows that people don't like **him***, the proform *him* can be interpreted as referring back to *John* (i.e. *John* can be the antecedent of *him* here): hence, this type of word is traditionally referred to as a **pronoun** because it is used 'on behalf of/in place of' (which is the meaning of the prefix *pro+*) a noun expression. However, in a sentence such as *Mary may have been tired, but she didn't seem **so***, the antecedent of the word *so* is the adjective *tired*: since it wouldn't be appropriate to use the term *pronoun* to describe this function of *so*, the more general terms *proform* or *proconstituent* have been devised in more recent work. We can then say that *him* is a nominal proform whereas *so* (in the use illustrated here) is an adjectival proform.

PROG Progressive auxiliary (e.g. *is* in *He is waiting*). See **aspect**.

PROGP Progressive phrase – i.e. a phrase headed by a progressive auxiliary.

Progressive See **aspect**.

Project(ion) A projection is a constituent which is an expansion of a head word. For example, a noun phrase such as *students of linguistics* is a projection of its head noun *students* (equivalently, we can say that the noun *students* here projects into the noun phrase *students of linguistics*). A *minimal projection* is a constituent which is not a projection of some other constituent: hence, heads (i.e. words) are minimal projections. An *intermediate projection* is a constituent which is larger than a word, but smaller than a phrase. A *maximal projection* is a constituent which is not contained within any larger constituent with the same head. So, for example, in a sentence like *He is proud of you*, the adjectival phrase *proud of you* is a maximal projection, since it is a projection of the adjective *proud* but is not contained within any larger projection of the same adjective *proud*. By contrast, in a sentence such as *He is proud*, the adjective *proud* is both a minimal projection (by virtue of the fact that it is not a projection of some other head) and a maximal projection (by virtue of the fact that it is not contained within any larger structure which has the same head adjective).

Pronominal See **pronoun**.

Pronoun The word **pronoun** is traditionally defined as a word used in place of a noun expression. For example, in a sentence such as *John thinks people dislike him*, the pronoun *him* can be used to replace *John* at the end of the sentence, in order to avoid repeating the noun *John*. (Of course, *him* could also refer to someone other than *John.*) Pronouns differ from nouns in that they have no intrinsic descriptive content, and so are **functors** (see §2.4). In much recent work, most types of pronoun are analysed as **determiners**: for example, *this* is said to be a prenominal determiner in a sentence such as *I don't like this idea* (since it modifies the following noun *idea*), but a pronominal determiner (i.e. a determiner used without any following noun expression) in a sentence such as *I don't like this* (see §4.8).

Proper noun   See **common noun**.

Proposition   A term used to describe the semantic content (i.e. meaning) of a sentence. For example, we might say that the sentence *Does John smoke?* questions the truth of the proposition that 'John smokes'.

Pseudo-cleft   *Pseudo-cleft sentences* are sentences such as *What he bought was a car, What I said was that I was tired, What I'm going to do is sell my car*, where the constituent following the verb *be* (viz. *a car, that I was tired, sell my car*) is said to have undergone pseudo-clefting. The different term *cleft sentence* is traditionally used for sentences like *It was a car that he bought, It was on Friday that I last saw her* (where the constituents *a car* and *on Friday* are said to have undergone clefting).

Psycholinguistics   The study of the psychological processes by which we produce and understand speech.

Q   In one use, an abbreviation for **quantifier**; in another use, an abbreviation for *question affix*. (On the possibility that COMP in questions may contain an abstract question affix **Q**, see §6.9.)

Quantifier   A quantifier is a special type of **determiner** used to denote quantity. Typical quantifiers include the universal quantifiers *all/both*, the distributive quantifiers *each/every*, the partitive quantifiers *some/any*, etc.

Quantifier floating   See **floating quantifier**.

QP/Quantifier phrase   A phrase whose head is a quantifier – e.g. an expression such as *many people, few of the students*, etc.

Question   This refers to a type of sentence which is used to ask whether something is true, or to ask about the identity of some entity. See **yes–no question** and **wh-question**.

Question operator   See **Op**.

Raising (predicate)   The term *raising* is used in two senses. On the one hand, it is used in a general sense to denote any movement operation which involves moving some word or phrase from a lower to a higher position in a structure. On the other hand, it can also be used with the more specific sense of a *subject-to-subject raising* operation by which an expression is moved from one subject position to another (e.g. from being the subject of VP to being the subject of IP). The term *raising predicate* denotes a word like *seem* whose subject is raised out of subject position in a complement clause to become subject of the *seem* clause. See ch. 8.

RECIPIENT   The name of the thematic role borne by the entity which receives (or comes to possess) something – e.g. *Mary* in *John gave Mary a present*. See §8.4.

Reciprocal   Expressions like *each other* and *one another* (in sentences like *They hate each other/one another*) are traditionally classified as reciprocal **anaphors**.

Recursive   A recursive operation is one which can be repeated any number of times. For example, the process by which an adjective comes to modify a noun might be said to be recursive in that we can position any number of adjectives in front of a noun (e.g. *a **tall**, **dark**, **handsome** stranger*).

Reduced form   A form of a word which has lost one or more of its segments (i.e. vowels/ consonants), and/or which contains a vowel which loses its defining characteristics and is realized as the neutral vowel schwa /ə/. For example, the auxiliary *have* has the full (unreduced) form /hæv/ when stressed, but has the various reduced forms /həv/, /əv/ (and has the **contracted form** /v/). See §8.5.

Reference/Referential   The reference of an expression is the entity (e.g. object, concept, state of affairs) in the external world to which it refers. A *referential expression* is one which refers to such an entity; conversely, a *nonreferential expression* is one which does not refer to any such entity. For example, the second *there* in a sentence such as *There was nobody there* is referential (it can be paraphrased as 'in that place'), whereas the first *there* is nonreferential and so cannot have its reference questioned by *where?* (cf. **Where was nobody there?*).

Reflexive   A reflexive is a *+self/+selves* form such as *myself, himself, ourselves, themselves*, etc. See also **anaphor**.

Relative pronoun/relative clause   In a sentence such as *He's someone [who you can trust]*, the bracketed clause is said to be a *relative clause* because it 'relates to' (i.e. modifies, or restricts the reference of) the pronoun *someone*. The pronoun *who* which introduces the clause is said to be a *relative pronoun*, since it 'relates to' the expression *someone* (in the sense that *someone* is the **antecedent** of *who*).

Relativized minimality principle   A principle proposed by Rizzi (1990) which amounts to the claim that a moved constituent moves to the nearest appropriate position (where what is an *appropriate* position is relative to the type of constituent being moved: e.g. a moved head will move to the next-highest head position, an argument will move to the next-highest A position, an operator will move to the next-highest operator position, etc.).

Representation   A **syntactic representation** (or **structural representation**) is a notation/ device used to represent the syntactic structure of an expression (typically, a tree diagram or labelled bracketing): an **LF representation** is a representation of the logical form of an expression; a **PF representation** is a representation of the phonetic form of an expression.

Restrictive   A restrictive theory is one which imposes strong constraints on the types of structures and operations found in natural language grammars. See §1.3.

Resultative   A verb such as *paint* in a sentence such as *John painted his house pink* is said to be a resultative verb in that the result of the action of painting is that the house becomes pink.

Rich   To say that a language has a *rich* system of verb inflections (of a given type) is to say that it has a large number of inflectional affixes (of the relevant type) which attach to verbs; to say that a language has an *impoverished* system of verb inflections is to say that it has only a small number of verb inflections.

Root	The *root* of a tree diagram is the topmost node in the tree. Hence, a **root clause** is a free-standing clause, i.e. a clause which is not contained within any other expression. In traditional grammar, a **root** clause is termed a 'principal clause', 'independent clause' or 'main clause'. By contrast, an **embedded clause** is a clause which is contained within some larger expression and a **complement clause** is an (embedded) clause which is used as the **complement** of some item. So, in a sentence such as *I think he loves you*, the *think*-clause (i.e. the expression *I think he loves you*) is a root clause, whereas the *loves*-clause (i.e. the expression *he loves you*) is an embedded clause. Moreover, the *loves*-clause is also a complement clause, since it serves as the complement of the verb *think*.
S	In one use, this symbol represents the category label *sentence*; in another use, it represents the number-feature [singular].
+s	In one use, this denotes the plural suffix found in plural nouns such as *dog+s*; in another use, it denotes the third person singular present tense suffix found in verbs such as *adore+s*.
Schwa	The neutral vowel [ə] – e.g. the vowel corresponding to the bold-printed letters in words like *about, affair, potato*, etc.
Scope	The **scope** of an expression is the range of constituents which it 'modifies' or which fall within (what we might call informally) its 'sphere of influence'.
Scrambling	A process which reorders maximal projections internally within clauses, moving them further to the front of the clause. For example, in an Early Modern English sentence like *The king your mote did see* (Boyet, *Love's Labour's Lost*, IV.i), we might say that *your mote* has been *scrambled* out of its normal postverbal position (after *see*) into a position in front of *did* (see §10.3).
SE	Standard English
Second person	See **person**.
Segment	In phonology, to say that a word like *man* comprises the three segments /m/, /æ/ and /n/ is to say that these are the three sound units which determine the phonetic form of the word. In syntax, to say that a category comprises two segments (and so is a *split-segment category*) is to say that it comprises a constituent to which some other constituent has been adjoined, so forming an even larger constituent of the same type (e.g. if we adjoin *n't* to an auxiliary like *could* we form the even larger auxiliary *couldn't*, and this contains two auxiliary segments since both *couldn't* and *could* are auxiliaries).
Select(ion)	When a word can have a particular type of **complement**, we say that it *selects* (i.e. 'takes') the relevant type of complement (and the relevant property is referred to as *complement-selection*). So, for example, we can say that it is a complement selection property of the verb *want* that it selects (i.e. 'can take') a *to*-infinitive complement (as in *I want to help you*).
Semantics	The study of linguistic aspects of meaning.
Sentence	This term denotes a free-standing **clause** which is not contained within some larger expression. In terms of the conventions of the English spelling system, a sentence might be defined (rather inaccurately) as a string of words which starts with a word

527

beginning with a capital letter and which ends with a word immediately followed by a full-stop, so that this entry for **sentence** contains two sentences.

Sentence fragment   See **fragment**.

Shared string coordination   This refers to coordinate structures such as *John is buying and Mary is selling a house*, where the expression *a house* at the end of the sentence functions both as the complement of *buying* and as the complement of *selling*, and so is in some sense 'shared' between the two verbs (so that *a house* can be said to function as the *shared string* in the coordinate structure).

Shell   This term is used in connection with the idea (discussed in chapter 9) that verb phrases comprise two different projections, an outer **vp shell** headed by a **light verb**, and an inner **VP** core headed by a lexical verb.

Shortest movement principle   A principle of grammar requiring that a constituent should move the shortest distance possible in any single movement operation.

Silent   See **covert**.

Simple coordination   This refers to simple **coordinate** structures such as *John and Mary* in sentences like *John and Mary are expecting you*.

Singular   A singular expression is one which denotes a single entity (e.g. *this car* is a singular expression, whereas *these cars* is a plural expression).

Sister   Two nodes are sisters if they have the same **mother**. See §3.6.

Small clause   See **clause**.

Spec   See **specifier**.

Spec-CP/Spec-IP/Spec-VP (etc.)   The specifier position within CP/IP/VP.

Spec–head   A *spec–head* relation is a relation between a **head** and its **specifier**. For example, we might say that subject–auxiliary **agreement** involves a spec–head relation in sentences like *He has gone*, since *has* is the head of the clause and agrees with its specifier *he*.

Specification   See **feature**.

Specifier   The grammatical function fulfilled by certain types of constituent which (in English) precede the head of their containing phrase. For example, in a sentence such as *John is working*, *John* is the specifier (and **subject**) of *is working* (see §3.3). In a sentence such as *What did John do?*, *what* is the specifier of the CP headed by the inverted auxiliary *did*. See ch. 7.

Specifier-features   Features which determine the kind of specifier which a given type of head can have. For example, the specifier-features of the auxiliary *has* are [3SNom], and these tell us that it requires a third person singular nominative subject like *he/she/it*. See §5.3.

Specifier-first/-last   A *specifier-first* language is one which normally positions specifiers before their heads; a *specifier-last* language is one which normally positions specifiers after their heads.

Spellout   The point in a derivation at which phonetic and semantic features are processed by separate components of the grammar (the **PF component** and the **LF component** respectively). See §5.2.

Split infinitive   A structure in which the infinitive particle *to* is separated from the verb with which it is associated: a sentence such as *It's important to **really** try hard* contains an example of a split infinitive, since the particle *to* has been separated from the verb *try* by the intervening adverb *really*.

Split-INFL hypothesis   The hypothesis that there is not just one auxiliary position in clauses (= **INFL**), but rather two (**T** and **AgrS**). See §10.2 and §10.3.

Split-segment category   See **segment**.

Split-VP hypothesis   The hypothesis that verb phrases have a complex internal structure comprising an outer **vp** shell headed by a light verb, **AgrOP/AgrIOP** projections, and an inner **VP** core headed by a lexical verb. See §10.4.

Stack(ing)   To say (for example) that prenominal adjectives can be *stacked* in front of a noun is to say that we can have an indefinitely large number of adjectives positioned in front of a noun (e.g. *a **big**, **red**, **juicy**, **ripe** apple*).

Standard language   The variety of language used by central government administration, taught in schools and used e.g. by the presenters of (nonregional) radio/television news bulletins.

Star   An asterisk (*) used in front of an expression to indicate that the expression is **ungrammatical**.

Stem   A **morpheme** which contains no inflectional or derivational **affixes**. For example, the stem form of the verb *going* is *go*.

Stranded   A stranded (or orphaned) preposition is one which has been separated from its complement (by movement of the complement). For example, in a sentence such as *Who were you talking to?*, *to* is a stranded/orphaned preposition by virtue of the fact that it is separated from its complement *who* (which has been moved to the front of the sentence). By extension, in a sentence such as *They have all left*, the quantifier *all* could be said to have been stranded, since it is separated from the pronoun *they* which it quantifies.

String   A continuous sequence of words contained within the same phrase or sentence. For example, in the phrase *a couple of drinks*, the sequences *a couple, couple of, of drinks, a couple of* and *couple of drinks* are all strings, whereas the sequences *a of, a drinks, a couple drinks, a of drinks* and *couple drinks* are not. Note that a *string* need not be a **constituent**.

Strong feature   A strong feature is one which can trigger movement; a weak feature is one which cannot trigger movement. For example, finite verbs carry strong agreement-features in Early Modern English, and so raise to INFL; but finite verbs carry weak agreement-features in Modern Standard English, and so cannot move to INFL but rather remain *in situ*. See ch. 5.

Structural learning   This term denotes what children learn about grammatical structure in the language they are acquiring. See §1.8.

Structural representation   See **representation**.

Structural uniformity hypothesis   The hypothesis that all clauses have a uniform **CP/IP/VP** structure. See §4.6.

Structure   See **constituent structure**.

Structure dependence principle   A principle which states that grammatical operations are sensitive to grammatical structure, so that whether or not a particular grammatical operation can apply to a particular expression depends on the syntactic structure of the expression. See §1.6.

Stylistic variation   Variation correlated with stylistic factors.

Subcategory   A subset of the members of some category which share one or more grammatical properties in common, but which differ in some way from other members of the category. For example, **count nouns** are a subcategory of the category **noun**, in that all (regular) count nouns are countable, but differ from other types of noun in that e.g. mass nouns are uncountable. See §2.8.

Subject   The subject is one of the major constituents of a **clause**, since the smallest type of clause which we can construct is one which comprises a **subject** and a **predicate** (the predicate in most cases being a verb). Thus, in a clause such as *John smokes*, the subject is *John* and the predicate is the verb *smokes*. In semantic terms, the **subject** of a clause is typically the entity performing the action described by the verb. In grammatical terms, the subject of a clause is typically the expression which (for example) **agrees** with the verb, which precedes the verb and which carries nominative **case** if the verb is **finite**: e.g. in *He smokes cigars*, *he* is the subject of the verb *smokes* by virtue of the fact that *he* is nominative, *he* precedes the verb *smokes* and *he* agrees with *smokes* (in that both are third person singular).

Subject-control predicate   See **control**.

Subjunctive   In a (**formal** style) sentence such as *The judge ordered that he be detained indefinitely*, the verb *be* is said to be a (present-tense) subjunctive form, since although it has exactly the same form as the infinitive *to be*, it has a nominative subject *he*, and hence is a finite form. In a sentence such as *If he were here, he'd tell you what to do*, the verb *were* is said to be a past-tense subjunctive form. (For all verbs other than *be*, there is no morphological distinction between past-tense **indicative** and past-tense subjunctive verb forms.) In present-day spoken English, constructions containing subjunctive verbs are generally avoided, as they are felt by many speakers to be archaic or excessively formal in style.

Substitution   A technique used to determine the category which a given expression belongs to. An expression belongs to a given type of category if it can be substituted (i.e. replaced) in the phrase or sentence in which it occurs by another expression which clearly belongs to the category in question. For example, we might say that *clearer* is an adverb in *John speaks clearer than you* because it can be replaced by the adverbial expression *more clearly*. See §2.3.

Successive cyclic movement   Movement in a succession of short steps. See §6.4.

Suffix   See **affix**.

Supercategory   A category whose membership comprises all the members of two or more other categories. See §2.9.

Superlative   The superlative is a form of an adjective/adverb which carries the suffix *+est* (e.g. *John is the **hardest** worker because he works **hardest***) to mark the highest value for a particular property in comparison with others.

Synonym/synonymous   Two expressions are said to be synonyms/synonymous if they have much the same **interpretation**: for example, *dad* and *father* are synonyms.

Syntactic representation   See **representation**.

Syntax   The study of how words are combined together to form phrases and sentences.

T/T̄/T-bar/TP   T is an abstract **tense** morpheme (considered as one of the head constituents in clauses); T̄/T-bar is an intermediate projection of T; TP (tense phrase) is a maximal projection headed by T. See §6.8 and §10.2.

Tacit knowledge   Subconscious knowledge.

Tag (question)   A *tag* is a **string** usually consisting of an auxiliary and a pronoun which is added onto the end of a sentence. Thus, the bold-printed string is the tag in the following: *The president isn't underestimating his opponents,* **is he?**, and the overall sentence is known as a *tag question*.

Tense   Finite auxiliary and nonauxiliary verbs in English show a binary (two-way) tense contrast, traditionally said to be between *present-tense* forms and *past-tense* forms. Thus, in *John hates syntax*, *hates* is a present-tense verb form, whereas in *John hated syntax*, *hated* is a past-tense verb form. (An alternative classification which many linguists prefer is to say that *hated* carries *past* tense, and *hates* carries *non-past* tense.) The present/past tense distinction correlates (to some extent) with time reference, so that (for example) past-tense verbs typically describe an event taking place in the past, whereas present-tense verbs typically describe an event taking place in the present (or future). However, the correlation is an imperfect one, since e.g. in a sentence such as *If I went there tomorrow, would you come with me?*, the verb *went* is a past-tense (**subjunctive**) form, but has future rather than past time reference.

Tensed   A *tensed* (auxiliary or nonauxiliary) verb form is one which carries (present/past) tense – e.g. *is*, *will*, *could*, *hates*, *went*, etc. So, in effect, a tensed form is a **finite** form. By extension, a *tensed clause* is one containing a tensed/finite auxiliary or nonauxiliary verb.

Terminal node   A **node** at the bottom of a tree (i.e. a node which does not **dominate** any other node).

Ternary   Three-way: for example, we might say that English has a ternary **person** system in personal pronouns, in that we find first person pronouns like *I/we*, second person pronouns like *you* and third person pronouns like *he/she/it/they*.

Thematic role/θ-role   The semantic role played by an argument in relation to its predicate (e.g. AGENT, THEME, RECIPIENT, etc.). See §8.4.

THEME   The name of a specific theta-role (sometimes also termed PATIENT) associated with the entity undergoing the effect of some action. For example, *Harry* is the THEME **argument** of the verb *kill* in a sentence like *John killed Harry*. See §8.4.

Theoretical linguistics   The study of the properties of the grammars of natural languages.

Theory of grammar   A theory which specifies the types of categories, relations, operations and principles found in natural language grammars. See §1.3.

Theta-bar position/θ̄-position   A position in which no theta-role is assigned.

Theta-criterion/θ-criterion   A principle of UG which specifies that each argument bears one and only one theta-role, and each theta-role is assigned to one and only one argument. See §8.7.

Theta-marking/θ-marking   The assignment of **thematic roles** by predicates to **arguments**. For example, the verb *arrest* assigns the θ-role of PATIENT to its complement and assigns the θ-role AGENT to its subject, and is said to (directly) θ-mark its complement and (indirectly) θ-mark its subject. See §8.4.

Theta-position/θ-position   A position to which a theta-role is assigned (directly or indirectly) – hence a specifier or complement position within a phrase headed by an appropriate item belonging to a lexical category (N, V, P or A).

Theta-role/θ-role   See **thematic role**.

Third person   See **person**.

Three-place predicate   A **predicate** which takes three **arguments** – e.g. the verb *give* in *John gave Mary something* (where the three arguments of *give* are *John, Mary* and *something*).

Top/Topic/TopP   A **topic** is a constituent which receives special emphasis by virtue of being positioned at the beginning of a clause, and which may be moved into that position by **topicalization**. One way of analysing topics (as in the model answer for exercise VIII in chapter 7) is as constituents occupying the specifier position within a TopP (= topic phrase) projection headed by an abstract Top constituent.

Topicalization   A process by which a constituent is made into the *topic* of a sentence by being moved into a more prominent position at the front of the sentence (e.g. *such behaviour* might be said to be topicalized in a sentence such as *Such behaviour we cannot tolerate in a civilized society*).

TP   Tense phrase – i.e. a phrase headed by an abstract tense morpheme **T**. See §6.8 and §10.2.

TP adverb   An adverb which adjoins to some projection of **T**.

Trace (theory)   A *trace* is an empty category left behind (as a result of movement) in each position out of which a constituent moves. *Trace theory* is a theory which posits that moved constituents leave behind a trace in each position out of which they move. See §6.3.

Transitive   A word is said to be transitive (in a given use) if it checks objective case. So, for example, *hate* is a transitive verb in sentences like *I hate him* because it checks the objective case of *him*. In much the same way, the preposition *for* is transitive in *He bought it for us*, since it checks the objective case of *us*. By contrast, words which (in a given use) don't check objective case are intransitive (in the relevant use): for example, adjectives (e.g. *fond*) are generally intransitive and so can't have an objective complement (cf. **fond him*), and likewise all nouns (e.g. *loss*) are similarly intransitive (cf. **loss earnings*). Simplifying somewhat, we can say that a word is intransitive if it has no complement (e.g. *leave* in *He may leave*), or if it has a complement which is not a D or DP (e.g. *got* in *She got angry*, or *spoke* in *He spoke to her*). However, this is oversimplistic in that it overlooks the fact that a word with a clausal complement is transitive if its clausal complement has an objective subject (e.g. *expect* is transitive in a sentence like *We expect him to win* since *expect* checks the case of *him*), but words are generally taken to be intransitive when they have other types of clausal complement (e.g. *expect* is generally considered intransitive when it has a *that*-clause complement, as in *Nobody expected that he would win*). See also **object**.

Tree (diagram) A way of representing the syntactic structure of a phrase or sentence. See ch. 3.

Two-place predicate A predicate which has two **arguments**. For example, *kill* is a two-place predicate in a sentence such as *John killed Harry*, because it has two arguments (*John* and *Harry*).

UG See **Universal Grammar**.

Unaccusative An unaccusative predicate is a verb like *come* which allows a postverbal subject (as in *From inside the house came a cry of anguish*), and whose apparent subject originates in **VP** rather than **vp**. See §9.9 and §10.9.

Unary A unary feature is one with a single value. A unary-branching node is one which has a single daughter.

Unbound A constituent is unbound if it has no appropriate **antecedent** in an appropriate position within the relevant structure. For example, the **anaphor** *himself* is unbound in a sentence such as **She helped himself*, since *she* is not an appropriate antecedent for *himself*, and there is no other appropriate antecedent for *himself* anywhere within the sentence.

Underlying structure A structure as it was before the application of some movement operation(s).

Unergative An unergative verb is a verb like *groan* in a sentence such as *He was groaning* which has an agent subject but seems to have no object. See §9.8.

Ungradable See **gradable**.

Ungrammatical An expression is ungrammatical if it contains a morphological error (e.g. if some word is in the wrong form) or syntactic error (e.g. if some word occupies the wrong position). Hence, a sentence like **He seed me* is ungrammatical because *seed* is in the wrong form (*saw* is required), and a sentence like **He me saw* is ungrammatical because *me* is in the wrong position (cf. *He saw me*).

Uniform(ity) See **chain uniformity condition**, or **structural uniformity hypothesis**, or **uniform theta assignment hypothesis**.

Uniform theta assignment hypothesis/UTAH This hypothesis (put forward in Baker 1988) maintains that each theta-role assigned by a particular type of predicate is canonically associated with a specific syntactic position: e.g. **spec-vp** is the **canonical** position associated with an AGENT argument. See §8.8.

Uninterpretable See **interpretable**.

Universal Grammar/UG The study of the common grammatical properties shared by all natural languages (and of the **parameters** of variation between languages).

Universality A criterion of adequacy for a theory of grammar, requiring that the theory be applicable to all natural languages. See §1.3.

Unlicensed An *unlicensed* constituent is one which is not allowed to occur in the relevant position in the relevant phrase/sentence (e.g. the objective subject *him* is unlicensed in a sentence such as *Him is kind, since it occupies a position in which only a nominative pronoun like *he* is licensed (i.e. permitted)).

Unreduced See **reduced form**.

Unspecified Containing no specification of its value with respect to a given feature. For example the determiner *the* might be claimed to be unspecified with respect to number (i.e. whether it is singular or plural) – though in §5.6 we suggested that *the* carries a variable number-feature (and hence can be either singular or plural).

UTAH See **uniform theta assignment hypothesis**.

V/V̄/V-bar/VP V is a lexical verb; V̄/V-bar is an intermediate projection headed by a lexical verb; VP is a maximal projection headed by a lexical verb. See **lexical** and **projection**.

v/v̄/v-bar/vp v is a light verb; v̄/v-bar is an intermediate projection headed by a light verb; vp is a maximal projection headed by a light verb. See **light verb** and **projection**.

Variable The category variable X is used to denote 'any category of head which you care to choose' (and similarly $\overline{X}$ denotes 'any type of intermediate projection', and **XP** denotes 'any type of phrase'). The feature-variable [α] is used to represent 'any value for the relevant feature which you care to choose' (so that e.g. [$\alpha Number$] in effect means 'singular or plural in number', and [$\alpha Person$] means 'first, second or third person').

Variation A term used to describe differences between languages or between different varieties of the same language.

Variety A particular (e.g. geographical, social or stylistic) form of a language.

Verb A category of word which has the morphological property that it can carry a range of inflections including past tense +*d*, third person singular present tense +*s*, perfective +*n* and progressive +*ing* (cf. *show/shows/showed/shown/showing*), and the syntactic property that it can head the complement of infinitival *to* (cf. *Do you want to **show** me?*). See §2.2.

Verb movement See **V movement**.

Verb phrase A phrase/maximal projection which is headed by a verb – e.g. the bracketed phrase in *They will* [*help you*] (see ch. 3). In terms of the **shell** analysis presented in ch. 9, there are two different types of *verb phrase* – a **VP** headed by a **lexical verb**, and a **vp** headed by a **light verb**.

V(-to-I) movement An operation by which a finite verb moves from V to INFL (e.g. in Early Modern English). See §6.4.

Vocalic Containing a vowel or diphthong.

Vocative A vocative expression is one which is used to address one or more individuals, and which is set off in a separate tone-group at the beginning or end of the sentence (separated from the rest of the sentence by a comma). So, for example, *Fred* is a vocative expression in *Fred, can you give me a hand?* and similarly *you two* is a vocative expression in *Come here, you two!*

Voice   See **active**.

VP   See **V**.

vp   See **v**.

VP adverb   An adverb (like *perfectly*) which adjoins to some projection of V.

vp adverb   An adverb which adjoins to a projection of **v**.

VP-internal subject hypothesis   The hypothesis that subjects originate internally within **VP/vp**: see chs. 8 and 9.

***Wanna*-contraction**   The process by which the string *want to* contracts to *wanna*.

Weak features   See **strong features**.

Wh   This is widely used as a feature marking some word, phrase or sentence as interrogative. In a different use, it is a feature carried by constituents which undergo **wh-movement** (hence e.g. the relative pronoun *who* in *someone who I think is lying* could be described as a wh-pronoun, even though it is not interrogative).

Wh-expression   An expression containing a **wh-word**.

Wh-movement   A type of **operator movement** whereby an expression containing a wh-word (i.e. a word such as *who/which/what/where/why/when*) is moved to the front of a particular clause. See ch. 7.

Wh-parameter   The parameter which determines whether wh-expressions can (or can't) be moved to the front of an appropriate clause (especially in relation to wh-questions). See §1.7.

Wh-phrase   A phrase containing a wh-word.

Wh-question   A question which contains a **wh-word**, e.g. *What are you doing?*

Wh-word   A word which begins with *wh* (e.g. *who/what/which/where/when/why*), or which has a similar syntax to wh-words (e.g. *how*).

Word formation   A term relating to the morphological processes by which morphemes are combined together to form words.

Word order   A term representing the linear sequencing of words within a phrase or sentence.

X/$\overline{\text{X}}$/X-bar/XP   The symbol **X** (and sometimes **Y** similarly) is used as a variable denoting 'any word category you care to choose' (so X could be a noun, verb, adjective, determiner, complementizer, etc.). $\overline{\text{X}}$/X-bar is an intermediate projection headed by a word category; XP is a maximal projection headed by a word category. See **projection**.

Y/$\overline{\text{Y}}$/Y-bar/YP   See **X**.

Yes–no question   A question to which *Yes* or *No* would be an appropriate answer – e.g. *Do you like syntax?*

REFERENCES

Abney, S.P. (1987) 'The English noun phrase in its sentential aspect', PhD diss., MIT.

Akmajian, A. and F. Heny (1975) *An Introduction to the Principles of Transformational Syntax*, MIT Press, Cambridge, Mass.

Aronoff, M. (1976) *Word Formation in Generative Grammar*, MIT Press, Cambridge, Mass.

Authier, J.-M. (1991) 'V-governed expletives, case theory and the projection principle', *Linguistic Inquiry* 22: 721–40.

Bailey, B.L. (1966) *Jamaican Creole Syntax: a Transformational Approach*, Cambridge University Press.

Baker, C.L. (1970) 'Notes on the description of English questions: the role of an abstract question morpheme', *Foundations of Language*, 6: 197–219.

Baker, M. (1988) *Incorporation*, University of Chicago Press.

Baker, M., K. Johnson and I. Roberts (1989) 'Passive arguments raised', *Linguistic Inquiry* 20: 219–51.

Baltin, M. (1995) 'Floating quantifiers, PRO and predication', *Linguistic Inquiry* 26: 199–248.

Belletti, A. (1988) 'The case of unaccusatives', *Linguistic Inquiry* 19: 1–34.

(1990) *Generalized Verb Movement*, Rosenberg & Sellier, Turin.

Berko, J. (1958) 'The child's learning of English morphology', *Word* 14: 150–77.

Berman, R. (1988) 'Word class distinctions in developing grammars', in Y. Levy, I. M. Schlesinger and M. D. S. Braine (eds.) *Categories and Processes in Language Acquisition*, Erlbaum, London, pp. 45–72.

Bishop, D.V.M. (1994) 'Grammatical errors in specific language impairment: competence or performance limitations?', *Applied Psycholinguistics* 15: 507–50.

Bobaljik, J.D. (1995) 'Morphosyntax: the syntax of verbal inflection', PhD diss., MIT.

Bolinger, D and D.A. Sears (1981, 3rd edn) *Aspects of Language*, Harcourt Brace Jovanovich, New York.

Bošković, Z. (1994) 'Categorial status of null operator relatives and finite declarative complements', *Language Research* 30: 387–412.

(1995) 'Principles of economy in nonfinite complementation', PhD diss., University of Connecticut.

Bowerman, M. (1995) 'Don't giggle me!', talk presented at the University of Essex, 30th November 1995.

Bowers, J. (1993) 'The syntax of predication', *Linguistic Inquiry* 24: 591–656.

Bresnan, J. (1972) 'Theory of complementation in English syntax', PhD diss., MIT.

Brown, K. (1991) 'Double modals in Hawick Scots', in Trudgill & Chambers, pp. 74–103.

Burton, S. & J. Grimshaw (1992) 'Coordination and VP-internal subjects', *Linguistic Inquiry* 23: 305–13.

Burzio, L. (1986) *Italian Syntax*, Reidel, Dordrecht.

Carnie, A. (1995) 'Non-verbal predication and head movement', PhD diss., MIT.

Carrier, J. & J.H. Randall (1992) 'The argument structure and syntactic structure of resultatives', *Linguistic Inquiry* 23: 173–234.

Cheshire, J. (1989) 'Social background to variation in British English syntax', chapter 1 of Milroy and Milroy.

Chomsky, N. (1955) 'The logical structure of linguistic theory', unpublished manuscript, subsequently published as Chomsky 1975.

(1957) *Syntactic Structures*, Mouton, The Hague.

(1965) *Aspects of the Theory of Syntax*, MIT Press, Cambridge, Mass.

(1966) *Topics in the Theory of Generative Grammar*, Mouton, The Hague.

(1968) Interview with S. Hamshire in *The Listener*, May 1968.

(1970) 'Remarks on nominalization' in R.A. Jacobs & P.S. Rosenbaum (eds.) *Readings in English Transformational Grammar*, Ginn, Waltham, Mass., pp. 184–221.

(1972a) *Language and Mind* (enlarged edition), Harcourt Brace Jovanovich, New York.

(1972b) *Studies on Semantics in Generative Grammar*, Mouton, The Hague.

(1975) *The Logical Structure of Linguistic Theory*, Plenum, New York.

(1980) 'On binding', *Linguistic Inquiry* 11: 1–46.

(1981) *Lectures on Government and Binding*, Foris, Dordrecht.

(1986a) *Knowledge of Language: its Nature, Origin and Use*, Praeger, New York.

(1986b) *Barriers*, MIT Press, Cambridge, Mass.

(1989) 'Some notes on economy of derivation and representation', *MIT Working Papers in Linguistics* 10: 43–74 (reprinted as chapter 2 of Chomsky 1995c).

(1993) 'A minimalist program for linguistic theory', in Hale & Keyser (eds.) *The View from Building 20*, MIT Press, Cambridge, Mass. (reprinted as chapter 3 of Chomsky 1995c).

(1995a) 'Bare phrase structure' in G. Webelhuth (ed.) *Government and Binding Theory and the Minimalist Program*, Blackwell, Oxford, pp. 383–439.

(1995b) 'Categories and transformations', chapter 4 of Chomsky 1995c.

(1995c) *The Minimalist Program*, MIT Press, Cambridge, Mass.

Chomsky, N. and H. Lasnik (1995) 'The theory of principles and parameters', in Chomsky 1995c, pp. 13–127.

Cinque, G. (1994) 'Evidence for partial N-movement in the Romance DP' in G. Cinque, J. Koster, J.-Y. Pollock, L. Rizzi & R. Zanuttini (eds.) *Towards Universal Grammar: Studies in Honor of Richard Kayne*, Georgetown University Press, Washington, D.C.

(1995) 'Romance past participle agreement and clause structure', talk presented to the Romance Linguistics Seminar, University of Cambridge.

Contreras, H. (1986) 'Spanish bare NPs and the ECP', in I. Bordelois, H. Contreras & K. Zagona (eds.) *Generative Studies in Spanish Syntax*, Foris, Dordrecht, pp. 25–49.

References

Contreras, J. (1987) 'Small clauses in Spanish and English', *Natural Language and Linguistic Theory*, 5: 225–44.

Culicover, P.W. (1992) 'Evidence against ECP accounts of the that-t effect', *Linguistic Inquiry* 23: 557–61.

Davis, H. (1987). 'The acquisition of the English auxiliary system and its relation to linguistic theory', PhD dissertation, University of British Columbia.

Emonds, J.E. (1976) *A Transformational Approach to English Syntax*, Academic Press, New York.

Ernst, T. (1991) 'On the scope principle', *Linguistic Inquiry* 22: 750–6.

Fabb, N. (1988) 'English suffixation is constrained only by selectional restrictions', *Natural Language and Linguistic Theory* 6: 527–39.

Fasold, R. (1980) 'The relation between black and white speech in the south', mimeo, School of Languages and Linguistics, Georgetown University, Washington, D.C.

Felser, C. (1995) 'The syntax of verbal complements: a study of perception verbs in English', PhD diss., University of Göttingen.

Fillmore, C.J. (1968) 'The case for case', in E. Bach & R.T. Harms (eds.) *Universals in Linguistic Theory*, Holt Rinehart & Winston, New York, pp. 1–88.

(1972) 'Subjects, speakers and roles', in D. Davidson & G. Harman (eds.) *Semantics of Natural Language*, Reidel, Dordrecht.

Gopnik, M. & M. Crago, (1991) 'Familial aggregation of a developmental language disorder', *Cognition* 39: 1–50.

Grice, H.P. (1975) 'Logic and conversation' in P. Cole & J. Morgan (eds.) *Syntax and Semantics 3: Speech Acts*, Academic Press, New York, pp. 41–58.

Grimshaw, J. (1991) 'Extended projection', draft manuscript, Brandeis University, July 1991.

(1993a) 'Minimal projection, heads, and optimality', draft manuscript, Rutgers University, June 1993.

(1993b) 'Minimal projection, heads, and optimality', conference handout, Rutgers University, November 1993 [revised version of Grimshaw 1993a].

Groat, E. (1995) 'English expletives: a minimalist approach', *Linguistic Inquiry* 26: 354–65.

Gruber, J.S. (1965) 'Studies in lexical relations', PhD diss., MIT.

Guéron, J. (1990) 'Particles, prepositions and verbs', in J. Mascaró and M. Nespor (eds.) *Grammar in Progress*, Foris, Dordrecht.

Guilfoyle, E. (1983) 'Habitual aspect in Hiberno-English', *McGill Working Papers in Linguistics* 1: 22–32.

Guilfoyle, E., H. Hung and L. Travis (1992) 'Spec of IP and spec of VP: two subjects in Austronesian languages', *Natural Language and Linguistic Theory* 10: 375–414.

Haegeman, L. (1992, 1st edn) *Introduction to Government and Binding Theory*, Blackwell, Oxford.

(1994, 2nd edn) *Introduction to Government and Binding Theory*, Blackwell, Oxford.

Hale, K. & S.J. Keyser (1991) 'On the syntax of argument structure', Lexicon Project Working Papers, MIT, Center for Cognitive Science, Cambridge, Mass.

(1993) 'On argument structure and the lexical expression of semantic relations', in K. Hale & S. J. Keyser (eds.) *The View from Building 20*, MIT Press, Cambridge, Mass., pp. 53–109.

(1994) 'Constraints on argument structure', in B. Lust, M. Suñer & J. Whitman (eds.) *Heads, Projections and Learnability*, Erlbaum, Hillsdale, N.J., vol. 1, pp. 53–71.

Halle, M. & A. Marantz (1993) 'Distributed morphology and the pieces of inflection' in K. Hale & S.J. Keyser (eds.) *The View from Building 20*, MIT Press, Cambridge, Mass., pp. 111–76.

Harley, H. (1995) 'Subjects, events and licensing', PhD diss., MIT.

Harris, J. (1986) 'Expanding the superstrate: habitual aspect markers in Atlantic Englishes', *English World-Wide* 7: 171–99.

Harris, M. (1991) 'Demonstrative adjectives and pronouns in a Devonshire dialect', in Trudgill and Chambers, pp. 20–8.

Henry, A. (1992) 'Infinitives in a *for-to* dialect', *Natural Language and Linguistic Theory* 10: 279–301.

(1995) *Belfast English and Standard English: Dialect Variation and Parameter-Setting*, Oxford University Press.

Hoekstra, T. (1984) *Transitivity: Grammatical Relations in Government-Binding Theory*, Foris, Dordrecht.

Huang, C.-T.J. (1982) 'Logical relations in Chinese and the theory of grammar', PhD diss., MIT.

(1993) 'Reconstruction and the structure of VP: some theoretical consequences', *Linguistic Inquiry* 24: 103–38.

Ihalainen, O. (1991) 'Periphrastic *do* in affirmative sentences in the dialect of East Somerset', in Trudgill and Chambers, pp. 148–60.

Jackendoff, R.S. (1972) *Semantic Interpretation in Generative Grammar*, MIT Press, Cambridge, Mass.

Johnson, K. (1991) 'Object positions', *Natural Language and Linguistic Theory* 9: 577–636.

Jones, M.A. (1994) *Sardinian Syntax*, Routledge, London.

Katz, J.J. and P.M. Postal (1964) *An Integrated Theory of Linguistic Descriptions*, MIT Press, Cambridge, Mass.

Kayne, R.S. (1982) 'Predicates and arguments, verbs and nouns', *GLOW Newsletter*, 8: 24.

(1984) 'Principles of particle constructions', in J. Guéron, H.-G. Obenauer and J.-Y. Pollock (eds.) *Grammatical Representation*, Foris, Dordrecht, pp. 101–40.

(1989) 'Facets of Romance past participle agreement', in. P. Benincà (ed.) *Dialect Variation in the Theory of Grammar*, Foris, Dordrecht, pp. 85–104.

(1994) *The Antisymmetry of Syntax*, MIT Press, Cambridge, Mass.

Keyser, S.J. & T. Roeper (1992) 'Re: the abstract clitic hypothesis', *Linguistic Inquiry* 23: 89–125.

Kitagawa, Y. (1986) 'Subjects in English and Japanese', PhD diss., University of Massachusetts.

Klima, E.S. (1964) 'Negation in English', in J.A. Fodor & J.J. Katz (eds.) *The Structure of Language*, Prentice-Hall, Englewood Cliffs, N.J., pp. 246–323.

Koizumi, M. (1995) 'Phrase structure in minimalist syntax', PhD diss., MIT.

Koopman, H. & D. Sportiche (1991) 'The position of subjects', in J. McCloskey (ed.) *The Syntax of Verb-Initial Languages*, Elsevier (published as a special issue of *Lingua*).

References

Kuroda, Y. (1988) 'Whether we agree or not', *Lingvisticae Investigationes* 12: 1–47.

Labov, W. (1969) 'Contraction, deletion, and inherent variability of the English copula', *Language* 45: 715–62.

Lakoff, G. (1971) 'Presupposition and relative well-formedness', in D.D. Steinberg & L.A. Jakobovits (eds.) *Semantics*, Cambridge University Press, pp. 329–40.

Larson, R. (1988) 'On the double object construction', *Linguistic Inquiry* 19: 335–91.

(1990) 'Double objects revisited: reply to Jackendoff', *Linguistic Inquiry* 21: 589–632.

(1991) '*Promise* and the theory of control', *Linguistic Inquiry* 22: 103–39.

Lasnik, H. (1981) 'Restricting the theory of transformations: a case study', in N. Hornstein and D. Lightfoot (eds.) *Explanation in Linguistics*, Longman, London, pp. 152–73.

(1992) 'Case and expletives: notes toward a parametric account', *Linguistic Inquiry* 23: 381–405.

(1995) 'Case and expletives revisited: on greed and other human failings', *Linguistic Inquiry* 26: 615–33.

Longobardi, G. (1994) 'Reference and proper names', *Linguistic Inquiry* 25: 609–66.

McNally, L. (1992) 'VP-coordination and the VP-internal subject hypothesis', *Linguistic Inquiry* 23: 336–41.

McNeill, D. (1966) 'Developmental psycholinguistics', in F. Smith and G.A. Miller (eds.) *The Genesis of Language*, MIT Press, Cambridge, Mass., pp. 15–84.

(1970) *The Acquisition of Language*, Harper and Row, New York.

Manzini, M.R. (1994) 'Locality, minimalism and parasitic gaps', *Linguistic Inquiry* 25: 481–508.

Marantz, A. (1984) *On the Nature of Grammatical Relations*, MIT Press, Cambridge, Mass.

Martin, R. (1992) 'On the distribution and case features of PRO', MS., University of Connecticut.

Miller, J. (1989) 'The grammar of Scottish English', chapter 4 of Milroy & Milroy.

Milroy, J. and L. Milroy (1989) *Regional Variation in British English Syntax*, Economic and Social Research Council, Swindon.

Ouhalla, J. (1991) *Functional Categories and Parametric Variation*, Routledge, London.

Pesetsky, D. (1995) *Zero Syntax: Experiencers and Cascades*, MIT Press, Cambridge, Mass.

Pierce, A. (1992) *Language Acquisition and Syntactic Theory: a Comparative Analysis of French and English Child Grammars*, Kluwer, Dordrecht.

Pollock, J.-Y. (1989) 'Verb movement, Universal Grammar, and the structure of IP', *Linguistic Inquiry* 20: 365–424.

Postal, P.M. (1966) 'On so-called pronouns in English', in F. Dinneen (ed.) *Nineteenth Monograph on Language and Linguistics*, Georgetown University Press, Washington, D.C., pp. 201–24.

(1974) *On Raising*, MIT Press, Cambridge, Mass.

Radford, A. (1981) *Transformational Syntax*, Cambridge University Press.

(1988) *Transformational Grammar*, Cambridge University Press.

(1990) *Syntactic Theory and the Acquisition of English Syntax*, Blackwell, Oxford.

(1992) 'The acquisition of the morphosyntax of finite verbs in English', in J. M. Meisel (ed.) *The Acquisition of Verb Placement: Functional Categories and V2 Phenomena in Language Acquisition*, Kluwer, Dordrecht, pp. 23–62.

Rickford, J.R. (1986) 'Social contact and linguistic diffusion: Hiberno-English and New World Black English', *Language* 62: 245–89.

Ritter, E. and S.T. Rosen (1993) 'Deriving causation', *Natural Language and Linguistic Theory* 11: 519–55.

Rizzi, L. (1990) *Relativized Minimality*, MIT Press, Cambridge, Mass.

Roberts, I. (1986) *The Representation of Implicit and Dethematized Subjects*, Foris, Dordrecht.

(1991) 'Excorporation and minimality', *Linguistic Inquiry* 22: 209–18.

(1993) *Verbs and Diachronic Syntax*, Kluwer, Dordrecht.

(1996) *Comparative Syntax*, Arnold, London.

Rohrbacher, B. (1994) *The Germanic VO Languages and the Full Paradigm: a Theory of V to I Raising*, GLSA Publications, Amherst.

Rooryck, J. (1994) 'On θ- and α-underspecification in syntax and phonology', *MIT Working Papers in Linguistics* 22: 197–216.

Rosen, S.T. (1990) *Argument Structure and Complex Predicates*, Garland, New York.

Rosenbaum, P.S. (1967) *The Grammar of English Predicate Complement Constructions*, MIT Press, Cambridge Mass.

Ross, J.R. (1967) 'Constraints on variables in syntax', PhD diss., MIT (published as *Infinite Syntax!* by Ablex Publishing Corporation, Norwood, N.J., 1986).

Rothstein, S.D. (1995) 'Pleonastics and the interpretation of pronouns', *Linguistic Inquiry* 26: 499–529.

Safir, K. (1993) 'Perception, selection and structural economy', *Natural Language Semantics* 2: 47–70.

Salles, H. M. P. (1995) 'Preposition pied-piping and preposition stranding; a minimalist approach', *Bangor Research Papers in Linguistics* 6: 97–123.

Schaeffer, J. (1994) 'The split INFL hypothesis: evidence from language-impaired children', talk presented to the Child Language Seminar, Bangor.

Sobin, N. (1985) 'Case assignment in Ukrainian morphological passive constructions', *Linguistic Inquiry* 16: 649–62.

Speas, M. (1986) 'Adjunction and projections in syntax', PhD diss., MIT.

(1995) 'Economy, agreement and the representation of null arguments', mimeo, University of Massachusetts.

Spencer, A.J. (1991) *Morphological Theory*, Blackwell, Oxford.

Sportiche, D. (1988) 'A theory of floating quantifiers and its corollaries for constituent structure', *Linguistic Inquiry* 19: 425–49.

Stowell, T. (1981) 'Origins of phrase structure', PhD diss., MIT.

(1982) 'The tense of infinitives', *Linguistic Inquiry* 13: 561–70.

Stroik, T. (1990) 'Adverbs as V-sisters', *Linguistic Inquiry* 21: 654–61.

Tieken-Boon van Ostade, I. (1988) 'The origins and development of periphrastic auxiliary *do*: a case of destigmatisation', *Dutch Working Papers in English Language and Linguistics* 3: 1–30.

Travis, L. (1984) 'Parameters and effects of word order variation', PhD diss., MIT.

Trudgill, P. & J.K. Chambers (1991) (eds.) *Dialects of English: Studies in Grammatical Variation*, Longman, London.

References

Ura, H. (1993) 'On feature-checking for wh-traces', *MIT Working Papers in Linguistics* 18: 243–80.

Uriagereka, J. (1995) 'Aspects of the syntax of clitic placement in Western Romance', *Linguistic Inquiry* 26: 79–123.

Vainikka, A. (1994) 'Case in the development of English syntax', *Language Acquisition* 3: 257–325.

Vikner, S. (1995) *Verb Movement and Expletive Subjects in Germanic Languages*, Oxford University Press.

Wakelin, M.F. (1977, 2nd edn) *English Dialects: an Introduction*, Athlone, London.

Watanabe, A. (1993) 'Agr-based theory and its interaction with the A-bar system', PhD diss., MIT.

Williams, E. (1994) 'A reinterpretation of evidence for verb movement in French', in D. Lightfoot & N. Hornstein (eds.) *Verb Movement*, Cambridge University Press, pp. 189–205.

Wolfram, W. (1971) 'Black-white speech differences revisited', in W. Wolfram & N. H. Clark (eds.) *Black-White Speech Relationships*, Center for Applied Linguistics, Washington, D.C., pp. 139–61.

Woolford, E. (1991) 'VP-internal subjects in VSO and nonconfigurational languages', *Linguistic Inquiry* 22: 503–40.

Zagona, K. (1987) *Verb Phrase Syntax*, Kluwer, Dordrecht.

INDEX

Index